The McGraw-Hill
Real Estate Handbook

OTHER McGRAW-HILL BOOKS BY ROBERT IRWIN

Timeshare Properties: What Every Buyer *Must* Know

The New Mortgage Game

The $125,000 Decision: The Older American's Guide to Selling a Home and Choosing Retirement Housing, Revised Edition

Riches in Real Estate—A Beginner's Guide to Group Investing

Protect Yourself in Real Estate: The Complete Beginner's Guide (paperback)

The Real Estate Agent's and Investor's Tax Book (with Richard Brickman)

How to Buy a Home at a Reasonable Price (paperback)

How to Buy and Sell Real Estate for Financial Security (paperback)

The McGraw-Hill
Real Estate
Handbook

Robert Irwin
Editor in Chief

McGraw-Hill Book Company

New York / St. Louis / San Francisco / Auckland
Bogotá / Hamburg / Johannesburg / London / Madrid
Mexico / Montreal / New Delhi / Panama / Paris
São Paulo / Singapore / Sydney / Tokyo / Toronto

Realtor® *is a registered trademark of*
the National Association of Realtors.

Library of Congress Cataloging in Publication Data

Main entry under title:

The McGraw-Hill real estate handbook.

   Includes index.
   1. Real estate business. I. Irwin, Robert,
date.

HD1375.M17   1984   333.33   83-14872
ISBN 0-07-032056-X

1234567890   DOC/DOC   8987654

ISBN 0-07-032056-X

The editors for this book were Bonnie Binkert and Christine Ulwick,
the designer was Jules Perlmutter, and the production
supervisor was Sally Fliess. It was set in Gael
by Com Com.

Printed and bound by R.R. Donnelley & Sons Company.

To the Real Estate Professionals

Contents

viii   **Contents**

INDEX

About the Editor in Chief

Robert Irwin is the editor in chief of the *McGraw-Hill Real Estate Handbook.* He is a California-licensed real estate broker, an investor, and an author. He has written seven books for McGraw-Hill on real estate, including *The New Mortgage Game* (1982); *The $125,000 Decision* (1982); *Riches in Real Estate* (1981); and *The Real Estate Agent's and Investor's Tax Book* (with Richard Brickman—1981).

Mr. Irwin received his B.A. in philosophy from California State University at San Jose and his M.A. in English from California State University at San Francisco. He operated his own real estate company for many years before turning his attentions to writing and investing.

Contributing Authors

Joseph D. Albert, Ph.D., is Assistant Professor of Real Estate and Urban Development, North Texas State University, Denton, Texas. He was formerly Assistant Professor of Real Estate and Economics, Oglethorpe University, Atlanta, Georgia.

Dr. Albert received his Ph.D. from Georgia State University, Atlanta, Georgia, in 1978 with a double major in real estate and economics. He received his B.S. from the University of South Florida, Tampa, Florida, in 1971 with a major in business administration and economics. He is a member of the American Real Estate and Urban Economics Association, senior member of the National Association of Review Appraisers, and recipient of the Certified Review Appraiser (CRA) Designation. He has published numerous articles in the fields of appraisal and real estate.

Michael Antin is an attorney who specializes in taxation and trusts. He has given numerous seminars for the American Bar Association, law schools, and other groups.

Mr. Antin is the senior partner of the Los Angeles law firm of Antin, Stern, Litz, and Grebow. He is also the author of *How to Operate Your Trust or Probate* (Layman, 1983). Mr. Antin has also authored dozens of articles for a wide variety of legal and lay journals.

He is a member of the American Bar Association's section of taxation and business law, the State Bar of California's section of taxation, probate and trust law and the Los Angeles County Bar Association. Mr. Antin served as vice-chairman of the Beverly Hills Bar Association tax committee in 1970 and as chairman of the probate and trust law committee in 1969. He is a member of the Western Pension Conference and the Beverly Hills Estate Planning Council.

Mr. Antin received his J.D. from Boalt Hall School of Law, University of California at Berkeley, in 1963 and received his bachelor's degree from U.C. L.A. in accounting in 1960. He has also passed a C.P.A. exam.

Dr. Wayne Archer has taught real estate at the University of Florida since 1971. His areas of expertise are real estate market analysis and real estate finance. He is a faculty member for schools of the Mortgage Bankers Association of America and for mortgage lending seminars of the Institute of Financial Education.

Dr. Archer's research experience includes assignments as a visiting researcher at the Federal Home Loan Bank Board and the Federal Savings and Loan Insurance Corporation as well as regular consulting assignments in private industry and state government.

He has published research in several major real estate–related journals, including the *Journal of The American Real Estate and Urban Economics Association,* the *Real Estate Appraiser,* and the *Federal Home Loan Bank Board Journal.*

Robert J. Bond is a teacher of real estate at Los Angeles Valley College. He formerly taught at California State University, Los Angeles, U.C.-L.A. Extension, and Pasadena City College.

Dr. Bond holds a Ph.D. in finance and urban economics from U.C.-L.A. and Kensington University. He has an M.A. in administration from California State University, Los Angeles, and a B.A. from California State University, Los Angeles.

Dr. Bond is self-employed as a consultant in real estate brokerage, banking, investments, tax accounting, and life insurance underwriting.

Dr. Bond was director of the Van Nuys Chamber of Commerce from 1977 to 1980 and director of Stephens & Stone from 1978 to 1980. At the present time he is the coordinator of the Real Estate Division of Los Angeles Valley College.

He is a member of the California Association of Realtors' finance committee, the California Association of Real Estate Teachers, the American Real Estate and Urban Economics Association, the California Business Education Association, the Pacific Southwest Business Law Association, and the National Association of Realtors.

Richard Brickman is a practicing attorney and certified public accountant in Thousand Oaks California. He is licensed to practice before the California Supreme Court, the U.S. Supreme Court, and the U.S. Tax Court.

Mr. Brickman received his bachelor's degree in business administration from the University of California, Los Angeles, in 1963 and his law degree from the same institution in 1966.

He has written numerous articles on real estate taxation and is coauthor of *The Real Estate Agent's and Investor's Tax Book* (McGraw-Hill, 1981).

Jim Brondino specializes in real estate investments and tax-deferred exchanges. He has been the recipient of the "Exchangor of the Year" award and has repeatedly earned the designation of "Million Dollar Exchangor."

Mr. Brondino conducts a nationally recognized real estate tax and exchange seminar approved as a qualifying course for the National Council of Exchangors Gold Card and a listing in *Who's Who in Creative Real Estate.* His articles have appeared in *Real Estate Today, Creative Real Estate,* and *Trader's Topics.*

Mr. Brondino holds a master's degree from the University of Redlands. He is a Realtor and serves on the board of directors of the Los Angeles County Apartment Owner's Association.

Thomas W. Dooley is proprietor and president of TWD & Associates, a real estate and general management consulting organization specializing in franchising, training, marketing, futurism, and company evaluation. He previously was a special representative for Homes for Living Network, St. Louis, Missouri; chief executive officer for Gallery of Homes, Inc., Elmhurst, Illinois; and executive vice president of the Realtor's National Marketing Institute.

Mr. Dooley is the author of two books: *Real Estate Brokerage in the '80s—Survival among the Giants* (Real Estate Education, 1980) and *How to Afford Your Dream Home in Bad Times as Well as Good Times* (Real Estate Education, in press).

Mr. Dooley is currently director of graduate studies at the College of Business and Teachers of Lewis University. He previously was with the Department of Management, College of Business, Northern Illinois University. He holds an M.B.A. in business administration-management from Xavier University, Cincinnati, an M.A. from the University of Toronto in philosophy, and an A.B. from Thomas More College in Lakeside Park, Kentucky.

Silas Ely is a private appraiser, instructor, and educational consultant. He serves as a panel appraiser for Crocker National Bank and a number of other lending institutions in the Los Angeles area. Previously, he was principal appraisor for the Los Angeles County Assessor's office, where he served as head of appraisal standards.

Mr. Ely is on the faculty of Santa Monica College and has been a senior faculty member of the University of Southern California College of Continuing Education. He is a past chairman of the California Association of Real Estate Teachers, past director-at-large of the California Association of Realtors, and past consultant and appraisal group leader for the California Department of Real Estate.

In 1979 Mr. Ely coauthored the California Department of Real estate instructor-student guides in real estate appraisal. He is also coauthor of *Basic Real Estate Appraisal* (Wiley, 1982).

Mr. Ely holds a B.A. in political science, a certificate in real estate from U.C.L.A., and the instructor credential for California Community Colleges. He received his appraiser certification from the California state board of equalization in 1967 and is a licensed California real estate broker.

William F. Friery, president of Watt & Friery Marketing Co., Inc., time-share division of Watt Industries, Inc., is a pioneer in U.S. time-sharing. His California projects include San Diego Country Estates, San Diego; Laguna Shores, Laguna Beach, and the Tennis Club Resort, Palm Springs. He was vice president of sales for Quechee Lakes Resort, Vermont. A native of Hartford, Connecticut, he spent four years in the U.S. Marine Corps.

H. James Griggs is president of Financial Investment Advisors in Sacramento, California. He formerly was president of Buhler Mortgage Company, Inc.

Mr. Griggs is on the board of directors of Point West Bank, Sacramento, California; is an associate member of the National Council on Teacher Retirement; and is a member of the Mortgage Bankers Association Project Loan Committee. He attended the University of California at Berkeley and has a B.S. in civil engineering, construction, and business.

Richard P. Halverson is executive vice president of the First Trust Company of Saint Paul. He is responsible for investment operations which handle more than $4.5 billion in fiduciary assets. Other responsibilities include supervision of employee benefit administration, real estate operations, marketing for employee benefit, economic forecasting, and corporate long-range planning and strategy.

Before joining First Trust Saint Paul in November 1977, Mr. Halverson was vice president of Waddell & Reed, Inc., a major mutual fund management complex with assets in excess of $2.2 billion. At Waddell & Reed Mr. Halverson managed two mutual funds and was extensively involved in the firm's portfolio strategy and implementation.

Mr. Halverson received an M.B.A. from Harvard University, where he graduated with distinction and was named a Baker scholar. He received his B.S. from the University of Utah where he graduated magna cum laude.

Mr. Halverson holds the respected Chartered Financial Analyst designation, has served as president of the Kansas City Society of Financial Analysts, and is active in the affairs of the International Financial Analysts Federation.

Mr. Halverson is the author of *Financial Freedom* (Harbor, 1982), a book describing successful personal financial management during the economic transition of the 1980s.

Louis B. Hansotte is a practicing attorney and the senior partner of the San Diego law firm of Hansotte, Nostrand and Lange. He teaches "Legal Aspects of Real Estate" for the Grossmont Community College and has coordinated the college's real estate program.

Mr. Hansotte has taught real estate licensing courses and has been part owner of two license training schools in addition to authoring four segments of the California Department of Real Estate's multimedia presentation on legal aspects of real estate.

Mr. Hansotte has lectured extensively and has presented continuing education seminars on many aspects of real estate. He is the author of *Legal Aspects of California Real Estate* (Wiley, 1982).

Mr. Hansotte received his B.S. in engineering from the U.S. Military Academy at West Point, New York. He has a C.L.U. designation from the American College of Life Underwriters, Bryn Mawr, Pennsylvania, and an L.L.B. from La Salle Extension University, Chicago, Illinois. He is a real estate broker and a member of the California Bar Association.

K. Reed Harrison is an attorney-at-law in Westlake Village, California. He is also chairman of the board of directors of the Village Bank, N.A.

Mr. Harrison is admitted to practice before all courts in the State of California; U.S. District Court, Central District; Ninth Circuit Court of Appeals; and the U.S. Supreme Court. His law practice emphasizes real estate and commercial law, and he has represented numerous clients in both residential and commercial landlord-tenant disputes.

He is also a licensed real estate agent and personally owns and manages income properties.

Dr. Thomas R. Harter is the chief economist and senior staff vice president of the Mortgage Bankers Association of America (MBA) in Washington D.C. As chief Economist and senior staff vice-president of the Economics and Education Department, Dr. Harter is responsible for MBA's economic and policy research. Dr. Harter also has overall responsibility for the MBA School of Mortgage Banking and the Correspondence Course Program and is the secretary of the Research and Educational Trust Fund as well as the Certified Mortgage Banker Program. A frequent speaker and lecturer at real estate industry meetings, conventions, and educational programs, Dr. Harter has published extensively on the subjects of capital formation, financial institutions, and economic forecasting.

Prior to joining the MBA, Dr. Harter was the senior economist and manager of program development at the Federal Home Loan Bank of San Francisco. From 1968 to 1974 he served as an associate professor of finance at the University of Colorado Graduate School of Business and worked as a private consultant to numerous financial institutions.

Dr. Harter received his Ph.D. in finance from Northwestern University in Evanston, Illinois, and he received his B.A. and M.B.A. from Washington University in St. Louis, Missouri.

Bruce B. Howey is a Realtor and speaker for the National Institute of Exchange Counselors, Inc. Mr. Howey is also a member of the National Association of Realtors, the Realtors National Marketing Institute ("certified commercial investment member"), the California Association of Realtors, and the Graduate Realtors Institute and is past president of the San Fernando Valley Exchangors and the National Council of Exchangors.

He holds a California life teaching credential in business education and is a graduate of Orange Coast College with a degree in real estate. Mr. Howey also graduated from the U.C.L.A./U.C.I./U.C.S.J. advanced teacher workshops and is coauthor with Evelyn Walsh of *Creative Communications* (California Association of Realtors, 1974).

James H. Koch publishes the monthly newsletter *Country Property*. He conducts popular seminars on country property investing and is an experienced investor in the field.

Mr. Koch has published six books: *Pitfalls in Issuing Municipal Bonds* (Moody's Investors Service, 1975), *A Selected Annotated Bank Marketing Bibliography* (American Bankers Association, 1971), *How Banks Can Use Direct Mail as an Effective Marketing Tool* (American Bankers Association, 1972), *Profits from Country Property* (McGraw-Hill, 1981), *How to Get the Most Profit from Your Collectibles* (ARCO, 1982), and *Profits from Small Town Property* (Van Nostrand, 1983). In addition he has written numerous articles, including a long series for the magazine *Country Living*.

Mr. Koch received his B.A. from Carleton College, Minnesota, and did graduate work as a Woodrow Wilson Fellow at Princeton. For many years he was with Dun & Bradstreet, Inc., as a reporter and middle-management executive and then was a senior partner and, since 1972, president of Aquarian Advertising Associates, Inc., of New York City.

Jerry Krantz has participated in the real estate market as a real estate broker since 1972 and as an investor since 1970.

As an investor, Mr. Krantz has owned and managed single-family homes, apartment buildings, and commercial properties. As a real estate broker, he has been involved primarily in residential investment and exchanging. He has served on the board of directors of several real estate exchange clubs and has been president of Central Coast Exchangors (the oldest real estate exchange club in California).

Prior to being in real estate, Mr. Krantz worked for 10 years in the engineering field. He holds a B.S. in physical sciences from California State University at Long Beach.

Norman H. Lane is a professor at the University of Southern California Law Center, Los Angeles. Dr. Lane received his A.B. in 1960 from Columbia University and his L.L.B. in 1963 from Harvard University. He was admitted to the New York Bar in 1965 and the California Bar in 1971. From 1963 to 1964 he was a law clerk for the Honorable Thurgood Marshall, U.S. Court of Appeals, Second Circuit. From 1964 to 1969 he was an associate with Carter, Ledyard & Milburn in New York City.

Dr. Lane has written on the subjects of accounting, corporations, estate planning, international transactions, taxation, federal trusts and estates, and employee stock ownership trusts. He is a member of Phi Beta Kappa, and he was a member and chairman of the Executive Committee Tax Law Section of the State Bar of California. He is on the Planning Commission of the U.S.C. Tax Institute.

Warren Lasko is executive vice-president of the Government National Mortgage Association (GNMA). He is responsible for administering the GNMA mortgage-backed securities program, which has financed over $130 billion in housing for moderate-income families. The program is the single largest element of the residential secondary mortgage market. He also oversees GNMA's Tandem programs, which finance some $2 billion annually in tent-assisted housing.

Mr. Lasko has made numerous contributions to housing policy at HUD, including major improvements in the GNMA mortgage-backed securities program, serving as a member of various task forces on the future of FHA, the development of HUD's section 8 rent subsidy programs and section 202 elderly housing program. As an economist he has done research on national housing needs and on the financing of national housing goals.

Mr. Lasko has degrees in economics from Columbia University in New York. He is an active participant in a number of community and conservation efforts and has published numerous articles relating to housing and mortgage financing.

Robert C. Mason is currently an independent appraiser working in Los Angeles. Previously he was chief appraiser of the Commercial Industrial Division of the Los Angeles County Assessor's Office. He is a member of the American Institute of Real Estate Appraisers and holds their M.A.I. designation. He is a senior member of the Association of Governmental Appraisers and is past president of the Los Angeles chapter of the International Association of Assessing Officers.

Mr. Mason has taught real estate appraisal at U.C.L.A., Santa Monica City College, El Camino Community College, and Pierce Community College. He holds a B.S. in economics from the University of Miami, a Certificate of Real Estate from U.C.L.A., a teaching credential in real estate appraisal from the state of California, and an advanced certificate from the California State Board of Equalization.

Mr. Mason is the author of numerous articles in appraisal and assessor journals.

Alfred Mattei Mingione graduated in 1959 from Florida Southern College with a B.S. Mr. Mingione has been directly involved with site selection and real estate department problems for the past 25 years. During this period, he has worked as a site selector, real estate supervisor, department manager, and real estate consultant. He presently operates his own real estate consulting business in Georgia.

Robert J. Mylod is president and chief operating officer of the Federal National Mortgage Association. He joined the corporation in January 1983. Mr. Mylod previously served as president of Advance Mortgage Corporation, Detroit, for 8 years. Prior to that, he was executive vice president of Advance for 2 years.

He began his career with Citibank in 1965, where he worked for 8 years, first in the mortgage and real estate loan department and later in the corporate planning department, where he was involved in the acquisition of Advance Mortgage.

During his nearly 10 years in Detroit, he served on the board of directors of the Detroit Symphony Orchestra, the board of trustees of the Henry Ford Hospital West Bloomfield (Michigan) Center, and the board of governors of the Mortgage Bankers Association of America.

Born in Brooklyn, Mr. Mylod earned a B.A. in English at St. John's University, New York. After graduating, he served 3½ years in the U.S. Navy.

O. Nicholas Ordway is the holder of the Hawaii Chair of Real Estate at the University of Hawaii. Previously he was associate professor of finance and real estate at the University of Texas at Arlington and Assistant professor of real estate, urban affairs, and business law at Georgia State University. He is also a real estate consultant throughout the United States, Canada, Latin America, and Asia.

Dr. Ordway has written numerous articles and scholarly papers for leading real estate publications. In addition, he has published seven books in the field including *Winning at Zoning* (with Dudley Hinds and Neil Carn—McGraw-Hill, 1979); *International Real Estate Investment* (with Dudley Hinds—Real Estate Education Company, 1983); *Real Estate Principles for License Preparation* (with Dennis Tosh—Reston, 1979, 1981); and *Income Property Appraisal and Analysis* (with Jack P. Friedman—Reston, 1981). He has received numerous recognitions for his writings including the Percy and Betty Wagner Award in 1982 from the American Institute of Real Estate Appraisers.

Dr. Ordway is a member of the Georgia Bar and the American Bar Association. He received his B.A. in political science from Emory University, Georgia, his Juris Doctor from the University of Georgia, and an M.B.A. and a Ph.D. from Georgia State University.

Thomas D. Pearson, Ph.D., is program director and associate professor of Real Estate and Urban Development, Department of Finance, Insurance, Real Estate, and Law, North Texas State University, Denton, Texas. He is currently writing *Real Estate Finance and Investments* for Reston Publishing Company and has published numerous articles in a variety of journals.

Dr. Pearson received his Ph.D. in economics from Georgia State University in 1974 and his M.A. in economics from Louisiana State University in 1966. He is a member of the American Real Estate and Urban Economics Association, Southwestern Society of Economists, the American Institute of Real Estate Appraisers and an affiliate member of the Denton Board of Realtors.

Barbara Phillips is a real estate broker and teacher in the Los Angeles area. She is currently acting as a real estate agent and teaching broker qualification courses at Pasadena City College (P.C.C.). Ms. Phillips was the 1981 "Teacher of the Year" at the P.C.C. real estate division. She is general manager for Real Estate Masters, a professional training school.

She has authored several continuing education courses for California Realtors, accredited by the state Division of Real Estate.

Ms. Phillips has owned and operated her own realty company, is guest speaker at many real estate boards, and is a trainer for several real estate companies.

Augustine Sodaro is the resident manager for Coldwell Banker's Claremont, California, office. He also teaches "prospecting" in the company's "fast start" training program. Previously he was director of administration for the Campus Crusade for Christ, San Bernardino, California.

Mr. Sodaro has received the following awards: *Wall Street Journal* "Student Achievement Award" (1971); "Community Leaders and Noteworthy Americans" award (1975); and the "Notable Americans of the Bicentennial Era" award (1976). He holds a B.A. in business administration from Asusa Pacific College.

James L. Sublett is the executive director of the State Teachers Retirement System of Ohio. Previously, he held the position of executive secretary to the Kentucky Teachers Retirement System.

Mr. Sublett is the past president and current secretary-treasurer of the National Council on Teacher Retirement. He is also a member and past president of the Southern Conference on Teacher Retirement. He has degrees from Transylvania University, Lexington, Kentucky, and the University of Kentucky and has done graduate work at Purdue University and the University of California. He holds an honorary L.L.D. from Eastern Kentucky University.

Beverly F. Tanner was named Certified Financial Planner of the Year, 1980–1981, by the Institute of Certified Financial Planners. She is senior vice president of Planned Investments, Inc., of San Francisco and president of Intravest Centaur Corporation, a financial planning service. A nationally recognized leader in the field, Ms. Tanner lectures at colleges and universities across the country and frequently gives interviews to the press on financial matters. Her latest book is *Shelter What You Make, Minimize the Take* (Reston, 1983).

William R. Thomas, Jr., was named executive vice president of mortgage services for the Federal Home Loan Mortgage Corporation in June 1982. He directs the corporation's regional operations; the development, implementation, and marketing of its mortgage loan purchase programs; and the administrative servicing of its mortgage loan portfolio.

Mr. Thomas previously was executive vice president of mortgage operations. He joined the Mortgage Corporation when it was created in July 1970. He was regional vice president in Indianapolis and Cincinnati, and he was senior vice president in Dallas from 1976 until his appointment as executive vice president in Washington, D.C., in 1977.

A graduate of the U.S. Naval Academy, Mr. Thomas served in the armed forces for 5 years and had a 10-year career in mortgage finance before joining the Mortgage Corporation.

Dennis S. Tosh is holder of the J. Ed Turner Chair of Real Estate at the University of Mississippi. A licensed real estate broker, Dr. Tosh received a Ph.D. in real estate from Georgia State University. He is the author or coauthor of six books, including *Real Estate Principles for License Preparation* (Reston, in press) *Real Estate Math Made Easy* (Reston, 1982), and *Guide to Examinations and Careers in Real Estate* (Reston, 1979).

Dr. Tosh was previously chairman of the Department of Economics and Finance at the University of Baltimore. He is currently a consultant on real estate licensing examinations for the Educational Testing Service (ETS) and the American College of Testing (ACT).

Dr. Tosh is a member of the Real Estate Educators Association, the Real Estate Centers Directors and Chairholders Association, the American Real Estate and Urban Economics Association, and the National Association of Corporate Real Estate Executives.

Maurice A. Unger, formerly a professor of Real Estate at the Graduate School of Business Administration, University of Colorado, is author of *Financial Planning for Retirement* (Dual Publications, 1983), *How To Invest in Real Estate* (McGraw-Hill, Revised edition in press), *Elements of Business Law* (Prentice-Hall, 1968), and *Elements of Real Estate Appraisal* (Wiley, 1982) and coauthor of *Real Estate Principles and Practices*, 7th edition (Southwestern, 1983), *Real Estate Finance* (Southwestern, in press), and *Personal Finance* (Allyn & Bacon, 1972).

Mr. Unger received his J.D. from Duke University, is a member of the New York Bar and the American Arbitration Association, and is past president of both the Denver chapter of the American Society of Appraisers and the Rocky Mountain Business Law Association. He is also a member of the Financial Management Association, the Midwest Business Association, and the Real Estate Educators Association. In addition, he has taught at the University of Idaho, the University of Massachusetts, and the University of Florida.

Ray Watt is chairman of the board and chief executive officer of Watt Industries, one of the country's largest Real Estate Development firms.

Mr. Watt has held prominent positions in the government as well as the private sector. He served in 1969 as a consultant to the secretary of the Department of Housing Partnerships, a corporation established by Congress to accelerate the development of housing for low- and moderate-income families; he still serves on its board.

From 1971 to 1978, Mr. Watt was chairman of the Federal Home Loan Bank of San Francisco. He is a trustee of the University of Southern California, where he received an honorary doctorate of law degree. In addition, he is a trustee of Wells Fargo Real Estate Trust and a member of the board of directors of The Wickes Corporation and holds leadership positions in many business and civic groups. He has been named "Builder of the Year" three times by professional organizations.

William C. Weaver is professor of real estate at North Texas State University. He received an M.B.A. from Loyola University in computer science and management and is a 1980 graduate of the School of Mortgage Banking. He is currently completing his Ph.D. in real estate and urban affairs.

Mr. Weaver has published in various real estate–oriented journals, including: *The Real Estate Appraiser & Analyst, The Mortgage Banker, The Real Estate Securities Journal, The Appraisal Journal, Real Estate Today, Real Estate Issues,* and *Real Estate Review.*

Mr. Weaver's consulting firm, Real Property Consultants, specializes in complex real estate problems.

Preface

You are holding in your hands the only book you may ever need to become successful in real estate.

Designed as an introduction to the field for incoming agents, investors, and those in associated fields as well as a ready reference for the experienced professional, this handbook covers all of real estate with both depth and clarity.

The idea for this book was first considered nearly 3 years ago. At that time several of us involved in real estate lamented the fact that there was no "special book" that would cover the most relevant real estate topics in a way that would give in-depth information and be simple to read.

Soon afterward, work was begun on this book. Dozens of experts endeavored to put their own special mark of excellence into concise chapters on their real estate specialties. The idea was to pack as much information as possible into as few words as possible, all the while maintaining a highly readable format.

The result is this authoritative book. I believe that whether you are an agent, broker, builder, lender, developer, attorney, accountant, appraiser, or investor, you will find true value here.

It is my hope that this book will become the Bible of the real estate industry—required reading, a solid reference for every desktop. If you have a question on real estate and want a detailed answer prepared by an authority on the subject, look in here first.

Robert Irwin

SPECIAL NOTE TO READER

The opinions and materials in this book were prepared by authorities who specialize in real estate. No one, however, can anticipate all the myriad financial situations that readers can find themselves in.

Therefore, this book is sold with the understanding that neither the editor nor any of the contributors is involved in providing accounting, legal, or other services of a professional nature. Before taking any legal, tax, or investment advice it is suggested that the reader consult with his or her own personal attorney.

The McGraw-Hill
Real Estate Handbook

Part **1**

Financing

Chapter 1

Sources of Real Estate Financing

Wayne Archer   Professor of Real Estate, University of Florida

T his chapter is about finding sources of real estate financing. Financing commonly is the element most critical to successful real estate transactions. Especially when interest rates are high, agents or investors who use more sources of money will see more of their transactions succeed!

DIRECT SOURCES OF RESIDENTIAL LOANS

Traditional Sources

Traditional direct sources (originators) of residential mortgage loans are mainly commercial banks, mortgage companies, and thrift institutions [savings and loan associations (S&Ls) and mutual savings banks]. Together they have originated over 95 percent of home first mortgage loans. The relative roles of these sources, shown in Table 1-1, have changed through the years. Savings and loan associations, especially, have increased their share of the market in recent decades thanks to their locations in growth regions and their effective lending programs.

Local Variation in Lenders

How these lenders vary by locality is even more important than the lenders' total market shares. For example, in many areas of the north-

TABLE 1-1 Home Mortgage Loan Originations*
Market Share of Major Lenders
(Percent)

	Commercial banks	Mutual savings banks	Savings and loan associations	Mortgage companies	Federal, state, and local credit agencies	Other	Total
1970	22	6	42	25	4	1	100
1971	22	6	46	22	3	1	100
1972	23	7	48	18	3	1	100
1973	24	7	49	16	3	1	100
1974	24	6	46	19	5	0	100
1975	19	6	53	18	4	0	100
1976	22	6	55	14	3	0	100
1977	23	5	53	16	3	0	100
1978	24	5	49	19	3	0	100
1979	22	5	44	24	3	2	100
1980	22	4	46	22	5	1	100

*One- to four-family nonfarm homes. Excludes loans originated by sellers and nonfinancial businesses, such as real estate brokers.
SOURCE: Office of Financial Management, U.S. Department of Housing and Urban Development.

eastern United States savings and loan associations are eclipsed in home lending by mutual savings banks and commercial banks. As for mortgage companies, their importance as home lenders will vary from city to city, depending on the history and character of the local firms.

Variation in Lending Activity

Lenders have different appetites for home loans. Some commercial banks limit home loans to their established business customers. At the other extreme, mortgage companies have been a steady source of loans on lower- and middle-price homes. Historically they have made government-insured [by the Federal Housing Administration (FHA)] or government-guaranteed [by the Veterans Administration (VA)] loans, which have appealed to first-time home buyers because of low down payments. In between these banks and mortgage companies have been some conservative thrift institutions. They have made conventional loans (not government-insured or -guaranteed) for homes of any price, but with loan-to-value limits suitable only to persons with equity or cash reserves, such as second-time home buyers.

Firms also differ in the variety of loans they offer. Depending on market needs and the style of the firm, the loans have ranged from little more than a single, standard home loan to a wide variety of choices. In the extreme, lenders might even offer "wrap-around" loans and second mortgage loans to supplement existing loans on older homes.*

Deregulation, High Interest Rates, and Revolution in Home Lending

In the past, traditional home lenders had to limit most of their loans to a narrow range of types and terms. But no longer. Financial institutions have seen the elaborate net of regulations that used to govern their actions fall away. This has resulted from the simultaneous impacts of the Depository Institutions Deregulation and Monetary Control Act of 1980 and of an upward surge in interest rates. The shock of these events has set in motion a dominolike tumbling of traditional constraints on real estate lending that will go on for years.

These changes have reached far beyond the thrift institutions and commercial banks. Mortgage companies, for example, have made parallel changes, forced by the competition of changing financial institutions and by the changing requirements of markets in which they resell home loans.

Deregulation and high interest rates have revolutionized the home loan industry. Thrift institutions are merging at unprecedented rates, producing for the first time interstate and even coast-to-coast firms. These mergers will open up new channels by which mortgage loan money can flow, perhaps making even more types of loans available.

In addition to consolidation, a second change in financial institutions is a shift in their real estate activity. Some thrift institutions will deemphasize real estate lending, and some commercial banks and even credit unions may concentrate more on home mortgage loans.

The revolution has been not only in the firms of the industry but also in the industry's product. The traditional fixed-rate level-payment loan has virtually been replaced by alternative mortgage instruments. Loans with adjustable rates, adjustable payments, and even a growing balance (negative amortization) already dominate the market, and still more new instruments are emerging. These include shared-appreciation mortgages (SAMs), price-level-adjusted mortgages (PLAMs), growing-equity mortgages (GEMs), reverse-annuity mortgages (RAMs), and a wider range of second mortgage loans.†

---

*Wrap-around loans, a special type of second mortgage loan, are explained on page 1-5.
†A SAM gives the borrower loan payments based on a below-market interest rate. In return, the lender gets a share of the property appreciation after, say, 10 years. A PLAM requires payments based on a real rate of interest of, say, 4 percent. However, each year the balance remaining is increased by the rate of inflation for the previous year. A GEM

Other Sources of Home Loans

Although thrift institutions, commercial banks, and mortgage companies have long originated the bulk of home loans, there are a host of
smaller sources as well. What is available depends on the locality, the
characteristics of the home, and the characteristics of the borrower.
Several important examples of special programs, including rural home
loans, "gap" financing for existing homes, and participation financing,
follow.

Rural Home Loans.   Rural home buyers may be eligible for a home
loan from either of two exceptionally low-cost programs. The first program operates through the Federal Land Bank. For an owner-occupied
residence on a full-time farm the program has provided 75 percent
loans up to $80,000 at 4 to 6 percentage points below the market rate
of interest. The second program operates through the Farmers Home
Administration (FmHA). This program restricts eligibility to households
with below-average incomes and also restricts house design (for example, no family room or air conditioner); it provides funds at several
percentage points below the market level.

Gap Financing of Existing Homes.   A buyer of an existing home may
want to preserve the old mortgage loan, either to avoid financing fees
or to preserve a favorable interest rate. This may be possible if the loan
is government-insured or if it otherwise lacks an enforceable due-on-
sale clause. However, the problem with preserving existing financing
is that there usually is a large gap between the sale price and the
existing loan balance.

The solution to this gap can be found through second mortgage
financing. Several forms of second mortgages are possible. One might
come from the seller through a purchase-money mortgage. This
amounts to either an installment payment or a delayed balloon payment of the gap difference. Normally it is secured by a second mortgage
executed simultaneously with transfer of title. Such loans have long
been the second largest method of home financing behind institutional
first mortgage loans.

A second gap arrangement might be a similar loan provided not by
the seller but by a third party. Third parties may be first mortgage
lenders wanting to negotiate compromise loans to improve their own
incomes, or they may be some other institutional lenders. Frequently,

---

starts out as would a standard fixed-rate mortgage loan. However, after each year the
payments increase by the previous year's rate of inflation. The effect is to shorten the loan
life as inflation increases. A RAM begins with no balance but accumulates one as the
borrower receives regular advances from the lender.

however, they are simply individuals investing through a trusted broker. (These persons will depend heavily on the broker to underwrite the loans adequately.) For some cases with FHA or VA loans a special source of second mortgage money is available. Since 1981, if the first mortgage loan on an existing home is held by the Federal National Mortgage Association (FNMA), a second mortgage loan on that home can be sold to FNMA. This provides an attractive solution to the gap problem for many sellers of homes financed by the FHA or the VA.

An especially attractive way to preserve an existing loan is by a so-called wrap-around loan. The glory of a wrap-around loan is that it looks and acts as a first mortgage loan. The borrower makes a single monthly payment to the second mortgage lender (possibly the seller of the home) that is sufficient to cover both old and new loan payments. The second lender, in turn, makes the payment to the original lender. Thus the second lender has security for its loan much as if by a first mortgage. The payments can amortize to the end of the old loan term, or they may partially amortize and then balloon at the end of the old loan term. The wrap-around loan could even have negative amortization until the old loan is paid off.

Wrap-around loans minimize stress of the loan on both buyer and lender (seller). They provide a single, level payment that covers both loans. They amortize over a longer period than do straight second mortgage loans. They provide low risk and high yield to the lender.

The greatest problem with gap financing is that the primary source (the seller) usually needs cash for a subsequent home purchase. However, this problem is not always severe, because the seller frequently can convert a well-made second mortgage loan to cash. Sometimes one can "discount" the loan to a third party, usually at some loss. More commonly, one can use the "paper" from the second mortgage loan as collateral for a bank loan. These recourses partially offset the illiquidity problem with seller gap financing.

Participation or Joint Venture Financing.   Home financing became an unsolvable problem for many when interest rates rose sharply in the late 1970s. Perhaps the most intriguing solutions to the interest payment problem have been through third-party participations in the financing and ownership, sometimes called "shared-equity mortgages" (SEMs). Under these plans a third-party investor becomes a co-owner as tenant in common along with the buyer. The investor makes part of or all the down payment for the home and possibly some portion of the monthly payments. In return, the investor gets a share of the interest and tax deductions plus a share of the equity at sale. Four items are divided between the owner and investor: down payment, monthly payment, tax deductions, and proceeds from the sale. The shares of each can be negotiated separately. In addition, the investor may be able to claim tax deductions for depreciation.

It is a potentially rewarding challenge during times of high interest rates to locate investors for participation home loans. The investor can be a parent or other relative, the seller, a broker, the primary lender, or any other person with a comparatively high marginal tax rate. In many instances the participation could offer the investor a very high yield asset that would also diversify his or her investment portfolio. Although shared-equity financing has several limitations (it is complex and it departs from the traditional notion of home ownership), it could be increasingly useful as a step between renting and ownership.

INDIRECT SOURCES OF RESIDENTIAL LOANS

The types and terms of home loans are quoted by the loan originators. But what they offer is heavily influenced by the ultimate sources of capital. This section introduces major indirect sources of home loan funds, including subsidized home mortgage loans, giving special attention to the emerging secondary mortgage markets, to mortgage-backed securities, and to retirement and pension funds.

Secondary Mortgage Markets

Since the late 1960s secondary mortgage markets have had increasing influence as sources of home loans. The key organizations involved are the FNMA, the Federal Home Loan Mortgage Corporation (FHLMC), and the Government National Mortgage Association (GNMA). Although these organizations do not originate mortgage loans, they do provide a secondary market where originators can turn over inventories of loans to originate new ones. Increasingly, these agencies have assumed major roles in a process called "mortgage banking," in which firms originate loans only to sell them to indirect investors with continuing loan servicing provided.

The institutions of the secondary mortgage market grew out of concern about the shortage of funds flowing to home loans. The concern motivated Congress, in 1968, to establish the legislative framework. In that year it reorganized FNMA, making it a quasi-private institution to buy and sell home mortgage loans. Also, it established GNMA as part of the Department of Housing and Urban Development, including in its powers the power to guarantee securities backed by pools of government-insured or -guaranteed home loans. Then in 1970 Congress created the FHLMC to purchase and sell conventional home loans and to issue participations in home loan pools.

Both FNMA and the FHLMC have grown rapidly and have responded to a deregulated industry by expanding the types of loans they accept. FNMA, for example, accepts all standard types of government-insured loans (their original specialty) plus a growing variety of variable-rate and graduated-payment conventional loans, various second mortgage loans for up to 15 years in term, loans originated with interest-rate "buydowns," and variable-rate graduated-payment loans secured by residences on leasehold estates. The FHLMC has expanded to purchases of home improvement loans; older low-yield conventional loans; and adjustable mortgage loans.*

The growth of mortgage banking and of secondary markets has given the policies of FNMA and FHLMC much weight in home mortgage lending. Many lenders now will originate loans only if the loans qualify for sale to FNMA and FHLMC. (The two organizations have gone far to jointly specify loan documentation that is used industrywide.) Thus, in many situations, what loans are available will depend on what can be sold through FHLMC or FNMA.

Mortgage-Backed Securities

An early step forward in secondary mortgage markets was the creation of mortgage-backed securities. The prototype was the GNMA pass-through security. Under this program, the originator of, say, a million-dollar pool of FHA or VA loans can sell undivided interests in the pool through GNMA certificates; GNMA guarantees timely payment of principal and interest to the purchaser, thus eliminating default risk. The originator usually remains the servicer and administrator of the loan pool.

Activity in mortgage-backed securities has been expanding. GNMA pass-through activity grew in the early 1970s; in the mid-1970s use of FHLMC participation certificates grew; and in the late 1970s several privately sponsored mortgage-backed securities were issued. In the early 1980s FNMA mortgage-backed securities for conventional mortgage loans have been introduced. Now that the patterns are well established, lenders and private mortgage insurance firms are issuing a new generation of specialized mortgage-backed securities.†

*The programs of FNMA and FHLMC are steadily evolving. Current descriptions are always available from regional offices or from the home offices in Washington, D.C.

†See Mark Korell, "Second Generation Mortgage Pass-through Certificates," *Pension World*, June 1982.

Pension and Retirement Funds

Private pension funds and government retirement funds are considered the growth source of the future in real estate finance. In assets, as shown in Table 1-2, they already surpass the life insurance industry. With their accelerating growth rate, they are expected soon to surpass the savings and loan associations. So far their investment in real estate has been small, averaging perhaps 2 to 3 percent of assets. But they appear to be increasing this commitment for the future to between 5 and 15 percent. Thus, by any estimate they will become a major source of funds for home mortgage loans.

These entities invest indirectly in home loans through mortgage-backed securities, and so the evolution of such securities is a key to their future investment in home loans. Special mortgage-backed securities programs are emerging in many states which enable state retirement funds, as well as private pension funds, to invest in pools of home loans originated within the state. In some cases the mortgages in the plan are experimental in design, such as growing-equity mortgages.

Subsidized Sources of Home Loans

Several special sources of home mortgage loans are available at subsidized rates. In a number of states and localities, public bond issues have been used to fund home loans at below-market interest rates for low- and moderate-income buyers. Usually the mortgages are originated through traditional home mortgage lenders.

The volume of these programs has been modest through mid-1981. At least forty-two states have operated tax-exempt programs for home mortgage financing, with average cumulative authorizations of slightly over $300 million per state. The activity has been concentrated, however. For example, Alaska, Connecticut, Kentucky, New Mexico, and

TABLE 1-2 Selected Sources of Funds for Home Mortgage Loans by Total Assets

(Billions of Dollars)

	Savings and loan associations	Total life insurance companies	Life insurance pension fund reserves	Retirement and pension funds*
1975	338.2	279.7	72.2	251.8
1980	629.8	469.8	165.8	484.9

*State and local retirement funds and private pension funds.
SOURCE: Federal Reserve Board, Flows of Funds Division.

Rhode Island have funded some of the larger programs despite their relatively smaller populations.*

In addition to home loan subsidy programs by states, there have been a number of municipal programs. However, political resistance to these programs appears significant because they tend to strain municipal credit to subsidize middle-income buyers. It does not seem likely that these local programs will grow.

In the past the U.S. government funded mammoth volumes of subsidized home purchases. The central program was the FHA 235 program enacted in the Housing and Urban Development Act of 1968. However, the FHA 235 program virtually had been closed down by 1982, along with most other U.S. housing subsidy programs.

SOURCES OF INCOME PROPERTY FINANCING

Compared to home financing, income property financing is a world apart. What separates it is its focus: it shifts from buyer affordability to investment return. In other words, the primary underwriting analysis shifts from income of the owner to income of the property. Thus income property financing calls for specialized lenders who have knowledge of income-producing real estate.

Savings and Loan Associations

The savings and loan associations are important income property financers.† Well over half make income property loans. About half of their loans are for multifamily residences. Another large portion is for subdivision development—presumably leading to subsequent loans on the homes to be built. The remainder cover the spectrum of income property loans from restaurants to warehouses.

Savings and loan associations have financed mainly smaller income properties, usually in their local area, but what they finance depends partly on their size. Although the typical savings and loan association will deal with properties involving, say, less than a million dollars, billion-dollar firms can handle loans of almost any size.

Most savings and loan associations have tended to follow conventional

*Data are from "1981 Survey of Housing Finance Agencies," Council of State Housing Agencies, Washington, D.C., 1981.

†Impressions reported here are based on a special survey of the Federal Home Loan Bank Board, which covered income property loans from savings and loan associations for 1975 through 1978.

practices in income property lending, but some of all sizes have been innovative and aggressive. These firms have readily entered into joint ventures, participation loans, and financing of unusual properties. Many have set up service corporations with broad freedom to develop and invest in income property.

Mutual Savings Banks

Mutual savings banks tend to be veterans at financing income property. They have long had greater freedom and greater size than the typical savings and loan association. Because of their location in the slower-growth, mature economy of the northeastern United States, they felt the need early on to expand their investments beyond traditional single-family home loans. Mutual savings banks have financed all types of income property in their home region, and larger ones have sought investments elsewhere, often by purchasing loans from distant mortgage companies who continue to administer the loan on their behalf.

Mortgage Companies

Mortgage companies have been trailblazers in income property finance. Early in the twentieth century they began by charting a network of correspondent relationships between farmers of the Midwest who needed capital and life insurance companies of the Northeast that needed investment opportunities. Following World War II the mortgage companies were at the forefront in exploring creative methods of financing income-producing real estate. In more recent times they have been early participants in secondary mortgage markets for home loans. Most recently they have been among the first organizations to seek new forms of real estate finance that will attract the interest of the swelling pension funds. Some mortgage companies limit their originations largely to single-family homes, but most provide a wide range of mortgage lending services.

Life Insurance Companies

Life insurance companies have been a prime source of funds for income-producing real estate, especially in the last two decades. After years of fruitful investment first in loans on farms and then in FHA and VA loans on homes, they recognized the premium opportunities emerging in loans for shopping centers and other large-income properties.

Generally, life insurance companies have shown sophistication in underwriting real estate investments. They have restricted their investment to large-scale, permanent loans, leaving small loans, construction loans, and most development loans to other lenders more suited to handling them. Their real estate sophistication was evident during the severe overbuilding of the mid-1970s; life insurance lenders appear to have anticipated the worst situations considerably better than most lenders.

The real estate investment policy of a life insurance company (or other insurance company) depends heavily on its size. A relatively small number of the largest companies hold the vast share of real estate investments in the industry. Small- and medium-size life insurance companies have quite varied interests in real estate, including loans to a particular highly creditworthy firm, loans on a particular class of properties, or little more than their own buildings.

Commercial Banks

Although they are a factor in all phases of income real estate finance because of their sheer volume of assets, commercial banks play a special role as construction lenders. They have provided the vast majority of construction loans for medium- to large-scale income properties. As with thrift institutions and life insurance companies, the form of commercial bank activities in real estate depends much on bank size as well as on the management and territory of the bank.

Real Estate Investment Trusts

For a while, real estate investment trusts (REITs) were an attractive source of funds for many swashbuckling developers. The rise and fall of REITs is the most sensational story in modern real estate finance. Investors began to form REITs in 1961 after Congress enacted a tax law treating them as nontaxed conduits similar to mutual funds. Through the 1960s REITs increasingly were thought of as mutual funds for real estate with near panacea potential. Through REITs the small investor could participate in the rich returns of real estate investment. Since REITs were unregulated in a world of highly regulated lenders, they could be the way, at last, to funnel large amounts of capital into the risky but high-return types of real estate finance.

And funnel they did! Two types of REITs were well established in time for the real estate boom of the early 1970s, and they flourished. The more deliberate of the two types was the equity REIT, acquiring ownership in a wide variety of income-producing real estate. The more sensational of the two was the mortgage REIT. Typically, it sold shares of beneficial interest and then leveraged the proceeds with massive bank lines of credit, investing the capital heavily in construction loans for commercial property. By the end of 1974 REIT assets had grown to over $21 billion, perhaps 20 percent of the amount of real estate assets held by life insurance companies at the time; 72 percent of these assets were held by mortgage REITs.

The balloon popped in 1974 and 1975 with the severe real estate recession. In a host of ways mortgage REITs had been reckless, and when demand for real estate fell as interest rates and costs rose, REITs reaped what they had sown.* They experienced massive defaults on loans that other lenders would not make in the first place.

Mortgage REITs are nearly a thing of the past, but equity REITs have survived. The REIT industry at the outset of the 1980s is experiencing moderate growth and generally is regaining its health. The mortgage REIT may yet reappear for special purposes. For example, a large mortgage banking firm recently considered establishing a REIT to fund shared-appreciation mortgage loans for apartment projects. Other special applications of the REIT vehicle seem plausible.

Pension Funds

In income property finance, just as with home finance, pension and retirement funds are considered the source of the future. The approaches to real estate by pension funds vary enormously. Further, changing state laws are opening the door to even greater diversity, through equity investments.

Many pension funds invest indirectly in real estate through a commingled real estate fund. An example is Prudential's PRISA. This pioneering open-ended fund has several hundred pension fund participants and, with over $3.7 billion, it holds a large number and large variety of real estate assets.

Commingled real estate funds come in many shapes and sizes. They are sponsored by most major life insurance companies and by major banks. The funds concentrate on income property investments, but their strategies are various. Some are diversified over the spectrum of equity, equity-debt, and debt investments, although most appear to concentrate on the mortgage end of this spectrum. Many invest in a wide range of property types and others specialize. Some seek large properties and others seek smaller investments such as neighborhood shopping centers or medium-size suburban office buildings.†

Pension and retirement funds frequently combine investment in a

---

*An excellent analysis of REIT errors is provided by Howard H. Stevenson in "Lessons from the Mortgage Trust Experience," *Real Estate Review,* Fall 1976, pp. 72–77.

†The activity of commingled real estate funds and other real estate investments of pension funds are regularly tracked in such publications as *Pension World* and *The Institutional Investor.*

commingled fund with their own direct investments. Once again, the direct investment can range widely by form of investment and type of property. One popular approach is the convertible mortgage, which gives the fund equity appreciation while it leaves the mortgagor with several years of tax-deduction benefits.*

Foreign Capital

Another source of real estate capital is foreign investment, although it appears to be mostly for equity. There are abundant impressions but few hard numbers concerning the patterns of foreign investment. Perhaps all that is clear is that it has come from many regions, including Canada, England, West Germany, the Netherlands, the Middle East, and Central and South America. How the money is invested varies somewhat by region as well as by source. For example, there appears to be a not-unexpected concentration of Latin American investment through Miami. As one observer has noted, whatever the source, once the money arrives in the United States, it appears to behave not unlike money from U.S. sources.†

Sources for Acquisition and Development

The world of income property finance has several specialized needs that require special loans. One example is acquisition and development financing. Institutional lenders historically have been unable to finance raw land being held for development, so other sources have had to be found. Perhaps the most common solution to this problem has been for the buyer-developer to purchase the land on a contract for deed. If this will not work, the developer has to turn to equity partners or find a source of funds both sufficiently knowledgeable and able to risk the loan. These have been scarce. However, one source that is becoming more common is the service corporations of some savings and loan associations. These entities have gained more latitude in recent years to undertake risky loans, and they should have an interest in acquisition loans because these loans could lead to subsequent investment opportunities by the service corporation and its parent. Mortgage companies are a second potential source of acquisition financing. Again, because the deal may lead to subsequent opportunities for investment, the

---

*The convertible mortgage converts to an equity interest, either automatically or at the option of the lender. The conversion can be gradual, or it can occur at one or more option dates at a predetermined price or a predetermined capitalization of income.

†Some impressions of foreign investments can be found in Jack Friedman, "The Truth about Foreign Investors in U.S. Real Estate," *Real Estate Review*, Fall 1980, pp. 13–15, and in Robert C. Jackson, "Foreign Investors Love New York," *Real Estate Review*, Summer 1981, pp. 55–61.

mortgage company often will try to maintain a source of acquisition financing.

Standby Sources

A second form of special loan is the standby commitment for a permanent loan. Often, to make construction loans, lenders will require advanced commitments by permanent lenders to "take out," or pay off, the construction loans when the projects are complete. If developers believe that they can negotiate more favorable permanent loans after construction begins, they will seek substitute "standby commitments" to qualify for the construction loans. They will pay a fee for the commitment, but they will use the commitment only if better financing fails to materialize. Standby commitments can come from many of the same sources as do permanent income property loans.

Sources of Gap Loans

A third specialized form of loan is gap financing. This becomes necessary when the long-term or permanent loan commitment that will pay off a construction loan pays only a "floor" amount—perhaps 80 percent of the total commitment—until a required occupancy is achieved. The gap between the floor amount and the construction-loan amount may be financed by a separate short-term lender until adequate occupancy brings about full permanent financing. In addition to traditional lenders, some major nonfinancial corporations have invested in these gap loans. At a surplus stage of their cash cycle they can realize a handsome short-term yield on the surplus by investing in these loans. Usually, they will make the loan through a mortgage company or other intermediary.

Sale Leaseback

For corporations that have strong credit but high cash needs (perhaps for expansion) one way to reduce borrowing is through sale leaseback of facilities. The simplest arrangement is to sell the land and building to, say, a life insurance company or pension fund and then to lease back net (the occupant pays all expenses). A more sophisticated sale leaseback involves the land alone. This arrangement preserves the tax-depreciation deductions of the building for the occupant, giving the land—with no depreciation—to the low- or zero-tax investor.

Tax-Exempt Financing

For projects which help build the economy of a local area, below-market financing may be possible through industrial-development bonds (IDBs). The bonds are issued under the auspices of state or local government and thereby have tax-exempt status. They are an obligation not of the government but rather of the project owner (who must be private). Still, they typically market at rates well below commercial mortgage rates.

IDBs can finance a wider range of projects than is apparent. In addition to manufacturing-related projects, they appear to be applicable, for example, to a wide range of downtown redevelopment projects, health care facilities, and education-related facilities. Currently, the maximum financing of $10 million (with limits on prior and subsequent use of IDBs by the borrower) is sufficient to finance a multitude of small- to medium-scale projects that contribute to a local economy.

Small Business Administration

Rapid property appreciation increases the incentive for businesses to own their facilities. Where a business chooses to own, it may find attractive financing of its facilities through loan guarantee programs of the Small Business Administration (SBA). Provided that the firm meets the requirements, it may be able to obtain a loan with up to 90 percent or $500,000 (1982) guaranteed for the lender. The loan can be for 20 years (in some cases, up to 25 years). It can cover the cost of expansion or acquisition of everything from land to equipment. The loan interest rate can be a fixed rate or based on the prime interest rate.

Eligibility for SBA guaranteed loans encompasses a wide range of firms. While the applicant must have a viable business, the firm can be surprisingly large, with up to 1500 employees in some cases of manufacturing firms, up to $8 million gross business for service firms, and up to $7.5 million sales for retailing.

CONCLUSION

Whether one is seeking home financing or income property financing, the sources and types of financing are anything but routine. In the turbulent financial climate of the 1980s the instruments and sources of finance are going through drastic, continuous change. So the real estate broker or investor who has always been a student of properties and potential buyers must also be a student of the marketplace for real estate finance.

The New Mortgages

Robert Irwin

A few years ago a chapter on new mortgages would have been unthinkable. Between the 1930s and 1980 there was virtually only one kind of mortgage—the fixed-interest-rate loan. It was a standard which everyone used and understood.

However, in 1980 with the emergence of very high interest rates paid on savings and a savings and loan association (S&L) industry stuck with a huge portfolio of old long-term low-interest-paying mortgages, things changed. Lenders no longer wanted to make 30-year loans at a fixed rate of interest. They were afraid that short-term costs to them (interest paid on savings) might rise before the loan was paid back, and thus they would lose huge amounts of money. And borrowers found that very often they could not qualify for mortgages at higher interest rates.

These two concerns—by the lender who did not want to be stuck with a portfolio of lower-than-market-rate loans and by the borrower who could not afford to purchase a house because of high interest rates—led to the creation of an "alphabet soup" of new mortgages. Each new form of mortgage can be viewed as an attempt to address the concerns of the lender and borrower. And each attempted to do this a bit differently.

FIXED-RATE MORTGAGE

The fixed-rate mortgage that was so widely accepted during the past 40 years really is not the old institution that most people think. The fixed-rate mortgage does not go back much beyond the Great Depression of the 1930s, when it was created with the help of the government-sponsored Federal Housing Administration (FHA). Prior to that time there were relatively few fixed-rate mortgages. In fact, prior to the 1930s, the mortgage market looked very much as it does today, with a wide variety of shorter-term or adjustable-rate instruments.

The fixed-rate mortgage is simply a loan in which the rate of interest is set, or fixed, when the mortgage is initiated and does not change during the life of the loan. For example, if the rate is set at 10 percent, then that is the interest that the borrower pays (usually only on the remaining balance of the mortgage, called "amortizing" the debt) for its entirety, up to 30 or 40 years. At year 27, for example, on a 30-year loan, the interest rate is still 8 percent, even if short-term interest rates happen to be 20 percent (or 3 percent).

The advantage to the borrower of the fixed-rate mortgage is enormous. The borrower can lock in an interest rate so that she or he will know in advance exactly what the monthly payment and debt reduction will be. Additionally, appreciation to the property benefits only the borrower, not the lender. For these reasons the fixed-rate mortgage was the foundation of the real estate boom that occurred after World War II and, in truth, continued until about 1980.

The disadvantages to the lender, however, are enormous. The lender is locked into receiving a fixed rate of interest for a very long time. Although this was not a problem while interest rates overall remained stable and savers were willing to, in effect, subsidize mortgages by keeping their funds in low-interest-paying savings accounts, it proved a disaster when rates shot up in 1980. Lending institutions in some cases were *paying out* interest on savings at 14 percent while their *income* from mortgages averaged closer to 9 percent.

In addition, in some fourteen states the due-on-sale clause, which allowed lenders to call in fixed-rate mortgages on the sale of the property, was declared unenforceable. This meant the lender was locked into a losing mortgage even if there was a new borrower. This inability to roll over portfolios from low-interest long-term debt to higher-interest short-term debt caused a financial crisis in 1981 to 1982 which threatened to bankrupt the savings and loan industry. Relief, however, was offered by the Supreme Court, which reinstated the enforceability of due-on-sale clauses for federally chartered S&Ls in 1982. Parity for state-chartered savings and loan associations followed in many states.

One would think that, given the turmoil in financial markets in recent years, the fixed-rate mortgage would be dead. That, however, is far from true. A great many lenders have discovered that borrowers balk at the other mortgages being offered. To maintain their business, many lenders have been forced to return to offering the fixed-rate mortgage, although usually at 1 point higher than its alternatives.

RENEGOTIATED MORTGAGE

The fixed-rate mortgage offered today by most institutions is a sort of hybrid. It does offer a fixed rate, and the monthly payback is calculated usually over 30 years, but the term of the mortgage is often set for a much shorter time. For example, one might have a mortgage for 10 percent over 30 years to be renegotiated in 5 years.

In other words, for the first 5 years, the mortgage is treated exactly as if it were a 30-year mortgage fixed at 10 percent. At year 5, however, the interest rate is renegotiated. It might be adjusted up or down either for another 5-year term or for the balance of the mortgage. For example, if rates were higher after 5 years, the mortgage might be renegotiated up to, say, 15 percent. The new rate is then amortized over the remaining term.

Note that "renegotiate" does not mean that the borrower and lender sit down and argue with equal strength on what the interest rate should be. Rather, the lender dictates the interest rate (almost any rate, but usually the mortgage market rate or a little lower) and may be committed to only one thing—guaranteeing to offer a loan to the borrower.

The borrower, however, has the option of taking what the lender offers or paying off the loan in full, usually without penalty. Assuming the lender offers the market rate or close to it, most borrowers accept the terms.

At the time of this renegotiation the lender may also offer the borrower other alternatives. These could include an adjustable-rate or a graduated-payment mortgage. In addition, the lender may agree to renegotiate the repayment period back up to a full 30 years, thus reducing the monthly payment.

ADJUSTABLE-RATE MORTGAGE

In an adjustable-rate mortgage (ARM) the interest rate is set only for a short time, typically 6 months. After that 6-month period, the rate is adjusted either upward or downward according to an index. The most commonly used indexes are mortgage rates on previously occupied homes, 3-year Treasury-bill (T-bill) rates, and 6-month T-bill rates.

If a lender, for example, used the 6-month T-bill rate and during the past 6 months that rate increased by 1 percentage point, the interest rate on the mortgage could be increased (at the lender's option) by 1 point. If the T-bill rate decreased, then the mortgage rate (in most cases) would have to decrease accordingly.

The adjustable-rate mortgage differs considerably from the older variable-rate mortgage (VRM). In a VRM, typically the mortgage rate could not be increased by more than 0.5 percent during each 6-month period and usually could never be increased by more than 2.5 percent over the original interest rate.

In an ARM, however, the mortgage rate can be increased by *any amount justified by the index.* If, for example, 6-month T-bill rates shot up by 5 percent, then the mortgage interest rate could also be raised by 5 percent.

One obvious thing about an ARM is its unpredictability. For example, a borrower whose initial interest rate was 10 percent, assuming a $100,-000 mortgage amortized over 30 years, would have a monthly payment for the first 6 months of the loan of about $875. If during that period the index to which the mortgage was tied jumped, say, 4 percent, then during the next 6 months the borrower might have a 14 percent mortgage. Again assuming a $100,000 loan for 30 years, the monthly payment would soar to about $1185! That's an increase of over 35 percent in monthly payment virtually overnight.

Of course, such dramatic fluctuations are highly unusual in the mortgage market interest rate. Changes have occurred during a 6-month period of as much as 7.5 percent in the 6-month T-bill rate and of nearly 4 percent in the 3-year Treasury rate.

Few, if any, borrowers are capable of absorbing such a dramatic change in monthly payments. Therefore, many lenders have voluntarily "capped" the monthly payment. Typically this cap specifies that within any given period (usually 6 months to a year) the monthly payment will not be allowed to rise by more than 7.5 percent. In the previous example, the initial monthly payment was $875, and 7.5 percent of that amount is about $66. The monthly payment, therefore, could not rise above $940 for that period.

$875	Initial monthly payment
66	Maximum 7.5% increase
$940	New monthly payment

Capping monthly payments may seem like an acceptable solution, since it does keep down the monthly payment for the borrower, but it really is merely a deferral of interest. Clearly, if the rate on the mortgage rises by 4 percent, an increase of $66 on the monthly payment will not cover it. Indeed, to fully amortize the mortgage at 14 percent, the payment must be $1185 per month. The payment of $940 is $245 per month short. What happens to this shortage?

In the case of an ARM it is added to the principal. In other words, in this situation, the amount the borrower owes increases! This is called "negative amortization." Thus if a borrower obtains a mortgage with an initially low interest rate and then finds that the index to which the ARM is tied rises, he or she could end up owing a great deal more than was originally borrowed. Ultimately, the borrower is placed in the position of paying interest on interest.

Another way of looking at this is to realize that with an ARM a lender is, in effect, participating in the future appreciation of the property. In an ARM in which negative amortization has taken place, when the borrower sells, she or he does not get *all* the benefits of equity increase. Some must go to the lender.

Prepayment of ARMs without penalty is allowed usually within 30 days of any interest adjustment; ARMs, however, normally have due-on-sale clauses and thus probably are not assumable.

GRADUATED-PAYMENT MORTGAGE

The ARM solves the liquidity problem for the lender, but it does next to nothing about reducing the monthly payment to affordable rates for the borrower. One answer has been the graduated-payment mortgage (GPM).

The GPM works as a trade-off. In exchange for lower payments in the first years of the mortgage, the borrower agrees to make higher payments in the later years. The actual amount by which the monthly payment can be reduced in the first few years can be quite substantial —in some plans 25 percent or more. For example, a $35,000, 30-year fixed-rate mortgage at 8.5 percent has a monthly payment of $269. Under one plan used by the FHA, in the first year the mortgage payment was reduced to $203. In each succeeding year it increased by about $16 per month until year 5, when it reached $291 and remained at that level for the remainder of the term.

The GPM is generally recommended for young couples who expect their incomes to rise in the near future. Presumably, as their incomes rise, they will be able to afford increasingly higher payments. It generally is not recommended for older borrowers or those on fixed incomes.

A GPM can be either a fixed-rate or an adjustable-rate mortgage. Some lenders in recent years have combined the GPM with the ARM to produce a mortgage whose monthly payments can fluctuate according to both an index *and* a predetermined graduated schedule.

SHARED-APPRECIATION MORTGAGE

At a time when housing prices were rising, some lenders proposed to share appreciation in the property with the borrower. These shared-appreciation mortgages (SAMs) typically would offer a substantial interest rate reduction, say 40 percent, for 40 percent of the profit when the property was eventually sold.

The subsequent downward performance of the housing market coupled with difficulties in operating SAMs (who is to determine when the house should be sold, who gets the benefits of improvements made exclusively by the borrower, and so forth) has made SAMs unpopular. The very few SAMs that were actually funded were mainly in Florida.

ACCELERATED-PAYMENT MORTGAGES

Over the past few years borrowers have discovered an interesting phenomenon with regard to long-term mortgages. In the initial years almost the entire monthly payment goes to interest. For example, for a $100,000 loan at 12 percent for 30 years, the first month's payment is roughly $1028. Of that amount $1000 goes to interest and only $28 to principal reduction! In the second month $999.71 goes to interest, and the amount that goes to principal is *increased* by only $0.29! Clearly, it will take a very long time (more than 20 years) before there is a substantial reduction in the principal.

If, however, the borrower pays additional amounts toward the principal (over and above what is called for in the amortized monthly payment), the loan can be paid off much faster. By simply doubling the principal payments (initially paying only about $28 more per month) the loan can be paid back in less than half the 30-year period at a reduction of more than half of the interest otherwise charged! Many borrowers, therefore, have been "accelerating" their mortgages, or paying them off earlier.

In response, lenders have begun offering a growing-equity mortgage (GEM). A GEM is nothing more than a shorter-term mortgage. Typically it is for 15 to 20 years. It offers rapid, or accelerated, payoff of mortgage debt—something both borrower and lender highly approve of.

GEMs also do not involve much higher monthly payments. For example, it takes $1028 to pay off a $100,000 mortgage at 12 percent interest for 30 years. In 20 years the same mortgage can be paid off at about $1100 per month. In 15 years it is $1200, and for 10 years it is about $1435.

Monthly payback of $100,000 at 12 percent (fully amortized)

$1028	30 years
1100	20 years
1200	15 years
1435	10 years

Note that to cut the length of the mortgage by one-third (from 30 to 20 years) increases the monthly payment by only $72. Cutting the length of the mortgage in half increases the monthly payment by only $172, or about 17 percent of the total monthly payment. From these figures it is easy to see why so many borrowers are opting for APMs.

FEDERAL HOUSING ADMINISTRATION

Federal Housing Administration (FHA) loans were extremely popular during the 1950s and early 1960s. A significant portion of homes that were sold had this type of financing. By the 1970s, however, less than 10 percent of all mortgages were FHA-insured. Their inconvenience, complexities, and high cost to sellers made them unpopular. Today the FHA operates under the Department of Housing and Urban Development (HUD) and FHA loans are again popular.

There have been numerous FHA programs in the past, including:

Title II

203(b)	Financing one-family to four-family dwellings
203	Special financing for veterans
207	Rental housing and mobile home parks
221(d)	Low-cost dwellings for one to four families
222	One-family homes for service personnel
234(f)	Condominiums
234(d)	Condominium conversions
235	Assistance to low-income families in the form of mortgage subsidies

In general, the FHA operates as a giant insurance company. In most cases, the FHA does not advance any money. Rather it insures a mortgage (of one of the varieties discussed earlier) to a lender. In other words, if the borrower defaults, the FHA ensures that the lender will not lose any money. To pay for this insurance, the FHA charges 0.5 percent, which is added to the interest rate and paid by the borrower.

Federal Housing Administration loans have certain advantages. For example, they have traditionally been fully assumable; there have been no prepayment penalties; and there is a very low down payment, as low as 3 percent in some cases.

There are also, however, certain disadvantages. *Both* the buyer and the property must meet rigid standards. Because the loans are often offered at below-market mortgage rates, the seller (the buyer is prohibited) must often pay many points to obtain the loan. (A "point" equals 1 percent of the total mortgage amount.) Occasionally in tight markets a seller pays 8 to 10 points. Also, the process of applying for and obtaining the FHA loan can be filled with red tape and can be discouraging.

The borrower must establish a "trust account" on FHA loans. This is an account administered by the lender in which the borrower pays enough each month that at year end the lender can pay both the taxes and the insurance on the property. In addition, to qualify for an FHA mortgage, the buyer must agree to live on the property.

More information on FHA loans can be obtained by checking with any local HUD office or almost any institutional lender.

VETERANS ADMINISTRATION LOANS

Veterans Administration (VA) loans continue to be popular. They are available to U.S. veterans. In general, to qualify a veteran must have been in the armed forces after January 31, 1955, and must have served continuously on active duty for at least 181 days. In addition, the veteran must have other than a dishonorable discharge. Special rules also apply to veterans of World War II and the Korean and Vietnamese wars.

As under an FHA loan, under a VA loan the government advances no money. Rather it "guarantees" (as opposed to "insures") the veteran's purchase. This amounts to guaranteeing to repay the lender a certain portion of the mortgage. In 1950 the amount guaranteed was $4000; more recently it was $20,000. The amount of the guarantee is frequently adjusted by the VA.

Lenders are willing to make, for example, an $80,000 mortgage with only a $20,000 guarantee because the VA guarantees against the loss of the *first* $20,000. In other words, if there is a foreclosure of a $80,000 mortgage and at auction sale the property brings only $60,000, the VA will make up the whole $20,000 difference. (Any additional amount will be a loss to the lender.) Since properties rarely sell for less than 20 to 25 percent of the loaned amount, even at auction sale, it is a fairly safe guarantee. Lenders have generally been willing to make VA loans equal to 4 or 5 times the guarantee amount.

Under a VA loan, typically the veteran does not have to make any down payment. The VA, however, approves the property and issues a certificate of reasonable value (CRV), which is the maximum mortgage amount it will allow. The veteran may pay more than the CRV but must do so out of personal funds.

The VA also has rigorous qualifications for veterans. However, the veteran may appeal a turndown, and the VA will listen to and sometimes act favorably on explanations of unusual circumstances.

As with the FHA loan, the owner must intend to occupy the property; the purchase cannot be for investment. Also a trust fund to cover taxes and insurance is mandatory.

One interesting aspect of VA loans is that the "entitlement," or the amount of guarantee to which a veteran is entitled, has increased over the years. The result is that veterans who still qualify and who originally were only entitled to, for example, $7500 may still have $12,500 of a $20,000 entitlement left. This means that they may be able to reuse their benefits on a new VA purchase. (All VA loans are fully assumable.)

For further information on VA loans, contact any office of the Veterans Administration.

PRIVATE MORTGAGE INSURANCE

Private mortgage insurance (PMI) has been available for over a decade and is widely used by lenders. A PMI loan is one in which a private insurer guarantees to repay the lender a certain portion of the loan amount in the event of default. Typically the amount repaid is 20 percent, and, as with VA loans, it is the top 20 percent.

To obtain PMI insurance on a mortgage, both the buyer and the property must qualify not only with the lender but also with the PMI company. Typically, only the best borrowers and the choicest properties meet PMI standards.

The cost of PMI insurance is usually about 0.25 percent of the mortgage amount, and it is tacked onto the mortgage interest rate and paid monthly by the borrower.

Chapter 3

Pension Fund Financing of Real Estate

H. James Griggs   President, Financial Investment Advisors

James L. Sublett   Executive Director Emeritus, State Teachers Retirement System of Ohio

For many years the typical sources for meeting most financial needs have been the time-tested institutions such as banks, savings and loan associations (S&Ls), other types of thrift institutions such as credit unions, and, particularly in the real estate field, insurance companies. However, increasingly in recent years, pension plans, both public and private, have become a major source of capital.

Currently the assets of U.S. pension funds equal about $750 billion, and soon they will pass $1 trillion, thus constituting the largest single pool of investment capital in the nation. The implications for all those who utilize institutional funds are obvious. For those entities seeking capital for real estate development, however, the growth of pension fund assets has particular significance.

Traditionally, pension funds have been very conservatively invested with heavy emphasis on fixed-income securities of the highest quality. Only in recent years has diversification into other investment media, such as common stocks, occurred, and only now are pension fund investors showing interest in equity real estate.

REAL ESTATE INVESTMENTS

Real Estate Loans

In discussing real estate loans, we can talk about both residential and commercial loans such as straight loans, participation loans, convertible mortgages, and participating convertible mortgages.

Straight Loan.   The straight loan is a payment which would provide for the repayment of the principal and interest. This loan might be insured by an agency of the federal government or by private mortgage insurance, and it would be used primarily for residential property.

Participation Loan.   The participation loan is used primarily for conventional commercial financing in which the lender, in addition to receiving a fixed principal and interest payment, would participate in any additional increases in net income to the property. These increases might come in the form of particular increased rents derived from the property in the form of indexed rent or increased market rents or, in the case of certain retail properties, in the form of percentage rents which are received in addition to the fixed monthly rental and would be a function of the gross sales of the tenant in the property.

Convertible Mortgage.   The convertible mortgage contains a feature that allows either the total of or a portion of the principal to be converted into an equity ownership interest at some future date. This enables the seller, who is frequently a developer, to retain the ownership provision, which allows the seller to retain tax considerations while allowing the lender to receive benefits of ownership as though she or he had a fee title to the property. This is particularly advantageous where the lender is a pension fund, because currently pension funds do not pay income taxes, and the tax benefit is of no direct value to them. They have the right, if they have a fee ownership, to sell the property to someone who can use the tax benefits and to take back a convertible mortgage.

Participating Convertible Mortgage.   The participating convertible mortgage has the advantages of both a participating mortgage and a convertible mortgage. When using a participating convertible mortgage, a property owner must recognize that he or she immediately has a partner in the property—a partner who ultimately will own all or a portion of the property with the owner. This type of loan can also be used with a management-intensive property when the investment criteria of the pension fund are such that involvement in the day-to-day management of the property is undesirable. Therefore, pension funds would make this type of a transaction when they want not only the advantages of ownership but also the expertise of an experienced developer and/or investor to manage the property.

Equity Ownership

Equity ownership exists when the pension fund buys the property outright and takes a fee ownership or leasehold ownership, in the case of a long-term ground lease. Funds typically do not like ground-lease transactions, but in the event that they would accept a ground lease, it would typically have to be 60 years or more and/or contain an option to purchase the property at some future date. Purchases made on lease-hold interest typically would require 25 to 50 basis points higher yields than with direct fee ownership. This same yield increase would be required if a loan were used.

Commingled Funds

Commingled funds can come in the form of open-ended funds. In open-ended funds there is a constant reinvestment process of the fund; there typically is no fixed termination date of the fund; participants come and go from the fund on the basis of a current valuation done on a periodic basis. In closed-end funds, specific assets are put into the fund and, at an agreed-on date, a majority or a fixed percentage of the participants in the fund elect to terminate the fund and to liquidate the assets of that fund at a future date.

Both these types of commingled funds offer the pension funds, partic-ularly the smaller funds, the opportunity for diversification in the form of different types of properties and/or geographic diversification as might be provided by the particular commingled fund. The problem with this vehicle is that too often pension funds invest in a commingled fund without investigating the actual assets of the fund and/or what form of diversification and liquidity it gives to the buyer. In fact, many pension funds have entered into these commingled funds thinking that they had a great deal of liquidity and have found in recent years that in fact there is not a strong form of liquidity in commingled funds. Typically they cannot get out of the fund unless there is another pur-chaser standing in the wings to acquire their interest. Therefore, the funds that are large enough to set up their own form of diversification of investments are turning to this approach rather than to the emphasis on commingled funds.

RESTRAINTS ON PENSION FUND INVESTMENTS

The investments of a pension fund are governed largely by two areas: (1) statutory or governmental restraints and (2) governing-body policy.

Governmental Restraints

The governmental restraints vary a great deal from state to state and according to whether it is a public or private pension fund. The types of investments that can be made have limitations relative to restraints, such as in stocks, where there must be a continuous period of net profit for a fixed number of years, a paid dividend for a fixed number of years, and a net worth with a minimum of so many dollars. There may also be other liquidity requirements in the law.

Also, many times under governmental restraints certain credit requirements exist for the financial strength of the borrower in the case of a bond, and they may require a rating by one of the major standard rating bureaus such as Moody's, Standard & Poor's, or Fitch. Typically, the bonds for public funds must carry an "A" rating or better. Typically such restraints are not put on the private funds by governmental statute.

Currently, the majority of states cannot make real estate equity investments. Some can make real estate loans on commercial properties, if the borrower has a certain rated credit, such as "A" or better, or commercial paper rating of "1," or something of that nature, a limiting criterion. Other states have commercial lending with no restraints other than a loan-to-value ratio whose value is established by an appraiser of a recognized national agency. Other funds have limitations for residential property in their own state, and some even have requirements in which the loans made on residential properties must be either insured or guaranteed by an agency of the federal government, such as the Federal Housing Administration (FHA) in the case of insurance and the Veterans Administration (VA) in the case of the guarantee.

Board Policy

Typically, the board policy is established to see that the lending requirements of the pension fund comply with any statutory limitations. They also tend to interpret and explain statutory intent and to be somewhat more restrictive than the statute. For instance, the statute might allow 10 percent of a fund's assets to be invested in real estate, whereas the board policy would restrict the investments in real estate to 5 percent of the total assets of the fund.

Therefore, the types of investments can be put into the following broad categories: (1) bonds; (2) equities/common and preferred stock; (3) real estate—real estate loans and real estate equity purchases; and (4) other investments such as commercial paper, certificates of deposit (CDs), and/or special-risk investments that may be carried in a special category of the assets such as a "prudent-man" investment. Risk capital in new ventures or corporate ventures could be classified in that category.

PENSION PLANS

An understanding of the types and organization of pension funds from the viewpoint of fund managers is essential in a successful approach to real estate investment.

Pension plans are either public or private, and private plans include both single-employer plans and multiemployer plans, commonly referred to as "Taft-Hartley plans." Both single-employer and multiemployer plans are subject to the provisions of the Employee Retirement Income Security Act (ERISA). Except in a very minor way, public plans are not controlled by this act. However, current congressional activity suggests that there soon will be similar regulatory measures for public plans.

Public Pension Plans

Studies have identified over 6000 public pension plans in the United States.* These range from small plans covering fewer than fifty employees to giants with more than a million participants. Regardless of size, these plans share certain common characteristics.

Statutory Basis.   All public plans have their origin in an enactment of some legislative body, be it a city council, county or parish commission, or state legislature. They derive their powers to accumulate funds, invest assets, and pay benefits from these provisions. Statutes governing public plans may be broad and general or detailed and specific. All too often the latter pattern prevails, particularly in the investment-authorizing sections.

Joint Contributory Structure.   Financing of public plans is different from that of private plans. The general pattern is to require both employer and employee contributions toward the funding of benefits. These contributions plus the income earned from asset investment create the reserves from which benefits are paid.

Organization and Control.   Again, unlike private plans, at least single-employer plans, the common practice in public plans is to lodge overall control in a board or commission. Typically, the makeup of such boards is provided in the governing statute. In size they range from as few as three to more than a dozen members. Members may derive their offices by appointment (usually by a governor or legislature), by virtue of holding a certain office (state treasurer, attorney general), or by elec-

*Report of the Pension Task Force on Public Employee Retirement Systems, Committee on Education and Labor, 95th Cong., 2d Sess., Mar. 15, 1978.

tions involving the plan participants. Within the framework established by statute, the board is responsible for establishing policies governing administration of the plan and for overseeing the general activities of staff, including the investment of plan assets.

Private Plans

Private plans consist of two basic types: single-employer and multiemployer. Both single-employer and multiemployer plans share some of the same characteristics, but in many aspects each is unique.

Single-Employer Plans. Single-employer plans cover the employees of a single employer. Included, however, may be the employees of subsidiary corporations or the employees in many plants scattered throughout the country or the globe, provided the same "umbrella" covers them all.

Typically, the cost of providing benefits in such plans is the sole responsibility of the employer. Pension benefits as well as other fringes usually are collectively bargained and constitute a business cost in the same manner as wages. Because every benefit dollar produced from asset investment increases corporate profitability, the investment philosophy of single-employer funds has often been more inclined to risk taking than that of the more conservative public sector. Coupled with the temptation to invest heavily in the securities of the employer, this riskier environment led to the enactment of ERISA.

Multiemployer Plans. Multiemployer plans also usually derive from collective bargaining. Their use is most widespread among industries employing large numbers of craftspersons, usually working for small employers.

Such funds are characterized by common pools into which contributions are paid and from which benefits are disbursed. Both contribution rates and benefit payments are uniform.

Multiemployer plans are controlled by trustees representing both employers and employees; in fact, they are sometimes described as "jointly trusteed plans." They resemble public plans in that they represent both employers and employees.

Plan Qualification

Whether public or private, single-employer or multiemployer, pension plans share a common thread, that of qualification. Qualification under Section 401(a) of the Internal Revenue Code requires that a plan not discriminate in favor of officers, stockholders, supervisors, or highly compensated employees. Securing a "determination letter" from the

Internal Revenue Service (IRS) yields some very important tax benefits and has unique investment implications. Employer contributions to a qualified plan are nontaxable, and normal earnings on investments enjoy similar treatment. Additionally, there is favorable tax treatment of certain benefits payable by the plan. The tax treatment of investment earnings gives qualified pension plans some very distinct advantages as compared to other financial institutions. This is nowhere more true than in equity real estate investment, as will be emphasized later in this chapter.

Employee Retirement Income Security Act

A growing concern about the financial stability of private pension funds gave rise to the enactment of the Employee Retirement Income Security Act in 1974. The contents of the act are both extensive and technical, and much too detailed to set forth here. However, the act did provide for fiduciary standards which have continuing implications for those involved in providing investment opportunities for pension plans.

The act establishes fiduciary standards and duties and sets forth certain requirements for the plan and for the establishment of the trust. It prohibits certain transactions between the plan fiduciary and a party of interest.

One important duty prescribed for plan trustees is the establishment and maintenance of an investment policy. The terms of this policy must be specific enough to offer guidance to the plan administrator and flexible enough to permit full utilization of available, viable investment instruments. Unfortunately, many plan trustees, and cofiduciaries employed by them, have backgrounds and philosophies geared principally to investment in bonds, stocks, and mortgages. They must be educated to the distinct advantages of substantial commitments to equity real estate.

Pension Plan Organization and Staffing

Background and Types.   Pension plans have been around a long time, first in the public sector, then in private or "corporate" plans, and finally in multiemployer funds. The first public system, created in 1857, covered New York police officers. Toward the end of the nineteenth century, a number of municipal plans evolved, particularly for teachers. In 1911 Massachusetts established a full program covering all state employees. The largest growth and development in the public sector took place in the late 1930s and throughout the decade of the 1940s. As a result, today over 90 percent of municipal and state-level employees are covered by pension plans other than Social Security.

Only within the last 25 years has similar development taken place in private or industrial plans. A smaller percentage of industrial workers derive benefits from private plans. However, as our population has become more and more "security" conscious, pensions and related benefits have become an ever larger component of compensation packages. The net result is a more rapidly increasing asset pool that is available for investment.

Whether public or private, pension plans fall into two basic categories: (1) defined-contribution plans and (2) defined-benefit plans. In defined-contribution plans, specified contributions (either a percentage of payroll or cents per hour) are set aside in a trust fund. These contributions plus income resulting from their investment provide the reserves to pay benefits at retirement. Obviously, increases in investment return will result in an improvement in benefits, a reduction in cost, or a combination of the two.

In defined-benefit plans, pensions are a product of years of service, average salary for a stated period (usually the 3 to 5 years of greatest earnings), and a "formula factor" (commonly 1 percent to 2 percent per year of service). Typically such a plan at normal retirement age of 60 or 65 would pay an employee with 30 years of service from 30 percent to 60 percent of salary.

In general, defined-contribution plans are most common in the private sector, and the majority of public employees participate in defined-benefit programs.

Organization for Asset Investment.   An employer, whether private or public, has available several types of organization for investing the plan assets. The least involved for the employer is the insured plan. Here the employer contracts with an insurance company to provide the benefits stipulated in the plan. The contributions to the plan equal the premiums paid, and the employer has no involvement with investing assets. Smaller companies are the most likely users of insured plans.

Sponsors of pension plans may elect to employ outside organizations to manage the investment portfolio. One manager or several may be employed, depending somewhat on the total size of the fund. Bank trust departments, investment advisory firms, and subsidiaries of investment banking firms are typical managers used. The sponsor may have an in-house organization to monitor performance of the several managers and make recommendations for change, but there is little direct involvement in the investment management process.

From the standpoint of those interested in the sale of real estate to pension funds, these two methods of investing assets offer distinct disadvantages. In the insured plan, typically the insurance company will develop its own real estate opportunities, and the contributions of a typically small pension fund will be commingled with other funds in company-originated projects.

Professional management companies, bank trust officers, and the like often have a considerable cash flow available for investment. Unfortunately, many such concerns are almost totally oriented toward the market in high-grade stocks and bonds, and they have little expertise in real estate–related opportunities. Recently there has been some effort to correct this situation, but professional money managers, as a group, have a long way to go to fully understand the mechanics and values of equity real estate acquisition.

A third type of investment management is the so-called in-house program. Here a staff of professionals in the direct employ of the sponsor, operating under policies established by the sponsor, manages the assets of the plan. Increasingly, both public and private plans have been adopting this type of organization, particularly the public plans. Almost every public plan in the nation with assets of $1 billion or more is currently managing internally all or a major portion of its assets, usually with marked success. Because this type of organization is relatively recent in origin, there is more of a tendency to be interested in and to be staffed for equity realty transactions. See Figure 3-1 for a typical in-house organization in a public retirement plan.

Use of Outside Consultants.   A properly staffed organization will, over time, achieve very satisfactory results. Typically, in addition to the in-house staff, a pension fund may employ outside advisors, not as discretionary money managers but rather as additional expertise in the selection of investment opportunity.

The use of such consultants is of particular significance in real estate acquisition because of the typical advisory firm's ignorance of investment opportunities. Real estate consultants *must* be selected with great care. Only those individuals with widely diversified experience in all phases of commercial real estate financing should be considered. Too often plan management succumbs to the temptation of using a local retired broker who has had a long successful career in residential housing sales. Such a person can do more to destroy an imaginative, dynamic program of creative real estate investment than can a major earthquake.

Developing the Real Estate–Investment Policy.   All investment of pension fund assets should be governed by a carefully formulated investment policy approved either by the corporate board of a private plan or by the trustees of a public or multiemployer plan. Once in place, this policy should be the rule and guide of those administering day-to-day investment.

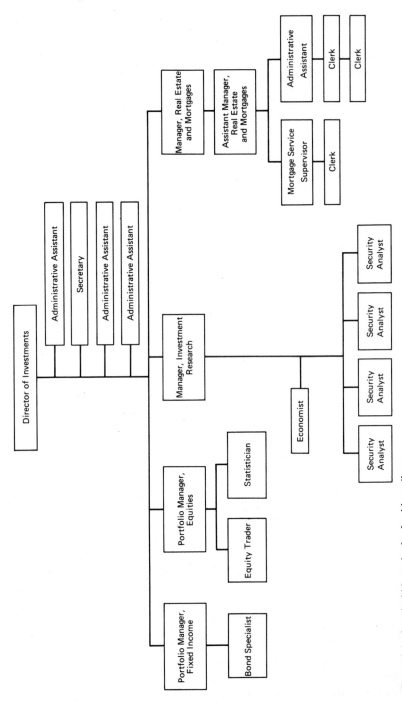

Figure 3-1 A typical hierarchy for fund investing.

Once again, guidelines for stocks and bonds usually are more clearly defined than those for real estate. For this reason, if no other, the real estate section of the policy should receive careful attention. A carefully developed policy will avoid future problems.

As a minimum, a policy governing the acquisition of real estate should include the following:

1. Types of property to be acquired
   a. Office buildings
   b. Retail outlets
   c. Distribution centers
   d. Apartment buildings
2. Properties to be avoided
   a. Single-use facilities (i.e., oil refineries, steel mills)
3. Investment objectives
   a. Return commensurate with risk
   b. Adequate cash-on-cash return
   c. Provisions for increasing cash flows
      (1) Percentage rents
      (2) Short-term leases
      (3) Cost-of-living tie-ins
   d. Diversification
      (1) Types of property
      (2) Geographical distribution
4. Investment vehicles
   a. Sale leasebacks
      (1) Triple-net leases
   b. Joint ventures
   c. Limited partnerships
   d. Participating or convertible mortgages
   e. Fee simple ownership
      (1) Professional building management

The investment policy should also set forth the minimum documentation that will be required in the case of property acquisition. Making these requirements clear will avoid misunderstanding by the buyer, the seller, the developers, brokers, or others involved in the transaction. Suggested minimum documentation is:

1. Building and systems evaluation by a qualified engineering firm
2. Appraisal by a qualified appraisal firm mutually selected by the buyer and seller

3. In the case of forward-purchase commitments, approval of plans and specifications by a qualified engineering firm
4. A financial analysis, including but not limited to the expected rate of return, appreciation potential, resale potential, and relationship of assets to the total portfolio
5. Legal review and approval of appropriate documents
6. Management by a firm with extensive experience and a proven capability in managing similar properties (no pension fund belongs in the property management business!)

Real estate is new to pension funds. It occupies the same position today that common stocks did 20 years ago. Therefore, it behooves everyone involved in the real estate–investing process to participate in an ongoing program of education designed to promote a thorough understanding of what real estate can do for a pension fund and, conversely, what it cannot do. This will help avoid the unwarranted expectations which have often plagued other investment media.

FOLLOWING A TYPICAL TRANSACTION

There are five steps in a real estate deal: (1) originating the transaction, (2) selecting the investment, (3) underwriting the transaction, (4) closing the transaction, and (5) managing the assets after the transaction is closed.

Originating the Transaction

Typically, the pension fund transaction is initiated by in-house staff, by a real estate advisory consultant, or through direct contact with real estate brokers and/or developers. In any case, the transaction is brought to the attention of and reviewed by the pension fund.

Selection of Investment

Selection of investment is made on the basis of three factors. The first factor is the type of property in which they are allowed to invest under their statutory requirements and the current board policy. The second factor is whether the investment currently meets the market-yield requirement. Today the most active approach to making that yield analysis for real estate is to determine the internal rate of return. Of course, the yield for the real estate must be on a favorable comparative basis with other investment opportunities which the fund has available in their allowable-investment categories. The portfolio balance is the third factor involved in the selection process. A typical pension fund will want to work with a percentage of different types of properties and a geographical balance. A typical fund portfolio distribution could be something along the following lines: office buildings, 50 percent; shopping centers, 15 percent; industrial, 10 percent; strip centers and freestanding retail, 20 percent; and residential multifamily projects, 5 percent.

Underwriting

The investment package is then analyzed by the fund-staff personnel, their outside consultant, or typically, a combination of outside consultant and staff. They review the investment for qualification criteria such as the property quality, the quality of the income stream, the quality of the tenants, yield comparisons, future holding periods, and loan commitments.

Tenant Quality.   The underwriting of tenants depends on the quality of the tenants, on their ability to produce the projected income stream in the market where the property is situated, and on how competitive the projected income stream was with the existing marketing conditions. Thus the durability of that income stream can be determined, and proper trend assumptions can be made from a realistic base rather than from an unrealistic assumption. The market is always there where the property is located, and one cannot assume that the property under consideration will be unaffected by the market today or at some time in the future. Too frequently an effort is made on the part of the seller and/or the borrower to create a case for the uniqueness of a property in order to justify proposed rental rates greater than those available in the current market for space. One must be careful of violating sound underwriting in this area. There is absolutely *no* substitute for a market comparison study to determine existing rents and to predict reasonable rent increases in the future. This is true for expenses as well as for rents, since both affect the net income, and that is what is available for the return on the investment. Accurate predictions of vacancies must be made, as must arrangements for leasing again if current leases are shorter than desired. Undoubtedly there will be additional tenant improvements that must be considered, and there will be carrying charges during this vacant period that must be considered in the analysis. There is no substitute if you are dealing with an existing property. Go directly to the books of the property in question and use the actual historical income and expense figures for the property and update them in view of today's very volatile economic conditions. Questions of taxation and utilities are two major areas of consideration.

Yield Comparisons. The most common yield comparison today for real estate transactions is the internal rate of return, which is the discounted rate of return. Also important is the average rate of return, since it is a simple arithmetical average and not a discounted rate that might allow proper comparison with another straight debt investment. In comparing yields one must make the equivalency test from a straight monthly payment to a bond-equivalent yield which might be received on an annual basis. Depending on what your beginning yield is, this basis-point differential in yield can be substantial. An understanding of compounding is essential to correct yield comparisons.

Interest is compounded whenever it is paid and collected, or added to the principal, which is the same thing. If you put $100 in a bank and the bank paid 5 percent interest annually, then you would have $105 in the bank at the end of the year; but, if the bank paid interest (i.e., compounded) semiannually, you would have $105.06. You could call the $0.06 the interest on interest. If the bank paid interest quarterly, you would have $105.09 at the end of the year. If it paid monthly, you would have $105.12. This shows the advantage of more frequent compounding. The effective rate is more than 5 percent when the compounding is more than once a year, thus

Compounding	Amount in bank	Effective rate (percent)
Annual	105.00	5.00
Semiannual	105.06	5.06
Quarterly	105.09	5.09
Monthly	105.12	5.12

But observe that on a mortgage with monthly payments, the interest is paid or collected (i.e., compounded) every month. Thus the effective annual rate is really more than the stated rate, and there is an advantage in investing in a mortgage with monthly payments rather than some other equally good investment which pays the same nominal interest rate only semiannually or annually.

In the United States almost all bonds pay interest semiannually. Therefore, when the Federal Housing Administration states a mortgage yield, it gives it as the equivalent of a semiannual interest investment. For example, the FHA would say that a 5 percent monthly mortgage purchased at face value of 100 would yield, not 5 percent, but 5.05 percent. These yields are not the same as in the *Insured Mortgage Yield Tables* (Form no. 2331) published by the FHA, which show that a monthly 5 percent mortgage at 100 yields 5 percent. The FHA deal is

5.05 percent, and thus a 5 percent monthly mortgage is really equivalent to a bond or other semiannual investment which paid 5.05 percent. (For the yield in semiannual compound interest, Table 2 in the FHA *Insured Mortgage Yield Tables* gives the extra yield to be added to any yield shown in the booklet up to 10.02 percent.)

Future Holding Period. In analyzing the investment we must consider the criteria for durability, quality, future economic obsolescence of the property, any functional obsolescence that might be inherent in a tenant with a short-term lease that would require substantial modification of the project to sustain an income stream, future competition that might come into the area, and the property's ability to compete in the marketplace in the future. A reasonable period of time should be considered in analyzing the investment, and it will vary depending on the type of property, whether it is in a growth area, and whether you intend to sell the property at an early date.

Loan Commitment. After the underwriting has been completed, the loan would then be subject to the commitment process, which will vary from fund to fund. Some funds have an investment officer with sufficient authority to commit a transaction; other funds have a committee. Some funds require that it go to the entire board for approval. When the process is most efficient, the board dictates policy to the investment department of the organization, and then the investment officer or a subcommittee of the board's investment committee meets periodically to approve the transaction. This same process is followed in the case of an outside consultant. Many consultants have the right to commit directly the purchases and/or loans. This is called "discretionary power." Whether this power is granted usually depends on the expertise of the staff and/or the fund. Some funds do not have authority for granting discretionary investment authority to an outside consultant not directly responsible to the plan trustees. Assuming that the transaction is approved, then it goes to the closing process.

Closing the Transaction

The loan closing can be handled by (1) staff in-house counsel, (2) the consultant setting up and handling the transaction with in-house counsel, or (3) in-house counsel and outside counsel, who work together to effect the closing of the transaction.

The form for closing the transaction, of course, will vary from state to state, and proper legal advice is important in each state in which the subject property is located. Do not assume that the laws in the state in which the pension funds are situated will govern in the event of discrepancies. The best approach is to use counsel who are very experienced in the field of real estate and to approve two or three outside counsel whose credentials are satisfactory to the lending and/or purchasing entity so that they are available to expedite transactions for the fund. A full legal checklist for closing will not be discussed in this chapter but should be developed by anyone entering the lending field. Anyone doing business with a fund should take the time to sit down and meet with staff and/or staff counsel to find out exactly what their closing procedures are, since each fund will have its own idiosyncrasies and procedures. Typically, pension funds are at no expense in connection with closing either a purchase transaction or a lending transaction. The fees are paid by the borrower and/or the seller for both the title company closing costs and legal fees. A lid should be negotiated on the legal fees so that there are no unfortunate surprises during or after the closing.

Asset Management

Asset management is probably the most important process of the entire chain of activities, since it ultimately will determine both where to put the profits for the fund and how to protect that income stream, including monitoring the asset once the transaction is closed. The basic steps in asset management, whether it be conducted by in-house staff, outside investment advisors, or a combination of the two, are as follows:

1. Set up the particular project into the portfolio-monitoring system, which is usually done by computers because of the magnitude of the project and the number of projects involved. All critical dates should be put into the tickler system. All critical information relative to the project should also be put into the system so that it is on call on a daily basis and so that a monthly report is available to the board and/or staff members. This process is critical, and any fund should monitor very carefully either its own or its advisor's ability to handle this portion of the work.

2. With this information in the computer, all critical dates should be reviewed regularly with a system for calling up these dates at least 45 days in advance to avoid expiration of lease options and fire insurance policies, to ensure collection of overage rents and rent increases, and so on.

3. In monitoring the periodic payments, which in real estate transactions typically are done on a monthly basis, assume that all increases in rent and/or loan payments are put into effect on the proper date and that all payments are received on time and, if not, that appro-

priate late charges are received with them. This also enables the staff or consultant to determine how closely the property is tracking, what the original estimates of income are, and, if the payment record of a particular tenant is poor at lease renewal time, whether to renew the lease or to get new tenants with a sounder credit position. In the case of a convertible mortgage, if the payments have not been satisfactory, then the probability of wanting to have this individual as a partner would be reduced considerably.

4. Regularly review the economic conditions in the property's area; thus you can determine whether the subject property is performing as it should in this particular economic environment. Examine whether the property is following the original economic trend line. These data can be used for future underwriting of new projects and for determining the disposition of existing projects.

5. In the case of owned real estate, the entire portfolio should be reviewed at least annually to determine which properties to sell, which properties to hold on to, and on which properties to change the form of ownership. (For example, to sell a property and carry back a convertible mortgage could have a favorable yield improvement of 200 to 250 basis points over original fee acquisition within a very short time after acquisition.)

SUMMARY

Pension funds are, and will continue to be, an excellent source of capital for the real estate market both for lending and for selling a finished product. Both pension funds and those doing business with them should recognize what a very special product real estate is and the importance of doing business with experienced individuals in the marketing stream such as brokers, developers, appraisers, consultants. Thus the key word for pension fund portfolios in real estate is *quality*.

PRESENT VALUE AND INTERNAL RATE OF RETURN

The timing of the cash flows is an important factor in the analysis of any investment. The sooner a cash flow is received the more weight it should have in the investment decision. For example, $100 received today is worth more than $100 received 10 years from now. Through the use of present value tables we can calculate how much a future cash flow is worth today given a certain discount rate.

The internal rate of return (IRR) calculation stresses the importance of the timing of cash flows of an investment. The IRR is the discount rate that equates the present value of future cash flows to the cost of the investment.

For an illustration of the IRR calculation, assume an investment of $1000 and the following cash flow: year 1, $500; year 2, $400; year 3, $300; and year 4, $100. Since the IRR calculation is a trial-and-error procedure, the first step is to try several discount rates that appear close to the IRR. Because the IRR is usually between 10 and 20 percent, we will initially try 10 percent, 15 percent, and 20 percent as discount rates:

Year	Cash flow	Discount factor at 10%	Discounted value
1	500	.9091	$ 454.55
2	400	.8264	330.56
3	300	.7513	225.39
4	100	.6830	68.30
			$ 1078.80
		Discount factor at 15%	
1	500	.8695	$ 434.75
2	400	.7561	302.44
3	300	.6575	197.25
4	100	.5718	57.18
			$ 991.62
		Discount factor at 20%	
1	500	.8333	$ 416.65
2	400	.6944	277.76
3	300	.5787	173.61
4	100	.4823	48.23
			$ 916.25

Clearly, the higher the discount rate that is used, the lower the present value of the cash flows will be. This relationship can be seen more clearly by graphing the data from the calculations (see Figure 3-2). The actual IRR is the intersection of the graph with a horizontal line drawn from $1000 on the Y axis. To calculate the IRR, different discount factors are tried until one is found where the discounted value of the cash flows is equal to the investment. In the example, the actual IRR is 14.49 percent:

Year	Cash flow	Discounted factor at 14.49%	Discounted value
1	500	.8734	$436.70
2	400	.7629	305.16
3	300	.6663	199.89
4	100	.5820	58.20
			$999.95

Formula for IRR Calculation

$$\text{Investment} = \frac{\text{Cash Flow Year 1}}{(1 + r)} + \frac{\text{Cash Flow Year 2}}{(1 + r)^2} + \frac{\text{Cash Flow Year 3}}{(1 + r)^3} + \frac{\text{Cash Flow Year } j}{(1 + r)^j}$$

$r = \text{IRR}$

Example   Investment = 1000   Cash Flows = Year 1: 500

Year 2: 400   Year 3: 300   Year 4: 100

$$1000 = \frac{500}{(1 + .1449)} + \frac{400}{(1 + .1449)^2} + \frac{300}{(1 + .1449)^3} + \frac{100}{(1 + .1449)^4}$$

$$1000 = 436.70 \quad + \quad 305.16 \quad + \quad 199.89 \quad + \quad 58.20$$

$$= 999.95$$

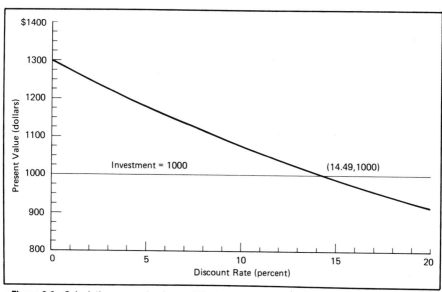

Figure 3-2 Calculating present value and the internal rate of return.

Chapter 4

Finance and the Lender's Viewpoint

Thomas R. Harter Chief Economist and Senior Staff Vice President,
Mortgage Bankers Association of America

SOURCES OF FINANCE AND THE LENDER'S VIEW OF THE BORROWER

A mortgage is a formal document that an owner of real property uses to pledge that property as security for payment of a debt. In common usage, the term refers to a first mortgage, or the claim that must be satisfied before any other claim is considered in the event of default and foreclosure. A second mortgage, then, is only secure to the extent that property value remains after a first-mortgage claim is fully satisfied. An owner of real property that makes use of a mortgage to finance the purchase of real estate is referred to as the "mortgagor," or the borrower. The entity that extends the borrower credit using the mortgage process is called the "mortgagee," or the lender.

Most people are familiar with the long-term fixed-rate self-amortizing mortgage. The term of a mortgage is the amount of time over which the debt is to be outstanding. A long-term mortgage is one that is paid off over an extended period, usually 20 to 30 years. A fixed-rate mortgage is a loan that carries the same rate of interest throughout the term of the loan. Fixed-rate loans are usually of the level-payment variety; the mortgage payment of principal and interest does not change over the term of the loan. In a level-payment mortgage, the amount of the payment is divided between interest (based on the amount of the loan still to be paid) and principal. The process of reducing the outstanding debt, or principal, is called "amortization." A mortgage that reduces the entire principal to zero over the original term of the mortgage is a self-amortizing loan.

However, many of today's mortgage loans deviate from the characteristics just discussed. A rollover mortgage, or Canadian rollover mortgage, is a type of loan that carries a shorter term, typically 3 to 5 years. At the end of this time the entire remaining principal is due and a new mortgage loan is issued. This new mortgage loan need bear no relation to the original loan and may well carry a different interest rate. The principal due at the end of the original term is referred to as a "lump sum" or "balloon" payment, and these loans are sometimes called "balloon loans" or "bullet loans."

Many mortgage loans bear interest rates that may vary over the term of the loan. These are adjustable-rate, or variable-rate, mortgages. The interest rate, and in most cases the monthly mortgage payment, depends on changes in market interest rates; adjustments in the interest rate update the rate according to the current market rate of interest. Adjustments are made on a prearranged schedule, and the new rate is often based on an index that represents the change in market interest rates since the last adjustment. The interest rate usually is adjusted every 6 months or every year, but some loans are adjusted as frequently as monthly, and others are adjusted after 3 years. Although the interest rate, and possibly the monthly payment, is changed in much the same manner as a rollover mortgage, it differs in that it still represents the same loan, since the original term and other characteristics remain unchanged.

One of the most widely used alternatives to the traditional mortgage is the graduated-payment mortgage. As its name suggests, this loan differs from a fixed-rate fully amortized mortgage in that the monthly payments are not fixed for the life of the loan, although the interest rate remains constant for the term of the loan. Monthly payments start below those of a comparable traditional loan but increase periodically (usually yearly) for some set period (typically the first 5 or 7 years of the loan), after which the payments are fixed for the remaining life of the loan. These lower payments at the beginning of the loan enable borrowers to qualify for loans that would result in monthly payments too high for current income under traditional conditions. The difference between the lower initial payment and the amount that would have been paid under a fixed-rate fully amortized loan is added to the principal of the loan, causing the payments in the latter (fixed-payment) portion of the mortgage to be above those of a comparable traditional loan because of the increased principal balance. This type of mortgage loan appeals to buyers that expect their income to increase enough to handle the increased payments in the later years of the term.

The process of adding to the outstanding principal balance of the mortgage is called "negative amortization," and it represents the opposite of the usual practice of reducing the principal amount as the loan progresses. This negative amortization can be applied to other types of loans, resulting in such mortgage hybrids as the graduated-payment variable-rate mortgage or the level-payment adjustable-rate mortgage, among others.

In the process of mortgage finance, one of the most important considerations is the amount of money the prospective home buyer can use as a down payment. The amount of the down payment represents the total equity, or price minus loan amount, at the time of purchase. The more equity home buyers have at the time of purchase the less likely they will be to miss mortgage payments (termed "mortgage delinquency"). This has a direct bearing on whether a prospective lender will make a mortgage loan available to a mortgagee and on what interest rate the lender will charge to adjust for the different levels of risk that correspond to different levels of down payment.

There are two components of the yield for mortgage loans. The first, the rate on which the monthly payments are based, is the contract interest rate. The other component takes any up-front loan fees that are paid and combines them with the contract rate to produce the annual percentage rate (APR). If there were no fees or charges for originating the loan, the contract rate and the APR would be equal. The up-front fees that are charged for making the mortgage loan are origination fees or discount points, and these funds, in part, reimburse the lender for the work that goes into making a mortgage loan, including document preparation, credit reports, and property inspection. This fee is usually 1 to 2 percent of the original loan amount. In addition, there may be fees for other specific services connected with the mortgage loan procedure.

The origination fee is only one part of the expense of arranging for a home purchase. Closing costs, or settlement costs, are all the expenses involved in completing the real estate transaction. These usually include discount points, title insurance fees, land survey fees, attorney fees, prepaid items such as property taxes and mortgage insurance escrow payments, and loan origination fees.

Points, or discount points, are paid to the lender to increase the investment value (or yield) of the mortgage loan. A point is 1 percent of the loan principal, so that a charge of 4 points on a loan of $50,000 would mean a payment of $2000. On Federal Housing Administration (FHA) loans, the borrower is prohibited from being charged the points involved. This may result in the seller attempting to recoup these charges in a higher selling price or refusing to become involved in a transaction that depends on the payment of points.

One of the most important details of a real estate transaction is the process of making sure that the property is free and clear of any liens or other claims of partial or total interest on the property. This specialized function is often performed by title insurance companies. These firms search the applicable records for any claims registered against the property under consideration, and they issue an insurance policy to cover the prospective lender against any claims that may have been overlooked in the title search. Many buyers also purchase title insurance to protect themselves from loss should the title prove to be defective.

Attorney fees and land survey fees are paid when the services are rendered. Mortgage insurance is usually required by a lender when the initial down payment is 20 percent or less. These policies ensure that, in the case of default by the borrower, the difference between the price that the property would command if sold in the market and the loan amount (if the loan amount is more than the selling price), would be paid to the lender to make the investor "whole." This enables lenders to make mortgage loans to buyers with low down payments without assuming a risky investment position. This type of policy should not be confused with mortgage life insurance, which is a type of term life insurance that pays off the remaining principal balance of the loan in the event of the borrower's death.

The mortgage insurance premium is usually part of the monthly mortgage payment, and it is calculated as a small percentage of the outstanding principal balance. As discussed previously, the outstanding principal balance declines as a mortgage loan matures, except in non-amortizing loans or loans that feature negative amortization.

There are other clauses in a mortgage loan that are extremely important when comparing different mortgages. Assumability, or the ability of the mortgage loan to be transferred to a new owner should the property be sold, has become a vital difference among mortgage types as interest rates have escalated. The ability of a seller to offer this older mortgage, which may bear an interest rate below that of current loans, as part of the financing package often allows the prospective buyer to afford the home when the monthly payments under a new loan would have been too high. In these cases, a knowledgeable seller may command a premium price for a property that was originally financed with an assumable loan. Loans that contain due-on-sale clauses prevent the loan from being transferred by allowing the lender to demand repayment of the outstanding principal balance when the property is sold or transferred.

The option to pay off the remaining principal balance before the scheduled date is a standard characteristic of most mortgage loans. Many loans have prepayment clauses, which state that the mortgagor is obliged to pay a fee if the loan is repaid before the original due date. This fee compensates lenders, since early repayment of principal and interest may reduce the yield they can earn on their capital.

Other nonstandard terms in a mortgage loan include the schedule of charges for late monthly payments, the deposit for the mortgage commitment, the method of handling persistent mortgage delinquency, and what constitutes default.

MORTGAGE CHARACTERISTICS AND THE INVESTOR

An institution or an individual who invests in a mortgage loan is primarily interested in a secure investment that provides a competitive return on the original capital. The underlying security of any loan lies in the collateral, which in the case of a mortgage loan is the real property under consideration. Additional security is provided by the ability of mortgagees to meet their mortgage obligations in the form of monthly payments.

Underwriting is the process of investigating the security of a prospective mortgage loan in order to assign it a certain risk factor and a loan term and interest rate based on this risk. One of the most basic steps in the underwriting process is the appraisal of the property under consideration. An appraisal is a qualified expert's estimation of the market value of the property. The document that reports the expert's findings to the mortgagor is also called an appraisal. The value of the property assigned by the appraiser may be different from the asking price, but the investor will be wary of making a loan in excess of the appraised value of the property. The appraised value should be the market value of the property, or the price that a theoretical buyer would be willing, but not compelled, to offer for the property in a reasonable amount of time.

The other major aspect of the underwriting process is the investigation of the creditworthiness of the prospective home buyer. The primary consideration is, of course, whether the income of the borrower is sufficient to handle the mortgage payments under question in addition to the borrower's other expenses. The income used in this calculation may be different from the borrower's understanding of personal income, since the lender will allow only income considered stable to be used in the calculation. Another indication of the creditworthiness of borrowers is their experiences with debt obligations. A credit check usually is performed at the request of the lending institution, and this results in a credit report that lists the success, or difficulty, that the borrower has had with credit in the past. This report is used to assign a credit rating to the prospective borrower, and this rating then is used as a factor in the calculation of the risk premium of the mortgage loan.

Another factor that may enter into the creditworthiness calculation is the overall net worth of the borrower. A person that has substantial assets other than the property under consideration is much less likely to default on the mortgage loan. Also, in the case of default these assets can be attached by the lender if the value of the property is less than the outstanding principal loan balance at the time of default.

The amount of the loan, in relation to the price paid for a property, is a key determinant of the lender's risk. This loan-to-value ratio represents the potential exposure of the lender if the borrower should default on the loan and force the lender to foreclose on the property to recoup the investment. A loan-to-value ratio of greater than 80 percent (meaning a down payment of less than 20 percent) is usually considered risky enough to warrant mortgage insurance coverage, and virtually all loans with loan-to-value ratios of 90 percent or more carry this protection. The return that a mortgage loan provides to an investor is the mortgage yield. This yield includes the return generated by the interest payments on the unpaid principal balance and any other lump-sum payments, such as up-front loan fees or discount points, that increase the return on the capital invested. If the lender is servicing (handling the payments) the mortgage loan for a separate investor, the yield to the investor is less than the interest rate on the mortgage, since there is a small charge to the investor for the servicing.

THE IMPORTANCE OF THE SECONDARY MARKET

The role of a strong secondary market is essential to the future success of the housing industry. The primary market exists where a lender makes a loan to a borrower, and the secondary market refers to the buying and selling of home loans among primary lenders and investors. This purchase and sale of mortgage credit instruments is important because it links the mortgage markets to the nation's capital markets. This link provides a liquid market for mortgages. This is particularly important for investors, such as pension funds, that have typically not invested in mortgages in the past. They now can achieve the higher yields associated with sound mortgage investments with the knowledge that a market exists where these investments can be liquidated quickly and with low transaction costs.

In addition to providing liquidity, the secondary market also acts as a conduit for capital to the housing markets during periods of tight credit. Traditionally, during these periods, mortgage money becomes scarce and real estate activity slows down. By selling mortgages in the secondary market during these periods, lenders can gain access to additional funds with which they can make more mortgages. This conduit process of the secondary market also allows for a flow of capital from surplus areas to deficit areas within the country. Historically this meant that investors in the capital-rich East invested in mortgages originated in the South and West.

Another important feature of the secondary market is its dependence on standardized mortgage documentation. The key to any efficient and liquid market is the knowledge that the product that you purchase or sell is fungible, that is, interchangeable with any other product on that market. This is especially true in the mortgage markets where the number of possible variations in mortgage terms and documents can be extreme. To have an efficient secondary market standard mortgage documents must allow investors to trade in the market without worrying about differences in the mortgages underlying their investments. The pioneer in the effort toward standardization was the FHA 30-year amortizing mortgage, which became the model for conventional mortgages. Now the advent of a number of adjustable-rate mortgages means that new standard instruments must be devised.

The building of the national secondary market began with the chartering of the Federal National Mortgage Association (FNMA) in 1938; FNMA was part of the Department of Housing and Urban Development until 1968, when it was spun off into a new public/private corporation. FNMA's primary role continues to be that of a major investor in the secondary market, with a portfolio worth almost $80 billion. These purchases are financed through the issuance of short-term obligations. Although its cost of capital has been above the return on its mortgage portfolio, FNMA has remained in the market and is attempting to focus its buying on adjustable-rate mortgages. It has also recently introduced its own form of mortgage-backed security based on conventional mortgages.

Another institutional factor in the secondary market is the Government National Mortgage Association (GNMA or Ginnie Mae). This agency, part of the Department of Housing and Urban Development, guarantees mortgage-backed securities based on FHA and Veterans Administration (VA) mortgages. These Ginnie Maes form the basis of the securement of the secondary market. Under this concept investors purchase securities rather than whole loans or participations. These securities represent an undivided interest in the underlying pools of mortgages. Trading in mortgage-backed securities is much quicker and more efficient than trading in the loans themselves. The success of Ginnie Maes has spawned a number of other mortgage-backed securities programs based on conventional loans. These conventional programs are expected to grow much bigger than the GNMA's.

As the traditional division between mortgage lender and investor continues to change, the secondary market will grow even more important. Mortgage finance, once just a grouping of local or regional submarkets, has become an integral part of a truly national capital market. Thus the prospective home buyer, once assured of a steady supply of cheap credit, must now compete for funds with the nation's large corporate borrowers. Only a functioning, truly national secondary market will keep mortgage credit flowing to the consumer. Conversely, it will be this national market that lures new investors into housing finance. These investors will be attracted by the high yields and low risks represented by home loans packaged as mortgage-backed securities. The future might even bring an international secondary market for mortgages in which U.S. home buyers secure at least part of their financing from foreign capital markets.

Chapter **5**

Fannie Mae—
The Federal National
Mortgage Association

Robert J. Mylod   President, Federal National Mortgage Association

T he Federal National Mortgage Association is the largest institution in the secondary mortgage market and the largest investor in home mortgages in the United States. Fannie Mae, as it has long been nick-named, owns one out of every twenty home loans in the nation. In terms of assets, it is the fifth largest U.S. corporation.

FUNCTION OF THE SECONDARY MARKET

Through the purchase of home loans, the secondary mortgage market provides liquidity to local financial institutions, which originate mort-gages in their communities. The need for liquidity may arise for several reasons.

Certain regions of the country, notably the South and West in recent years, have experienced growth and in-migration, which create de-mand for more mortgages than local savings institutions can meet. Thus lenders in California, Texas, and Florida have been most active in sell-ing loans to Fannie Mae, and lenders in New England have been more able to meet housing demand with local capital.

Not all mortgages are provided by depository institutions. Mortgage bankers, most notably, do not have deposits; instead, they function as brokers between investors and people who need home loans. Historically, a large share of Fannie Mae's customer base has been mortgage bankers, although depository institutions have expanded their use of the secondary market in recent years.

Traditionally, the need for secondary market support has increased when money was in short supply and its cost rose. Other sources of funds for mortgages, particularly deposits in savings institutions, tend to shrink or to be diverted during periods of tight money. Lenders who ordinarily invest their own deposits in mortgages, therefore, turn to the secondary market when credit is restricted. Because of depository institution deregulation in the early 1980s, however, all kinds of mortgage originators will rely more on the secondary market throughout economic cycles.

As a result of deregulation, savings and loan associations (S&Ls)—traditionally the major sources of mortgage money—will have to pay market rates of return on savings deposits, whose interest rates used to be capped by federal regulation. The cost of money will continue to rise as a result. To enable S&Ls to pay these higher rates, they have been given expanded investment authority. More of their deposit funds will be invested in nonmortgage instruments which have shorter terms and produce higher rates of return. Thus S&Ls probably will act more like mortgage bankers, originating mortgages for sale in the secondary market. (In 1981, savings and loan associations for the first time sold more than half the dollar volume of their mortgage originations.)

Finally, the secondary market functions as a backup to all mortgage lenders. Without it, mortgage loans would be essentially illiquid and thus a much less attractive investment for lenders. Even those lenders who originate home loans intending to hold them in their portfolios can do so with the knowledge that, should their financial situation or asset management objectives change, they could sell the loans into the secondary market.

THE ORIGINS OF FANNIE MAE

The Federal National Mortgage Association was the first institution established for the sole purpose of providing liquidity to U.S. home mortgage lenders. Today a private corporation owned by its shareholders, Fannie Mae was originally a part of the federal government, a wholly owned subsidiary of the Reconstruction Finance Corporation (one of the New Deal initiatives to restore the housing industry after its collapse during the Depression).

Prior to the Depression, most home loans were for short terms, usually 5 years. Borrowers paid only interest during the term of the loan, and the principal was still owed at the end of the term. In practice, the loans were usually renewed, but, when the Depression hit, many lenders lacked the funds to refinance the loans. More than 30 percent of the mortgage loans in the nation went into default, and hundreds of lending institutions failed.

The long-term fully amortized mortgage was introduced in 1934 by the newly created Federal Housing Administration (FHA). Thus home buyers were promised that they could not lose their homes so long as they met their mortgage payments, and lenders were protected by federal insurance on the loans. However, this did not give lenders money to loan.

This problem was addressed by the establishment of the Federal National Mortgage Association in 1938 to buy the new FHA mortgages, replenishing lenders' funds so that they could make more loans.

Fannie Mae evolved with the housing market in the years after its establishment. It began to purchase loans guaranteed by the Veterans Administration (VA) in 1952.

As prosperity returned to housing in the years after World War II, the need for government-funded support diminished. In its place grew the need for a corporation which could respond to the demands of the now-active housing marketplace rather than for one which operated within the confines of the government appropriation process. Fannie Mae, as a result, became a private corporation through a series of steps taken over a 20-year period.

In 1968, Fannie Mae was completely rechartered, and its government-related functions were assigned to a new agency, the Government National Mortgage Association (promptly nicknamed Ginnie Mae). Under the new charter, Fannie Mae's purpose is to provide liquidity for housing through the purchase of mortgages. It is dependent on its own earnings and borrowing capacity to do that. The new Fannie Mae is shareholder-owned, privately managed, and tax paying.

The charter specifies certain ties to the U.S. government. The secretaries of the Treasury and Housing and Urban Development have certain regulatory authority over the corporation. Also, the Treasury has discretionary authority to purchase up to $2.25 billion in Fannie Mae debt. This "backstop" has not been exercised since the corporation became private.

The corporation's board of directors is comprised of fifteen members; ten members are elected by shareholders, and five are appointed by the President of the United States. The corporation currently has 65 million shares of common stock outstanding. It is actively traded on the New York Stock Exchange and on several regional exchanges.

The corporation has two primary sources of income: (1) the spread, or the difference between the cost of the money it borrows and the return on mortgages in which it invests those funds, and (2) the fees it charges lenders for its services.

In 1972, Fannie Mae began buying conventional (nongovernment-backed) mortgages, which now account for about four-fifths of new home mortgage originations. To create a market for loans not insured by the government, Fannie Mae fostered the development of national uniformity in home loans; in cooperation with the Federal Home Loan Mortgage Corporation (Freddie Mac), Fannie Mae drew together thousands of legal and lending forms in use across the nation and produced the uniform documents used by most home lenders today. The corporation's purchase of nongovernment loans grew steadily; by 1981, 34 percent of its portfolio was invested in conventional mortgages.

THE LINK BETWEEN MORTGAGE AND CAPITAL MARKETS

Once its ties to the federal budget were severed, the rechartered Fannie Mae became essentially a channel through which funds were attracted from the money and capital markets to housing finance.

The corporation has been the second largest borrower in the United States (after the U.S. Treasury); it borrows funds through the issuance of intermediate-term debentures and short-term notes. Although its debt issues are not insured or guaranteed by the government, the capital market has afforded them federal agency status, which results in a broader market and therefore in a larger capital resource for housing. The corporation borrowed $55 billion in 1982, of which $11.3 billion purchased additional mortgages and $43.7 billion refinanced older borrowings that had matured.

HOW FANNIE MAE PURCHASES MORTGAGES

Fannie Mae buys mortgages from all types of institutions, including savings and loan associations, mortgage bankers, commercial banks, mutual savings banks, and credit unions. A lender first obtains a "commitment," for which it pays a fee, under which Fannie Mae is obligated to purchase a specified dollar amount of mortgages, in many cases at a specified yield.

Commitments may be for different periods—for example, 2 months or 12 months—which assures lenders that funds will be available for loans that they originate within that period. Commitments may be for a specific type of loan; examples would be FHA and VA loans or adjustable-rate mortgage loans. They may provide for optional or mandatory delivery of mortgages. In a mandatory commitment, a lender must deliver the volume of loans specified. Under an optional commitment, the lender may choose to deliver loans elsewhere if a better price can be obtained once they have been originated.

Even after it sells loans to Fannie Mae, the lender continues to service them, collecting monthly payments and the like. Fannie Mae pays the lender a fee for this service, which provides that institution with a steady source of income.

Fannie Mae's purchase function is unique in several ways. Most important, Fannie Mae is always there—unlike most other mortgage investors, it invests only in mortgages. It does not divert funds to other investments when their yields rise above those on mortgages. Fannie Mae's enormous borrowing capacity dwarfs any other investor's capacity for mortgage purchases. Through recessions, periods of tight credit, and other difficult market conditions, Fannie Mae can tap large sources of funds and thus can always support housing by making mortgage funds available.

Second, Fannie Mae purchases a wider array of mortgage loans than does any other investor. It purchases fixed-rate and adjustable-rate loans; first and second mortgage loans; FHA, VA, and conventional loans. It is one of the few investors to routinely purchase loans with down payments as low as 5 percent. For several years Fannie Mae has been the largest single investor in FHA and VA graduated-payment mortgages, which have been popular with young families. It has also designed a number of new types of loans, which will be detailed later, to assist with the nation's growing problem of housing affordability. In many cases, Fannie Mae is the *only* national market for these loans. The corporation also buys loans on some multifamily and nonowner-occupied housing.

Third, the corporation offers alternative approaches for mortgage originators seeking secondary market support. Lenders may sell whole loans to Fannie Mae or partial participation interests in pools of loans. Or, they may put together pools of mortgages against which Fannie Mae will issue and guarantee securities the lenders can sell to other investors. They may use Fannie Mae's services on a regular basis, relying on the corporation as a primary source of funding for their business, or they may transact sales to Fannie Mae only during periods of particular stress on their business.

The corporation is headquartered in Washington, D.C. Policy, planning, and program development are managed primarily in the headquarters office. Purchase and marketing functions are carried out in five regional offices in Philadelphia, Atlanta, Chicago, Dallas, and Los Angeles. The addresses and service areas for the regional offices are listed at the end of this chapter.

GROWTH OF THE CORPORATION

The corporation grew rapidly throughout the 1970s, during a period of unprecedented housing—and mortgage—activity. Its portfolio grew from $15.9 billion at the end of 1970 to more than $74 billion by mid-1983. By late in 1978, however, the corporation and other portfolio investors in mortgages began to experience the pressures of rising interest rates which afflicted the U.S. economy for several years thereafter: the cost of short- and intermediate-term debt rose more rapidly than did the return on longer-term assets.

At the same time, Fannie Mae was confronted with an unprecedented need for support by the housing and home finance markets. The nation's thrift institutions were under severe stress, victims of the same pressures suffered by Fannie Mae compounded by a decrease in the supply and increase in the cost of consumer savings deposits. Fixed-rate 30-year mortgages, for decades the standard instruments used to finance U.S. home purchases, were pushed beyond the financial reach of most families by interest rates of 16 percent and higher. Home sales, new construction, and mortgage originations slowed to a trickle throughout 1981 and 1982. A system of housing that had produced a 65 percent national rate of ownership of the highest quality housing in world history no longer worked.

NEW DIRECTIONS IN THE 1980S

Changes in the marketplace and changes in its own situation prompted Fannie Mae to revamp and expand its secondary market operations in the early 1980s.

Nearly all mortgages purchased by the corporation in the 1970s were whole fixed-rate first mortgage loans. In 1981 the corporation opened up its purchases to a wide range of alternatives.

The majority of lenders actively using Fannie Mae services in the past had been mortgage bankers, whereas depository institutions were more inclined to hold their loans in portfolio. Economic strain led thrift institutions to turn to the secondary market, and Fannie Mae introduced several new purchase methods in 1981 to serve the needs of thrift institutions.

Fannie Mae began to purchase participation interests in pools of loans, which many thrift institutions prefer to the sale of whole loans. The corporation also greatly expanded the array of mortgages it would buy on a regular basis and began to purchase nonstandard loans on a negotiated basis. In addition, Fannie Mae offered to purchase older loans to provide lenders, and thrift institutions in particular, with additional sources of liquidity. In 1981 alone, FNMA tripled its volume of purchases from thrift institutions.

A LEADER IN INNOVATION

The need for alternatives to the standard fixed-rate mortgage—to make mortgages more affordable for consumers and better long-term investments for money suppliers—had become unarguable by 1981.

When federal regulators approved the origination of adjustable-rate mortgages (ARMs) in early 1981, Fannie Mae moved rapidly to provide a national market for them, opening its window for commitments to purchase several ARM varieties in July.

Also in 1981, the corporation initiated a number of new standard mortgage plans aimed at addressing the affordability dilemma posed by high interest rates. The common characteristic of these plans was that, in one way or another, they lowered monthly payments during the early years of a mortgage. Although Fannie Mae did not invent these concepts, it was the first to provide national acceptance for them. For instance, it began buying buydown mortgages, in which a third party, such as a home builder or seller, makes a lump sum payment when the loan is originated to reduce the home buyer's effective interest rate in the early years of a mortgage loan. The option of combining graduated-payment features with ARMs was another FNMA innovation aimed at making mortgages more affordable.

Fannie Mae also began to purchase second mortgage loans in 1981. Second mortgages had been considerably more expensive than first mortgages prior to Fannie Mae's entry into the market, and their availability was limited in many areas of the country. Several factors contributed to an increase in demand for second mortgages; for one, home sellers combined assumable mortgages, take-backs, and other forms of so-called creative financing with additional second mortgage financing to transact a sale under distressed market conditions. Also, many families with older low-rate mortgages turned to second mortgage financing to tap the equity in their homes to improve their property or for other purposes.

Largely as a result of all these innovations, Fannie Mae purchased $6.1 billion in mortgages in 1981 (most in the second half of the year after the new plans were introduced) and $15 billion in 1982. It remained, throughout that troubled period for the industry, a primary source of mortgage funds and the only source of funding for many of the new mortgages.

CONVENTIONAL MORTGAGE-BACKED SECURITIES

Even as it and the rest of the housing industry grappled with the immediate problem of making home ownership affordable in a high-interest-rate environment, Fannie Mae undertook to address the longer-range necessity of bringing new investors into the mortgage market. In October of 1981, the corporation introduced its guaranteed, mortgage-backed certificates—securities backed by pools of conventional mortgages which could be sold by originators of the mortgages to nontraditional investors.

A decade earlier Ginnie Mae had begun guarantying securities backed by FHA and VA mortgages. These securities, which offered investors high yield, security, and liquidity, generated the largest new infusion of capital into housing in the 1970s. But FHA and VA mortgages make up only one-fifth of the nation's outstanding home loans; the far larger share is in conventional mortgages.

Fannie Mae modeled its securities after those of Ginnie Mae, which had succeeded in attracting new mortgage investors. Of the FNMA securities sold during the first 12 months after their introduction, more than half were purchased by pension funds, the largest new source of funds for housing.

Through FNMA's mortgage-backed securities operation, lenders obtain commitments from the corporation for the issuance and guarantee of a specified dollar amount of securities sometime during the next 6 months. The lender then puts together a pool of mortgages—either new originations or old loans—and premarkets the securities to investors. When the loan pool is completed, Fannie Mae issues the securities to the investors and provides a 100 percent guarantee of the full and timely pass-through of principal and interest payments. Fannie Mae receives a fee for this guaranty, and the lender gets a fee for continuing to service the loans.

GREATER RELIANCE ON THE SECONDARY MARKET

Throughout the 1970s, the ratio of mortgages written each year to those sold into the secondary market was between 31 and 38 percent. In

1981, it topped 50 percent for the first time in history. This trend is expected to continue throughout the 1980s, making the secondary market the primary source of funds for mortgages.

Offices of the Federal National Mortgage Association

Home Office

3900 Wisconsin Avenue, N.W.
Washington, D.C. 20016

Southwestern Regional Office

2001 Bryan Tower
Suite 1200
Dallas, Texas 75201

Serving Arkansas, Colorado, Kansas, Louisiana, Missouri, New Mexico, Oklahoma, and Texas

Western Regional Office

P.O. Box 24019
10920 Wilshire Boulevard
Suite 1800
Los Angeles, California 90024

Serving Alaska, Arizona, California, Guam, Hawaii, Idaho, Montana, Nevada, Oregon, Utah, Washington, and Wyoming

Midwestern Regional Office

150 South Wacker Drive
Chicago, Illinois 60606

Serving Illinois, Indiana, Iowa, Michigan, Minnesota, Nebraska, North Dakota, Ohio, South Dakota, and Wisconsin

Southeastern Regional Office

100 Peachtree Street, N.W.
Atlanta, Georgia 30303

Serving Alabama, Florida, Georgia, Kentucky, Mississippi, North Carolina, South Carolina, and Tennessee

Northeastern Regional Office

510 Walnut Street
Philadelphia, Pennsylvania 19106

Serving Connecticut, Delaware, District of Columbia, Maine, Maryland, Massachusetts, New Hampshire, New Jersey, New York, Pennsylvania, Puerto Rico, Rhode Island, Vermont, Virgin Islands, Virginia, and West Virginia

Fiscal Office
100 Wall Street
New York, New York 10005

Freddie Mac— The Federal Home Loan Mortgage Corporation

William R. Thomas, Jr. Executive Vice President, Marketing and Mortgage Operations, Federal Home Loan Mortgage Corporation

In the late 1960s, the home-building and real estate markets were in serious trouble. Interest rates were high, and mortgage credit had virtually disappeared as new savings deposits at thrift institutions declined from $6.1 billion in 1967 to a negative $1 billion in 1969.

Congress searched for measures to stimulate the housing industry. A critical need existed for a secondary market function to serve originators of conventional mortgage loans. Conventional loans are those mortgage loans with no federal government guarantee or insurance. Both the Government National Mortgage Association (GNMA) and the Federal National Mortgage Association (FNMA) already were in operation to support the government's housing objectives by providing a secondary market for Federal Housing Administration (FHA) and Veterans Administration (VA) mortgage loans.

Through the Emergency Home Finance Act of 1970, Congress created the Federal Home Loan Mortgage Corporation (also known as "Freddie Mac"). Its major goal, as outlined in its charter, was to develop a national secondary market for conventional home mortgage loans. It was also authorized to purchase FHA and VA loans to get established as a secondary market entity while formulating programs for conventional loans. Today the corporation's programs are designed exclusively for conventional loans, and its total annual purchases of these loans amount to billions of dollars.

The corporation received initial capital of $100 million through the sale of nonvoting common stock to the twelve Federal Home Loan banks. The three members of the Federal Home Loan Bank Board (FHLBB), serving in a separate capacity, were designated as the corporation's board of directors.

Management at the corporation made two important operating decisions in its early years. First, the corporation decided that its efforts to initiate a market in which lenders could sell conventional mortgage loans should support development of a larger market with many participants. The corporation wanted to promote wide development of secondary market programs, both public and private, since demand for housing was great and demographics proved that it would steadily increase. The corporation knew that it could not meet all the nation's housing needs.

Second, the corporation designed a financial structure for its operations that was inherently different from any other secondary market entity. Rather than accumulate mortgages it purchased from lenders, it would pool the loans into securities for resale to investors. These mortgage securities are known as "pass-through" securities because a borrower's mortgage payments are passed by an original lender to a conduit like Freddie Mac, which in turn passes the payments through to an investor. The corporation's pass-through security, the mortgage participation certificate (PC), was introduced in 1971 and was the first conventional mortgage pass-through security. This method of financing has enabled the corporation to make a profit every year of its existence.

ACCOMPLISHMENTS

Because of these two major operating decisions, along with the corporation's intent to increase the availability of funds for the conventional mortgage market, the corporation has realized several accomplishments.

First, the corporation offsets the effects of disintermediation. Disintermediation is a primary cause of an economic slump within the housing industry. It is a phenomenon which occurs during periods of high interest rates, when savers take their deposits out of thrift institutions and place them in more lucrative investments. Lenders then face a demand for mortgage money that is greater than the money available from the resources of their own institutions. With a secondary market operation like Freddie Mac in place, lenders can sell mortgage loans they originate to regain funds for more lending or other investment opportunities.

Another of the corporation's accomplishments is the nationwide standardization of lending practices. Uniformity within the conventional mortgage market did not exist prior to 1970 , and the corporation had to tackle this lack if it wanted to promote national circulation of funds from capital surplus areas to capital deficit areas. The corporation, working with FNMA, developed standard mortgage documents that have been accepted by the mortgage finance industry. It created standard loan application forms and appraisal forms and procedures. It put in place underwriting guidelines and procedures.

The corporation also succeeded in building a bridge between the traditional mortgage market and the capital investment market through the sale of its mortgage pass-through securities. When first introduced, PCs found their largest investment market among thrift institutions such as savings and loan associations, which were able to use the PCs to meet their real estate investment requirements. Today, purchasers include a wide range of institutional investors, including pension funds and insurance companies. Figure 6-1 provides a composite of PC investors for the years 1977 through 1981. During that period, nonthrift institutions made up almost 60 percent of all PC investors, bringing new money from the capital market to the mortgage market. The attraction of these new funds has meant billions of dollars for housing finance which would have been invested elsewhere.

METHODS OF OPERATION

Freddie Mac buys conventional residential mortgage loans, principally from savings and loan associations. It is also authorized to buy from other institutional lenders, including commercial banks, credit unions,

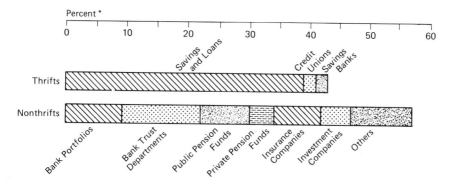

*Does not include PCs sold in the guarantor program.

Figure 6-1 Composite PC buyer profile (1977 to 1981).

mortgage bankers, and mutual savings banks. Figure 6-2 shows the percentage breakdown in 1980 and 1982 of Freddie Mac commitments to buy loans by types of institutions seeking to sell loans.

To make an offer to sell mortgages, lenders telephone Freddie Mac on any business day between 10 AM and 2 PM (EST); offers are accepted on a first come, first served basis. Sellers can also obtain commitments for an 8-month forward program each Tuesday.

A lender considers several factors before deciding to sell loans in the secondary market. These factors include (1) the dollar amount of eligible mortgages that the lender is able to sell, (2) a net yield at which the lender is willing to sell the mortgages, (3) whether to negotiate an individual deal, and (4) whether to bid for an immediate-delivery contract, for a forward-delivery commitment, or for both. Other factors, such as interest rate trends, mortgage demand, internal cash flow, and other investment opportunities are also important considerations in a lender's decision to sell.

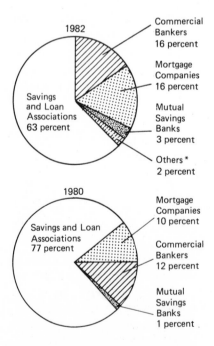

* Includes life insurance companies, private non-insured pensions funds, REITs, and state and local retirement funds.

Figure 6-2   Freddie Mac's commitments by types of sellers in 1980 and 1982.

The first factor, the dollar amount, is based on the amount of loans a lender has originated or believes it can originate within a given time. Loans must be closed before a lender can deliver them for purchase by the corporation.

The second factor a lender considers is what workable net yield to offer the corporation. A lender reviews the interest rates of the mortgages to be sold, the net yields at which other conventional mortgages are trading in the secondary market, and any other relevant information. A lender must determine that the amount of interest generated by the mortgage loans it offers for sale is sufficient to meet the required net yield to the corporation and to allow adequate servicing compensation to its institution.

A decision on the final factor, whether to bid for an immediate-delivery contract or for a forward-delivery commitment, is based on a lender's needs for funds. Before placing a bid for an immediate-delivery purchase contract, the lender must remember that delivery of closed mortgage loans is mandatory within a specified number of days after the purchase contract's date of acceptance. The lender must have a sufficient dollar amount of eligible mortgages either in its portfolio or ready to close to meet the terms of an immediate-delivery purchase contract. However, a bid under the forward program is based on a lender's anticipated lending needs, and delivery is optional. A lender does not have to deliver any loans if conditions do not develop as anticipated. In addition, large-volume lenders are encouraged to contact Freddie Mac's offices to negotiate terms for individual deals.

A package of loans delivered to the corporation must include the documentation prescribed by the corporation for each purchase program.

Underwriters review and evaluate the documents submitted by the sellers. They evaluate the loan application and analyze the credit of the borrower, the loan-to-value ratio, the ratios of income-to-total-debt obligations, housing expenses, and any other significant credit factors. Properties are physically inspected when possible adverse conditions warrant such a review.

Once reviewed, loans are purchased or rejected. If purchased, funds are transmitted from the corporation to an account specified by the seller.

Loans are usually serviced by the seller. A servicing fee, if any, paid by the corporation to the servicer varies by program and type of sale. Monthly accounting and servicing reports must be submitted by servicers to the corporation's regional offices for processing. Figure 6-3 outlines the corporation's mortgage-purchasing process.

The corporation publishes a *Sellers' Guide,* which outlines the corpo-

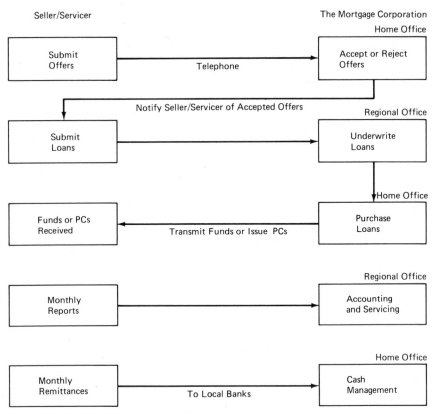

Figure 6-3 Freddie Mac's mortgage-purchasing process.

ration's requirements for loans that lenders submit for purchase; loans sold to the corporation must satisfy these requirements to be of investment quality. Investment quality of loans underlying PCs is emphasized by the corporation, because the corporation must attract buyers for its PCs.

PURCHASE PROGRAMS

A new projection of market needs for the 1980s by Regional Data Associates predicts that the secondary market will have to provide $1.17 trillion in this decade under a "most likely" economic scenario. The secondary market must expand to compensate for an erosion of the traditional savings deposit base as a source of mortgage funds. The market will have to meet new loan demand generated by changes in demographics: 42 percent of growth population in the 1980s will be among 35- to 44-year-olds, a group traditionally with the largest demand for home ownership and mortgage funds.

Freddie Mac continually works to anticipate market fluctuations and to structure programs to meet changing needs of home buyers, lenders, and investors. As of this writing, the corporation operates programs for several types of mortgage loans: (1) conventional single-family loans for fixed-rate and adjustable-rate mortgages; (2) conventional multifamily mortgages; and (3) second mortgage home improvement loans.

The corporation issues commitments to lenders to purchase these different types of loans on a daily basis. The corporation specifies the yield at which it buys loans.

Through June 1983, Freddie Mac committed to purchase about $70 billion of loans under its purchase programs. Figure 6-4 shows the yearly commitment volumes.

PURCHASE PROGRAM DEVELOPMENTS

According to the National Association of Realtors, monthly payments for principal and interest rose from $382 in 1978 to $885 in 1981 for the average-price existing single-family home financed with a down payment of 20 percent and a 30-year mortgage. Mortgage rates rose so high and so fast that most home buyers were forced out of the market; however, rates did not rise fast enough to keep pace with the cost of funds to lenders. The net worth of the nation's federally insured savings and loan associations—which make the bulk of conventional home

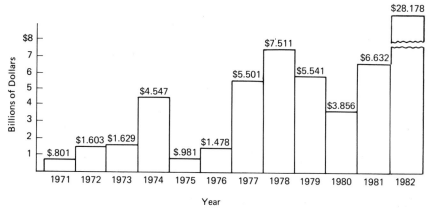

Figure 6-4 Freddie Mac's commitments (1971 to 1982).

mortgages—eroded significantly. Early in 1981 traditional mortgage lenders realized that they could no longer afford to make only 30-year loans with fixed interest rates while the interest rates they paid to borrow short-term funds continued to rise. Therefore, the corporation added new programs and enhanced its existing programs to adapt to this volatile economy.

In January 1981 the corporation inaugurated the first nationwide secondary market program for home improvement loans (HILs). The HIL program was introduced in response to a growing awareness that, as both home costs and energy costs increase, more and more home owners are choosing to improve their present housing rather than to purchase new homes.

The FHLBB issued regulations in April 1981 which permitted federal savings and loan associations to originate mortgage loans with adjustable rates. An adjustable-rate mortgage allows lenders to adjust rates on loans in their portfolio to protect them when their cost of funds changes.

Freddie Mac introduced its adjustable-rate mortgage (ARM) program for lenders, consulting with both the lending industry and consumers to identify appropriate program characteristics. The creation of a secondary market for adjustable-rate mortgages enabled lenders to originate ARM loans, secure in the knowledge that the mortgages could be sold to the corporation and the funds regained.

Also during that year, the corporation adapted its programs to permit purchases of mortgage loans with "buydown" and "shared-equity" features. Buydowns and shared-equity plans involve financing arrangements between home buyers and sellers or outside investors to help buyers qualify for mortgage loans. Although strict underwriting standards were maintained, the corporation revised its requirements to allow home buyers, sellers, and lenders additional flexibility for financing arrangements.

The corporation unveiled a quick funding program in mid-1981. The program streamlined processing requirements and cut by half the time required to deliver funds to lenders. Under the program, sellers who meet sales volume requirements and demonstrate satisfactory performance in origination, servicing, and accounting are permitted to deliver conventional fixed-rate mortgages with substantially reduced documentation.

In August 1981 the corporation began its guarantor program. Under this program, lenders are able to exchange fixed-rate mortgages, either newly originated or in portfolio, for PCs representing an interest in those same loans. Lenders who participate in the guarantor program cite improved liquidity as a key reason for their participation; PCs are more marketable than underlying mortgages. Lenders can offer PCs as collateral for certain types of borrowing rather than individual mortgages, reducing the documentation which is normally required by investors. The PC is attractive because timely payment of interest and full collection of principal are unconditionally guaranteed by the corporation. Also, lenders can arrange in advance to sell the PCs they receive from such a swap, thereby reducing the risk of an adverse interest rate movement.

The actual yield received by an owner of a PC depends on three factors: (1) the PC rate, (2) the specific timing of principal payments and prepayments of the mortgages represented by the PC, and (3) the price at which the PC is purchased. The certificate rate on a PC is set when the PC is issued. This is the rate at which interest on the unpaid principal balance will be passed through to a certificate holder.

Within its early months of operation the need of primary lenders for such a program was confirmed by the amount of activity conducted. Within 12 months of its implementation, lenders committed to exchange $22 billion of conventional fixed-rate mortgages for Freddie Mac PCs.

In 1983 Freddie Mac began purchasing ARMs tied to 3- and 5-year U.S. Treasury securities and 15-year conventional fixed-rate mortgages. The corporation also began purchasing non-owner-occupied mortgage loans under its standard and guarantor programs.

METHODS OF FINANCING

Freddie Mac uses a mix of financing alternatives to accomplish its objectives and remain profitable. It finances most of its mortgage purchases through PC sales. The corporation can also finance its operations through the issuance of debt obligations—long term through debentures and short term through discount notes, PC reverse repurchase agreements, and lines of credit obtained from commercial banks. In 1982 Congress authorized Freddie Mac to issue preferred stock.

Normally, Freddie Mac sells PCs daily through the corporation's thirteen-member group of investment bankers and its own retail sales operation. Figure 6-5 illustrates the corporation's mortgage-selling process.

Investors offer to purchase PCs at par, at a discount, or at a premium. The price at which investors purchase PCs is affected by the price offered for similar investments in the capital market.

PCs have proved to be attractive investments for capital market investors because they return a high yield relative to the level of risk.

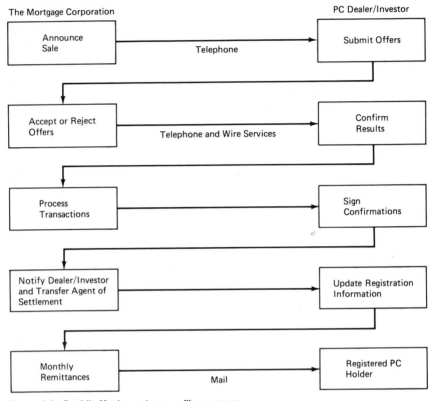

Figure 6-5 **Freddie Mac's mortgage-selling process.**

They carry the corporation's guarantee and are backed by investment-quality mortgages on residential properties.

Investors receive monthly cash flow from the mortgages through the remittance they receive from their PC investment. This frequent cash flow permits investors to reinvest the monthly remittance at market rates.

Freddie Mac periodically issues Collateralized Mortgage Obligations (CMOs), which are debt obligations secured by conventional mortgages. CMOs employ short-, intermediate-, and long-term maturities and provide long-term financing.

CONCLUSION

The Federal Home Loan Mortgage Corporation has pioneered the secondary market in conventional mortgages since 1970. The cumulative

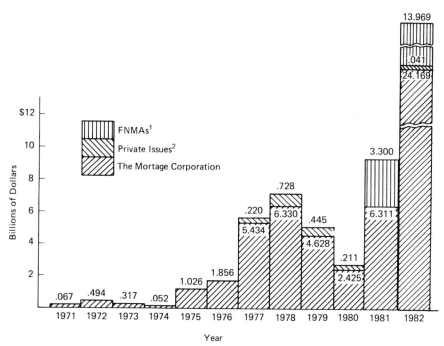

Figure 6-6 Sales of Freddie Mac's, private issues', and FNMA's pass-through securities (1971 to 1982). (¹Courtesy of FNMA. ²Courtesy of Blythe, Eastman, Paine, Webber as printed monthly in *National Thrift News.* Numbers shown include all issuers who have publicly marketed pass-through securities but do not include private placements. There were no private issues prior to 1977 or after August 1980.)

total of mortgages purchased by the corporation as of mid-year 1983 exceeded $60 billion, representing more than a million individual mortgage loans. The total mortgage portfolio—consisting both of mortgages which have been pooled into mortgage securities and of mortgages which have been retained—totaled $53 billion through the first quarter of 1983.

The corporation's PC was the industry's first conventional mortgage security. Approximately four-fifths of the corporation's purchases have been financed by selling these mortgage pass-through securities to investors. With approximately $60 billion in PC commitments since 1971, the corporation is the largest buyer-seller of conventional mortgages. Figure 6-6 compares issues of Freddie Mac securities, FNMA's conventional mortgage-backed securities, and private pass-through securities from 1971 through 1982.

The corporation's practice of buying and selling mortgages at a positive spread and with minimal market risk has maintained its profitability during both peak economic times and times of severe stress for the housing industry. The corporation has always kept its programs functioning, adapting them to current needs.

Thus the reputation of Freddie Mac is built on its leadership role in the secondary mortgage market; on the regard of investors for its financial strength; and on the convenience, quality, and liquidity of its mortgage participation certificates.

Chapter 7

Ginnie Mae— The Government National Mortgage Association

Warren Lasko Executive Vice President, Government National Mortgage Association

The marriage of the mortgage and securities markets was made complete in 1968 with the creation of the Government National Mortgage Association (GNMA)—frequently referred to as "Ginnie Mae." After years of flirtation—throughout the 1960s new ways were sought to tap the bond markets for housing loans—the Congress brought together these two major sectors of the capital market in a single financial instrument, the Ginnie Mae mortgage-backed security.

GNMA was established through amendments made to the National Housing Act in 1968. The agency, a part of the U.S. Department of Housing and Urban Development, administers two major programs: the mortgage-backed securities program, the subject of most of this chapter, and the mortgage purchase programs. The latter programs were inherited from the Federal National Mortgage Association (FNMA) when that agency was converted to a privately owned corporation in 1968.

Thus GNMA was created as much to accommodate the so-called privatization of FNMA as it was to establish a major new avenue of federal support for the housing markets. That is, a government agency was needed to carry on those functions which the newly private FNMA could not take with it to the private sector, namely, making subsidized loans and exercising the federal guaranty of securities. Surely no one then anticipated that Ginnie Mae would finance nearly twice as many housing loans as does the FNMA.

THE MORTGAGE-BACKED SECURITIES PROGRAM

Program Purpose

During the 1960s, much thought was given to finding ways to stream-line the mortgage debt instrument to make it a more attractive invest-ment to a broader base of investors. In particular, ways were sought to tap the huge volume of financial resources in the bond and securities markets. These resources never found their way into the mortgage market because of the complex legalities involved, the need for knowl-edge of local housing markets, the need for underwriting (appraise, analyze credit, and inspect) of each individual mortgage, and the need for servicing of individual mortgages. The major result of these efforts, the creation of GNMA and its mortgage-backed securities program, provides a means for channeling funds from the nation's securities markets into the housing market.

Through the vehicle of the federal guaranty (pledging the full faith and credit of the U.S. government), securities backed by mortgages became as safe, as liquid, and as easy to hold as Treasury securities. The federal guaranty made the securities acceptable to those sectors of the capital markets that otherwise would not supply funds to the mortgage market. The funds raised through the securities issued are used to make residential and other mortgage loans. Through this process, the pro-gram increases the overall supply of credit available for housing and ensures that this credit is available at reasonable interest rates.

Securities dealers have a saying for selling things to the investing public: "Keep It Simple, Stupid," known as the KISS principle. GNMA securities couple absolute security with simplicity. Investors in GNMAs can be told in a simple sentence the terms of the investment: interest at the stated rate and a full recovery of principal, both guaranteed by the federal government. More than anything, this simplicity and zero risk of loss of principal have made bond market investors on a massive scale willing to channel into the mortgage market funds that heretofore would not have gone into housing. Thus the program made the mort-gage market for the first time a truly national market, accommodating a ready interregional flow of funds for housing. In the process, the program makes the capital market more efficient through standardiza-tion, improved flow of information, and a better understanding of risks.

What Is a Ginnie Mae?

A Ginnie Mae is a privately issued security based on and backed by a pool of residential mortgages. Holders of the securities (the investors) receive a pass-through of the principal and interest payments on the pool of mortgages, less amounts to cover servicing costs and certain GNMA fees. GNMA guarantees the securities, assuring the registered holders of the security certificates of receiving the timely payment of scheduled monthly principal and interest and of certain prepayments and early recoveries of principal on the underlying mortgages. If borrowers fail to make timely payments on the mortgages, under the modified pass-through approach the securities issuers must make timely payments to the registered holders, using their own resources. It is the issuer's responsibility to originate and service the mortgages.

The securities have maturities equal to those on the underlying mortgages, usually 25 to 30 years. Because of prepayments, most of the mortgages are repaid in a much shorter period; thus the principal amount outstanding on pass-through certificates is repaid at an accelerated rate, especially in the initial years. By convention based on experience, yields on new securities often are quoted on a 12-year maturity basis. Although all the mortgages in the pools backing the securities are guaranteed by the federal government, the attractiveness of Ginnie Maes is enhanced by a further guarantee which commits the full faith and credit of the U.S. government for the timely payment of interest and principal.

Over $130 billion in GNMA securities has been issued in the 12-year history of the program. Some 3.5 million homes have been financed. The following is a summary of the principal provisions of the GNMA securities program.

Mortgage pools may consist of the following types of mortgages:

- Single-family level-payment mortgages [Federal Housing Administration (FHA), Farmers Home Administration (FmHA), or Veterans Administration (VA) loans on one- to four-family properties]
- Single-family graduated-payment mortgages (FHA or VA)
- Single-family buydown mortgages (FHA or VA)
- Mobile home loans (FHA or VA)
- Project construction loans, including multifamily residential, hospital, nursing home, and group practice facility loans (FHA)
- Project (permanent) loans, including multifamily residential, hospital, nursing home, and group practice facility loans (FHA)

Any one pool must consist of mortgages within just one of these categories. Recent levels of program activity in the several different types of pools are shown in Table 7-1.

Minimum pool sizes are $1 million for single-family mortgages and $500,000 in the other instances. Minimum amounts for certificates are $25,000 per certificate, and they may increase in $5000 increments.

TABLE 7-1   GNMA Mortgage-Backed Securities Issued, by Program Type
(Millions of Dollars)

Program	1979	1980	1981
Total GNMA securities issued	24,940	20,647	14,258
Single-family level payment	22,153	17,366	11,449
Single-family graduated payment	1,879	2,353	1,861
Mobile home loans	409	484	524
Buydown loans	—	—	32
Multifamily project loans	499	444	392

(One certificate in each issuance may be in an amount which is not a multiple of $5000.)

Program Participants

The Issuer.   The mortgage-backed securities program creates a unique role for the mortgage lender. As an issuer of GNMA securities, such a lender can create the vehicle for transferring funds from the securities market into the mortgage market. The process for becoming an issuer is illustrated in Figure 7-1.

To start this process, the lender applies to GNMA for approval to become an issuer and, simultaneously, for a commitment for guaranty of a security. Once approval of issuer status is granted, subsequent commitments are issued through a modified process.

To be eligible to issue GNMA securities, a firm must:

1. Be an FHA-approved mortgagee in good standing.
2. Be an FNMA- or GNMA-approved mortgage servicer in good standing.
3. Have the origination or servicing of mortgage loans as a principal element of its business operation.
4. Have a net worth (based on an audited financial statement) in assets acceptable to GNMA. The minimum net worth required is based on formulas relating to the volume of securities issued.

With the commitment in hand, the issuer proceeds to originate or acquire mortgage loans and to package a pool of mortgages. Typically, the issuer also makes arrangements with a securities dealer, through a "forward market" commitment, to market the mortgage-backed securities when they become available. Arrangements also must be made for a custodian to maintain possession of the mortgage and other documents and for the holding of principal and interest and tax and insurance funds at a financial institution in custodial accounts.

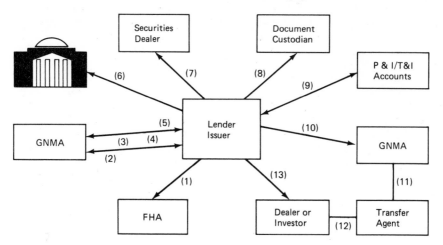

1 Lender obtains FHA mortgage approval
2 Lender applies to GNMA to become an approved issuer
3 GNMA approves lender as an issuer (based on FHA status and net worth)
4 Lender applies to GNMA for a "commitment to guarantee" securities
5 GNMA approves "commitment"
6 Lender originates FHA-VA-FmHA mortgages*
7 Lender "markets" securities *
8 Lender places loan documents with a document custodian
9 Lender establishes P & I and T & I custodial accounts
10 Lender submits "pool" documents to GNMA (includes guaranty agreement and instructions for preparing securities)
11 GNMA approves issuance and instructs New York agent to prepare certificates
12 Transfer agent delivers securities
13 Lender-Issuer administers securities

*These steps need to be coordinated to minimize market risks.
Figure 7-1   Steps to becoming a GNMA securities issuer.

When a pool of mortgages is assembled, the issuer submits to GNMA all the documents needed for final approval of the issuance. On approval of the pool documents, GNMA instructs its transfer agent to prepare and deliver the certificates in accordance with instructions provided by the issuer. With the timely delivery of the certificates ensured, the issuer can make firm plans for the sale of the certificates to investors (holders).

Once the securities are issued, the issuer thereafter is responsible for passing through to the holders the monthly payments provided for in the securities. The issuer also is required to provide for the servicing of the mortgages, for administration of the securities, and for periodic reporting to GNMA. Figures 7-1 and 7-2 outline the relationships among the various participants in the program.

There are about eleven hundred issuers active in the GNMA pro-

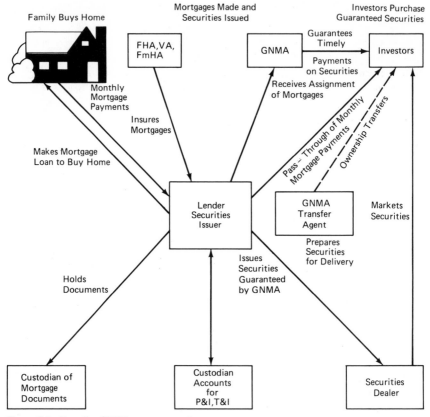

Figure 7-2 How the GNMA program works.

gram. About two-thirds are mortgage companies. The rest are primarily commercial banks and savings and loan associations (S&Ls).

The inducement for mortgage lenders to enter the program for the most part involves the fees to be earned on mortgage servicing. In the single-family securities programs, for instance, the interest rate on the securities is required by GNMA to be ½ percent (50 basis points) below the rate on the mortgages in a pool. Of these 50 basis points that the issuer earns annually over the life of each pool, 6 basis points are paid to GNMA as a guaranty fee, and the remaining 44 are retained as servicing compensation.

Securities Dealers and Investors. Most GNMAs are sold by issuers to dealers who in turn resell them to final investors. There are approximately twenty major dealer firms that account for most of the distribution and trading of GNMAs, but there are about sixty firms throughout the country that make a market in the securities.

Thrift institutions were by far the largest investors in GNMA pass-throughs when they were first issued in 1970. In recent years, however, the investor base for GNMAs has broadened substantially. As seen in Table 7-2, in addition to S&Ls, mutual savings banks, commercial banks, pension funds, state and local governments, and private businesses have become important acquirers of these instruments. Credit unions and individuals also hold significant amounts.

Origination and Trading Arrangements

GNMA securities are traded both on an immediate-delivery basis, generally involving delivery within 30 days, and on a delayed-delivery or forward basis. The former involves trades of outstanding issues as well as sales of newly issued pass-throughs. Trading on a forward basis involves the purchase and sale of securities for delivery often 3, 4, or more months in the future. There are two types of forward-delivery securities, those calling for mandatory delivery (the predominant form) on a specified forward date and those with an optional delivery before a specified date (standbys). Most of this trading occurs among the dealer firms, but permanent investors and mortgage originators also trade forward contracts to improve yields on portfolio positions or in some cases to profit from expected movements in market prices. Trading on both a regular-delivery and forward-delivery basis is done on an over-the-counter basis with dealers standing ready to add to their position (or sell from their position) at quoted-bid and asked prices.

TABLE 7-2   Holdings of GNMA Securities by Type of Holder*
(As of March 31, 1982)

Holders	Amount (billions)	Percent of total
Savings and loan associations	$ 23.6	18.1
Pension funds (public and private)	12.1	9.3
Mutual savings banks	11.5	8.8
Corporations and partnerships	8.0	6.1
Commercial banks	6.6	5.1
State and local governments	5.7	4.4
Securities dealers	5.3	4.1
Nominees†	42.3	32.4
All others	15.3	11.7
Total issues	130.4	100.0

*Based on original amounts of issuances.
†Held in nominee names for the accounts of others.

GNMA Securities and the Mortgage Production Cycle

There are fundamental economic reasons for forward transactions in mortgages and mortgage-related securities. Contracts for the sale of existing properties usually require buyers to secure mortgage commitments from lenders 2 or more months before the property is transferred and the mortgage loan is closed. Advance commitments also are essential for the construction and sale of new properties. Before making a construction loan, institutions ordinarily require developers to arrange commitments for permanent mortgage financing; in fact, the permanent mortgage commitment usually forms the basis for the construction loan commitment. The production periods for single-family structures typically range from 3 to 6 months—although periods as long as 1 year are not uncommon—and the production periods for multifamily structures are even longer.

Most parties that commit to make mortgages are also mortgage investors (such as thrift institutions) who will ordinarily take these loans into their own portfolios. Accounting conventions allow institutions to enter mortgages so acquired at par on their books, even if at the time of closing they technically have a market value below par because interest rates have risen above the rate specified in the mortgage. Given that the institution generally can also count on cash flow to make the mortgage, it is, in a sense, screened from the interest rate risk associated with entering into forward mortgage commitments.

However, a substantial volume of mortgage commitments is originated by mortgage bankers—or by thrift institutions in excess of their prospective cash flow—who do not intend to hold them permanently in portfolio. In these cases, originators must decide whether to risk a loss if market rates rise (relative to a commitment rate) in the hope of gaining a profit if rates fall or to hedge their exposure to rate fluctuation. Traditionally, the originator obtains such a hedge by arranging to sell the mortgage once it has been consummated at a specified price to a final investor.

Clearly the delayed-delivery and optional-delivery characteristics of GNMA forward-delivery contracts are the natural outgrowths of the mortgage production cycle. A mortgage originator who has committed to make a block of mortgages or who expects to enter into such commitments in the future may seek GNMA securities' optional, delayed-delivery coverage for one or both of two reasons. Originators may view the GNMA market purely as permanent investors, using the commitment as an insured source of funds at a given interest rate once loans are closed. Or originators may purchase GNMA commitments purely as standby coverage for loans they are uncertain about being able to close or for loans they may sell to others.

The price of an optional-delivery commitment will be higher than the price for mandatory-delivery commitment, reflecting the risk of nondelivery, which in today's environment is difficult to hedge. Therefore, mortgage originators will find it practical to seek optional-delivery commitments only for that portion of their mortgage originations that they are uncertain about closing or delivering.

Futures Market

An organized futures market in GNMA-guaranteed securities has been in operation at the Chicago Board of Trade since late 1975, providing a hedge against interest rate changes for GNMA issuers, investors, and dealers. Generally, actual delivery is not made on the futures market, because positions usually are offset before the futures contracts expire.

Mortgage lenders may sell GNMA futures contracts as a temporary substitute for a sale in the cash market. This short hedge balances the risk of a long position in the cash market associated with the accumulation of mortgage inventory for later sale; losses incurred in the cash market when mortgage prices are falling should be approximately offset by gains realized on the futures contracts when the mortgage banker closes out its futures market position by buying back the contract at a profit. (If mortgage prices are rising, the situation is reversed.) On the other hand, companies committing to sell GNMAs in the forward market may simultaneously secure a long hedge in the futures market by buying an equivalent amount of futures contracts. Indeed, any institution committed to buying or selling Ginnie Maes in the forward market may hedge this position by taking a position in the futures market equal to and opposite from its forward market position.

Trading, Settlement, and Clearing Facilities

Ginnie Maes worth about $53 billion were reregistered in 1981. Moreover, dealers estimated that the actual volume of secondary market trading was substantially larger due to trades involving assignment but not registration—primarily among the securities dealers. Until recently there was no central clearinghouse, and most transactions in Ginnie Maes have been settled by individual dealers, either by delivery or by pair-offs and difference checks to settle trades.

In 1979, the MBS Clearing Corporation (MBSCC) was established to offer services providing risk reduction and settlement cost savings to firms active in the GNMA forward market. Mortgage bankers, investors, and dealers participate. Settlement cost savings for participants result from MBSCC's ability to net trades each settlement month into a substantially fewer number of balance order deliveries than a firm would achieve by pairing off open trades with another firm. MBSCC routinely nets over 90 percent of all trades, while firm-to-firm pair-offs normally net only 50 to 60 percent.

MORTGAGE PURCHASE PROGRAMS

Program Purpose

Under its mortgage purchase programs GNMA, as a secondary market facility, purchases certain types of mortgages to fulfill various national housing objectives, ranging from support of particular kinds of residential construction activity to general support of the mortgage and housing markets during periods of decline in those industries.

Mortgage purchase authority has existed since 1954 as one of the types of secondary mortgage market operations carried out by FNMA. When GNMA was created in 1968, it was given authority to carry out the functions. Two purposes are provided for by statute: (1) to provide financing for special housing programs designed to serve segments of the population not adequately served otherwise and (2) to counter declines in mortgage lending and residential construction activities.

A variety of different purchase programs have been implemented: some serve the special housing needs category and others the counter-cyclical goal. With respect to the first goal, the authority has provided financing for HUD-subsidized housing programs for a long time. For example, Program 17, which began in 1970, provides financing, at below-market rates if necessary, for section 236 and rent supplement projects. Such projects receive interest rate subsidies or direct rent assistance for low-income tenants. Over $6 billion in mortgage purchase commitments was issued under that program.

Most recently, GNMA's mortgage purchase authority has been used primarily to finance HUD's rental assistance projects under the so-called Section 8 program, which provides project owners with rent subsidies for low-income tenants. GNMA, in turn, provides permanent financing for the projects, at rates as low as 7.5 percent, on new and substantially rehabilitated projects in which at least 20 percent of the units are under contract for housing assistance payments (Section 8). A total of over $8.2 billion in commitment authority was committed for such projects through mid-1982. Federal budget plans call for the termination of the mortgage purchase programs.

Once purchased, the loans generally are held in GNMA's portfolio for a relatively short period and then are resold into the private market. The sales are made at so-called prices (percentage of par value) set by the marketplace to generate a market yield to the purchaser. The purchasers frequently are pension funds and other investors of long-term funds.

Program Mechanics

GNMA operates its mortgage purchase programs through the issuance of advance commitments to purchase mortgages at below-market interest rates; these mortgages must meet specified eligibility criteria. These commitments for permanent financing enable the project sponsors to proceed with construction. Once a project is completed and the mortgage is closed, GNMA purchases—takes delivery of—the long-term loan. A Ginnie Mae's purchase price is typically 97.5 percent of par. The difference between this price and the amount subsequently realized by GNMA on sale of the mortgage represents the federal subsidy. That is, GNMA's subsidy is effected by buying high and selling low. The GNMA mortgage purchase programs are popularly known as the "tandem" or "tandem plan" programs. Specifically, the terms refer to arrangements developed in 1970 to reduce federal budget outlays for mortgage purchase activities to the subsidy amount and substituting private financing for the remainder. Initially, the tandem plans provided for the assignment to a private investor (usually FNMA) of GNMA's commitment to purchase the mortgage. Thus, when the mortgage was purchased, private rather than public funds provided the financing. GNMA would make a payment to the investor to cover the subsidy, that is, the difference between the commitment price and the market price.

Generally, GNMA now accomplishes the substitution of private capital by purchasing whole loans and disposing of the loans after purchase. The mortgages are sold, usually at periodic public auction, and the government recovers the major portion of the amount spent to purchase the mortgage.

TABLE 7-3   GNMA Mortgage Purchase and Sales Activity by Fiscal Year*
(Millions of Dollars)

	1975	1976	1977	1978	1979	1980	1981
Single-family homes							
Loan purchases	2878	6932	1457				
Loan sales	1126	6399	3094	334			
Multifamily projects							
Loan purchases	726	663	648	1115	1492	1996	2168
Loan sales	170	860	577	244	1463	835	2019

*Fiscal years 1975 and 1976 ran from July through June; for 1978 through 1981, the period is October through September. The figures shown for fiscal year 1977 include a transition quarter and hence cover the period July 1976 through September 1977.

Table 7-3 shows the volume of activity in purchases and sales in recent years; as indicated, volume has been by no means constant. Purchases increased dramatically in 1976 as part of a countercyclical program to support single-family home construction. More recently, purchases of project loans have risen primarily in response to programs aimed at financing construction under the Section 8 rental assistance program.

Mortgage Instruments

Maurice A. Unger Professor of Real Estate, Emeritus, The Graduate School of Business Administration, University of Colorado

B asically, there are three types of mortgages and a number of mortgage instruments. The three types of mortgages are the mortgage proper, the deed of trust, and the installment land contract, which for some strange reason the Idaho Supreme Court has seen fit to label "the poor man's mortgage."

THE MORTGAGE

By definition the mortgage is the creation of an interest in property as security for the payment of a debt or the fulfillment of an obligation. In early England, there were two forms of mortgage. The first was the *mortuum vadium,* which entitled the lender to the rents and profits of the pledged land; therefore the land was considered "dead" to the debtor. The second form of mortgage was the *vivum vadium,* which applied the profits of the land to the debt. For all practical purposes the two forms amounted to the same thing. Eventually there developed the "common law" mortgage, calling for the debtor to pay a sum named at a certain time. In essence this is a modern mortgage, namely, there are two parties, and one agrees to pay another a sum of money, using real property as the security for the obligation.

THE DEED OF TRUST

The deed of trust is used in a number of states in place of the mortgage.*
It evolved as the result of default on railroad bonds in the late 1800s.
For example, if a corporation sold an individual a bond valued at $1000
and then defaulted, each bondholder had to sue as an individual. As a
result bonds became almost impossible to sell. To overcome this, a
corporation (as trustor or grantor) transferred the security for the debt
to a trustee who held for the benefit of the bondholders. Then, on
default, the trustee could foreclose on the security for all the bondholders. This developed into the real property deed of trust whereby the
borrower (trustor or grantor) conveys to a trustee for the benefit of the
lender. There are three parties here instead of two.

In both a deed of trust and a mortgage a note is signed, and the
property is used as security for the note.

Most of the institutional lenders, both in those states using the mortgage and in those using a deed of trust, have standardized the residential forms insofar as the first seventeen clauses are concerned. This was
at the insistence of both the Federal National Mortgage Association and
the Federal Home Loan Mortgage Corporation, who are by far the
largest purchasers of mortgages on the secondary market.

CONTRACT FOR DEED

The contract for deed or installment land contract also employs three
parties and is most frequently used as a seller financing device. The
three parties are the seller, the buyer, and the escrow agent. Under the
terms of the contract, the seller agrees to sell the buyer a parcel of real
property. However, legal title to the property is not to be transferred
to the buyer until the terms of the contract have been fulfilled. To
ensure this both the contract and a deed signed by the seller are delivered to an escrow agent, typically a bank. The escrow agent is given
instructions to receive payments and to deliver the deed to the buyer
after the terms of the contract have been fulfilled. The contract will
contain many of the provisions of a mortgage, namely, that the buyer
must pay the real property taxes, must keep the property insured
against fire, and so on.

Legal title remains with the sellers, and equitable title is given to the

*These states are: Alabama, Alaska, California, Colorado, Delaware, District of Columbia,
Illinois, Idaho, Mississippi, Montana, Nevada, New Mexico, Oregon, Tennessee, Texas,
Utah, Virginia, Washington, and West Virginia.

buyers during the term of the contract. Because buyers have equitable title, they are entitled to possess and to do with the property what they wish, except, of course, to commit waste.

It should be noted that the land contract calls for any payments made by the buyer to go to the seller as liquidated damages (damages decided on beforehand) in the event of default by the buyer. Whether this is enforceable depends on how much the buyer has actually paid to the seller. For example, in a contract calling for payments of $100,000 over time, assume that the buyer defaults after having paid $99,000; the question is whether the courts would permit the seller to keep the $99,000 and also get the property back. The answer is probably not. This would be labeled a forfeiture rather than liquidated damages, and a foreclosure sale would be necessary.

The foregoing is an outline of what might be termed the "garden variety" of mortgage instruments. The real question remains: how can these instruments be manipulated or used to achieve various financing ends?

THE PURCHASE MONEY MORTGAGE

The purchase money (PM) mortgage is used in seller financing, for both residential and nonresidential purposes.

Residential Financing

Assume that a seller owns his or her property free and clear. If money is tight with consequent high interest rates, the seller may agree to take back a PM mortgage as part of the purchase price. The buyer simply gives the seller a down payment and signs a note and mortgage payable to the seller.

There may also be a second PM mortgage. For example, assume a $100,000 piece of property with a $60,000 assumable mortgage. The seller may agree to take $20,000 down, a second PM mortgage in the amount of $20,000, with the buyer assuming and promising to pay the existing $60,000 mortgage.

Nonresidential Financing

Nonresidential financing generally arises in one of two ways: either a builder-developer is building tract homes or a builder-developer is engaged in what might be called "commercial development," for example, a shopping center.

From the viewpoint of the builder-developer one of the objects of the game is to use as little of his or her own money as possible. For example, in the case of tract homes, assume a seller has 100 lots valued at say $10,000 each for a total of $1 million. A sale might take place wherein the buyer (builder-developer) puts down $100,000 and the seller takes back a PM mortgage (or deed of trust) in the amount of $900,000. In this case the PM mortgage will contain a *partial release* clause whereby the seller agrees to release certain lots from the PM mortgage on payment of a certain sum of money. For example, it might read that on payment of $10,000 a certain lot will be released from the mortgage. The seller probably will require that somewhat more must be paid for the buyer to obtain the release, for example, $11,000, with the additional $1000 used to reduce the total indebtedness. This means that at some point the entire indebtedness will have been paid, and all the lots will then be released from the mortgage.

Any form of loan given to a builder-developer involves a two-step procedure: interim financing (construction loan) and permanent financing. If a builder-developer seeks a construction loan, it will be refused unless the land is free and clear of any encumbrances, therefore it must be released. When a tract home is sold, the permanent lender in effect substitutes the permanent loan for the construction loan.

If a builder-developer wants to build a shopping center, she or he may still put down $100,000 with the seller taking back a PM mortgage in the amount of $900,000. In this case the PM mortgage will contain a subordination clause in which the seller agrees that at the request of the builder-developer the first PM mortgage of $900,000 will move into second position under any construction loan. To effect this a subordination agreement is signed by the seller when the construction loan is obtained by the builder-developer.

In recent years, a new clause has been added to this type of agreement. This clause provides that the PM mortgage will automatically be subordinated to any construction loan. This automatic clause results from some builder-developers having been forced to pay additional sums to sellers who have refused to honor the subordination clause in their mortgages. Although the subordination clause is legally enforceable, builder-developers have paid rather than become involved in costly law suits.

Balloon Mortgage

To understand some of the material that follows, it is necessary to understand the so-called balloon mortgage. It is in fact a "garden variety" mortgage with a special proviso. In general it calls for periodic payments that do not amortize the loan by its termination date, at which time a lump sum payment is made. The notes which are secured by mortgages generally are considered *interest-only notes* or *straight notes.*

With an interest-only note, the borrower pays interest only for the term of the note, paying the principal at the end of the term. For example, an individual borrows $20,000 at 14 percent, interest only for 5 years. Typically, the interest is payable monthly, semiannually, or annually. At the end of the 5-year period the $20,000 is due and payable. This was the most common form of mortgage prior to the depression of the 1930s.

The straight note is only slightly different. With a straight note there are periodic payments of principal and interest. However, the payments of principal and interest do not amortize the mortgage over the term, and at the end of the term there is a balance due and payable.*

The Gap Mortgage

A gap or "bridge" mortgage is the "garden variety" of mortgage or deed of trust with a difference. It is in reality a second mortgage to be paid off when a permanent lender disperses the full amount due under the terms of a commitment for a first-mortgage loan.

Assume, for example, that a builder-developer has obtained both a construction loan and a commitment for a $5 million office building from a permanent lender. Among other things, the permanent commitment will provide for what is called a "platform" and a "floor" amount. In effect, permanent lenders state that if the project is 100 percent rented on completion of the project, they will buy the loan for $5 million from the construction lender. The agreement will also state, however, that if the project is not 100 percent rented (normally a percentage lower than 100) that they will only buy, say, $4.5 million on completion of the project. Further, the permanent lender states that the builder-developer generally has from 1 to 3 years to rent the project up to whatever percentage the permanent lender requires. The $500,000 that is missing is the "gap."

Where does the money to finance the gap come from? It comes from either a private investor or from the construction lender. In most cases it is the construction lender.

The Private Lender. In the case of a private lender, the $500,000 gap is obtained from a private investor. Generally, the mortgage takes the form of an interest-only mortgage with a balloon running between 1

---

*In California private lenders should seek legal counsel before becoming involved in the balloon mortgage. The court there has held that if the borrower's financial net worth has not declined and the value of the security is not threatened by waste or depreciation, the lender cannot foreclose merely because the borrower has not made or cannot make the balloon payment. Pas. v. Hill, 87 Cal App. 3d. 503, 530 (1978).

and 5 years. The interest rate is exceedingly high, and the mortgage contains a provision that the permanent lender can pay off the "gap" at any time. It should be added that the high rate of interest is an additional incentive for the builder-developer to rent the property as rapidly as possible. Of course the investor has only a junior lien against the property.

The Construction Lender.   In most cases the money for the gap is supplied by the construction lender. This is provided for in a previously executed buy-sell agreement signed by the builder-developer, the permanent lender, and the construction lender. A *buy-sell agreement* is a three-party agreement nearly always entered into when large sums of money are involved. Basically the permanent investor agrees to buy the loan from the construction lender on completion of the project. Another function served by the buy-sell agreement, at least from the viewpoint of the permanent lender, is that it prevents the builder-developer from shopping around for a better interest rate during the construction period. For example, the permanent lender might agree to take the loan at, say, 13 percent; without the buy-sell agreement if rates went down to 10 percent the builder-developer might obtain another permanent investor. Of course, were interest rates to rise, the builder-developer would be protected by the buy-sell agreement.

THE PIGGYBACK MORTGAGE

The so-called piggyback mortgage consists of a loan made jointly by two or more lenders. Sometimes it is called a "shared loan" or a "participation loan." In its simplest form two investors chip in to make a single loan. For example, A may need a $50,000 mortgage. A approaches C and B, who agree to make the loan. A note and mortgage is signed by A for $50,000 with C and B as mortgagees. C and B enter in an agreement called a "participation agreement" in some states and in others an "ownership agreement." The instrument defines the ownership or shares that two or more persons have in the same mortgage. Both parties may have put in an equal amount, and the participation agreement will so state. If the amount is unequal, this too will be spelled out, and conceivably one of the parties will agree to be a junior participant in the loan or to take the place of a second mortgagee.

   The piggyback mortgage is often used by institutional lenders to allow borrowers a higher loan-to-value ratio than may be permitted by law. Assume a borrower needs a 90 percent loan of $1 million, or $900,000, and an institution cannot make a loan greater than 75 percent, or $750,000. The institution can participate with "approved lenders." [These are federally and state-chartered insured savings and loan associations (S&Ls), insured banks, lenders approved by the Federal Housing Administration (FHA), and government secondary market agencies.] In this case, the institution agrees to take five-sixths of $900,-000, or $750,000, the maximum it can lend. (This institution is called the "lead" lender.) The participant then takes one-sixth of the $900,000 loan, or $150,000. The total amount of the loan is $900,000, or the 90 percent loan-to-value ratio needed by the mortgagor.

When two institutions are involved, the participation agreement spells out the shares of each in the mortgage and generally calls for each to be co-first mortgagees.

Sometimes the piggyback loan is made by an institution and a private investor. However, this is possible only when a participation agreement calls for the lead lender (the institution) to be the senior participant (first mortgagee) and for the private investor to be the junior participant (second mortgagee). In some strange fashion this has been ruled not a participation and hence approved (see Opinion of the General Counsel, Federal Home Loan Bank Board, June 3, 1969).

The Backup Contract Mortgage

The backup contract mortgage consists of a mortgage on a parcel of real property with a contract which guarantees the monthly payments. If a mortgage is sought for a special purpose building (for example, a building which might contain indoor tennis courts), the problem from the viewpoint of a proposed lender is that in the event of foreclosure a property of this nature might prove to be unmarketable. Consequently, in addition to the mortgage the proposed lender will require that either a corporation or an individual with an extremely high credit rating enter into a contract with the institution agreeing to guarantee the monthly payments on the mortgage for the term of the mortgage loan.

The Collateralized Mortgage

Rather than get involved in a participation loan, a lending institution might require a collateralized mortgage. The ultimate goal is the same as in the participation loan, namely, to enable a lender to make a loan with a higher loan-to-value ratio than permitted either by law or by institutional policy. Assume that legally an institution is permitted to make only a 75 percent loan and that a borrower requests $1 million. Because the institution can only lend $750,000, the additional $250,000 will be loaned only if it is secured by something other than the real property—generally time deposits of the borrower or a guarantee of another financial institution (national banks legally are permitted to make this type of guarantee).

The Buydown Mortgage

In the final analysis the buydown mortgage is in a real sense a collateralized mortgage, but the reasons for it are quite different from those for a commercial collateralized loan. First, it involves a loan on the purchase of a residence; second, the institution can legally make the loan. The purpose behind the buydowns is to lower monthly payments to the buyer during the first few years of the mortgage, thereby enabling more persons to qualify for such loans.

The seller pays the buydown. This lowers the interest rate and hence the monthly payments. The money paid for the buydown is placed in escrow at the closing and is added on to the monthly payments paid to the lender. Although generally the seller, often a builder, pays for the buydown, the payments for the buydown can be made by anyone, a buyer or a third party.

The Sale-Buyback

The sale-buyback involves both the use of the installment land contract or contract for deed and very large sums of monies. Assume that a builder-developer has built a project of $1 million; the project is then sold to an investor for $1 million. Simultaneously, the builder-developer and the investor enter into a long-term installment contract whereby the builder-investor agrees to repurchase the property. Under an installment contract title is split between legal title (in the investor) and equitable title (in the builder-developer). A number of things have taken place: (1) the builder-developer has achieved 100 percent financing; (2) as the equitable title holder, the builder-developer is entitled to depreciation [c.f. J.I. Morgan Inc., 30 T.C. 881 (1958)]; and (3) the builder-developer can deduct real property taxes and interest paid under the terms of the contract.

With regard to the investor, there also are three pertinent points: (1) In addition to interest, these transactions call for the investor to receive a percentage of the builder-developer's net income after the payment of the installment payment. (2) There is generally a 15-year "lock-in" provision, which prohibits the builder-developer from paying off the contract during that period, and generally, too, there are termination options at 5-year intervals. (3) The yield to an investor is greater than it would be under the terms of a mortgage.

For example, assume a 35-year contract of $1 million. On an annual basis the amortization is found by dividing the total amount by the number of years, or $28,571. As a percentage of $1 million this amounts to 0.03 percent. Thus the *principal* is paid off at the rate of 3 percent per year. Naturally the lender has to be paid a rate of interest on top of that, say, 8 percent, and 8 percent of $1 million is a payment of $80,000 per year. The total payment is 8 percent plus the 3 percent paid on principal, or an 11 percent annual constant. The annual payments then amount to $110,000.

Assume that the net income from the property is $200,000, which is to be split between the investor and the builder-developer. If the investor is to get 10 percent, then

Net income	$200,000
Less installment	110,000
Cash flow	$ 90,000
The split would be:	
Investor-seller	$10,000
Builder-developer–buyer	80,000
	$90,000

Under this situation the investor-seller receives $120,000 per year. If it were a mortgage at 8 percent interest, the yield would be much less. To find the mortgage payment the loan is divided by the present-value annuity interest factor for 35 years at 8 percent, which is 11.654. Thus: $1 million divided by 11.654 equals $85,807. Of this amount $80,000 is interest ($0.08 \times \$1,000,000$) for the first year only. After that the interest declines. The installment in the sale-buyback is $220,000, of which $80,000 is also interest, but the interest does not decrease each year; consequently, over the life of the contract the investor receives a larger amount in interest than under the terms of a mortgage.

The Wrap-around Mortgage

The wrap-around mortgage is a junior lien given as security for a note. The face value of the note is the sum of the balance of a first mortgage plus the amount due on a second mortgage. For example, assume a first mortgage of $50,000 and a loan to be given for $25,000—the total amount of the note will be $75,000. In states using a deed of trust, the wrap-around mortgage is called an "all-inclusive deed of trust."

Originally the wrap-around mortgage was developed to circumvent usury laws. At one time, for example, in the State of New York any rate of interest greater than 6 percent was considered usury, and 4 percent interest or less was considered normal. For example, assume an existing first assumable mortgage at 4 percent for $50,000. Assume a selling price of $75,000 with a wrap-around mortgage of $25,000 plus the

$50,000 at 6 percent. The total amount of interest to be paid to the holder of the mortgage is $4500 (0.06 × $75,000); out of this $4500, $2000 must be paid to the holder of the first mortgage, giving the holder of the mortgage a net of $2500, amounting to a 10 percent return on the $25,000 at risk, thereby circumventing the 6 percent usury law.

In recent years the wrap-around mortgage has been used to circumvent the nonassumption or due-on-sale clause that was inserted in conventional mortgages. The due-on-sale provision states that if the home is sold, the lender may modify the mortgage loan terms (interest) or call the loan due and payable in full. Over time, seventeen states either by legislative action or judicial decree declared the due-on-sale clause unenforceable. However, savings and loan associations who made most of the loans containing the clause are either federally chartered or state chartered. The federal courts, including the U.S. Supreme Court, have ruled that the federal courts can preempt the state courts with regard to any rulings on the due-on-sale clause where the institution is federally chartered. More important, in October 1982, President Reagan signed federal legislation making due-on-sale clauses enforceable.

Interestingly enough, while the various states were declaring the due-on-sale clauses unenforceable, the Federal National Mortgage Association (Fannie Mae), to protect itself from the wrap-around mortgage, in 1980 required a provision in all new fixed-rate conventional mortgages purchased that gave the holder of the mortgage a one-time right to call the mortgage due and payable at its seventh anniversary.

When President Reagan signed the legislation making the due-on-sale clauses enforceable, Fannie Mae announced that it would no longer require the 7-year call provision in fixed-rate conventional mortgages that it purchased effective October 15, 1982.

The Contract for Deed as a Wrap-around Mortgage

The contract for deed or installment land contract has been used as a wrap-around mortgage for many years, especially with regard to the purchase of farms and ranges. For example, assume that a property has a mortgage against it for $200,000 at 10 percent. A small down payment has been made, and the buyer owes $100,000 on the contract plus the $200,000 to the institution. The entire amount calls for the buyer to pay the seller 12 percent. Generally the buyer makes payment to an escrow agent (as in most wrap-around mortgages). The escrow agent then makes the payment on principal and interest to the holder of the first mortgage and goes to the seller under the terms of the contract.

Mortgage on a Lease

The mortgage on a lease, or leasehold mortgage, develops where a lease is mortgaged as security for a debt. Very frequently it is used in the sale of a business where the real property itself is not conveyed. For example, assume that a seller owns a business valued at $100,000. The seller does not own the real property but has a 12-year assignable lease. The fixtures are valued at $25,000. A buyer appears with $25,000 down payment. The buyer signs a note for $75,000. The $25,000 worth of fixtures is secured to the buyer as provided for by the Uniform Commercial Code. There still remains $50,000 which is unsecured. To secure this a mortgage on a lease is executed by the buyer in favor of the seller. The seller assigns the lease to the buyer. Under the terms of the mortgage on the lease, even in lien theory states is transferred back to the seller, on the condition that if the buyer pays the indebtedness, then the instrument will become void (nothing); if the buyer does not pay the indebtedness, then the seller is entitled to regain possession of the premises.

Often the mortgage of the fee plus a leasehold mortgage is used in high-ratio financing for commercial development. It arises under this kind of situation: assume that a builder-developer owns a parcel of land for which he or she paid $500,000 which is now worth $1 million. The builder-developer decides to construct a $2 million commercial property and after completion the total value of the land plus the building would total $3 million. The builder-developer could sell the property and lease it back under a straight sale-leaseback. In this case the $500,000 profit from the sale of the land would be a taxable event to the builder-developer. A second alternative could be a subordinated ground lease, subordinated to a first mortgage placed on the property by a permanent lender. On completion, the total value of the project is $3 million. In all probability, the best the builder-developer could hope for would be a 75 percent loan or $2.25 million.

Because the builder-developer's object is to get as much leverage as possible, she or he may look to the fee mortgage plus the leasehold mortgage. Therefore, the builder-developer forms a corporation called Builder-Developer, Inc. Then the builder-developer leases the $1 million piece of land to Builder-Developer, Inc. The lease is long-term, which is immediately recorded. At this point the builder-developer has the lease as owner-lessor plus the land that he or she is the owner of the fee simple in the leased land.

At this point two separate mortgages are negotiated: (1) an unsubordinated mortgage on the fee owned by Builder-Developer, Inc., for a 90 percent loan-to-value, or $900,000; (2) a mortgage on the lease for a 75 percent loan-to-value secured by the $2 million of improvements for $1.5 million, the total of the two mortgages amounting to $2.4 million.

Most of these loans are entered into by life insurance companies, using state laws permitting what is called a "basket loan." A basket loan allows insurance companies to place a percentage of their admitted assets in otherwise unauthorized or illegal investments. The percentages range from 3 percent to a high of 20 percent.

In this situation, the lender is protected in three ways: (1) The $900,-000 mortgage on the fee simple is secured by both the $1 million value of the land and by the rent from Builder-Developer, Inc., payable to the builder-developer (owner-mortgagor). (2) If the mortgage on the lease of $1.5 million is foreclosed, the builder-developer still has the fee simple, because the fee is unsubordinated. (3) If there is a foreclosure by the mortgagee on the fee simple, the mortgagee winds up with the land subject to the leasehold rent and the leasehold mortgage.

Part **2**

Real
Estate
Investing

Real Estate Investment Analysis

Richard P. Halverson   Executive Vice President, First Trust Company of Saint Paul

T he bottom line of any real estate investment is making money—making more money than can be made in alternative investments. But, investing is uncertain; the ultimate outcome is always unknown, and the investor must make decisions based on careful analysis.

Today, perhaps more than ever, careful, sophisticated analysis is the key to successful investing. But appropriate analysis can vary greatly depending on the investor and his or her circumstances. Traditionally, real estate investments have been the province of the wealthy: investors in high tax brackets who can use the substantial tax shelter frequently associated with real estate ownership. Today, however, a major new investor is on the scene—an investor who pays no taxes and cannot use any tax shelter. This investor, pension funds, is growing rapidly in size and influence.

TAXABLE AND NONTAXABLE INVESTORS

Comparing the taxable with the nontaxable real estate investor can clarify the fundamental differences between these two major sources of equity real estate investment and can help investors understand what the market for real estate is today and what it will be in the future. As we explore the differences between taxable and nontaxable investors, it is important to remember that perfect generalizations are impossible. Each investor is different, and each real estate deal is unique.

Individual versus Institutional

Taxable investors are customarily individuals. Pension funds, and other nontaxable investors, are customarily large pools of funds managed by financial institutions. Individuals invest for themselves. Institutions invest for others, and their clients are often represented by committees and boards of directors. Individuals make their own decisions and take their own risks. Institutions are paid professionals who make decisions and take risks for their clients. The institution is concerned not only about how well the investment might do but also about how its clients will feel about the investment. An individual can respond to hunches and intuition. An institution finds it difficult to explain hunches and intuition to clients. This does not mean that institutions are unwilling to take sizeable risks on behalf of clients. It does mean that institutions want to carefully quantify risks in their analysis.

The Prudent Man Rule

Most pension funds have trustees. A trustee is a person or a corporation charged with the responsibility of taking care of someone's property. In a pension fund the property belongs to beneficiaries. If imprudent decisions are made, the trustee can be sued.

In large pension funds the trustee is usually a bank and/or the institution investing the money. All trustees are subject to the so-called prudent man rule. Trustees have learned from sad experience that the only time their prudence is called into question is after a loss has occurred—an investment always looks like a bad idea after a loss. The only defense a trustee has after a loss is the ability to demonstrate that she or he acted with diligence and prudence before the investment was made. There are several things a trustee can do: First, carefully research and document judgments before investments are made. This prolongs the analysis and rules out investments that cannot be well analyzed. Second, invest in assets commonly used by other respected trustees. This slows the momentum for unusual, new, or creative investment concepts. Trustees usually want some other trustee to go first. Third, avoid investments with high potential risks even though there might be high potential rewards. Fourth, subject the potential investment to the scrutiny of many people. The institution may examine an investment all the way to its board of directors before committing. This results in time delays and increases the likelihood of rejection.

Another important issue with respect to prudence is that in the past

the courts have been willing to examine the prudence of a single investment among a whole portfolio of investments. A trustee may have fifty
investments of which forty-nine are wonderful. But, if one fails, the
trustee can be sued.

This individual investment concept is important when applied to real
estate. Each piece of real estate—no matter how desirable—is a small
business. Like any small business it faces high specific risks. That means
the trustee is likely to consider the risk of buying a shopping center
anchored by a J.C. Penney store as being substantially higher than the
risk of buying J.C. Penney stock. If traffic projections at the shopping
center fail to materialize, the shopping center may go broke and the
Penney store may close, but J.C. Penney as a company will continue.

Legislators are making some effort to switch the prudence tests from
individual investments to the total portfolio results. But most attorneys
feel it will be many years before the courts fully subscribe to this concept.

Prudence concerns are very real to all trustees. Institutions know this
and react accordingly. Individual investors who are not trustees have
no such concern. Prudence concerns have retarded the growth of equity investments in real estate by pension accounts. The concerns are,
however, being overcome. Nevertheless, for a considerable time to
come, when real estate is considered institutions will be most interested
in established, well-run, profitable properties with straightforward
financing. Institutions will shy away from development projects, heavily leveraged projects, projects without positive cash flow, and projects
containing unusual financing or other terms.

The Entrepreneur versus the Institution

To be successful the taxable real estate investor must be a tough-
minded investor and a creative entrepreneur. Frequently, the purchase of real estate puts him or her close to the running of a small
business, a business that may require substantial entrepreneurial management. A building or a piece of land can only make money for the
investor if it is earning an economic return.

The entrepreneur makes decisions, solves problems, and sees that
things happen. For example, the owner must lease space, collect rents,
and provide maintenance. And even though the investor may employ
professionals to handle these affairs, the professional is an extension of
the investor's entrepreneurial responsibilities. The more successfully
the entrepreneur manages a property, the greater the investment return.

In many cases, the actual success of the investment depends directly on the entrepreneurial skills of the investor. This means that a key decision in the analysis of taxable investors is how well they can handle the entrepreneurial aspects of real estate.

Nontaxable investors, on the other hand, are not entrepreneurs, they are institutions. Typically, institutions want to stay as far away as possible from entrepreneurial decisions. Institutions do not want to make operating decisions regarding a property. They do not want to worry about leasing properties, developing properties, or maintaining properties. Their fees rarely include such services, and consequently they are not staffed to perform them. Part of the analysis of an institution includes how well the property is managed by some other entrepreneur.

Pride of Ownership

Individuals frequently develop a pride of ownership for real estate. Institutions do not. Pride of ownership can color an investor's analytical objectivity for a purchase or a sale. An institution will frequently be much more statistical in its approach and very dispassionate in its ownership.

Time Horizon

Taxable individuals frequently have time horizons that extend only until the major tax or financing benefits run out. This time horizon is frequently less than 10 years. Further, individuals may come under pressure to sell when market conditions are poor.

Pension funds are capable of taking time horizons that are almost perpetual, and thus the pension fund can buy and sell when the market is right.

Tax Shelters

Taxable individuals usually want all the tax shelters they can get. This frequently leads taxable investors to new and development projects with heavy depreciation schedules and to heavily financed projects. Pension funds cannot use tax shelters, and therefore they lean toward investing in established projects with established positive cash flows. Usually the pension fund buys the property with no financing. Further, if possible, the institution will arrange for taxes and other deductibles to become the property of tenants who may be able to deduct them.

Investment Goals

Taxable and nontaxable investors are fundamentally different. It is reasonable that their investment objectives should also be different.

The investment goals of individuals include tax shelters and wealth accumulation. Much of their investment return comes from the government, in the form of tax savings, and from real estate appreciation. Often this appreciation is attractive only through the use of heavy financial leverage. The leverage allows the individual to buy the property with a small investment and to enjoy a substantial increase in wealth even with modest appreciation. But the pursuit of both large tax shelters and leveraged wealth accumulation substantially raises the potential risk of investment failure. Entrepreneurs are willing to take such risks.

The goals of pension funds are to achieve a total rate of return equal to or better than alternative investments. The pension fund also seeks diversification of its investments and an inflation hedge.

Professional money managers with large investment pools believe strongly in diversification. Increasingly, equity ownership in real estate is being recognized as an appropriate diversification to equity ownership in common stocks.

Despite the diversification argument, professional money managers want each investment to appear attractive relative to alternative investments. If the investment manager can earn more buying corporate bonds, why not buy the bonds and forget the real estate?

Inflation is a problem for pension funds. Pension fund managers would like to see the value of the pension assets increase at least as much as inflation. This helps the pension fund increase payments to beneficiaries in line with inflation. Real estate is one of those assets that has historically appreciated along with general inflation.

Inflation hedges and adequate rates of return can be achieved without tax shelters and financial leverage, and the risk of investment failure is reduced. Trustees prefer lower-risk situations.

Analysis by the Numbers

Differences between taxable and nontaxable investors lead to differences both in the properties to which each is attracted and in the type of analysis each will do. Suggested approaches follow. Each represents considerable effort, but since real estate investments tend to be large, the effort is justified.

The following are examples of appropriate analytical techniques. The figures in these examples are illustrative only, and they should not be considered typical of all real estate deals.

Assume that a taxable individual is anticipating the purchase of a duplex. The price is $150,000. The investor can finance the property with a $90,000, 25-year, conventional mortgage at 15 percent. Further, the seller is willing to take back a $45,000 contract for deed at 12 percent. The contract is due in 8 years in one lump sum. The investor puts in $15,000 equity.

Assume that the investor's combined federal and state tax rate is 60 percent. (State taxes are usually important and worth considering in the analysis.) The first step in the analysis is to estimate the cash flow for the first year in detail (Table 9-1).

A. Gross Rent. Gross rents are the total rents the investor can plan to receive if the unit is fully rented and everyone pays on time. To esti-

TABLE 9-1 Cash Flow Projection

	Revenues		
A.	Gross rent	$12,000	
B.	Less vacancy time	368	
C.	Net revenues (A − B)		$11,632
	Tax-deductible cash expenses		
D.	Manager's fee	$ 0	
E.	Regular maintenance	2,250	
F.	Rerent maintenance	400	
G.	Rental expense	160	
H.	Miscellaneous expenses	180	
I.	Utilities	676	
J.	Property taxes	3,000	
K.	Special assessments	0	
L.	Insurance	600	
M.	Interest payments (no principal)	18,876	
N.	Total tax-deductible cash expenses (D to M)		26,142
O.	Profit (loss) before noncash expenses (C − N)		$ (14,510)
	Tax-deductible noncash expenses		
P.	Depreciation		$17,500
Q.	Taxable profit (loss) (O − P)		($32,010)
	Taxes		
R.	Taxable profit (loss) (line Q)	($32,010)	($32,010)
S.	Tax rate	×60 %	
T.	Less tax liability		(19,206)
U.	Net profit (loss) (R − T)		($12,804)
	Cash flow		
V.	Profit (loss) before noncash expenses (line 0)		($14,510)
W.	Subtract tax liability (line T)		(19,206)
X.	Total cash flow (V − W)		4,696
Y.	Subtract principal payment on financing		357
Z.	Net cash flow		$ 4,339

mate this, examine the rental history of the property and the experience of other units in the area. Rental rates tend to increase 5 to 10 percent a year. In this example, assume that the investor can get $500 a month for these units or $12,000 a year for both units.

B. Vacancy Time. Renters do move around, and a turnover of 100 percent is not at all uncommon in some places, despite leases. Study the local area to make an estimate. In this example, assume a 50 percent turnover. With a 50 percent turnover, one tenant will leave every year. Then the investor must estimate how long the apartment will stand vacant before it is rented again. There are two variables to consider: (1) How long will it take to clean the unit for rerent? (2) How long will it take to get a suitable tenant? In our example assume 2 weeks, which is not bad for a part-time owner-landlord. At 2 weeks, this unit may be vacant 3.8 percent of the time. The expected lost rent due to vacancies is $230 (3.8 percent × $6000 per unit = $230).

Lost rental due to vacancies is not the only possible loss of rent. Renters are sometimes slow in paying. In fact, sometimes they get behind a couple of months and then leave. Estimating this loss is difficult, but assume it to be $138. Total lost rent due to vacancies is $368 ($230 vacancies + $138 losses = $368).

C. Net Revenues. Net revenues are line A minus line B.

D. Manager's Fee. Many investors hire professional managers to run their apartments. Managers take care of rentals, show the apartments, collect the rents, dun the slow payers, handle complaints, enforce the rules, maintain the property, and so on. Obviously managers want to be paid for all this. Compensation varies from reductions in rent to outright salaries.

Naturally, many real estate owners want the joy and headaches of managing their own units, which is what we are assuming here. Usually the reason they want the joys and headaches is because they do not want to pay a manager. Managing your own units is okay if you love self-inflicted torture, but if you do manage your own units and use $0.00 in the analysis, remember that your time is worth something.

E. Regular Maintenance. All buildings need maintenance: painting, filters, drains, yard work, and so on. There is more maintenance on a rental unit than on your own home. Renters do not take care of things as well as owners, and maintenance is more frequent and more significant. Figure 1.5 percent of the value of the property each year for maintenance, or $2250 in this case ($150,000 × 1.5 percent = $2250). Obviously the real figure may vary substantially. If this is a used building, some insight might be gained from the previous owner's records.

But do not accept previous records completely. Small real estate owners are notorious for bad records, and big real estate owners are notorious for changing records to make properties look good to potential buyers.

F. Rerent Maintenance.   There is always extra maintenance to get the apartment ready to rent again after a tenant moves out. Good operators usually repaint, clean the drapes, clean the cabinets, and shampoo, if not replace, the carpets. Usually a security deposit is collected when a renter first moves in. Part of this deposit can be kept if the apartment is left dirty or damaged. But the deposit cannot be used for normal wear and tear. On those occasions when you get a house wrecker for a tenant, the security deposit will only be a dent in a demolished apartment. In this case, estimate $400 per move.

G. Rental Expense.   Advertisements in the paper, or even commissions to rental agents, are part of doing business. The cost depends on the rental market. Figure $160 per move.

H. Miscellaneous Expenses.   Miscellaneous expenses may include licenses to be in business, termite inspections, legal fees for an eviction, office supplies, and so on. Estimate 1.5 percent of your gross rent in this case ($12,000 × 1.5 percent = $180).

I. Utilities.   Some landlords pay all the costs of utilities, some pay none. Others pay something in between. Assume that part of the costs, equalling $676 a year, will be paid.

J. Property Taxes.   Taxes are inevitable. Contact the local taxing authorities for an estimate. In this example, assume 2 percent of market value (2 percent × $150,000 = $3000).

K. Special Assessments.   Special assessments may include new sidewalks, sewer hookups, road repairs, and all sorts of political improvements. The estimate will be based on local conditions. In this case assume no assessments are pending.

L. Insurance.   A broad fire, physical damage, and liability policy will be necessary. Estimate $600 in our example.

M. Interest Payments (No Principal).   Mortgage payments are mostly interest for about the first three-quarters of the mortgage's life, and the contract for deed is all interest for 8 years. In this case the mortgage payment is $13,833 a year on this $90,000, 25-year, 15 percent first mortgage. Of these payments, $13,476 is interest the first year; only $357 will apply toward principal. Interest on the $45,000, 8-year, 12 percent contract for deed is $5400 a year. Total interest paid the first year is $20,660. Fortunately interest is tax deductible, and payment on principal, of course, is not.

N. Total Tax-Deductible Cash Expenses. For total tax-deductible cash expenses, add lines D through M. This figure represents all the expenses that must be paid in cash that also can be deducted from taxes.

O. Profit (Loss) Before Noncash Expenses. Subtract cash expenses (line N) from cash revenues (line C). This is the amount the investor's checking account should increase (or decrease) before considering income taxes. It is nice if this figure is positive. But, as in this example, it certainly does not always work out that way, especially in the early years. Usually operating cash flows improve as the project gets older. The rents tend to go up, and the debt repayments remain constant.

P. Depreciation. Depreciation is a noncash tax-deductible expense. It is one of the most important items of consideration for a taxable investor. (Depreciation rules are covered in detail elsewhere in this handbook.) For this example, assume that the investor is using accelerated depreciation of 175 percent of 15-year straight-line depreciation. Depreciation in the first year will equal $17,500. This figure will decline in subsequent years.

Purchase price	$150,000
Recovery period (years)	÷ 15
Straight-line depreciation	10,000
Accelerated depreciation	× 175%
First-year depreciation	$ 17,500

Q. Taxable Profit (Loss). Subtract line P from line O. A loss on this line is normal. In fact, if there is a positive figure here many taxable investors will feel that either they are not getting enough depreciation or they are not using enough financial leverage. Line Q is repeated and recorded in both columns as Line R.

S. Tax Rate. The investor is interested in his or her combined federal and state marginal tax bracket. Assume 60 percent here.

T. Tax Liability. If there is a profit on line T, a tax liability occurs. If there is a loss, the investor has a tax shield to apply against other taxable income.

U. Net Profit (Loss). Line U is the taxable profit minus the tax liability, or line R minus line T.

V. Profit (Loss) before Noncash Expenses. Line V is line O repeated. This is the operating cash flow.

W. Subtract Tax Liability (Line T). Line W is the cash flow generated by tax consequences.

X. Total Cash Flow. To get total cash flow, subtract line W from line V. (Remember when subtracting to change the sign. A minus sign becomes a plus sign.)

Y. Subtract Principal Payment on Financing. Principal repayments are a cash outflow, but they cannot be deducted from taxes.

Z. Net Cash Flow. The net cash flow is the number we have been working for. It is the amount that the owner's checkbook balance will increase (or decrease) after all the rents are collected, bills are paid, and taxes are settled. It is what real estate people consider their profit. Be glad if it is positive.

Having estimated cash flow for one year, the investor will be tickled to learn that cash flow should be estimated for a number of years into the future, since the cash flow will change every year. In this example assume that the investor plans to sell in year 8 before the contract for deed comes due.

To estimate future cash flows start with the figures developed for year 1. Then make adjustments for inflation or payments in future years. The adjustments used in this example include rent increasing every year at 6 percent and all expenses subject to inflation increasing 7 percent a year. Debt repayment (in this example) and depreciation do not change with inflation.

Some may question the assumption that rents rise more slowly than expenses. This relationship is not unusual. Renters will not pay as much to live in an old building as they will to live in a new one. But expenses do not care about the age of the building. In fact, if anything, an older building is subject to more expense than is a new one.

Rents often do not rise very fast because of the nature of the rental market. Most cities have thousands of rental units owned and operated by nonprofessionals. These people generally own a few units. Often they get to be friends with their tenants. The owner-landlords do not like to raise rents very fast on friends. This creates a drag on the whole market.

Big professional managers are not usually considered a drag on the rental market. Usually they want to get rents up as fast as possible. But in recent years the threat of rent controls in big cities has caused even the professionals to drag the increases.

With all these drags, it is not surprising that rents often lag behind inflation, generally, and behind the cost of being in the rental business, specifically. Sometimes rents will not increase for several years, then suddenly they will jump 10 to 20 percent in a year. Predicting rents is not entirely easy, but estimates of future rents are required to make estimates of future cash flows.

TABLE 9-2 Cash Flow Schedule*

Year	(1) Net Revenues (line C)	Minus	(2) Expenses before interest and depreciation (lines D to L)	Minus	(3) Interest (line M)	Equals	(4) Profit (loss) before depreciation (line O)	Multiplied by	(5) 1 minus tax rate (1 − line S)	Equals	(6) Operating cash flow	(7) Depreciation (line P)	Multiplied by	(8) Tax rate (line S)	Equals	(9) Depreciation tax shelter	(10) Debt principle repayment (line V)	(11) Net cash flow (col. 6 + col. 9 − col. 10 = col. 11)
1	$11,632	−	$ 7,266	−	$18,876	=	$(14,510)	×	.40	=	$(5,804)	$17,500	×	.60	=	$10,500	$ 357	$4,339
2	12,330	−	7,775	−	18,819	=	(14,264)	×	.40	=	(5,706)	16,563	×	.60	=	9,938	414	3,818
3	13,070	−	8,319	−	18,752	=	(14,001)	×	.40	=	(5,600)	15,607	×	.60	=	9,364	481	3,283
4	13,854	−	8,901	−	18,675	=	(13,722)	×	.40	=	(5,489)	14,632	×	.60	=	8,779	558	2,732
5	14,685	−	9,524	−	18,585	=	(13,424)	×	.40	=	(5,370)	13,634	×	.60	=	8,180	648	2,163
6	15,566	−	10,191	−	18,481	=	(13,106)	×	.40	=	(5,242)	12,611	×	.60	=	7,567	752	1,573
7	16,500	−	10,904	−	18,361	=	(12,765)	×	.40	=	(5,106)	11,560	×	.60	=	6,936	873	957
8	17,490	−	11,668	−	18,220	=	(12,398)	×	.40	=	(4,959)	10,477	×	.60	=	6,286	1,013	314

*Refer to table 9–1 for description of lines designated by letters.

See Table 9-2 for the cash flow schedule. The cash flow estimates developed represent green money in the bank if they are accurate. They are not the only source of green money, however. With luck, the duplex will appreciate and be worth more when it is sold or refinanced. In this case, assume that the duplex will increase in value 8 percent a year. Again, some people might think that it will appreciate faster than 8 percent a year, and it might. There are many examples of faster appreciation. But rental units often do not appreciate as fast as homes, in part because of depreciation rules and maintenance factors. Thus the investor will probably be disappointed if she or he counts on increases like those for single-family homes. We will also assume that the property will be sold in 8 years for $277,640. Of course, there will be $84,904 left to pay on the mortgage and $45,000 left on the contract for deed, a total of $129,904. The cash difference will be:

Selling price	$277,640
Remaining mortgage	129,904
Cash difference	$147,736

The investor must also consider taxes, since the government will tax the gain.

Selling price		$277,640
Less: cost	$150,000	
Depreciation taken	112,584	
Tax basis		37,416
Taxable gain		$240,224

A portion of the taxable gain will be treated as a long-term capital gain, and a portion will be subject to ordinary income taxes. The ordinary taxes arise from the recapture rules of accelerated depreciation. In this case ordinary income taxes are due on the amount of accelerated depreciation actually taken less the depreciation that would have been taken using 15-year straight-line depreciation.

Accelerated depreciation	$112,584
Less straight-line depreciation	80,000
Depreciation subject to recapture and ordinary income tax	32,584
Tax rate	60%
Ordinary income tax	$ 19,550

Capital gains taxes will apply to the remaining gain.

Taxable gain	$240,224
Less: recaptured depreciation	32,584
Capital gain	$207,640
Capital gain tax rate	
[40% × tax rate (includes state income tax)]	24%
Capital gain tax	$ 49,834
Total taxes:	
Ordinary income tax	$ 19,550
Capital gain tax	49,834
Total tax on gain	$ 69,384

The taxes, of course, are paid out of the cash received.

Cash difference	$147,736
Less taxes	69,384
Net cash gain on sale	$ 78,352

This investment looks pretty good. The original investment was $15,-000. In 8 years the investor has received $19,179 in total cash flows from operations and tax shelters. Then the investor received $78,352 more when the property was sold. The grand total is $97,531. It looks good, and it is good—but it is not quite as good as it first appears. Most of the dollars will not be received until sometime in the future—the biggest portion will not come for 8 years.

Dollars 8 years in the future are not as good as dollars today. Sophisticated real estate people discount the dollars they will get in the future, and, indeed, the investor has to discount the future cash flows to do a decent analysis. The discount rate should be equal to the interest rate available on alternative investments with about the same amount of work and risk. Usually there are no perfect comparisons, but, since tax shelter income is important to this investor, municipal bonds might be a place to start. Assume that 12 percent is available on municipal bonds. Municipal bonds require no work and a minimum of risk, and real estate requires a lot of work and plenty of risk. So the discount rate on real estate should be more. In this case assume that the investor thinks 3 percent is enough to compensate for the extra work and risk, which results in a 15 percent discount rate. To complete the analysis the investor must discount all the estimated cash flows as in Table 9-3. If the discounted cash flows add to more than the original investment, then the project is a good one. However, if column 3 adds to less than the original investment, the investor should forget the project and look elsewhere.

The investment in this example looks excellent. The discounted cash flows add up to $38,223, considerably more than the original invest-

TABLE 9-3 Discounting the Cash Flow

Year	(1) Total cash flow	Multiplied by	(2) Discount factor	Equals	(3) Discounted cash flow
1	$ 4,339	×	.870	=	$ 3,775
2	3,818	×	.756	=	2,886
3	3,283	×	.658	=	2,160
4	2,732	×	.572	=	1,563
5	2,163	×	.497	=	1,075
6	1,573	×	.432	=	680
7	957	×	.376	=	360
8	314	×	.327	=	103
Subtotal	$19,179				$12,602
8 (project sold)	78,352	×	.327	=	25,621
Total	$97,531				$38,223

ment of $15,000. Of course the cash flow along the way is low and will actually turn negative in year 9 if the project is not sold. The investor has to wait a long time to get most of the money back, but this is often the case when wealth creation is a major objective.

It is also worth noting that this project looks good because the investor's earnings are taxable. The tax shelter here turns operating cash losses into positive cash flows. This particular project would not look attractive to an investor in lower tax brackets or to a nontaxable investor.

THE NONTAXABLE INVESTOR

The nontaxable investor's objectives are substantially different from those of the taxable investor. Consequently, the type of project this investor analyzes will be quite different.

For illustration purposes, assume that a pension account is considering the purchase of a $5 million office building. The space is completely leased by a major corporation with a good credit rating. This is a triple net lease, which is a requirement of many pension accounts. The corporation is responsible for all maintenance, taxes, insurance, and utilities. All the pension account must do is collect the lease payments.

The building is now 5 years old. The original lease was for 10 years. At the end of 10 years the corporation has the option to renew for 10 more years. When the lease expires, the building, land, and all improvements will belong to the leaseholder. At years 5, 10, and 15 of the lease the leaseholder may—at its option—increase the rent by a factor of 50 percent of the increase in the consumer price index (CPI). No reduction is required if the index declines. The rent has just been increased to

$550,000 per year under the first rent escalator clause. Also assume that the building is in good repair and in an excellent location.

These terms are fairly straightforward. Many leases are substantially more complex, including such things as participations in the revenues of the occupying business, sharing of certain expenses, split ownership between land and building, and so on. Two points must be made here: First, a careful legal reading of the lease and a thorough understanding of its terms are musts. Second, today's analysis must be based on a number of future events which are difficult to predict. For example, will the company exercise its option to renew the lease? How much can lease payments be increased? What will the value of the building be when the lease expires?

To analyze this property the investment manager must choose an appropriate target rate of return, estimate the probable cash flow, and, finally, discount the cash flows by the required rate of return to see what an appropriate purchase price might be.

To select an appropriate rate of return, one must look at rates of return available on alternative investments. Assume that this tenant is a corporation with an AA bond rating. Assume that the pension manager can buy this corporation's bonds today at a yield of 14 percent. A 14 percent rate of return is a good place to start. But there is more uncertainty associated with this lease than with a bond. Assume that the fund feels that 2 percent will compensate it for the uncertainty. The appropriate discount rate then becomes 16 percent.

There are many approaches to the rate-of-return problem, some of which lead the analyst to a rate of return that is too low. Some use government bonds as the benchmark. But there is little justification for the use of government bonds, since the corporation is not as good a credit risk as the government. If the corporation fails, the building owner will lose the cash flow for a time.

Some analysts use discount factors even below bond rates. They argue that the risk is below that of a bond because of the value of the property. These analysts are double counting. The estimated value of the property is a key part of the cash flow analysis. Finding the appropriate target rate of return is important to a sophisticated analysis.

Cash flow analysis depends on judgments surrounding several events. We shall divide the events into discrete functions and use Bayesian statistics, or probability theory, to arrive at the numbers.

Event A

Assume that the property is purchased. One of two things may then occur: the lessor will receive the $550,000 annual rental payments for each of the next 5 years as scheduled, or the corporation will default and stop making lease payments. The analyst must assess probabilities for each of these alternatives. There is always a small chance of disaster, but in this case assume that there is no significant probability that the corporation will fail in the next 5 years or any time during the life of the lease. Hence a 100 percent probability is assigned to the event of payments being made (see Figure 9-1).

Event B

Five years from today the lease will expire, and the corporation will or will not exercise its option and renew the lease. The corporation may have a number of reasons for not renewing the lease. Assume that there is a 75 percent probability assigned to renewal and a 25 percent probability to nonrenewal (see Figure 9-2).

Event C

The analyst must make an estimate of what the building would be worth if the lease is not renewed 5 years from now. There are many possibilities for value, of course, but to keep the problem manageable the analyst looks at three values: an upper range based on 15 percent annual appreciation, a middle range based on 8 percent

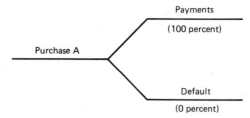

Figure 9-1   Event A: Return on lease—100 percent probability of payment.

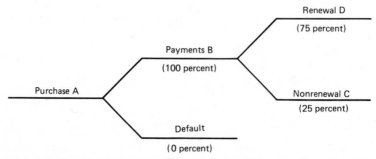

Figure 9-2   Event B: 75 percent chance of lease renewal.

appreciation, and a lower range based on no appreciation at all. The actual appreciation 5 years from now will depend on the economy of the location, the property, local vacancy rates, and so on. Such events are not easy to predict, but the consideration is unavoidable. Assume that best judgments lead one to assign a 20 percent probability to 15 percent appreciation, a 70 percent probability to 8 percent appreciation, and a 10 percent probability to 0 percent appreciation. This leads to the event fork in Figure 9-3.

Figure 9-3 can be reduced to one fork by taking the weighted average of the future value.

Potential annual appreciation	Compounding factor, 5 years	Multi- plied by	Original value	Equals	Future value	Multi- plied by	Proba- bility	Equals	Weighted value
15%	2.01	×	$5,000,000	=	$10,050,000	×	20%	=	$2,010,000
8	1.47	×	5,000,000	=	7,350,000	×	70	=	5,145,000
0	1.00	×	5,000,000	=	5,000,000	×	10	=	500,000
Future expected value									$7,655,000

The expected future market value of the property after 5 years is $7,655,000 (see Figure 9-4).

Event D

If the corporation does renew the lease, the pension fund does not have to worry about the value of the building, but it must analyze whether it can raise the rent. This depends on inflation. Again, it is difficult to predict what inflation will do for the next 5 years, but the escalators in this lease are a potentially valuable feature. They must be quantitatively analyzed to determine how much can be paid for them.

Suppose that we choose three typical inflation ranges out of many possibilities: A 12 percent annual inflation rate over the next 5 years is a 15 percent probability; a 7 percent annual inflation rate is a 70 percent probability; and finally, a 2 percent inflation rate is a 15 percent proba-

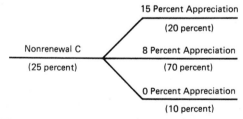

Figure 9-3 Event C: Appreciation 5 years in the future.

bility. This can be graphed as in Figure 9-5. This fork can be weighted and reduced to a single event:

Estimated inflation rate	Compound factor, 5 years	50% rent adjustment factor	Multi- plied by	6–10 year rent	Equals	11–16 year rent	Multi- plied by	Event proba- bility	Equals	Expected annual rent
12%	1.76	1.38	×	$550,000	=	$759,000	×	75%	=	$113,850
7	1.40	1.20	×	550,000	=	660,000	×	70	=	462,000
2	1.10	1.05	×	550,000	=	575,500	×	15	=	86,625
Expected annual rent years 11 through 15										$662,475

This event can now be added to our figure (see Figure 9-6).

Event E

At the beginning of year 16, the pension fund may be able to raise rent payments again, depending on inflation. One may assign different probabilities to different inflation ranges, but in this case assume that years 16 through 20 will be about the same as years 11 through 15. In this case the new event will be calculated and plotted just as event D was but with new rent levels.

Estimated inflation rate	Compound factor, 5 years	50% rent adjustment factor	Multi- plied by	11–16 year rent	Equals	16–20 year rent	Multi- plied by	Event proba- bility	Equals	Expected annual rent
12%	1.76	1.38	×	$662,475	=	$914,216	×	15%	=	$137,132
7	1.40	1.20	×	662,475	=	794,970	×	70	=	556,479
2	1.10	1.05	×	662,475	=	695,599	×	15	=	104,340
Expected annual rent years 16 through 20										$797,951

Event F

The analyst is now at the end of year 20 for the lease and year 15 for the ownership of the building. The lease will expire, and the pension fund will have to do something with the building.

There are a great many options open to the pension fund at this point. They can best be summarized by estimating the market value of the property. It is extremely difficult to know what things will look like near the end of the century, but the ultimate value of this property is the key to whether the pension should make the investment today.

Once again, out of nearly infinite possibilities, assume a high, moderate, and low range for compound appreciation over the 15 years the pension fund holds the building. We will assign a 20 percent probability

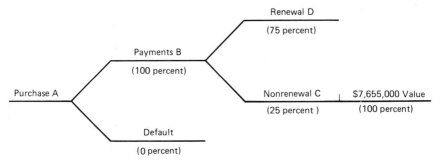

Figure 9-4   Event C reduced to weighted average of future value.

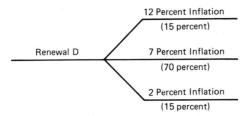

Figure 9-5   Event D: Future inflation possibilities.

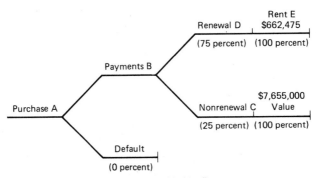

Figure 9-6   Event D reduced and added to figure.

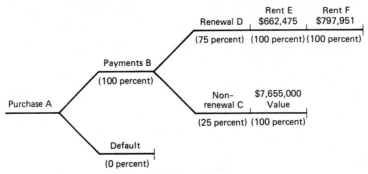

Figure 9-7   Event E reduced and added to figure.

that the building will appreciate at 10 percent annually, a 65 percent probability to 5 percent compound annual appreciation, and a 15 percent probability that the property will appreciate only 2 percent a year for the next 15 years. These possibilities may be reduced to a single fork as in the past:

Potential annual depreciation	Compounding factor, 15 years	Multiplied by	Original value	Equals	Future value	Multiplied by	Probability	Equals	Weighted value
10%	4.18	×	$5,000,000	=	$20,900,000	×	20%	=	$ 4,180,000
6	2.40	×	5,000,000	=	12,000,000	×	65	=	7,800,000
2	1.35	×	5,000,000	=	6,750,000	×	15	=	1,012,500
Future expected value									$12,992,500

The completed decision tree is shown in Figure 9-8. On the decision tree are the numbers to complete the analysis. Expected cash flows must be discounted by the analyst's target rate of return of 16 percent

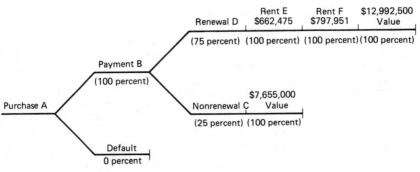

Figure 9-8   Completed decision tree.

TABLE 9-4 Probability-Weighted Present Value Analysis of Decision Tree

| Year of | | Discount factor | Multi- | | | Present |
Original lease	Current ownership	of current owner at 16%	plied by	Cash flow	Equals	value
		Present value analysis of event F				
20	15	.108	×	$12,992,500	=	$1,403,190
Present value of event F						$1,403,190
		Present value analysis of event E				
20	15	.108	×	$ 797,951	=	$ 86,179
19	14	.125	×	797,951	=	99,744
18	13	.145	×	797,951	=	115,703
17	12	.168	×	797,951	=	134,056
16	11	.195	×	797,951	=	155,600
Present value of event E						$ 591,282
		Present value analysis of event D				
15	10	.227	×	$ 662,475	=	$ 150,382
14	9	.263	×	662,475	=	174,231
13	8	.305	×	662,475	=	202,055
12	7	.354	×	662,475	=	234,516
11	6	.410	×	662,475	=	271,615
Present value of event D						$1,032,799
		Present value of renewal event				
Add:	Present value of event F					$1,403,190
	Present value of event E					591,282
	Present value of event D					1,032,799
						$3,027,271
	Times: Probability of renewal					× 75%
	Total weighted present value of renewal					$2,270,453
		Present value of "nonrenewal event				
11	6	.410	×	$ 7,655,000		$3,138,550
	Times: Probability of nonrenewal					× 25%
	Total weighted present value of nonrenewal					$ 784,638
		Present value of event A				
Add: Total weighted present value of renewal and total						$2,270,453
weighted present value of nonrenewal events						784,638
Present value of event A						$3,055,091

and then weighted according to the analyst's probability judgments at key events. The problem can be laid out as in Table 9-4.The figure of $3,055,091 represents the discounted, probability-weighted, total expected present value of the building to the pension account. This figure must be compared with the current value of the investment, or $5,000,000. Obviously the present value of the investment is well below the current value of the money. Thus the pension fund manager would be substantially better off buying a 16 percent bond with the same risk than buying the real estate offered, even though the property will probably appreciate in value and rents may be raised along the way. In the end the analysis suggests that the price of the purchase is too high. Given alternative investments, the pension fund would be unwilling to pay more than $3,055,091 for this property.

Sometimes the analyst is surprised by the results. In this case the deciding issue has been high current cash flow that would be available with a 16 percent bond versus high value in the real estate later on. With the high rate of return required, the ultimate value of the property could not offset the attractiveness of a cash flow along the way.

If the analyst is uncomfortable with the apparent conclusion, he or she will find great advantage in having laid the analysis out in decision tree form. The analyst may reexamine any of or all the assumptions to determine what impact they have on the answer. She or he may test what inflation of property and/or rents would be necessary to make this a good buy. This may be helpful in explaining the conclusion to others who have an interest in the pension fund.

Real estate investments are usually large. Further, they are normally very illiquid, especially in bad markets, and they carry risks that are frequently sizeable and always unique to the property. Hence, both taxable and nontaxable investors need to do careful detailed analysis before moving ahead. Taxable and nontaxable investors have substantially different objectives and may use substantially different analytical techniques, but in the end they have the same purpose—to make money.

The Residential Real Estate Market

Jerry Krantz Real Estate Broker and Investor

T he residential real estate market was the center of the real estate boom which occurred in the late 1970s. Prices doubled, tripled, and in some cases quadrupled in only a few years. Then came the recession of 1981 to 1982, and this market almost completely shut down.

Since most investors today are familiar with the residential market, the question of most concern is not "how to" but "when?" When will the boom days return? Let us consider each of four market elements (single-family housing, condominiums, apartments, and conversions) with regard to this question.

SINGLE-FAMILY HOUSING

Single-family houses appreciated enormously during the last decade. The median price nationwide went from the mid-$20,000 range to the high-$60,000 range. In some areas, such as California, the price soared to a median of well over $100,000.

Speculators bought single-family homes as a sure bet, expecting this appreciation to continue unabated. Unfortunately, this did not prove to be the case. With the 1980s came recession and high interest rates. At rates over 14 percent, most buyers balked, stalling the market. Sales were still made using creative financing techniques in which the sellers carried part of or all the mortgage. However, most of these depended on the buyer assuming an old low-interest-rate existing mortgage. When the Supreme Court handed down the *De La Questa* decision in 1982 making due-on-sale clauses enforceable for federally chartered lenders (in effect enforceable for nearly all lenders), the assumption of existing loans at the old low interest rate became difficult if not impossible. The slumping housing market virtually collapsed.

The volume of sales in some areas was cut in half. Prices in some areas began to decline. The old truism that if you bought a house, *any* house, you could make a profit in a short time went out the window. Housing, in general, became a much poorer investment than it had been for some time.

In some select areas, however, housing prices continued to move upward and sales continued to be brisk. In these areas the benefits of investing in single-family homes (rapid price appreciation, tax write-off, ease of financing and resale) may have slowed down, but they continued to make houses a strong investment.

Investing in houses for the future, therefore, becomes a matter of selecting the right areas. No longer can an investor buy simply any house. Today an investor has to buy a house in the right area.

Which are the right areas? Generally they are the areas of the country that were least hit by the recession of 1982 to 1983. They include the West, especially southern California; parts of Texas, such as the Fort Worth/Houston area; major western cities, including Phoenix, Denver, and Salt Lake. Also a good bet are the newer areas of Florida, some portions of the South, and a few scattered parts of the East Coast. Areas hardest hit by the recession, such as Michigan and much of the Midwest and Northeast, may see the housing market take a long time to recover.

In addition, even within a given city, there will be certain areas of growth and other areas of decline. Although location has always been the single most important aspect of real estate, today it is even more important than it was. In a tight market the very best locations become only adequate. Those locations which are only slightly less than best become undesirable.

CONDOMINIUMS

The condominium (condo) market today is almost identical to the single-family housing market. The onus that once applied to condos is completely gone—nearly everyone accepts them as a true home alternative.

Owning a condo involves a trade-off. In exchange for giving up some privacy and control over property, one usually gets amenities (such as a pool, tennis court, spa, and so on) and maintenance-free property.

One of the biggest problems with the condominium concept, however, has to do with participation in management. In a condo, each owner is a member of and represented by a home owner's association (HOA). In general, the HOA makes all the day-to-day decisions as well as long-term plans for the entire project.

However, if a condo investor-owner wants some control over this decision making, he or she must spend an increasing amount of time at meetings and planning sessions. If you do not want the HOA to put in a spa for $10,000 (it will not benefit you at all since you are renting out your unit and tenants will pay the same, spa or no), you have to attend the HOA meetings to add a note of moderation and reason.

Typically, the best owner-managers take over during the first year or two, and they end up spending long thankless hours. Eventually they give up in disgust—the burn-out rate for owner-managers is very high in condo developments. Eventually, less qualified people take over, and, typically, that is when investor-owners must step in to protect their investments.

In other words, as the development ages, one spends an increasing amount of time on management. Frequently, instead of the carefree management anticipated, there are more problems running the condo than there would have been with investing in a single-family home.

APARTMENTS

For years apartments were an underpriced investment. There were times when builders would plead with anyone to buy their apartment buildings. Then came the real estate boom of the 1970s.

Apartment buildings are bought and sold on the basis of their income, and the price is a factor of income. Typically, apartment buildings are sold at a price that is anywhere from 7 to 14 times their gross annual income. Price divided by income is the gross annual multiplier.

Sophisticated investors use gross multipliers only as a rule of thumb. They go on to compute the capitalization rate (CR), which is determined by dividing the net operating income (which is simply the income received minus the expenses paid out for 1 year) by the asking price. Previous to the boom, investors were looking for CRs of approximately 10 percent. The recent speculation boom resulted in properties selling at a CR of 3 to 5 percent.

With real estate escalating in price and with an obvious housing shortage occurring, investors poured into the apartment market. The gross income multiplier went from around 7 or 8 in the mid-1970s to 14 in some areas of the country by 1980. Thus in the past a person might have paid $700,000 for a building bringing in $100,000 per year, but now the buyers were paying $1,400,000 for the same building bringing in the same $100,000 per year.

The reason investors bought was price escalation. It was anticipated that the price of apartment buildings would continue to skyrocket. However, high interest rates, tight money, and the recession hit apartments harder, perhaps, than any other segment of the market. The high interest rates and tight money made it virtually impossible to finance the sale of apartment buildings. In addition, the hard times (and rent controls) made it virtually impossible to raise rents significantly.

Those who had bought at high gross annual multipliers (or low CRs) were stuck with illiquid investments, and they had huge negative cash flows. Thus, today the owners do not want to take a huge loss, but they cannot sell at a realistic price.

For new investors it is almost impossible to find an apartment building which can be purchased and operated at an economic profit (even with tax advantages). The apartment market, for practical purposes, is shut down until financing becomes easier, prices drop, or rents go up.

Of course, in any given area there will be exceptions. There will be buildings that are offered at reasonable prices. When this happens they will be gobbled up by alert investors.

CONVERSIONS

Many investors who were stuck with an apartment building that was losing money opted to convert to condominiums. The conversion, in the past, could be done fairly quickly and inexpensively, and the units could then be sold for hefty profits.

As apartments, the price of the structure was limited by the gross income or maximum rent. Raising rent and thus raising price, as we have seen, has been increasingly difficult in troubled times. However, if the owner goes from an apartment building to a condominium, she or he also moves from a price determined by income to a price determined by comparable values. And, with the increase in housing prices overall, an apartment building which might sell for $1 million can often be converted to a condominium whose total price could be closer to $2 million.

Recently, however, the conversion market has become much tighter. Government regulation has been increased in many areas, and now up to a year's care may have to be given to displaced tenants. In addition, the converter may have to pay for the tenants' moving expenses, and getting approval from regulatory bodies to convert can take as long as 4 years!

As if these were not enough problems, once conversion has taken place the sluggish market may make it difficult to sell the condominium units. Some conversions have converted back to apartment buildings when the units could not be sold.

Of course, the incentive of a big profit is still there, and an increasing housing shortage, as small numbers of residential units are built each year, puts more and more pressure on buyers. Therefore, the residential market, although not what it used to be, is certainly not dead. Selected investments in selected areas will do well.

As to the future, predictions I have seen indicate a strong economy by the mid-1980s. In addition, with the large number of singles and married "baby boom" couples entering the market and with the recent very slow pace of building, the long-term demand for residential property should become very, very strong in the not too distant future.

However, in all the residential markets previously discussed there is as of this writing the highest foreclosure rate since the Great Depression. The investors who still have cash with which to operate are able to glean handsome profits at some foreclosure proceedings. Even so, many investors hesitate to become involved because existing high interest rate loans or balloon payment loans on the property make purchasing difficult. Investing today requires careful analysis of the risks taken for the rewards expected.

Investing in Commercial Real Estate

Thomas D. Pearson Associate Professor of Real Estate and Urban Development, Department of Finance, Insurance, Real Estate, and Law, North Texas State University

Joseph D. Albert Associate Professor of Real Estate and Urban Development, North Texas State University

C ommercial real estate investment analysis requires an investment decision approach that incorporates property and market analytics to demonstrate their effect on cash flows and, hence, on investment value. This chapter will discuss the analytics of commercial property as they relate to investment decisions.

In a general sense we may define commercial real estate as land uses involving distribution, wholesale, retail, and service activities, including retail stores, shops, and shopping centers as well as certain types of warehousing and office space. Usually, the largest single concentration of commercial property in an urban area is found in the central business district. Commercial properties, however, spread out from the core along urban arterials, clustering in specialized commercial groups and nucleations in suburban areas. Recognizing the broad nature of commercial property, this chapter will focus on retail space such as freestanding stores and shopping centers. The analytics discussed are appropriate for any type of commercial property, but their applications vary from one commercial property type to another.

Any investment approach involving commercial property markets must focus on the investment decision-making process. Analytics of this process may be grouped under three headings: (1) property-specific analytics such as the physical, legal, and location characteristics of the property; (2) the market supply and demand features bearing on a point in geographic space; and (3) the finance investment analysis, including tax consequences and risk management considerations.

WHAT MAKES VALUE IN COMMERCIAL REAL ESTATE?

Supply and demand create value. Thus commercial property value is determined by the interaction of supply and demand forces. Perfect competition as written up in economics textbooks demonstrates the mechanism by which economic forces of supply and demand establish price, or value. Of course, this is a highly abstract and generalized theory, far removed from the imperfect competition of the workaday world. Nevertheless, the perfectly competitive model can teach us much.

First, we recognize that value depends on the supply of resource inputs of land, labor, capital, and entrepreneurial abilities. Land, labor, and capital can be acquired in various quantities and qualities which, in turn, will influence the size and quality of the commercial structure and transaction. The entrepreneur is the person who gathers these resources and "puts the deal together," whether it be a new development, a syndication, a tax-free exchange, or some other type of deal.

Second, value depends on the demand for commercial real estate. However, the demand for commercial real estate is indirectly derived from the business operations to be housed in the structures. Therefore, to understand the demand for a commercial property, we must recognize the demand for the products and services of the businesses operated from the real estate.

The perfectly competitive model of the academic economist teaches us that either an excess supply of or demand for commercial real estate is going to create price movements. To forecast these price movements we need to examine the independent variables in the demand and supply functions and identify forces that may affect them. However, we live in an imperfectly competitive world, and the insights of the competitive model are general in nature. Thus we must bring our reason and experience to bear on the various observable characteristics that affect commercial real estate values. These characteristics can be grouped under five major headings: (1) physical, (2) legal, (3) location, (4) market, and (5) investment.

THE PHYSICAL CHARACTERISTICS ANALYSIS

Commercial real estate consists of soil, brick, mortar, steel, and many other physical components. The size of the building, the quality of the materials and of the construction, the physical design, amenities, and parking facilities all have a significant bearing on the productivity and value of the real estate. These are items that determine the efficiency and capacity of the property to serve the needs of the property users. Thus, the person wishing to invest in commercial real estate must analyze carefully the physical attributes of the site and its major improvements.

Physical Characteristics of the Site

Site analysis for an existing commercial property is straightforward, and common sense and experience play a large role in the examination. Generally, one wishes to determine whether the shape, size, or topography of the site will have any adverse, or positive, effects on the intended use of the property. For example, if there exists a strong possibility of growth within the trade area, will the site's size and shape permit an expansion of facilities? The site may be large enough in gross square footage, but an irregular shape might limit its usefulness for expansion purposes. Similarly, the topography of a shopping center site may consist of aesthetically pleasing rolling terrain and may be considered a benefit. However, closer examination may indicate drainage problems that create water pooling and traffic problems during rainy weather.

Another site characteristic that should be evaluated is the microclimate. Microclimate analysis is taking on new significance today because of the rising energy costs of sustaining the controlled climate environments of large structures. Placement of the structure with respect to wind, trees, sun, and other natural elements can help to reduce energy costs.

If the proposed investment is an existing, fully operational concern, utilities supplying the property will be adequate. However, if the property is vacant land, or if substantial expansion at the site is expected, it must be determined whether utilities can accommodate the proposed facilities.

Physical Characteristics of Improvements

Analysis of the improvements to the site must be tailored to the type of structure and its possible uses. A vacant freestanding retail store with a wide variety of uses must be examined somewhat differently from an operating regional shopping center. In either case, certain physical attributes of the property should be evaluated: (1) construction quality, (2) functional utility, (3) support systems, and (4) parking facilities.

The construction quality and condition of the structural components of the building need to be evaluated relative to the original character and workmanship. High-quality materials and workmanship that have been well maintained obviously add to the value of the property. Poor workmanship coupled with lower-quality materials will detract from the value.

The building may be viewed as a set of systems, for instance: (1) structural system, (2) mechanical systems, (3) foundation, (4) floor, (5) wall, and (6) roof systems. In addition, the analyst should carefully examine the doors, windows, the moisture and thermal protection systems, and especially the finish work. Each of these systems contributes to the productivity of the property by influencing how well the building performs for its users.

Functional capability hinges on the exterior and interior design and amenities of the property. The architect played an important role in designing the exterior features of the building. The architect designed the building's shape, pattern, and facilities to be constructed from specific materials, all of which work together to create a visual image. Features such as landscaping, signage, night lighting, and truck service areas should be evaluated to determine how they contribute to or detract from the value of the property.

Interior features play an equally important role in determining the functional utility of the building. Current trends are to design the size, shape, and arrangement of interior commercial space with a great deal of flexibility. The analyst, to evaluate the appropriateness of the space, must be familiar with prospective tenant requirements regarding size, width, depth, height, and removability of wall partitions.

Heating, air conditioning and ventilation, plumbing, electrical and lighting systems, and escalators and elevators comprise the support systems of the building. Modern well-maintained support systems contribute to the overall productivity of the property. Because these systems have to be replaced several times over the life of the property, they should be examined with respect to their quality, chronological age, and future capability. The analyst must estimate their remaining functional lives.

Finally, the analyst must evaluate the parking facilities available for the commercial property. Again, different property uses have different parking requirements: A regional shopping center's parking needs will differ considerably from those of a freestanding pharmacy. The main point is for the analyst to recognize the parking needs, given the anticipated use of the property.

THE LEGAL CONSTRAINTS ANALYSIS

Real estate is a highly regulated form of business operation. Therefore, the commercial property investor must explore the regulatory environment of the property to identify legal constraints that may affect (1) the uses of the property, (2) the business operation to be located at the site, and (3) the investors in the real estate.

Legal Constraints on the Use of the Property

Real estate investor-analysts must be aware of the range of public and private restrictions placed on land and related resources. Identification of these constraints is fundamentally a matter of investigation and research. Interpretation of the factual information requires judgment based on experience. For example, what is the likelihood of obtaining a variance in a zoning classification, given the current makeup of the planning and zoning (P&Z) board and city council? If the zoning variance is requested, how will the residents of an adjoining subdivision react? Given the P&Z board, the council, and the residents, can the zoning change be obtained? If so, how long will it take? A list of the more common public and private constraints on property use is provided in Table 11-1.

Legal Constraints on Business Operations
Located at the Site

A potential investor must anticipate what prospective business operations will be housed in a commercial property and investigate restrictions that limit or modify the proposed business activities. An existing building, for example, may appear ideal for an exclusive restaurant and club. City ordinance may require facilities serving alcoholic beverages to be at least 1500 feet from any churches or schools. Careful measurement discloses that a church building is located 1682 feet away but that the church's land extends to within 1432 feet of the proposed club. If this restriction is not examined prior to creation of the club, the stage is set for litigation between the church and restauranteur.

TABLE 11-1   Public and Private Constraints on Commercial Property

Public constraints to examine:
1. Zoning classifications, master plans, and land use maps
2. Building codes and commercial district ordinances
3. Access controls such as signalization and turn lanes
4. Local, state, or federal easements for scenic views, avigation, urban renewal, and so on

Private constraints to examine:
1. Deed restrictions, covenants, and life estates
2. Merchants' association controls
3. Existing leases
4. Recorded liens such as mortgages, tax, mechanics, and the like

Thus a commercial facility may have a number of alternative business uses. Some uses may be affected by local, state, or federal regulations; others may not be constrained. Prior analysis aimed at profiling the potential space users is important if negative effects of legal constraints on the business operations are to be avoided.

Constraints on the Investors

Another facet of the analysis must be the constraints on the financial participants of the transaction. Given the hybrid financial arrangements available today, the investor may be a pension fund or a life insurance company as well as the traditional equity investor.

The traditional equity investor must conform to underwriting manual specifications and lender preferences. These are not legal requirements in a strict sense, but they do govern the nature of the project. The equity investor, therefore, must be aware of lender standards and screening techniques.

Lenders have been taking equity positions in shopping centers and other commercial property investments. Typically, these lenders are financial institutions, but they may be corporations, public utility companies, or other private or public business enterprises. To the extent that their activities are influenced by corporate charters, security laws, and regulatory commissions or other agencies, critical legal and regulatory constraints should be carefully identified and examined.

Legal constraints may inhibit or prevent a specific property from being as productive as it might be without them. Such constraints may affect (1) the uses of the site, (2) the business activities at the site, or (3) the investors. Thus the prospective commercial real estate investor should carefully identify and examine the potential consequences of these legal factors.

THE LOCATION ANALYSIS

"Location" is a widely used word among real estate practitioner-analysts. All recognize its importance to real estate values. However, few have examined the concept of location or broken it into its component parts. The following discusses several features of location at both the micro and macro levels.

The microlocation analysis should focus on access, linkages, and the commercial neighborhood environment. These features should be examined as they are during the immediate time period and as they may change over time. To better evaluate prospective microlocation changes, the analyst must become involved with macrolocation analysis—that is, how the urban area evolves over time causing access and linkages to be modified and how the anticipated changes will affect the property's productivity and value to the investor.

The Microlocation Analysis

Microlocation elements can be separated into three sets of features: (1) access, (2) linkages, and (3) the neighborhood environment. There is some overlap between these concepts. Also, the inclusion of the neighborhood environment as part of the micro features is arbitrary, but, given the continuous nature of spatial differentiation, it provides a convenient breaking point between micro- and macrolocation characteristics.

"Access" is defined as route environment characteristics which influence the ease and safety of transporting people and goods to and from a given commercial property. Thus, access refers to the roadway quality, traffic flows, turning lanes, signalization, visibility of entrances and exits, health and safety of the transport route environment. To the extent that traffic flows smoothly with coordinated signals, appropriate turn lanes, and well-marked entrances and exits, and without going through dangerous intersections or neighborhoods, it may be stated that the property has ease of access. If these characteristics do not exist, then the property does not have ease of access.

A commercial property has regular associations with other land uses both within and outside the immediate neighborhood. These associations are linkages. Linkages arise because there is a need to convey goods, services, people, or information between separate parcels of real estate. Thus, it may be said that "linkages" refer to the property's ties to its customers, suppliers, and to complementary land uses.

Access and linkage are important considerations to the commercial property analyst, because there are costs attached to overcoming the friction of space. First, there are out-of-pocket money costs for gasoline, tolls, fares, and so on. In addition, there is a convenience cost—that is, the degree of convenience in terms of time and distance to be traveled. We may reverse the time value of money and state that there is a money value of time and as travel time and distance rise, the costs also rise. Finally, trip frequency is a cost multiplier—a frequently made trip will multiply costs compared to an infrequently made trip of the same length and duration.

The function of the commercial property investor is to examine the various linkages and to identify the most important ones. The analyst must then assign weights based on alternative, likely property uses. Thus, for a retail business housed in a building the inward-oriented linkages of customers may be of greatest relative importance. However, for a commercial office building which houses high-income professionals and support staff, the inward orientation of employees may carry greatest relative importance. Outward-oriented linkages may carry significant weight for commercial buildings housing shopping types of goods.

Individual commercial property sites are integral parts of the surrounding neighborhood. Space users have substantial contact with the neighborhood, and it is therefore incumbent on the property investor to carefully analyze the forces and trends influencing the neighborhood. These include (1) the physical environment, (2) the economic environment, (3) the social environment, and (4) the institutional environment.

The physical environment of the commercial neighborhood includes many features. Among these are the quality of construction and maintenance of buildings, streets, common areas, landscaping, terrain, and microclimate. We may also include the design and aesthetic qualities of structures as well as the design and layout of the neighborhood.

The economic environment of a commercial district is functionally related to the income characteristics of the surrounding residential areas and the market the commercial district serves. Thus, market potential as represented by gross revenues for the space user is the decisive factor. The analyst should evaluate the prospect of changing markets and the impact these changing markets may hold for the space user and the user's ability to pay rent. Additional economic factors are trends in property taxes, insurance costs, the availability and quality of public services, and parking expenses.

The social environment is the most difficult element of a neighborhood to evaluate and interpret. For example, retail goods, services, and office space users sometimes appeal to customers or business peer groups where prestige and status attitudes are important. Therefore, a location in a high-status neighborhood may be important. For the commercial operator serving lower-income clientele, the exact opposite may be the case.

Finally, the institutional environment, consisting of public and private land use controls, must be examined by the investor-analyst. To the extent that other environmental variables have changed greatly while institutional variables have changed only little, distortions in commercial land uses and values will occur.

The Macrolocation Analysis

The investor must be cognizant not only of microlocation features but also of the relationship of the subject property and the neighborhood to the rest of the urban area. This is the concern of the macrolocation analysis.

Succinctly, the commercial property investor is seeking a rate of return on a long-term asset. Resale value of the property and the rate of return will be a function of the direction and rate of urban growth during the holding period. The rate of urban growth will depend on the dynamic features of the city's economic base. The geographic direction of urban growth will result in a modification of existing access, linkage, and neighborhood features. Thus, ultimately, the rate of return attained will be influenced by the direction and rate of urban change. Forecasting such change, therefore, is important to the investor.

An understanding of urban growth or decline can be acquired by reviewing the fundamentals of economic base analysis. Simplified, economic base theory states that an urban economy may be analyzed by categorizing firms as basic or nonbasic. Firms in the basic group generate employment which produces exportable goods and services, thereby causing an inflow of money to the city. An influx of basic-type firms attracts new employees and households. These, in turn, create a demand for the goods and services of nonbasic firms, which may be said to serve the needs of basic companies' employees. As nonbasic enterprises, such as grocery stores, physicians, and so forth, move into the community, additional employees are attracted to the city. Thus, once an urban area begins growing, a cumulative sequence may be released from which additional growth is derived.

The purpose of an economic base study is to accumulate data which will demonstrate the growth potential of the city and the related social and economic characteristics of the incoming population (Table 11-2 provides a checklist).

Assuming that the economic base study indicates that a community

TABLE 11-2 Economic Base Checklist

1. Master plans and land use maps for the city
2. Population and employment statistics such as totals; breakdown by age, sex, industry; income levels of population; trends in new industry location, types, and wage scales; basic industry trends in the city; ratio of basic employment to total; and ratio of total employment to total population
3. Community growth trends—population, employment, schoolchildren, utilities, payrolls, retail sales, bank deposits, and the like
4. General data—history of the city, climate, soil characteristics, and so on

will grow, the next step is to examine the direction of the corridors of growth. Because commercial real estate movements follow transportation and residential real estate development patterns, the most appropriate urban land use model is the sector theory of Homer Hoyt. This model states that high-income households establish a pattern of growth in a specific sector from which all residential land values scale downward. Once a high-, moderate-, or low-income residential sector becomes established, new development occurs at the urban fringe resulting in predictable directional growth. Commercial land values located in the path of such directional growth are influenced by the social and economic characteristics of the surrounding population. Thus, economic base analysis provides insights to the growth potential of the community and the income levels of in-migrants. The sector theory provides a framework for anticipating where these people may settle in a city. With this understanding, the commercial property investor has an intuitive and quantitative basis on which to make investment decisions concerning longer-term property values.

THE MARKET ANALYSIS

A market study is a critical part of the commercial real estate investment analysis. It is the purpose of the market analysis to delineate the trade area and to quantitatively evaluate demand and supply variables which will affect the performance of the prospective investment. Depending on the specific requirements of the study, forecasts of expected market variables such as prices, rents, operating expenses, space needs such as square footage, amenities and design, occupancy rates, and absorption rates may be critical. To make reliable forecasts, the investor-analyst should remember that the demand for commercial space is derived from the demand for commercial business operations that will operate from the real estate. Ultimately, the investor-analyst must evaluate the prospects for the various types of businesses that may use the property.

Defining the Trade Area

Delineation of the trade area involves identifying the geographic area in which the space user will have no preference when comparing alternative sites. Commercial retail space users primarily will be concerned with the linkages and accessibility of the potential shoppers.

The size, shape, and boundaries of the trade area will be a function of the type of goods or services offered by the business housed in the property. Typically, convenience goods stores will want to be located within 1.5 miles of or 5 minutes driving time from customers. Shopping goods stores will have a market area that ranges out to 10 or more miles and a 30-minute journey to shop. Thus convenience stores are densely distributed over geographic space because they rely on frequent visits from a small, local population. Shopping goods stores cater to a more widely distributed population making only occasional shopping trips.

Trade area shape is influenced by a wide range of physical, psychological, and political elements such as rivers, freeways, land formations, customer perceptions of the store and neighborhood, route environment, and city limits. Boundaries should be thought of as zones that shift seasonally, weekly, daily, and, in some cases, hourly.

Estimate Demand in the Trade Area

Retail property demand is derived from customer demand for goods and services. The demand for goods and services must be segmented and examined with respect to population, economic, and demographic variables. High incomes and dense populations imply a high potential for sales which can translate into high rent potential. Additional demographic information pertaining to age, sex, education level, race, household size, and so on can give additional insights into the type of goods and services demanded and, therefore, the prospective tenant for the property.

The geographic market area should be divided into primary, secondary, and tertiary trade areas. The primary area is the geographic core from which the store draws its greatest share of customers. Typically, this is 65 to 80 percent of gross sales. The secondary trade area may be defined as the area from which the next 15 to 25 percent of gross sales is drawn, and the tertiary area is the fringe from which the remainder of sales is taken.

To convert household densities and income into gross sales, the analyst must determine the capture rate of potential sales in the market. Given trade area population and income figures, the percentage of household income spent on goods sold by the prospective tenant, and the probable capture rate, a potential gross income figure can be obtained:

Estimating Potential Gross Income for a Commercial Property

The fundamental equation is

$$PGI = r(H \times I \times I_g \times C)$$

where H = number of households in trade area
  I = median annual household income
  I_g = percentage of I spent on goods and services sold by business in subject property
  C = capture rate of potential market sales
  r = percentage of gross revenues designated for rent

This can be refined to show primary, secondary, and tertiary areas as follows:

$$PGI = r[R_p(H \times I_p \times I_{gp} \times C_p)$$
$$+ R_s(H_t \times I_s \times I_{gs} \times C_s)$$
$$+ R_t(H_t \times I_t \times I_{gt} \times C_t)]$$

where R = percentage of sales deriving from respective submarket
  p = primary market
  s = secondary market
  t = tertiary market
  r = 0.03
  H_p = 2000 households
  H_s = 6500 households
  H_t = 10,000 households
  I_p = \$24,000 I_{gp} = 0.10 C_p = 0.65 R_p = 0.70
  I_s = \$21,000 I_{gs} = 0.10 C_s = 0.15 R_s = 0.25
  I_t = \$18,500 I_{gt} = 0.10 C_t = 0.02 R_t = 0.05

$$PGI = 0.03 \ [0.70(2000 \times \$24,000 \times 0.10 \times 0.65)$$
$$+ 0.25(6500 \times \$21,000 \times 0.10 \times 0.15)$$
$$+ 0.05(10,000 \times \$18,500 \times 0.10 \times 0.02)]$$
$$= 0.03 \ (\$2,714,375)$$
$$= \$81,431.25$$

The investor-analyst can now develop an estimate of gross revenues that each of several lines of business may generate. If each of the businesses can successfully operate from the real estate product, the analyst can concentrate efforts on attracting the business that will maximize rents.

Evaluate Competition in the Trade Area

The investor-analyst should assess the strengths and weaknesses of properties housing competitive businesses. To do so will require a field survey of the existing stock of properties in the appropriate market segment. In addition, information concerning proposed new construction and additions to the existing stock should be gathered.

Market Conditions and Equilibrium

Given the number of stores and the accumulated data, the questions become: Can I purchase (or build) this property and lease (or sell) it to an appropriate store owner? What is the appropriate type of store? With respect to the appropriate stores, is this market saturated? overstored? understored?

Two of the best indicators of market conditions are the vacancy rate and the absorption rate of new and existing space. If absorption rates are exceeding 100 percent, the vacancy rate is declining; if the absorption rates are less than 100 percent, the vacancy rate is rising. Trends in absorption and vacancy rates are ultimately translated into rent rates, terms, and property values. Table 11-3 provides a list of market conditions and equilibrium data needed for market surveys.

THE INVESTMENT ANALYSIS

Analyzing the desirability of the commercial real estate investment is in form no different from analyzing any other type of real estate. In substance, however, many differences exist between commercial real estate and other types of real estate investment, particularly when compared to residential projects. The cash flows of commercial projects tend to be more volatile than those of residential projects because of the relatively greater exposure to business risk. For example, rental revenues of a shopping center with participation leases show much greater sensitivity to economic fluctuations than do those of an apartment complex. Because of this higher-risk profile of commercial real estate, additional care in forecasting the investment cash flows must be taken. In addition, risk management tools and techniques must be employed wherever possible.

TABLE 11-3 Market Conditions and Equilibrium Checklist

1. Comparable property rents, prices, lease terms, operating expenses, and their trends
2. Stock of existing competing properties or space
3. Additions to the stock of properties or space and their trends
4. Current mortgage and financing rates, conditions, and terms
5. Vacancy rates
6. Absorption rates
7. Number of persons per retail establishment
8. Available retail expenditures per establishment
9. Parking ratios
10. Sales per square foot of gross leaseable area

Relationship of the Property and Market Analytics to the Investment Analysis

Examination of property and market analytics helps determine whether a commercial facility in geographic space can be translated into dollars and be a viable investment. Often the physical, legal, and location features interact in such a manner as to affect the capital budget, operating budget, or both, thereby rendering the project infeasible. An example can demonstrate this process.

Assume that an investor owns a freestanding commercial building. A prospective tenant wants to operate a bakery shop from the property. Physical modifications to accommodate the bakery may include extending natural gas utilities to the shop, modifying the floor supports for heavy ovens, installing insulation and heavy-duty air conditioning for the kitchen, and inserting a large plate glass showcase window. Parking space will be to the rear of the building, necessitating curb cuts from the main street. A large neon sign will be needed to permit motorists to see the shop from a block away. Further, a traffic light and turn lane are deemed desirable.

Investigation of legal considerations finds that current zoning restrictions will not permit parking at the rear of the building because of proximity to residential properties. Nor will the city traffic engineers agree to the curb cuts, extra traffic lights, or turn lane, and therefore accessibility will be reduced. With appropriate capital expenditures the building can be modified, and it is possible to operate a bakery from the building; however, legal constraints and impaired access definitely will have an impact on bakery revenues and potential for rent payments.

This example illustrates how real estate cash flows may be affected during operations, assuming some level of bakery goods demand. The capital outlays by the owner-investor for the signage, kitchen, and window modifications and the reworked heating–air-conditioning system are a cost to be covered by property rents. Negative legal and access features lead one to believe that bakery sales will be impaired, reducing net operating income, given an operating expense picture. Note that systematic examination of property and market analytics can indicate potential effects on cash flows at each stage of the investment cycle. These phases are (1) origination phase, (2) operating phase, and (3) termination or disposition phase. Further, each phase has unique tax consequences and risk management considerations.

Cash Flows at Origination

At every phase of the cycle we seek the bottom line, the after-tax cash flow. The cash flow at this phase is an outflow; once the price of the asset has been negotiated, little can be done to further minimize the outflow. However, at this point crucial decisions are made relative to allocating front-end transaction costs which can have a significant impact on the overall profitability of the investment. Almost none of the costs of acquiring real property can be expensed in the year of acquisition. These costs are usually recovered for tax purposes over periods applicable to the terms of the mortgage loan or the tax life of the recoverable basis in the property. Assignment of such costs to recovery periods is not as cut and dried as it may seem.

Typically, when commercial real estate is acquired the investor will find front-end transaction costs such as those indicated in Table 11-4 associated with the transaction. In many cases these costs are for services which serve a dual purpose. Initially, these services may be to ensure the financial soundness of the investment or validity of title, in which case their cost would be recovered over the tax life of the investment. However, the loan package submitted to the lender may also require such inputs, in which case their costs would be recovered over the term of the loan. For such dual function services the costs should be allocated to the shortest recovery period with emphasis placed on their necessity for that function. For example, it is easily argued that a construction engineer's inspection of the physical attributes of the building and a market study by a professional analyst were needed to determine the economic viability of the project. It is just as easily argued that these were commissioned in response to the lender requiring their inclusion in the loan submission package. The cost of the reports should be deemed by the investor a cost of acquiring financing only if the loan term was less than the 15-year write-off period for the property. In all such cases the assignment would be made to the shorter write-off period, which today tends to be the loan term. Currently, most nonparticipatory loans are written for relatively short periods (typically 10 years) with a 20- to 25-year amortization schedule. Cost recovery of front-end loan costs is based on the loan term and not on the amortization period, which tends to make the assignment of front-end costs as a cost of obtaining financing more attractive.

TABLE 11-4   Typical Front-End
Transaction Costs

1. Appraisal fees
2. Survey fees
3. Document stamps
4. Attorneys fees
5. Brokerage fees
6. Market and feasibility studies

An even more crucial element of the origination phase than allocating transaction costs is negotiating the debt financing. In today's market the number and diversity of financial arrangements challenge the comprehension of the real estate investor. The appropriate choice of the financial package can be the key to a successful investment, particularly in commercial real estate.

Although seemingly a straightforward process, an initial task confronting the investor is the computation of the cost of the debt alternatives. Two loans with equivalent stated rates may have significantly different costs when all requirements are examined. For example, a 14 percent 25-year loan which requires 1.5 percent of gross income to be contributed to a reserve for replacement account is cheaper than a 14 percent 25-year loan which requires that 2 percent be placed in reserve. Such seemingly innocuous items can substantially differentiate debt packages with respect to cost. Table 11-5 contains a list of the items that can increase the cost of debt.

The type of debt arrangement is also significant in commercial real estate investment. As previously indicated, commercial real estate, and particularly shopping centers, tends to be more sensitive to economic environment factors than does residential real estate. For this reason, participation financing may be preferable to fixed-rate financing, since some of the business risk is shifted to the lender. A more detailed discussion of financing as a risk management tool is presented later in this section.

Cash Flows from Operations

Investment analysis requires that forecasts about future events be made on the basis of reasonable assumptions and the best available information about physical, legal, location, and market attributes of the property. The basics of property and market analyses for commercial projects were presented earlier in this chapter, and it is from these analyses that the cash flow estimates during the operations phase are generated. The pro forma of the operations phase can be considered a year-to-year series of operating, income, and cash flow statements. Of these three statements, the one which sets off commercial real estate from other types of real estate is the operating statement.

TABLE 11-5 Contributors to Cost of Debt

1. Level and rate of contributions to reserve accounts
2. Costs of preparing the loan submission package
3. Prepayment penalties on refinancing fees
4. Loan origination fees
5. Loan points

Estimating operating cash flows for commercial projects depends on leasing terms and periods as well as future market conditions. For retail space in particular leasing arrangements can become diverse and complex. A typical shopping center will have numerous lease periods and rental rates across its tenants, depending on quantity of space occupied, financial strength of tenant, desirability of tenant, and type of retail activity. In many cases concessions on lease terms and rates to some tenants must be recouped from others. Percentage leases which call for investor participation in tenant revenues will be commingled with fixed-rate leases on the same project. Different degrees of sharing operating expenses with tenants will be encountered. The frequency and level of rental increases will differ between leases. Such differences make the projection of operating cash flows quite difficult but, as will be explained later, also provide for an impressive array of risk management tools for the investor.

Once operating revenues and expenses are estimated, the primary task remaining during the operations phase is the choice of depreciation method. The current tax law allows the use of accelerated depreciation on commercial property, but it institutes a substantial penalty for its use. When the asset is sold, all depreciation taken will be recaptured as ordinary income, which, for most investors, presents a prohibitive cost for the luxury of increased tax savings in the early years of the investment. A simple technique for determining the desirability of accelerated versus straight-line depreciation is available and should be applied at the beginning of the investment. The technique simply compares the present value of tax savings during the early years of operation to the present value of the tax penalty upon disposition. The steps are:

1. Determine the excess of accelerated depreciation over straight-line depreciation in years where applicable and multiply the excess by the marginal tax rate.

2. Determine accumulated depreciation over the holding period if accelerated depreciation is used and multiply times the tax rate.

3. Determine accumulated depreciation over the holding period if straight-line depreciation is used and multiply times 40 percent and then times the tax rate.

4. Subtract the result of step 3 from the result of step 2. (This is the difference in the tax liability at sale.)

5. Discount the results of steps 1 and 4 with an appropriate discount rate. If the present value of step 1 is greater than the present value of step 4, use accelerated depreciation; if it is not greater, use straight-line depreciation.

It is assumed that the forecasted selling price is greater than the purchase price of the project. If such is not the case, reduce the accumulated depreciation in both steps 2 and 3 by the amount which the purchase price exceeds the forecasted selling price.

During the analysis of the operations phase an anticipated holding period must be determined. This requires a year-to-year computation of the profitability of remaining in the investment. It should be recognized that financial leverage will decrease over time due to increases in the value of the project and amortization of the mortgage debt. Also, a downward pressure on return will be evident due to an erosion of the tax shelter components of interest expense and to depreciation if the accelerated method is chosen. However, the appropriate measure of equity at any given point is the after-tax cash flow which a sale of the project would generate and not simply the beginning equity adjusted for before tax increases in value and amortization of mortgage principle. The optimal holding period for the project is that in which the return on current after-tax equity in the project was greater than that possible in an alternative investment.

Cash Flows from Disposition

The final phase of the investment is the termination phase, the last entry on the pro forma. This is also the most difficult phase to forecast. The difficulty arises from the necessity for forecasting a disposition value and a disposition method.

To estimate the disposition value, the best approach is to extrapolate price trends in the local area using an extended data period which incorporates more than a single phase of the real estate market cycle. In most cases a 10- to 12-year data history is sufficient, although it still may not represent an accurate picture of the future. An examination of the economic base with careful thought given to corridors or sectors of growth may provide insights into anticipated changes in access, linkages, neighborhood environments, and other market variables that will have an impact on future value.

Related to the assumed project value at disposition is the method of disposition. The alternatives include an outright sale for cash, a sale on the installment basis, and an exchange for other real estate. The method of disposition which maximizes the present value of the sale of the asset should be used to determine the after-tax cash flow at termination.

Risk Management for the Commercial Investor

Commercial real estate has a relatively greater degree of business risk than do some other types of real estate. Because of this greater exposure risk management becomes an integral part of the thinking of the commercial real estate investor. We will highlight financing and lease arrangements as risk management tools.

The lease is the classic risk management tool, designed to provide a stable revenue stream and therefore a lower level of risk for the real estate investor. Such stability, however, does not come free of sacrifice. Invariably, increased stability in the income stream obtained through lease arrangement also calls for lower rent levels, less frequent rent increases, or a greater burden of operating expenses. Even so in many cases the decreased risk exposure is well worth the sacrifice. We will examine such trade-offs and discuss the strategy for negotiating the lease arrangement from the investor-landlord point of view.

Escalation clauses have become a common element in commercial leases due to the inflationary environment of recent years. These clauses allow the investor to transfer purchasing-power risk to the tenant at the price of concessions in the initial base rent. Assuming that both parties to the negotiations are rational economic beings, the risk-return trade-off will depend on their relative expectations about inflation. Investors who anticipate lower rates of inflation than do their tenants should be able to improve their perceived wealth positions by negotiating away escalation clauses in the lease. If perceptions run in the opposite direction, investors will improve their perceived positions by including these clauses. With numerous leases on a single project, investors should keep abreast of price forecasts to enhance their relative position in these negotiations.

Operating risk can be transferred to tenants through the use of net lease arrangements, again at the expense of lower rental rates. Net leases allow the investor to transfer a large portion of operating expenses to the tenant. The desirability of net rents relative to gross rents will depend on the management expertise of the investor and the anticipated ability to maintain low operating expenses. If operating expenses are expected to increase by a greater absolute amount than gross rents, then net lease arrangements are more beneficial for the investor. If absolute rent increases are expected to exceed operating expense increases, then leases calling for gross rents would be preferred.

Traditionally, leases are tools for transferring business risk from the investor to the tenant. In so doing the investor gives up greater initial rents for longer periods of assured income. In general the longer the lease period, the lower the initial rent. Determining the optimal trade-off between stability and rents is the most difficult of lease strategies. The degree to which rents are sacrificed for stability should be a function of the phase of the market in which the leasing is occurring. In a tight-space market premium rents can be commanded, but tenants are wary about locking themselves into high rents for an extended period.

Since tight markets are generally followed by intense building, which leads to more of a buyers market, it should prove beneficial to accept something less than premium rents for a longer commitment from the tenant. The extended lease period should ideally carry through the soft market period and come up for renegotiation after the market has come full circle to an excess demand condition. For these strategies to pay off the investor should carefully analyze the historical data on the market in the area with an eye toward identifying the periodicity of the market cycle.

Debt financing is generally thought to increase the risk of the investment for the equity position. This is true, but similar degrees of financial leverage may bring about substantially different levels of risks. Although not well perceived by many real estate investors, participation financing can decidedly lower the exposure to business risk. On a participatory debt arrangement the investor normally gets a significantly lower fixed interest rate in return for lender participation in the cash flows generated by the property. The lower interest rate allows a much larger cushion between net operating income (NOI) and debt service, thereby diminishing the possibility of negative cash throw-off. Potential variation in the cash flows going to the equity position is diminished by the fraction to which the lender is participating in the cash flow. With the larger cushion and diminished variation, equity investing is less risky than it would be with a straight fixed-rate loan. The participation arrangement has allowed the shifting of a portion of the business risk in the investment to the lender.

The strategy for negotiating the debt arrangement on the part of the equity position is straightforward. If the forecasted income stream is perceived to be extremely stable, the fixed-rate arrangement would most likely be preferable for the investor. If the income stream is perceived to be quite volatile, the shifting of risk allowed by the participation loan would make it the preferable arrangement.

The volatility of real estate markets over the past decade has highlighted the necessity of risk management in real estate investments. Leasing and financing are two areas where fundamental risk management techniques can be used to enhance the risk-return profile of the commercial real estate investment.

SUMMARY

Commercial real estate markets determine the prices paid for commercial properties. Markets, however, are a function of property attributes, supply and demand variables, and investment considerations.

Property attributes may be divided into physical characteristics, legal constraints, and location features. The physical characteristics include the land and all improvements as they function as a unit to satisfy the space user needs. Public and private legal factors most frequently serve to limit use of the property. Location analytics may be categorized as either microlocation or macrolocation characteristics. Microlocation analysis involves examination of the route (linkage) connecting the subject property with other, separate parcels as well as the environment of the route (access) and the various commercial neighborhood environments.

The macrolocation study focuses on the rate and direction of change in the urban scene to forecast microlocation changes and their effects on property prices. The rate of urban growth can be evaluated by the urban economic base method; the sector theory may aid in forecasting the direction of growth.

The market study is designed to identify critical supply and demand variables. The investor-analyst must gather data to evaluate market operations by defining a trade area and attempting to quantify demand and supply to determine if excess demand, excess supply, or market equilibrium exists.

Assuming that both property-specific and market analyses are positive, the final step is the investment analysis. Keeping in mind all property and market considerations as they influence cash flows, the analysis is then evaluated with regard to the investor's financing arrangements, tax consequences, and risk management considerations.

Investing in Raw Land and Farm Acreage

James H. Koch, Publisher, *Country Property*

THE VALUE OF LAND

O ver the centuries, ownership of well-situated land has been the foundation of many a fortune in the United States. It endures, still, as a good medium for accumulating wealth, as a final, great land boom continues.

The size of this land boom depends, in large part, on the persistence of inflation. The reasons for continuing inflation are global and based on economics largely out of the control of any government or groups of countries (such as the Common Market or the Organization of Petroleum Exporting Countries). The worldwide interdependence of various national economies precludes any one country from eliminating inflation for any length of time, even though international cooperation may bring it down to manageable limits. Concurrent with these interdependencies, there are demands for substantial capital to develop the Third World and to refashion economic structures of the developed nations for the postindustrial age of high technology and of sophisticated financial, business, and personal services on earth as well as for extensive exploration of space for both military and economic reasons.

The rising expectations of the developing countries, spread by mass communication now available throughout the world via satellite, ensures a heavy demand for capital to provide food, computerized services, capital goods, and weapons.

With the demographic trends of rising population, particularly in the underdeveloped countries, added to this basic economic demand, the need for land and housing, and financing of these, will become even more of a political factor than today. No matter how hard governments temporarily apply the brakes on money expansion, they will eventually have to give in, for political reasons, to at least moderate growth over the long term.

Under these circumstances the economic factors which affect the value of raw land and farm acreage, subject to the laws of supply and demand as capital assets, have special upward pressures. They form, literally, the base of more sophisticated assets such as the buildings and equipment of an agribusiness or the construction of a residential development, a manufacturing or distributing plant, a shopping center, or a warehousing complex.

One cannot stress too often that land has *relative value*. It is expensive or cheap depending on its present and potential use. The fortunes in land made by entrepreneurs during the course of U.S. history were made because certain individuals had the foresight or the luck to own land in the path of spreading population and business. This land was a strategic part of a growing city, or it was needed by railroads, by farmers expanding their holdings, or by corporations to extract natural resources or to manufacture goods.

Thus, in addition to the general rise in value of all capital assets, land can increase in value because of many special situations. It is not surprising that the most valuable land is (1) land used by businesses in the largest cities of greatest population density, (2) land in areas which have rich mineral resources, or (3) the most fertile agricultural soil. Land in the second and third categories may cause villages and towns to spring up in the vicinity to provide shelter, trading, and recreational facilities for the surrounding miners and/or farmers.

Ownership of land in strategic places was and is an intelligent person's way to a fortune. Good land judgment, coupled with sound financing, generates capital gain with a minimum of further physical effort. Sometimes a good buy requires only the passage of time to accumulate in value. Holding such a parcel is a wise (and lazy!) path to wealth, and the process can be hastened through creative and energetic improvements (which will be discussed later).

THE SUPPLY OF RAW LAND AND FARM ACREAGE IN THE UNITED STATES

Of the 2.264 billion acres of land in the United States, approximately 742 million (or about one-third) are federally owned and 1.522 billion are in state, Indian, or private hands (see Table 12-1).

TABLE 12-1 Ownership and Use of Land
(Millions of Acres)

Ownership	Cropland	Grassland, pasture, and range	Forest land	Special uses and miscellanous land	Total land area
Federal	1	150	285	306	742
State and other public owners	2	41	39	73	155
Indian	2	32	13	5	52
Private	466	364	400	85	1,315
Total	471	587	737	469	2,264

SOURCE Soil Conservation Service, U.S. Department of Agriculture, *National Resource Inventories,* Washington, D.C., 1977, p. 5.

Most federal lands are held in reserve. Some acres are leased for grazing, and timber companies enter into agreements to cut some of the federal timber, but by and large one-third of the U.S. land is used only recreationally, if at all. Some of the largest tracts are seldom seen by human eyes because the public has no convenient access to them.

A limited amount of federally owned land and unused buildings will be sold under a new policy announced in 1982 by the Bureau of Land Management of the Department of Interior. This program has already encountered opposition from environmentalists who prefer a no-growth policy to letting private individuals use (they would say exploit) federal lands. It is probable, in the long run, that a gradual release of only a small fraction of federal lands will take place under some form of compromise. According to the intention of the program, the proceeds of such sales will reduce the national debt.

Most of the acres, comprising one-third of the U.S. land area, will never come to market during the next two or three decades at least, and most will never come to market at all. That leaves about two-thirds of the national land area for practical discussion.

Table 12-2 shows how much of this nonfederal land is available for agriculture, how much is not, and for what other purposes it is being used. Note that most of it (90 percent) is available for agriculture, either as cropland, pastureland, rangeland, or forestland. Actual farmsteads (farm buildings and residential amenities) cover less than 1 percent of the total land available for agriculture. Table 12-3 identifies the amount of agricultural land that has been converted to other uses.To understand these tables the following definitions are in order.

Cropland is used to grow crops, either alone or in rotation with grasses and legumes. Cropland production includes row crops, field crops, hay crops, rotation hay and pasture, nursery crops, orchard crops, and other similar specialty crops and summer-fallow lands.

TABLE 12-2 Status of Use for Nonfederal Land Available for Agriculture
(Thousands of Acres)

Farm production regions and states	Cropland		Pastureland		Rangeland		Forestland		Other Land in Farms		Farmsteads	Total
	Nonirrigated	Irrigated	Total	With cropland conversion potential	Total	With cropland conversion potential	Total	With cropland conversion potential	Total	With cropland conversion potential		
Northeast												
Connecticut	193	8	12	30	0	0	1,416	55	50	15	16	1,795
Delaware	505	37	23	19	0	0	360	93	4	2	13	942
Maine	885	22	249	83	0	0	16,520	161	39	10	45	17,770
Maryland	1,638	39	486	187	0	0	2,148	325	74	6	91	4,476
Massachusetts	264	18	91	38	0	0	2,756	104	38	6	24	3,191
New Hampshire	273	0	95	53	0	0	3,976	160	7	4	12	4,363
New Jersey	622	155	144	81	0	0	1,965	230	81	52	52	3,019
New York	5,894	75	2,286	726	0	0	15,445	444	609	240	215	24,524
Pennsylvania	5,651	10	1,797	599	0	0	14,349	540	531	160	257	22,595
Rhode Island	30	0	18	4	0	0	301	12	3	0	3	355
Vermont	590	7	534	119	0	0	3,928	73	22	6	16	5,097
Total northeast	16,545	371	5,835	1,939	0	0	63,164	2,197	1,458	501	744	88,127
Appalachian												
Kentucky	5,419	9	5,735	2,424	0	0	10,648	644	130	28	282	22,223
North Carolina	5,926	271	2,030	978	0	0	16,813	3,893	114	92	328	25,482
Tennessee	4,902	26	5,474	2,363	0	0	11,638	1,319	64	60	287	22,391
Virginia	3,127	82	3,274	823	0	0	13,233	1,262	83	32	208	20,007
West Virginia	981	10	2,037	299	0	0	9,805	113	25	19	76	12,934
Total Appalachian	20,355	398	18,550	6,887	0	0	62,137	7,231	476	231	1,181	103,037

State											
Southeast											
Alabama	4,462	37	4,122	2,360	0	0	19,792	1,763	96	24	231	28,740
Florida	1,469	1,720	5,483	2,121	3,017	640	12,140	814	238	38	117	24,184
Georgia	5,851	636	3,234	1,888	0	0	21,566	3,861	41	29	242	31,570
South Carolina	3,287	44	1,242	700	0	0	10,770	1,515	33	29	121	15,497
Total southeast	15,069	2,437	14,081	7,069	3,017	640	64,268	7,953	408	120	711	99,991
Lake states											
Michigan	9,256	228	1,230	642	0	0	15,323	894	962	278	315	27,314
Minnesota	22,518	398	2,889	1,463	110	15	13,806	1,919	1,080	314	698	41,499
Wisconsin	11,401	340	2,738	1,116	4	0	13,259	1,353	1,275	127	350	29,367
Total lake states	43,175	966	6,857	3,221	114	15	42,388	4,166	3,317	719	1,363	98,180
Corn belt											
Illinois	23,770	66	3,070	1,226	0	0	3,028	497	527	212	501	30,962
Indiana	13,180	140	2,147	1,001	0	0	3,534	596	418	197	384	19,803
Iowa	26,356	75	4,530	1,803	0	0	1,487	183	215	179	708	33,371
Missouri	13,797	776	12,823	5,764	35	23	10,832	727	216	86	422	38,901
Ohio	11,719	43	2,615	1,077	0	0	5,865	629	384	162	366	20,992
Total corn belt	88,822	1,100	25,185	10,871	35	23	24,746	2,632	1,760	836	2,381	144,029
Delta states											
Arkansas	5,547	2,443	5,628	1,966	248	47	14,072	1,194	99	74	197	28,234
Louisiana	4,738	1,161	2,945	1,344	326	0	12,595	1,550	58	26	162	21,985
Mississippi	6,948	354	4,041	1,806	30	0	14,412	1,916	92	44	246	26,123
Total Delta states	17,233	3,958	12,614	5,116	604	47	41,079	4,660	249	144	605	76,342
Northern plains											
Kansas	25,631	3,175	2,701	1,356	16,276	3,992	788	115	328	95	378	49,277
Nebraska	13,794	6,905	2,899	1,253	22,001	2,499	444	36	253	157	478	46,774
North Dakota	26,835	78	1,544	816	10,564	1,913	366	62	1,010	91	397	40,794
South Dakota	17,684	472	2,413	1,289	22,198	4,101	330	20	531	83	477	44,105
Total northern plains	83,944	10,630	9,557	4,714	71,039	12,505	1,928	233	2,122	426	1,730	180,950

TABLE 12-2 Status of Use for Nonfederal Land Available for Agriculture *(Continued)*
(Thousands of Acres)

Farm production regions and states	Cropland		Pastureland		Rangeland		Forestland		Other Land in Farms		Farmsteads	Total
	Nonirrigated	Irrigated	Total	With cropland conversion potential	Total	With cropland conversion potential	Total	With cropland conversion potential	Total	With cropland conversion potential		
Southern plains												
Oklahoma	11,073	710	8,713	2,785	14,566	2,709	4,931	253	82	47	274	40,349
Texas	22,510	7,929	18,768	4,781	95,401	8,781	9,240	524	874	140	619	155,341
Total southern plains	33,583	8,639	27,481	7,566	109,967	11,490	14,171	777	956	187	893	195,690
Mountain												
Arizona	145	1,167	11	9	35,091	313	1,803	1	17	14	17	38,251
Colorado	7,699	3,394	1,598	254	23,801	2,408	3,343	30	225	42	183	40,243
Idaho	2,743	3,547	1,109	500	6,589	793	4,230	144	51	4	126	18,395
Montana	13,294	2,061	2,647	1,136	38,834	4,476	6,341	55	194	32	162	63,533
Nevada	4	1,103	298	24	7,351	231	230	0	19	7	17	9,022
New Mexico	1,203	1,079	382	33	42,096	1,249	3,426	1	191	4	76	48,453
Utah	655	1,160	626	145	9,385	363	1,071	0	23	10	33	12,953
Wyoming	1,320	1,650	736	254	26,169	1,600	1,164	4	9	7	52	31,100
Total mountain	27,063	15,161	7,407	2,355	189,316	11,433	21,608	235	729	120	666	261,950
Pacific												
Alaska	46	0	1	0	6,276	0	6,900	124	0	0	1	13,224
California	1,920	8,153	1,127	613	17,554	1,789	9,855	63	281	112	257	39,147
Hawaii	139	154	992	74	0	0	1,443	11	90	3	3	2,821
Oregon	3,139	2,009	1,767	512	10,110	390	10,066	219	127	12	151	27,369
Washington	6,179	1,772	1,252	480	6,041	605	12,382	430	173	33	234	28,033
Total Pacific	11,423	12,088	5,139	1,679	39,981	2,784	40,646	847	671	160	646	110,594
Total												
All regions	357,212	55,758	132,706	51,417	414,073	38,937	376,135	30,931	12,086	3,444	10,920	1,358,890

SOURCE: Soil Conservation Service, U.S. Department of Agriculture, *National Resource Inventories*, Washington, D.C., 1977.

Pastureland produces forage plants, principally for animal consumption. In addition to regulating the intensity of grazing, management practices typically include mowing, weed or brush control, and liming or fertilizing. Pastureland may be on drained or irrigated lands. Also included in pastureland, regardless of treatment, is land managed to establish or maintain stands of grasses such as bluegrass, brome grass, or Bermuda grass, either alone or in mixtures with clover or other legumes.

Rangeland features vegetation which is predominantly grasses or grasslike plants. Included are lands planted either naturally or artificially to duplicate native vegetation. Rangelands include natural grass lands, savannahs, shrublands, most deserts, tundra, alpine communities, coastal marshes, and wet meadows. They include land less than 10 percent covered by forest trees of any size. Rangelands in Alaska are primarily tundra and alpine meadows. There is some use of this rangeland by caribou and for limited reindeer herding.

Forestland (or woodland) has at least a 25 percent natural tree cover or has been at least 10 percent stocked by forest trees. It includes land that formerly had such a tree cover and is now suitable for natural or artificial reforestation.

Other land in farms includes tracts reserved for wildlife and windbreaks, land not directly associated with farmsteads. It includes commercial feedlots, greenhouses, and nurseries.

Farmsteads include land for dwellings, buildings, barns, pens, corrals, windbreaks, family gardens, and other similar uses connected with operating farms and ranches.

Agricultural potential for various types of land A high-potential evaluation suggests favorable physical characteristics and also evidence of similar land that was converted to cropland during the previous 3 years. A medium-potential evaluation suggests favorable physical characteristics but with conversion costs expected to be higher than those for soils with a high-potential rating. Areas with either high or medium potential were included in the tables as having "cropland potential." They represent a part of pastureland, rangeland, forestland, and other farm acreages but are not included in the total of nonfederal land presently available for agriculture.

Urban and built-up land has been used for residences, industrial sites, commercial sites, construction sites, railroad yards, small parks of less than 10 acres within urban and built-up areas, cemeteries, airports, golf courses, sanitary land fills, sewage treatment plants, water control structures and spillways, sport-shooting ranges, and the like. The right-of-ways of highways, railroads, and other transportation facilities are

TABLE 12-3 Conversion of Agricultural Land
(Thousands of Acres)

Farm production regions and states	Agricultural land converted to urban and built-up, transportation, and water 1967–1977	Prime farmland Total	In cropland use
Northeast			
Connecticut	360	394	133
Delaware	60	350	276
Maine	< 1	853	324
Maryland	780	1,262	814
Massachusetts	300	448	169
New Hampshire	190	144	86
New Jersey	140	1,249	502
New York	810	4,000	2,286
Pennsylvania	1,280	4,448	2,351
Rhode Island	150	84	23
Vermont	220	374	128
Total northeast	4,290	13,606	7,092
Appalachian			
Kentucky	760	5,994	3,334
North Carolina	1,280	5,606	2,729
Tennessee	770	6,447	3,078
Virginia	1,400	4,324	1,508
West Virginia	480	502	285
Total Appalachian	4,690	22,873	10,934
Southeast			
Alabama	890	7,856	2,913
Florida	3,470	1,417	404
Georgia	1,400	7,767	3,655
South Carolina	920	3,484	1,543
Total southeast	6,680	20,524	8,515
Lake states			
Michigan	1,220	8,382	5,695
Minnesota	490	19,513	15,302
Wisconsin	190	10,319	6,475
Total lake states	1,900	38,214	27,472
Corn belt			
Illinois	1,060	21,400	19,100
Indiana	740	14,162	11,515
Iowa	440	19,127	16,875
Missouri	480	15,067	9,544
Ohio	1,310	11,280	9,216
Total corn belt	4,030	81,036	66,250
Delta states			
Arkansas	370	13,250	6,633
Louisiana	250	9,353	5,267
Mississippi	720	10,227	5,200
Total delta states	1,340	32,830	17,100

12-8

TABLE 12-3   Conversion of Agricultural Land   *(Continued)*
(Thousands of Acres)

Farm production regions and states	Agricultural land converted to urban and built-up, transportation, and water 1967–1977	Prime farmland Total	In cropland use
Northern plains			
Kansas	<1	27,318	19,520
Nebraska	250	14,203	11,899
North Dakota	320	13,915	12,701
South Dakota	530	5,071	4,312
Total northern plains	1,100	60,507	48,432
Southern plains			
Oklahoma	250	15,622	8,390
Texas	2,260	37,498	17,631
Total southern plains	2,510	53,120	26,021
Mountain			
Arizona	320	1,161	1,086
Colorado	400	1,760	1,613
Idaho	190	3,512	2,998
Montana	350	1,240	889
Nevada	<1	303	243
New Mexico	290	524	504
Utah	290	650	641
Wyoming	<1	259	224
Total mountain	1,840	9,409	8,198
Pacific			
Alaska	0	0	0
California	1,500	7,805	6,545
Hawaii	60	227	184
Oregon	270	2,373	1,823
Washington	630	2,016	1,453
Total Pacific	2,460	12,421	10,005
Total All regions	30,840	344,540	230,011

SOURCE: Soil Conservation Service, U. S. Department of Agriculture, *National Resource Inventories,* Washington, D.C., 1977.

included if they are within urban and built-up areas. In 1977 this category accounted for 4 million acres of small built-up areas of from ¼ to 10 acres in size.

Rural transportation land is land designated for use as roads and railroads in rural areas. This usually includes the entire right-of-way.

Other nonfarm land is used for greenbelts, large unwooded parks, and other nonfarm uses not elsewhere defined. This category also includes land in strip mines, quarries, gravel pits, and borrow pits that has not been reclaimed for other uses. Of this type of land, between 2 and 3 million acres have cropland conversion potential.

Water constitutes bodies of water less than 40 acres in size and streams less than ⅛ of a mile wide.

Prime farmland is the best land for farming. Prime acres are flat or gently rolling and susceptible to little or no soil erosion. These acres are the most energy efficient and produce the most food, feed, fiber, forage, and oil-seed crops with the least amount of fuel, fertilizer, and labor. Their soil quality, growing season, and moisture supply enable high, continuous productivity without damaging the environment. Prime farmland includes cropland, pastureland, rangeland and forestland. It does not include land converted to urban, industrial, transportation, or water use.

Classes of Agricultural Soils

The U.S. Department of Agriculture has set up eight soil classifications based on use. The risks of soil damage or the limitations in use become progressively greater from class I to class VIII. Under good management practice, soils in the first four classes are capable of producing forest trees, range plants, and the common cultivated field crops and pasture plants.

Soils in classes V, VI, and VII are capable of producing adapted *native* plants. Some soils in classes VI and VII can also produce specialized crops, such as certain fruits and ornamentals and even field and vegetable crops under highly intensive management which includes elaborate procedures for soil and water conservation. Soils in class VIII do not support crops, grasses, or trees without major reclamation effort, which is usually uneconomical.

Notes on Various Classes of Soil

Class I soils represent prime agricultural land. They have few limitations and are suited to a wide range of plants. These soils may be used profitably and safely for cultivated crops, pasture, range, forest, and wildlife. They are nearly level, and the erosion hazard (wind and water) is low. They are deep, generally well drained, and easily worked. They hold water well, and either they are well supplied with plant nutrients or they respond vigorously to fertilizers. Overflow does not damage these soils; they are productive and can be cropped intensively. The local climate favors the growth of many of the common field crops, and, when so used, these soils need only routine management to maintain productivity. Irrigated soils fall into class I if the limitation of the arid climate has been offset by relatively permanent irrigation systems. But if there are recurring limitations, such as salt accumulation, high water table, overflow, or persistent erosion, these soils fall into a lower class.

Class II soils have some limitations that reduce possibilities of plant choice or require moderate conservation practices. They require careful management and conservation practices to prevent deterioration or to improve air and water supply when the soils are cultivated. The limitations are relatively few, however, and remedial measures are easy to apply. The soils can support cultivated crops, pasture, range, forest, or wildlife habitat. They may require special soil conservation practices, water control devices, or tillage methods when used for cultivated crops.

Soils in class III have severe limitations that can reduce the choice of crops and/or require special conservation practices. When these soils are used for cultivated crops, the conservation practices are usually more difficult to apply and to maintain. With these reservations, they can support cultivated crops, pasture, forest, range, or wildlife habitat.

Soils in class III through class VIII are affected by difficulties which restrict the amount of cultivation, timing of planting, tillage, harvesting, and/or choice of crops. The negative factors include:

1. Degree of slope
2. Susceptibility to water or wind erosion or lasting effects of past erosion
3. Frequent flooding causing crop damage
4. Slow permeability of the subsoil which inhibits drainage and root penetration
5. Wetness or persistent waterlogging after drainage
6. Shallow depth to bedrock, hardpan, fragipan, or claypan that limits the rooting zone and water storage
7. Low capacity for holding moisture
8. Low fertility not easily corrected
9. Salinity or alkalinity
10. Inhospitable climate

Although soils in class IV can support a limited number of crops, they require very careful management, and conservation practices are more difficult to apply and sustain. They are used more frequently for pasture, forest, range, or wildlife habitats.

Class V soils have little or no erosion hazard but have other substantial defects which cannot be corrected economically. Soils in this class, with substantial management, can support good pastures or tree crops.

Soils in class VI have further limitations and are generally not suited to growing crops. With extraordinary management, they might support tree crops, orchards, blueberries, and similar semiwild growth. They are used primarily for pasture, range, forest, and wildlife habitats.

Class VII soils have such severe limitations that they are unsuited to cultivation, even as pasture, in most circumstances. Under proper management, they can be used for grazing, forest, or as a wildlife habitat. Depending on local climate, they may support the growing of certain trees.

The worst soils form class VIII. They do not support commercial crops or, even under expert management, grasses or trees. They can, however, be used for recreation, wildlife habitat, watershed protection, and scenic values, but some of these minor benefits may even require protective management.

Except for class I, each of these classes has subclasses representing dominant limitations to agricultural use. The others fall into one or more subclasses, depending on the specific limitation.

Subclass w, excess water, for example, consists of soils in which excess water is the dominant hazard or limitation in use. Poor soil drainage, wetness, high water table, and overflow put soils into this subclass.

Subclass e, erosion hazard, consists of soils for which susceptibility to erosion or past erosion damage is the dominant problem or hazard in use.

Subclass s, other unfavorable soil conditions, includes soils in which the characteristics of the root zone limit uses. These may be shallowness, stoniness, low-moisture retention, low fertility difficult to correct, and salinity or sodium content.

Subclass c, limitation by climate, includes soils threatened by temperature extremes and lack of moisture. When one or more limitations influence the classification, the subclasses are assigned by priority c, e, w, and s, in that order. For example, in a grouping of soils in very humid regions, climate gets first priority but the erosion hazard takes precedence over wetness.

Zoning and Its Limitations on Land Use

In addition to these natural land classifications established by the U.S. Department of Agriculture, states and municipalities may pass laws that affect land use and erect a superstructure of regulations atop the natural strictures for agriculture. These can severely limit possible economic return from any acreage purchased for speculation or development. Any prospective buyer of acreage must investigate uses of the land before closing on the purchase. The local farm agent or equivalent should be able to identify its soil classification; a town clerk can assist in determining the applicable zoning that affects building or other potential improvement of the parcel.

As mentioned before, the value of land is relative to its actual and potential legal use. Improved land, such as land with buildings on it, irrigation systems, sewage systems, a convenient supply of water, electricity, communications, and access via good roads, will have greater value, acre for acre, than unimproved land. And a building lot of 0.25 acres zoned for industry or business in an attractive town has a greater value than 0.25 acres of farmland which does not have conveniences such as community water and sewer systems, electricity, telephone, well-kept roads, fire and police protection, and school systems. The commercial land has, in short, a higher economic use.

Some communities have erected barriers to impede further development within community limits by requiring so much land for the site of a house that it is prohibitively expensive or it cannot be found at all. Such a town has, in effect, legislated zero growth by requiring more acreage per building than is available. In these cases, either zoning regulations have to be changed to allow a smaller acreage or square footage per family home, or the community will hold, for a time, to a zero-growth pattern, and the prices of existing homes will rise according to demand for such exclusive property. Such a freeze in one community eventually stimulates growth in similar neighboring communities, simply because there is no other economic alternative. This principle applies to Peoria, Illinois, and Portland, Oregon, as well as to New York City.

If you doubt the steadily growing value of U.S. land, consider Tables 12-4 through 12-7, which demonstrate values in dollars per acre (not adjusted for inflation). Of course, farmland can be leased as well as purchased, and Tables 12-5, 12-6, and 12-7 give an idea of current income that can be expected from such land arrangements.

VALUES VARY WITH AGRICULTURAL ECONOMY

In addition to the degree of inflation of the national economy, the value of farm acreage fluctuates with the prices farmers get for their produce, the expense of their equipment and its financing, the cost for storing crops, and the interest they must pay on their loans for equipment, materials, and purchase of additional land. When these are high in

TABLE 12-4 Average Value of U.S. Farmland by State and Region, 1970–1982
(Dollars per Acre)

State	1970	1973	1975	1976	1977	1978	1979	1980	1981	1982
Northeast										
Maine	161	253	341	375	414	464	538	579	612	636
New Hampshire	239	404	564	625	696	787	919	988	1,045	1,087
Vermont	224	346	462	496	533	584	660	710	751	781
Massachusetts	565	766	961	1,044	1,138	1,261	1,443	1,552	1,641	1,707
Rhode Island	734	1,124	1,500	1,650	1,821	2,045	2,370	2,548	2,696	2,804
Connecticut	921	1,229	1,525	1,645	1,780	1,960	2,227	2,395	2,533	2,634
New York	273	356	510	553	587	600	670	708	749	786
New Jersey	1,092	1,337	1,807	2,106	2,211	2,386	2,701	2,926	2,998	3,118
Pennsylvania	373	491	734	820	994	1,115	1,273	1,404	1,447	1,332
Delaware	499	645	971	1,114	1,250	1,350	1,500	1,755	1,843	1,659
Maryland	640	843	1,060	1,280	1,353	1,579	1,800	2,251	2,556	2,416
Lake states										
Michigan	326	444	553	609	778	877	975	1,082	1,232	1,192
Wisconsin	232	328	434	496	598	718	856	980	1,105	1,073
Minnesota	226	269	429	529	672	761	901	1,061	1,231	1,197
Corn belt										
Ohio	399	505	706	846	1,099	1,224	1,483	1,678	1,727	1,474
Indiana	406	494	720	888	1,188	1,357	1,589	1,833	1,972	1,715
Illinois	490	567	846	1,062	1,458	1,625	1,858	2,013	2,133	1,940
Iowa	392	466	719	920	1,259	1,331	1,550	1,811	1,941	1,802
Missouri	224	294	396	456	548	641	726	878	941	872
Northern plains										
North Dakota	94	108	195	236	274	300	347	399	423	436
South Dakota	84	94	145	163	194	227	256	273	290	291
Nebraska	154	193	282	363	420	412	525	600	660	626
Kansas	159	199	296	342	398	418	501	573	590	585

Appalachian										
Virginia	286	391	558	633	701	774	930	1,009	1,080	1,040
West Virginia	136	204	300	393	430	459	592	704	751	829
North Carolina	333	461	590	676	759	830	1,051	1,215	1,331	1,284
Kentucky	253	327	427	514	619	715	861	955	991	996
Tennessee	268	346	467	528	618	736	860	953	1,024	972
Southeast										
South Carolina	261	336	467	515	600	653	773	879	930	918
Georgia	234	329	474	507	581	685	777	868	915	842
Florida	355	464	685	763	861	981	1,149	1,352	1,507	1,432
Alabama	200	267	364	425	477	527	639	792	935	922
Delta states										
Mississippi	234	270	379	408	461	567	681	825	1,047	1,000
Arkansas	260	337	419	475	542	606	770	921	1,061	1,104
Louisiana	321	403	512	575	665	818	1,001	1,288	1,519	1,511
Southern plains										
Oklahoma	173	219	302	345	394	450	512	604	662	696
Texas	148	196	243	274	299	337	386	448	492	576
Mountain states										
Montana	60	76	112	134	157	176	196	229	239	254
Idaho	177	229	339	386	454	515	585	669	717	753
Wyoming	41	55	80	98	110	121	144	153	164	170
Colorado	95	137	188	219	256	273	322	376	412	419
New Mexico	42	56	78	86	101	112	143	190	203	211
Arizona	70	91	111	122	138	154	199	264	282	294
Utah	92	141	188	227	271	308	400	530	567	590
Nevada	53	74	85	98	112	140	191	253	271	282
Pacific states										
Washington	224	273	350	438	535	602	692	725	854	888
Oregon	150	205	250	294	342	414	504	556	605	611
California	479	509	653	711	759	914	1,186	1,426	1,735	1,905
48 states	196	246	340	397	474	531	628	725	795	788

SOURCE: Soil Conservation Service, U.S. Department of Agriculture, National Resource Inventories, Washington, D.C., 1982.

TABLE 12-5 Farms Rented for Cash

	Rent in dollars				Ratio of rent to value (percent)			
State	1979	1980	1981	1982	1979	1980	1981	1982
Northeast								
New Jersey	31.80	35.80	37.40	44.10	1.4	1.5	1.5	1.8
Pennsylvania	29.40	31.20	35.20	37.60	2.3	2.1	2.4	2.5
Delaware	41.70	49.60	57.10	57.50	2.9	3.1	3.0	3.5
Maryland	37.10	40.20	43.60	47.40	2.8	2.3	2.5	2.6
Lake states								
Michigan	40.00	46.40	51.00	50.20	4.5	4.5	4.2	4.2
Wisconsin	42.00	45.00	49.10	53.30	5.6	5.1	5.2	5.3
Minnesota	53.80	59.50	63.30	68.30	5.3	4.9	4.8	4.9
Corn belt								
Ohio	69.00	72.00	78.60	80.80	4.1	4.0	4.2	4.7
Indiana	85.00	94.00	101.00	98.70	5.2	4.9	5.1	5.4
Illinois	92.00	99.00	106.80	112.80	4.3	4.3	4.4	5.0
Iowa	89.00	96.00	101.80	106.10	5.0	4.7	4.7	5.0
Missouri	44.30	50.50	52.90	52.70	5.9	5.8	5.9	5.8
Northern plains								
North Dakota	22.40	24.10	25.50	27.30	6.2	6.0	5.9	5.8
South Dakota	17.20	19.20	20.90	21.30	5.9	5.7	5.8	5.7
Appalachian								
Virginia	28.00	27.80	31.10	36.60	3.6	3.3	3.7	3.7
North Carolina	34.40	32.90	37.80	39.40	4.5	3.8	4.1	3.9
Kentucky	40.10	45.80	48.00	52.30	4.7	4.8	5.0	5.0
Tennessee	37.00	41.00	43.80	45.00	4.9	4.8	5.0	5.0
Southeast								
South Carolina	23.70	24.60	27.00	25.80	3.9	3.8	3.7	3.5
Georgia	29.40	30.70	32.60	29.90	4.7	4.3	4.4	4.1
Alabama	25.60	28.30	29.00	30.10	5.2	4.9	4.2	4.0
Delta states								
Mississippi	30.50	34.90	37.00	39.10	5.3	5.1	4.5	4.5
Arkansas	33.30	39.70	40.80	45.40	4.7	5.2	4.6	4.3
Southern plains								
Oklahoma	19.50	18.90	20.40		3.8	3.2	3.3	

SOURCE: Soil Conservation Service, U.S. Department of Agriculture, *National Resource Inventories*, Washington, D.C., 1982, p. 38.

relation to income, as in the years since 1979, farmers suffer a financial squeeze between lenders' rates and seasonal needs for loans. They stop buying additional land and tend to sell part of what they own to pay off past debt. Since farmers are the major buying influence in the farmland market, their relative absence as buyers and presence as sellers caused acreage prices to decline slightly (1 percent) in 1982. No significant decline has occurred, however, since the Great Depression in the early 1930s.

Prices of other rural land in the vicinity of farms tend to follow acreage prices because farmland's fortunes follow rather than diverge

TABLE 12-6 Cropland Rented for Cash

State	Rent in dollars per acre				Ratio of rent to value (percent)			
	1979	1980	1981	1982	1979	1980	1981	1982
Northeast								
Vermont	22.40	24.90	28.00	25.60	3.6	3.5	3.7	3.6
Massachusetts	30.40	29.90	35.00	32.10	2.3	2.0	2.4	2.1
New York	30.90	32.80	35.20	34.20	7.1	7.5	6.5	6.5
New Jersey	34.40	36.40	40.30	48.90	1.7	1.6	1.6	2.0
Pennsylvania	32.60	36.60	37.50	39.50	2.2	2.2	2.3	2.5
Delaware	45.60	51.90	59.30	60.50	3.0	3.0	3.4	3.6
Maryland	40.80	42.80	46.70	51.00	2.9	2.3	2.2	2.6
Lake states								
Michigan	41.60	49.40	51.90	55.40	4.6	4.6	4.2	4.4
Wisconsin	48.00	51.90	55.70	58.10	5.6	5.1	5.2	5.1
Minnesota	58.30	62.90	68.80	72.40	5.3	4.9	4.8	5.1
Corn belt								
Ohio	76.80	81.80	87.70	88.40	4.2	4.1	4.3	4.9
Indiana	91.70	101.90	106.30	104.90	5.3	5.0	5.1	5.3
Illinois	99.00	107.00	113.80	119.40	4.3	4.3	4.5	5.0
Iowa	98.50	107.10	113.60	118.80	5.1	4.7	4.8	5.2
Missouri	57.80	66.70	68.80	70.00	6.5	6.1	6.1	6.3
Northern plains								
North Dakota	27.80	30.40	31.60	32.90	6.4	6.4	6.1	6.1
South Dakota	25.20	27.30	29.50	31.10	6.1	5.9	5.9	5.9
Nebraska (nonirrigated)	41.00	46.30	48.20	52.10	6.1	5.8	5.7	5.9
(irrigated)	91.60	100.20	109.00	111.00	7.0	6.3	6.5	6.8
Kansas (nonirrigated)	27.90	30.60	31.70	34.00	5.4	5.2	4.9	5.2
(irrigated)	58.80	60.90	64.00	62.80	7.3	7.2	6.9	6.9
Appalachian								
Virginia	33.20	37.10	41.10	42.00	3.6	3.5	4.3	3.6
North Carolina	37.10	38.40	44.40	48.30	4.1	3.9	4.1	4.0
Kentucky	51.90	57.40	62.30	64.00	5.0	4.8	5.6	5.1
Tennessee	47.10	51.00	50.90	54.60	5.5	5.4	5.4	5.5
Southeast								
South Carolina	27.60	27.30	29.20	27.80	4.0	3.7	3.8	3.4
Georgia	36.10	35.00	35.20	33.10	4.7	4.5	4.4	4.1
Alabama	31.60	35.00	35.30	36.10	5.4	5.0	4.6	4.4
Delta states								
Mississippi	38.60	41.60	44.90	46.10	5.7	5.2	4.7	4.7
Southern plains								
Oklahoma (nonirrigated)	28.00	26.50	29.90	32.30	4.3	3.5	3.7	4.0
(irrigated)				51.60				5.3
Texas (nonirrigated)	18.30	21.10	22.50	25.20	3.6	3.4	3.5	3.3
(irrigated)	47.30	52.70	54.80	54.50	6.5	6.0	6.0	5.8

SOURCE: Soil Conservation Service, U.S. Department of Agriculture, *National Resource Inventories*, Washington, D.C., 1982, p. 39.

TABLE 12-7   Pasture Rented for Cash

State	Rent in dollars per acre				Ratio of rent to value (percent)			
	1979	1980	1981	1982	1979	1980	1981	1982
Northeast								
Vermont	9.60	13.30	12.00	11.60	3.3	3.3	3.3	2.7
Pennsylvania	14.10	15.50	14.90	16.50	1.8	1.7	1.7	1.9
Lake states								
Wisconsin	20.10	21.10	22.70	23.60	5.0	4.6	4.8	4.8
Minnesota	21.10	24.20	20.40	22.10	4.9	4.7	4.4	3.9
Corn belt								
Ohio	24.90	27.80	27.30	28.10	3.1	3.1	3.1	3.4
Indiana	26.30	32.30	36.60	34.20	3.5	3.4	3.8	3.4
Illinois	30.20	34.40	35.20	33.70	3.2	3.4	3.4	3.4
Iowa	35.00	36.20	39.40	44.00	4.6	4.3	4.4	4.5
Missouri	22.60	26.50	27.70	26.00	4.5	4.4	4.8	4.4
Northern plains								
North Dakota	7.80	6.70	9.10	9.20	4.4	4.6	4.3	4.4
South Dakota	9.20	9.50	10.00	9.50	3.6	3.3	5.2	5.0
Nebraska	10.20	10.20	12.90	12.60	5.0	4.4	5.1	4.7
Kansas	11.60	12.40	12.60	12.80	3.8	3.5	3.4	3.4
Appalachian								
Virginia	17.10	17.70	20.80	17.70	3.0	2.6	2.7	2.3
North Carolina	15.60	18.80	19.70	21.00	2.5	2.7	2.6	2.6
Kentucky	22.50	24.10	27.50	28.20	3.6	3.7	3.8	3.9
Tennessee	20.30	22.50	24.40	24.70	3.3	3.1	3.5	3.4
Southeast								
South Carolina	14.20	15.20	20.50	17.00	2.7	2.7	3.4	2.7
Georgia	19.00	19.80	20.00	19.60	3.2	3.0	3.0	3.0
Alabama	13.60	16.10	17.10	17.40	3.3	3.3	3.1	3.0
Delta states								
Mississippi	13.70	14.40	15.40	15.70	3.7	3.0	2.9	2.9
Arkansas	15.30	14.90	18.00	15.80	3.6	2.9	3.4	2.4
Southern plains								
Oklahoma	9.80	11.00	10.90	11.60	2.7	2.5	2.4	2.4
Texas	6.00	6.40	6.90	7.90	1.8	1.7	1.6	1.5

SOURCE: Soil Conservation Service, U.S. Department of Agriculture, *National Resource Inventories*, Washington, D.C., 1982, p. 40.

from the basic economy. Residential land prices participate in this rise and fall and also in the fortunes of the housing industry. It is significant, however, that shelter sales (land and homes together) declined drastically in the double dips of the 1979 to 1982 recession, yet prices, partly because of creative financing techniques, continued to rise to record levels. Corrections occurred only selectively in areas where previous run-ups had been excessive.

Because of the nationwide shortage of housing, single-family home prices are expected to move up strongly. With farm prices also in a recovery phase, land and shelter prices should stimulate one another and move ahead smartly later in the 1980s.

WHERE AND HOW TO BUY LAND

There is a simple answer to the question of where to buy land as an investment. Buy where there is population and business growth. Buy it where you have analyzed that a change will take place that causes increased land values because of rising demand. Perhaps a major corporation plans to relocate its headquarters in the vicinity or intends to build a plant. Perhaps the climate attracts people thinking of retirement. Perhaps recreational possibilities are opening up. You may not buy the exact land the corporation finally decides it wants, but the purchase will cause *all* land values in the vicinity to rise in addition to the gradual surge caused by inflation.

Table 12-8 shows areas of the country which are growing faster than others. Note that for the first time in 160 years rural counties (those counties with no towns larger than 50,000 people) are growing faster than urban counties.

Other sections in this handbook will tell you how to buy real estate and what experts to use in the process, such as accountants, lawyers, appraisers, bankers, brokers, and developers. All these professionals can help the individual investor make a good and profitable deal. Their expert opinions are usually worth their fees, particularly when the investor is new to the process of buying land.

HOW TO IMPROVE YOUR RAW LAND AND FARM ACREAGE

To improve raw land and farm acreage, make it support a higher economic level of use. The classifications of farmland do not condemn the land to its class. Land can gradually reach a higher classification, just as neglect can cause a lower classification.

An investor can improve nonfarm land and request a change in its zoning to a higher and more profitable economic use, but this is a speculative move. A lawyer and local realtor can advise you whether plans for a parcel are likely to be allowed by the local planning commission. Be sure to get clearance before much money is put into improvements. That necessary variance may not be granted, and the improvements already made could be declared illegal according to local building codes!

Some experienced developers with sound ideas for higher levels of economic use take options, say for a year or two, on likely land and then work out the legal details, submitting plans for approval by the pertinent local planning bodies. Once this is obtained, they sell this option on the land to another developer who perhaps has better financing and know-how in actual building.

TABLE 12-8 State Population Changes, 1970–1980

Area	Total 1980 preliminary (thousands)	Total 1970 (thousands)	Total Change (percent)	Metropolitan 1980 preliminary (thousands)	Metropolitan 1970 (thousands)	Metropolitan Change (percent)	Nonmetropolitan 1980 preliminary (thousands)	Nonmetropolitan 1970 (thousands)	Nonmetropolitan Change (percent)
United States	225,299	203,302	10.8	162,494	148,880	9.1	62,805	54,422	15.4
Northeast	49,011	49,061	-.1	41,614	42,480	-2.0	7,397	6,580	12.4
Maine	1,124	994	13.1	344	307	12.0	780	686	13.6
New Hampshire	919	738	24.6	466	363	28.5	453	375	20.8
Vermont	511	445	15.0	—	—	—	511	445	15.0
Massachusetts	5,728	5,689	.7	5,502	5,523	-.4	226	166	36.3
Rhode Island	946	950	-.4	864	855	1.0	81	94	-13.6
Connecticut	3,097	3,032	2.1	2,848	2,804	1.6	249	229	8.9
New York	17,533	18,241	-3.9	15,445	16,290	-5.2	2,087	1,951	7.0
New Jersey	7,336	7,171	2.3	6,707	6,756	-.7	629	415	51.5
Pennsylvania	11,818	11,801	.1	9,437	9,581	-1.5	2,381	2,220	7.3
North Central	58,602	56,590	3.6	39,752	39,107	1.6	18,850	17,483	7.8
Ohio	10,758	10,657	1.9	8,508	8,596	-1.0	2,250	2,061	9.2
Indiana	5,454	5,195	5.0	3,468	3,349	3.6	1,987	1,847	7.6
Illinois	11,326	11,110	1.9	9,061	8,956	1.2	2,266	2,154	5.2
Michigan	9,237	8,882	4.0	7,400	7,354	.6	1,837	1,528	20.2
Wisconsin	4,689	4,418	6.1	2,652	2,578	2.9	2,037	1,840	10.7
Minnesota	4,069	3,806	6.9	2,591	2,417	7.2	1,478	1,389	6.4
Iowa	2,908	2,825	2.9	1,084	1,033	4.9	1,824	1,792	1.8
Missouri	4,899	4,678	4.7	3,067	3,042	.8	1,833	1,636	12.0
North Dakota	652	618	5.6	88	74	19.8	564	544	3.7
South Dakota	688	666	3.3	110	95	15.6	578	571	1.3
Nebraska	1,565	1,485	5.3	689	637	8.2	876	849	3.2
Kansas	2,356	2,249	4.7	1,035	977	5.9	1,321	1,272	3.8

South	74,734	62,813	19.0	47,268	39,353	20.1	27,466	23,460	17.1
Delaware	595	548	8.5	399	386	3.3	196	162	20.9
Maryland	4,192	3,924	6.8	3,529	3,357	5.1	663	567	16.9
Dist. of Col.	638	757	-15.7	638	757	-15.7	—	—	—
Virginia	5,321	4,651	14.4	3,483	3,074	13.3	1,839	1,577	16.6
West Virginia	1,931	1,744	10.7	683	664	2.8	1,248	1,080	15.5
North Carolina	5,842	5,084	14.9	2,652	2,285	16.1	3,190	2,799	14.0
South Carolina	3,061	2,591	18.2	1,472	1,223	20.3	1,589	1,367	16.2
Georgia	5,396	4,588	17.6	3,106	2,594	19.8	2,290	1,994	14.8
Florida	9,579	6,791	41.1	7,951	5,711	39.2	1,629	1,080	50.8
Kentucky	3,642	3,221	13.1	1,620	1,511	7.2	2,022	1,710	18.3
Tennessee	4,539	3,926	15.6	2,692	2,365	13.9	1,847	1,561	18.3
Alabama	3,867	3,444	12.3	2,390	2,129	12.3	1,476	1,316	12.2
Mississippi	2,503	2,217	12.9	560	455	23.1	1,943	1,762	10.3
Arkansas	2,281	1,923	18.6	715	606	18.0	1,566	1,317	18.9
Louisiana	4,194	3,644	15.1	2,660	2,262	17.6	1,534	1,382	11.0
Oklahoma	2,999	2,559	17.2	1,688	1,412	19.5	1,311	1,148	14.2
Texas	14,153	11,199	26.4	11,031	8,563	28.8	3,122	2,636	18.4
West	42,952	34,838	23.3	33,859	27,939	21.2	9,092	6,899	31.8
Montana	784	694	12.9	188	169	11.3	595	525	13.4
Idaho	944	713	32.3	173	112	54.0	771	601	28.3
Wyoming	469	332	41.1	—	—	—	469	332	41.1
Colorado	2,878	2,210	30.3	2,057	1,597	28.8	821	613	34.1
New Mexico	1,295	1,017	27.4	449	333	34.7	847	684	23.8
Arizona	2,714	1,775	52.9	2,037	1,323	54.0	677	453	49.5
Utah	1,459	1,059	37.7	1,153	843	36.7	306	216	41.7
Nevada	800	489	63.8	656	394	66.4	144	94	52.8
Washington	4,110	3,413	20.4	2,927	2,491	17.5	1,183	922	28.3
Oregon	2,617	2,092	25.1	1,566	1,281	22.3	1,051	811	29.6
California	23,517	19,971	17.7	21,717	18,638	16.5	1,800	1,333	35.0
Alaska	400	303	32.3	174	126	37.7	226	176	28.5
Hawaii	965	770	25.3	762	631	20.9	203	139	45.4

SOURCE: U.S. Department of Commerce, Bureau of the Census, *1980 Census of Population*, Washington, D.C., pp. 49–58.

The option approach has two major advantages: it offers the investor maximum leverage and profit while minimizing risks. And it saves the investor the trouble, time, and financing expense required to build and sell the actual development. Nonetheless, it requires specialized experience and a knack for sensing what higher, feasible use can be created for a given parcel of land.

Wealthy private and—including pension funds—institutional investors also use professional management to help them select and operate farms and other land suitable for upgrading and/or development. With the growing interest in U.S. land as a valuable investment, professional consultants have also emerged and, if they have proven track records, are worth their fees.

A PYRAMID OF HIGHER ECONOMIC USE

There are many factors that increase the value of raw land, but they are all variations on improving the land for a higher and better economic use of its features. They make idle land the least valuable, although it, too, during a period of general inflation, will rise in price per acre (perhaps enough to make up for its annual real estate taxes and the expense of meeting local regulations concerning weeds and trash).

Listed in descending order of value based on use, the following typical kinds of improvement can produce profits for an investment in land:

1. Industrial park
2. Shopping mall
3. Condominium development
4. Resort hotel
5. Development of small lots for single families
6. Development of large lots for single families
7. Campground for recreational vehicles
8. Working farm
9. Cropland leased out
10. Pastureland leased out
11. Woodlands and/or wetlands leased out to a hunting club
12. Hilly or mountainous acreage for scenic value, hiking, backpacking, or family camping (personal pleasure rather than economic reward)

An investor may find it infeasible to aim for the top of the pyramid by starting with an industrial park. Land used for a time as a working farm, as cropland, or as pastureland can, as urban civilization spills over into the area, move up to higher uses. Meanwhile, if well managed, the land produces income, makes its taxes and minor expenses, and provides a profit.

HOW LAND COMPARES IN RETURNS WITH OTHER INVESTMENT MEDIA

Farm acreage and residential housing have done very well compared with the performance of stocks and bonds, for example, over the past 10 years. Only certain collectibles and commodities have outgained it. Land grew in value at an average rate of 13 percent a year, housing at a rate of 9.9 percent; the average price of stocks increased 3.9 percent and of bonds 3.6 percent. Meanwhile the consumer price index (CPI) went up an average of 3.6 percent. Details are shown in Table 12-9.

WHEN TO INVEST IN RAW LAND OR FARM ACREAGE

Because the current U.S. land boom has great sustaining power and will affect values well into the next century, *now* is a good time to act. During recessions, land prices pause; sometimes they even dip in areas where there have been unusual previous gains. Thus buyers have rela-

TABLE 12-9 Land's Performance Compared to Other Investment Media, 1972–1982
Compound Annual Rates of Return

	10 Years	Rank	5 Years	Rank	1 Year	Rank
Oil	29.9%	*1*	21.2%	*4*	6.3%	*3*
U.S. coins	22.5	*2*	21.4	*3*	−27.8	*13*
U.S. stamps	21.9	*3*	26.6	*1*	−3.0	*9*
Oriental rugs	19.1	*4*	17.1	*6*	−16.2	*11*
Gold	18.6	*5*	17.3	*5*	−34.0	*14*
Chinese ceramics	15.3	*6*	23.7	*2*	−0.5	*6*
Farmland	13.7	*7*	10.7	*9*	−0.9	*7*
Silver	13.6	*8*	5.5	*13*	−44.5	*15*
Diamonds	13.3	*9*	13.7	*7*	0.0	*5*
Housing	9.9	*10*	10.0	*10*	3.4	*4*
Old masters	9.0	*11*	13.7	*8*	−22.0	*12*
CPI	8.6	*12*	9.6	*11*	6.6	*2*
Stocks	3.9	*13*	7.7	*12*	−10.5	*10*
Foreign exchange	3.6	*14*	1.6	*14*	−1.9	*8*
Bonds	3.6	*15*	0.6	*15*	11.4	*1*

SOURCE: Salomon Brothers Inc.

TABLE 12-10 Land Evaluation Chart

Parcel's identity and address ——————— Date ————————————————

Parcel's address ———————————————————————————————

Parcel's present owner —————————————————————————————

Owner's address ———————————— City/Town —————————— State ————————

Owner's telephone number ——————————————————————————

Characteristics of parcel ————————————————————————————

	Point score 1 to 4 for important features				
	4	3	2	1	Parcel's score
General features (maximum of 20 points)					
Distance from major population centers	Under 50 miles	50–100 miles	100–150 miles	Over 150 miles	
Distance from major highway	Under 10 miles	10–20 miles	20–30 miles	Over 30 miles	
Distance from major airport	Under 10 miles	10–20 miles	20–30 miles	Over 30 miles	
Major recreation areas within 20 miles	More than 4	2–4	0–2	None	
Distance to lake or ocean	Under 5 miles	3–10 miles	10–20 miles	Over 20 miles	
Physical features (maximum of 60 points)					
Distance from access road	Through site	Under 1 mile	1–5 miles	Over 5 miles	
Condition of access road	Paved—good	Paved—fair	Gravel—good	Poor	
Acreage (total)	100	500–1000	250–500	Under 250	
Topography (general character)	Gentle	Rolling	Hilly	Mountainous	
Extent of slopes over 20%	Less than 25%	25–50%	50–75%	Over 75%	
Woodlands (extent)	Over 75%	50–75%	25–50%	Under 25%	
Woodlands (type and condition)	Excellent	Good	Fair	Poor	
Extent of tract with good soils	Over 75%	50–75%	25–50%	Under 25%	
Rock and ledge occurrence	None	Occasional	Frequent	Extensive	
Water (pond and/or brook) on site	Good	Small	Possible	None	
Gravel—distance to source	On site	Under 1 mile	1–5 miles	Over 5 miles	
Existing buildings	Excellent	Fair	Poor	None	
Electric power	On site	Under 1 mile	1–2 miles	Over 2 miles	
Public water supply	On site	Within 1 mile	Over 1 mile	None	
Public sewers	On site	Within 1 mile	Over 1 mile	None	
Miscellaneous features (maximum of 20 points)					
Percent of tract usable	Over 75%	50–75%	25–50%	Under 25%	
Zoning controls	None	Limited	Average	Rigid	
Subdivision controls	None	Limited	Average	Rigid	
Environmental controls	None	Limited	Average	Rigid	
General character of land	Attractive	Pleasant	Average	Poor	

Total score for land's features

Deduct results of environmental impact study or practical effect of zoning regulations			
Make no change if effects are minor; deduct 20 points for moderate impact; 50 points for substantial impact	Deduct		———————————
			———————————
			———————————

12-24

TABLE 12-10   Land Evaluation Chart (*Continued*)

Net Score

Details of possible financing	
Asking price	$
Possible mortgage	$
Required down payment	$
Notes on financing details	
Notes on zoning and/or soil classification	

tive bargains at those times and should pounce on land that may become available at slightly distressed prices. This is particularly the case with farmland where the original owner may have overextended his financing and decides to sell some of his acreage at less than premium prices simply to pay off obligations at onerous interest rates.

In the long run, purchase of well-situated land will seem a profitable investment 10 years hence and even more in 20 years. Get the expert advice you need to fill gaps in your knowledge and jump aboard the boom. Your profits will be limited only by the amount of energy and concentration you supply to the project. Land will work for you if you are willing to do the modest amount of homework it requires.

Table 12-10 is a chart for comparing various properties. Note that it provides three types of characteristics with weighted scoring for each: *general factors,* worth a maximum of 20 points; *physical factors,* worth a maximum of 60 points; and *miscellaneous factors,* worth a maximum of 20 points. Each determining factor should be rated on the basis of a scale of 1 to 4 with the most favorable characteristic given a 4. Thus the highest-scoring property presumably is the best buy. Make notes, too, on the possible financing, either through a bank or, what is most likely in the case of acreage and raw land transfer, through financing by the seller. This is a factor removed from the land itself, but even the most attractive parcel may have an owner unwilling to finance the sale attractively. Perhaps the local bank does not want to extend itself further nor let you assume a possible previous mortgage—with difficult financing, it is possible that the owner will lower the price to facilitate the sale.

Chapter 13

Time-Shares

William F. Friery   President, Watt & Friery Marketing Company, Inc.

WHAT IS TIME-SHARING?

Time-sharing is a relatively new concept that has revolutionized the vacation real estate market. It is a technique for the multiple ownership and/or use of resort and recreational properties. Used for what it was intended, it provides annual vacation housing in a strong resort market. Time-sharing permits the purchase of only that interval of time, that piece of the clock, actually used for vacations. And it is a way of paying for tomorrow's vacation with today's money.

Various Types of Time-Shares

Time-sharing has been applied to hotels, motels, condominiums, townhouses, single-family dwellings, campgrounds, boats, motorhomes, and yachts. It can involve new construction, conversion of existing structures, properties solely devoted to time-sharing, and multiple-use resort properties.

There are two major types of time-sharing, an ownership interest in the real estate and the right to use. Time-share ownership assures the buyers, who receive a deed or title to the property and title insurance, the right to use, will, lease, or sell their interest and occupancy rights. Those who purchase pay the property taxes and are able to deduct interest in taxes, pro rata. (Bear in mind that business and corporation purchases may be tax deductible if the time-share units are used for employee incentive or other business use.) The right-to-use formula offers a lease to use the living space for a specified number of years without residual benefits.

In both types of time-sharing there are fixed or floating time spans, depending on the facility. Fixed time allows buyers to have the same week or weeks each year for as long as they have the property. Floating time allows the buyers to reserve their time any time within the season they purchased.

Some facilities allow bonus time, and thus after the buyers have reserved their time, they can, for a nominal fee and on 24-hours notice, stay in the facility for two nights or more depending on vacancy availability.

In addition, there are club membership or vacation license time-shares, which entail the purchase of a club membership which offers the right to occupy a living space for a specified length of time annually. Many developers initially selected the right-to-use or the club membership because there were no state or federal jurisdictions. But it also became obvious that the consumer was not being adequately protected under certain forms of lease contracts. In all but the ownership plan the tenant does not have to worry about taxes, management of the property, or forming a property owners association. But the property reverts to a builder or seller when the use privilege expires.

Time-sharing or interval ownership merely breaks resort home ownership into smaller, more affordable segments. In fact, it is the new dimension of real estate after the land, the house on the lot, and the condominium.

Historically, private real estate ownership is a recent phenomenon. In Europe, where time-sharing started about 20 years ago, land ownership did not extend to the masses until the early 1700s. Settlers brought to the United States the British recorded deed system to show ownership, measured by length and width in feet, with no pressing need to consideration of height. Later came the one deed for each building with neither height nor numbers of units considered.

The convenience of apartment living and the tax benefits of home ownership created the third dimension of real estate, the condominium. The condominium revolution allows for as many deed and title insurance policies on one piece of property as there are living units. Thus, the fourth dimension, interval ownership, with one deed for each 1-week or 2-week interval in 52 weeks per year, was evolved. The deed shows ownership for the apartment on a weekly interval, permitting the owners use only at the time specified on the deed.

Advantages of Time-Sharing

Generally, time-share resorts are located in the major resort communities of the world. The buyer pays a one-time price of anywhere from $2500 to $20,000 for a 7-day period in a condominium unit that can be used every year without additional payment or rental fees (other than nominal prorated home owners dues and maintenance fees).

For those who do not have the desire or resources to buy a vacation or second home, time-sharing properties offer the popular option at a fraction of the purchase price of the entire unit. Also, a well-located and designed time-share facility can be a hedge against inflation in resort accommodations.

Experts have long agreed that a time-share is a good value if the savings on rent, meals, and recreational expenses equal in 10 years the amount paid for the time-share. If, for example, a 1-week time-share is purchased for $5000 and the assumed maintenance fee is $200 annually, and assuming that the resort unit would rent for a minimum of $800 per week ($115 per night), in 10 years the buyer would have expended $7000 under a time-sharing plan ($5000 plus ten times $200). However, if the rental for 1 week each year would have totaled $8000 (ten times $800), it would have cost $1000 more than the purchase. In future years the savings would be much greater because, with this example, the entire cost of the time-share has been amortized over the initial 10 years.

Time-share units with kitchens offer both a convenience and a savings. Generally, the family on vacation spends three to four times more for food because they are eating out than when at home. Also, the time-share facility usually offers all the individual, personal comforts of a luxury resort hotel or condominium, providing complete services such as maid service and linens as well as the amenities unique to the area.

The annual maintenance fee, which covers the upkeep of buildings and grounds, interiors, repairs, replacement of furnishings, appliances, dishes and decorations, is shared by all the owners. This prevents the problems of deferred maintenance and protects the real estate asset. This is significant because where an owner may put off or defer maintenance the time-share budget provides adequate fees to ensure continuity. The majority of quality time-share facilities offer year-round maintenance and security and are staffed 24 hours a day, 365 days per year.

Among the more interesting benefits is the guarantee of a vacation destination. If the vacation week or weeks are not used during a particular year, those weeks do not accrue. However, time-share owners can generally sublease or rent or allow family or friends to use the time-share in their absence. The opportunity to trade on an informal or formal basis through trading networks or exchange programs is also an option to owners. There are voluntary exchange programs, offered for a nominal fee, to over thirty countries with more than 650 other resorts.

Who Buys Time-Shares?

With an estimated 350,000 families owning time-shares in the United States, the profile of the time-share buyer ranges the gamut in profession and age. Based on a survey taken at the Laguna Shores time-share facility in Laguna Beach, California, after 942 buyers had purchased a portion of the total offering of 1700 unit weeks, we found the following: the highest percentage of buyers were self-employed, 22 percent; people in sales numbered 14.4 percent; managers, line supervisors, and so on, accounted for 10.3 percent; engineers and technicians, 9 percent; electricians, nurses, carpenters, business administrators, and other executives, 7 percent; secretaries, 6.4 percent; doctors, lawyers, and certified public accountants, 6.2 percent; retirees with no occupation listed, 6.2 percent; school principals, and teachers, 4.7 percent; banking, office, savings institutions, and insurance workers, 4.1 percent; professors and associate professors, 3.6 percent; people employed in military, sports, and theology, 3.1 percent; construction administrators and contractors, 0.6 percent.

Married buyers outnumbered single buyers 67.96 percent to 32.04 percent. Those over 50 years old and not quite 60 numbered the most buyers with 42.90 percent. Next were the 40 to 49 year olds with 26.32 percent. The 30 to 39 age group was third with 21 percent, and those 60 and over made up 15.59 percent of the buyers. Those 20 to 29 bought the least number of units in that property.

Most of the sales were to buyers within a radius of 150 to 300 miles of the site, 2 to 3 hours of driving time. More than 60 percent of the buyers bought more than one unit, and eleven buyers bought more than four units each.

This survey is more or less typical, but the age groups vary according to the resort locations and amenities. For instance, sailing and ski areas tend to attract a somewhat younger age group.

How Time-Sharing Differs from Other Real Estate

Time-Sharing is a creative sale rather than a need sale, which generally applies to housing. One must create the need by pointing out the advantages, such as cost savings and convenience.

Time-share is such a specialty that it demands an expertise that is quite different from that needed in general real estate. The standards of excellence for time-share resorts, both in careful site selection and good management, must be maintained: Owners must feel that their share of the resort is *new* every time they enter it.

What Time-Share Means to a Community

A truly representative time-share project affords benefits to communities. The very nature of the product stabilizes the tourist and traveler use pattern. For those communities that have experienced fluctuating cycles of economy the time-share facilities have been a boon. In Hawaii, for example, where tourism is the chief industry, when the economy slowed down and tourism decreased, people took a second look at the time-share visitors. They found there had been no drop in their visits. Time-share owners are going to be there, good times, bad times, and in all kinds of weather, as the saying goes. And they tend to stay longer and spend slightly more money than does the average tourist.

Studies have consistently proved that the influx of time-share vacation owners has increased the economic base of these communities by as much as 20 to 30 percent overall. This is especially beneficial because most time-share facilities are used on a year-round basis. This has accounted for a new appreciation of the new breed of vacationers.

HISTORY OF TIME-SHARE

Europe to the United States

The idea of time-sharing originated in Europe about 20 years ago when inflation-cautious Europeans discovered that vacations could become affordable by buying only that portion of vacation time that they could use in a resort they would most like to frequent. Several families then purchased a villa, or resort house, on the Riviera and mutually agreed on the choice of the weeks used. This enabled them to share the costs of maintenance, purchase money, debt service, and replacement items.

Eventually, the idea was expanded in certain geographic locations, and the concept of exchanges was born. For example, if the owners wished to spend time at a coastal resort during the summer, they would make equal time available at a ski lodge during the winter. It was all very informal and sometimes led to misunderstandings because no one was actually responsible for equality in the exchange.

Time-sharing moved to the Virgin Islands about 1968 and eventually to the coast of Florida. This was approximately the same time that the Florida condominium building boom was experiencing grave difficulties caused by overbuilding for a nonexistent market. This started the great "bail-out program" of 1974 and 1975, when the time-sharing concept became the panacea for careless development and marketing planning. It was moderately successful. About the same time time-sharing spread northward along the East Coast and was introduced in the Hawaiian Islands with a new wave of interest. But it was not until

1976 that the industry really started to mature, so that in early 1977 the beginning of a solid industry was evident.

Some Time-Share History on the West Coast

Early in 1977, shortly after I joined the California-based Watt Industries, discussions began in earnest as to the marketability and feasibility of a time-share product in California. After 8 months of planning, we launched the first Watt Industries time-share as well as California's first major time-share offering, 1600 shares of 2-week intervals on a portion of the San Diego Country Estates property.

While we were not the first in the West, it was a new concept to most Californians and we soon realized that traditional marketing techniques were not sufficient to educate and attract the consumer.

In 1978 we embarked on an intensive consumer education program, and sales increased tremendously. Watt & Friery Marketing Company is successfully marketing three major time-share developments in new and different markets. They have become models for future developments: San Diego Country Estates in the inland coast; Laguna Shores on the West Coast; and The Tennis Club Resort in the Palm Springs desert.

These projects provided valuable insight into consumers' desires for time-sharing resorts and have produced valuable data analysis regarding the vacation use patterns of buyers. This is invaluable when structuring the use system of a new project.

Exchange Programs

Perhaps one of the greatest attractions of time-sharing to buyers is the exchange possibilities. Should time-share purchasers want to add even more variety to their vacations they can book other holiday stops through one of the world's resort exchange services.

There are several exchange services now in operation; the largest and best known is Resort Condominiums International (RCI), based in Indianapolis. RCI started in condominiums in 1972 and expanded into time-sharing in 1975. Through their computer operation and flexibility RCI handled more than 33,000 exchange vacations for time-share owners in 1981. RCI now offers more than 650 resort exchange opportunities in over thirty countries. Vacation Horizons International, a subsidiary of RCI, also offers about 100 top of the line resort exchanges throughout the world. Interval International, another experienced, worldwide exchange service is the second largest exchange system; it has more than 350 resorts available to time-share owners. Network One, a new service, has about thirty worldwide resorts at present. The cost of belonging to an exchange averages about $50 per year per owner family.

Exchange services are good for those vacationers who want a changing pattern of vacations or for those who are subject to transfer away from the area where they purchased their time-share.

Most time-share exchanges are made on the level of the purchase. It is seldom possible to trade up or for a higher resort accommodation than the one purchased. One of the biggest mistakes developers can make today is sticking with the efficiency units rather than offering the larger one- and two-bedroom suites. This is because the smaller units cannot be upgraded to regular exchanges, which limits who will buy the studio-type units.

In reserving exchange space it is wise to make reservations at least 90 days in advance to ensure the resort destination desired.

WHAT MAKES UP A GOOD TIME-SHARE?

Location

Location should be the first consideration in choosing a time-share. A tremendous amount of research goes into the location of a time-share project. The site should be identified with a resort destination that has one and preferably three or four seasons. If the location is only desirable for 6 months of the year, it will be difficult to sell with such limitation on the buyers. If it is a known resort area and attracts people 12 months of the year, it could be the ideal time-share site.

The facility should be located with accessibility to a primary market for both the convenience of the eventual owner and the conveniences of marketing, since time-sharing involves multiple sales.

The facility should have amenities on the property and/or within close proximity, such as water or snow sports, athletic activities, scenic beauty, popular stores, good restaurants, and sightseeing possibilities.

Size

The size of the facility is a major factor. Experience has shown that the small offerings of ten, fifteen, or twenty units prove unprofitable in the long run because an additional ten or fifteen units can be marketed for the same costs as the smaller facility. On the other extreme, the major offerings of 6000 to 10,000 weeks, particularly in a regional marketplace and in a volatile economy, can experience periods of extremely slow sales. (Developers can get deed backs, foreclosures, and resales occurring in the middle of a selling period.) To be of optimal size, a time-share offering should be between fifty and eighty units. This puts the offering around 2500 to 4000 weeks. I think that a variety of desirable locations rather than massive undertakings has less problems, can be sold faster, and is easier to control and manage.

Owners often show more pride of ownership and get to know one another and the resort staff in a smaller project.

Interiors

The interior furnishings of a time-share unit should be something that an owner would consider "an experience." Quality should be stressed since people on vacation want to have a full range of conveniences and luxuries which they may or may not have in their own homes. Washers and dryers, blenders, electric barbecues, microwave ovens, regular ovens, trash compactors, dishwashers, vacuum cleaners, televisions, ironing boards, steam irons, and telephones should all be considered. It is important to maintain a standard of excellence without burdening the owners association with expensive replacement. Therefore practicality is equally important in selecting items.

Property Management

After the acquisition, construction, and marketing of a project, the next phase is property management. The first rule for the property manager is to educate the staff to understand that the buyers are owners—not guests. Time-share management is actually hospitality, property management, and hotel/condominium management.

An agency can be hired to manage a time-share property. The agency would be responsible for the total package—the front of the house, which includes the front desk, the switchboard, reservations and manager, to the back of the house, which includes maintenance, refurbishing, repairs, laundry, grounds, housekeeping, and all owner relations. The agency acts for the property owners or home owners associations, setting up the annual meetings, preparing the monthly statements for home owners dues, preparing the annual report, and handling legal affairs.

MARKETING TIME-SHARES

The quality of a time-share project is directly related to the marketing concept. And the development of a marketing plan should start right at the beginning of the project.

First, a definition of marketing as it regards time-sharing is appropriate. Every decision in the course of the project's development involves marketing. It is the who, what, where, why, and when of the business. Even if there is a mediocre job in the development and finance of a project, a good marketing program can often make it a success. However, a poor marketing program, even with good construction and finance, can cause a project to fail.

The need for vacations and the fact that the vast majority of the population perceives vacations as a necessity and not a luxury support the product. Identification of where the market is and of what the buyer in the market for that product looks like are required, as are methods used to reach the buyer profile in that market. This all has to be done before the finite adjustments such as pricing, terms, and the use factor are built into the product. The application of marketing science will determine the cost and effective absorption rate for the product.

Cost of Marketing

The most significant cost in time-share development is the marketing cost. It is a combination of many factors, a total approach, that determines a successful sales absorption rate. It defines the buyer, the marketplace, and the approach to the marketplace. It also is the pricing, financing, the use system, the property management function, and more. If only one of these facets is out of balance, it will affect the success of the entire program.

Unlike high-demand consumer products, which do not have to rely on the critical aspect of the total approach, the synchronization of a time-share marketing approach can be very critical. Today in the United States approximately one in ten to one in twelve client visits to a time-share resort results in a sale. The cost of providing this prospect ranges anywhere from as little as $50 in a densely populated area to as high as $250 for the most remote time-share destinations. A generally accepted average would be $80 to $100.

Following the formula through, it looks like this: If a developer has 100 units to sell and is offering 51 weeks, there are 5100 time-shares to sell. This means that 5100 buyers must be sold. To sell 5100 buyers, 51,000 prospects (one buyer for every ten prospects) must come through the door at a cost of $80 per prospect. The generation cost would therefore be $4,080,000 to sell out the project. This is just the direct marketing cost.

It is conceivable that with the advent of a broad consumer awareness and acceptance of the time-share product, the marketing costs will be reduced considerably. Once the acceptance and motivation of the consumer to buy the product reaches a sufficient level, and time-sharing becomes a generic word, then different marketing approaches will become more cost effective. Currently this is not the case. The selling process relies on people being exposed to the product.

It should be pointed out that there is a great deal of expense and risk involved for the developer and the marketer before any profit can be realized. Often an average time-share prospect does a quick mathematical equation, such as multiplying the cost of the unit being offered to him or her by 51 weeks, and quickly concludes that the developer is realizing a tremendous profit. The prospect does not realize that it costs 27 percent to 50 percent of that sales volume to market the product, not including the cost of acquiring the property, the cost of renovating, or the costs for legal and financial assistance. Until time-sharing becomes an accepted household word, the major challenge facing the industry is the ability to attract a sufficient number of potential prospects to the resort.

The most effective way to achieve this objective is to utilize a variety of programs. The best market penetration is achieved by the marketers who are constantly creating and implementing a tremendous variety of sales programs to produce large numbers of qualified prospects. It is not unusual for a marketer of a major time-sharing facility to use ten or fifteen different generation programs at the same time. Because these programs can be very expensive, they must be monitored on a daily basis.

Advertising

Since the beginning of time-sharing, the print media, radio, television, direct mail programs, owner referral programs, mass mailings, sweepstakes, premium offers, and off-site locations have been used to entice a prospect to book a trip to the project. A new method is the use of off-site public contact locations, which is showing some success, but it is still difficult to convey the thought that time-sharing is an effective, simple, urgent matter to the consumer. It is obvious to the developers, lenders, and marketers that time-sharing is a complex, sophisticated business that is not easily explained to the buying public. On the bright side, however, is the fact that the time-sharing concept is familiar to at least three out of ten people today, compared to one out of twenty in 1976 to 1977.

Time-share marketing programs must be continuously monitored. A developer of residential real estate may prepare an advertising campaign that is good for 12 months, but the time-share campaign can change every 30, 60, or 90 days.

Public Relations

In 1976 to 1977, I was involved in an effort to market a time-share resort. We realized at that time that traditional methods of resort marketing were not effective and went heavily into public relations for consumer acceptance. We devoted a large part of our efforts, energies, and marketing dollars to an aggressive public relations campaign. The traditional public relations effort, which involves the planting of stories in certain publications, was supplemented with an all-out campaign to educate people about the new real estate concept. Our time-share articles and stories were directed not only to the real estate sections but also to travel, features, human interest, and local news editors. We relied heavily on regional and national media as well as industry distribution of information and features. This public relations effort proved critical. The importance of public relations participation in the overall marketing plan from the very initiation of the concept, through the planning stages, to the ultimate successful completion of sales cannot be overstressed. Public relations is an image builder and a liaison with community and business leaders, and it can provide a positive environment for the creation of the product.

Pricing

Perhaps the single most important aspect of time-share selling following location and seasonability is the pricing of the product. The attractiveness of the pricing is a critical factor in successful sales penetration, especially in a recessionary period. Earlier the prices set did not relate to the marketplace in which the product was being sold. From late in 1980 up to 1982 time-share prices nationally appeared to be much higher per unit than they were four years earlier, and a slowdown resulted. Pricing must relate to marketing analysis, the demographics of location, the terms, the down payment, and the anticipated sales absorption rate. It has become increasingly clear that time-share inventory must be sold on a constant and expeditious basis. It is important that the pricing relate to the quality and the location as well as to the consumer's conception of value and affordability. As with any form of real estate, the worth of a particular time-share product is exactly what the consumer will pay for it at the time you want to sell it.

FINANCING

What the Lender Looks for

The lender primarily looks for collateral, such as a hotel or condominium, or the ratio value of paper in making a loan to time-share. Also, the lender wants to know whether the cash flow of the project is adequate to support a loan and if the timing of the cash flow meets requirements.

Financing can be difficult in times of recession, and the problem is exacerbated by the overall educational process a lender has to go through to learn about time-share, especially if the loan is a first and there is no past experience. No changes in lending are expected in the foreseeable future or through 1983. The current prime plus 2 to prime plus 4 is expected to continue. In fact, a developer generally pays 3 to 10 points up front to the banker or possibly to the mortgage banker.

Due to the tight money market the lenders are getting more involved in the overall marketing programs of the time-share projects. They now consider marketing the chief area of scrutiny, since it is important that they understand where and how the dollars are being spent, where the benefits, if any, are derived, and what type of programs are in operation. The lender wants to know where the prospects are coming from and what percentage of the walk-through prospects actually buy. Most lenders also want to know whether there is a manager and a property management program in existence and whether they will remain after sellout. A final question in the minds of lenders is whether the developer has the financial capability to see a project through to completion.

How to Obtain Financing

The simple rule in obtaining financing is to make the yield attractive enough to the banker. The easiest method is to go to the right lender, one who knows about and understands time-sharing and is already in the business of lending money to time-shares.

To have any chance of obtaining financing, a time-share developer needs a background, a track record of at least four or five projects. As in all loans today, it is difficult to get financing if it is a "first" for the developer or the project. One of the few ways to get a favorable loan response is to joint venture a project with a lending institution so that the institution can share in the profits.

Early Lender Involvement

Sometimes the developer can carry his or her own paper and will also carry back the paper. Other developers have to tie in with major lenders and will hypothecate (pledge) the notes receivable. But, if a lender is needed, that person or institution should be determined well before any other steps are taken. In fact, the lender should be determined by the time the formal project loan application is prepared. Early lender involvement generally means better loan timing and better loan structure. Policy decisions can often be made at this stage that save both the lender and the builder valuable time.

Method

After the project submission stage is completed, there is sufficient preliminary information available to involve a prospective lender. This information would include: (1) a general project concept, (2) a plot plan location map, (3) a summary profit analysis, and (4) a project timetable.

A Lending Example

The Laguna Shores project was financed outside the property; we bought the property with no mortgage on it. The encumbrances or borrowings that we made to finance the project were done outside the property so there was no blanket encumbrance and no mortgage on the property. The property was then put into a trust, free and clear of all encumbrances. The reason this is done is to satisfy all Department of Real Estate requirements and also to provide what we believe is a major requirement for selling fee title. The consumer is generally protected when buying fee title in real estate.

Lender Relations

The chief financial officer and other company principals of a developer or development should maintain regular contact with various lenders. Current knowledge of funds, availability, interest rates, preferred geographical areas of lending, and actual loan structure must be maintained to expedite specific loan approvals. If the builder has an existing relationship with one or more lenders, these sources should be coordinated through the chief financial officer for the maximum overall benefit.

THE FUTURE OF TIME-SHARE

The Growth of Time-Share

As of early 1978, the United States had 240 resort condominiums and hotels and approximately 160 developers involved in time-sharing plans. About fifty locations with two or more projects accounted for 60 percent of new inventory and were part of the multiproject programs. Six organizations accounted for forty-eight separate facilities: Holiday Clubs International (twenty-three locations), Vacation Internationale (ten), Sweetwater Park (six), Captran (four), Carriage House (three), and Playboy (two).

Outside the United States there were about one hundred time-share facilities operated by approximately seventy organizations. That included Europe with about fifty locations and twenty time-share developers. In Mexico there were over thirty locations and some twenty developers. The Caribbean accounted for another fifteen to twenty locations and nearly the same number of developers. South America, Australia, and some other parts of the world had a few time-share facilities.

By 1979 there were 350 time-share projects in the United States. That figure grew to 425 in 1980, 600 in 1981, and between 775 and 825 in 1982. Forty or more of the multiple location developers were selling $10 million a year by 1982. Even with an early start Europe's time-share did not keep pace with the time-share growth in the United States.

The time-share sales volume in the United States:

1975—$50 million	1980—$900 million
1976—$75 million	1981—$1.3 billion
1977—$150 million	1982—$1.5 billion
1978—$300 million	1983—$3.5 billion
1979—$650 million	(projected)

Although time-share development and sales have been slower than expected, it must be remembered that a new entrant into the time-share business needs at least 12 months to start up. Once a developer is in the business the test is to stay in business and expand.

Despite the recessionary problems more than 70 percent of today's time-share developers believe sales will increase in 1983 to 1984. Less than 4 percent expect a sales decline. Unlike previous years more new construction and fewer rehabilitation projects are expected in the coming years. There will be more off-site marketing and a much bigger role for the brokers in 1983 to 1984.

The Time-Share Industry and Regulation

Along with the recession there has been another negative factor in time-share sales—a series of anti-time-share stories by the media. This was caused in part by the activities of a few developers and marketers who used unscrupulous sales techniques, but it also was caused by a few uninformed, so-called investigative reporters who failed to educate themselves about the new field and its benefits to the communities. As more reliable editors are stepping in to analyze the product, uninformed reporting is less of a problem.

However, the presence of unscrupulous developers and sellers in the industry continues to be an ongoing problem in a few isolated cases around the country. These unacceptable practices in the industry are under severe scrutiny by the industry. In 1982 the National Timesharing Council (NTC), a division of the American Land Development Association, set up several programs to educate and influence time-share developers, state regulatory bodies, and the buyer. Since more than 75 percent of the nation's time-share developers are members of the NTC, a code of ethics for time-share projects has been adopted by the membership. This was known as the NTC/NARELLO (National Association of Real Estate License Law Officials) Model Time-Share Ownership Act, designed to ensure consumer protection while preserving a reasonable commercial atmosphere. The act has been promoted in every state, the U.S. territories, and several Canadian provinces. It either has been adopted in total or has influenced legislation in Nebraska, California, Hawaii, Florida, Virginia, and Tennessee. With this act the states can create a climate where quality in time-sharing programs can flourish and projects and practices that do not live up to quality and regulatory and legislative standards can be weeded out.

There are no federal agencies specifically responsible for the regulation of time-sharing, but there are several agencies that administer laws, rules, and guidelines which affect how time-sharing can be structured, marketed, and sold. The three federal agencies that play a role are the Federal Trade Commission, the Department of Housing and Urban Development, and the Securities and Exchange Commission.

For more information on time-sharing the consumer can write for *Resort Timesharing—A Consumers' Guide*, published by the NTC, 604 Solar Building, 1000 16th Street, N.W., Washington, DC 20036. The professional can obtain copies of the NTC's code of ethics, *Standards for Admission and Continuing Membership*, and *Disclosure Standards for Exchange Companies* at the same Washington address. Also, the professional can glean up-to-date time-share information on a regular basis by subscribing to the industry publication *Resort Timesharing Today*, published by Carl Burlingame, CHB Co., 1101 North San Antonio Road, Suite 303, Mountain View, CA 94043. Of special interest is Robert Irwin's *Timeshare Properties*, McGraw-Hill, 1983.

Why Time-Share Owners Buy

Most time-share owners buy for several reasons: (1) they want to use their vacation unit for future vacations, (2) they see the units as sound business investments, (3) they buy with a view to selling in the future,

(4) they like the resort exchange opportunities, and (5) they like owning a part of a favorite resort.

Based on a survey taken of the Watt & Friery time-share buyers we found that the majority of the owners are enthusiastic about their purchases of time in the leisure homes.

More than 80 percent of the owners (84.3) expressed satisfaction with their purchases and a like figure (85.1) were satisfied with the resort unit maintenance. They also liked the communications between management, the developer, and the owner. And 89.3 percent said they have recommended time-sharing to others.

There also was enthusiasm over the owners' future plans. More than 19 percent (19.2) said they intend to buy more time intervals in the same resort. Another 41.3 percent said they plan to purchase additional time-shares in another development. And 41.3 percent requested exchanging their units with owners at other time-share developments.

While most had confidence in the future resale value of their time-share unit, 27.8 percent said they don't intend to sell. Only 8.6 percent said they plan to sell within the immediate future. Another 16.4 percent said they would sell after 5 years. And 75.6 percent said they favor an on-site professional resales program to help them if they decide to sell.

The vast majority (86.2) said they are using and enjoying their time-share units. Some 46 percent have used their units three or more times.

Changes in Time-Share Sales Techniques

There are five good reasons why the marketing techniques for time-share will experience significant changes in 1982 to 1983: Product pricing, increased cost of sale, the economy, increased competition, and consumer resistance. Price is a major concern. Now more than ever the time-share concept calls for a product structured and designed for quality and affordability for a large segment of the marketplace. The increasing cost of many time-share projects seems to be more reflective of the developers' return on investment than a function of the supply and demand of the marketplace. Pricing must be realistic.

Early buyer profiles consisted of a family with an income of $30,000 a year with a husband and wife, both working, and 2.5 children, normally vacationing 2.5 weeks every year and spending an average of $2500 per year. The broad spectrum of buyers has been narrowed by about 20 percent of the previous figures and now includes the affluent young families who understand and appreciate the modern concept and the medium- to high-income middle-aged and older couples who appreciate the convenience of a time-share over a second home and who consider the estate value for their heirs.

Most developers and marketers recognize that the chief reason to change the marketing strategies is the economy. Although 66 percent of the working population enjoys a lifestyle that provides the financial capability to "own" a vacation, and they would readily spend $2500 to $3500 on a vacation, they are not willing to assume any type of long-term financial commitment. On the other hand, there are a significant number of people who recognize that the present economic conditions do not last forever—they can be convinced to consider a recessionary period as an opportunity to purchase not only real estate but other luxury items as well.

As the economy softened in 1980 and 1981 and stagnated in 1982, the picture changed drastically within the industry. The one-facility owner, new to the business, can no longer solve all the problems now facing the time-share industry and all real estate. The cost of sales has risen from about 27 percent in May of 1981 to almost 42 percent in 1982. The significance of increased marketing costs has limited the number of new entries in the time-sharing field.

In addition, major lenders today are no longer satisfied with what many call obscene interest rates—they want a major piece of the action. If it starts to make more sense for developers to invest their capital in money market funds than to become involved in venture capital opportunities, we could begin to see a rapid decline in future time-share development. Thus there will be a kind of weeding out of less than responsible time-share entrepreneurs. Those with poor location quality and product amenities will, even at low prices, have difficulty competing.

There also is a need for the development of some professional time-share management talent. Right now the industry sadly lacks this type of individual. Professional time-share management institutions are needed in which the science and the skills that are necessary for successful time-share development can be taught. Some hotel management schools and others will ultimately develop an educational format to train people to handle the aspects of time-sharing.

On the bright side, time-sharing still remains the number-one positive scene in the real estate picture. Further, more and more members of the fourth estate are taking time to learn the truth about time-sharing and some are becoming buyers as well.

The product must be of a quality that can withstand all scrutiny. Assuming that the project is well situated and adequately financed and meets the criteria of a destination or regional resort—and the price is right—the following can be done to brighten the sales picture: Examine and improve packaging, improve and maintain an image that is conveyed to the consumer in as many ways as possible, and maintain the spirit of success throughout your entire organization, including subsidiary offices. It might be wise to affiliate with regional and national broker outlets, pump new vitality into referral programs, and consider implementing a vacation store.

Vacation stores in strategic locations will eventually revolutionize the industry. These franchised outlets will provide to large numbers of consumers a relaxed opportunity to shop for a desired beach, mountain, or urban vacation destination. In one location and in one sitting, consumers will be able to complete their travel arrangements for a visit to the resort they have selected. Time-share selling will then be a streamlined, computerized occurrence of simplicity and selectivity by the consumer.

As the American consumer becomes more familiar with the logic and advantages of time-share vacation ownership, the industry will enter into a period of enlightenment. A substantial amount of marketing dollars will be better utilized in providing an interested prospect with sufficient facts and information about vacation ownership—relating to his or her desires and socioeconomic needs—to allow the prospect to exercise his or her own process of selectivity.

The role of the salesperson and brokers will essentially change in the area of primary emphasis. Rather than trying to convince a disinterested prospect—who primarily responded because of an exciting premium offer—of the benefits of time-sharing, they will be able to direct their expertise and knowledge toward helping an informed consumer with the particular resort he or she has selected.

Site Selection

Alfred Mattei Mingione   Real Estate Consultant

MATCHING THE SITE TO THE OCCUPANTS' NEEDS

The importance of proper site selection may at first appear obvious, that is, to what extent the site location is profitable and measures up to the needs, goals, and objectives of the buyer and/or the user. Unfortunately, a great deal of time and money is usually spent prior to evaluating any particular location from a profitable standpoint. In other words, retail sales, for example, can be estimated but are not established as a statistic until the sales are actually made and substantiated. The property is purchased, and the building is built—all on sales estimates. The following information is a detailed guide for all those involved or who wish to be involved in buying, selling, or obtaining control of real estate. In addition, this information would be extremely useful to those desiring employment as site selectors or in real estate–related jobs. Thousands of corporations have real estate departments and provide outstanding career opportunities. In general, universities and real estate–related schools do not teach any type of user-oriented site selection. It is therefore somewhat of a lesser-known field, although it can be lucrative and satisfying.

Many promising ideas, operations, and entrepreneur projects have failed because of poor initial site selection. The very first locations of any company should be super winners, to complete the initial growth stages successfully.

In the past three decades, the demand for prime lucrative site locations has increased, and prime first-choice locations have decreased. To say the least, this imbalance of supply and demand has created today's highly competitive market for first-choice, prime locations.

Since the 1950s and 1960s profound changes in lifestyles have occurred along with such things as the construction of the interstate system, more jobs for women and blacks, increases in leisure time and travel, increases in per capita and median family income, the overwhelming growth experienced by the airline companies, and so on. Out of the changes in people's lifestyles arose a tremendous increased demand for service stations, fast foods, motels, shopping centers, convenience markets, recreational areas, and, in general, all prime retail and commercial site locations.

Clearly, second, third, and fourth choices of locations often must be sought in lieu of the prime, sometimes obvious, locations. It therefore follows that in today's market and economy one must be able to locate, evaluate, and obtain productive site locations. The following serves as a guide toward these goals, whether you are a buyer, seller, investor, broker, speculator, user, or seeking to establish a career.

Not all the following information is always required for proper site location; one must tailor the following information, guidelines, and principles to one's particular needs. For example, various large corporations fostering muffler shops, fast food stores, service stations, and various franchises vary greatly in the format and criteria required in a site package submitted for their approval. This is due to company policies and procedures and also to the major factors which they have found to produce the highest sales volume for their own particular operation. For example, a doughnut shop produces higher sales, in general, by locating on the "breakfast" side of the street, and fried chicken sales will be higher on the "going home" side. These factors reiterate our first point—the importance of matching the site to the occupant's needs. Bear in mind, however, that should unforeseen circumstances arise, and a site should lose its original purpose and usefulness, the potential for optional uses can provide excellent insurance against loss. Therefore, the prudent investor will obtain as much information as possible before making substantial capital investments. The following is a brief look at some additional unique requirements.

Sales	Unique Requirements
Breakfast-type sales	Going to work side or breakfast side of street. Heavy early morning traffic.
Fried chicken and other take-out	Going home side of the street. Ethnic makeup of surrounding area (certain ethnic groups will provide more demand for fried chicken than will others).

	Operation close to nearby homes due to the limited time product will stay warm and fresh. Walkup trade (a big plus, will be medium- to lower-income groups and middle-age groups).
Fast foods, burgers, hot dogs, ice cream, pizza, and so on	Neighborhoods with large numbers of children.
Service stations	Sales on corner locations (particularly far corners and turn corners, depending on traffic flow). Interstate highway locations with good visibility (most preferable are pin locations at full-diamond interchanges).
Convenience markets	Heavy density of population nearby, multifamily and apartment units, high rise, and so on.
Hardware and do-it-yourselfers	Backed up predominantly by single-family dwellings and higher median age groups.
Small warehouses	Excellent visibility and exposure.

This list merely scratches the surface, but it should stimulate your creative thought process in regard to site selections.

The Approach and Purpose

Due to the tremendous amount of information to be gathered, it is often difficult and somewhat confusing for the novice to know exactly where to begin. Here again experience is the teacher. Once you have a thorough understanding of what market the site is to be located in, why, the requirements involved, and budgets and time schedules, it is then best to plan and organize the ways to gather and substantiate this information in the quickest and most efficient manner. First obtain that information which is free or at little expense and close at hand. In this way, you can begin to evaluate the site as information is obtained. Save the more expensive and costly items for last in case your preliminary findings should deem the site undesirable (this becomes even more important if there is extensive travel involved).

Criteria and Information Required for Approval

In general, the following material is in the order which company approval committees would prefer to review the site package.

Cover Letter.   The cover letter is merely a brief outline letter covering the major contents of your site package. It should first identify the type of site, such as an interstate location, neighborhood, highway, or shopping center pad. The letter should be very careful to point out any adverse conditions prevailing and any factors which would be a departure from company policy. A sample letter for a service station site might start out with the following paragraphs.

Sample Letter.   Subject site is located on the far corner of the traffic-controlled intersection of First Avenue and Main Street in Norcross, Georgia. Both roads are major highway arterials and are heavily travelled, lending support to our recommendation for a 24-hour location. First Avenue has 24,000 ADT (average daily traffic), and traffic counts on Main are 38,000 vehicles per 24-hour period. The traffic is made up primarily of local commuter, commercial, and tourist.

The surrounding neighborhood (as per attached aerial photos) consists primarily of single-family dwellings in the $90,000 range. The population within a 2-mile radius of site is 22,400 people; median family income is $43,000.

The self-service operation on the southeast quadrant of subject intersection is presently doing 60,000 gallons per month (according to the meter readings and backed up through conversations with the local operators). It is a 7-day, 24-hour operation with 20 percent of the volume being done between 12:00 P.M. and 6:00 A.M. No other services are offered.

Our nearest unit is 4 miles west on the opposite side of Main Street and is presently averaging 80,000 gallons per month. We definitely need representation in this area, and, as per attached maps, this is the best available site in the marketing area. It is 200 feet by 200 feet on the northwest quadrant and accessibility, ingress, and egress are more than adequate. Visibility is excellent from all directions.

Subject site falls directly in the path of our distribution and delivery objectives, and an average operation should produce a minimum of 40,000 gallons per month.

I strongly recommend that we secure this site as soon as possible, and I await your approval.

Traffic Counts.   Traffic count maps can be obtained in various ways depending on the size of the city or area and how sophisticated its information systems are. The best sources are departments of transportation, regional and local planning centers, and traffic departments. Naturally you will seek all the information you can while visiting these various departments. Normally, a good regional planning center can supply you with a wealth of information pertaining to your criteria.

Traffic count maps are usually the best for analyzing purposes, since they will give you counts within a radius around your site. This is excellent for comparison purposes. You can back up these maps with your own periodic counts. For example, you can count the number of vehicles going past a site 10 minutes out of every hour for an 8-hour period. This will give you an excellent feel for the site's peak high and low periods and for the type and general speed of the vehicular movement. Keep in mind that, although little traffic is undesirable, it is possible that too much heavy traffic can make ingress and egress difficult, making your site traffic-bound. Some companies actually purchase traffic count meters and take their own counts. This indicates the importance of substantiating accuracy.

Photography.

Ground.   The old saying that a picture is worth a thousand words is true now more than ever. Some companies will take panoramic shots which show the site and its relationship to adjoining sites. A slide presentation can show shots taken from all directions and starting about ¼ mile from the site and then every 50 to 100 feet to the site. This gives an excellent windshield view of the site. It will also show many important factors such as visibility, accessibility, competition, road condition, and so on, and it is an excellent aid in describing the site to others. This and all presentations should be good enough to sell the site to those who have never physically been to it and who may never actually see it. A modern videotape will carry this even another step forward.

Other ground photographs should be taken of the entire site from a construction standpoint. These will point out rises and dips, curbs and gutters, utility poles, sewer and storm drains, manholes, and so on, and will be a tremendous help in preparing cost estimates, site preparations and layouts, and so forth.

Aerial.   Aerial photos show the site and its relationship to the entire trading area. They should be marked to point out residential areas, commercial areas, main roads and arteries, growth areas, generators, competition, and other company outlets.

Topography.   Photos of the topography are taken only when there are unusual circumstances which could present obstacles to the construction or the operation departments such as underground rock in the area, unusual foliage indicating swamp or high water table, drainage problems, and severe changes in elevation. These photos can also be used as indicators to construction such as where you recommend placement of some items such as buildings, dumpster, telephone booths, poles, curb cuts, underground tanks, parking lot striping, and required landscaping.

Trading Area.   Photographs of competitors' operations, general retail outlets, generators, current or proposed construction areas, traffic controls, and so on, will help management to better understand the proposed location and marketing area.

Maps and Diagrams.   I cannot conceive of finding or selling an adequate site without proper maps. Maps contain a good deal of important information that is unavailable elsewhere. They will help you find sites and help you sell the site package. Every site locator will find maps one of the most useful of tools.

The following procedure offers one of the better ways to begin to locate and evaluate good sites. This procedure is particularly useful when your objectives are to locate sites in marketing areas which you have never been to and know nothing about.

1. Obtain good understandable maps of the proposed marketing area. Different maps can be obtained by phone or mail; select the best-suited ones. They can be obtained through chambers of commerce, banks, map stores, mapping companies such as Dolph and Champion, local book stores, office supply stores, local and regional planning centers, drug stores, the superintendent of documents in Washington, D.C., or local government printing offices, and so forth. Probably you will need several different maps for various purposes.

2. Take a colored marker and draw lines along all barriers, whether natural or synthetic, including rivers and streams, railroad tracks, limited access routes, and any obstacle making it more difficult to travel from one side of the site to the other. The map will now be sectioned into several different areas, some of which will ultimately become trading areas for proposed sites.

3. Put the following information into each one of the trading areas or sections. The information can be derived from your U.S. census tracts.
    a. Population and numbers of people living in that section, including ethnic breakdown.

Example:

1400	Blacks
1300	Whites
1540	Spanish
700	Chinese
4220	Italian
9160	Total

I would like to point out there is no bias or prejudice involved, just a simple fact that some groups will not go for certain items, and others will. Lower-income groups will naturally be more price conscious. Salami and provolone sandwiches will sell better in an Italian neighborhood; older groups will not be receptive to items which are hard to chew, since they have a higher incidence of false teeth; and so on. In effect, the principles of supply and demand operate to bring products to those who most want them.

b. Median age. Record the median age into each section. The median age is that at which there is the same number of people older as there are younger.

c. Median income.

d. Number of households in each section.

e. Average family income.

f. Retail sales. If updated census tracts are unavailable, various computer companies sell demographic information. One creative way to obtain information would be to secure a zip code map of your area. The main post office can supply you with this and the number of residential mail deliveries in each zip code area. This number times the number of people per household will give you an update on population.

4. Indicate on your maps all competitors, larger shopping centers and malls, other generators, and the downtown section. You now have an idea of what your marketing area looks like without ever having been there.

5. Go to the marketing area. Drive all major arteries marking work maps and reconfirming and updating your initial information. You should now be able to pick the prime trading area sections in which you would like to locate sites.

6. Continuing on a process-of-elimination basis, you should now determine exactly from which point to which point you want your site to be in for each trading area. For example, you might want a company operation on Market Street between First and Tenth avenues. You can now draw a strip map of this 10-block area from First to Tenth. The map should show every parcel of property, the actual property owner, name and address, telephone number, and what business there is on the parcel or if it is vacant. You can now contact each property owner requesting information as to the availability. You can update your strip as you begin your negotiations, prior to final evaluations and recommendations.

To emphasize again, the more you know about a site and the surrounding area, the more comfortable and confident you will feel with your recommendations. Remember, one so-called "dog," or poor location, will nullify the benefits from several good sites.

Demographics.   Statistics can be purchased. Most larger companies have small libraries containing the majority of required information. There are several excellent marketing guides, available from your local book stores, which break down the marketing areas into number of households, population breakdown, automobiles registered, medium and median income, and retail sales. Also, recent U.S. census tracts are most useful, and one should become as familiar as possible with them.

Competition.   In general, competition is anyone vying for a share of the same spendable dollar that you want. More specifically, there is direct and indirect competition. Direct is that competition serving the same trading area selling the same products or services that you are, under the same or a different brand name. Indirect competition would be anyone offering a different product or service but satisfying the same customer needs. In other words, X fried chicken unit would be in direct competition with Y fried chicken unit. X fried chicken unit would be in indirect competition with Y pizza parlor, since they are seeking the same food dollar and satisfying like demands.

Generators.   Generators are businesses, attractions, or situations which draw people and traffic past or near your site. Some excellent generators are shopping malls, large discount stores, tourist attractions, interstate access, and large factories and plants. Good generators are permanent. There are also top of the mind generators such as post offices, fire stations, libraries, etc. These are places with familiarity and are useful in giving directions, such as, "We are located next to the post office" or "We are across the street from the fire station."

Physical Characteristics.   *Ingress and Egress.*   Ingress and egress are the physical entering and exiting of the site, which should be simple and easy for the customer. The driver has to either stop or park to make a purchase. The less congestion there is and the smoother traffic flows, the more convenience for the customer. Customer satisfaction should always be one of the main considerations when making preliminary layouts and recommendations. In general, the larger the site is, the better the chances are for securing wide curb cuts, adequate parking, good traffic flow, smooth entering and exiting, proper surface drainage, and so on. For example, if the site elevation is much higher than the street grade, the driveways can be lengthened to provide a greater graduated ratio, if the additional square footage is available. This will give the customer a smoother and more comfortable access.

Accessibility. Difficulty in getting to a site can prove to be disastrous. Quick, convenient access should be a major consideration in site location for any sales outlets. However, in the case of a small warehouse or a muffler shop, for example, access becomes less important. Customers are going to a specific place for a predetermined reason. Even if the location is passed, they will probably turn around and come back. In the case of fast foods, gasoline, coffee, and so on, impulse plays a larger role. If you pass one, there will probably be another one up the street.

Careful attention should be paid to the ease of access from all directions. This and turn lanes, speed of traffic, traffic lights, congestion, number of traffic lanes, median or road dividers and cuts should all be considered when rating accessibility. When rating accessibility, however, remember to consider the competition's position. If your accessibility or any other factors are extremely poor, weigh them in comparison with the competition—if you are going to sell hot dogs, and all other food locations in the trading area have just as poor or poorer access than your site does, you would not lose a competitive edge. You and the customers have no choice but to put up with the situation.

Visibility. Visibility obviously is of the utmost importance. What good is any retail location if no one can see it? In general, visibility factors should be used and upgraded to the maximum. From the customer's standpoint, it is important to determine where you are, what you are selling, and how to get to you soon enough to make a decision before he or she is on top of you or has passed by. Visibility is even more important on interstate and highway locations, where limited access traffic is moving at 50 to 70 miles per hour. Modular and directional signs are necessary tools but cannot replace the value of building visibility.

Distribution. Distribution refers to the layout of units (retail outlets), or where they are in relationship to each other. Distribution also refers to the transporting of products and merchandise from their original destination, usually through various warehouses and transportation systems and on to the units. The total distribution picture should be evaluated carefully, particularly for newer and younger companies. This will give direction as to where new sites are feasible and how any new site will fit into a distribution pattern. Obviously, if there were eight company units within 3 miles of each other, the ninth location would present problems if it were 40 miles down the road, since the cost of doing business per unit increases. (Consider, for example, the per unit increased time and travel for the multiunit manager.)

Keep in mind that distribution does not necessarily mean a cluster of units. Some companies find it more profitable to have a string of units from one point to another. For example, an oil company may locate service stations along Interstate 95 every 40 miles from New York to Florida. The traveler can then purchase the same brand of gasoline on the entire trip from New York to Florida. Larger companies which have successfully completed their initial growing pains will combine distribution patterns and become very flexible as to where new outlets can be located and still be properly stocked and served.

Hours of Operation.   The number of hours of operation is an important consideration in evaluating any location. It may at first seem that an increase in hours necessarily will produce more profits. However, in some cases increasing the operational hours will simply produce more costs and less profit. Naturally the longer the unit can stay open on a profitable basis, the better the site. Many companies desire nothing but 24-hour, 7-days-a-week continuous operations, and others want a 12- or 14-hour operation. In other words, some companies are geared to a specific time period, and others are flexible and have varied operations.

The proposed site should be physically checked, double-checked, and then checked again at all proposed operating hours. One cannot accept the accuracy of traffic count maps and other information. The key here is to become as familiar as feasible with the off hours and nighttime activity and traffic surrounding a site. It may sound great from a competitive standpoint to be the only store open at night, but locating a store in such a place might be creating a target for crime.

Profitability.   Too often companies have purchased high-priced sites with overinflated sales estimates. Most companies will have their own forms for projecting return on investments and profit and loss, but these are only as good as the accuracy of the sales estimates. In addition, there are usually cost estimates to be provided such as the cost of site preparation and construction. These must not be underestimated. Although a book could be written on estimating and profitability factors alone, for the purpose of this chapter, let us just say that any inaccuracies will come back to haunt you. Your track record and/or income will be directly related to the actual performance of the unit. There is no substitute for good information, knowledge, and experience.

Appraisals.   All sites should be formally appraised prior to securing. In the interim, it should suffice to know that your negotiation prices will be in the ball park. The best way to arrive at a value for vacant or conversion-type properties is by comparison. Get the address or legal description of similar sites in the same trading area. Most people working at the courthouse will be glad to show you how their appraisal system works. These systems will give all the information you need to find the property owners, dimensions, purchase price, and so on.

Next, rate each parcel with pluses or minuses depending on how that site compares with yours. This will give you an excellent feel for the trading area prices. The sites used for comparison are called "comparables" and are dealt with in greater detail in the chapter on appraisals. The comparables may also be your best source of second, third, and fourth choices of locations.

General Site Information. Utilities, zoning, site dimensions, and other general site information must be substantiated. Do not believe anything anyone tells you; to be on solid ground, you *must* document for yourself. Many sites have been purchased at which the owners could not establish their original enterprise. Zoning codes are readily available from the zoning departments, utility information from the utility departments and companies, and so on. There really is no excuse for incorrect information. Surveyors, title insurance companies, construction people, operations people, and many others will rely on your information.

MARKETING ANALYSIS

We have now covered the basics in finding and evaluating individual sites. The following is a brief outline of the basics in determining desirability of a marketing area—that is, whether you even want to establish sites in any particular marketing area. This will also indicate how heavy of an investment would be practical should you decide to establish locations in a given market.

The same basic principles apply when weeding out marketing areas as in finding site locations. The major difference is that you will be dealing with larger areas (called "marketing areas") rather than smaller areas ("trading areas"). A trading area might consist of a 3-mile radius around a shopping center, and the marketing area might consist of eight or ten trading areas. In general, the larger towns and cities will constitute a marketing area within which will be several trading areas. Usually there will also be a certain amount of overlap.

The foregoing definitions are general and used primarily for comprehension of this chapter. Real estate site selection and evaluation has somewhat of a language of its own, but one can easily pick up the "lingo" with a little on-the-job training and experience. The following is a general list of things to look for and information that will be helpful in evaluating an entire marketing area. This is food for thought rather than an attempt to cover every possible situation.

Economy

One of the first priorities in evaluating a new market or marketing area is to determine the strength and soundness of its economy. As a site selector you will not have time to attempt any elaborate profile, but there are certain basic pieces of information and facts which can be learned fairly easily. (The company may wish to seek more detailed information, either through their own or outside marketing departments.) Your information should simply back up and verify the company's conclusions. If it does not, a red flag is raised, and mistakes and misinformation can then be corrected. Inaccurate information can result in a poor location, and mistakes in marketing analysis can result in several poor locations. Information may be obtained through various government agencies, marketing guides, economic profiles and booklets, census tracts, and the like. Looking over and riding the entire area is most helpful in gaining a quick overview. Talking with cooperative well-established merchants in each trading area will uncover a wealth of information. Naturally, the more time you spend in an area with your eyes and ears open, the better feel you will have for that market. The economy should be strong and stable.

Competition

When dealing with an entire marketing area the picture is broader in scope. Retail sales information should be obtained and broken down by amounts and categories. Comparisons can be made with other successful marketing areas of the same relative size.

Take a look at the competition: how successful do they appear, how busy are they at different time intervals, are their parking lots full or empty, what are their hours of operations, and so forth.

Growth Factors

Population breakdowns and facts will be done in conjunction with the demographic information in your site approach. However, additional statistics should be included in the initial marketing analysis. Some of these are growth history; population shifts; projection of future population factors; possible effects of future construction, road changes, annexing, change in government, and so on; and effects of larger employers laying off or shutting down, status of present and prospects for new industry, and reliance of area's economy on any one industry.

Government Bodies

It is advisable, prior to spending too much time in one area, to check with governmental bodies and authorities to determine how well your particular operations will be accepted from a political standpoint. The receptiveness and general feelings of people in key positions can make a big difference in your approach, objectives, and ultimate achievements in the area. Obtaining zoning, variances, liquor permits, and the like can be extremely difficult, time-consuming, and expensive, or it can be relatively easy with good cooperation. Keep in mind that you have something to offer—purchasing property, paying taxes, stimulating growth, new modern construction, serving the community, and so forth.

LEASES AND CONTRACTS

The contents and main bodies of instruments used for obtaining control of properties vary greatly, and we will not attempt detailed descriptions. Familiarity with the basic types of instruments used is important. You should, of course, fully understand any particular contracts or documents which are to be used in any negotiations. A general knowledge of real estate law is extremely helpful. When negotiating, paragraphs, clauses, statements, and so on, can be added, deleted, or amended to achieve desired results. Naturally the more knowledge you have, the better your results. Most large companies have their own printed forms prepared by lawyers, and the reasons for and possible ramifications of each clause should be understood.

Purchase and/or Lease Options and Contracts

Purchase and/or lease options and contract forms give the potential buyer the right to purchase or lease a determined property under certain terms, covenants, and conditions, as stipulated in the option or contract, in return for certain considerations. For example, a company may have a 120-day option to purchase X property for $200,000, in consideration for $5000. In other words, the owner will keep the $5000 if the property is not purchased within 120 days for $200,000. The $5000 consideration pays the owner for taking the property off the market for 4 months; normally it will become part of the purchase price when the option is exercised. The 120 days gives the company time to put their site package together to determine the desirability of the property. As stated in our opening paragraphs, much time and money can be spent prior to developing actual sales.

Letters of Intent

Letters of intent serve the same purposes as purchase or lease options, but they are generally easier to write and save the time of detailed negotiations. The letter will highlight the major intentions of the parties involved. In most cases the letter of intent is somewhat ambiguous and generally difficult to enforce. However, it is stronger than a handshake or oral agreement and can be easily recorded in the public records.

Ground Lease

A ground lease, sometimes referred to as a "land lease," is used when the leasee leases the ground and pays for construction thereon. This is usually least desirable from the buyer's standpoint, since financing becomes difficult unless the owner or lessor will subordinate the property. However, if the leasee should go bankrupt, the landowner, or lessor, may be stuck with an undesirable building. Although a "triple A" tenant is most desirable to the landowner, from the leasee's standpoint, more capital is tied up in unfinanceable construction, making expansion more difficult and costly. In connection with site selection, a prime site can be strong enough to attract triple A tenants on a net net ground lease—net meaning that the tenant leasee pays all taxes, insurance, maintenance, and so on. Remember that the leasee is obligated to the terms of the lease whether or not the outlet is successful.

Build to Suit

A build-to-suit lease is sometimes referred to as a leasor built lease. This is basically a lease of the land and the building or facilities as one package. The leasor pays for the construction of the facilities.

HOW TO BECOME A SITE SELECTOR

Education

A good site selector will need some practical working knowledge in various areas. A college or some type of equivalent degree is most helpful in opening doors. Many companies hesitate to grant interviews to those who lack experience or degrees, even though those companies may have their own training programs. Some courses, which are readily available to all, that would be most helpful in developing a strong background are as follows:

Real estate—commercial and residential
Construction
Architecture
Real estate law
Leases and contracts
Communications

Appraising
Math and algebra
Government systems
Surveying
Marketing
Sales
Economics
Management
Geography

Companies Using Site Selectors

Most expanding larger companies have real estate departments. The following are some examples of industries to consider:

Grocery chains
Oil companies
Restaurant chains
Fast food chains
Department stores
Real estate companies
Real estate consulting firms
Convenience store chains
Trucking companies
Auto manufacturers
Developers and builders
Motel chains

These companies are constantly looking for sharp real estate–oriented people. Many have their own training programs, and, often, for those starting out, a good attitude and willingness to learn can offset lack of experience. The personnel departments are very receptive and will be happy to answer questions, correspond, and supply necessary information for employment.

There are, of course, also classified advertisements, employment agencies, and mailing lists of companies who employ real estate personnel.

Meeting and talking with people in the business can be a tremendous asset. Their opinion and advice can help you make the right decision.

Part 3

Taxation and Real Estate

Chapter 15

Introduction to Real Estate Tax Shelters

Beverly F. Tanner Senior Vice President, Planned Investments, Inc.

WHAT IS A TAX SHELTER?

Many people bandy about the term "tax shelter" as if tax shelters were as common and understandable as a toothbrush or a glass of milk. My experience, however, has been that relatively few of us truly know just what a tax shelter is. Even those who participate in shelters are sometimes surprised at tax results which should have been evident from the outset.

A tax shelter, in general, is an umbrella that shelters income from *current* taxation. The word "current" is important here—most tax shelters do not avoid taxes. Rather they transfer taxation from the present to the future.

THE DEFERRAL OF TAXES

The vast majority of tax shelters are a transfer or a *deferral* of taxes from the present to the future. Simply, we do not pay today, but we will have to pay tomorrow.

The easiest to understand tax deferrals are the common Keogh or individual retirement account (IRA) plans. Each dollar placed into a Keogh or IRA (up to the limits allowed by law) is tax deferred. If we place $2000 into such a retirement plan, that money is not taxable in the year in which we place it.

Assume that our taxable income in a given year is $30,000. ("Taxable income" is the amount we have to pay taxes on after all deductions.) We place $4500 into a Keogh plan. That $4500 can be subtracted from our otherwise taxable income of $30,000 to give us an adjusted taxable income of $25,500. Thus the effect of placing the money in the Keogh plan is that it reduced the amount on which we would have to pay taxes in the year we placed the money. Once in the Keogh plan, the $4500 is allowed to grow and the income it produces is not taxed in the current year.

However, eventually, probably at retirement, we will withdraw our money from the Keogh plan. At that time we will have to pay taxes on it. We may add the amount we get from our retirement plan to our other ordinary income for that year and pay taxes on it. (There are special income-averaging methods to reduce taxes on large lump sum payments from retirement plans.) Thus we simply deferred payment to a future year.

Investors defer tax payments with the anticipation that in a future year they will be in a much lower tax bracket and, thus, will end up paying a much lower tax. In addition, since the income on the money is not taxed while it is in the Keogh (or IRA) plan, these funds can grow at a much faster rate than if they had been invested outside.

REAL ESTATE DEFERRALS

When purchasing real estate we typically have two goals in mind. The first is to make a profit on the investment. The second is to create a tax shelter. How do we accomplish the second goal?

Depreciation

Tax shelters in real estate are accomplished largely because of depreciation. Depreciation is writing off or deducting a portion of the loss in value of a structure (land is not depreciable).

All buildings deteriorate over time. Rather than wait until that eventuality, however, the government allows the owner to depreciate each year a portion of that loss, on certain types of buildings and according to strict rules (see Chapter 18 for specifics on depreciation). For example, an apartment building may be valued at $300,000. Its life span may be 15 years. Rather than wait until year 15 to claim a loss of $300,000 (when, presumably, the building's useful life would have ended), we take a loss each of the 15 years. One method of calculation is called "straight-line depreciation," or claiming an equal amount each year. (Accelerated methods are also allowed on some types of structures.) Thus we would divide $300,000 by 15 and take a loss of $20,000 each year.

It is important to recognize that this so-called loss does not physically take place until, presumably, year 15. That is, we continue to receive income from the property while we are writing off the $20,000. The loss, for practical purposes, appears only on paper. It is this loss, however, that gives us our real estate tax shelter.

Moreover, let's assume that our rental income is $20,000 per year from our apartment building. In addition, all taxable expenses, including mortgage interest, property taxes, insurance, maintenance, and so forth, also come to exactly $20,000: Our apartment building is a "wash." From a cash flow position, it exactly breaks even; it makes just enough money to pay its own way.

Now, let's consider the building from a tax viewpoint rather than a cash flow viewpoint. Remember the depreciation—in this case a loss of $20,000 per year from this cause. On paper our building, instead of breaking even, now shows a loss. (Note that depreciation does not affect cash flow. The building still makes just enough money in cash to pay its own way.)

As the building owners, when we file our federal income taxes we may now list this apartment building as a loss. We write off $20,000 from our taxable income. If we happen to be in the 50 percent tax bracket, we save $10,000 in taxes we otherwise would have to pay that year.

This is the first step of a real estate tax shelter. Too often, however, unwary investors think it is the only step. It is not. The $20,000 we did not pay taxes on was not tax-free. It was instead tax-deferred.

Adjusting Basis

Assume that our building's costs (including purchase price, fees, closing costs, and so on) came to $300,000. That becomes our basis in the building, or what we have invested. When we write off $20,000 we lower that basis. After 1 year our basis is down to $280,000. Since we have deducted a loss of $20,000, we have that much less invested in the structure. At the end of 10 years our loss would be $200,000 and our adjusted basis would be only $100,000.

Now we sell. Our sales price is $600,000. Obviously we made a profit, and we will have to pay taxes. How much will our taxable gain be? We subtract our adjusted basis ($100,000) from our adjusted sales price ($600,000) and we find we have a taxable gain of $500,000.

For those familiar with tax laws this will be obvious. For others, however, it might appear a sleight of hand. After all, didn't we pay $300,000? Subtract that from our sales price and we show a profit of $300,000. How did we get to $500,000? Where did the extra $200,000 come from? It came from the amount we depreciated each year (a loss of $20,000 a year for 10 years or $200,000).

Thus we come full circle. That money that we wrote off for tax savings for 10 years comes back as a taxable gain; we did not avoid paying taxes on the money, we simply deferred that payment to a future year. (Of course, there are many methods of continuing to defer that taxable gain such as exchanging the building or taking payments over several years.)

THE BOTTOM LINE

If we have to pay taxes either way, what is the advantage to deferral? There are many advantages. For one, most real estate qualifies for capital gains treatment. If we hold the property for the required period (currently 1 year), when we sell we do not pay at the ordinary tax rate but at the advantageous capital gains rate, which is currently at a maximum of 20 percent. If one is in a 50 percent tax bracket, that is a savings of 30 percent in taxes—a considerable amount. Second, we can pick and choose the year in which we sell. If we sell in a year in which we have a much lower ordinary income, because of the way capital gains is calculated, we may end up paying even less than 20 percent (see Chapter 16 for calculations). Third, we have use of the money for the 10 years. We can invest it and reap additional benefits.

TYPES OF REAL ESTATE TAX SHELTERS

Equity Builders

Typically, equity builders are apartment buildings that are purchased with the anticipation that the equity build-up will be great because of mortgage reduction and price inflation. The hope is usually to sell in a relatively short time, say 5 to 10 years, for a substantial profit. Here the tax shelter is an added incentive but not the sole motive for the investment.

Deep Shelters

Deep shelters typically are government-subsidized housing opportunities in which the investor intends to hold the property for a long time—upward of 20 years or longer. Typically these properties do not appreciate, and there is small equity build-up. There is, however, a continuing strong write-off year after year. These are purchased primarily as tax shelters, usually by high-income individuals.

Syndications

A syndication, typically a limited partnership, is formed by a group of individuals who gather together to buy a property too large for any one of them to afford individually. The tax advantages are usually identical to an individual investing. The investment may be either an equity builder or a deep shelter.

A WORD OF CAUTION

Real estate tax shelters are some of the oldest and most desirable tax shelters. When properly understood, they can provide exactly the kind of write-off that many investors desire. A word of caution, however: An individual should never buy real estate *only* for the tax shelter. The long-term economic viability of the investment should always be of greater concern.

Chapter 16

Capital Gains and Tax Aspects of Real Estate Sales

Norman H. Lane   Professor, University of Southern California Law Center

T he income tax rules concerning the disposition of real property are very complex, because they incorporate a large number of relevant factors. Tax consequences will depend on, among other things, (1) the character of the property in the seller's hands, that is, whether it is held primarily for personal purposes such as a family residence, as a long-term investment, as part of an active business, or in a dealer status; (2) the nature of the disposition, whether it was a voluntary sale or an involuntary conversion, such as a condemnation or sale under threat thereof; (3) the type and value of consideration received, that is, "like kind" property, notes or contract indebtedness of the buyer, or anything else, such as cash, nonqualifying property (known as "boot"), or relief from indebtedness owed to others; (4) the period for which the seller held the property before sale (more or less than 1 year); and (5) the period over which payments from the buyer will be received, if the seller finances the sale to any extent. All these points must be addressed in planning the sale or disposition of property.

Although the answers can be very complex, the *questions* one should ask concerning a disposition are somewhat simpler. The first issue is to determine whether gain or loss has been realized and what the relevant magnitude is. In general, gains will increase a taxpayer's overall liability, and losses will, if deductible, reduce it. If a gain has been realized, when must, or may, it be reported (currently or on a deferred basis) and what is the character of the gain—fully taxable ordinary income, short-term capital gain, or lightly taxed long-term capital gain? If a loss has been realized, the investor will want to know whether it is deductible or must be treated as nondeductible personal expense; whether it is fully deductible as an ordinary loss or is subject to the less favorable rules affecting capital losses; and whether the loss may be claimed in the year of sale or must be deferred until some later date.

DETERMINING THE AMOUNT OF GAIN OR LOSS

A taxpayer gains from a sale or exchange if the amount realized on the sale exceeds the adjusted basis of the property; an excess of adjusted basis over amount realized produces a loss. The amount realized is the amount of cash received plus the fair market value of any other property received. Forgiveness or discharge of the seller's indebtedness is usually treated as equivalent to cash; this rule can produce a "phantom gain" in the event of foreclosure if the amount of debt satisfied in the foreclosure exceeds the taxpayer's adjusted basis.

If the seller finances the buyer's purchase by taking back notes or evidences of indebtedness of the buyer (whether secured by mortgage or deed of trust or not), some special rules apply. As will be discussed later, if a gain is realized on the sale, a fraction of the total gain equal to the fraction that the buyer's indebtedness bears to the total consideration may be deferred by the seller. It may be reported for taxation when payments on account of the buyer's indebtedness are received, under the installment method of reporting. When the taxpayer uses the installment method, the face amount of the note is used to compute reportable gain, even though the fair market value of the note is lower (because of a below-market interest rate or a buyer's doubtful financial responsibility). An exception to this rule, as will be discussed later, will come into play if the stated interest rate on the buyer's note is less than 9 percent.

Taxpayers can elect *not* to report on the installment method of accounting; they can instead report the sale as a closed transaction in the year of sale. In this situation, all consideration, including the buyer's indebtedness, is reduced to fair market value for purposes of determining gain or loss. These rules lead to an interesting paradox: In some situations, the sale of property may produce a gain if the installment method is elected (because the face amount of the note is ultimately treated as an amount realized in determining gain) but a loss if the installment method is not elected (because the fair market value of the note is lower than its face amount and may be less than basis.

Determining the fair market value of noncash property is often quite difficult, and this is one of the justifications for permitting tax-deferred exchanges of real property to occur. All relevant facts are considered, including comparable sales, value of the property disposed of, capitalization-of-income approaches, and the like. These issues frequently produce heated controversy between taxpayers and the Internal Revenue Service (IRS).

Can there be property which has no fair market value? According to the IRS, this will be true only in "rare and extraordinary cases," but some courts have found such circumstances to exist. If property can be treated as having no fair market value, then the tax consequences may be deferred until the property is disposed of or collected. Treating a receipt as having no fair market value is sure to provoke controversy with the IRS and should not be attempted without obtaining competent professional tax advice.

The concept of basis, which is subtracted from the amount realized to determine gain or loss, was discussed in Chapter 15. Upon sale of property, the adjusted basis is used as the offset, so that any depreciation deductions or cost recovery allowances previously claimed by the taxpayer (or a donor to the taxpayer) which reduced basis ultimately increase the gain or decrease the loss reportable on sale. If the taxpayer disposes of less than the entire interest in property, he or she will have to allocate basis, claiming only the portion of the total adjusted basis which is reasonably attributable to the interest disposed of. In a few rare cases, however, a reasonably accurate allocation could not be made, and courts have permitted the proceeds of sale or other disposition to be offset against all the taxpayer's basis, without requiring allocation. Allocation is typically based on the relative values of the portions sold and portions retained at the time of acquisition rather than the time of disposition. Customary methods are based on square footage or acreage, adjusted for such attributes as road or beach frontage, improvements, and the like.

If the interest retained by a seller has certain characteristics, the whole transaction may be treated as something other than a sale, with distinctly unfavorable tax consequences (notably, inability to offset any receipts by basis or to report the transaction as a capital gain). Suppose, for example, that an owner of property leases it for 25 years, and receives a lump sum advance payment equal to the discounted value of 25 years worth of rent. Courts have held that this transaction amounts merely to receipt of prepaid rent and is not a qualifying sale. The consideration received is ordinary income, fully taxable, even though the seller has clearly parted with a valuable interest in the property which will reduce whatever consideration she or he may receive on future disposition.

Similarly, payments received on the lease of mineral rights in a tract of land will be treated as ordinary income, not sale proceeds, if the seller-landowner retains a royalty interest in future production (as is customary). However, a conveyance of acreage in fee or the conveyance of a tenant-in-common interest in particular property where the buyer's rights have no time limitation will qualify as a sale. Also, if the lessee of property receives consideration for the total assignment of an interest, his or her receipts qualify for sale treatment so long as the term granted is as long as the original lease. If the lessee subleases for a shorter period, retaining a reversionary interest, however, the transaction will probably produce ordinary income.

Sometimes taxpayers will wish to avoid characterizing a transaction as a sale, although the IRS will insist that this treatment is proper. For example, suppose that a property owner leases to a tenant at a high rental and gives the tenant an option to purchase the property in the future for a relatively small amount. The owner may want to treat the transaction as a lease-with-option until the option is actually exercised, thereby continuing to claim depreciation on the property. If the transaction looks suspicious, the IRS may claim that the purported option was virtually certain to be exercised and thus that the sale should be treated as having occurred when the arrangement was entered into. This is especially likely to happen if the lessor is in a substantially higher tax bracket than the lessee so that the IRS would lose less tax revenue when the deduction for cost recovery is allocated to the lessee-buyer. Similarly, purported sale leaseback arrangements can sometimes be recharacterized as mere loans by the buyer-lessor, meaning that no new basis for the property is achieved, and depreciation or cost recovery stays in the hands of the original owner.

EXPENSES OF SALE

Sellers incur many costs when they sell real estate, of which the most important are brokerage commissions, attorneys' fees for complex transactions, escrow charges, and title insurance costs. In general, these expenses of sale are treated as offsets to the selling price, reducing the gross amount realized to a figure net of selling costs. The difference between the net amount realized and the adjusted basis is the gain or loss.

TIMING OF INCOME AND LOSS

Gains or losses are normally taken into account in the seller's taxable year in which the sale is made. This is not necessarily the year that legal title passes to the buyer, because sellers often retain legal title to secure the buyer's payment of deferred purchase price installments. Nor is it necessarily the year that a contract for sale is entered into, since numerous conditions may exist before the buyer is obligated to pay the purchase price and the seller obligated to convey possession of the property. A sale for tax purposes occurs when the burdens and benefits of ownership pass to the buyer and is usually considered complete when escrow closes. However, if a buyer goes into possession before close of escrow and is free to use the property in any reasonable way, the IRS may argue that the sale occurred when the buyer took possession, especially if there is no apparent nontax reason to defer close of escrow and the arrangement seems designed merely to defer the seller's liability.

Although gain is technically realized in the year of sale, its taxability may be wholly or partially postponed. The three major ways of effecting postponement are tax-free (more accurately, tax-deferred) exchanges, discussed in detail in Chapter 25; sales of principal residences, discussed in Chapter 17; and the installment method of reporting gain. Some less common methods will be noted later in this chapter.

INSTALLMENT SALES

Rules relating to installment sales of real estate were substantially rewritten in 1980, in an effort to make them somewhat fairer and simpler. For those who recall the old rules, probably the most important change was the elimination of the old requirement that no more than 30 percent of the total consideration could be received in the year of sale, followed by the rules which extend the availability of installment reporting to cases where the purchase price is not completely fixed at the time the sale occurs. Another significant change is that, under the new legislation, installment method treatment is automatic when deferred payments are received, unless the taxpayer rejects this method. Under the old law, a taxpayer had to specifically elect use of the installment method when the return for the year of sale was filed (subject to certain rules which permitted retroactive election of the method if failure to make the election on the return was due to reasonable cause).

In general, use of the installment method means that the gain realized, computed when the sale occurs, is reported for tax purposes only as actual payments are received from the buyer rather than when the seller acquires the buyer's notes or other evidences of indebtedness. Consider a simple case in which the sale is for a total stated price of $100,000, payable $35,000 in the year of sale, $5000 for the next 5 years, and $10,000 for the following 4 years, plus interest on the unpaid balances. Assume that the property's adjusted basis was $40,000. In this situation, the total profit to be reported is $60,000, of which $21,000 will be reported in the first year, $3000 in each of the next 5 years, and $6000 in each of the last 4 years. Of course, interest on the notes will also be taxable as ordinary income.

The general formula is that a fraction of the total profit is taxable in each year that payments on account of principal are received, in the proportion that the payment in the particular year bears to the total payments to be made. In other words, a fraction of each year's payment constitutes gain in the ratio that the total profit realized bears to the total selling price.

Of course, life is not always that simple, and a number of possible contingencies must be provided for. Suppose, for example, that part of the purchase price is not paid directly to the seller but is in the form of an assumption (or taking subject to) by the buyer of existing indebtedness on the property. As we saw earlier, relief from indebtedness is normally considered an amount realized by the seller. However, when the installment method is used, the seller's liability on the relief from indebtedness may be deferred. This is accomplished by deducting the amount of the existing loans from the payments to be received from the buyer, although they still figure in computing the profit realized by the seller. To return to our illustration, suppose that the buyer assumed an existing $20,000 mortgage, reduced the down payment to $25,000, and lopped off the last year's payment to the seller. That is, the buyer agrees to pay the seller $25,000 down, $5000 in each of the next 5 years, and $10,000 in each of the last 3 years, plus interest. In this case, the profit on sale remains $60,000; 25/80 of it will be reported in the year of sale (that is, $18,750); 5/80 in each of the next 5 years ($3750 per year, or $18,750); and 10/80 in each of the last 3 years ($7500 per year, or $22,500).

If the amount of debt on the property at the time of sale exceeds the seller's adjusted basis, then the excess is treated as a payment in the year of sale, and the seller will have to recognize some gain. For example, suppose that in the prior example, the seller had an adjusted basis of only $10,000 rather than $40,000, so that the total gain to report was $90,000. Under the governing IRS regulations, payments in the year of sale are $35,000 (the actual $25,000 down payment plus the $10,000 excess of mortgage over basis), and additional payments of $5000 for 5 years and $10,000 for 3 more years will be made. All such payments will be considered taxable gain, since the seller's basis is fully recovered by offsetting half of the mortgage debt against it. The gain ratio, in other words, is 100 percent.

In the past, taxpayers have tried to defer taxation of the excess of mortgages over basis by using the device of a wrap-around note or an all-inclusive trust deed. Using the figures of the last paragraph, if the sale were made on a wrap-around basis, the buyer would sign a note to the seller for $75,000 rather than $55,000, and the seller would agree to "service," or pay off, the underlying $20,000 loan with the additional payments made by the buyer. (Normally, the extra payments totaling $20,000 in principal plus interest would be made at times closely related to the times that the seller is required to pay off the underlying note.) Suppose, for simplicity, that the underlying debt was payable in four annual installments of $5000 each (plus interest), and so the buyer's payments were increased to $30,000 in year 1, $10,000 in years 2 through 4, $5000 in years 5 and 6, and $10,000 in years 7 through 9. Under some court decisions, it was arguable that the seller could report 30 percent of the total profit in year 1 (gain of $27,000), 10 percent in each of years 2 through 4 ($9000 each), 5 percent in years 5 and 6 ($4500 each), and 10 percent in each of years 7 through 9 ($9000 each). This is a better result, in most cases, for the seller than the non-wrap-around computation. Note that, in this case, the seller reports more gain in years 1 through 4 than the amount of net payments he or she keeps. Wrap-around financing is sometimes used for nontax reasons, of course, notably in cases where the existing loans on the property are at low interest rates but are due on sale and all nonassumable by a buyer. Under some state laws, if the buyer-seller arrangement took the form of a contract for deed (land sale contract) with wrap-around financing, the nonassumability feature could be overcome.

Under new regulations prescribed by the IRS, however, the tax deferral formerly available through wrap-around financing would be largely eliminated. The excess of underlying financing over adjusted basis would always be treated as a payment in the year of sale, and hence would be subject to immediate taxation; the balance of the seller's gain can be deferred. Some taxpayers believe that these regulations are invalid, but it would be best to obtain professional advice before proceeding to report inconsistently with them.

In most instances, installment sales are the result of the buyer's needs, rather than the seller's preferences, since the buyer may or may not have full cash available or be able to obtain third-party financing on acceptable terms. This has been especially true in the past few years, when institutional lenders such as banks and savings and loan associations have charged very high interest rates. Sometimes, however, buyers are able to come up with the full cash price, or something similar to it, but sellers are unwilling to sell for cash, preferring to use the installment method to defer their tax liability. Can this be done?

Two major techniques were available, before the new installment sale legislation took effect, that enabled the seller to get cash (or its equivalent) from the buyer while deferring tax liability. The first was a sale to a related person, such as a family member or family trust, on the installment method, followed by the buyer's resale to the third party for cash. Under this pattern, the seller would pick up his or her gain only as payments were made by the intermediary, and the intermediary would have little or no tax consequences (since the intermediary's basis would include the obligation given to the original owner). A second approach was to have the buyer secure the obligation, by depositing cash in escrow or with a bank or financial institution. Case law, in this area, frequently found the second type of transaction a tax-avoidance sham, and it was not reliable.

Under the new legislation, the consequences of the two methods are reversed: In general, installment sales to family members or related parties will not permit the original seller to defer reporting gain beyond the time that the intermediary receives payments from the ultimate buyer, unless the intermediary holds the property for at least 2 years before resale and is at risk during that period. However, the term "related party" is somewhat narrowly drawn and does not include, for example, the seller's brothers, sisters, son-in-law, daughter-in-law, or corporations in which the seller (and close relatives) hold less than 50 percent of the stock. Certain other exceptions to the rule also exist; for example, if the second disposition is an involuntary sale (that is, a condemnation), the seller's gain is not accelerated. Professional advice should be sought when considering how and whether to structure transactions involving this approach.

However, the new law specifically permits the buyer's obligation to be secured by a "standby letter of credit" or other form of guarantee, issued by a third party such as a financial institution. This rule probably applies even if the guarantor, for example, requires the buyer to deposit the unpaid purchase price with it before it issues the guarantee. However, the guarantee must be nonnegotiable and nontransferable for value by the seller (except in conjunction with a transfer of the buyer's note) prior to the existence of a default by the buyer.

In some cases, taxpayers who engage in a nontaxable exchange of like kind property also receive the buyer's note as additional consideration in cases where the value of the property they give up exceeds the value of the property they receive. Under the new method, the installment method is available with respect to the note, but the computations must reflect the receipt of the nonrecognition property. (This matter is discussed in greater detail in Chapter 17.)

DISPOSITION OF INSTALLMENT OBLIGATIONS

If sellers of real property on the installment method get tired of waiting for buyers to make their payments and decide to cash out notes, their gain will be accelerated, reduced by any discount on the note they are required to accept. To illustrate, suppose that Ms. Brown had a basis of $40,000 in her real property, and sold it to Mr. Jones for total consideration of $100,000, payable $25,000 in the year of sale and thereafter in five equal installments of $15,000 (plus interest). After collecting two of the installments she sells the note, with a remaining balance of $45,000, to Mrs. Green for $35,000, accepting a $10,000 discount. Of Ms. Brown's original anticipated gain of $60,000 ($100,000 minus $40,000 basis), she reported $15,000 in the year of sale and $18,000 when she collected the first two installments. The note in her hands has a basis of $18,000, its $45,000 remaining face less the $27,000 anticipated profit not yet reported. Thus, her gain on disposition will be $17,000. The $10,000 discount is not reported by Ms. Brown, but Mrs. Green will report it when she collects the remaining installments from Mr. Jones.

The rule that disposition of an installment note triggers recognition of previously deferred gain also applies to some transactions where nothing is received by the disposing party (the original seller), notably where he or she makes a gift of the note to a family member. In this case, the fair market value of the note is deemed "constructively received" by the seller at the time of disposition, and gain will be computed accordingly.

If a person holds an unpaid installment obligation when she or he dies, the deferred gain is not accelerated unless the obligation is bequeathed to the obligor or otherwise canceled at death (which might occur, for example, if the buyer was the seller's child). The recipient of the obligation under the decedent's will, state intestacy laws, or other arrangements will pick up the remaining gain as payments are actually made by the buyer. Installment obligations do not get a new "stepped-up" basis at death, because they are considered income in respect of a decedent.

ALTERNATIVES TO INSTALLMENT REPORTING

Closed Transaction Method

Sellers can elect to report the sale as a closed transaction, taking into account the fair market value of all consideration received, including the buyer's obligations, and determining gain or loss accordingly. According to the regulations, this election must be made on a timely filed return for the year of sale, and the election must be unconditional. Late elections "will be permitted only in those rare circumstances when the Internal Revenue Service concludes that the taxpayer had good cause for failing to make a timely election." An election may be revoked only with the consent of the IRS.

If the fair market value of the buyer's notes is less than their face amount, so that reporting on the closed transaction method produces an amount realized less than the total of principal payments plus down payment to be made by the buyer, the seller will have additional income, in the nature of discount, as future payments occur. If the payments are received from the buyer, these payments will constitute ordinary income, unless the buyer is a corporation, in which case they probably will constitute capital gain. Caution is advised before treating sales in this fashion.

Open Transaction Method

Prior to the new installment sale legislation, taxpayers could occasionally qualify for reporting sales of property on the so-called open transaction method. This method produces a longer period of deferral of the tax liability than even the installment method, since all payments received from the buyer are first offset against the taxpayer's basis and gain is recognized only when payments exceed that basis. The exact conditions under which the open transaction method was authorized were the subject of lively controversy between taxpayers and the IRS, and case law was not entirely consistent. One circumstance in which the right to report on the open method was reasonably clear, however, was when payments were largely contingent on the results of future operations of the property by the buyer, for example, some or all payments were dependent on sales, profits, or rental income. One reason for allowing this was that the installment method could not be used, before 1980, unless the sale was for a fixed price.

Under the new legislation, contingent payments may be reported on installment principles, although the exact rules for determining the timing of gain are very complex. As a result, both the IRS regulations and the congressional committee reports on the new law indicate that the open transaction approach to reporting gain on sales will almost never be allowed. The regulations state that "only in those rare and extraordinary cases involving sales for a contingent payment obligation in which the fair market value of the obligation . . . cannot reasonably be ascertained will the taxpayer be entitled to assert that the transaction is 'open.' Any such transaction will be carefully scrutinized to determine whether a sale has in fact taken place." The regulations also state that under no circumstances will an installment sale for a fixed-amount obligation be considered an open transaction.

The installment method cannot be used to report a loss. Losses are always reported on the closed transaction approach. However, as noted earlier, in some cases a transaction may produce gain when the installment method is used but a loss when the closed transaction approach is used. In such cases, the taxpayer may well have an election.

OPPORTUNITIES FOR DEFERRAL

In addition to the deferral of tax liability provided by the installment sale treatment, like kind exchanges and sales of principal residences are important planning opportunities. These aspects are covered in Chapter 17 of this book. A third type of deferred gain transaction which is elective with taxpayers is a sale of property pursuant to or under threat of condemnation and certain other dispositions which qualify as "involuntary conversions." In general, if a gain is derived from an involuntary conversion, liability may be deferred by timely reinvestment of the full proceeds of conversion, within a prescribed time limit. Currently, the time for replacement begins on the earliest date that a threat of condemnation occurs, and usually ends 3 years after the close of the first year in which any part of the gain was realized. In some cases, this period may be extended with IRS consent. To qualify for deferral, the taxpayer must acquire either property which is similar or related in service or use to the former property or 80 percent control of a corporation which holds such property. In the case of condemnations (but not other involuntary conversions) the taxpayer may also acquire property which is of like kind with the property converted. As defined by the courts, the term "like kind" gives more flexibility than "similar or related in service or use." For example, almost any parcel of real property is "of like kind" with any other, but courts have held that hotels and office buildings are not, in general, similar or related in service or use.

If the cost of replacement property is less than the net proceeds of conversion, then gain must be recognized to the extent of the unreinvested proceeds. The basis of replacement property will be reduced from its actual cost by the amount of any deferred gain. Gain that is recognized will usually be eligible for treatment under section 1231 of the code, as will be described.

CHARACTER OF GAIN AND LOSS

To determine the character of gain and loss on dispositions of property, assets are classified into three distinct types. These are (1) inventory or dealer property, on which gains and losses are both ordinary, regardless of how long the property may have been held; (2) true capital assets, gains which usually qualify for favorable long-term capital gains rates (maximum 20 percent) if held for more than 1 year, but losses on which enjoy only severely restricted deductibility; and (3) trade or business property, often called "quasi-capital assets" or "Section 1231 property," which generally is treated most favorably. Net gains are taxed as capital gains (except for depreciation recapture), and net losses are allowed full deductibility against ordinary income. Investors in real property, therefore, usually try to classify their holdings as trade or business property (Section 1231) assets, and the IRS frequently alleges that they are inventory-type property when gains are realized and "true" capital assets when losses are involved.

In deciding the issue of inventory versus trade or business property, the major issue is whether the particular asset sold was "property held by the taxpayer primarily for sale to customers in the ordinary course of his trade or business"; if so, then it is inventory-type property and does not qualify for reduced tax rates. With one narrow exception involving subdivided (but not otherwise improved) land held for at least 5 years before sales of lots occur, there are almost no statutory rules for interpreting this language. Instead, the law consists of hundreds if not thousands of court decisions and IRS rulings involving the so-called dealer issue. As one might expect, these decisions do not form a wholly consistent body of law, and any principles extracted from them are very general in nature. Courts have identified dozens of factors that are relevant in deciding whether a particular taxpayer is considered a dealer who holds land parcels as inventory or a long-term investor or operator of real property. No single factor or combination of factors is determinative of the issue.

In general, the most important factors that show dealer status (which taxpayers usually wish to avoid) are the frequency and continuity of sales; the extent of improvements made to the property; the length of the period (beyond 1 year) that the property was held before sales commenced; the extent to which the taxpayer or taxpayer's employees devoted time, effort, and expense to marketing the property; and the homogeneity of the property (selling 100 identical lots from a single large tract is more likely to lead to a finding of dealer status than selling 100 separate, previously constructed residences each with diverse characteristics). If no more than three or four sales of real property are made in any year, it is unlikely, although not impossible, that the IRS will assert that the taxpayer is a dealer in property. Once again, it is important for taxpayers who engage in a substantial volume of real estate transactions over a period of years to obtain competent professional advice to minimize the risk of dealer status for their gains.

Whether the taxpayer held real property as a pure investment, that is, as a true capital asset, or as property used in a trade or business (although not held for sale to customers in the ordinary course of business) usually is relevant only when losses are involved, since gains will be favorably treated in either case (assuming that the 1-year holding period is met). In general, improved real estate which is rented out to tenants or held for the purpose of rental is considered trade or business property under Section 1231. The major exception is when the owner's responsibilities with respect to the property are very nominal. For example, if the building is rented for a long term to a tenant under a triple net lease, so that the tenant bears all costs of maintenance, insurance, and so forth, and the owner has few or no managerial duties, it will probably be considered a true capital asset. Also, if there is a very small scale rental operation—say, ownership and rental of just one single-family house—some courts have held that the activities were in the nature of investment rather than business activity. A special definition of "net lease"—leading to a finding of investment—is found in certain code sections, but it is not directly applicable in this context. In general, normal ownership and operation of a multifamily dwelling, multiunit shopping center, or office structure with numerous tenants under reasonably short-term leases and numerous expenses borne by the owner will probably lead to a finding that the owner was in the business of owning and operating improved real estate. Real estate held as an incident to some other business, such as manufacturing or retailing, will also be treated as business use property eligible for favorable treatment.

RECAPTURE RULES

Two principal rules provide for treatment of some proceeds as ordinary income even if the assets ordinarily qualify for favorable capital gains treatment. These are (1) the recapture rules, which relate to gains where depreciation has previously been taken, and (2) the imputed interest rules applicable when stated interest on a purchase money note to the seller is less than a minimum prescribed by the IRS.

Recapture of Cost Recovery Allowances

Gains on the sale of property subject to the accelerated cost recovery system (ACRS)—in general, that acquired after 1980—will be treated as ordinary income up to the full amount of allowances taken during the holding period, if (1) the taxpayer has elected an accelerated method of cost recovery for 15-year property, and such property is commercial or industrial in nature rather than residential, or (2) the property is treated within the 5-year or 10-year class, rather than the 15-year class for cost recovery purposes. If the property is 15-year residential property with respect to which the owner has used the statutory accelerated method, then any gain will be treated as ordinary income only to the extent of the "additional depreciation," that is, the amount of the cost recovery allowance in excess of what would have been permitted using the straight-line method. (This is similar to the pre-1981 rules which governed all buildings.) Therefore, if property is 15-year life property and straight-line cost recovery is elected, no portion of the taxpayer's gain on sale will be treated as ordinary income. If it is commercial or industrial property and an accelerated method is chosen, then the full allowance claimed may be recaptured as ordinary income, up to the total gain realized.

It seems advisable for taxpayers who purchase commercial or industrial properties subject to ACRS to elect straight-line cost recovery rather than the accelerated method. Those who purchase residential property usually should elect the accelerated method, since this will reduce taxable income currently. However, if the gain is taxed in the year of sale, taxpayers may be subject to a bunching effect which increases the effective rate of tax paid. Some may therefore prefer to use the straight-line method even in the case of residential property.

A few types of property, mostly low- and moderate-income projects subsidized in one form or another by the federal government, qualify for more favorable recapture rules. In general, the portion of the gain taxable as ordinary income declines once the property is held more than 100 months, thereby reconverting some ordinary income into capital gain. However, depreciation allowances for low-income rehabilitation projects (written off over 5 years) and certain other types of fast write-off property are subject to full rather than limited recapture.

To illustrate the basic recapture rules, suppose that Ms. Green buys an apartment house on March 1, 1981, and sells it on September 30, 1988, claiming the fastest available cost recovery. Her total purchase price was $500,000, of which $400,000 was allocable to the building and eligible for cost recovery. Her total cost recovery allowances under the accelerated method during the 7.5-year holding period amounted to $246,000. Had she claimed straight-line depreciation, her total cost recovery allowance would have been $200,000. Therefore, the first $46,000 of her gain will be taxed as ordinary income, and only the balance will be eligible for capital gain or Section 1231 treatment. If Ms. Jones's property had been a commercial or industrial building rather than apartments, the first $246,000 of her gain (i.e., the full gain up to the amount of the cost recovery allowances claimed) would be ordinary income, and only the portion of her selling price which exceeds the original purchase price would qualify for capital gain or Section 1231 treatment.

If the property is not subject to the ACRS system, because it was acquired before 1981 or is subject to the antichurning rules discussed in Chapter 18, ordinary income recapture depends primarily on whether an accelerated method of depreciation was used. So long as the property is held more than 1 year before sale, gains will be recaptured as ordinary income to the extent of excess depreciation but not to the extent of straight-line depreciation. In some cases, notably low-income housing and other buildings originally acquired by the seller before 1976, these rules are relaxed somewhat further, with a forgiveness of some of the recapture where the property is held more than 100 months before sale. If the property was acquired by the seller before 1969, the forgiveness begins as early as 20 months after the date of acquisition. Taxpayers in these situations should consult competent accountants for further guidance.

When an installment sale of real property occurs and recapture rules are involved the portion of the gain treated as ordinary income is taxed first. Only after the applicable amount is fully recaptured will additional principal payments qualify for capital gains treatment.

Certain dispositions, notably transfers to controlled corporations, to partnerships, and transfers by gift do not trigger ordinary income recapture or capital gain. Instead, the transferee inherits the property's adjusted basis and its recapture potential. If a taxpayer dies holding real property subject to recapture, the recapture potential is eliminated in the hands of the estate, heir, or legatee, since the property will have a new basis after death.

Sale to Related Parties.   Gain on the sale of depreciable property will be treated as ordinary income, if the buyer of the property is either the taxpayer's spouse or a corporation of which more than 80 percent of the stock is owned by the seller or seller's spouse. Certain sales incident to a divorce, however, are not subject to this rule, even if the parties are technically still married when the sale occurs.

Determining Holding Period.   The benefits of both long-term capital gains status and Section 1231 status depend on the property having a more than 1-year holding period in the hands of the seller. This requirement may, in some cases, be satisfied through a "tacking" concept. For example, if property is acquired through a tax-free exchange, the replacement property's holding period is deemed to include the period for which the former property was held. This rule applies even if the owner had given boot to obtain the new property or had received boot on the former exchange. Also, the holding period of property acquired by gift will include the donor's time of ownerships. However, property acquired through exercise of an option to buy does not include the period for which the option was held; a new holding period for the property begins on the day after the exercise of the option. Under a special rule, property acquired from a decedent is always deemed long-term property, whatever the actual holding periods of the decedent, the heir, or the estate may be.

Note that favorable long-term treatment depends on a holding period of more than 1 year. The holding period begins on the day following acquisition of ownership and ends on the date of sale. Thus, if property is purchased on January 15, it should not be sold before January 16 of the next year. If property is acquired on the last day of any calendar month, it should not be sold before the first day of the thirteenth month thereafter, if long-term treatment is desired.

Sometimes property has a split holding period, part of it being considered long term and part short term. This is especially likely to occur when construction of improvement activity is undertaken, since each element of cost is deemed to be acquired when the work to which it pertains is completed. If a building is constructed during 1982 at a total cost of $500,000, for example, and sold on February 15, 1983, one would try to determine the portion of the $500,000 represented by work done before February 15, 1982, to decide how much gain is long term.

Netting Concepts.   A number of different so-called netting rules can enhance or reduce the benefits of long-term capital gains treatment. For example, if the taxpayer in 1 year sells one piece of Section 1231 property at a $100,000 gain and another at a $75,000 loss, in general, long-term capital gain and loss treatment applies to both transfers. If the gain and loss are taken in different years, however, and no other transactions of this type occur in either, then the taxpayer's gain will enjoy long-term capital gains treatment, and the loss will be a fully deductible ordinary loss. Similarly, true long-term capital gains are usually most efficiently used if they are not offset by capital losses, which may call for staggering the timing of gains and losses in different years. However, if a taxpayer has a long-term capital loss, short-term capital gains realized in the same year may offset it in full, although long-term capital gains must be offset first. Careful planning of gains and losses and year-end reviews of an investor's situation are therefore highly desirable.

Imputed Interest Rules

If property which would normally qualify for capital gains treatment is sold, and part of the purchase price is in the form of notes or other indebtedness of the buyer, the law usually requires part of the proceeds of sale to be recharacterized as ordinary income, in the nature of interest, unless the notes call for stated interest at a rate prescribed by the IRS. For sales made after July 1, 1981, the minimum rate is 9 percent per annum, simple interest; for sales before that date but after July 24, 1975, the minimum rate was 6 percent. If stated interest is not provided at this rate, then the imputed rate becomes 10 percent (or 7 percent) per annum, compounded semiannually, a significantly higher rate. Thus, notes should always carry a 9 percent interest rate or higher. Even if the market rate of interest is higher than 9 percent, no additional interest will be imputed, unless the IRS changes the rates. Such changes will be prospective only, that is, they will not affect sales made before the effective date of the change, even if payments are received afterward.

Special Limitations on Deduction of Losses

Although gains are at least partially taxable, currently or on a deferred basis, regardless of the character of the property sold, losses are not deductible unless they are incurred in a business or other transaction "entered into for profit." Thus, losses on a personal residence are not deductible at all, since ownership of such a residence is not considered a transaction entered into for profit. Similarly, losses of property deemed acquired as a "hobby" may not be deductible. If property is converted from personal use to income-producing purposes, loss incurred after the date of conversion may be deductible, but for this purpose, the taxpayer's basis is limited to the lesser of the actual adjusted basis on the date of conversion or the fair market value at that time. The IRS will frequently challenge claims that property has been "converted," unless there is a reasonably extended period during which net rental income from the property is received before the sale occurs.

Also, losses are not deductible if the purchaser is within a defined class of related persons, for this purpose defined to include spouse, ancestors, lineal descendants, brothers and sisters, as well as various nonindividual taxpayers such as trusts created by the taxpayer and corporations which are controlled by her or him or members of the family. If a nondeductible loss is incurred because of the identity of the buyer, the buyer will secure some benefits from the seller's higher basis, but a complete carry-over is not authorized.

If the property sold at a loss is a true capital asset, rather than property described in Section 1231 of the code, then losses are allowable, if at all, only as capital losses. This means, in the case of individual sellers, that the deduction may be taken only to the extent of capital gains realized in the same year plus up to $3000 of ordinary income. Excess capital losses may be carried over until the taxpayer either offsets them against capital gains or dies. Long-term losses may be further restricted. It takes $2 of long-term loss to offset $1 of ordinary income; long-term losses can be deducted in full, however, against current or future capital gains. Long-term losses first offset long-term gains, then short-term gains, and then the ordinary income allowance. Short-term losses, in contrast, first offset short-term gains, then long-term gains, then the ordinary income allowance of up to $3000. Carry-overs of both types of losses retain their long-term or short-term character. These rules are substantially modified for corporate taxpayers who incur capital gains and losses; competent advice should be sought if questions arise in this area.

Sales of Partnership Interests and Corporate Stock

Many persons hold interests in real estate through ownership of interests in partnerships or stock in corporations which hold title to the underlying property. (Partnership ownership is more common, for reasons described in Chapter 24. Such persons may, accordingly, realize gain or loss by selling their partnership interests or corporate stock to other investors, even though the underlying partnership or corporation continues to hold the assets. When this occurs, a number of complex rules may apply. In general, a partnership interest is considered a true capital asset, and gains are treated as capital gains and losses as capital losses, with long-term or short-term treatment depending on how long the interest or stock was held before sale (rather than on how long the partnership or corporation held its assets). However, in some cases the sale of a partnership interest at a gain, or the receipt of payments in retirement of a partnership interest, may be partly or fully treated as ordinary income, especially when the partnership holds assets subject to depreciation recapture or treatment as inventory. Also, certain sales of stock and similar transactions can be treated as ordinary income if the corporation is determined to be "collapsible," that is, holds property which it has improved or constructed but from which little profit has been realized when the sale of stock occurs. Competent professional advice should be sought should issues of this kind arise.

Deferral on Home Sale

Richard Brickman   Attorney-at-Law, Certified Public Accountant

Perhaps the most frequently asked question with regard to real estate and federal income taxes concerns the common deferral of taxes on the sale of a principal residence (technically called a "non-recognition of gain on sale of a principal residence"). Unfortunately, this happens to be one of the most misunderstood areas of the tax law.

THE CONCEPT

The concept, basically, is that an owner can defer the payment of taxes resulting from gain on the sale of a principal residence. The deferral can be made indefinitely, as long as certain rules are followed.

Time

To qualify for indefinite deferral, the taxpayer must purchase a new principal residence within 24 months before or 24 months after the sale of the old residence. This gives the taxpayer great opportunity to use the rule. There is actually a broad 4-year period of time when it applies.

Principal Residence

Both the old property sold and the new property bought must be the taxpayer's principal residence. "Principal" here means the taxpayer's primary residence. It need not be limited to a house—a house trailer, houseboat, or even stock in a tenant-owned stock cooperative may qualify. What is excluded is investment property owned by the taxpayer in which he or she does not reside. (Note that simply because a property is residential *does not* mean that it qualifies. A taxpayer owning a duplex and living in one side may have the side lived in qualify and the side rented out not qualify.)

The rule is mandatory, not optional. All the gain must be deferred if the new principal residence costs more than the old. However, if the new residence costs less than the old, then only a portion of the gain may be deferred.

It is important to understand that it is not necessary to buy a new residence costing more than the old for the rule to apply. With a new residence costing less than the old, a portion of the gain may still be deferred (the remaining portion having a recognized gain).

Under the deferral rule the profits from the old property do not have to be invested in the new. All the gain can be withdrawn and spent as the taxpayer wishes (assuming that the new principal residence costs more than the old). The emphasis is not on equity but on price.

DEFERRALS

The taxpayer should understand that, under the tax deferral rule, the gain is not excused. It is simply deferred. Eventually, if the taxpayer sells the new property and does not replace it, all the gain will become taxable (at the end of the 24-month period).

A taxpayer may defer the gain on the sale of a principal residence unlimited times. It is possible to go from residence to residence, almost indefinitely deferring gain (as long as the replacement property costs more than the old—for full deferral).

Only one sale and purchase of a residence is allowed every 24 months. In the case of more than one purchase and sale during that period, only the last residence purchased is counted. The purchase and sale of any other residences during that period will be treated as normal investment with no deferral permitted.

SPECIAL RULES

However, if the taxpayer should move because of a change in employment, then more than one rollover every 24 months is allowed, provided that certain conditions are met. These include distances from the old residence to the new and certain full-time work qualifications. Since these rules are relatively complex and may change with new tax acts, they should be discussed with an attorney.

In addition to allowing for more than one rollover every 2 years, job movement may also entail certain deductions which could be applied against an individual's ordinary income. The decision on whether to take these as such or to use them as deductions against the property is difficult and should be made with the advice of an attorney.

For taxpayers in the military, the replacement time is extended to 4 years and is totally suspended if the individual is in a combat zone. During the time the taxpayer is in the military, it may be possible to rent the property out and still have it qualify as a principal residence (depending on the military placement and housing opportunities of the individual).

COST DEDUCTIONS

Improvements to property increase its tax basis. For example, we might buy a home for $80,000. Later we put in a swimming pool for $20,000. Our tax basis now totals $100,000. As long as the purchase *and* improvement was done within the specified time limits (2 years before or after sale of the old residence), the increased tax basis may be used for calculating the amount of the deferral. In this example, the new property therefore would have a tax basis of $100,000 when calculating new purchase price.

Certain costs incurred in fixing up the old residence for sale can be deducted. In general, these are costs for fixing up the property where work started no more than 90 days before a sales contract is signed and where the work is paid for no more than 30 days after a sale has been completed. The work must be for repairing existing property and cannot be for improvements. The amount is deducted from the sales price. The calculation would be made in the following manner:

Selling price	$75,000
Less commission and costs	−5,000
Adjusted sales price	70,000
Less basis (original cost plus cost of improvements)	−35,000
Gain realized	$35,000
Deduction for fixing-up:	
Adjusted sales price	$70,000
Less fixing-up expenses	−1,500
New adjusted sales price	$68,500

This example gives the method of calculating both the gain realized and the fix-up costs. Note that although the fixing-up expenses are deductible when figuring the amount to be deferred under the rule, they cannot be used when figuring a recognized gain. In other words, in this example, $68,500 would be used for calculating whether or not the purchase price of the new residence was higher, but the basis would still be $70,000.

Taxpayers may exclude up to $125,000 of the gain when they reach age 55. This exclusion means that up to $125,000 may be tax free, but there are certain specific conditions which much be met. The fine book *The $125,000 Decision* by Robert Irwin (McGraw-Hill, 1982) carefully outlines all of these conditions. It points out that this exclusion is available only once in a lifetime, that the person must be 55 years old or older, that the property must be a principle residence for the last 3 out of 5 years, and that there cannot have been a previous election. This exclusion may be combined with the deferral of gain on sale, which can provide an additional benefit.

The gain on sale may be deferred even if it is not a cash sale. The rule applies to those situations in which there is an installment sale, that is, the seller does not receive his or her money in a single payment.

NOTIFICATION TO THE INTERNAL REVENUE SERVICE

When a principal residence is sold and the seller intends to replace it with a new one, the Internal Revenue Service (IRS) must be informed in the year of sale (IRS form 2119). A special statement may also be required (check with your attorney or tax accountant).

As noted at the beginning, the deferral of gain is one of the most common tax rules applied in real estate. Virtually anyone who has sold their home and bought another has run into it. However, it does have, as noted here, certain specific rules.

While we've covered most of the rules relative to the nonrecognition of gain on sale of a principal residence, we have not covered all, nor have we in detail described how the actual calculations are made. This is the proper realm of a qualified accountant or attorney.

The deferral remains a popular tax rule. But it is not a simple one.

Chapter 18

Depreciation (Cost Recovery Deductions)

Norman H. Lane Professor, University of Southern California Law Center

Probably the most significant tax characteristic of investments in improved real property is that the net rental income does not completely increase an owner's income tax liability, as is true of most dividends and interest income. It may be offset by a deduction for cost recovery, better known as "depreciation." In fact, the cost recovery allowance deduction will often exceed the net rental income, especially when the property is acquired with substantial seller or third-party financing, so that the property operations result in a tax loss which reduces the owner's liability on unrelated sources of income such as wages and salary. The tax benefits from real estate investment, unlike vehicles such as pension and profit-sharing plans, do not require that the owner refrain from using the savings to satisfy current consumption desires; any net cash flow realized can be saved, spent, or reinvested in other property by the owner, without current tax cost. To complete the picture, one should note that claiming cost recovery allowances will result in a reduction in basis of the property subject to the allowance, thereby increasing the gain or decreasing the loss realized on a subsequent sale of the property. In many cases, however, the gain on disposition can be deferred, through so-called tax-free exchanges, subjected to the very favorable long-term capital gain treatment with a maximum federal liability of 20 percent, or even eliminated completely if the owner dies while holding the property on which deductions have been claimed.

The treatment of cost recovery was extensively changed by the Economic Recovery Tax Act of 1981, even down to the name of the concept. The act drastically simplifies the process of determining the "useful life" of property, which formerly was often the subject of heated controversy between taxpayers and the Internal Revenue Service (IRS). It provides a fixed 15-year life for almost all property which taxpayers are free to use; they may also use two longer lives if they choose, although this will be rare in practice. The act also simplifies the methods by which the cost recovery allowances are computed, since only two approaches are authorized by its terms, in contrast to the large number of methods applicable before 1981. Moreover, the act prohibits the formerly common practice of assigning different useful lives to various structural components of a building; the 15-year period (or longer elective lives) will apply to everything.

However, many important rules were not significantly altered by the act. Thus, only property with a limited ascertainable useful life is eligible for cost recovery; land, most intangible assets such as goodwill, and certain improvements which are considered permanent are not eligible for cost recovery under either the old or new rules except at the time of sale. Furthermore, the total cost recovery allowance that may be claimed for a property is limited by the "historical cost" or other basis of the property without adjustment for the effects of inflation. Thus, the taxable gain on the sale of property can still exceed what most people view as the real gain.

DETERMINING PROPERTY BASIS

The word "basis" is a tax term which means, roughly, the amount of a taxpayer's investment in property which can, at some time during its holding period or at the time of sale, be recovered "tax free." That is, basis is offset against income from, or proceeds of sale of, property to reduce taxable income. The "unadjusted basis" is the basis established when the property is acquired; the "adjusted basis," which is more important, is the basis of a property thereafter, which is both increased and decreased by various transactions such as improvements (which increase basis) and cost recovery allowances (which reduce basis).

Most commonly, the unadjusted basis of property is determined by its cost to the taxpayer, assuming that it was purchased in an arm's-length transaction. In general, cost includes not only the down payment but also ancillary costs paid by the buyer, such as attorney and escrow fees, broker's commissions if any (usually these are borne by the seller), and the price paid for any option to buy which is exercised. It also usually includes indebtedness incurred to purchase the property. For example, if Mr. Jones buys a piece of real property, paying $50,000 down, assuming an existing first mortgage of $180,000, and giving a note for $70,000 to the seller secured by a second mortgage or trust deed, his total unadjusted basis for the property will be $300,000. Depreciation will normally be computed on the fraction of this amount which represents the value of the buildings only, rather than the buildings and the underlying land.

It is important to note, however, that the IRS may attack the purchase price of property as being inflated, especially when the seller takes back a large note on which little or no payments are due for many years and for which the buyer has effectively no personal liability. In other words, if the cost of property significantly exceeds its fair market value, and the buyer has little or no reason to actually come up with the total purchase price, the basis may be limited to fair market value. Thus, even though investments in real property are not subject to the strict at-risk rules applicable to such investments as equipment leasing, farming operations, and the like, very similar results may occur as a result of IRS rulings and court decisions in the area.

Since purchase money financing generally is included in basis from the beginning, owners do not obtain an increase in basis by paying off debt. However, failure to pay off significant amounts of debt may increase the gain reported on disposition, as we saw in Chapter 17.

Normal operating expenses of property also do not increase basis; rather, such costs are treated as current deductions against operating income received. This is usually a desirable result. Controversy arises frequently regarding costs which in a taxpayer's opinion constitute fully deductible expenses but which the IRS considers capital improvements which must be added to basis and recovered only through the cost recovery system.

In resolving questions in this area, the courts and the IRS examine whether the expenditure significantly adds to the expected life of the property, adapts it to a new function, or increases its capacity in some way, all of which point toward capitalization. If, however, the expenditure is designed simply to maintain property in ordinary efficient condition or to remedy damages caused by unexpected events such as water leaks, oil seepage, and the like, the expenditure will qualify for current deduction.

If the repair results from a casualty loss which itself qualifies for a deduction, the taxpayer will be limited to one deduction; one cannot deduct both the loss in value resulting from the casualty and the cost of repairing it. Whether repairs are currently deductible or capitalized additions to basis is often a difficult question, and results are hard to predict.

Property Not Acquired through Purchase

Sometimes people acquire property in transactions which are not ordinary purchases. Most common are bequests or inheritances, gifts, tax-free exchanges, tax-free distributions from entities such as trusts and partnerships, and interests which are obtained as the result of, or compensation for, personal services rendered to another. In all these cases, special basis rules apply.

Acquisitions through Bequest or Inheritance.   If an interest in property is included in the gross estate of a decedent, its unadjusted basis in the hands of the heir or legatee is generally the fair market value of the property at the date of death, or, in some cases, an alternate valuation date, which may be up to 6 months following the date of death. This rule is of great practical importance, since any gain accrued in the property during the decedent's ownership is, in effect, never subject to income tax liability. However, any loss accrued during this period is never deductible.

The law presently requires only that the property be included in the gross estate, not that any estate tax liability actually be imposed on its transfer to the heir or legatee. As a result of the new tax law, only a small percentage of estates will actually incur federal estate tax liability, because of the increased exemption levels and, even more significantly, the unlimited marital deduction for property transferred to or for the benefit of a surviving spouse. Nevertheless, such property presently receives a new basis at the death of the deceased owner. Furthermore, if a couple resided in a community property state and held interests in real property as community property, then both halves of the community receive a new basis at death, although only one half is actually included in the gross estate of the first spouse to die. This rule is an important consideration in deciding how title to property acquired by a married couple should be registered.

The gross estate of a decedent is different from the probate estate. The latter is, typically, only property held at death in the sole name of the decedent, or, in some states, property held at death as community property of a husband and wife. However, the gross estate includes property held in revocable living trusts, many joint tenancies (although only half of the value of joint tenancies between husband and wife is normally includable), and various other arrangements. This property will usually receive a full stepped-up basis at death, but only half of interspousal joint tenancies gets a new basis.

Transfers by Gift.   When property is transferred by inter vivos gift, rather than at the death of the owner, the basis of property in the donee's hands is normally the donor's basis, increased by any gift taxes paid by either party to effect the transfer. If, however, the value of the gifted property at the time of the gift is lower than the donor's basis, then the donee's basis for purposes of computing loss is limited to the fair market value at the time of the gift. Cost recovery, however, may be determined using the donor's basis. As an illustration, suppose that a parent bought income property for $500,000, took $50,000 of depreciation or cost recovery, and gave it to a child when its fair market value was $400,000. The child's unadjusted basis for purposes of determining gain or depreciation is $450,000, but for purposes of determining loss is only $400,000. Thus, if the child shortly afterward sells the property for $375,000, the deductible loss is only $25,000; if the child sells it for $525,000, however, the gain is $75,000. (If the property sells for anything between $400,000 and $500,000, the child has neither gain nor loss.) This rule is designed to block attempts to maximize loss deductions through transfers to related parties in higher tax brackets.

Sometimes donors make "bargain sales" of property to donees, receiving a price which is less than market value. In such cases, there is a conflict between the rules relating to the basis of property acquired by purchase and those that relate to the basis of property acquired by gift. The applicable regulations say that, in such cases, the donee will take the higher of the price paid or the donor's basis as the basis for determining gain and depreciation, adjusted by adding back any gift taxes paid.

Before 1981, if property were given to a donee and the donor died within 3 years after the gift, then the value of the property at the time of death would be included in the gross estate of the donor, and the donee would thus normally get a new basis for it. This rule was largely eliminated by the new tax law, so that, today, the gift rules rather than the death rules for determining basis apply. Also, the new law provides that if one person gives appreciated property to another, the latter dies within 1 year after the gift, and the decedent leaves the property back to the original donor or donor's spouse, then the property will not get a stepped-up basis but will be limited to the basis in the hands of the decedent immediately before death. This rule is designed to block efforts to obtain "cheap" basis step-ups through transfers to persons who are likely to die in the near future and who do not themselves have substantial estates on which taxes will be due.

Tax-Deferred Exchanges. Because one can defer capital gains tax through exchanging one piece of investment or business real property for another, many such transactions have taken place. (The general subject is taken up in Chapter 25.) For our purposes, the effect of making a tax-deferred exchange is important. In general, the replacement property's basis is equal to the basis of the property given up in the exchange, plus any new consideration furnished to the other party by the investor in question. For example, suppose that Albert owns investment property on Oak Street that has an adjusted basis of $200,-000 and a fair market value of $500,000. Betty owns property on Elm Street that has an adjusted basis of $350,000 and a fair market value of $600,000. (Both properties are free and clear.) Albert and Betty make an exchange, and Albert pays Betty an additional $100,000 to balance the values. In Albert's hands, the Elm Street property will have a basis of $300,000, that is, his adjusted basis in the Oak Street lot plus the $100,000 additional consideration. Betty's basis in the Oak Street lot will be $350,000, the same as her former basis in Elm Street; she will also owe tax on the $100,000 cash she received in the exchange, probably at capital gains rates. If any mortgages are involved in the exchange of one or both of the properties, the exchangor who increases net mortgage indebtedness may generally increase basis by the net difference, and the exchangor who reduces net mortgage indebtedness must usually pay tax on the reduction, which is treated much as though he or she actually received cash in an amount equal to the net reduction.

Various provisions of the Internal Revenue Code provide for tax-free rollovers of gains on certain transactions in which the taxpayer receives cash and then reinvests the same or a larger amount in qualifying replacement property. Most important are the provisions relating to the involuntary conversion of property, for example, through destruction by fire (with receipt of insurance proceeds in excess of adjusted basis), and condemnation or the threat thereof, and for sale of a principal residence if the net proceeds are reinvested in a similar residence. Property acquired pursuant to the rollover provisions generally has a basis equal to its cost *minus* the amount of deferred gain on the disposition of the original property. For example, if the taxpayer's original property had an adjusted basis of $150,000 when it was destroyed by fire, but the taxpayer received $250,000 in insurance proceeds based on replacement cost and then purchased a new piece of property for $275,000 within the qualifying period, the basis of the new property will be $175,000—a cost of $275,000 less $100,000 of unrecognized gain. If the replacement property cost less than the net proceeds from the disposition of the old property, some tax will be paid on the net cash withdrawal, and the basis of the new property will generally be the same as the basis of the old property. Thus, in the prior example, if the cost of the new property was only $230,000, then its adjusted basis will be $150,000, and the taxpayer would owe tax on the net withdrawal of

$20,000 ($250,000 insurance proceeds less $230,000 reinvested). Note that qualifying new investment need not be made in cash; acquisition indebtedness will usually count as well, unless it is deemed excessive under the rules discussed earlier.

Real property is often held by legal entities such as corporations, partnerships, and trusts. In most cases, transfers to such entities by individuals who thereafter hold interests in the entity are tax free or tax-deferred. Except in the case of corporations (and organizations treated for tax purposes like corporations), tax-free transfers of property held by such entities to their members or beneficiaries individually are also commonly made. In general, the basis of property acquired by an entity in exchange for issuing interests in the entity (such as stock certificates or partnership interests) will be the same as it was in the transferor's hands, and the basis of property distributed tax free by an entity to an individual member or investor will be equal to its basis in the entity's hands. In some cases, however, these rules are modified, and competent legal or accounting advice usually should be obtained before engaging in any such transaction, to ensure that there will be no adverse tax consequences. This is especially true when the transfer is made by a corporation to one or more shareholders, since there is often a serious risk that the distribution will be treated as a fully taxable dividend to the recipients.

Property interests are occasionally acquired as compensation for personal services, such as might be rendered by an employee to an employer or an agent or broker to a principal. When this is established, the employee or agent's basis in the interest will usually be equal to its fair market value at the time of receipt, at least if his or her right to keep the property is no longer subject to a substantial risk of forfeiture. Although this seems like a favorable rule, it is actually often disadvantageous, since the consequence of acquiring a cost basis will be that the value of the interest received is included in the employee's gross income, at its fair market value without the benefit of the special capital gains rates. This result is especially adverse if the employee does not have cash available to bear the tax burden and no convenient way of obtaining it short of a forced sale.

Often, it is better for the employee or agent to borrow the money to make an outright purchase of the interest from the employer or principal; such loans can be made at below-market rates or on an interest-free basis and may not have to be repaid until sale of the property or some time long in the future. When a taxpayer contemplates negotiating a deal which may involve acquisition of a property interest for services, she or he should obtain competent professional advice. It will often be possible to structure the transaction in a fashion which will produce much more favorable tax results, but care and caution are always indicated in doing so.

ALLOCATION OF BASIS—LIMITING NONDEPRECIABLE INVESTMENT

As stated earlier, once the basis of property as a whole is determined, it is usually necessary to allocate the total basis between nondepreciable land and depreciable buildings and associated personal property such as furniture and furnishings. The allocation is a question of fact on which the taxpayer bears the burden of proof in any contest with the IRS. Sometimes, the assessed valuations on recent real property tax bills are accepted as evidence of the property allocation, but appraisals by one or more competent professionals are probably the best evidence of relative values, although they are often costly to obtain. A taxpayer's unsupported estimate of relative values will usually be given little weight, either by the IRS or any court in which the issue will be tried.

To minimize nondepreciable investments in land, various techniques are possible. Instead of acquiring title to the property in fee simple, the investor may obtain a long-term ground lease or may purchase a lessee's interest. If an investor deals directly with the owner of the fee title and leases the ground from him or her, then normal periodic ground rents will be fully deductible as operating expenses. Of course, when the lease expires, the property, including any improvements thereon, will revert to the lessor, usually with no obligation to compensate the lessee for any improvements made. Therefore the value of a leasehold interest—the right to occupy land for a stated term—will decline as the term of the lease approaches its expiration, unless the lessee's interest is protected by options to renew the lease at fixed rents or by options to buy the land. If, however, such options are deemed "bargains" by the IRS, that is, are exercisable at substantially lower than a reasonable estimate of fair market value, then the IRS may contend that the purported lease is really a purchase of the land and deny some of or all the deduction for rent. (Some of the rent paid may be recharacterized as deductible interest in this situation.) If an investor purchases a lessee's interest in a ground lease, in effect becoming an assignee of the leasehold interest, or gives the ground lessor a "bonus" for signing the lease, then the front-end payments made will be amortized in equal installments over the remaining term of the ground lease, with each year's amortization deductible as an expense. In some cases, however, the IRS may assert the right to require amortization over a term which includes optional renewal periods as well, thereby reducing the annual amount of the amortization deduction. This is particularly likely to occur if the basic lease term has only a short period left to go or if the lessee and lessor are treated as related parties.

If land is purchased with long-term financing, most of the payments in the early years may be deducted as interest if the financing is of the usual level payment variety. These deductions are similar in effect to the rent deductions mentioned earlier.

In addition to land and buildings, allocations of basis may sometimes be necessary to certain other categories of assets, notably goodwill or going-concern value, which most taxpayers seek to minimize, and tangible personal property acquired with the real estate. Most buyers seek to maximize the personal property acquired, since its cost may be recovered over a 3- to 5-year period, and they may also be eligible for a partial or full investment tax credit when it is purchased. Tangible personal property will be significant when the real property consists of furnished apartments or is used as a hotel or motel. In general, however, buyers of commercial real estate, such as stores, offices, and warehouses, do not acquire much tangible personal property when they buy a building, since this is generally furnished by each lessee.

ELIGIBILITY FOR COST RECOVERY

Property is eligible for cost recovery allowances only if it is considered held for use in a trade or business or for investment. Excluded from depreciation are personal use property, owner-occupied residences, for example, and property which is considered inventory, that is, is held for sale to customers in the ordinary course of a trade or business. For example, a developer who puts up a housing tract and sells off individual homes or who constructs a condominium project and immediately begins to sell the units will not be eligible to claim cost recovery allowances as long as she or he is actively engaged in marketing. Property can, however, change its character from one use to another; if the new use is an eligible one, the cost recovery period begins with the date of conversion. Thus, if an individual moves out of a house and rents it to a tenant, the owner may claim the allowance when the property is offered for rental in a bona fide fashion, even if the owner is unable to secure a tenant immediately. It should be noted that, when conversion occurs, the basis for depreciation is the lesser of the property's previous basis or its fair market value at the time that conversion occurs. In general, merely offering a personal residence for sale, rather than for rental, does not effect a conversion, and no cost recovery or depreciation allowance will be deductible during the period that it is on the market, even if the taxpayer is no longer living in the property.

When property is held partly for personal use and partly for income-producing purposes, basis must be further allocated between the two components in proportion to their respective fair market values. Thus, if a triplex building has three identical apartments, one of which is occupied by the owner, two-thirds of the cost of the building will be eligible for cost recovery allowances.

If property is rented to a family member, at a fair arm's-length rental charge, a law passed at the end of 1981 permits the owner to take full deductions for cost recovery and other expenses and to deduct any operating loss from the property, just as if the tenant were unrelated. However, special rules apply if the lessee also has an ownership interest in the unit. If the rental is below market value, a number of complex limitations on deductions apply; the most important is that no net loss will be deductible from outside income.

If property is rented out temporarily, as when the taxpayer is away from home on a temporary job or for educational purposes, the same new law specifically removes any restriction on the deduction of reasonable expenses, including the appropriate cost recovery allowance. The basis for cost recovery will be, as described earlier, the lesser of the property's previous basis or its fair market value at the time rental use commences.

PERIOD FOR COMPUTING COST RECOVERY ALLOWANCES

Under the new legislation, buildings acquired after 1980 are generally eligible for full cost recovery over a 15-year period, unless the acquisition was made from a person related to the taxpayer (under rules to be described). Buyers or other new owners may also write off the cost over either 35 or 45 years. Separate choices are permitted for each building. Ordinarily, taxpayers will use the longer optional recovery periods only if they are currently in a very low tax bracket and expect to remain there indefinitely, and thus they wish to preserve as much of their basis as possible to offset future sales proceeds. The minimum 15-year recovery period applies whether the building is new or used. A shorter write-off is permitted in only a few special circumstances, which will be noted later in this chapter. Once taxpayers elect a particular write-off period, they may change the election only with the consent of the IRS, which is likely to be difficult to obtain.

The statutory write-off period chosen applies, in general, to all structural components of a building, including its shell, roofing, electrical systems, heating and air conditioning systems, plumbing, and even the paint in place at the time of acquisition. Routine postacquisition replacements of these components may, in most cases, be deducted when made as an operating expense; they need not be written off over a new 15-year period. Other improvements must be recovered over the period chosen for the basic building. However, if substantial work is done on a property, after it is acquired, for instance, if it is significantly enlarged, then the new work may qualify as a separate building and its cost may be recovered over a 15-year (or longer) period, without regard to the treatment of the original structure. This rule applies only to improvements made during a 24-month period after the building is at least 3 years old and only if the cost of such improvements equals or exceeds 25 percent of the building's adjusted basis on the first day of the 24-month period.

If a building is not located within the United States, the minimum recovery period is 35 years, and the taxpayer may elect a 45-year recovery period.

METHODS OF DEPRECIATION

Taxpayers may choose one of two methods for recovering their investment in property subject to the new accelerated cost recovery system. One is the straight-line method, in which an equal fraction (generally 6.67 percent of the cost of the property) is deducted in each full year of ownership; the deduction for the first and last years of ownership is prorated based on the number of months in the year that the property was held. The second method specified in the statute is an accelerated method; the deductions for the early years of ownership are higher and for later years of ownership are lower than under the straight-line method. The exact fraction for each year depends on what month during the year the property was acquired and on whether the property constitutes qualified subsidized low-income housing. The relevant fractions are found in tables promulgated by the IRS. For reasons discussed in Chapter 16, most taxpayers will find it advantageous to use the accelerated method for residential property such as apartment houses and the straight-line method for commercial and industrial buildings such as stores, offices, and factory buildings.

BUILDINGS INELIGIBLE FOR ACRS SYSTEM

If a building was owned by the taxpayer, or a statutorily described related person, at any time during 1980, it is ineligible for the ACRS system. Furthermore, if the taxpayer acquired the building in 1981 or thereafter but leases it to a person who owned it at any time during 1980 (or to a person related to such owner), it is ineligible. If it was acquired after 1980 in a nonrecognition (tax-free) exchange, for property owned by the taxpayer or related persons during 1980, only the new money invested, not the carry-over portion of the basis, is eligible for the new system. Similarly, if it is acquired in a tax-free transaction between corporation and shareholder, partner and partnership, or the like, the portion of the basis which carries over from the prior owner is not eligible for the new system.

The term "related person" is defined quite broadly in the statute. It includes, for example, the current owner's spouse, ancestors, lineal descendants, and siblings (by the whole or half blood); an individual and a corporation in which that individual, or members of her or his family, own 10 percent or more of the value of stock outstanding; corporations which are under generally common control; partnerships and partners who have a 10 percent interest in either capital or profits; and numerous other categories of persons and legal entities. Relationships must be carefully checked, preferably with competent professional advice, any time sales or purchases are made between two persons or entities which might conceivably be considered related. Moreover, the IRS is granted broad authority to prescribe regulations which would catch transactions if one of the principal purposes is to avoid the special "antichurning" rules described, and such regulations may well be retroactive when they are issued.

If property is not eligible for the new system, then the old, that is, pre-1981, rules will apply. Under these rules, there was no fixed period for cost recovery of buildings, although the IRS did promulgate some nonbinding guidelines. Useful life became a matter of separate proof in each individual case. The method for computing depreciation depended on the character of the building at the time of acquisition, whether it was new or used, residential or commercial, and so forth. The rules differed, moreover, for property acquired at different times, since they were extensively changed in both 1969 and 1976. However, separate component depreciation was generally permitted, which resulted, typically, in useful lives averaging about 25 to 30 years for new structures and less than that for older buildings.

SPECIAL CATEGORIES OF PROPERTY

A few types of structures are eligible for faster write-offs because they are not deemed "buildings." These include structures which are used as an integral part of a manufacturing, construction, or production activity, such as blast furnaces, machinery housings (which do not provide work space for operators), and electrical transmission lines; structures used for bulk storage of fungible commodities such as grain elevators and petroleum storage tanks; and single-purpose agricultural or horticultural structures such as livestock pens, poultry coops, and greenhouses. The taxpayer who owns these special purpose structures need not operate the related business.

All these structures may be written off over a 5-year period (in a few cases, a 3-year period) under a method which provides, except in the first year, for somewhat accelerated cost recovery compared to the straight-line method. (Note: It is to be remembered that new tax bills may be expected from Congress by 1985 on 1986 and they could change current write-offs.) Taxpayers may use the straight-line method and may also elect 12- or 15-year lives in lieu of 5 years (using the straight-line method only).

Some assets found in certain types of buildings probably will not be considered structural components and thus will be eligible for the 5-year life and the other rules outlined. Furniture and appliances in furnished apartments or motel rooms and certain movable partitions installed by the owner of a building are examples of this category. Fine distinctions are often drawn: For example, under analogous IRS rulings in a different context, window-type portable air conditioners are probably eligible for 5-year write-off, but through-the-wall units are considered structural components. So-called antichurning rules, designed to block application of the new ACRS system to property acquired before 1981, also apply to the 5-year property. In fact, the rules are stricter than those applicable to buildings, since they apply when the use, as well as the ownership, of property remains in the same person who used the property in 1980 or earlier. For example, if some 5-year property was leased by a former owner to a tenant throughout 1980 and the first owner sells to a new owner but the same lessee remains in possession throughout, the new owner will not be eligible for the ACRS system. In contrast, the new owner of 15-year property leased under the same circumstances would normally be eligible for the ACRS system.

LOW-INCOME HOUSING

Through 1983, taxpayers who own residential units whose tenants are persons with low or moderate incomes (as determined by the Department of Housing and Urban Development) may elect to recover rehabilitation expenses on each such unit over a 60-month period using the straight-line method. The amount eligible is generally limited to

$20,000 per dwelling unit, although in some cases the limit can be raised to $40,000; moreover, at least $3000 in rehabilitation expenditures must be made for a dwelling unit to qualify. The term "dwelling unit" means an apartment or furnished room used to provide living accommodations, but it does not apply to any unit in a building in which more than half the units are used on a transient basis.

LEASEHOLD IMPROVEMENTS

When a lessee or tenant of land constructs an improvement on the property, the cost recovery or depreciation allowance belongs to the tenant, even though under state law the property may be treated as a "fixture," title to which vests in the landlord or lessor. The period for write-off depends on the term of the lease. Assuming that the transaction would normally be subject to the new ACRS system, if the unexpired term of the lease exceeds the statutory write-off period (usually 15 years), then the normal cost recovery rules apply. However, if the remaining term of the lease is less than the statutory life at the time the improvements are constructed, then the tenant may recover the cost of the improvements through periodic amortization deductions over the unexpired term of the lease, using only the straight-line method. In certain situations, the term of the lease must be computed by including any optional renewal or extension periods, especially when the lessor and lessee are related. It should be noted that when the lease term expires and the lessor acquires possession of the lessee's improvements their value will not generally be income at that time, but she or he will not usually obtain any basis in the improvements recovered.

Suppose that a tenant has constructed leasehold improvements and then the landlord sells his or her interest in the property to a buyer who purchases the land and the "reversionary interest" in the improvements. May the buyer claim depreciation or cost recovery deductions and, if so, when? If the lease has only a short time to run at the time of the sale, then the buyer may be paying a substantial amount, based on the projected rental value of the improvements. An early case gave buyers the right to claim depreciation immediately, based on the market value of their interest in the building, but more recent decisions have held that no depreciation is allowable until the expiration of the lease, and it will start then based on the portion of the purchase price properly allocable to the improvements. These decisions seem more sensible.

The purchaser of a manufactured home which otherwise qualifies for depreciation may recover its cost over a 10-year period, rather than the normal 15-year period, using a somewhat accelerated method. A manufactured home is basically a traditional 8-foot or wider mobile home designed for long-term use on a fixed site.

INVESTMENT TAX CREDITS

Most real estate investors will not benefit from the tax law's allowance of an investment credit, equal to a percentage of qualifying expenditures, against tax liability, because buildings and structural components usually are not eligible for the credit. However, there are numerous exceptions to this rule, so that in particular situations credit may be allowed for certain costs incurred by the owner of a building or similar structure.

The most common situation where an investment credit may be allowed to a real estate investor is in the area of rehabilitation of existing structures. If a building is at least 30 years old when a rehabilitation program is commenced, if it is used for commercial or industrial rather than residential purposes by the occupant or occupants, if it is rehabilitated pursuant to a program which leaves 75 percent of the existing external walls in place as external walls, and if the cost of rehabilitation exceeds the adjusted basis of the property immediately before rehabilitation commences (or $5000, if basis is less than $5000), then a credit is generally allowable for qualifying expenditures. The amount of the credit depends on the age of the building at the time rehabilitation commences; if it is more than 30 but less than 40 years old, the credit is 15 percent of qualifying expenditures; if it is more than 40 years old the credit percentage is 20 percent. Note that a credit against a tax differs from a deduction; it directly reduces the tax liability dollar-for-dollar, whereas a deduction reduces taxable income and saves taxes only to the extent of the applicable marginal rate. Investment credits, including the rehabilitation credit, may not exceed the first $25,000 of tax liability in any year plus 85 percent of the tax liability in excess of $25,000; however, unused credits may be carried back 3 years and forward 7 years to offset tax liability in those years. Allowable rehabilitation credits reduce the taxpayer's adjusted basis in his or her property, although only half of the investment credit on other types of property has this effect.

Some other rules applicable to the rehabilitation credit are as follows:

1. Depreciation on the rehabilitated building may only be claimed under the straight-line method.

2. The cost of acquisition or enlargement of a building does not qualify for the credit.

3. Taxpayers generally have 24 months to accumulate sufficient rehabilitation expenditures to meet the minimum, but in some cases involving phased rehabilitations under architectural plans the period is extended to 60 months.

Even more favorable rules are applicable to rehabilitations of "certified historical structures" designated in accordance with regulations of the Department of the Interior. The credit is 25 percent of qualifying expenditures, and residential properties are eligible.

Another category of property eligible for investment credit, in general at the rate of 10 percent of qualifying expenditures, is the special purpose structures mentioned earlier (such as power lines, wind tunnels, grain elevators, and poultry coops). Also, the cost of an elevator or escalator in a commercial or industrial building, but not a residence, is eligible for the 10 percent credit, as are movable partitions and similar nonpermanent nonstructural components of commercial and industrial buildings. However, air conditioning and heating units are not now eligible for the credit, even if they are portable.

Still another category of investment credit eligible property is various types of energy-saving equipment which may be installed in buildings. Only a few categories were eligible after the end of 1982, however.

Investment tax credits of all types are subject to partial or full recapture if the taxpayer disposes of part of or all of the interest in the property within 5 years after making the qualifying expenditure. Similarly, if an investment is made by an entity such as a partnership and a partner who has enjoyed the benefit of the credit reduces her or his interest substantially within the 5-year period, the credit may also be recaptured. Exceptions are made for certain dispositions which are more like changes in form than substance, such as the transfer of individually owned property to a controlled corporation.

Investment tax credits other than the rehabilitation credit are sometimes disallowed if the owner does not use the property directly, instead leasing it out.

Investment tax credits earned in years after 1980 are allowable only to the extent of the taxpayer's at-risk amount in the property subject to the credit. This means, in general, that the credit is not allowed if the qualifying expenditures are financed with nonrecourse loans (those on which the taxpayer has no personal liability), although they may be allowed at the time and to the extent that such loans are actually paid off. Certain complex and limited exceptions to the at-risk rules do apply.

Individuals are entitled to a limited credit, distinct from the investment tax credit, for certain energy-saving expenditures they make on their principal residence (whether they own or lease it). Landlords are not eligible for the residential energy credit. The maximum credit in any one year is $300, except that the credit is increased to $4000 in connection with projects employing solar or wind energy. The residential energy credits are scheduled to expire at the end of 1985.

Part **4**

Real
Estate
Law

Chapter 19

Real Property Ownership

Robert J. Bond   Professor of Real Estate, Los Angeles Valley College

"**C**ujus est solum, ejus est usque ad coelum et ad inferos"—whose is the soil, his it is also unto the sky and the depths. This was once the commonly accepted notion of landownership, owning not only the soil itself—the surface—but also all the way to the core of the earth and to the periphery of the skies, as far as the naked eye could see and beyond.

All this changed as modern technology set in, particularly with aircraft. Today landowners have no right to possession of the airspace over their land above the minimum altitudes for normal aircraft flights (excluding landing and takeoff). Under a U.S. Supreme Court decision, *(U.S. v. Cousby)* such upper airspace is a "public highway" to which no private right of possession exists. In effect, the airspace required as "navigable airspace" to accomplish maximum flight paths for climb and descent is in the public domain.

The interest in the possession of land also extends below the surface and presents similar problems to those of airspace. Questions frequently arise in connection with mining laws, for instance. In most states it is a trespass to mine under another's land in the absence of an agreement to the contrary. Again relying on the maxim "Cujus est solum," the owner of realty is entitled to the free and unfettered control of her or his land above, on, and beneath the surface. So whatever is in a direct line between the surface of the land and the center of the earth belongs to the owner of the surface. The major exception is when, as in so many cases, one or more previous owners reserved part of or all the subsurface rights when they transferred title.

CLASSIFICATIONS OF PROPERTY

All property can be divided into two classes: real, or immovable, property and personal, or movable, property.

Real Property

Real property consists of land, that which is affixed to land, that which is incidental or appurtenant to land, and that which is immovable by law. There are no absolute rights to real estate as such. There are rights of public agencies that are paramount, and there are private restrictions which limit ownership rights. Hence, real property refers to the so-called bundle of rights which one has with respect to the real thing, the physical tangible substance we know as "real estate." These rights include the right to:

Possess the property
Encumber the property
Use the property exclusively
Transfer or convey the property
Lease the property
Transfers the property by testamentary disposition
Improve the property
Enjoy the property
Voluntarily dedicate the property for public use

State and/or local governments can set limitations which are paramount to the individual's rights. They can, for example, tax, to pay for government services; condemn, under eminent domain; regulate, under the police power of the state, through zoning, building restrictions, subdivision regulations, health and safety code, noise abatement, pollution control, and other ecological controls; escheat, when no will is left and when there are no heirs to succeed to the property. In addition, there are private restrictions imposed by deed, through so-called covenants, conditions, and restrictions, or "Cs, Cs, and Rs," for short. Similarly, restrictions may be imposed through various liens (whether voluntary or involuntary), easements, encroachments, leaseholds, licenses, emblements, and so on.

Personal Property

Personal property is anything that is not real property. It may be tangible, such as furnishings, equipment, and stock in trade found in a business opportunity, or intangible, such as notes and trust deeds, leaseholds, and choses in action or in possession.

Fixtures

"Fixtures" are defined as items which were once personal property or chattel but which became reality through attachment to the land or structure. The reverse is also true: realty may become personalty. For example, when a house is elevated on cribs to be moved, such as through condemnation action, it then becomes chattel. The tests applied to determine whether an item is a fixture are:

1. Agreement of the parties to the transaction

2. Intention of the parties if no agreement

3. Adaptability to use (for instance, screens or tacked-down wall-to-wall carpeting are regarded as fixtures)

4. Degree or method of attachment or affixation to the land or structures

5. Relationship of the parties [in the event of a dispute, the courts generally favor the buyer as against seller; beneficiary (lender) against trustor (borrower); and lessee (tenant) as against lessor (landlord)]

6. Trade (if used in one's trade or business, the item is usually regarded as personalty)

ESTATES IN LAND

An estate is ownership interest or possessory rights in real property. Estates may also be nonpossessory, such as easements, reservations, and restrictions contained in a deed, reparian rights, trusts, future interests, licenses, profits, and emoluments.

Possessory Estates

Possessory estates are those involving a right to possession. These may be broken down into the following categories:

I. Freehold
   A. Estates in fee
      1. Absolute
      2. Qualified
         a. Condition precedent
         b. Condition subsequent
         c. Special limitation
         d. Executory limitation
            (1) Remainderman
                (a) Vested
                (b) Contingent
   B. Life estate
      1. Reservation
      2. Others
      3. Operation of law
II. Less than freehold
   A. Leaseholds
      1. Estate for years
      2. Estate from period to period
      3. Estate of sufferance
      4. Estate at will
   B. Nonproperty interests
      1. Invitee
      2. Licensee
      3. Tolerated intruder
      4. Trespasser

Freehold Estates

Freehold estates are real property rights of indefinite duration which are freely inheritable and which are therefore not capable of precise measurement. Smaller estates in fee may be carved out of the original larger estate, namely, separate fee interests in the land, in the airspace above the land, and in the subterranean strata, for purpose of extracting minerals, oil, gas, and other subsurface substances. One may own one or any combination of these interests through sale or reservation of one or more of such interests. Hence, fee interests may be viewed as measured in terms of the quantity of the estate granted.

Fee Absolute Estates.   Fee absolute estates are the highest form of ownership possible. By contrast, qualified fee estates can be defeated or set aside. Qualified fees are therefore also referred to as "defeasable," or determinable, fees. If there is no "condition precedent," the fee transfer commences upon the occurrence of some contingent event.

For example, title to the property may transfer when the grantee marries or reaches a particular age.

Condition Subsequent. A fee on "condition subsequent" vests immediately, subject to termination on the occurrence of a later, or subsequent, event. The fee is transferred to a person so long as that person does not violate a particular restriction imposed in the deed (e.g., "so long as he remains unmarried"). There is no automatic right of reentry if the condition is broken; instead, there remains the power of termination, or the right of reversion by the grantor when the restriction is violated. For this reason, it may be said that fees on condition subsequent and condition precedent, as well as on special limitation and executory limitation, measure the quality of interest in the fee: each may be terminated by the grantor under varying circumstances.

Special Limitation. A fee on "special limitation" transfers title immediately but stipulates that the fee will expire automatically upon the occurrence of some stated event. For example, the fee is to vest in the grantee so long as the property is used as a church, school, or for some other stated purpose. The interest of the grantor is called a "possibility of reverter" and is transferable by the grantor during his or her lifetime and on the grantor's death passes to the heirs or devisees.

Executory Limitation. In contrast, a fee on "executory limitation" provides for title transfer to a designated person on the death of the grantee. Such remaining interest does not ever revert to the grantor but to a party referred to as a "remainderman." The remaining interest may be either vested or contingent. If a "vested remainderman," the third party receives the "estate in expectancy" even if he or she dies before the grantee. Under such circumstances, the third party's heirs would succeed to her or his interest. However, if a "contingent remainderman," the third party must survive the grantee; otherwise, with the third party's death the estate in expectancy also dies.

Life Estates

Life estates are those created for the grantor, another party, or by operation of law. They may be created by grant, will, or deed. Although they are of indefinite duration, since it is not possible to determine how long the holder, or life tenant, will live, they are not estates of inheritance. That is, they cannot be transferred to the life tenant's heirs. The length of time for the estate is measured by the lifetime of the life tenant. With the tenant's demise, the tenancy also dies.

Reservation.   A life estate may be created in favor of the grantor, who conveys title to another but reserves the right of possession for as long as she or he lives. For example, a father desiring to minimize the impact of estate taxes may transfer title to a house to his son but retain the right to live in the home for the rest of his life.

Remainder and Reversion.   The life estate may be created in favor of others. For example, a mother may desire to retain ownership in the home but give up possessory rights to a needy child or other relative. Or a daughter may give up possession of property owned by her to her elderly parents, thus providing them with a home for their joint lives.

Dowry and Curtesy.   Creation of a life estate by operation of law is acknowledged by many states. A "dower" consists of the rights a married woman is entitled to on death of her husband when no will exists or when she is left out of his will. Similarly, "curtesy" is the life estate owed the husband when his wife dies.

Rights of Life Tenant.   The owner of a life estate, or life tenant, has the power to encumber, lease, convey, or otherwise dispose of his or her interest as long as such interests do not extend beyond the life of the tenant. The tenant is under legal duty not to commit waste or otherwise injure the rights of the owner of the remainder or reversion. The life tenant is also under a duty to pay real estate taxes, interest on mortgage loans, costs of ordinary repairs to improvements on the property, and an apportionment of extraordinary assessments. In turn, the fee owner or remainderman is obligated for the cost of capital repairs, a portion of assessments, and the amortization, or principal, due on secured loans against the property.

Less-than-Freehold Estates

Less-than-freehold estates are treated under the laws governing personal property. They consist principally of leaseholds, comprising one of the following:

Estate for Years.   An "estate for years" is also known as a "tenancy for years," or "fixed period" in which the lease is granted for a fixed term, up to 99 years (the maximum allowed), or even a term less than a year, such as for 25 days (as illustrated by a lease of a lot to be used for the sale of Christmas trees).

Estate from Period to Period.   An "estate from period to period," or "periodic tenancy," is a lease given from month to month, week to week, or some other designated period. It is renewable by both parties, subject to termination by either party by complying with the notice requirements to cancel, in general, 30 days. Regardless of the type of lease, however, a tenant may be forced out much sooner, through issuance of a 3-day notice to pay or quit in event that the tenant does not pay or violates one of the other leasehold covenants (in which case a simple notice to quit will suffice).

Estate of Sufferance.   An "estate of sufferance," or "tenancy of sufferance," occurs when the tenant remains on the premises after the lease has expired. She or he is technically then a hold-over, trespasser, or tolerated intruder. If the landlord or lessor accepts the tender of a rent payment, however, the tenancy converts to a periodic or fixed term, depending on the circumstances.

Estate at Will.   An "estate at will," or "tenancy at will," is one which is terminable at the will of either lessor or lessee. However, most states require a notice to terminate, generally measured by the term of the leasehold itself (i.e., month to month requiring 30 days), therefore such estates are not recognized in those states.

Nonproperty Interests

Nonproperty interests consist of those merely entering on the land of another. Different duties or obligations are owed to such parties, depending on their classification.

Invitee.   An invitee is a person who enters on the land by invitation of the owner, express or implied, such as guests, workers, prospective tenants, or customers of a store, for a mutual benefit. The owner owes a duty to exercise ordinary care in keeping the premises in a reasonably safe condition and to warn the invitee of any known dangers.

Licensee.   A licensee is one who enters the property of another by permission, for purposes benefiting the licensee, such as a door-to-door salesperson. The owner owes a duty only slightly less than that of the invitee, namely, to maintain the premises in a safe condition and to refrain from active misconduct which might result in injury.

Tolerated Intruder.   A tolerated intruder is a trespasser whose presence is known to the owner but is tolerated, even though the intruder constitutes a nuisance. The owner owes a duty to warn the intruder of possible hazards and to abstain from conduct that could result in personal injury.

Trespasser.   A trespasser enters the land of another without express or implied consent of the owner. Although no affirmative duty to maintain the property in safe condition is owed such person, the owner or occupant must not intentionally harm or create traps or hazards which could injure. However, if the trespasser is a child, the "attractive nuisance" doctrine will generally apply, whereby the owner owes an affirmative duty to protect children against foreseeable dangers, such as swimming pools.

Easement

An easement is an interest one has in the land of another. Easements are created for an almost infinite number of purposes, chiefly to create a right of way; to conduct sports; receive air, light, and heat; to use party walls and fences; to retrieve errant golf balls; and so forth.

Appurtenant Easements.   Literally meaning "belonging to," appurtenant easements run with the land and therefore bind all future owners. A "dominant tenant" and "servient tenant" exist in all such easements. The former designates the party who benefits from the easement, such as the right of cross-over on an adjoining parcel where the dominant tenant is landlocked; the latter designates the tenant whose land is burdened for the enjoyment of the dominant tenant.

Gross Easements.   An easement in gross is a personal right attached to the holder rather than to any particular parcel of land. As such it exists without a dominant tenant and must be expressly transferred with each new owner of the underlying land. Examples include every kind of public utility installation, such as for telephone poles and wires, oil pipe lines, electric lines, water conduits, and the like.

Affirmative Easements.   Affirmative easements require the doing of a thing, such as the granting of a right to have water flow without disturbance of any kind or the right to maintenance of a division fence by a coterminous owner. All easements in gross are by nature affirmative, whereas appurtenant easements may be either affirmative or negative.

Negative Easements.   A negative easement is a right *not* to do a particular thing. For example, the owner of a lot may purchase from an adjoining owner the right not to erect a structure above a certain height, in order not to obstruct air, light, or view. By definition all negative easements are appurtenant to the land to which they attach, although they may be terminated by later agreement, by a cutoff point specified in the original agreement, or by other methods.

Easements may be *created* in a number of ways:

1. *Express grant*—usually executed by a deed or other instrument in writing. It is voluntarily, or contractually, established by the parties to the easement.

2. *Implied grant*—although nothing is stated in writing, such easement arises out of the original unity of ownership due to necessity, continued use, or by any other means showing an intent to be permanent.

3. *Express reservation*—arises out of the withholding for the benefit of the grantor a portion of the property conveyed to the servient tenant usually for purposes of ingress and egress.

4. *Implied reservation*—similar to the express reservation, only this easement is created out of the implied acts of the parties, where a former unity of title is divided into the requisite tenements, with a portion of the land excepted for the benefit of the dominant tenant.

5. *Prescription*—a prescriptive easement may be created by meeting five tests:
   a. open and notorious use
   b. continuous and uninterrupted use for a period of years (five in most states)
   c. hostile to the true owner
   d. exclusive to the adverse claimant
   e. under some claim of right
   Such an easement cannot be claimed where the right is permissive and by definition cannot be created against a public property.

6. *Necessity*—established by court order, if necessary, due to a property that is, for example, landlocked and therefore inaccessible. Courts have held that an implied right of necessity passes to the grantee as appurtenant to his or her land.

7. *Miscellaneous*—other methods of creating easements include those of eminent domain, dedication, estoppel, and by reference to map or plat.

Easements may be *terminated* by any of the following methods:

1. *Deed*—usually a quitclaim deed is utilized to expressly release the easement by the dominant in favor of the servient tenant.

2. *Merger*—when the two estates are merged, that is, when the same person becomes the common owner of the easement and the servient tenement, on the grounds that a person cannot have an easement over her or his own property.

3. *Nonuse*—when an easement was acquired by prescription, nonuse for a period of years (determined by each state) will extinguish it.

4. *Court order*—through a quiet title suit, foreclosure of a senior encumbrance, or condemnation action.

5. *Abandonment*—where an intent to relinquish the easement is shown, expressly or implicitly.

6. *Miscellaneous*—other methods of terminating an easement include those of destruction of the servient tenement, excessive or unauthorized use, adverse possession for at least 5 years by the servient tenant, eminent domain, expiration of the agreed term, and by cessation of necessity when the easement was originally created by necessity.

Restrictions

Restrictions on property may be of two types: private or public. Public restrictions are created by zoning, building, and other public controls. Private restrictions are set out by deed. They may be general, as when they affect an entire tract, or specific, as when they affect only a particular parcel. The seller or grantor may, for example, impose a restriction that the property is to be developed only as a church and that the grantor may take back the property if it is converted into a theater. Because of this harsh remedy, the courts will construe a restriction as a covenant and not a condition, unless it can be unequivocally demonstrated that a condition was imposed.

Reparian Rights

Reparian rights are the rights of a landowner to water on, under, or adjacent to the owner's land. Although the owner of land bordering on a river or other watercourse has no absolute ownership of the waters, the owner has the right to the reasonable use of waters flowing past her or his land.

Licenses, Profits, and Emoluments

License.   License is a personal, revocable, and nonassignable permission or authority to enter on the land of another for a particular purpose. No possessory interest is created in the land. An example would be tickets purchased to a sports event, concert, or theater, authorizing the holder only to view the performance.

Profits.   A "profit a prendre" is the right to take something from the land, such as soil, timber, or produce. Such rights are usually sold apart from the land itself, although they may be created in favor of a lessee or reserved for the benefit of the grantor.

Emoluments and Emblements.   A special kind of profit, an emolument is a right given as compensation for services rendered. In exchange for tilling the soil, for example, an employee may be granted the right to some of or all the production from the farm for a specified time.

METHODS OF OWNERSHIP

"Ownership" is defined in *Black's Law Dictionary* as "Collection of rights to use and enjoy property, including rights to transmit it to others. The right of one or more persons to possess and use a thing to the exclusion of others." This section concerns how title to real property can be taken and transmitted.

All property is either separate or community. Similarly, title to all property can be taken either individually or in coownership.

Severalty

Severalty is ownership by one party only.

Individual Ownership. Individual ownership is by either a single person or a married person taking title in his or her own name alone. When single people die, their property is distributed to those named in their respective wills; if no will is left, such person is said to die "intestate," in which case her or his estate passes to the heirs by "operation of law," that is, according to the probate code. However, when a married person who owns property in his or her name alone dies, the property also passes to those designated in the will unless the property was purchased with "community funds," in which case the surviving spouse is entitled to half the property. In the absence of a will, the heirs succeed to the property by operation of law; in California, for example, all the property goes to the spouse if no children are left; otherwise one-third goes to the surviving spouse and two-thirds is distributed equally to the children, or "issue."

Corporation. In the eyes of the law, a corporation is treated as a separate entity, or legal person, apart from its owners. A corporation was described in a U.S. Supreme Court decision over a century ago as "an artificial being, intangible, invisible, and existing in contemplation of law." Its creation comes from the corporate charter issued by the state in which it incorporated, and it is said to have perpetual existence. It is vested with essentially the same powers and authority as natural persons, including the right to purchase and sell property in its own name. Since it is an artificial being, a principal officer, usually the corporate secretary, signs on behalf of the corporation.

Unincorporated Associations. Many associations are organized for the purpose of fostering and promoting the beneficial interests of the members. Realty boards, labor unions, church and charity groups, clubs, credit unions, and medical societies are all examples of such associations, which are endowed with powers similar to the corporation. The association's charter and bylaws will usually specify one or more persons authorized to act on behalf of the group.

Syndicates and Investment Trusts. Both syndicates and investment trusts involve the pooling of assets or resources by more than one party for the purpose of investing in real estate or security instruments, that is, trust deeds and mortgages. One or more persons act on behalf of such business organizations. For example, the most common form of syndicate structure is established as a "limited partnership," described as an association of one or more general partners and one or more limited partners. The general partner acts as spokesperson for the group. In the case of the investment trust—whether a real estate investment trust or mortgage trust—a trustee acts on behalf of the trust.

Cooperatives. Cooperatives, or "own-your-own apartments," are a form of ownership in severalty. A corporate organizational structure is set up for title vesting, which contemplates ownership of an undivided interest but with exclusive occupancy rights on the part of the various owners in designated portions of the multiple project. By way of contrast, condominium ownership involves undivided ownership of common areas, plus a divided interest in the cubicle occupied by the owner. In the case of either the cooperative or the condominium project, the individual occupiers may hold title to their separate interests under severalty or under some form of joint ownership.

Coownership

Various forms of multiple ownership, or coownerships, are available to two or more owners.

Joint Tenancy. A joint tenancy may be created if four "unities" are present at the time of creation:

1. Time. Unity of time occurs only when all the joint tenants take title to the property at the same time. Another tenant cannot be added at a later time. Similarly, cotenants who transfer their interests to another are said to have destroyed the joint tenancy with respect to their status, although the remaining joint tenants remain joint tenants with respect to each other.

2. Title. Unity of title means that all the joint tenants must acquire the property under the same single instrument, usually a grant deed. Each must be so named in the deed.

3. Interest. Unity of interest requires equal fractional interest in the whole of the property. None of the tenants may own more or less than her or his fellow tenants.

4. Possession. Unity of possession specifies that each tenant have equal and coextensive rights to possess all the property. If, for example, there are two joint tenants, they cannot split the property with exclusive right of possession in only half the property.

The principal characteristic of joint tenancy is the right of survivorship. That is, when one tenant dies, the surviving cotenant automatically succeeds to the decedent's share, without the necessity of probate to establish the rights of survivors. Prior to death, a joint tenant may do almost anything with her or his interest, except leave it to someone else by will. The deed supersedes a will, by operation of law. Note that multiple ownership may exist without destruction of the joint tenancy. Thus, a Mr. Smith may own a one-fourth interest in a property in severalty, and a Mr. and Mrs. Jones might own the remaining three-fourths as joint tenants. When Smith dies, his interest passes to his devisees or heirs; if either of the Joneses dies, the surviving spouse succeeds to the decedent's (three-eighths) interest.

Tenancy in Common. Tenancy in common is ownership by two or more persons without right of survivorship, normally created by un-related parties who do not desire to leave their respective interests to the surviving cotenants. Although each tenant in common receives an undivided interest described in a single deed, only one unity is required, that of possession. Thus Ms. Able may own 60 percent of the property, with Mr. Baker owning the remaining 40 percent. Baker may in turn sell a portion of his interest by a second deed to Ms. Charley. However, each is entitled to use all the property, not a fractional portion as each interest may appear. When a tenant in common dies, her or his interest passes to those designated in the will, or to his or her heirs, should the tenant die intestate. Any instrument transferring title to more than one person which does not specify a joint tenancy, community property, or tenancy in partnership is presumed to create a tenancy in common.

Community Property. Community property is ownership of property acquired by husband and wife during marriage, except that which is obtained by devise or descent, awards for personal injury, and gift.

The interest each spouse has in one-half of the community estate is called "separate property," the same given to property owned by each prior to marriage. Assets that are acquired during marriage or property that was owned separately prior to marriage that is commingled after marriage is presumed to be community property.

Both spouses have equal right of management of the community.

As such, each may do anything with the community property, except to sell or convey realty belonging to the community, encumber it, or to lease community real property for over 1 year. Of course, each spouse may perform any of these acts with the consent of the other spouse.

Since the interest of each spouse is deemed to be separate, either may dispose of his or her interest by will to whomever he or she wishes. If no last will is left, the surviving spouse takes all. If separate property other than community interest is owned and one dies intestate, half will go to the surviving spouse, and half to an only child; if more than one child, one-third goes to the surviving spouse, and two-thirds is shared equally by the children.

Tenancy in Partnership.   As defined in the Uniform Partnership Act, a partnership is "an association of two or more persons carrying on a business as co-owners for profit." Each person is entitled to share in the profits and losses as their interests may appear, whether equally or unequally. On the death of a partner, the heirs succeed to the decedent's right in the form of accrued profits and proportionate property owned but not in the business of the partnership as such. Surviving partners may sell the partnership real property but must account to the heirs for their share of the proceeds.

Each partner is deemed to be an agent for the partnership and for each other, as long as the partner is operating within the course and scope of the partnership business. Therefore, in the absence of contrary evidence, any one partner may buy or sell for the benefit of the partnership. Title may be acquired in the name of one or more of the partners or in the name of the partnership. Any general partner who is authorized to do so may act for the business. Regardless of how title is vested, as long as it was acquired with partnership funds, or interest is shown, it is deemed to be partnership property. If acquired in the partnership name, however, the legal title can be conveyed only in the partnership name.

A partner's interest as a tenant in partnership is not subject to attachment or execution based on a claim against a partner individually as long as the suit was not the object of partnership activity. However, a partner's interest in the partnership can be reached by a creditor's proceeding based on a claim against the partner who was acting within the course of scope of the partnership which gave rise to the claim.

When a partnership is dissolved, the partnership is not terminated as such but continues until the winding-up of the partnership affairs and a complete accounting. Such winding-up includes the conveyance or distribution of the partnership property.

ENCUMBRANCES AND LIENS

Encumbrances

An encumbrance is anything that affects the title of use of property. It is sometimes described as anything that loads or burdens title, or it may be defined as a charge or limitation on ownership. However, as can be seen from the following discussion, it may be both a benefit as well as a burden, depending on the relationship of the parties affected. Although many variations of encumbrances exist, there are four principal types.

Encroachment. An encroachment is the building of a structure or construction of any improvements partially or wholly on the property of another. Such extension onto another's property constitutes a trespass, which may be enjoined either by mutual agreement of the parties involved or by court action. Unlike liens, encroachments restrict the use and enjoyment of the affected property to the extent that one's property is effectively reduced in size and therefore limited in its potentially full development.

Easements. Easements are nonpossessory, and the types, methods of creation, and their termination were discussed previously. To the extent that one's property is used in some way for the benefit of another, the result is an encumbrance to the so-called servient tenant.

Restrictions. Restrictions consist of covenants and conditions found in deeds and other instruments. The owner of real property may be restricted or prohibited from doing certain things relating to the property or from using it for certain purposes. For example: "the lot may be used only for the construction of a single family dwelling of at least 1000 square feet and at a cost of no less than $50,000."

Covenants are restrictions wherein a promise to do or not to do certain things to the property is found in deeds. If broken, the remedies available to the party who had imposed the covenant are either an injunction against continued breach or an action for money damages.

Conditions are restrictions that are treated more stringently by the grantor than a mere covenant. In addition to the two remedies available for violation of a covenant, the grantor may seek a third: recover the property through reversion, called a "right of reverter." Because of its harshness, amounting to a forfeiture, the courts are hesitant to interpret a restriction as a condition. Therefore, unless clearly set forth in unambiguous terms, restrictions are generally viewed as covenants and not as conditions.

Liens

Liens constitute a class of encumbrance which does not restrict the use and enjoyment of property. A lien is a charge against property, representing a debt or legal procedure by which to collect money for which realty is security. Liens may be classified as general liens, affecting all property owned by the debtor, and specific, affecting only one parcel; they may also be classed as voluntary or involuntary.

Voluntary. Voluntary or contractual liens are created by the voluntary acts of the parties to a contract. Most of these are in the nature of a security device and therefore constitute a lien.

Mortgages. Mortgages are two-party instruments: the borrower is called the "mortgagor," the lender the "mortgagee." Like the deed of trust, a mortgage is a contract whereby property is hypothecated for the purpose of securing a debt or obligation. However, no title is transferred, and the mortgage could outlaw, that is, become uncollectable, after 4 years if the lender takes no action to recover the debt during this period. In contrast, because legal title rests in a third party in the case of a trust deed, such instruments do not bar beneficiaries from pursuing legal action even after 4 years, even though the promissory note—the primary evidence of the debt—outlaws after 4 years.

Very few mortgages exist in some states. Because of the ease of foreclosure, the elimination of redemption rights following a trustee's sale, and the indefinite continuance of the third-party interest as long as the debt remains unpaid, the deed of trust is obviously favored.

Trust Deeds. Trust deeds are three-party instruments: the borrower is called the "trustor," the lender the "beneficiary." A third party, "the trustee," ordinarily a corporation, stands between the trustor and beneficiary and is vested with the legal title with "power of sale." That is, the trustee is empowered to sell the property given as security for a loan only in the event that the debt is not paid and then only on instructions from the beneficiary.

Similarly, after the loan has been fully paid, the trustee is instructed to reconvey legal title to trustor, accomplished through a "reconveyance deed." Because the trustee can act under only these two circumstances, it is said to have a mere naked, or bare, legal title which lies dormant ("inchoate") until the debt is repaid.

If the loan is not paid according to the terms of the trust deed, the trustee will ordinarily be instructed by beneficiary to sell the property at auction to raise funds to pay off the unpaid debt. Such a "trustee's sale" must be accomplished in accordance with prescribed legal procedures, which typically involve a term of not less than 3 months and 3 weeks. A 3-month period of reinstatement exists following the recordation of a "notice of default" in the county in which the property is located. Advertising for such sale must then take place for no less than 20 days, during which time the trustor may redeem by paying the entire unpaid balance of the loan, plus penalties and costs.

Following a sale, the successful bidder receives a "trustee's deed," and the sale is said to be "absolute," that is, no right of redemption exists for the trustor. However, if the trustee pursued the sale by "court action," or suit tried in a superior court, the trustor is allowed a period of up to 1 year to redeem, just as is allowed under a mortgage foreclosure.

Land Contracts. Land contracts, or whatever other name they may be designated, were discussed in the section on contracts. A land contract creates a voluntary lien, since the buyer, or vendee, agrees to purchase real property under terms that provide for the ultimate delivery of a deed only after the vendee has fulfilled certain conditions of the contract, namely, the payment of all or a certain part of the purchase price through regular installments. Meanwhile, as "equitable owner" the vendee is given possession of the property.

Involuntary Liens. Involuntary liens are those not voluntarily created by debtors. They become a charge against property by operation of law. Hence, they are also referred to as statutory liens.

Mechanic's Liens. Mechanic's liens are those created by the state constitution in favor of contractors, subcontractors, laborers, and the like who have contributed to a work of improvement on real property and have not been paid for their labor or materials. The law in most states prescribes that a prelien notice in the form of a "notice of intent to lien" must be filed with the county recorder's office within so many days (20 in California) of commencement of work. The period of filing a lien varies from as few as 30 days to not more than 90 days after completion of a building or other work of improvement.

Many states provide for two recordings of a notice of completion by the owner after the work of improvement is completed. In California, if a notice of completion is filed by the owner within 10 days after the job is completed, the original contractor has 60 days in which to file a lien, and all others have 30 days. If no notice of completion is recorded, all parties have 90 days.

Should a job not be completed due to acts of God, strikes, impossibility of performance, disagreements causing work stoppage, or any other reason, then a notice of cessation of labor or notice of abandonment may be filed. This has the same time effect as the recording of a completion notice.

A mechanic's lien may take priority over other liens which were placed on the property after the job was started. This is referred to as the "doctrine of relation back," and all others furnishing labor or materials thereafter will share on par, as their financial interests may appear, even though they appeared subsequent to the creation of trust deed or other liens. For this reason, construction lenders and others making loans will carefully check to determine that no work has been started before committing themselves to a loan.

Anyone filing a mechanic's lien must institute a suit for foreclosure of the lien within the statutory number of days (90 days in California) after recordation of said lien. The suit is similar to a mortgage foreclosure, resulting in a court-ordered sale to satisfy the claims. In event of insufficient funds following the sale, the court may award a deficiency judgment against the debtor for the balance.

Sometimes a lien is filed against property whose owner did not contract for the improvement, as when a tenant negotiates a contract for major repairs or alterations to a leasehold. For protection, the owner may repudiate responsibility and liability by recording a "notice of nonresponsibility" within so many days (10 in California) of the time he or she acquired knowledge. In addition, a copy of the notice must be posted on the property. The contractor would then have to look to the contract for remedy, that is, sue the contracting party for collection.

A mechanic's lien may be discharged by the running of the statute of limitations, that is, after 90 days if no foreclosure action is commenced; by written release, through the recordation of a "release of mechanic's lien"; by the issuance of a bond to release the lien; by satisfaction of the judgment lien against the debtor; by foreclosure of a prior lien; and by dismissal of the action when the court is convinced that a valid claim is not sustainable.

Assessment Liens. Assessment liens are imposed on properties benefitting from improvements that are classified as "off-site" improvements, such as street widening, installation of street lights, gutters, curbs, storm drains, sewers, and drainage. A number of laws allow for the imposition of this special kind of tax on the benefitted property, such as California's Street Improvement Act of 1911. This state law provides that adjoining owners are to be assessed or charged a proportionate share of the costs, depending on how much their properties benefit. They can either pay the assessment in full within 30 days after completion or pay the lien in installments over a period not to exceed 15 years through an assessment bond.

Property Taxes. Property taxes are the main source of revenue for local governments. They become a lien on the same day of each year, and the property that does not "pay its way" may be sold to the state and ultimately auctioned off at public sale to discharge the debt.

Sales Taxes. Should a merchant not remit sales or use taxes required on certain retail sales transactions, her or his property may be liened for the amount of taxes owed plus penalties.

Income Taxes. When a property owner fails to pay income taxes due to federal, state, or local governments, the property can be encumbered with a lien as in the case of sales taxes.

Attachment Lien. An attachment lien is a form of encumbrance that applies on unsecured transactions. It is seizure of property by court order to make the property available if a judgment is obtained in a pending lawsuit.

Gift Taxes. Gift taxes are due on transfer of property exceeding the statutory exemptions. Once gifts exceed the allowable exemptions, taxes are due. If not paid, they constitute a lien against the real property of the donor, who is responsible for filing a return and for payment of the taxes due.

Estate Taxes. Estate taxes are due on the net estate of a decedent, subject to exemptions which increase each year. A marital deduction is allowed for married couples.

Inheritance taxes are levied against the heirs to the estate on their respective distributive shares. The amount due depends on the relationships of the devisee or heir, since exemptions are also provided and the exact amount is determined by the relationship of the heir to the testator.

As with other taxes, such federal and state liabilities may become a charge against the property of the estate and against the devisees.

Execution Liens. Execution liens are levied against a property which is ordered sold by court for nonpayment of a debt. In general, an execution follows a judgment rendered against the property, paying in full the amount for which the property was sold with interest and expenses.

CHANGES IN LAND USE

Now that we have a fundamental understanding of property, estates in land, ownership, and encumbrances, we shall examine how some of these fundamentals apply to changes and trends in land use.

Trends in land use can evolve slowly or swiftly depending on a great number of factors: the influx of people to a given area; changing public tastes in housing and shopping preferences; customs and habits of people in the community; an increase or decrease in spendable income in an area; costs of land, money, materials; gradual changes in the age of residents; local taxing methods; and local requirements (or lack of them) to maintain property in a safe, neat condition. Local building codes also change requirements for use of materials, types of structures allowed, types of uses permitted, and control of off-site advertising signs and new industries. Planners, demographic specialists, census analysts, large lending institutions, major builders, and suppliers will try to project trends as accurately as possible so that changing needs and desires can be met in an orderly fashion.

Residential Land

Laws are expanding to accommodate a greater variety of houses and apartments. Governing bodies seek ways to encourage the development of new housing stock at a greater variety of prices, to streamline the processing of the various permits, and to encourage the rehabilitation of older housing stock. Many cities have declared a willingness to work with developers and the housing industry to find new ways to provide desperately needed moderately priced housing. Real estate professionals must keep abreast of these constantly changing regulations, since ignorance can prove very costly if building plans have to be redrawn to accommodate new standards of insulation, fire resistant materials, hard wire smoke detectors, and so on. Another example of a change that will have great impact on real estate activity is the state provision that mobile homes can no longer be automatically barred from land zoned for single-family dwellings.

Frequent changes in government housing subsidies must be followed diligently. Newspapers, trade periodicals, and industry newsletters are the best sources for this information.

New types of home ownership also have had an impact on the housing industry. Among the most frequently encountered types are condominiums, stock cooperatives, own-your-own apartments, and planned residential developments.

Condominiums

The condominium method of ownership is the separate, fee simple ownership of individual units (interests in space) with tenancy in common ownership of common areas. Owners of condominium units receive deeds giving them absolute ownership of their units. Occupants own their own units, secure their own financing, receive individual tax bills, and may acquire title insurance policies on the property. Separate mortgages and other liens attach to the unit and may be foreclosed and the unit sold separately from other units in the condominium. Normally, an elected governing board performs the management function, and monthly assessments are made to cover the costs of maintenance for the common areas. The sale of the condominium does not require the approval of the other owners, and the owner's easement in the common areas passes to the new owner.

The condominium plan and the covenants, conditions, and restrictions must exist and be recorded. Also, if a condominium project has a certain number of units, some states will regulate it as a subdivision.

All states have enacted legislation authorizing condominium ownership. As long as legal requirements are met, a condominium project can take any form, from single-story townhouse to high-rise, and be for any lawful use, from residential to industrial to commercial.

Condominium units are conceived as cubes of space bounded by floor, ceiling, and wall surfaces. The common area, title to which is held by all owners as tenants in common, is ordinarily composed of the land together with all structural portions of the buildings, including plumbing, electrical pipes and conduits, as well as all bearing walls, roofs, and foundations. Basically, only the enclosed cube of space above the surface of the land is separately owned.

With respect to the duration of its enjoyment, a condominium estate or interest may be (1) an estate of inheritance or a perpetual estate; (2) an estate for life; or (3) an estate for years, such as a leasehold or a subleasehold.

Normally, there are three minimum requisites for every condominium deed, as follows: (1) The description must include an interest in the common area. By statutory definition, the common area is presumed to be owned in equal shares by the various condominium owners. Essentially, the common area is the entire project except the units owned in severalty. (2) The deed must include a description of the unit or units to be acquired in severalty. It will usually be sufficient to refer to the unit designations as they are shown on the diagrammatic map or on the subdivision map. (3) The deed must also include the imposition of the declaration of restrictions. It is the customary practice to incorporate and impose the declaration of restrictions in every deed by reference to the record of the declaration.

In summary, the nature of a condominium gives to each buyer in a multiple development an undivided interest in the land on which the structure is built and, in addition, gives the buyer a fee interest in a cube or unit of airspace, that is, the space or apartment enclosed by four walls, the lower surface of the ceiling, and upper surface of the floor.

Ownership of such a dwelling unit is a divided interest, and each owner is entitled to a separate tax bill and can obtain a separate encumbrance and a separate policy of title insurance covering his or her interest. The concept of condominium applies not only to single-family homes but also to office buildings, industrial parks, shopping centers, and other commercial developments.

Stock Cooperatives

A form of multioccupant project often confused with condominium is a stock cooperative. The latter is distinguished from a condominium in that the legal title to the entire project is vested in a single entity, which may be a cooperative association, a nonprofit corporation, or a cooperative housing corporation. An individual purchaser does not receive a deed but instead receives a share of stock or a certificate of beneficial interest, with the right to occupy a particular apartment. The purchaser has a proprietary lease and is sometimes referred to as a "tenant stockholder."

Such projects are normally financed by a blanket encumbrance constituting a lien on the entire project. Heretofore, the real property taxes were assessed to the title-holding entity and were a lien on the project as a whole. Now it is possible for the owners of stock cooperatives and other forms of multiple ownership to obtain separate assessments and tax bills.

The management of the title-holding entity is generally exercised by a board of directors composed of and elected by the owner-tenants. A disadvantage of the cooperative plan in the minds of some prospective residential owners is the fact that the purchaser has no evidence of title, such as a deed. Nor do owners have a land interest to hypothecate (offer as security) for their own mortgages—unless the lender is willing to accept a stock pledge or an assignment of the tenant's beneficial interest. Frequently, however, such stock or beneficial interest is subject to a prohibition against hypothecation.

Since the corporation or association is the sole legal owner of the entire cooperative project, it alone can mortgage the property, customarily under a "blanket" loan covering the land and the building, which includes all the living units. The corporation, being the owner, has the direct responsibility for payments of all encumbrances, which may include unsegregated taxes and assessments as well as mortgages. Thus, the purchaser in a cooperative project may be concerned about a possible loss of investment through the foreclosure of an obligation arising out of defaults other than her or his own. Although such purchaser agrees to pay a proportionate amount of the mortgage and tax payments, the failure of any one to pay his or her share may result in burden to be assumed by the other purchasers if foreclosure of the lien on the whole property is to be avoided. Hence, the reason for obtaining separate tax assessments.

Differences between Condominiums and Cooperatives

The major difference between a condominium and a cooperative is that in a condominium each unit is owned individually. In a cooperative, a corporation owns the project, and the tenant has a proprietary lease and owns shares in the corporation.

In a condominium, owners can usually sell their units to anyone who can pay for them, and in a cooperative the corporation must approve of the proposed tenant. Sometimes a condominium owner holds a unit subject to a right of first refusal in the other unit owners. The other owners have the first opportunity to purchase the unit.

Many cooperative agreements contain a "right of first refusal." Hence, if you wished to sell your unit, the corporation's bylaws would specify that an option be granted for some specified time—usually 30 days—in which the corporation may buy the stock for a price that is determined according to a formula set out in the bylaws. By contrast, such right of first refusal options are accorded to condominiums only when an apartment house is being converted to condominiums. In such cases, the tenants are ordinarily given the first right to purchase their apartment unit.

Community Apartments

Community apartments can be distinguished from a stock cooperative because they have no single title-holding entity. The occupants usually own an undivided interest in the entire project as tenants in common with the other owners and an exclusive right to possession of a specific unit or apartment. Each purchaser receives a deed describing his or her undivided or fractional interest in the whole project.

The control and management are generally provided for in a declaration of restrictions, which may also provide for maintenance assessments, voting rights, and so on. As with condominiums and stock cooperatives, an association serves as a forum and governing body for the community apartment.

Although the apparent intent of the own-your-own plan was to provide an arrangement by which purchasers could deal with their titles independently, the plan does not fully satisfy some prospective buyers. Although the purchasers can offer what they own in the land and building as security for an individual mortgage, some institutional lenders have been unwilling to make loans on fractional interests.

Also, the advocates of these plans have not been able to segregate satisfactorily blanket encumbrances for the benefit of individual owners and lenders. Thus, as in the case of a stock cooperative, the purchaser of an own-your-own apartment could face a possible loss of the investment through foreclosure of obligations arising out of the other people's defaults on the unsegregated taxes and assessments as well as blanket encumbrances.

Planned Residential Developments

The ingenuity of real estate developers has been responsible for the creation of as many varieties of planned developments as there have been developers. These developments are designed to meet individual needs in areas of diminishing available land. Such projects have been designated by many names, such as "townhouse development" and "postage stamp subdivisions." Also called "planned unit developments" (PUDs), this type of subdivision provides for high-density housing, often with as many as eleven to fifteen or more units per acre. The more common form consists of separately owned parcels with additional parcels owned in common.

Usually, the commonly owned parcels are the areas or facilities shared and enjoyed by all residents, such as recreational areas. The management and control of the common areas is usually handled by an owners' association created in accordance with the provisions of a recorded declaration of restrictions, with each owner holding stock, shares, or a certificate of membership in the association.

Such projects are similar to a condominium in that the units are generally owned in severalty, and ownership of the common area is shared.

The following is a list of the characteristics of planned residential developments:

- Usually the boundaries of each owner's small lot coincide exactly with the limits of his or her apartment, which is in a building located on several of these small lots.
- A purchaser of any one such small lot acquires, in addition, title to that portion of the improvement located on that lot (i.e., the apartment and that part of the structure enclosing it).
- Side, rear, and front yard areas, which would otherwise be required for building setbacks under local ordinances, are usually pooled within large "green area" lots shown separately on the map.
- Since these green area lots are designed for the common use and benefit of all residents in the development and include within their confines the general landscaping, recreational, and service facilities, it is customary that they be jointly owned.

• Titles or ownerships in a planned residential development are vested in individual purchasers, such as in a conventional subdivision. Each such purchaser receives a grant deed describing a full interest in her or his particular lot (apartment), together with an undivided interest in the green area lots.

The difference between a unit in a planned residential development and a condominium is based on the structural characteristics of the two parcels. In a unit of a PUD (a "townhouse"), no one else owns an interest above or below the structure; therefore, the owner also holds title to the ground on which the structure rests. However, a condominium may have individual owners living above or below each, as in an apartment house, so the land under the structure must be considered part of the commonly owned area.

Townhouses

The term "townhouse" was first used to describe the city residence of one whose main house was in the country. Today, a typical townhouse is a two-story structure containing multiple units joined together physically as an apartment, but for which an owner holds title to the land under the unit.

Whether part of a 2-unit building or a 200-unit building, a townhouse has a certain basic structure. Townhouse residents have no one living above or below them. The unit and the land on which a townhouse rests are conveyed together to an owner. Depending on the provisions in the deed, a townhouse may take on the form of a "townhouse condominium," or it may be part of a planned unit development. When the units are connected to each other by common walls, forming one continuous building—such as those found in San Francisco or New York—the term "row houses" may be used.

Sometimes the word "plex" is used. If two units are connected to each other, the structure is a duplex; if three, a triplex; if four, a four-plex or quadraplex. A person may own an entire "plex," occupying one unit and renting out the others.

Time-Sharing

Time-sharing is a form of ownership that is receiving increased attention, particularly in resort areas, and many states are therefore requiring that when there are a certain number of time-share ownerships contained in a given project the subdivision act applies. Under time-sharing, a person acquires the right to exclusive use of a unit in a condominium or other multiple-housing development for a specified period of time each year. In effect, each unit is owned by a number of persons, the number depending on the number of time periods that make up a year. For example, if a unit is purchased on a 2-week time-share plan by twenty-six people, each of the owners has an exclusive right to occupy the premises during his or her 2-week ownership period.

There are two kinds of time-sharing. One is the time-sharing *estate*, where the investor is given an ownership interest for a fractional period of the year. The other is time-sharing *use*, where one buys a membership or license but not an interest in the land; here the buyer would not have any equity in the unit, and therefore such units would be lower priced.

The traditional forms of buying, selling, leasing, and renting have been around for centuries, but time-sharing is relatively new and untested. Buyers and sellers should therefore seek competent advice of counsel when investing.

Chapter 20

Real Estate License Law

Dennis S. Tosh   J. Ed Turner Chair of Real Estate, University of Mississippi

oday, if you live in any one of the fifty states, the District of Columbia, the Canadian provinces, Guam, or the Virgin Islands and you engage in real estate brokerage activities, you must be licensed. To broker real estate and/or engage in similarly defined activities without first obtaining such a license can result in very serious consequences.

During the early years of this century many states began to recognize the need for regulating certain real estate activities by imposing rules and regulations for anyone engaged in such activities. At the same time, the National Association of Real Estate Boards (today known as the National Association of Realtors) took the position that people engaged in these activities should indeed be regulated by the states in which they were doing business. Accordingly, jurisdictions began to regulate via the same means, namely, the issuing of a real estate license to those persons defined as being engaged in real estate brokerage. The state of Oregon in 1913 passed the first real estate license law later upheld in the courts as being constitutional.*

*Robert W. Semenow, *Questions and Answers on Real Estate* (9th ed.), Prentice-Hall, Englewood Cliffs, N.J., 1978, p. 553.

WHY LICENSE BROKERS?

The justification for requiring a real estate license is the same in every jurisdiction—*the protection of the public.* The purpose is not, as some people may think, to raise money for the state treasury or real estate commission. As jurisdictions have enacted real estate license law, people have challenged the constitutionality of requiring an individual to obtain and maintain a license to engage legally in real estate activities. The argument commonly used is that a person without a license is being deprived of the opportunity to make a living. Yet time and time again courts have ruled that states do have such power as provided for under the police power reserved to each state by the Constitution of the United States. This power permits states to do whatever necessary to protect the health, safety, morality, welfare, and property of the citizens of that state. Thus states have the power to restrict real estate brokerage activities to those people who meet and maintain certain minimum standards.

WHO MUST BE LICENSED?

In general, anyone defined as "brokering" real estate must be licensed. The term "brokering" is broadly defined as: "That part of the real estate business concerned with the bringing together of parties involved in a real estate transaction." Examples of brokering include selling, buying, leasing, renting, and exchanging property.

Real Estate Broker

A real estate broker is defined as: "Any person, association, partnership, or corporation *who for another* and for a *fee, commission* or any other *valuable consideration* performs any of the following acts: sells, purchases, exchanges, leases, rents and or who attempts to do any of these acts." Note that a broker does not have to be a natural person; a corporation or a partnership can be a broker. Also, observe that one does not have to be successful to be included in the definition. If you do it, attempt to do it, or hold yourself out as doing it, then in terms of definition, and thus regulation, you have done it and are subject to regulation.

Real Estate Salesperson

A real estate salesperson is defined as: "Any *person* licensed to perform *on behalf of a real estate broker* any act or acts authorized to be performed by the real estate broker." A salesperson, then, must be a natural person, not a corporation or partnership, and such a person is only licensed to work on behalf of someone else, namely, a real estate broker. A real estate salesperson is not licensed to work on his or her own behalf or on behalf of just anyone, specifically, just any broker. Rather, a salesperson is licensed to work on behalf of one broker.

A common practice, particularly in residential real estate transactions, is to refer to a real estate salesperson as an "agent." For example, "I'm a real estate agent with ABC Realty." While such casual reference may be all right when introducing yourself or explaining your occupation, the use of the word "agent" has an entirely different meaning within a real estate context.*

Others

In addition to those defined as real estate brokers or real estate salespersons, persons engaged in numerous other related activities must also be licensed. This varies somewhat from state to state, but activities requiring a real estate license include the following:

Property managers—All but seven states require that anyone who manages real property belonging to others be licensed as a broker.†

Seller of cemetery lots—Six states require a broker's license for selling cemetery lots.

Appraisers—Nine states require an appraiser to be licensed as either broker or salesperson. In addition, four states require a special license for appraisers of real estate.

Mortgage bankers and mortgage brokers—Fourteen jurisdictions require mortgage bankers and mortgage brokers in their jurisdiction to be licensed as real estate brokers, and twelve jurisdictions have a separate license for anyone defined as such.

People dealing in mineral, oil, and gas leases—Only six states require a broker's license, for people who deal in mineral, oil, and gas leases, and four other states have a separate license requirement.

Auctioneers—Twenty-nine jurisdictions require that auctioneers be licensed as real estate brokers.

*For a discussion of the term "agent," see Chapter 21.
†Summary information on persons required to be licensed in each jurisdiction is available in the National Association of Real Estate License Law Officials, *Annual Report of the Interstate Corporation Committee.* Copies of this report may be obtained at a cost of $15 per copy from Robert H. Peterson, executive vice-president, NARELLO, Sunset Valley Law Building, 2580 South 90 Street, Omaha, Nebraska 68124.

Subdividers, developers, and builders—The regulation of subdividers, developers, and builders varies greatly from jurisdiction to jurisdiction. In some states a builder is exempt from being licensed when selling his or her own homes. However, anyone else attempting to sell the homes would have to be licensed. Subdividers and developers fall under a great deal of regulation, from both the real estate agency as well as other state agencies. In addition, federal agencies are also involved in the regulation of subdividing and developing land.

Anyone currently engaged in any of these activities or contemplating beginning one of them is advised to check with the appropriate state authorities as to whether a real estate license or any other license is required prior to commencing work.

Exemptions

As noted, persons engaged in particular real estate activities may need a license in one state but not in another. Although exemptions vary from jurisdiction to jurisdiction, the following are among the more common:

Persons appointed by or acting under court order to oversee the property of another, such as a trustee, administrator, or guardian

Public officers, such as housing officials or tax assessors, while performing their official duties

Financial intermediaries such as commercial banks or savings and loan associations involved in managing and selling property acquired by them through foreclosures

Individual owners of real estate who wish to sell their own property

Home builders selling homes constructed by them for sale to the general public

Persons holding a power of attorney from someone who has authorized her or him to represent the owner in a single transaction for the purpose of buying or selling real estate.

WHO ISSUES REAL ESTATE LICENSES?

Included in the licensing law in every jurisdiction are provisions for the creation of a real estate board or commission. These regulatory bodies carry out the statutory provisions of the licensing law. In addition, a real estate board or commission implements the rules and regulations needed to carry out the responsibilities of the commission, namely, the regulation of real estate activities. Thus, a commission has state statutes that it must uphold, such as the minimum age requirement for a real estate broker's license, as well as rules and regulations that it chooses to establish to perform its duties. For example, by statute a particular state may require that a written examination be passed prior to the issuing of a real estate license, and thus the commission is required by law to administer such an exam. The particulars as to how long the exam will last, the minimum passing score, and where the exam will be given are generally not included in the statutes; rather, such specifics would be established by the commission as part of its rules and regulations. Such regulations are not law, but, as long as they do not conflict with statutes, they have the same effect on licensees as if they were law.

The names and addresses of all state and province officials follow. Anyone with particular questions about the requirements or licensing laws in a particular jurisdiction should contact the appropriate commission.*

State and Province Administrative Officials

Alabama

Mrs. M. L. Goodwin, Director
Real Estate Commission
State Capitol
Montgomery, Alabama 36130
205-832-3266

Alaska

James L. Magowan, Executive Secretary
Department of Commerce & Economic Development
142 East Third Avenue
Anchorage, Alaska 99501
402-276-7969

Alberta

R. A. Nolan, Superintendent of Real Estate
Department of Consumer and Corporate Affairs
9th Floor, Capital Square
10065 Jasper Avenue
Edmonton, Alberta, Canada T5J 3B1
403-427-2244

Arizona

R. B. Nicholls, Commissioner
Department of Real Estate
1645 West Jefferson
Phoenix, Arizona 85007
602-255-4345

Arkansas

Roy L. Bilheimer, Executive Secretary
Real Estate Commission
1 Riverfront Place, S. 660
North Little Rock, Arkansas 72114
501-371-1247

*Real estate commissions publish their rules and regulations in text or pamphlet form. In the majority of states free copies are available, although in some a minimal fee is charged.

British Columbia

P. Dermot Murphy, Secretary
Real Estate Council
608-626 West Pender Street
Vancouver, British Columbia
  V6B 1V9
604-683-9664

California

David H. Fox, Commissioner
Department of Real Estate
714 P Street
Sacramento, California 95814
916-445-3996

Colorado

Keith T. Koske, Director
Real Estate Commission
110 State Service Bldg.
Denver, Colorado 80203
303-839-2633

Connecticut

Laurence L. Hannafin, Executive
  Director
Real Estate Commission
90 Washington Street
Hartford, Connecticut 06115
203-566-5130

Delaware

Sue Stiers, Administrative Assis-
  tant
Real Estate Commission
P.O. Box 1401
Dover, Delaware 19901
302-678-4186

District of Columbia

Clara Doleman
D. C. Real Estate Commission
614 H Street, N.W., Rm. 109
Washington, D.C. 20001
202-629-4543

Florida

C. B. Stafford, Executive Director
Real Estate Commission
400 West Robinson Street
P.O. Box 1900
Orlando, Florida 32802
305-423-6053

Georgia

Charles Clark, Commissioner
Real Estate Commission
40 Pryor Street, S.W.
Atlanta, Georgia 30303
404-656-3916

Guam

Johnny S. Chaco
Real Estate Examiner
Department of Revenue and Tax-
  ation
Division of Insurance, Banking &
  Real Estate
P.O. Box 2796
Agana, Guam 96910

Hawaii

Yukio Higuchi, Executive Secre-
  tary
Professional & Voc. Licensing Di-
  vision
Department of Regulatory Agen-
  cies
Real Estate Commission
P.O. Box 3469
Honolulu, Hawaii 96801
808-548-7464

Idaho

C. Julian Welke, Executive Secre-
  tary
Real Estate Commission
State Capitol Building
Boise, Idaho 83270
208-384-3363

Illinois

Val J. Budd, Jr., Commissioner
Real Estate Commission
17 North State Street
Chicago, Illinois 60602
312-341-9810

Indiana

Gary A. Price, Executive Director
Real Estate Commission
100 N. Senate Ave., Room 1022
Indianapolis, Indiana 46204
317-633-5386

Iowa

Eugene O. Johnson, Director
Real Estate Commission
Executive Hills, Suite 205
Des Moines, Iowa 50319
515-281-3183

Kansas

J. Paul Flower, Director
Real Estate Commission
Room 1212, 535 Kansas
Topeka, Kansas 66603
913-296-3411

Kentucky

Marcella W. Horney, Administrative Director
Real Estate Commission
100 E. Liberty, Suite 204
Louisville, Kentucky 40202
502-588-4462

Louisiana

Harry M. Hollins, Executive Director
Louisiana Real Estate Commission
P.O. Box 14785
Baton Rouge, Louisiana 70808
504-389-7755

Maine

Paul A. Sawyer, Director
Department of Business Regulation
Real Estate Commission
4th Floor, State Office Building
Augusta, Maine 04333
207-289-3735

Maryland

Charles G. Chambers, Executive Director
Real Estate Commission
One South Calvert St.
Room 600
Baltimore, Maryland 21202
301-383-2130

Massachusetts

Angela M. Mullins
Head Administrative Assistant
Board of Registration of Real Estate Brokers and Salesmen
100 Cambridge Street
Boston, Massachusetts 02202
617-727-3055

Michigan

Dwight A. Snyder
Deputy Real Estate Commissioner
Department of Licensing & Regulation
P.O. Box 30018
Lansing, Michigan 48909
517-373-0490

Minnesota

Barbara M. Kivisto, Real Estate Director
Real Estate Commission
500 Metro Square Building
St. Paul, Minnesota 55101
612-296-6319

Mississippi

Phillip D. Hardwick, Administrative Officer
Real Estate Commission
1920 Dunbarton Street
Jackson, Mississippi 39216
601-292-7656

Missouri

Roger M. Doyle, Executive Secretary
Real Estate Commission
3523 North Ten Mile Drive
P.O. Box 1339
Jefferson City, Missouri 65101
314-751-2334

Montana

Michael A. Devich, Administrator
Board of Real Estate
1424 9th Avenue
Helena, Montana 59601
406-449-2961

Nebraska

Paul Quinlan, Director
Real Estate Commission
301 South Centennial Mall
Lincoln, Nebraska 68509
402-471-2004

Nevada

R. Lynn Luman, Administrator
Real Estate Division
Department of Commerce
201 South Fall Street
Carson City, Nevada 89710
702-885-4280

New Hampshire

Alice C. Hallenborg, Executive Director
Real Estate Commission
3 Capital Street
Concord, New Hampshire 03301
603-271-2701

New Jersey

Joan Haberle, Secretary-Director
Real Estate Commission
201 East State Street
Trenton, New Jersey 08625
609-292-7656

New Mexico

Robert P. Harrelson, Executive Secretary
New Mexico Real Estate Commission
4000 San Pedro, N.E.
Albuquerque, New Mexico 87110
505-842-3226

New York

Donald L. McManus
Director of Regulated Affairs
Department of State
270 Broadway
New York, New York 10007
212-488-3670

North Carolina

Phillip T. Fisher, Secretary-Treasurer
Real Estate Commission
1200 Navaho Drive
P.O. Box 17100
Raleigh, North Carolina 27619
919-833-2771

North Dakota

Dennis D. Schulz, Secretary-Treasurer
Real Estate Commission
410 East Thayer Avenue
P.O. Box 727
Bismarck, North Dakota 58501
701-224-2749

Ohio

Charles H. McClenaghan, Superintendent
Department of Commerce
Division of Real Estate
180 East Broad Street, 14th Fl.
Columbus, Ohio 43215
614-466-4100

Oklahoma

Charles C. Case, Jr., Executive Director
Real Estate Commission
4040 North Lincoln Blvd., Suite 100
Oklahoma City, Oklahoma 73105
405-521-2187

Ontario

J. P. Cox, Registrar
Ministry of Consumer and Commercial Relations
Business Practices Division
555 Yonge Street
Toronto, Canada M7A 2H6
416-963-0406

Oregon

William F. Gwinn, Commissioner
Real Estate Commission
158 12th Street, N.E.
Salem, Oregon 97310
503-378-4170

Pennsylvania

Pierce L. Clouser, Jr., Administrative Secretary
Department of State
Professional & Occupational Affairs
Real Estate Commission
P.O. Box 2649
Transportation & Safety Building

Harrisburg, Pennsylvania 17120
717-787-2121

Quebec

Real Martel, Superintendent
Service du Courtage Immobilier du Quebec
Ministere des Consommateurs Cooperatives et Institutions Financieres
800 Place d'youville
Quebec City G1R 4Y5
418-643-4597

Rhode Island

Donald L. Medici, Deputy Administrator
Real Estate Division
100 North Main Street
Providence, Rhode Island 02901
401-277-2255

Saskatchewan

E. M. Saunderson, Superintendent of Insurance, No. 308
1919 Rose Street
Regina S4F 3P1
306-565-2957

South Carolina

Fred B. Beall, Commissioner
Real Estate Commission
2221 Devine Street
Suite 530
Columbia, South Carolina 29205
803-758-3981

South Dakota

Jack C. Burchill, Executive Secretary
Real Estate Commission
P.O. Box 490
Pierre, South Dakota 57501
605-733-3600

Tennessee

Ann Tuck, Executive Director
Real Estate Commission
556 Capitol Hill Building
Nashville, Tennessee 37219
615-741-2273

Texas

Andy James, Administrator
Real Estate Commission
P.O. Box 12188, Capital Station
Austin, Texas 78711
512-475-4250

Utah

Stephen J. Francis, Director
Department of Business Regulation
Real Estate Division
330 East 4th South St.
Salt Lake City, Utah 84111
801-533-5661

Vermont

Nelda G. Rossi
Executive Secretary
Real Estate Commission
7 East State Street
Montpelier, Vermont 05641
802-828-3228

Virginia

David W. Seitz, Assistant Director
Real Estate
2 South 9th Street
Richmond, Virginia 23219
804-786-2161

Virgin Islands

Leonard Monsanto, Director
Division of Licensing
P.O. Box 2515
St. Thomas, Virgin Islands 00801
809-774-5024

Washington

Gordon L. Smith, Administrator
Real Estate Division
P.O. Box 247
Olympia, Washington 98504
206-753-6681

West Virginia

Donald E. Portis, Executive Secretary
Real Estate Commission
1033 Quarrier Street
Suite 400
Charleston, West Virginia 25301
304-348-3555

Wisconsin

Cletus J. Hansen
Bureau Director
Room 281, 1400 E. Washington
Madison, Wisconsin 53702
608-266-5450

Wyoming

Connie K. Anderson
Director of Real Estate
Supreme Court Building
Cheyenne, Wyoming 82002
307-777-7141

HOW TO OBTAIN A LICENSE

Every jurisdiction has very specific requirements for the issuance of either a real estate broker's or salesperson's license. Such requirements vary from state to state, but the following are common throughout the United States and Canada.

Age

Every jurisdiction has a minimum age requirement for both a broker's and salesperson's license. In the majority of states the minimum age is 18 years, although in some states, due to the experience requirement for a broker's license, the minimum age becomes 21.

Minimum Experience

States do not require any experience prior to obtaining a salesperson's license. By definition a real estate salesperson is licensed to work on behalf of someone else, and thus experience is acquired on the job. The majority of jurisdictions do, however, require a minimum amount of experience prior to the issuing of a broker's license. Such experience can be as high as 5 years as an active salesperson with proof of your activities during that period of time. Currently, only nine states do not require experience for someone seeking a broker's license.

Character

Since the purpose of licensing law is to protect the public, anyone licensed must be of good character and reputation. Jurisdictions often require an applicant to include the names and addresses of residents of the state who, if contacted, can verify the character of the applicant. In addition, included in the licensing law in most states is a code of ethics which all applicants agree to abide by and uphold. The code of ethics includes the licensee's relationship with the public, the client, and other licensees. In some states the code of ethics adopted by the National Association of Realtors is used, and in others a specific code of ethics is included as part of the licensing law.

Prelicensing Education

Prelicensing education varies greatly between jurisdictions. Almost all states have a statutory requirement for a minimum amount of formal education such as elementary school or high school for either a salesperson's or broker's license. Beyond the minimum formal education requirement, jurisdictions vary as to how much, if any, prelicensing real estate preparatory work is required. Currently, ten states do not have any such preparatory requirement for a salesperson's license, and nine states require none for a broker's license.

For the majority of states the means by which such preparatory courses can be met varies greatly. In all jurisdictions such courses can be completed through the completion of approved college and university courses. In addition, numerous states accept course work completed through the Realtor Institute Program offered by the state Realtor associations. Finally, some jurisdictions allow prelicensing courses to be offered through proprietary schools located within the state. Often such schools offer real estate courses geared specifically toward the licensing examinations.

Of all the prelicensing requirements, none changes as often as this one. Anyone seeking a real estate license should contact the state licensing agency to ascertain the latest prelicensing education requirements.

Written Examination

Every jurisdiction requires some proof that an applicant has a basic understanding of real estate principles and practices prior to the issuing of a license. In addition, the statutes and rules and regulations of the particular state in which the licensee is going to operate must be understood. Thus, a written examination is given, and an applicant must obtain a minimum passing score.

Even though the subject matter included is basically the same, all states do not use the same examination. Various examinations currently being used include the Real Estate Licensing Examinations, the ACT National Real Estate Examination, and others.

Real Estate Licensing Examinations

Approximately thirty jurisdictions use the examination developed and administered by the Educational Testing Service (ETS) in Princeton, New Jersey. Commonly referred to as the "ETS" exam, this examination consists of multiple choice questions developed to test the applicant's knowledge of basic real estate topics.

Broker Examination.   The broker examination consists of two separate tests, a uniform test and a state test. Eighty questions are asked on the uniform test and thirty to forty are included on the state test. Depending on the jurisdiction, the exam can last up to 4½ hours. The eighty questions cover topics within four broadly defined areas: real estate brokerage, 35 percent; contracts and other legal aspects, 27 percent; pricing and valuation, 15 percent; and financing and investment, 23 percent.

Approximately 20 percent of the questions on the uniform test require some type of mathematical calculation—real estate math is an important topic on the ETS examinations. The questions on the state test deal with specifics in that state. Topics include licensing requirements; hearing procedures; fair housing; code of ethics; and refusal, suspension, and revocation of a license. In most states a minimum passing score is required on the state exam as well as the uniform exam. Partial retake of one of the two examinations is permitted in the majority of jurisdictions.

Salesperson Examination. The salesperson examination also consists of two separate tests, a uniform test and a state test. The eighty questions on the uniform test cover topics in five broadly defined areas: real estate contracts, 13 percent; financing, 24 percent; real estate ownership, 22 percent; real estate brokerage, 24 percent; and real estate valuation, 17 percent. Approximately 20 percent of the questions on this exam also require some type of mathematical calculation. As is true with the state test for the broker's examination, the salesperson exam includes a thirty- to forty-question state examination. The state exam for each state is different for those applicants seeking a salesperson's license than for those sitting for a broker's license; however, the general topics covered on the two state exams are basically the same.

ACT National Real Estate Examination

More than ten states use the licensing examination developed by the American College of Testing (ACT) in Iowa City, Iowa. The format of the examination is all multiple choice questions and, as is true with the ETS examinations, the ACT questions cover the common body of knowledge that a prospective licensee is expected to understand.

Uniform Tests. Both salesperson and broker examinations consist of one hundred questions covering five subject areas. These five areas along with the percentage of questions within each area are as follows:

	Broker (%)	Salesperson (%)
Real estate transfer and law	50	50
Real estate valuation	15	17
Real estate finance	10	15
Specific fields	25	18

Although certain questions on the uniform exams require mathematical calculations, the emphasis on math is less on the ACT examinations than on the ETS examinations.

State Tests. Approximately one-third of the questions on the examinations cover topics peculiar to the licensing laws and statutes of each jurisdiction. Each jurisdiction participating in the ACT National Real Estate Examination determines both the number of questions to be included in this part of the examination and the minimum passing score that must be obtained.

One feature present in many jurisdictions using the ACT exam concerns reciprocity agreements. The majority of states currently using this exam have established either full or partial reciprocity with the other states using the examination. This means that a person licensed in one state who moves to another state using the same exam may not have to take all the examination prior to being licensed in his or her new state. In the majority of jurisdictions, the applicant need only pass the state examination to meet the examination requirement for a license.

Others

A few states do not participate in either of the national examination programs. In those states the examinations are developed and administered by various means. In most instances, the real estate commissions have staff personnel who oversee both the development and the administering and grading of the examination. The types of questions and topics covered on these exams vary greatly, although the general subject areas tested are the same as with the national examinations.

In two jurisdictions the real estate commissions work with a university in that state in the development and administering of the examination. As is true with those states who have personnel within their commissions to develop the examination, the real estate commission determines the topical areas and the type and number of questions to be included on these examinations.

Fees and Application Forms

Various fees must be paid prior to the issuing of either a salesperson or a broker license. These fees cover the processing of the license, examination, issuing of the license, and contributions to a recovery fund. In addition, all applications must be on the proper forms as provided by the particular jurisdiction in which one is seeking to be licensed.

Photograph and Fingerprints

The majority of jurisdictions require that an applicant include a current photograph as part of the application for a license. In addition, some states require the submission of fingerprints with the application.

Sponsor

As noted earlier, a real estate salesperson is defined as someone licensed to work on behalf of a real estate broker. Thus, to acquire a salesperson's license, one must have a licensed broker who is willing to hold the license. Jurisdictions normally require the broker of record to submit the application of anyone seeking a salesperson's license under that broker. Included in the application is a statement signed by the broker in which the broker agrees to abide by the rules and regulations governing the relationship between the broker and salespersons licensed under her or him.

Minimum Residency

In some jurisdictions an applicant must prove that he or she has been a resident of that state for a minimum period of time prior to applying for a real estate license. Such proof may come in the form of the establishment of a mailing address, the paying of income tax, or the registration of an automobile. Residency requirements vary greatly between states.

Recovery Fund or Bond

As part of the application fee, many jurisdictions require a contribution to a recovery fund maintained by the real estate commission. Such a fund serves people who have suffered a financial loss resulting either directly or indirectly from action or inaction of a licensee. In those states that have such a fund, the contribution of each licensee is usually a one-time payment, made at the time of application. In a few states, a minimum bond must be acquired by all licensees.

WHAT ACTIONS CAN RESULT IN LOSS OF LICENSE?

Anyone who does not meet the minimum prelicensing requirements as established by a particular real estate commission may be refused a license. Such is the power of the real estate commission. In addition, for all persons currently licensed, certain actions or inactions may result in either the suspension or revocation of an existing license. Among the more common reasons for having a license suspended or revoked are the following:

Willful misrepresentation or knowingly making a false promise either directly or through someone else.

Using any contract form or any advertising matter which includes the name of any association or professional organization of which the licensee is not a current member. For example, advertising as a Realtor when you are not.

Retaining the services of a person as a salesperson on a purely temporary or single-deal basis to evade the law in regard to paying a commission to a nonlicensed person.

Acting for more than one party in a transaction without the knowledge and consent of all parties in the transaction (note that the illegality is in the fact that the parties are unaware rather than in the representation of more than one party).

Representing or attempting to represent any other real estate broker as a real estate salesperson without the express knowledge and consent of the broker named in your salesperson's license.

Failing to account for and remit as soon as possible any moneys coming into your possession which belong to others.

Failing to promptly furnish a duplicate copy of all listings, leases, or sales contracts to all parties to the transaction.

Misleading or untruthful advertising, including advertising property for sale or for rent or offering to buy property as an agent or broker without disclosing in the advertising the name of the advertiser, the fact that she or he is an agent or broker, or, when such advertising is published over the name of a licensed salesperson, failure to disclose in the advertisement the name of the broker.

Paying or receiving any rebate, profit, compensation, or commission to an unlicensed person.

Soliciting or inducing any party to a contract, lease, or agreement to break such contract for the purpose of substituting a new contract, lease, or agreement where the soliciting or inducing is motivated by anticipating personal gain by the licensee.

Forgery, embezzlement, obtaining money under false pretenses, larceny, extortion, conspiracy to defraud, or other such offenses where the licensee has been convicted of such actions in a court of law.

Negligence or failure to disclose or to ascertain and disclose to any person with whom the licensee is dealing any material fact, data, or information concerning or relating to the property with which the licensee is dealing, which the licensee knew or should have known.

Any act or conduct which constitutes or demonstrates bad faith, incompetency, or untrustworthiness or dishonest, fraudulent, or improper dealings.

PENALTIES FOR LOSS OF LICENSE

Anyone holding either a real estate salesperson's or a broker's license undoubtedly acquired the license with the full intent and expectation of holding the license for as long as he or she should choose. However, as can be seen from the previous discussion, any number of activities or inactivities can, and often do, result in the loss of a license. The penalties for losing a real estate license can be quite severe.

Certainly the most obvious and indeed most severe penalty is the loss in your ability to engage in those activities which require a real estate license. Accordingly, a person is no longer able to earn the income associated with those activities. Real estate brokerage is the type of profession in which, with a great deal of hard work and effort, a person can make a great deal of money. Perhaps because of this some people believe that a real estate license is too easily obtained. However, for those people who believe this, let them be reminded that the same license which is "so easy to get" can also be quickly taken away and with that taking goes the ability to earn the income resulting from real estate brokerage activities.

In addition to loss of income, the suspension or revocation of a license may also result in either a fine, imprisonment, or both. The licensing law in each jurisdiction specifically states the dollar fine (generally the wording is: up to a maximum of so much) which shall be imposed if a licensee is deemed guilty of any activity which results in the suspension or revocation of his or her license. Further, provisions are included for the sentencing of a certain amount of imprisonment due to action or inaction on the part of a licensee.

For this reason, any person licensed as a real estate broker or salesperson should strive to stay abreast of the license law requirements in jurisdictions where he or she is engaged. The violation of real estate license law is certainly a good example of where "ignorance of the law is no excuse." As a professional agent,* a licensee is expected to keep informed and in cases where real estate brokers or salespersons have found themselves in a court of law as a result of a dispute or misunderstanding, courts have often ruled against the licensee on the grounds that he or she should know better and as a professional agent had the responsibility of being informed.

FUTURE OF LICENSE LAW

Although it is very difficult, if not impossible, to predict the future of any real estate–related activity, a few observations can be made in regard to the future and direction of real estate licensing law. In retrospect, less than 70 years have passed since the first real estate license law was enacted. During that period every jurisdiction has enacted some form of licensing law. Included in these laws have been increased

---

*A "professional agent" is defined as someone who is normally employed in a principal-agent relationship.

minimum educational requirements, additional prelicensing course work, and more and more postlicensing requirements. In short, states have continued to push for a better-educated and more knowledgeable real estate practitioner. The result has been a decrease in errors both of omission and of commission by real estate brokers and salespersons. Certainly the public has benefitted from these stricter requirements.

Jurisdictions continue to require additional amounts of continuing education for the licensees in their jurisdiction. Currently, more than twenty states have some type of continuing education for both brokers and salespersons. Such requirements have continued to increase, and many of the states who presently do not require any such continuing education are taking steps to require it in the near future. Such action raises the professional level of people engaged in real estate as a profession. Again, the main beneficiary is the general public.

If you are a licensee, keep yourself informed of the license law. The well-informed person is better able to serve her or his clients as well as more likely to succeed at whatever is undertaken.

Chapter 21

Agency Role of Real Estate Brokers

B. Nicholas Ordway Associate Professor of Finance and Real Estate, University of Texas at Arlington, and 1983–1984 Hawaii Real Estate Chairholder, University of Hawaii

A real estate broker acts as a special and professional "agent" for a client, known as a "principal." An agent is anyone who has the authority to act in the place of another. If the "scope of authority" is broad enough, the agent can bind the principal to contracts, sell and purchase property, or perform other business transactions. Normally, a real estate broker's scope of authority is very limited and usually restricted to finding a qualified buyer or property, but the real estate broker can be delegated very broad powers by the principal.

Accepting the role of an agent places special duties on the broker to act as a "fiduciary." A fiduciary is anyone on whom the law imposes special obligations to act in the best interests of another person. Examples of other fiduciary relationships include trustee-beneficiary, lawyer-client, and banker-depositor. Failing to fulfill one's fiduciary responsibilities can result in money damages, suspension or loss of license, imprisonment, and destruction of a business reputation in the community.

The agent has authority to create legal relationships on behalf of the principal. This agent can be employed by the principal as a "servant" or can be an "independent contractor." A person is considered a servant if the employer has the right to control the details of the person's work. An independent contractor contracts for certain results and retains control or discretion over how these results will be achieved.

This distinction between the servant and the independent contractor is important for several reasons. If a person is classified as a servant, then the employer is responsible for any civil damage which occurs while the servant is working within the scope of activities that are part of the employment. The employer is also responsible for worker's compensation and the withholding of social security and income taxes. The independent contractor—not the employer—is responsible for civil wrongs (torts). Likewise, an independent contractor is responsible for his or her own taxes.

There has been controversy in recent years as to whether salespersons working for a broker are servants or independent contractors. If a broker retains too much control over the details of a salesperson's work, the courts would ordinarily classify that salesperson as a servant.

There are several sources of law or business custom that define the agency role of the real estate broker. The most important of these include:

1. Common-law agency and contract principles
2. State licensing laws
3. Other state laws
4. Federal laws
5. Professional codes of ethics

Although these sources interact to create rights and duties of brokers and salespersons, for the purpose of analysis, this chapter will consider each source separately.

COMMON-LAW AGENCY AND CONTRACT PRINCIPLES

Real estate brokers must analyze principal-agent issues on several levels. First, there are issues associated with the employment of the broker by the client; second, there are the relationships formed by the employment of salespersons by the broker; and third, there are problems resulting from cooperative ventures with other brokers. Many of these issues or problems can be understood by applying common-law agency and contract principles.

The Agency Relationship

A threshold question that must be answered is whether an agency relationship has been created. Although there are other ways that an agency can be created, an ageny usually is created by an express appointment by the principal. An express agency may be created either orally or in writing. Some states require that a real estate broker be employed by a written agreement; other states will recognize oral appointments.

Most real estate agency relationships are formed when a seller employs a broker to find a qualified buyer for a property. The agreement to pay a commission is found in a "listing contract." There are three basic types of listing contracts that are common in this country: the open listing, the exclusive agency listing, and the exclusive right to sell.

Open Listing.   The open listing (also known as the "simple listing" or the "general listing") is an agreement that the broker will earn a commission if he or she is the efficient and procuring cause of a sale during a listing period. In this situation, the broker has a nonexclusive right to find a buyer who is ready, willing, and able to purchase the property. In other words, the seller retains the right to employ other brokers or to sell the property without the assistance of any broker. A commission will be earned only if the broker is the one who actually makes the sale. A broker is usually reluctant to accept an open listing. This is because the broker may spend a great deal of time and money trying to market the property only to discover that no commission has been earned because another broker has found a buyer or the property has been sold by the owner.

Exclusive Agency Listing.   An exclusive agency listing is one in which the broker is the exclusive agent for the owner. The broker is entitled to a full commission if the property is sold through the efforts of any other broker. Only if the owner is the procuring cause of the sale does the listing broker not earn a commission.

Exclusive Right to Sell.   Under an exclusive-right-to-sell listing, a broker is entitled to a full commission if anyone, including the owner, is the procuring cause of the sale during the listing period. What happens if a sale is imminent and the owner delays accepting an offer until after the listing period has expired? Unless the listing contract contains an extender or carry-over clause, the broker cannot collect a commission in most states. An extender or carry-over clause says that a broker is entitled to a commission for a specified period (for example, 90 days) from the expiration date of the listing if the property is sold to anyone who was shown the property during the listing period.

To facilitate marketing of properties, many brokers enter into a joint effort called a multiple listing service (MLS). Under an MLS, brokers agree to pool all their listings to allow any broker to show any properties that are in the pool. If a broker, other than the listing broker, is able to facilitate a sale, there is a prearrangement as to how the commission will be split. Normally, the selling broker receives a larger percentage of the commission than the listing broker. The selling broker is technically a subagent. Unlike a salesperson, who is the agent of a broker and who is solely responsible to the broker, the selling broker has a fiduciary relationship with the original broker's principal. This means the subagent may sue the seller in the subagent's own right. The original listing broker is not normally liable for the acts of the subagent. However, the listing broker is responsible for the acts of her or his salespersons.

In addition to the express appointment, an agency can be created by estoppel, by implication, by necessity, and by ratification. No agency can be created solely by the acts of the agent. For an agency to exist, the principal must have performed some action, made some statement, or failed to speak when there was a duty to do so.

Agency by Estoppel.   An agency by estoppel is created when the principal negligently leads a third person to believe that someone is an agent or that an agent with limited authority has more authority than was expressly given. Such an agent is called an "ostensible" agent. Agency by implication occurs when a reasonable person would believe from the conduct of the principal that an agency existed. For example, assume that Mr. Smith advertises that he will pay a 10 percent commission to any broker who finds an acceptable buyer for a warehouse. If a broker introduces a buyer who purchases the warehouse, a commission will have been earned even though no listing contract had been signed.

Agency by Necessity.   Agency by necessity occurs in emergency situations where the principal cannot be reached and a reasonable person would normally believe that a principal would have appointed an agent if he or she had known about the emergency. For example, assume that water caused erosion that could lead to the collapse of a building unless immediate steps are taken to prop up the building with jacks and reinforcing pillars. A broker who had been employed to sell the building might believe that there was an emergency and might, if the seller could not be found, reasonably employ workers to prevent the collapse.

Agency by Ratification.   Agency by ratification occurs when a principal accepts the benefits of a contract negotiated by someone who was not an agent. Assuming that the principal is made aware of all material facts pertaining to the transaction, once the contract is accepted the principal becomes bound by any statements of the ratified agent.

A principal is only bound by the action of an agent who is acting within the scope of actual or ostensible authority. Agents can be classified on the basis of how much authority is delegated to them. An agent who has complete authority to do anything that the principal could do is called a "universal agent." Such an agent is usually appointed by a written power of attorney. An agent who has authority to transact a broad range of contracts within a commercial endeavor is called a "general agent." One who has very limited authority is called a "special agent." In most cases a broker is authorized to act only as an intermediary to bring together a buyer and seller or lessor and lessee. Therefore, the broker normally would have to be classified as a special agent.

If an agent acts beyond the scope of his or her authority, the principal is not bound. A third person who reasonably relied on the agent's statement that she or he had sufficient authority may sue the agent for damages. The legal basis for the suit is that the agent breached an "implied warranty of authority."

The Fiduciary Relationship

As noted previously, an agent is a fiduciary. This relationship creates a number of duties. Violation of these duties can lead to civil penalties and possible loss or suspension of a broker's or salesperson's license. In most cases, violation of these duties can lead to the loss of the real estate commission. A description of some of the more common duties follows.

Duty to Perform Competently. A broker must not neglect to perform services contracted for in the employment contract. The broker must meet the standard of performance that is customary of other professional agents in the same market.

Duty to Perform Personally. Normally an agent may not delegate the performance of duties to another person unless it is customary in the trade or industry. In real estate, brokers can normally work through their salespersons. However, the brokers remain personally liable for any negligence of their employees.

Duty to Be Loyal. A broker cannot receive compensation from two opposite sides of a transaction without disclosure and the prior approval of both parties. Also, the broker may not take advantage of confidential information or compete with the principal.

Duty of Fidelity. A broker cannot make any secret profits or accept kickbacks. The broker must disclose to the principal any direct or indirect conflicts of interest. For example, if the broker has a property listed, it is improper to urge the principal to sell the property to a partnership or corporation in which the broker owns an interest without first disclosing that interest. The broker must also disclose to any principal any family ties he or she has with others in the transaction.

Duty to Obey Legitimate Instructions.   Unless instructions are illegal or unethical, the broker must obey all instructions given by the principal. If the broker does not want to obey instructions, the employment should not be accepted.

Duty of Accounting.   A broker is responsible for all money or checks deposited to him or her on the principal's behalf. Insurance should be carried to cover any losses. Any checks given to the broker should be immediately cashed and put into a trust account. A broker may not put the money into a personal account: Putting money into a personal account is referred to as "commingling" and can result in the loss of the real estate license.

Duty to Inform of Material Facts.   A broker must advise the principal of any material facts that become known to the broker. A fact is considered material if the knowledge of it could affect the client's judgment. One reason for this duty is that the principal is presumed, by law, to know any facts that are brought to the attention of the agent.

The principal also has duties to the agent. A basic duty is to compensate the agent for fulfilling the terms of the agency. In real estate, this usually pertains to the earning of a commission, although it can also include finder's fees and fees for other services.

A broker has generally earned a commission when a buyer who is ready, willing, and able is found. A buyer is ready if there exists a present contractual intent to purchase the property within the time parameters stated in the listing contract. A buyer is willing if all the terms set by the seller are unconditionally agreed to by the potential buyer. A buyer is able if he or she has the financial resources to purchase the property. Once this ready, willing, and able buyer is found, the broker is entitled to a commission even if the property never closes for some reason such as a title defect. However, the original listing contract may state that the commission is payable only out of the proceeds received at closing or may contain other stipulations. In such a situation, a commission is not earned until the stipulations are met. Further, before a broker is entitled to a commission, she or he must be properly licensed in the state where the brokerage services are provided.

STATE LICENSING LAWS

A more detailed discussion of state licensing laws appears in Chapter 20. This section is concerned with how the state licensing law affects the agency role of the broker.

The licensing law defines a broker, an associate broker, and a salesperson. A "broker" is usually broadly defined and typically includes any person, association, partnership, or corporation who provides any of a wide range of real estate services for a fee or commission. These services include listing, selling, purchasing, exchanging, leasing, renting, collecting rents, or any other activity dealing with the transfer of real property interests. An "associate broker" is one who has all the qualifications of a broker but is employed by another broker. A "salesperson" is typically one who is licensed to perform on behalf of any licensed broker. For all practical purposes, in most states the salesperson does not have an independent legal existence. The salesperson is a mere extension of the broker.

The state licensing law creates a real estate commission to administer the law and to create necessary regulations. The commission issues licenses, collects annual fees, and hears complaints against brokers or salespersons.

The licensing law describes what can lead to suspension or revocation of a license; included is a discussion of hearing procedures and methods of appeal. Some typical violations of the licensing law that can result in a loss of commission or suspension or revocation of license are:

- Accepting a commission or valuable consideration as a real estate salesperson from any person except the employing broker
- Paying or receiving any undisclosed rebate on expenditures made for a principal
- Inducing any party to a contract to break the contract for the purpose of substituting a new contract which would result in personal gain for the licensee
- Guaranteeing future profits which may result from the resale of real estate
- Net listing contracts which provide for a "net" return to seller, leaving the licensee free to sell the property at any price and retain the full amount of the excess as compensation.*

Additional violations include discrimination on the basis of race and other reasons and failure to fulfill agency duties. (Discrimination is discussed in a subsequent section of this chapter.) Other violations include criminal conduct like fraud and embezzlement. Finally, there may be technical violations such as the failure to provide duplicate copies of contracts to all parties to a real estate transaction.

*For a more comprehensive listing of violations, see Dennis S. Tosh and Nicholas Ordway, *Passing Your Real Estate Exam,* Reston Publishing, Reston, Virginia, 1981, pp. 18–19.

OTHER STATE LAWS

In addition to specific state licensing laws and regulations passed by the licensing commission, states can pass general laws that affect the liability or duties of real estate agents. This section concentrates on two types of such laws: consumer protection legislation against deceptive trade practices and legislation concerning the unauthorized practice of law.

Deceptive Trade Practices

Some states have passed laws to make it easier for consumers to collect against merchants and providers of services who engage in deceptive trade practices. These laws are often applicable to real estate brokers and salespersons.

Normally, to recover damages for false information, a consumer must file a lawsuit and prove either fraud or misrepresentation. It is necessary to prove that a material misrepresentation of fact was detrimentally relied on by a "reasonable person," resulting in economic damage. Further, to show fraud, the consumer must also demonstrate intent or gross negligence. This is difficult, and often the consumer's legal expenses exceed the ultimate recovery. A deceptive trade practices law changes this.

A deceptive trade practices law loosens these legal standards. Normally, it must be shown that the real estate broker committed an unlawful business practice. Under some of the state laws there is no longer a need to show detrimental reliance by a reasonable person, nor is there a need to show economic damage.

Disputes involving deceptive trade practices laws have included incorrect statements of the square footage in a home, misquoted lot size, failure to inform buyer that a house has been rejected by an FHA appraiser, termite damage, cracks in foundation, lot drainage problems, and facts omitted that might have influenced a purchaser's judgment.*

If a real estate agent is found guilty of violating the law, the consumer is usually able to recover actual damages, court costs, reasonable attorney's fees and, under some laws, punitive damages that may be as much as three times the actual damages. Real estate agents can often avoid the punitive damages by making a good faith effort to settle the dispute out of court.

Unauthorized Practice of Law

Brokers or salespersons who are found guilty of the unauthorized practice of law may find themselves fined, in jail, and subject to a contempt

---

*See A. L. Wright, "An Analysis of the Deceptive Trade Practices Act in Texas," R-379-5C-183, Texas Real Estate Research Center, College Station, Texas, March 1979.

of court citation and possible civil damages. Exactly what constitutes the unauthorized practice of law differs from state to state. Some states are stricter than others. In many jurisdictions, the state board of Realtors has reached an agreement with the state bar association defining what constitutes unauthorized law practice.

Most states permit agents to prepare listing contracts, sales agreements, and leases. Some states have forms approved by the state licensing commission that may be filled out by brokers and salespersons. Ordinarily, the agent may only fill in the blanks and perform other mechanical tasks. Clauses involving substantive legal issues should be drafted by an attorney. Also, more specialized documents such as options, mortgages, and deeds of trust should normally be completed by attorneys, although a number of states permit brokers to complete these documents as well.

A broker who is not acting in the role of an agent or does not have an involvement in a transaction should not prepare legal documentation. Further, receipt of a fee or other compensation above the sales commission for preparing paperwork might be viewed as evidence of the unauthorized practice of law. Giving of legal advice involving the interpretation of contracts, quality of title, or other such opinions should be left to a qualified attorney.

There is sometimes a conflict between the agent's duty to disclose material facts or information that may affect the principal's business judgment and the rules against giving legal advice. Where such a conflict exists, the client should be advised to seek legal assistance. Some state laws make it a requirement for the broker to suggest that the client seek additional legal counsel on certain matters such as title opinions. It is also an ethical standard of the National Association of Realtors to recommend that legal advice be sought where parties to a transaction need it. To avoid future disputes, the broker should put in writing the recommendation to consult a lawyer.

Such rules exist to protect the public. Normally a broker does not have the necessary expertise to give comprehensive legal advice on complex real estate matters. Bad advice can lead to financial losses by the client and can harm the integrity of the profession.

FEDERAL LAWS

Until recent years, the federal government did not become involved in the regulation of the real estate brokerage industry—such regulation was left to the states. This is no longer the case. Federal agencies have been authorized to regulate a broad range of activities commonly entered into by real estate brokers. This section will concentrate on three major areas of concern: (1) fair housing laws, (2) antitrust legislation, and (3) other federal laws.

Federal Housing Laws

It is the stated policy of the federal government to eradicate discrimination in real estate markets on the basis of race, color, religion, national origin, or sex. To accomplish this purpose, two laws are enforced: the Civil Rights Act of 1866 and the Federal Fair Housing Act of 1968.

The Civil Rights Act of 1866 prohibits discrimination on the basis of race in all real estate transactions. After Reconstruction this law was ignored until 1968, when the U.S. Supreme Court revived it in *Jones v. Alfred H. Mayer Co.*, 392 U.S. 409 (1968). This case involved a builder who, in 1965, refused to sell a house to a person on the basis of that person's race. In 1968, the builder was ordered to sell a house to the plaintiff at 1965 prices and to absorb the price difference.

The 1866 law is enforced by bringing a civil suit in U.S. District Court. The suit must be brought within the time period permitted by a state's statute of limitations for torts. This would normally be 2 to 4 years, depending on the state. Brokers found guilty of violating this law pay actual damages, court costs, and punitive damages and, possibly, lose their real estate licenses.

The Federal Fair Housing Act of 1968 specifies seven basic violations. An individual or firm cannot use race, color, religion, national origin, or sex to discriminate in the following acts:

1. Sale or rental of housing
2. Modifying terms, conditions, or privileges in the sale or rental of housing
3. Discriminatory advertising in the sale or rental of housing
4. Refusing to make a dwelling available for inspection if it is for sale or rent
5. Blockbusting (inducing owners to sell by making representations that a neighborhood is becoming occupied by people of a different race, color, and so on)
6. Modifying the terms or conditions of a loan used to buy, build, or repair a dwelling
7. Participation in a multiple listing service

Although there are some exceptions to this law, these exceptions do not apply to real estate brokers or salespersons. Further, courts have tended to interpret this law very broadly. It is thus advisable not to give even the appearance of discrimination against individuals in the protected classifications.

The 1968 law can be enforced in three ways. First, a complaint can be filed with the Department of Housing and Urban Development (HUD). Currently, HUD has limited powers and cannot issue cease and desist orders or levy fines. HUD is restricted to "informal conciliation" and tries to settle the dispute privately among the parties. Second, a civil suit can be filed in U.S. District Court within 180 days of the alleged violation. The court may issue an injunction and award actual damages, up to $1000 in punitive damages. Third, in major matters, where there is a pattern of discrimination or where large numbers of people are involved, the U.S. attorney general may file a civil suit.

Antitrust Legislation

Congress has passed legislation that prohibits unreasonable restraints on trade and monopolization. The key legislation that defines these violations is the Sherman Antitrust Act. Violations of the Sherman Antitrust Act result in both criminal and civil liability. Criminal sanctions include up to 3 years in prison, up to $100,000 penalty for an individual, or up to $1 million for an organization or firm. Civil liability can result in the wrongdoer paying three times the amount of actual damages proven in court.

Real estate brokers are likely to violate antitrust legislation in two areas: rate fixing and access to multiple listing. Brokers cannot collude to fix uniform brokerage commission rates. (Collusion can be actual or inferred from circumstances.) For example, in one city, major brokerage firms raised the residential commission rates from 6 percent to 7 percent within a short time. Most of the other firms followed the lead of the major firms. This was found to be rate fixing by the federal courts, and heavy fines were imposed on the firms that had led the rate increase.

Multiple listing services (MLS) are often established by a local board of Realtors. Firms that are not members of an MLS soon find themselves at a competitive disadvantage. Courts have ruled, in some states, that these firms cannot be prevented from participating in MLS even if these firms do not wish to join the local board.

Other Federal Laws

The scope of federal laws and legislation is constantly expanding. Old laws are being reinterpreted, and new laws are being passed. Two sets of laws have become important to brokers who deal in the sale of lots and in syndications.

The Interstate Land Sales Full Disclosure Act applies to any lots in a subdivision of fifty or more lots that are being sold as part of a common marketing plan. A purchaser can void the purchase of such a lot unless certain requirements are met. The first requirement is that a statement of record must be filed with the secretary of HUD. This statement of record contains details about title, infrastructure (roads, utilities, and so on), and certain financial information. The second requirement is that the purchaser be furnished a property report at least 3 business days before the sales contract is signed. A property report must contain disclosures about material facts such as those involving physical, legal, or financial aspects of the property which can influence the consumer's judgment. Violation of this law can result in both civil and criminal penalties.

A syndication is considered to be a security under federal law and under most state laws. A security is any investment contract or any investment with which one expects to make a profit solely from the efforts of anyone other than the investor. This definition is broadly construed by the courts. Unless one is exempt from the provisions of the securities acts of 1933 and 1934, a broker who sells a security must be appropriately licensed as a securities dealer.

There are two general exemptions from the SEC regestration requirements. The first is the private offering exemption under rule 146 of the Securities and Exchange Commission (SEC). This is an offering to so-called knowledgeable investors through a private offering memorandum. The offering must be restricted to no more than thirty-five purchasers, and general solicitation or advertising is forbidden. The second exemption is the intrastate offering under rule 147 of the SEC. Strictly enforced, this exemption is lost if an offering is made to even one out-of-state resident. If an offering is a security, a broker must qualify as a security dealer, even if the offering is exempt from registration.

If a syndication is not exempt, then it is necessary to register the offering with the SEC. This is likely to be expensive and time-consuming. Along with the registration, the broker is obligated to provide various disclosures in a prospectus to any potential investors. There is also a short-form registration for offerings under $1.5 million. This is provided by SEC regulation A and simplifies the difficulties and expenses of registration. Failure to register will require the broker to refund any payments made by investors. Any misrepresentations associated with the offering can lead to serious criminal and civil penalties.

PROFESSIONAL CODES OF ETHICS

Many real estate brokers and salespersons belong to professional associations such as the National Association of Realtors (NAR) or the

National Association of Real Estate Brokers (NAREB). Members of these organizations pledge to adhere to professional codes of ethics. The ethical standards in the codes have been established to guide members in their conduct with the public, their clients, and their fellow members.

In some states, the standards of these ethical codes are incorporated as part of the state licensing laws. Further, courts often look to these codes to determine what is customary practice within a particular profession. For these reasons, real estate agents should be familiar with these codes even if they are not members of a professional organization.

The professional codes incorporate the basic duties of the agent to the principal that have been previously described. Further, professionals are urged not to disparage the reputations of fellow professionals. Disputes and controversies among members of the profession should be avoided or submitted to private arbitration. Although the broker or salesperson must be faithful to the client, all parties in a real estate transaction should be treated with fairness. These codes also contain prohibitions against discrimination and the unauthorized practice of law.

CONCLUSION

The agency role of the real estate broker is complicated by the various sources of law and custom that help define it. As society has changed, there has been a tendency to impose increasing responsibility on the broker and salesperson. The largest expansion of legal liability has come from the federal and state governments—the federal government has been concerned primarily with major social issues concerning human rights and economic concentrations of power, and state governments have expanded their laws to create new protection for consumers. The growing complexity of the agency role makes it essential for brokers to stay current by participating in continuing education programs or seminars offered by professional trade associations and universities.

Real Estate Contracts

Louis B. Hansotte   Senior Partner, Hansotte, Nostrand and Lange

Virtually every official act in the life of a real estate licensee, from the licensee's own contract of employment to the negotiation and implementation of an agreement between buyer and seller, borrower and lender, or any parties to an exchange, involves some aspect of the law of contracts.

The ability to write a contract which clearly represents the parties' intent, often under circumstances when no professional assistance is available, therefore becomes one of the most significant attributes of a successful broker or salesperson.

A contract may be defined as a legally enforceable agreement between two (or more) parties to do (or to refrain from) a specific act or acts. Implicit in this definition are the following:

1. The parties have met and discussed an agreement (privity).

2. The agreement was made with an intent to perform (not just to discuss preliminary matters or to make promises in jest).

3. The parties are legally competent and have reached a "meeting of the minds."

4. There is a mutual obligation supporting the promises to be performed.

5. There are no defenses to performance (all technical requirements of law have been met).

22-1

6. An appropriate action is timely and properly brought either to compel performance of the agreement or to seek damages for its breach.

INVITATION TO MAKE AN OFFER

Common law recognized the retailers' practice of displaying goods or merchandise without intending to become bound to the advertising, or "puffing" (exaggeration) accompanying the display.

A customer entering a store could not normally create a valid and binding agreement with the merchant by "accepting" the merchant's advertised price for an item; rather the merchant's display would be considered preliminary in nature, or an invitation to make an offer. The customer would make an offer (if desired), which the merchant could then either accept, counter, or reject without liability to the customer.

Although current truth-in-advertising laws may modify this common-law concept to some extent, the general practice of the law today is still to consider advertising, or displaying merchandise, as an invitation to offer rather than a firm offer to sell.

In real estate transactions, a prospective seller frequently engages the services of a licensed broker to help find a buyer and handle the details of the sale. The contract of employment between the seller and broker is a *listing agreement,* and later we will examine in detail some of the current forms of listing agreements.

Although a seller, in entering into a listing agreement with a broker, is generally manifesting a sincere desire to sell the property being listed, a listing agreement is *not* an offer to sell. In addition to serving as the source of the broker's compensation, it is an *invitation* to submit offers.

The significance of this difference is that a prospective buyer cannot "accept" a seller's offer in the listing agreement, even if the buyer is willing to meet all the terms and conditions set forth in the listing. Rather the buyer is (usually) the one who makes the offer, and it is then the seller's choice to accept, modify, or reject the buyer's offer.

PRESENT CONTRACTUAL INTENT

The difference between a preliminary inquiry and a firm offer lies in whether the "offeror" intends to become bound by an acceptance of that "offer." In law, the moving phrase is "present contractual intent."

You and Jean are standing on a lot that you own. There has been no prior discussion of a sale of that lot between you. Jean asks, "Do you want to sell this lot?" Even if your answer is "yes," it is clear that no contract results. Not only did neither of you intend to become bound to that agreement (no present contractual intent), but none of the terms of the sale has been discussed or agreed to, and a court could not enforce it.

Instead, suppose Jean says, "I'll give you $20,000 for this lot." Again, even if you said "OK," there probably would not be an enforceable agreement. It would not appear that Jean would intend to be contractually bound by that statement, and even discounting the effect of the statute of frauds (which requires contracts for the sale of real property to be in writing to be enforceable), it is not likely that a court would find the presence of a contractual intent.

But Jean and you (unless you want to sell for that price) have to be careful. Many states apply the "objective" theory of contracts. The court will consider not what the parties may have subjectively intended but rather what a reasonable person observing the conduct of the parties would have assumed. If a reasonable person would have felt bound by the agreement, a contract would be formed, assuming that all other elements of a valid contract were present.

What if Jean wanted her offer to be taken seriously and wanted to create a binding obligation? She should word it in a manner which objectively would leave no doubt about what was intended: "I am writing down an offer to purchase your lot (legally describing it) for $20,000 cash, and if you will write your acceptance of my offer below it, and sign it, we will have a deal." Thus:

1. Offers should not be confused with preliminary "invitations to make an offer."

2. An enforceable offer requires an intent to become bound, or present contractual intent.

3. The intent to be bound may be objectively determined, even if the party did not intend to enter into an enforceable agreement.

ELEMENTS OF A VALID CONTRACT

An agreement, to appear as a legally enforceable contract, must at the very least evidence a meeting of the minds and an underlying mutual obligation. The first of these elements is called "mutual assent"; the second, "consideration."

Mutual Assent

Mutual assent is found in an *offer* and an *acceptance*. A communicated offer creates the privity previously referred to, and, assuming objectively determined present contractual intent, will be valid if it is reasonably definite and certain as to parties, price and terms, subject matter, and time for performance.

Parties and Title. The identities and capacities of the parties are not problems when the parties are specifically named and legally competent. Use of a "nominee" can invalidate an offer since a nominee cannot be identified, and specific performance will usually not be granted if the buyer is not known. If the buyer's identity is not known, it is better for the offer to set forth the offeror's name as buyer, with that buyer reserving the right to assign his or her interest to another before the close of escrow. Specific performance could therefore be obtained, at least in the name of the offeror. A clause to accomplish this result might read as follows:

> Title to be taken as JOHN HUGHES and MARY HUGHES, Husband and Wife, as Joint Tenants. Buyers reserve the right to assign their interest in the subject property by a writing delivered to escrow prior to the close thereof.

Another problem concerning parties can arise if the buyer is a partnership or a corporation. Except for statutes specifically authorizing a partnership to receive, hold, and convey titles to real property, a partnership in law is not considered to have an existence separate from its partners. Therefore, agreements conveying real property to either general or limited partnerships must be carefully prepared in accordance with applicable statutes, or they may be invalid. A partnership offer when the partnership entity is recognized by statute might be as follows:

> Title to be taken as ABCD, a Limited Partnership.

An offer from a partnership entity *not* recognized by statute might be as follows:

> Title to be taken as A, B, C, and D, General Partners in the ABCD General Partnership.

Corporations can take title to real property in their own names. A corporation is a single, artificial entity. Although there may be many shareholders of the corporation, the entity itself is treated like a single person. Care must be taken in the case of a newly formed corporation that escrow does not close, and title pass, before the corporation's articles are filed. If the corporation is not in existence at the time of the conveyance, no title will pass. It might also be noted that title may be passed *to* a corporation with relative ease, but usually it may not be transferred out *from* a corporation without adequate consideration. Tax counsel should be consulted prior to the delivery of a conveyance of real property into a corporation to avoid serious tax and legal problems. If it is later determined, for example, that the title should have been held in individuals' names and leased to the corporation or that the transfer constitutes a dividend to shareholders, distribution of the property out of the corporation would not provide for a tax deduction, but receipt by the shareholders could constitute a taxable receipt of income.

Finally, problems may result from individuals who do not have the legal capacity to receive or convey legal title to real property. Persons who are mentally incompetent, and minors, are examples.

Those persons who are adjudicated (judicially determined) incompetent have no capacity to enter into valid contractual agreements, and, although they may be grantees in real property conveyances, they may not be grantors. That is, they may receive, but not give, good title to realty.

Real property transactions in behalf of both categories of grantors lacking legal capacity must be handled for them by court-appointed guardians or conservators. A minor, however, who has been emancipated may deal with real property in most states. California recently adopted legislation making it relatively easy for an emancipated minor to go before the court and obtain a judicial declaration proving emancipation. However, dealing with a minor who claims to be emancipated, but who has not complied with the statutory requirements to prove capacity, would not be prudent. Generally, a court will approve a sale of real property belonging to an incompetent but will not approve a purchase of such property.

An agreement on behalf of such a person should contain language advising all parties that court approval of the transaction is, or may be, required:

> Purchase (or sale, or encumbrance) of this property (and commissions payable thereon) is subject to approval of the court in the (conservatorship) (guardianship) (estate) of HENRY BELLOWS, Case #123 456.

Price and Terms.   The element of price should not create a problem in a real estate agreement, since price is always extensively discussed before the agreement is reduced to writing.

Terms, on the other hand, frequently present problems. Availability of loans, conditions not yet known, results of inspections, investigations and tests, zone changes, and other matters may affect the buyer's willingness to agree to an initial large cash outlay. Also, a review of the tax consequences of the transaction to both parties may affect the ultimate terms of an agreement.

Too often, the parties (and their advisors) will take the easy way out, leaving these matters to future agreement. It is a fundamental principle of law that a court will not make an agreement for the parties. It will interpret or enforce an agreement or declare that there is no agreement, but it will not create one in the absence of one or more essential elements of an agreement. An agreement to agree is no agreement at all. To say, therefore, that the price of the subject property is $250,000, with $50,000 cash down and the balance to be paid "on terms to be mutually agreed on later," is to omit an essential element from the contract. The court will not insert the term of the loan, the monthly payment, or the interest rate, if the parties do not agree on them later. If an all-cash payment for the property is not to be made, one must specify in the agreement, in detail, each essential element of the terms of payment in the agreement.

Subject Matter.   The subject matter of a contract to purchase real property is, obviously, the real property. It must be *legally described.* That means it must be described with sufficient certainty as to allow a court to determine what specific property the parties contemplate by their agreement.

There are three methods by which property generally is legally described: metes and bounds; U.S. government survey; and reference to a recorded map. It is not essential to use one or a combination of these methods, since real property may be adequately described in other ways. It is desirable to do so, however, because they are accepted methods and avoid ambiguity. A proper legal description can be obtained by referring to the deed by which the present seller acquired the property, to the title report issued at that time, or to the preliminary title report if one has been received in the present transaction.

It is not good practice to refer to real property by its street address alone, since that does not describe the quantum, or extent, of the property. Nor is it desirable to use the commonly accepted practice of referring to the tax parcel number. Tax assessors are concerned about not missing any parcels of property on their assessment rolls—not necessarily about the exactitude of their descriptions. If a street address or tax parcel number is used at all, it should be in addition to a legal description, not instead of one.

Time for Performance.   In an all-cash transaction, performance of the conditions of an agreement are concurrent. The seller does not relinquish the deed until the buyer relinquishes the purchase money.

Most real estate transactions are not all cash. Many times agreements are conditioned on the happening, or nonhappening, of one or more events. Under these circumstances it is important to spell out who does what, when it is to be done, and what happens if it is not done.

Consideration

"Consideration" is the obligation which underlies an enforceable agreement. It is that which is bargained for. It must be "mutual," that is, both parties to an agreement must be bound to its performance, or neither party will be bound.

In the typical "bilateral" contract, the obligations of the parties are found in their mutual promises to do (or refrain from doing) something. An agreement to purchase a specific parcel of real property for $100,-000 is a promise on the part of the buyer to buy, and a reciprocal promise on the part of the seller to sell the property for the agreed upon price. It is the exchange of a promise to buy for a promise to sell that creates the obligations, or consideration, in a bilateral contract. It is *not* the payment of the $100,000, although that is frequently stated to be the consideration. It is the *promise* to buy, given in exchange for the *promise* to sell. Thus, in a bilateral contract, consideration is found in a promise for a promise.

In the typical "unilateral" contract, the obligations of the parties are found in the promise given by one party in exchange for the act of the other—a *promise* for an *act*.

"Here is $10,000 cash which I will give you if you will sell this lot to me," Henry tells Arthur, handing over the money at the same time. Henry's obligation is found in his *act* of handing over the money; if Arthur agrees, he will be making a *promise* to sell the lot.

Options

Consider an offer to enter into an option agreement: "I will give you $1000 if you will agree to sell me your house for $100,000 and give me the right to buy the house for 30 days."

Such an *option* agreement is frequently referred to as a unilateral contract, with the explanation that it binds only one party (the optionor), since the optionee is not obligated to buy and therefore is not bound to the contract. An option agreement is unilateral, but not for that reason. It is unilateral because it is an exchange of a promise for an act.

The optionee is bound to pay the $1000 if the option is to be created, so both parties are bound—one to pay the money, the other to keep open for 30 days the offer to sell. The agreement is unilateral because it represents the exchange of a promise for an act, instead of a promise for a promise.

An example of the importance of the distinction between unilateral and bilateral contracts may be seen in examining more closely the listing agreement. In the typical listing agreement, the seller employs a licensed broker to find a ready, willing, and able buyer for the seller's property. To ensure the broker's right to compensation, the broker should use a bilateral contract—a promise for a promise. But what can the broker promise? If the broker promises to find a buyer for the property, but cannot find one, the broker may be sued for breach of contract! If the seller agrees to pay the broker only after the broker has found a buyer (a promise for an act), until the buyer is found, the seller is not liable to the broker and may cancel the listing without liability for a commission! Liability may exist, however, for expenses incurred by the broker up to the time of termination of the listing.

The problem may be resolved by creating a bilateral contract wherein the broker promises to use due diligence in trying to find a buyer. As long as the broker does use due diligence, even if a buyer is not found, the seller is bound to recognize the contract for the duration of its term. Many listing agreements thus contain a provision which recites in part: "In consideration of the broker's *due diligence.*"

Once the courts have established the appearance of a valid agreement, they will enforce it unless one or more defenses are available to prevent its enforcement.

DEFENSES

If the foregoing elements of a valid contract are present, a court should find an existing, valid agreement unless one or more defenses are available to preclude its enforcement.

There are, of course, many possible defenses which could be raised in any given case. Some of the more commonly asserted defenses, particularly in real estate agreements, include the following.

Lack of Real Consent

Consent, or mutual assent, is found in an offer and an acceptance. If there is no consent, there is no so-called meeting of the minds, and there can be no enforceable agreement.

Sometimes consent is given, so that element is present. But if the consent was not freely given, or real, this lack then becomes a matter of defense, meaning the burden of proceedings is on the defendant to show that the consent, although given, was improperly obtained, for example, when misrepresentation, fraud, concealment, coercion, or undue influence has been used by one party against the other.

Fraud and Misrepresentation. Fraud and misrepresentation differ only in the element of knowledge, actual or constructive. Each requires a misstatement of a material fact by one party (the defendant in a lawsuit) and the reasonable reliance on that misstated fact by the other party (the plaintiff) to their economic detriment.

If the truth of the stated fact was unknown to the defendant, the misstatement is classified as a negligent misrepresentation. If the misstated fact was known to the defendant to be false when it was made, *or if there were circumstances whereby the defendant should have known* (is charged with the knowledge) of the fact misstated, then the wrong is classified as a fraudulent misrepresentation. Under circumstances where the defendant had a special fiduciary relationship with the plaintiff, the law may find that the defendant's conduct was fraudulent even in the absence of knowledge of the misstatement. This is called "constructive fraud."

In addition to an expressed wrongful statement is the failure to make a statement when there is a duty to make one. This is known as a "concealment" and, as with an affirmative misstatement, may be negligent or fraudulent.

The primary significance of the distinction between fraud and misrepresentation is that in cases of fraud the law not only allows the plaintiff to recover the plaintiff's provable losses (actual damages) but also may permit an award of "punitive" or "exemplary" damages. In cases where the actual amount of loss was slight, if a finding of fraud is made in the case, the court may award substantial damages as punishment or by way of example to others, and, in some states, from the state real estate recovery fund.

Undue Influence or Coercion. Lack of real consent also occurs when there is actual or constructive force used to obtain that consent. Obviously, an agreement entered into at gunpoint would not be enforceable, even though the element of consent was technically present.

Sometimes the relationship between the parties, although not amounting to the use of physical force or its threat, may be such that one of the parties was guilty of "overreaching." If one party is in a superior legal position to another, such as where the attorney-client, broker-client, or trustee-beneficiary relationship exists, that position of superiority may result in obtaining consent which a court would not consider to have been freely given.

Void versus Voidable.   Agreements obtained in this manner are not void, but they are *voidable*. It sometimes happens that the innocent party wants to be bound to the bargain entered into, notwithstanding the possibility of their having been unfairly influenced. To avoid the unjust result which would obtain if all such agreements were automatically cancelled, the law allows the aggrieved party to elect either to retain its benefits or to avoid being bound to the agreement. After the parties are restored to equal footing (all elements of the transaction have been fully and fairly disclosed, competent advice has been obtained for the unsophisticated party, or one lacking capacity has regained that capacity), the contract can be voided or affirmed. A voidable agreement, then, is one which is valid and enforceable until the person who has the right to do so elects to void it.

Statute of Frauds

Contracts for the sale or purchase of real property or any interest in it (such as an easement) are required by the statute of frauds to be in writing to be enforceable. Conversely, when such agreements are not in writing they are unenforceable.

In general, the law will not permit one to take unfair advantage of the statute. If one promises to reduce an agreement to writing, allows the other party to rely on the promise to their detriment, and then claims that their failure to create the writing defeats the agreement, an "estoppel" may arise. The wrongdoer may not take advantage of their own wrongdoing by claiming the statute of frauds as a defense. Naturally, each case involving an estoppel must be judged on its own merits, and it is never a wise practice to assume that the defense of estoppel will be a viable one. Agreements required to be in writing by the statute of frauds should always be reduced to writing promptly after being created.

Statute of Limitations

The statute of limitations requires that a legal action be brought, if at all, within a certain period of time after the right to bring it arises. The law does not help those who "sleep on their rights." Since most real property agreements must be in writing because of the statute of frauds, the most frequently applicable time period for such transactions is usually 4 years.

The right to bring a legal action does not arise when the contract is entered into, but when it is first breached. That starts the "tolling" of the statute of limitations, and any legal action not brought within the applicable time period will be dismissed by the court, if the statute is properly raised as a defense.

Bankruptcy

A discharge in bankruptcy is a legal defense to the performance of an agreement. Although the obligation may be valid in all other respects, and even though the debtor acknowledges that a debt is proper and unpaid, it cannot be collected if the debt has been discharged in bankruptcy.

The effect of filing a petition in bankruptcy is to stay (stop) collection or foreclosure actions that have already been started and to prevent the filing of new actions.

Such a stay can have a disastrous effect on a secured creditor who may have been told that, if the debt is not paid according to its terms, the creditor can always resort to the security through foreclosure. Remember that all loans, secured or not, are made subject to the operation of the bankruptcy laws. Although possibly sympathetic to the creditor's position, courts will not disregard the legal effect of the debtor's bankruptcy and allow collection of the debt except in compliance with all the provisions of the Bankruptcy Act.

PERFORMANCE AND BREACH

A contract performed according to its terms, if one assumes that all parties agree that is has been properly performed, obviously does not give rise to an action for its breach. A real or imagined breach usually will result in one of two possible actions: damages or rescission. When more than one remedy is available to a party to a lawsuit, the law frequently requires the plaintiff to make an "election of remedies," which is the choice between two or more remedies, stated and communicated to the other party early in the proceedings.

For example, suppose Barney Buyer and Sally Seller have executed a contract to purchase and sell a parcel of real property. After escrow has closed, Buyer takes possession and discovers that the water table which Seller had represented to be at 30 feet below the surface was, in fact, 50 feet below the surface.

Buyer may not then want the property, because the cost of drilling and pumping the water may make a commercial enterprise economically infeasible. Buyer's remedy would be to bring an action for "rescission" (cancellation) of the agreement. The first step in the rescission action would be to promptly and personally deliver a written notice of rescission to Seller.

Such a notice might be drawn along the following lines:

Notice of Rescission

BARNEY BUYER *(Buyer)* hereby notifies SALLY SELLER *(Seller)* that that certain agreement to Purchase Real Estate entered into by and between the above-mentioned parties and covering property commonly known as 3333 Main Street, City, and legally described as (enter legal description) is hereby rescinded.

Rescission is based on Amended Statutes, Section XXX of the State of Confusion, and misrepresentation of one or more material aspects of the referenced agreement, namely: (enter facts to support the rescission action).

Dated: _____

_____

Barney Buyer

However, each state's statutes must be consulted before preparing an actual notice to ensure compliance with specific statutory requirements as to the form and contents of the notice.

Perhaps Buyer really wants the property, notwithstanding the alleged misrepresentations. Buyer could then affirm the contract and sue Seller for (monetary) damages. The amount of damages being sought would probably be the difference between the contract (agreed-on) price and the value of the land considering the lower water table. If Buyer were successful in his suit, he would then have acquired the property for the proper price based on its actual value rather than on the agreed-on value set forth in the contract, and Buyer would be "made whole" by the judgment.

This choice, or election, of remedies must usually be made as the first step in the action, and subsequent steps must be consistent with the choice that was made. The courts will not allow Buyer to waver back and forth as the case progresses—or to have the best of both worlds. The election, once made, is usually irrevocable.

It must be remembered that, as a general rule, defenses not raised will be waived. It is not up to the court to raise a defense for a party; it is up to that party. A defense which could have been raised at the time of trial but was not will usually not become the basis for a successful appeal if raised for the first time on appeal.

SPECIFIC REAL ESTATE CONTRACTS

Having reviewed some of the legal principles applicable to contracts generally, it is now appropriate to take a more detailed look at three of the commonly used contracts related to real property transactions: (1) listing agreements, (2) offers to purchase (deposit receipts), and (3) escrow instructions.

Listing Agreements

A listing agreement may be viewed as a contract of employment between a seller and a real estate licensee hired to find a buyer for the seller's property. As in any employment contract, it spells out the essential elements of the hiring—the term and conditions of the employment and the compensation of the licensee.

Listings, like most real estate contracts, are not required to be on prescribed forms. However, in many states by agreement between the Realtor associations and state bar associations, forms have been preapproved for licensee's use. Although not legally required, the forms will avoid many questions about the unauthorized practice of law and will provide convenient checklists for vital information. In California, the law requires that a statement concerning commissions be included in all listing agreements advising the principal that commissions are not fixed by law but are subject to negotiation between the parties.

Listings may be grouped into three general categories: (1) an exclusive-right-to-sell listing; (2) an exclusive agency listing; and (3) an open listing.

Each has the common characteristics of identifying the parties (the seller and the broker), the subject matter of the contract (the real property), and the compensation to be paid if the licensee successfully locates an acceptable buyer (the commission).

The types of listings differ primarily as to the conditions under which the licensee is entitled to receive the commission. In an exclusive-right-to-sell listing, the broker is paid if the property sells during the term of the listing, whether the buyer was obtained through the broker holding the listing, through another broker, or through the efforts of the seller directly. In an exclusive agency listing, the broker is paid if the property sells through the efforts of the listing broker or any other broker (agent) used by the seller. If the property sells to a buyer produced by the seller (and not through any broker, whether the listing broker or another), *no* commission is payable. In an open listing, the listing broker earns a commission only if the property sells *and* the broker can establish that

that broker was the procuring cause of the sale. "Procuring cause" is a technical term which requires that, to be compensated, the broker must do more than show that the broker first introduced the buyer and seller to each other. The broker must show a "causal connection"—an unbroken chain of events—which led from the broker's introduction of the parties to the ultimate sales agreement. There are many situations in which the broker can show the former but not the latter, and therefore the broker will not be compensated even though the sale was completed.

The Safety Valve Clause.   Listings frequently include language to the effect that, if the seller enters into a contract with a prospective purchaser furnished by the broker during the term of the listing, the broker will be entitled to a commission even after the term of the listing has expired. Such a clause is called a "safety valve" clause and is designed to give the broker some measure of protection against the seller who tries to avoid the broker's right to compensation by delaying the sale until the listing has expired. It is important to review and comply with the exact language of the safety valve clause to be in a position to enforce it later if necessary. For example, it may provide that the list of prospective purchasers be furnished to the seller in writing at or prior to the expiration of the listing agreement. If the broker fails to follow the language of this provision, the right to a commission after the listing expires will probably be lost.

It is easy to understand why a broker would prefer an exclusive-right-to-sell listing and why the seller would probably prefer an open listing. It is one of the broker's burdens to convince the seller that the broker will be more productive, more willing to spend time and money, and more likely to produce an acceptable buyer if given an exclusive-right-to-sell listing. Figure 22-1 is an example of a typical exclusive-right-to-sell listing. Note some of the important elements of contract validity previously discussed in the form of listing shown.

Parties.   The listing agreement is a contract (of employment) between the seller and the broker. The buyer is *not* a party to it. Sometimes a buyer makes a "full-price" offer—one exactly on all the terms and conditions of the listing agreement—which the seller subsequently rejects. (Not often, but sometimes!) The buyer may then threaten to sue for breach of contract or to bring an action to compel the seller to sell (specific performance). It is difficult for the buyer to understand why a favorable judgment would not be forthcoming under those circumstances, but if there is no contract, damages will not lie for its breach and an action cannot be successfully maintained for its performance. The listing is not an offer to sell, which the buyer can accept. It is only when the buyer makes an offer which the seller, in turn, accepts, that a contract is formed. The fact that the buyer made a full-price offer does not compel the seller's acceptance, although it could give rise to a breach of the (employment) contract in an action brought by the broker. The broker has performed, and is entitled to compensation. But the buyer does not yet have an enforceable contract.

Terms and Conditions.   As in any enforceable agreement, all the essential terms and conditions under which the broker earns a commission should be spelled out. The property should be properly described. Price and manner of payment must not be left to future agreement. The expiration of the listing period must be set forth with certainty; in some states it is a license violation to permit the execution of an exclusive listing without setting forth a definite and determinable time at which the listing expires.

In this connection, the broker might lose part of the time period of the listing if a buyer were produced, an escrow opened, and for some reason the escrow failed to close. If by then the listing period has expired, the broker did not have the full time originally agreed on to try to find a buyer. The broker may be protected by providing that the term of the listing agreement shall be extended by any such period that the property is off the market because it is in escrow. But the broker must be careful not to violate the definite termination date rule in allowing for such an extension. One way of protecting both parties is to provide that: "The term of this listing shall be extended by any period during which the property is in escrow. Notwithstanding the foregoing provision, however, this listing shall expire in any event not later than (enter a certain date)."

Note the language at the bottom of the listing agreement, wherein the broker agrees to use "due diligence" in procuring a buyer. Do you remember the reason for that? It is intended to make the contract bilateral, vesting the rights of the parties immediately, as opposed to unilateral, where the rights of the parties do not vest until there has been performance of the act constituting the consideration for the contract.

At least three other listing forms are frequently used, but really do not constitute additional classes of listing agreements.

Net Listings.   In a net listing, the seller asks for a stated sum and allows the broker to retain, as a commission, everything received from the sale over the stated sum. Net listings in most states are frowned on but not illegal. The fear is that a broker, having found a seller willing to accept less than market price for the property listed, will keep a disproportionately large amount of the selling price as the broker's compensation.

EXCLUSIVE AGENCY LISTING

The undersigned Owner hereby GRANTS the undersigned Broker the EXCLUSIVE AGENCY, for a period commencing this date and terminating at midnight of ...., 19......., to sell the real property situated in the City of ...., County of ...., State of..,

described as: ....

....,

consisting of: ....,

at the price of: $...

....DOLLARS),

on the following terms:..

....

....

....

or at such price and terms as shall be acceptable to Owner, and to accept a deposit thereon.

Owner reserves the right to sell the property during the term hereof, without incurring liability for any compensation to Broker, provided that the sale shall not be made to a person with whom Broker shall have negotiated during the term hereof, and provided that Broker, prior to any such sale, has not become entitled to compensation in accordance with the terms hereof. In the event that Owner shall sell the property, he shall immediately notify Broker in writing. specifying the name of the purchaser and the purchase price to be paid. In the event that Broker does not advise Owner, in writing, within 7 days, that he has negotiated with said purchaser, it shall be conclusively presumed that he has not. Upon the receipt by Broker of such notice, the agency granted hereby shall terminate, provided, however, that in the event the sale is not made in accordance with the notice, the rights of Broker hereunder shall continue for the balance of the term hereof.

Owner agrees not to publicly offer the property for sale at a lower price than that stated hereinabove. Owner agrees further to notify Broker within 24 hours of any change in price or terms.

In the event the property is sold subject to FHA or VA financing, Owner agrees to pay up to .... discount points necessary to obtain such financing.

Owner agrees to transfer the following personal property, included in the above price, by a Warranty Bill of Sale in favor of purchaser at close of escrow: ....

NOTICE: The amount or rate of real estate commissions is not fixed by law. They are set by each Broker individually and may be negotiable between the Seller and Broker.

Owner agrees to pay Broker as compensation for services rendered a fee of...

....per cent of the selling price, IF:

1. Broker procures a purchaser during the term hereof on the terms specifed herein or on any other terms acceptable to Owner.
2. The property is sold, exchanged, or otherwise transferred during the term hereof, through any other agent.
3. The property is withdrawn from sale, or if this authorization is revoked during the term hereof, or if the Owner otherwise prevents the performance hereunder by the Broker, except as provided for herein.
4. A sale, exchange, or other transfer of said property is made within twelve (12) months after the termination of this authorization to persons with whom Broker shall have negotiated during the term hereof and whose names the Broker shall have submitted in writing to Owner within ten days after termination of this authorization.

If suit is brought to collect the compensation or if Broker successfully defends any action brought against Broker by Owner relating to this authorization or under any sales agreement relating to said property, Owner agrees to pay all costs incurred by Broker in connection with such action, including a reasonable attorney's fee.

Owner agrees to make available to Broker and prospective purchasers all data, records and documents pertaining to the property, to allow Broker, or any other broker with whom Broker chooses to cooperate, to show the property at reasonable times and upon reasonable notice and to commit no act which might tend to obstruct the Broker's performance hereunder. Broker may furnish such information to third parties, and after sale of the property, may disclose the terms of sale to interested parties.

In the event of a sale, Owner will promptly, upon Broker's request, deposit in escrow all instruments necessary to complete the sale.

Owner warrants the accuracy of the information furnished herein with respect to the above described property and agrees to hold the Broker harmless from any liabilities or damages arising out of incorrect or undisclosed information. Owner agrees to notify Broker within seven days of any changes in rentals and/or expenses of the property. The undersigned Owner warrants further that he is the owner of record of the property or has the authority to execute this agreement.

Receipt of a copy of this authorization is hereby acknowledged.

In consideration of the execution hereof, the undersigned Broker agrees to use diligence in effecting a sale of said property.

Dated:..Seller

....Broker ....Seller

....Address....................Phone ....Address....................Phone

By.. Date property was purchased:...

Address:...Price..

Corner..Between..and..

District..Lot Size/Acreage..Zoning..

Taxes $....................................... Allocated to Land:..Allocated to Improvements:..Bonds $..

Existing Encumbrances:

1st Loan $......................................., $........................... Mo. @........................%, Including Impounds ☐, Lender..Loan No........................

2nd Loan $......................................., $........................... Mo. @........................%, Due on Sale ☐, Due Date..

3rd Loan $......................................., $........................... Mo. @........................%, Due on Sale ☐, Due Date..

Reason for Selling:..

Exchange for: ....

Remarks: ....

PROPERTY INFORMATION ON REVERSE SIDE

Figure 22-1   An exclusive-right-to-sell listing. (Reprinted by permission of Professional Publishing Corporation. Copyright © 1969 by Professional Publishing Corporation, 122 Paul Drive, San Rafael, California 94903.)

22-16

SINGLE FAMILY DWELLING

FLOOR PLAN	BED ROOMS	SIZES	BATH ROOMS	SHOWERS Stall	SHOWERS O-Tub	LIV.R. SIZE	DIN.R. SIZE	KIT-CHEN	OTHER ROOMS	STOR-AGE	KITCHEN	GARAGE	GROUNDS
3rd Floor											Blt-In R&O	No. Cars	Improved
2nd Floor											Disposal	Side by Side	Fenced
1st Floor											Dishwash	Tandem	Sprinkler
Street Lev											Fan	Attached	Patio
Cellar											Hood	Detached	BBQ
TOTAL											Bkfst Area	Car Port	Pool

No. Stories		Floors		Transp. Blks.		Cond. Grounds
Attached		Fireplace		Shops Blks.		Cond. Exterior
Detached		Heat		Elem. School		Cond. Interior
Style		Air Cond.		Jr. High School		Occupant
Year Built		W/Stripped		High School		Owner ☐ Tenant ☐
Builder		Insulated		Paroch. School		Phone
Exterior		Interior Walls		Carpets		To Show
Roof		Laundry		Drapes		Lock Box
Sq. Ft.		220 Wiring		Inter-Com		Key At
Level/Slope		Copper Pipes		Possession		
View		Sewer		Rental		

MULTI-FAMILY DWELLING

Units	Rms	Bdrms	Baths	Furn	Refr	Sq.Ft	CONDITION	TENANTS	Phone Nos.	Lease E/D	Monthly Rent	ANNUAL STATEMENT
												Taxes
												Insur.
												Licenses
												Util/Wat
												Trash
												Mgr/Jan
												Elev Serv
												Gardener
												Pool Serv
												Mangmnt.
												Legal/Acct
												Maint.
												Gross Inc
						INCOME FROM: LAUNDRY ☐ GARAGES ☐						Less Exp
UNITS				SQ. FT.					TOTAL MONTHLY INCOME			Net Inc.

RES. MGR.   APT. #   PHONE: TO SHOW:

No. Stories	Floors	Laundry Rm.	Fire Sprinklr.	Transp. Blks.
Elevator	Carpets	Washr-Dryer	Copper Pipes	Freeway Blks
Type Constr.	Drapes	Owned/Lease	Sep.Gas Meters	Shops Blks.
Exterior	Fireplaces	Storage	Sep.Elec.Meters	Cond. Ground
Year Built	Inter-Com	Recreatn. Rm.	Lawn Sprink.	Cond. Exter.
Builder	TV Outlets	Hall Floors	Pool	Cond. Halls
Level/Slope	Blt-In R & O	Heat	Garages	Cond. Apts.
View	Fan & Hood	Car Ports	Parking Lot	
Basement	Garb. Disp.	Air Cond.		
Roof	Dish Washer	Garb. Chutes		

COMMERCIAL-INDUSTRIAL

LESSEE	TYPE BUSINESS	Sq. Ft.	Rent P/Sq. Ft.	OVERAGE	Tax Clause	Lease E/D	INCOME	ANNUAL STATEMENT
								Taxes
								Insur.
								Utilities
								Services
								Salaries
								Mangmt.
								Legal/Acct
								Maint.
								Gross Inc
								Less Exp
								Net Inc.

Advert. Value	Load Access	Type Constr.	Amps	Fire Sprinklers
Dist. Main Highw.	Room F/Expans	Exterior	Voltage	Load. Dock
Trans. Blks.	Size Bldg.	Roof	Plumbing	Spec. Equipmnt
Spur Track	No. Stories	Height Clear.	No. Toilets	Front Ft.
Traffic Count	Basement	Floors	Heat	Square Ft.
Parking	Age Bldg.	Load Factor	Air Cond.	Office Area
Restrictions				

LAND

HIGHEST & BEST USE:	DISTANCE TO:			
Farm	Transp.	Easements	Storm Drain	Bonds
Ranch	Main Highway	Restrictions	Sewerage	Front Ft.
Timber	Railroad	View	Water	Square Ft.
Industrial	Metrop. Area	Above Grade Ft	Gas	Dedication
Commercial	Bus. Distr.	Below Grade Ft	Power	Fire Hydrant
Motel	Shop. Center	Contour	Phone	Traffic Count
Resort	Schools	Fill Required	Street	
Subdivision	City Limits	Depth Bedrock	Sidewalks	
Building Lot		Sub-Soil	Curbs	
		Zoning	Gutters	

The Owner of the herein property verifies the accuracy of the information contained herein .... Owner

22-17

Those states, as opposed to making a net listing illegal, require the broker to disclose to the seller, in writing, before the seller becomes bound to the sale, the exact amount of compensation which the broker will earn as a result of that transaction. The feeling is that when the seller sees the amount for which the property is actually being sold, the compensation agreement will not be approved, and the seller will not then be subject to the broker's overreaching.

Option Listings. Option listings, like net listings, are frowned on but not necessarily illegal. In an option listing, the seller offers the broker an option to purchase the listed property, usually net of the broker's commission. In theory, the seller is not concerned with the source of the purchase price, whether it comes from a bona fide buyer or from the broker. Therefore, a sale to the broker at a price net of the commission theoretically puts as many dollars in the seller's pocket as a sale to a third person would, out of which the commission would then have to be paid.

The reason for the concern about an option listing is that the broker may find a prospective buyer willing to pay considerably more for the property than the broker's option requires the broker to pay for it. Under those circumstances, the broker's fiduciary duty would require the broker to obtain the higher offer for the benefit of the seller. If the broker sees an opportunity to increase the broker's compensation by instead exercising the option to purchase and then reselling the property at the higher price to a prospective purchaser, the broker may be tempted to disregard the duty to get the best possible price for the seller. For this reason, many states which do not outlaw the use of option listings require the same written disclosure to be made by the broker to the seller before the seller becomes bound to the sale. If the seller approves, the broker may go ahead and exercise the option to purchase; otherwise, the seller gets the benefit of the broker's efforts in producing a higher purchase price for the property.

Guaranteed Purchase Agreement. Under a guaranteed purchase agreement the broker agrees, before finding a buyer, that, if the property does not sell within the term of the listing, the broker will buy it. This assures the seller that the property will be sold, one way or the other. The broker in this instance does not violate any fiduciary duty, unless the broker conceals the existence of a prospective purchaser from the seller until the listing period ends, to take advantage of the higher purchase price.

Multiple Listing. A multiple listing is not a different kind of listing but rather is the result of an association of brokers who agree to share their listings under prescribed conditions. Using the services of a multiple listing association enables all participating brokerage offices, regardless of size, to participate in listings obtained by others and exposes properties listed by one broker to all other broker-members of the multiple.

Most multiple listing associations require that only exclusive-right-to-sell listings be forwarded for publication in the multiple listing service. This is to ensure that commissions will be earned without the necessity of proving the element of procuring cause. Conversely, all exclusive-right-to-sell listings obtained by participating members must be forwarded to the association within a set period of time such as 48 hours after the listing is obtained. This is to prevent the use of the multiple only for listings which members feel they cannot easily market themselves, a practice that, if permitted, would soon result in only the poorest listings ever being forwarded to the service.

Net listings, option listings, and multiple listings are, in fact, not different kinds of listings; rather, they represent different uses for existing types of listings. A net listing, for example, could be taken using an exclusive-right-to-sell, an exclusive agency, or an open listing.

DEPOSIT RECEIPT

After the property is listed, and preferably soon after, an offer may be obtained to present to the seller. Offers are presented on the typical real estate form called a "deposit receipt," a copy of which is shown as Figure 22-2.

Although not legally necessary to constitute a binding contract, most real estate practitioners feel that a "good faith" deposit of money should accompany an offer. The deposit receipt evidences the terms of the agreement for which the deposit was made.

Some states require that some *caveat,* or warning language, be placed prominently on the document to advise the purchaser that the document represents something more than just a receipt for the deposit. One complaint which used to be made somewhat frequently was that the purchaser did not believe a binding agreement would necessarily result from the acceptance of the offer contained in the deposit receipt. The caveat suggests that the document is more than just a receipt for the deposit and that a binding agreement may result from its acceptance.

Parties

Remember that the parties to the listing agreement were the seller and the broker. The buyer, not one of the parties, could not insist on the

RESIDENTIAL PURCHASE AGREEMENT AND DEPOSIT RECEIPT

RECEIVED FROM ....

.... hereinafter designated as PURCHASER,

the sum of $ .... (.... DOLLARS)

evidenced by Cash ☐, Personal Check ☐, Cashier's Check ☐, Other ☐ .... to be deposited in trust upon acceptance of this offer,

as deposit on account of the PURCHASE PRICE of $ .... (.... DOLLARS)

for the real property situated in the City of .... County of .... State of ....,

described as ....

.... **upon the following TERMS and CONDITIONS:**

1. DEPOSIT INCREASE. The deposit shall be increased to $ .... within .... days from acceptance, evidenced by ....

2. CLOSING COSTS. Escrow fees, if any, and other closing costs shall be paid in accordance with local custom, except as otherwise provided herein.

3. PRORATIONS. Rents, taxes, premiums on insurance acceptable to Purchaser, interest and other expenses of the property to be prorated as of recordation of deed. Security deposits, advance rentals or considerations involving future lease credits shall be credited to Purchaser.

4. CLOSING. On or before .... or within .... days from acceptance, whichever is later, both parties shall deposit with an authorized escrow holder all funds and instruments necessary to complete the sale in accordance with the terms hereof. Thereafter any party, including Agent, may disclose the terms of sale. The representations and warranties herein shall not be terminated by conveyance of the property.

5. OCCUPANCY. Possession shall be delivered to Purchaser *(check either item [1] or [2]):*

☐ 1. *Upon recordation of the deed.*

☐ 2. *After recordation, but not later than midnight of* .... Unless Seller has vacated the premises prior to recordation, Seller shall pay Purchaser
.... per day from recordation to date of possession and leave in escrow a sum equal to the above per diem amount multiplied by the number of days from date of closing to date allowed for delivery of possession. Said sum to be disbursed to the persons entitled thereto on the date possession is delivered.

6. EVIDENCE OF TITLE in the form of ☐ a policy of title insurance, ☐ other: .... to be paid for by ....

7. EXAMINATION OF TITLE. 15 (fifteen) days from date of acceptance hereof are allowed the Purchaser to examine the title to the property and to report in writing any valid objections thereto. Any exceptions to the title which would be disclosed by examination of the records shall be deemed to have been accepted unless reported in writing within said 15 days. If Purchaser objects to any exceptions to the title, Seller shall use due diligence to remove such exceptions at his own expense before close of escrow. But if such exceptions cannot be removed before close of escrow, all rights and obligations hereunder may, at the election of the Purchaser, terminate and end, and the deposit shall be returned to Purchaser, unless he elects to purchase the property subject to such exceptions.

8. ENCUMBRANCES. In addition to any encumbrances referred to herein, Purchaser shall take title to the property subject to: (1) Real Estate Taxes not yet due and (2) Covenants, conditions, restrictions, rights of way and easements of record, if any, which do not materially affect the value or intended use of the property. The amount of any bond or assessment which is a lien shall be ☐ paid, ☐ assumed by ....

9. FIXTURES. All improvements, fixtures, attached floor coverings, draperies including hardware, shades, blinds, window and door screens, storm sash, combination doors, awnings, outdoor plants, potted or otherwise, trees, and items permanently attached to the real property-are included, free of liens, unless specifically excluded.

10. PERSONAL PROPERTY. The following personal property, on the premises when inspected by Purchaser, is included in the purchase price and shall be transferred in normal working order, unless otherwise stated herein, by a Warranty Bill of Sale to Purchaser at close of escrow: ....

11. MAINTENANCE. Until possession is delivered Seller agrees to maintain the heating, sewer, plumbing and electrical systems, including the water heater and any built-in appliances and equipment, as well as all outside locks and window hardware in normal working order, to maintain the grounds and to deliver the property free of debris and with no broken windows or shower glass, except as listed in an Addendum of same date, initialed by Purchaser and Seller.

12. NOTICES. By acceptance hereof, Seller warrants that he has no notice of violations relating to the property, from City, County, or State agencies.

13. DEFAULT. In the event that Purchaser shall default in the performance of this agreement, unless the parties have agreed to a provision for liquidated damages, Seller may, subject to any rights of the agent herein, retain Purchaser's deposit on account of damages sustained and may take such action as he deems appropriate to collect such additional damages as may have been actually sustained, and Purchaser shall have the right to take such action as he deems appropriate to recover such portion of the deposit as may be allowed by law. In the event that Purchaser shall so default, unless Purchaser and Seller have agreed to liquidated damages, Purchaser agrees to pay to the brokers entitled thereto such commissions as would be payable by Seller in the absence of such default. Purchaser's obligation to said brokers shall be in addition to any rights which said brokers may have against Seller in the event of default. In the event legal action is instituted by the broker or any party to this agreement to enforce the terms of this agreement, or arising out of the execution of this agreement or the sale, or to collect commissions, the prevailing party shall be entitled to receive from the other party a reasonable attorney fee to be determined by the court in which such action is brought.

14. PROVISIONS ON THE REVERSE SIDE. The provisions on the reverse side which are initialed below by the Purchaser are included in this agreement:

.....14-A PEST CONTROL INSPECTION PAID BY BUYER
.....14-B PEST CONTROL INSPECTION PAID BY SELLER
.....14-C EXISTING PEST CONTROL REPORT
BY .... DATED ....
.....14-D PURCHASE AS IS, SUBJECT TO APPROVAL OF REPORT
.....14-E WAIVER OF PEST CONTROL INSPECTION

.....14-F MAINTENANCE RESERVE $.............
.....14-G HOME PROTECTION CONTRACT
PAID BY.................
.....14-H ROOF INSPECTION
.....14-I VA APPRAISED VALUE CLAUSE
.....14-J FHA APPRAISED VALUE CLAUSE
.....14-K CONTINGENT UPON SALE of ...., hereinafter called "Purchaser's Property."

15. ADDENDUM. The following addendum of same date, signed and attached hereto is included in this agreement: Addendum No. ....

16. EXPIRATION. This offer shall expire unless a copy hereof with Seller's written acceptance is delivered to Purchaser or his Agent within .... days.

17. TIME. Time is of the essence of this agreement.

18. Additional TERMS and CONDITIONS: _____

_____

_____

_____

_____

_____

_____

The undersigned Purchaser has read both sides of this agreement and acknowledges receipt of a copy hereof. Purchaser acknowledges further that he has not received or relied upon any statements or representations by the undersigned Agent which are not herein expressed.

.... Real Estate Company   DATED: ....   TIME: ....

By .... Agent   .... Purchaser

Broker's Initials: .... Dated: .... Purchaser

ACCEPTANCE

The undersigned Seller accepts the foregoing offer and agrees to sell the herein described property for the price and on the terms and conditions herein specified.

COMMISSION. Seller hereby agrees to pay to ....

the Agent in this transaction, from proceeds at the close of escrow, the sum of $ .... or .... % of the sale price, whichever is the lesser, for services rendered. In the event that Purchaser defaults and fails to complete the sale, Agent shall be entitled to receive one half of Purchaser's deposit, but not more than the commission earned, without prejudice to Agent's rights to recover the balance of the commission from Purchaser. The mutual recission of this agreement by Purchaser and Seller shall not relieve said parties of their obligations to Agent hereunder. This agreement shall not limit the rights of Agent provided for in any listing or other agreement which may be in effect between Seller and Agent, except that the amount of the commission shall be as specified herein.

The undersigned Seller hereby acknowledges receipt of a copy hereof. DATED: ....   TIME: ....

.... Real Estate Company   .... Seller

By .... Seller

Figure 22-2 A typical residential deposit receipt. (Reprinted by permission of Professional Publishing Corporation. Copyright © 1982 by Professional Publishing Corporation, 122 Paul Drive, San Rafael, California 94903.)

......**14-A. PEST CONTROL INSPECTION.** The main building and all attached structures to be inspected by a licensed pest control operator. Purchaser to pay for inspection. Seller to pay for: (1) Elimination of infestation and/or infection of wood-destroying pests or organisms, (2) For repair of damage caused by such infestation and/or infection or by excessive moisture, (3) For correction of conditions which caused said damage and (4) For repair of plumbing and other leaks affecting wood members, including repair of leaking stall showers, in accordance with said pest control operator's report.

Seller shall not be responsible for any work recommended to correct conditions usually deemed likely to lead to infestation or infection of wood-destroying pests or organisms, but where no evidence of active infestation or infection is found with respect to such conditions.

If the inspecting pest control operator shall recommend further inspection of inaccessible areas, Purchaser may require that said areas be inspected. If any infestation or infection shall be discovered by such inspection, the additional cost of such inspection and additional required work shall be paid by Seller. If no such infestation or infection is discovered, the additional cost of inspecting such inaccessible areas and the work required to return the property to its original condition shall be paid by Purchaser.

Funds for work to be done at Seller's expense shall be held in escrow and disbursed by escrow holder upon receipt of proof of completion of said work or upon close of escrow, whichever occurs later.

As soon as the same are available, copies of the report, and any certification or other proof of completion of the work shall be delivered to the agents of Purchaser and Seller who are authorized to receive the same on behalf of their principals.

Seller reserves the right to perform all or part of the work in accordance with above pest conrol operator's report; provided that, upon completion of Seller's work, the property be re-inspected by a licensed pest control operator of Buyer's choice, but at Seller's expense and the report recommends no further work.

......**14-B. PEST CONTROL INSPECTION.** The main building and all attached structures to be inspected by a licensed pest control operator. Seller to pay for inspection and for: (1) Elimination of infestation and/or infection of wood-destroying pests or organisms, (2) For repair of damage caused by such infestation and/or infection or by excessive moisture, (3) For correction of conditions which caused said damage and (4) For repair of plumbing and other leaks affecting wood members, including repair of leaking stall showers, in accordance with said pest control operator's report.

Seller shall not be responsible for any work recommended to correct conditions usually deemed likely to lead to infestation or infection of wood-destroying pests or organisms, but where no evidence of active infestation or infection is found with respect to such conditions.

If the inspecting pest control operator shall recommend further inspection of inaccessible areas, Purchaser may require that said areas be inspected. If any infestation or infection shall be discovered by such inspection, the additional cost of such inspection and additional required work shall be paid by Seller. If no such infestation or infection is discovered, the additional cost of inspecting such inaccessible areas shall be paid by Purchaser.

Funds for work to be done at Seller's expense shall be held in escrow and disbursed by escrow holder upon receipt of proof of completion of said work or upon close of escrow, whichever occurs later.

As soon as the same are available, copies of the report, and any certification or other proof of completion of the work shall be delivered to the agents of Purchaser and Seller who are authorized to receive the same on behalf of their principals.

Seller reserves the right to perform all or part of the work in accordance with above pest control operator's report; provided that, upon completion of Seller's work, the property be re-inspected by a licensed pest control operator at Seller's expense and the report recommends no further work.

......**14-C. EXISTING PEST CONTROL REPORT ACCEPTED BY PURCHASER.** Purchaser accepts existing pest control report on the property by the licensed pest control operator whose name is listed under Item 14-C on the reverse side hereof. Purchaser has read and understands said report and acknowledges receipt of a copy thereof.

......**14-D. AS IS, BUT SUBJECT TO PURCHASER'S APPROVAL OF INSPECTION REPORT.** Property to be purchased in its present condition with no charge to Seller for any pest control work. However, Purchaser shall have the right to have the property inspected and to obtain a report from a licensed structural pest control operator. In the event the report indicates the necessity for repair of damage caused by infestation of wood-destroying pests or organisms and for correction of its causes, Purchaser may terminate all obligations of the parties hereunder by delivering a written notice to do so, together with a copy of said report, within ten business days from acceptance hereof, unless Seller notifies Purchaser within two business days thereafter of this agreement to pay for the work recommended by said report.

Purchaser acknowledges that he has not received or relied upon any representations by either the Agent or the Seller, with respect to the condition of the property.

......**14-E. WAIVER OF PEST CONTROL INSPECTION.** Purchaser has satisfied himself about the condition of the property and agrees to purchase the property in its present condition, without the benefit of a structural pest control inspection.

Purchaser acknowledges that he has not received or relied upon any representations by either the Agent or the Seller, with respect to the condition of the property.

......**14-F. MAINTENANCE RESERVE.** Seller agrees to leave in escrow a maintenance reserve in the amount specified under Item 14-F on the reverse side hereof.

If in the reasonable opinion of a qualified technician any of the terms listed under Item 11, MAINTENANCE, on the reverse side, are not in normal working order, Purchaser shall furnish Seller a copy of said technician's inspection report and/or submit written notice to Seller of non-compliance of any of the conditions of said Item 11, within ten (10) business days from date occupancy is delivered.

In the event Seller fails to make the repairs and/or corrections within five (5) business days from receipt of said report or notice, Seller herewith authorizes the escrow holder to disburse to Purchaser against bills for such repairs or corrections a total sum limited to the amount reserved. Said reserve shall be disbursed to Purchaser or returned to Seller not later than fifteen (15) business days from date occupancy is delivered.

......**14-G. A HOME PROTECTION CONTRACT** paid for by the party specified under Item 14-G on the reverse side shall become effective upon close of escrow for a period of not less than one year.

......**14-H. ROOF INSPECTION.** Within two (2) business days following acceptance hereof Purchaser, at his expense, may order a roof inspection report from a licensed general or roofing contractor. Copies of the report shall be delivered to the agents of Purchaser and Seller who are authorized to receive the same on behalf of their principals.

Within three (3) days following receipt of the report, Seller may (a) elect to pay the cost of all work recommended by such report; or (b) elect to pay none or only a portion of the cost of such work. Written notice of such election shall be delivered to Purchaser or his agent.

In the event Seller shall not have agreed to pay for all such work, Purchaser may elect to pay the balance of the cost of such work or terminate all rights and obligations to the parties under this agreement. Written notice of such election shall be delivered to Seller or his agent within seven (7) days following receipt of Seller's notice. In the event of such termination, Purchaser shall be entitled to a full refund of all deposits excluding the cost of the above roof inspection report. If no written election is made within seven (7) days, Purchaser shall have no right to terminate this agreement, and Seller shall be responsible for the cost of that portion of the work which he elected to pay.

In the event Seller shall have elected to pay the cost of all such work, Seller shall have the right to have the work performed by any licensed general or roofing contractor of his choice.

......**14-I. VA APPRAISED VALUE CLAUSE.** It is expressly agreed that, notwithstanding any other provisions of this Contract, the Purchaser shall not incur any penalty by forfeiture of earnest money or otherwise or be obligated to complete the purchase of the property described herein, if the contract purchase price or cost exceeds the Reasonable Value of the property established by the Veterans Administration. The Purchaser shall, however, have the privilege and option of proceeding with the consummation of this contract without regard to the amount of the Reasonable Value established by the Veterans Administration. Escrow Fee to be paid by Seller.

......**14-J. FHA APPRAISED VALUE CLAUSE.** It is expressly agreed that, notwithstanding any other provisions of this contract, the Purchaser shall not be obligated to complete the purchase of the property described herein or to incur any penalty by forfeiture of earnest money deposits or otherwise unless the Seller has delivered to the Purchaser a written statement issued by the Federal Housing Commissioner setting forth the appraised value of the property for mortgage insurance purposes of not less than $...................., which statement the Seller hereby agrees to deliver to the Purchaser promptly after such appraised value statement is made available to the Seller. The Purchaser shall, however, have the privilege and option of proceeding with the consummation of this contract without regard to the amount of the appraised valuation made by the Federal Housing Commissioner. The appraised valuation is arrived at to determine the maximum mortgage the Department of Housing and Urban Development will insure. HUD does not warrant the value or the condition of the property. The Purchaser should satisfy himself/herself that the price and condition of the property are acceptable.

......**14-K. CONTINGENCY RELEASE CLAUSE.** Subject to the sale and conveyance of "Purchaser's Property," described in Item 14-K on the reverse side hereof, within the time specified for closing of Seller's property. Seller shall have the right to continue to offer the herein property for sale and to accept offers subject to the rights of Purchaser. Should Seller accept such an offer, then Purchaser shall be given written notice of such acceptance. In the event the Purchaser will not waive this condition in writing within three (3) calendar days of receipt of such notice, then this agreement shall be terminated and all deposits be returned to Purchaser and escrow cancelled. Said notice may be personally delivered or mailed by certified mail and addressed to Purchaser, in care of his agent identified herein. In the event of mailing, such notice shall be deemed to have been given on the day following the date of mailing evidenced by the postmark on the envelope containing such notice.

____

____

____

____

____

____

The undersigned Purchaser hereby acknowledges receipt of a copy of the accepted agreement on the reverse side.

Date .... Time ....

.... Purchaser .... Purchaser

Purchaser's address .... City .... Zip .... Phone ....

FORM 101 (2-82)

existence of a contract binding the seller to sell, even if it were a full-price offer. But the parties to a deposit receipt are (primarily) the buyer and the seller. Once the seller accepts the offer made by the buyer and assuming that all other elements of a valid contract exist, the parties are bound to the agreement.

The part of the deposit receipt which is usually the most difficult for a licensee to complete involves the conditions, or contingencies.

Contingencies

A buyer, for example, does not want to become bound to the purchase of property if satisfactory arrangements for financing cannot be made. The existing loan, perhaps, must be one which the buyer can take over. A new loan might have to be arranged which has parameters that the buyer can afford (e.g., monthly payment, interest rate, balloon payment). The buyer cannot make an unconditional offer to purchase the property without the knowledge that these matters can be adequately resolved. Thus the buyer will want to "condition" the obligation on the buyer's ability to either "assume" or "take subject to" the existing loan on the property, or, alternatively, to obtain a new loan within limits established by the buyer.

Sometimes this is accomplished by a very general phrase, such as "subject to financing, or obtaining new loans, satisfactory to the buyer."

This kind of language is dangerous to both parties. The buyer may be bound to an unacceptable loan, or the seller may not be able to hold the buyer to reasonable loan terms if they are offered.

"Satisfaction" Problems

Courts frequently hold parties to a reasonable and objective standard whenever "satisfaction" or "personal satisfaction" language appears in an agreement. As in the element of mutual assent in a contract, this means that, even though the buyer may not be personally satisfied with loan terms that are offered, the buyer may nevertheless be required to accept them if a "reasonable person" under the circumstances would have found them acceptable.

The buyer may also find that, if the language is too loose, the element of consideration required for an effective agreement is missing. The law requires a "mutuality of obligation," or the consideration may be "illusory" and therefore missing. Mutuality of obligation means that both parties to an agreement must be bound to it or neither party will be bound. If the pure personal satisfaction of one party is really the essence of the agreement, it is possible that a court will conclude that that person is not bound to do anything. All that is necessary to avoid liability is for that person to say that she or he is not satisfied, no matter how reasonable the offered conditions might be.

Contingencies, to be effective, should be worded so that objective determination of compliance can be made while still protecting the legitimate interests of both parties. The contingency stated earlier concerning financing could be restated as follows: "This offer is conditioned on the buyer's obtaining a new loan in the principal amount of forty-five thousand dollars ($45,000.00), with monthly payments not to exceed eight hundred dollars ($800.00) including interest at fourteen percent (14%) per annum, or less, and for a term of twenty (20) years or more." Any loan commitment obtained can then easily be measured against those objective standards to bind the parties or to excuse performance if those terms cannot be obtained.

The contingency should set out the manner in which it is to be either satisfied or waived. It should also be specific as to which party or parties it is to benefit. The general rule is that a contingency may be waived by the person for whose benefit it is inserted into the agreement, but it is not always easy to determine which of the parties that is. To avoid disagreement later, the contingency should state that it is for the benefit of the buyer (or the seller, or both parties, as applicable).

Although the deposit receipt, when executed by both parties, is a contract between the buyer and the seller, the broker frequently becomes a party to it with respect to the broker's compensation.

Broker's Compensation

If the agreement provides that the commission is to be paid out of the proceeds available to the seller upon the close of escrow, or similar language, the broker may not be able to recover a commission if there are not sufficient funds available at the close of escrow with which to pay them. Although the buyer and the seller alone could not have agreed to deprive the broker of compensation, if the broker becomes a party to the agreement such a provision can be enforced against the broker.

A broker may be compensated by the seller (the usual provision), by the buyer (a "buyer's broker" agreement, as in Figure 22-3), or by the parties jointly. If compensation is coming from both parties, the broker has a duty to inform each of the principals that the other is also compensating the broker. This is especially important in an exchange transaction (which is really two sales); many times the transaction is handled by one broker who is compensated by each of the parties for services rendered in selling, or exchanging, their properties.

Although the seller usually hires the broker to find a buyer and there-

COOPERATION AGREEMENT BETWEEN BROKERS

The undersigned brokers, hereinafter referred to as Listing Broker and Selling Broker, desiring to cooperate in the sale of the real property, situated in the City of ....,

State of ...., described as...

....agree as follows:

(1) The Listing Broker hereby authorizes the Selling Broker to offer the above property ☐ for sale, ☐ for exchange, ☐ for lease and to accept a deposit thereon.

(2) Selling Broker agrees to submit all offers to Listing Broker and agrees further that he shall not present any offers direct to the Owner, without Listing Broker's prior written consent. Listing Broker agrees to present to the Owner any reasonable offer which Selling Broker shall obtain.

(3) In the event a sale, exchange or lease of the above property is made to an offeror produced by Selling Broker, Listing Broker agrees, upon completion of the transaction, to pay to Selling Broker ....% of the total brokerage fee received. Listing Broker may, in his sole discretion, modify his agreement with the Owner with respect to the brokerage fee payable and such modification shall be binding upon Selling Broker.

(4) Selling Broker agrees, to use courtesy and consideration for the Owner in showing the above property and to follow Listing Broker's instructions for showing the property.

(5) Selling Broker shall not solicit offers for the property through written advertisements.

(6) Selling Broker shall not accept any Authorization from the Owner to sell, exchange or lease said property within 12 months from this date.

(7) It is expressly understood that this agreement does not extend to brokers other than the undersigned.

Dated:...   Dated:...

....Listing Broker   ....Selling Broker

By..   By..

Figure 22-3   A broker cooperative agreement. (Reprinted by permission of Professional Publishing Corporation. Copyright © 1971 by Professional Publishing Corporation, 122 Paul Drive, San Rafael, California 94903.)

fore owes a commission if the broker performs, some agreements provide that the broker may seek a commission directly from the buyer on the buyer's default in the purchase agreement.

Other matters which might appear in the deposit receipt include: (1) provisions for the inclusion of any personal property or fixtures which might be involved in the sale; (2) qualification of an exchange as "tax-deferred" (frequently but erroneously referred to as "tax free") under the provisions of Section 1031 of the Internal Revenue Code; and (3) qualification of the sale as an "installment" sale, also under applicable provisions of the Internal Revenue Code.

When the contract has been formed by an acceptance of an offer contained in a deposit receipt, the parties should move quickly to the next step, which is to open an escrow to consummate the sale.

ESCROW INSTRUCTIONS

Conditions Concurrent

When the order in which conditions are to be performed in agreement is not specified in the agreement, the law considers that they are conditions "concurrent," to be performed simultaneously. But real estate transactions generally are too complicated for the performance of simultaneous conditions. Financing arrangements must be completed; title problems must be researched and, if necessary, cleared; and inspection of the property is frequently made a condition of the purchase and must be completed, either by the buyer alone or by various experts acting on the buyer's behalf. Most of these conditions take time to arrange and complete.

The device most frequently used to ensure that title does not pass until the seller's conditions have been met and that the purchase price is not released until the buyer's conditions have been met is an "escrow." An escrow is a process wherein each party deposits funds and documents as they become available. When all the conditions have been fulfilled (or waived by the party for whose benefit they were inserted), then title is ready to pass and the escrow closes, delivering title documents to the buyer and funds and loan documents to the seller.

Requirements for Valid Escrow

The escrow holder must be an independent third party with no financial interest in the outcome of the transaction, sometimes referred to as a "stake holder" for obvious reasons.

Escrow instructions are executed by the buyer and seller separately, but are read together as though they were a single instrument in determining the agreements of the parties. If there is a disagreement in the interpretation of the instructions, the escrow holder will usually not honor the demands of either party for fear of being sued by the other. Rather, if the problem cannot be resolved amicably, the escrow holder will file a lawsuit called an action in "interpleader." In effect, the escrow holder deposits the funds and documents it has into court, joining the principals as defendants in the litigation and telling the court that conflicting demands have been made and that the escrow holder is unable to determine which of them to follow. The court then listens to each party's argument and orders whatever relief appears to be appropriate under the circumstances. By instituting an interpleader action, the escrow holder is protected, since the court's decision will be binding on both principals.

Interpretation of Escrow Agreements

Certain rules regarding the interpretation, or construction, of contracts are frequently applied when escrow instructions are not clear. For example, later agreements usually supercede prior agreements. Therefore, if it is *not* the intent of the parties to do so, they should express a contrary intent: "These instructions supercede the prior agreement(s) of the parties only to the extent of a conflict between them. In all other respects, the prior agreement(s) of the parties remain(s) in full force and effect."

Typed-in portions of the escrow instructions usually take precedence over preprinted portions. The preprinted portions should therefore be reviewed carefully so that a desired provision will not be deleted.

If ambiguous, contracts will usually be construed the most strongly against the party who prepared them. In a case where two parties are equally free from wrongdoing, the one who had control over the preparation of the agreement (and could have been more careful in its preparation) is the one to suffer if there is an ambiguity or uncertainty. For this reason, unusually complicated portions of the agreement should be drafted by the party who is most interested in ensuring their enforceability. Conversely, the blame for provisions inserted for a party's benefit which are later found to be invalid will frequently fall on the person who drafted that portion of the party's agreement. Frequently, that person is the licensee.

Limitations of Escrow Instructions

Contrary to common practice, escrow instructions should not be used in place of a formal agreement between the parties. This is especially true when there are complicated or unusual provisions to be included in the agreement, such as release clauses, subordination agreements, or various forms of releases or disclaimers. The primary purpose of the escrow instructions is to satisfy the escrow holder's need for directions from the principals. These matters are usually well covered by the instructions, which for the most part are prepared by and for the escrow holder. Other matters not connected with the mechanics of the escrow are not the direct concern of the escrow holder and are frequently not well covered or provided for in the instructions. In fact, they will frequently contain an exculpatory provision stating that a given condition is inserted for the benefit of the parties but is one "with which the escrow holder is not to be concerned."

"Surviving" the Escrow

Some matters normally included in escrow instructions cease to be of importance when the escrow closes. Failure to comply with them will prevent the escrow from closing, but on closing the events become history and of no further concern to the parties. Other matters, such as warranties, may become important after the escrow closes. It is then that some failure of title, encroachment, or claim will be raised, and the only expressed statement as to how those matters should be handled is found in the escrow instructions. In this situation, the instructions should state that these conditions are to "survive" the closing of escrow: "The foregoing warranty is to survive the closing of this escrow."

When all the conditions set forth in the instructions have been met or waived by the party or parties entitled to their benefit, the escrow is ready to close. At that time, it is said to be a "perfect" escrow. Documents evidencing the parties' interests are forwarded to the respective parties or to the recorder's office in their behalf, and the funds available from the escrow are disbursed appropriately. The escrow is then closed, and the transaction has been concluded.

Chapter 23

Landlord-Tenant Relations

K. Reed Harrison   Attorney-at-Law

CONVEYANCE VERSUS CONTRACT

Historically, the lease of real property was regarded as a conveyance of an interest in land. However, the trend today is to apply modern contract principles to the landlord-tenant relationship. The relationship of the landlord and tenant is based on contract, express or implied. Their respective rights and duties are determined by such contract, which is usually in the form of a lease, together with the law of the jurisdiction where the real property is located, which may be read into the contract.

NECESSARY FORMALITIES

Oral leases are normally valid and binding on the landlord and tenant if the period specified in the oral agreement does not exceed the local statute of frauds. In most jurisdictions, under the statute of frauds, an oral lease is not enforceable if it exceeds the period of 1 year.

A written lease is preferable to an oral lease: the term may exceed 1 year, and the respective parties more clearly understand their respective rights and duties under a written lease. At a minimum, a written lease should contain a correct designation and identification of the parties and/or their respective agents; an accurate description of the premises, including parking arrangements if applicable; the term of the lease; the landlord's duty in delivering the premises to the tenant at commencement of the term; the party responsible for paying various expenses and repairs associated with the property; and who may use the property and for what purposes. The lease should be signed by the parties. A complete checklist is provided at the end of this chapter.

An oral modification of a lease is invalid if both the original and remaining periods of the lease exceed the local statute of frauds. For example, in most jurisdictions, a lease which exceeds 10 years could not be orally modified. Likewise, an agreement to make a lease would be valid (if the lease is to be over 1 year) where the agreement is in writing and contains the essential elements set forth previously.

INVALID LEASES

The parties may inadvertently create an invalid lease. If the tenant pays rent to the landlord pursuant to an invalid lease, he or she may create a periodic tenancy, that is, a tenancy which is valid for the period for which the landlord accepted rent. Such a lease will remain in effect for successive periods until one of the parties gives notice of the lease's termination for a period equal to the period for which the tenant paid rent. If the tenant enters into possession without paying rent, a tenancy at will is created and the landlord may immediately bring an action to evict the tenant. If the parties to the lease fully perform as if the lease was valid, some authorities argue that the lease should be given full force and effect.

PERMITTED USES

A tenant has the right to use and occupy the premises described in the lease and to use any personal property included therein. In absence of a restriction in the lease, the tenant has the right to occupy and use the land demised in the same manner that the owner might have done for any lawful purpose or business which does not injure the landlord's interest in the property. The parties to a lease may, however, by express provisions in the lease, restrict the uses to which the tenant may put the leased premises, so long as such restrictions are not for the purpose of creating a monopoly, restraining trade, or otherwise contrary to public law or policy. A tenant generally has no right to remove, destroy, or alter buildings or to make other improvements on the leased premises without the express consent of the lessor.

LANDLORD'S DUTIES TO TENANT

Unless specified otherwise in the lease, the landlord has an obligation to maintain the property in a reasonable manner. Such agreements are binding on the parties unless there is an overiding social policy which would prohibit placing the obligation to maintain and repair on the tenant.

Normally the tenant has the right of quiet use and enjoyment of the demised premises, and the landlord (unless specified otherwise) has the duty and obligation to maintain the premises. An actual or constructive eviction of a tenant occurs when any act of the landlord deprives the tenant of the right to quiet use and possession of the demised premises, expels the tenant from the premises, or denies the tenant use thereof. An eviction of the tenant must be distinguished from a voluntary abandonment of the premises by the tenant. Any disturbance of the tenant's right to quiet use and possession by the landlord (or someone acting under the landlord's authority) which renders the premises unfit for their intended occupancy or which deprives the tenant of the beneficial enjoyment of the demised premises and causes the tenant to abandon the premises amounts to a constructive eviction. Thus, the failure of the landlord to furnish heat, light, water, elevator service, sewage services, means of ingress and/or egress, or any other act which deprives the tenant of the beneficial enjoyment of the premises in the manner contemplated by the parties may amount to a constructive eviction.

It should be remembered that an eviction of a tenant may also occur where there is a breach of a covenant to title or quiet enjoyment. Normally, a covenant of title and quiet enjoyment exists in a lease either expressly or implicitly. Therefore, when the landlord either intentionally or negligently disturbs the quiet use and possession of the tenant or where some third person who claims a paramount or superior title to the landlord in the property disturbs the tenant's right to possession, an unlawful eviction occurs, and the tenant can make legal claims against the landlord.

Where the landlord is obligated to make repairs and an unsuitable condition arises after the tenant enters into possession, the landlord has an obligation to promptly repair the demised premises. In such a situation, the tenant should notify the landlord promptly and in writing of the required repairs.

The wrongful eviction of a tenant by a landlord, whether actual or constructive, may terminate the tenant's obligations under the lease; in certain situations it may also entitle the tenant to recover damages against the landlord. Such damages may include the actual or rental value of the unexpired lease term, costs of leasehold improvements, costs of moving to new premises, and other expenses associated with the landlord's breach. In addition, the tenant may have the right to discontinue paying rent or to terminate the lease and move. The tenant may be entitled to an abatement of the rent based on the fair market value of the lease, may use the rent to eliminate or repair the default, may place the rent in escrow pending the abatement of the offending condition, or, as indicated, may sue the landlord for damages.

Many jurisdictions have now enacted ordinances which impose on the landlord a duty to maintain the property "in a reasonably good state of repair," "maintain the property in a clean and sanitary condition," "maintain the property in reasonably good working condition," or other general terms which leave a great deal of discretion to enforcing the local codes and ordinances. Certain local codes and ordinances provide monetary penalties, imprisonment, or other penalties for the violation of these laws. In addition, certain laws confer on the tenant the right to withhold payment of rent, the right to terminate the lease, the right to collect damages, or the right to repair and deduct the repairs from the rental payment.

ASSIGNMENT AND SUBLETTING

Questions frequently arise in the landlord-tenant relationship as to whether the tenant has the right to assign or sublet the demised premises. An assignment of a leasehold interest is a transaction whereby the tenant transfers his or her entire interest in the demised premises, or a part thereof, for the entire unexpired term of the original lease. A sublease contemplates that the tenant retain some interest in the demised premises even though a third party has leased the property. In the absence of a statutory provision to the contrary or, as is more normally the case, a restriction on the right of assignment in the lease, a tenant has a right to assign her or his leasehold interest in the demised premises without the consent of the leasor. Frequently, a lease will contain a provision indicating that the tenant may not assign or sublet the lease without the consent of the landlord, "which consent shall not be unreasonably withheld." If such a reasonableness provision is contained in the lease, the landlord may deny assignment or subletting only for a reasonable good faith business reason. If, however, the lease gives the landlord unfettered and absolute discretion to prohibit assignment or subletting, the landlord may prohibit them, giving no justifiable reason for denying permission.

Most jurisdictions hold that the owner or landlord may validly impose a restriction against the assignment of the term or any part thereof by the tenant. In addition, in some jurisdictions the right of a tenant to assign is restricted by statutory provisions.

The assignee of a lease receives all the benefits that the tenant would have otherwise enjoyed in the property. In addition, the law implies a promise on the part of the assignee to perform all the duties which had been previously imposed on the former tenant. The former tenant or assignor retains an obligation to the landlord to perform all the terms and conditions of the lease. If the assignee fails or refuses to perform the conditions of the lease and the original tenant or assignor is obligated to pay rent, taxes, or other sums of money to the original lessor under the covenants and promises in the lease, the original tenant or assignor may pay such sums and recover from the assignee. Normally, however, the duties of an assignee terminate when he or she assigns the lease to some third party. In such a situation, the original tenant or assignor remains liable for all the terms and conditions in the lease.

RETALIATORY EVICTION

Many jurisdictions have by statute or by common law developed laws prohibiting retaliatory eviction. The main purpose of the prohibitions against retaliatory eviction is to prevent the landlord from evicting a tenant because of the tenant's complaint to an appropriate government agency as to the inhabitability of a dwelling where the tenant is not in default in the payment of rent. Normally such antiretaliatory eviction laws also apply where the tenant has made repairs to the demised premises and deducted the amount of such repairs from the amount of the rental due the landlord. Also, the landlord usually may not retaliate by increasing the rent or decreasing services to the tenant where the tenant has, in addition to complaining to a governmental agency with regard to housing or health code violations, complained to the landlord of violations or organized to become a member of a tenant's union. Such laws are not totally one-sided, and the landlord may bring an action for possession if the violation was caused by the tenant or some other person in the tenant's household or on the request of the tenant, if the tenant is in default of rent, or if the landlord evicts the tenant to comply with applicable building or housing code ordinances requiring alteration, remodeling, or demolition.

RENT

Leases normally require the payment of rent. "Rent" may be defined as the usual price or consideration paid by a tenant to a landlord for the use and occupation of real estate under a lease. If the lease or contract between the parties fixes the amount in terms of payment of rent, such provisions will control. Where the relation of landlord and tenant is established without any express agreement as to the amount of rent to be paid, the law will imply a promise by the tenant or occupant to pay the reasonable value of the use and occupation of the premises. Unless there is a provision in the lease or custom to the contrary, the rent is payable at the end of the term by which the rent is measured. However, the lease will usually provide for payment of rent at the beginning of the term, and that is when the rent is due.

EMINENT DOMAIN

An eviction of the tenant by the landlord, whether actual or constructive, normally relieves the tenant of the duty to pay all or part of the rent during the time the tenant has been evicted. The taking of the demised premises under the power of eminent domain likewise terminates the liability for future rents. A well-drawn commercial lease will specify the respective rights and liabilities of the parties in the event the property has been taken by eminent domain.

DESTRUCTION OF THE PREMISES

In the absence of agreement or a statute to the contrary, the accidental destruction of a leased building by fire or other casualty does not affect the liability of a tenant for future rents. Again, a well-drawn lease will define the tenant's rights and liabilities on the destruction of the demised premises.

INJURIES TO THIRD PERSONS

The landlord is not generally liable for the acts of the tenant when injuries result to others from the tenant's negligent use of the premises. However, the landlord may be liable to persons outside the demised premises for injury or damage resulting from his or her negligent maintenance of the premises or from a nuisance existing thereon at the time of the lease. This liability may extend to owners or occupants of adjoining or neighboring premises or to users of adjacent public ways. The duties and liabilities of a landlord to persons on the leased premises by the consent of the tenant are the same as those to the tenant. This rule applies to members of the tenant's family as well as invitees and subtenants. If the property is leased for use by the public and such property is not safe for the purpose intended and the owner knew or by the exercise of reasonable diligence should have known of such dangerous conditions, the owner will be liable to patrons or customers on the premises for injuries resulting from such conditions. In addition, if the owner leases premises to different tenants and expressly or implicitly reserves common areas such as entrances, halls, stairs, elevators, and walkways for the common use of the various tenants, it is the duty of the landlord to exercise reasonable care to keep such places safe, and the owner is liable to a tenant or a person who is injured on the premises.

EXPIRATION OF TERM

The parties to a lease may, either in the original lease or by a subsequent agreement, agree to renew or extend a lease after the expiration of the original term. Such provisions for renewal or extension are frequently in the form of an option to the tenant. If a general covenant to renew or extend the lease makes no provision as to terms, a renewal or extension on the same terms as provided in the original lease, including the amount and terms of payment of the rental and the duration of the lease, will be assumed. Under such a covenant to renew, the tenant is not entitled to have inserted in the renewal lease a covenant for further renewal. In the absence of a statute to the contrary, it is generally held that a provision in a lease clearly giving the lessee and her or his assigns the right to perpetual renewals is valid. Most leases contain a notice procedure whereby the tenant must give the landlord notice of intent to renew.

The tenant has no right to hold over or remain in possession of the demised premises after the termination of the lease without the agreement of the landlord. The landlord has the option to treat a tenant who has wrongfully held over after the termination of the lease as a trespasser or as a periodic tenant. The tenant may become a tenant at sufferance, at will, month to month, year to year, or some other definite term depending on the circumstances of the case and the statutes involved.

A tenancy for a fixed term terminates without notice to the tenant at the end of the specified term. If the tenant fails to vacate the demised premises, the landlord may commence a summary proceeding to recover possession from the tenant.

OPTIONS—RIGHT OF FIRST REFUSAL

An option to purchase the demised premises is often contained in a lease. The purpose option contained in a lease is subject to the same rules applicable to options generally. The option is actually an irrevocable offer by the landlord to sell the property which is accepted by the tenant's exercise of the option. Therefore, the option must contain the complete terms of purchase with definiteness and certainty. As a minimum, the option should contain an adequate description of the parties, of the property, of the purchase and loan terms, of any warranties of seller, and of conditions of buyer's obligation to purchase, if any. Some leases will also give the tenant the right of first refusal to purchase the demised premises. If the tenant has the right of first refusal, such right is conditional on the landlord's willingness to sell. The tenant merely has a preference over other prospective purchasers if the landlord decides to sell the demised premises. Should the landlord decide to sell the demised premises, either to a third party or to the tenant, the tenant's right of refusal ripens into an option.

TERMINATION

A tenancy at will is terminated by either party giving that notice required by local statute. A tenancy for an unspecified term is deemed to be renewed for the period (periodic tenancy) for which the tenant pays rent. The periodic tenancy may be terminated by giving notice equal to the period or as required by the local jurisdiction. The most common type of periodic tenancy is the month-to-month tenancy. The month-to-month tenancy is terminated by either party giving 30 days written notice to the other.

EVICTION

Most jurisdictions provide for a summary remedy when the landlord becomes entitled to possession of the premises because of termination of the lease, passage of time, forfeiture, conditions subsequent, after foreclosure or sale by trustee, failure to pay rent, breach of a condition or covenants in the lease, or other reason. The statutory remedy provided in most jurisdictions is usually summary in nature, that is, it is designed to simplify and expedite the proceeding by which the landlord may recover possession of the property. Typically, the summary and proceeding available to the landlord may recover possession of the property, recover unpaid rent, recover for damages to the property, and other related claims.

The summary procedure for possession and damages by the landlord may be maintained against a tenant only where the conventional relationship of landlord and tenant exists between the plaintiff and the person the landlord is seeking to evict. The summary procedure cannot normally be maintained where the landlord-tenant relationship no longer exists.

The normal summary procedure requires that as a condition precedent to bringing the action the landlord must serve on a tenant a notice to perform the covenants or conditions contained in the lease, pay rent, perform some other act, or quit the premises. The notice should state that the landlord elects to terminate the lease. A defect in the notice will normally be a valid defense to the summary dispossession action.

The action can normally be brought by the landlord, the landlord's personal representative, a colessor, a cotenant, a successor to the landlord, and a tenant who has assigned or sublet the demised premises. No person other than the tenant, subtenant, or assignee of the demised premises need be made parties defendant to the lawsuit.

The normal statute providing for the summary dispossession procedure requires that the complaint in unlawful detainer allege the existence of the landlord-tenant relationship, contain an adequate description of the premises, determine termination date of the tenancy, and state the exact amount of rent alleged to be due from tenant. The complaint should describe the neglect or failure to perform some covenant or condition of the lease agreement other than the payment of rent, an unauthorized assignment or subletting of the demised premises, the maintenance of a nuisance or use of the premises for an unlawful purpose, or failure by the tenant to deliver possession as specified in the written notice of termination or offer to surrender which is accepted in writing by the landlord. In addition, the complaint must allege that the defendant has been served the required notice requiring him or her to pay rent or to perform covenants or conditions for possession of the premises and that the defendant refused to comply. Certain statutes will also allow the landlord to seek treble damages.

Most jurisdictions provide a shortened period of time for the defendant to answer the suit and for preference in setting the case for trial. After trial of the matter the court will, if plaintiff is entitled thereto, give judgment for possession, rent, and damages. Thereafter, the landlord may obtain a writ of possession which authorizes the sheriff to move the tenant forcibly from the property.

As affirmative defenses to the landlord's suit, the tenant may allege that the landlord has breached a covenant in the lease, that the property is uninhabitable, that the tenant has complied with all terms and conditions of the lease, or other authorized affirmative defenses. The landlord may not personally evict the tenant unless specifically authorized to do so by local statute.

MITIGATION OF DAMAGES

In most jurisdictions, the landlord is not required to make a reasonable effort to minimize damages (loss of rental income) by leasing the property to another after the lease is executed by the parties and subsequently breached by the tenant. This rule is based on the theory that the lease of real property is a sale of an interest in land and not merely a contract and that, therefore, the tenant's breach does not terminate the lease but gives rise to the landlord's cause of actions for damages. Should the landlord elect to do nothing, she or he may sue the lessee as each installment of rent matures or for the whole amount when it becomes due. The landlord can retake possession, treating the lease as terminated, or the landlord can retake possession for the account of the tenant and hold the tenant liable for general damages for the difference between the stipulated rent and what in good faith the landlord can recover from reletting.

More and more jurisdictions, applying modern contract principles, provide by statute that a tenant's breach of the lease and abandonment of the property operates to automatically terminate the lease absent a provision to the contrary in the lease agreement. The present law in the minority jurisdictions further provides that the landlord has the affirmative obligation to make a reasonable and good faith attempt to mitigate damages by subletting the property at the fair market rate. As a result, the tenant is entitled to offset against the unpaid rent which accrues after the date of termination the amount of rent actually received by the landlord from subletting as well as the amount of rents the tenant is able to prove the landlord could have obtained by acting reasonably in subletting the property. In these jurisdictions, the landlord may be able to stand by and collect rent from the breaching tenant if the lease so provides, as long as the landlord does not terminate the tenant's right to possession and only if the lease expressly permits the tenant to mitigate damages by subletting or assigning her or his leasehold estate. The affirmative obligation is thereby shifted from the landlord to the tenant. Should the property be relet, the landlord's right to recover rent from the original tenant is terminated at the time the landlord terminates the tenant's right to possession.

CHECKLIST FOR REVIEWING LEASES

1. **Parties**
   a. Are the parties named correctly? ( )
   b. If the landlord or tenant is an agent, is evidence of authority indicated? ( )
   c. Is either party's performance guaranteed? ( ) Should it be? ( )

2. **Premises**
   a. Is the description of the premises adequate? ( )
   b. Is a plot plan necessary? ( ) Should a legal description be included? ( )
   c. Is parking provided for? ( )

3. **Term of Lease**
   a. Are the commencement and termination dates specified or determinable? ( )
   b. Is the date on which tenant is bound by the terms of the lease specified or determinable? ( )
   c. Is there a renewal provision? ( ) If so, are the provisions the same as those in original agreement? ( ) Is the method for determining rent on renewal adequate? ( ) May tenant renew if in default? ( )
   d. Is there a holding-over provision? ( ) Are the terms and rent the same? ( )

4. **Delivery of Premises**
   a. Is the building completed? ( )
   b. Is there work to be done in readying the premises? ( ) Is such work described in the lease or letter agreement in sufficient detail? ( )
   c. Must landlord proceed with due diligence in completing work on the premises? ( )
   d. If tenant requests or does work, must the plans be approved? ( )
   e. Is the lease void or voidable if not ready on the commencement date? ( ) If not, is the rent adjusted? ( )
   f. Does the lease terminate if occupancy does not commence within a specified time? ( )
   g. Is a certificate of occupancy required? ( )

5. **Rent**
   a. Is the amount of rent clearly set forth? ( )
   b. Is proration provided for? ( ) For what purpose? ( )
   c. Is it clear where the rent is to be paid? ( )
   d. Are set-offs permissible? ( )

e. Are interest and penalties payable on late payments? ( ) How much? ( )

f. Is there a deposit? ( )
   (1) If so, is interest payable on the deposit? ( )
   (2) Is the deposit to be returned? ( )
   (3) Applied against rent? ( )
   (4) In the event of a transfer of landlord's interest, does the lease specify what happens to the deposit? ( )

6. **Rent Adjustment—Expenses**
   a. Is there a rent adjustment clause? ( )
   b. Is the determination of expenses a function of the first year of operation of the building? ( ) Is the base year adequately defined? ( )
   c. Is the statement of expenses prepared by a C.P.A.? ( ) If not, may tenant examine the books? ( )
   d. Does tenant have a right to object to such statement? ( )
   e. Is the tenant's pro rata share the same as the floor space occupied? ( ) Is this percentage specified in the lease? ( )
   f. Are the expense factors specified? ( ) Which of the following are expenses of the building for this purpose:
      (1) Real estate taxes ( )
      (2) Personal property taxes ( )
      (3) Building employees' wages ( )
      (4) Assessments ( )
      (5) Utilities ( )
      (6) Repairs ( )
      (7) Remodeling ( )
   g. If increased taxes are paid on a pro rata basis, are the base assessment and tax fiscal year adequately specified? ( ) If the building may be remodeled, are the provisions adequate? ( )
   h. May tenants challenge increased tax assessments in name of landlord if landlord fails to do so? ( )

7. **Taxes**
   a. Is tenant liable to pay real estate taxes on the premises? ( ) Personal property taxes? ( )
   b. Is tenant required to pay the taxes attributable to tenant improvements or fixtures? ( ) If so, must tenant request separate billing? ( )
   c. Is tenant required to pay taxes on any other areas of the building? ( )
   d. Must tenant pay assessments? ( )
   e. Does landlord have the right to pay taxes for tenant and require

repayment from tenant? ( ) Is this payment designated as additional rent? ( )

f. If tenant pays taxes or assessments, may he or she challenge assessment in name of landlord? ( )

8. Use of Premises

a. Is tenant's use of premises sufficiently broad or sufficiently restricted? ( )

b. Must tenant comply with laws and public regulations? ( )

c. Does tenant's business involve any risk of violating such laws or regulations? ( )

d. Is there a no-competition business clause? ( )

9. Repairs and Alterations

a. Does tenant accept "as is"? ( )

b. Who must repair? ( ) Must tenant repair for damage not caused by misuse or neglect? ( ) Must landlord repair:
   (1) Plumbing? ( )
   (2) Heating and air conditioning? ( )
   (3) Windows? ( )

c. Are repairs distinct from restoration after casualty? ( )

d. Must repairs be made if insurance proceeds are insufficient? ( ) Must reconstruction? ( )

e. If so, who pays the difference? ( )

f. After a casualty is landlord responsible for any repairs other than for reconstruction? ( )
   (1) Must the landlord ʀrepair tenant's alterations or fixtures? ( ) Reconstruct? ( )
   (2) Are the circumstances requiring reconstruction sufficiently defined? ( )
   (3) Does landlord have the option to terminate if reconstruction is not possible? ( ) If it is not desired? ( )
   (4) Does tenant have the option to terminate if reconstruction is not completed within a specified period? ( )
   (5) Is the rent adjusted pending reconstruction? ( )

g. May tenant make any alterations? ( )

h. Does tenant's business suggest that alterations are necessary? ( ) If so, are they to be made prior to tenancy? ( ) If they are to be made after tenancy:
   (1) Must tenant pay for alterations? ( )
   (2) Do alterations belong to landlord? ( )
   (3) Must landlord approve the plans or contractor? ( )
   (4) Are there restrictions on tenant's right to alter? ( )

    i. Must the tenant restore the premises at the conclusion of the tenancy? ( ) Is fair wear and tear accepted? ( )

    j. Does the tenant have trade fixtures? ( ) May they be removed after the surrender of the premises? ( ) Must they be removed? ( )

10. **Assignment and Subletting**

    a. Is landlord's consent required? ( )

    b. Does landlord agree not to unreasonably withhold consent? ( )

    c. Are standards for assignment or subletting specified? ( ) Does landlord have the option to terminate the lease if consent for assignment or sublease is requested? ( )

    d. Can assignment or subletting take place by operation of law? ( ) By mortgage ( ), pledge ( ), hypothecation ( ), encumbrance ( ), bankruptcy ( ), death ( )?

    e. Is the sale of stock in a corporate tenant covered by this provision? ( ) Is a merger ( ), sale of assets ( ), attachment ( ), execution ( )?

    f. Does landlord share in any increased rent under subletting? ( )

11. **Transfer of Landlord's Interest**

    a. Is landlord relieved of liability on the lease? ( )

    b. Is there a clause requiring attornment to landlord's successor? ( )

    c. Must landlord's transferee assume the obligations of the lease in writing? ( )

    d. May transferee terminate the lease? ( )

12. **Indemnification of Landlord**

    a. Must tenant indemnify landlord for causes other than tenant's negligence? ( ) Are injuries caused by landlord's negligence or willful misconduct excluded? ( ) Is there a waiver of subrogation? ( )

    b. Must tenant indemnify landlord for injuries sustained by third parties in common areas? ( ) For breach of its obligations under the lease? ( )

13. **Services and Utilities**

    a. Is landlord's duty to supply utilities to the premises sufficiently defined? ( )

        (1) Must utilities be supplied on weekends? ( )

        (2) Nights? ( )

        (3) Include elevators? ( ) Air conditioning? ( )

        (4) Janitorial services? ( )

    b. Is tenant required to pay for utilities either directly or by reimbursing landlord? ( )

    c. Is tenant's use of certain apparatus on the premises restricted? ( )

        (1) Is tenant anticipated to use apparatus which will require large amounts of utility services? ( )

    d. Is landlord liable for damage caused to anyone by operation or nonoperation of services and utilities? ( )

    e. If services or utilities are not provided, is rent ever abated? ( ) For interruption due to labor disputes? ( ) For casualties? ( )

14. Common Areas

    a. Are there common areas? ( )

    b. Are there restrictions on tenant's right to make use of the common area? ( )

    c. Are the common areas sufficiently defined? ( )

    d. Does tenant bear any costs in the operation or maintenance of the common areas? ( )

15. Reentry by Landlord

    a. Is reentry by landlord specifically permitted? ( )

        (1) To carry out landlord's obligations? ( )

        (2) To show the premises? ( ) Is this limited to a specified period before the end of the term? ( )

        (3) To make repairs? ( )

    b. Does tenant specifically waive claims for damages caused by reentry? ( ) For use of scaffolding, and so on? ( ) Is blockage of entrance or unreasonable interference with business excepted? ( )

    c. Is unlawful entry, detainer, or eviction excepted? ( )

    d. Are there any areas landlord does not have a right to enter? ( ) Should not have a right to enter? ( )

16. Default

    a. Are defaults adequately specified? ( )

    b. Is abandonment a default? ( )

    c. In the event of abandonment does landlord have the right to remove and store personal property for tenant's account? ( ) To appoint a receiver? ( )

    d. May landlord use tenant's fixtures in the event tenant abandons the premises? ( )

    e. May the landlord reenter upon default? ( ) Lease the premises for the account of the tenant? ( ) Terminate the lease? ( ) Are liquidated damages provided? ( )

17. **Eminent Domain**
  a. Does the landlord have the option to terminate the lease for a taking of less than all the premises? ( ) Does the tenant? ( )
  b. Does tenant share in the condemnation award if the entire premises are condemned? ( ) For a partial taking? ( ) For improvements and moving expenses? ( )
  c. Does tenant waive all claims against the landlord for the value of the unexpired term? ( )
  d. In event of partial taking is there a proportionate reduction in the rent? ( )

18. **Attorney's Fees**
  a. Are they provided? ( )
  b. Limited to court action? ( ) To actions resulting in judgment? ( )
  c. Do both parties have a right to attorney's fees? ( )
  d. Does tenant have a right to attorney's fees? ( )
  e. Must amount be reasonable? ( ) Determined by court? ( )

19. **Waiver**
  a. May a waiver by landlord constitute a later waiver on identical matters? ( )
  b. Does subsequent acceptance of rent by landlord constitute a waiver of anything but that rental payment? ( )
  c. Is it provided that a surrender of the premises can be accepted only in writing? ( )

20. **Insurance**
  a. Does tenant have a duty to maintain insurance in specified types and amounts? ( ) If so, specify amounts and types:

  _____

  (1) Are amounts adequate to protect landlord? ( )
  b. Is approval of insurer by landlord required or are standards set forth in the lease? ( )
  c. Do landlord and tenant waive subrogation? ( ) Does tenant waive as to other tenants? ( ) Are these waivers conditioned on not incurring an additional premium? ( )

21. **Notices**
  a. Must all notices be written? ( )
  b. Must all notices be served by registered or certified mail, postage paid, return receipt requested? ( )
  c. May notices be served upon tenant by leaving them at the premises? ( )

22. **Abandonment**
  a. Is abandonment a breach of the lease? ( )
  b. Does abandonment terminate the lease? ( )

23. **Subordination**

   a. Are the lease and tenant's interest therein expressly subordinated to mortgages and deeds of trust? ( ) To other leases? ( )

   b. Does tenant have a duty to execute instruments evidencing the lease? ( )

   c. Is there a requirement that mortgagees or master lessors execute nondisturbance agreements? ( )

   d. Does the purchaser have the right to attornment? ( ) To terminate the lease? ( ) To require a new lease? ( )

24. **Miscellaneous**

   a. Does invalidity of one section affect the remainder of the issue? ( )

   b. Does the lease constitute the entire agreement between the parties? ( )

   (1) Are there other agreements? ( ) If so, what:

   _____

   c. Is the manner of amending specified? ( )

   d. Is time of the essence? ( )

   e. Is the landlord's performance excused by labor disputes?

   f. Is a governing law specified? ( )

   g. Are the signatures properly executed and notarized where required? ( )

Chapter 24

Syndication

Michael Antin   Senior Partner, Cruikshank, Antin, Stern, Litz and Grebow

GOALS

A syndication is an investment vehicle that allows an aggregation of investors to join together to exploit a business opportunity for profit. To fully understand a syndicate's function as well as its advantages and drawbacks, one must examine syndication from two viewpoints. The first is that of the passive investor, or limited partner. The second is that of the active investor, or general partner.

Passive Investor

In addition to participating in a larger investment than would otherwise be possible, the passive investor in a syndication often also has one or more of the following goals:

1. Greater safety
2. Better management
3. Market for later resale
4. Expertise in selecting an appropriate investment
5. Market entry (might not be able to get into a particular market at all, if not for the syndicate)
6. Tax benefits

24-1

7. Opportunity to be a passive investor (no midnight calls that the roof is leaking)
8. Limited liability

Active Investor

From the viewpoint of the active investor who is also the general partner, the developer, or the syndicator, the benefits are one or more of the following:

1. Additional capital
2. Compensation for his or her skill in attracting capital
3. Opportunity to deal with property with a much greater value than would be possible if only his or her money were invested
4. Control—investment without interference of other partners
5. Free ride—often the benefits come to the syndicator without putting up capital of her or his own

LIMITED PARTNERSHIP

A variety of entities can be used to achieve the above goals, including a corporation or even taking title to property as tenants in common. However, because a limited partnership is eligible for special tax treatment, can separate passive and active investors, and is a familiar form in the marketplace, it is the vehicle most commonly used.

Under the Uniform Limited Partnership Act, specialists in the field have developed a law which defines and addresses the concept of a limited partnership. Each state has either adopted or amended this act.

In general, the act specifies what should go into a limited partnership agreement, when and where to file, and so on. Creating the limited partnership documents is the proper domain of an attorney familiar with the relevant state laws. Certain elements, however, are common to most limited partnership agreements:

1. Centralized management (general partner)
2. Limited liability (limited partners)
3. Continuity of life (in some states)
4. Free transferability of shares

These characteristics are 100 percent present in a corporation. In a limited partnership, they are each present to some extent. For tax purposes the limited partnership must have less than a majority of these elements. Thus it is important, for tax purposes, that the person drafting the documents be both skilled and knowledgeable in tax law.

TYPES OF LIMITED PARTNERSHIPS

A number of types of limited partnerships are available. These generally fall into two categories: large partnerships listed with the Securities and Exchange Commission (SEC) and the smaller "friendly" partnerships found in most states.

Friendly Partnerships

Certain partnerships are called "friendly" because the partners involved are presumed to have a relationship in addition to the business relationship involved in the partnership. Perhaps they all belong to the same church or synagogue, or they might all be members of a fraternity or sorority. It is assumed that because they are friends, they will be inclined to protect one another in the investment area.

In California, for example, a limited partnership in the realm of not more than thirty-five people comes under an exemption from the "blue sky" laws. (The Department of Corporations does not require qualification of the partnership until there are more than thirty-five nonaccredited investors.) Again, the thinking here is that the people investing have some sort of friendly relationship with one another.

However, if the partnership has more than thirty-five nonaccredited investors and is one that would require SEC regulation, state securities processing may be required. In addition, if the partnership is involved in real estate it may also be subject to regulation by the real estate department of the state. In California, however, all offerings are now with the Department of Corporations.

Finally there is the matter of partnerships which are interstate. Interstate means crossing state lines. If investors are in more than one state, or if investors are in one state and the property is in another, then the partnership is subject to SEC regulation.

One must secure SEC approval for interstate offerings. The application and follow-up is both time-consuming and expensive. An SEC registration could cost upward of $50,000. Thus, most small syndicators strive to have a small number of limited partners to avoid the SEC registration procedure. (There are some waivers of the SEC registration such as a "private offering exemption" or other exemptions which may waive anywhere from 0 to 100 percent of the full registration process.

The SEC rules, however, are complex and are the fit domain of a specialist in the field.)

DISADVANTAGES OF A SYNDICATION

The limited partners in a syndication have to have enormous faith that the syndicator has integrity; is honest, conscientious, experienced; and effectuates her or his expertise to their benefit in the project. In other words, the passive partners put up the money, and the general partner handles the investment. The success or failure, therefore, rests entirely with the general partner. The obvious disadvantage is that the general partner could fail in one or more areas.

TAXES

Tax advantages acquired from the property will flow directly through the partnership vehicle to the individual investors. In other words, if there should be a write-off caused by leveraging through financing and from depreciation, that write-off would not be captured by the partnership itself but would pass through. If the partnership, for example, had a $100,000 write-off and there were ten partners, each partner might get a $10,000 write-off on personal income taxes.

In general, a tax write-off or deduction occurs because there is a leveraging or a financing of property. There are two different types of financing: recourse and nonrecourse. With "recourse" financing the person who borrows the money is at risk: We borrow $50,000 to buy into a motion picture. The picture flops. We still have to pay back the $50,000. With "nonrecourse" financing, however, there is no risk. For example, if I endorse someone's check on the back "without recourse," if that check should bounce, the bank or other cashers of it cannot come back to me for the money.

In a syndication, typically, the partnership borrows money with nonrecourse to the partners. This means that the individual partners are not liable, but the partnership is. (Since the partnership really has no assets other than those contributed by the partners, it is essentially a risk-free note.)

In general, a write-off cannot be achieved when there is a nonrecourse note. However, in those situations when recourse notes are obtained, a deduction or write-off can be achieved. The singular exception here is real estate. As in our example, a nonrecourse note can be used to give a raised basis for depreciation which will result in a write-off. (See Chapter 18 for further discussion.)

A-B PARTNERSHIP

The purpose of an A-B partnership is to separate the tax advantage to be obtained from a partnership from the economic gain to be obtained. One category of partner (A for example) gets the tax leverage. Another category of partner (B) gets the economic gain.

As an example, think of a partnership where the limited partners include a retirement plan and a corporation. The retirement plan, since it pays no taxes, does not need tax benefits. It only wants income. The retirement plan might be designated "A" and receive a guaranteed return, say 12 percent. The corporation, on the other hand, pays lots of taxes, and it wants a deduction. Hence the corporation might be designated "B" and receive all the write-off.

This can be accomplished by having A own the land and B own the building. Since only buildings (not land) can be depreciated, the tax advantages thus flow to B.

Today syndication is one of the most popular vehicles for raising capital to invest in real estate. Although there have been some notable syndication failures, thousands of investors and syndicators have had successful experiences with them.

Part 5

Exchanges
of Real Estate

Chapter 25

Introduction to Real Estate Exchanges

Bruce B. Howey   Realtor and Speaker for the National Institute of Exchange
Counselors, Inc.

More and more frequently one hears the following comment: "I want to exchange my property." Why are so many people making real estate exchanges? Although many reasons exist for exchanging investment property, three basic factors motivate investors: investment, tax advantages, and psychological or personal factors.

Some investment advantages include the restructuring of an equity position, leveraging of the equity, consolidation of properties, division of properties, and the dissolution of partnerships and joint ventures.

Tax advantages are a consideration in almost every exchange; some primary reasons include the avoidance of immediate capital gains tax, restructuring of depreciation, increasing basis, restructuring financing, or taking advantage of new tax laws.

The psychological aspects of making an exchange are almost endless. Primarily investors are looking for benefits such as the following: to relocate property to a more active area, to change types of property, to reduce or eliminate debt, to increase appreciation potential or income or spendable, to reduce or eliminate management problems, to maintain a continuity of income, or to diversify investment holdings.

MECHANICS OF EXCHANGING

Exchanges will fit one of three major categories: (1) two-way exchanges, (2) two-way and cash out, and (3) multiple exchanges. Each portion of an exchange is composed of the property and/or the client, acting as an entity, and is called a "leg." Since exchanges are always made in couplets, no matter how many legs are in an exchange only two legs are worked on at any one time.

One of the larger exchanges a few years ago had forty-three legs, but it was put together two legs at a time, each one adding to the other until there was a "taker" for every leg (or property/client). The exchange agreement only provides for two parties to the contract, and not until a meeting of the minds has been achieved between those two parties can the next leg of the transaction be negotiated.

Although all exchanges are made between two parties, it is rather difficult to put together a two-way exchange. In daily practice the chances of discovering two properties with two owners whose equities can readily be balanced and who each desire to own the other's property are exceedingly slim. Consideration must always be given to the locations, financing, types of properties, and motivations of each of the parties. The complexities involved usually will send the agent searching for one or more legs to effect a closing. But for purposes of illustration, in a two-way exchange we would have two takers as follows:

$$A \rightleftarrows B$$

A will take B and B will take A, thereby culminating the exchange.

A variation of this straight two-way transaction would be a "cash out": the finding of a buyer for one of the two properties. Here we find A is the taker for B, but B only wants cash. In this case, B does take A, subject to a buyer being found for A's property and to the concurrent closing of the escrows, so that a tax-deferred exchange can take place. B takes the cash, and C (the cash buyer) takes A. Here is an example of this type of transaction:

A		B	C
$20,000	Market value	$80,000	$20,000 cash
0	Loan	$45,000	
$20,000	Equity	$35,000	
$15,000	Difference		
$35,000	Needed to balance		

The first step in this transaction is that A takes B and B takes A with $15,000 note to balance. Next, B sells A's property to C for $20,000 cash, retaining the $15,000 note.

This transaction could also be reversed so that C (the cash buyer) takes A and A then takes B's property with A's cash. One basic rule of a tax-deferred exchange is that the taxpayer (A) must never have unilateral control of the cash in the transaction. This can be avoided by having an escrow handle the transaction and thereby have two parties in contract at all times.

Multiple exchanges are complex transactions, yet they are arrived at by merely adding on one or more legs until a taker is found for each of the properties offered.

Three-Way Exchange	Five-Way Exchange
A takes B	A takes B
B takes C	B takes C
C takes A	C takes D
	D takes E
	E takes A

Each leg in an exchange is assembled through the use of three fundamental rules needed for every successful transaction. These are most easily symbolized by a triangle (Figure 25-1). As illustrated in Figure 25-1, we must have sufficient *time* to locate a suitable property for exchanging; there must be sufficient *money* in the transaction to pay the escrow closing costs and agent's commissions; and the taxpayer must be seriously *motivated* to make an exchange.

The true exchange broker is construed as a problem solver, because the transactions frequently are very complex, and all these factors must be considered or much time will be lost. Since a successful broker's stock-in-trade is time and knowledge, neither should be frittered away on an unmotivated client. Anyone entering the exchange field should thrive on attacking problems and arriving at solutions and also should have a working knowledge of psychology and a knack for applying it in subtle and meaningful ways.

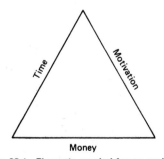

Money

Figure 25-1 Elements needed for an exchange.

INTERNAL REVENUE CODE, SECTION 1031

The primary law governing the deferment of property taxes is less than 2 pages long and is very basic. The first rule is the nonrecognition of gain or loss from exchanges which are solely of like kind. Properties must be held for productive use in trade or business or for investment reasons. This does not include any stock-in-trade or property held primarily for sale, or stocks, bonds, notes, or certificates of trust.

Gain from exchanges which are not solely like kind would be taxable to the extent of their fair market value. No loss is recognized in an exchange, at any time. It must be remembered that in an exchange the basis of the like kind property carries over to the new property, and any unlike property would add to that basis.

What is "like kind" property? It includes land and improvements, all fixtures (under certain circumstances), and leases which have a remaining term at closing of the exchange of at least 30 years. Only like kind property can be exchanged "tax free," which is a euphemism used by many people when they actually mean tax-deferred, since taxation is merely postponed. It is in no sense avoided or escaped forever.

Examples of exchangeable properties which qualify as like kind would be ranches, industrial buildings, office buildings, commercial buildings, residential income units, mobile home parks, and land held for investment.

To achieve the desired tax deferment in an exchange, certain requirements must be met: there must be no cash, no boot, and no net mortgage relief.

One of the first things to consider is whether the client needs or can effect a full tax deferment or a partial one. To postpone taxation completely there must be no cash, boot, or net mortgage relief. If any one of these accrues to the client, then a partially taxable event has occurred. Should the client receive all cash, all boot, and complete mortgage relief, then a fully taxable event has taken place. But in no event will the client ever pay more than the indicated gain, which would be the difference between the adjusted cost basis and the market value of the property conveyed. Remember that transaction costs must be considered when computing the taxability of each transaction. Mortgages assumed will add to basis, and mortgages relieved are subtracted from basis to determine the new adjusted cost basis.

Assume that a taxpayer has a free and clear lot that was acquired for $50,000. The lot is exchanged into a property at an acceptable value of $250,000. The taxpayer adds $125,000 cash to balance equities. Disregarding transaction costs what would be the new adjusted basis? (See Figure 25–2.)

	LINE NO		(1) PROPERTY			(2) PROPERTY		
INDICATED GAIN	1	Market Value of Property Conveyed	125	000				
	2	Less: Adjusted Basis	50	000				
	3	Less: Capitalized Transaction Costs	-0-					
	4	INDICATED GAIN	75	000				
BALANCE EQUITIES	5	Equity Conveyed	125	000				
	6	Equity Acquired	250	000				
	7	Difference	125	000				
	8	Cash or Boot Received	-0-					
	9	Cash or Boot Paid	125	000				
DETERMINE RECOGNIZED GAIN	10	Old Loans	-0-					
	11	Less: New Loans	-0-					
	12	NET LOAN RELIEF	-0-					
	13	Less: Cash or Boot Paid (L9)	125	000				
	14	Recognized: Net Loan Relief	-0-					
	15	Plus: Cash or Boot Received (L8)	-0-					
	16	TOTAL UNLIKE PROPERTY RECEIVED	-0-					
	17	Recognized Gain LESSER OF L4 or L16	-0-					

Transfer of Basis

	LINE							
TRANSFER OF BASIS	18	Adjusted Basis (L2) Plus (L3)	50	000				
	19	Plus: New Loans (L11)	-0-					
	20	Plus: Cash or Boot Paid (L9)	125	000				
	21	Plus: Recognized Gain (L17)	-0-					
	22	Total Additions	175	000				
	23	Less Old Loans (L10)	-0-					
	24	Less: Cash or Boot Received (L8)	-0-					
	25	NEW ADJUSTED BASIS	175	000				

DATE_____

NAME____TAXPAYER

PROPERTY CONVEYED____LOT

Original Cost: $50,000

TAXPAYER

Gives		Gets
125,000	MV	250,000
-0-	LN	-0-
125,000	EQ	250,000
125,000	DIF	→

MV = Market Value

LN = Loan

EQ = Equity

DIF = Difference

Old ACB = Substitute Basis

ACRS = Accelerated Cost Recovery System

Old ACB		ACRS	
50	000	125	000

Figure 25-2 Exchange basis worksheet.

THE PROBLEMS AND BENEFITS OF MOTIVATION

The degree of the client's motivation is a key to problem solving. Extensive counseling is a must for every exchange broker. If the true problem is not identified and understood, then the solving of the problem becomes very complex, if not altogether impossible.

In counseling clients it has been found that all parties who are in title to the property presented for exchange must be present during the discussions. Often the parties in title are not all aware of the problems or view them in divergent and contradictory ways. Only by the agent's proper counseling techniques can all parties be in accord and the correct property be found that will give them the benefits they all desire. Depending on the complexity of the problem, it might take several counseling sessions to ultimately satisfy the needs of all the owners.

"Benefits" are what we and our clients are seeking. The properties are vehicles used to solve certain problems and to arrive at desired benefits. By keeping benefits foremost in mind, the exchange broker can come up with workable solutions and can assist the client in seeing the property as an investment vehicle. Viewing the property as an investment vehicle can avoid obstacles of personal preference and prejudice about the properties.

THE CLOSING TEAM

Once the true motivation of the client is discovered it is time to form "the team." The two primary members will be the client's attorney and certified public accountant (CPA). The broker does *not* give legal or tax advice but acts as the catalyst for making things happen which will benefit the investor-client. Additional team members are lenders, appraisers, termite specialists, the property management personnel, and the escrow officer who later effects the closing of the transaction. Each of these people furnishes a specialized service which is vital to the successful culmination of the transaction, and each must be chosen with care. It is only when the escrow has closed that the investor-client can begin to reap the benefits of the exchange.

MARKETING PREPARATION

During the counseling process various items of documentation are gathered to build the "homework" file. Such items as (1) income tax returns, (2) statement of income and expenses for income-producing properties, (3) copies of notes and mortgages or trust deeds or contracts, (4) copies of leases and/or rental agreements, (5) photographs of the offered property, (6) inventory of personal property remaining with the property when transferred to new owner, (7) title policy or abstract or new preliminary title report, (8) rental schedule, (9) copy of front page of the existing insurance policies, (10) current tax bill, and (11) all information appropriate to the agent's complete knowledge of the client's property, especially including any adverse conditions which might present problems for any new owner and must be made known to same prior to execution of the exchange agreement.

When the broker has assembled and analyzed a complete homework file the property can be presented in the marketplace.

ANALYSIS OF THE CLIENT'S PRESENT POSITION

With all the data now available to the broker, the first order of business is to develop the net operating income of the property. This includes all the income and expenses attributable to the property, whoever owns it. Interest on loans and depreciation schedules are personal items, and as such they are reported differently by different owners. The net operating income would be the gross scheduled income as of today's date minus a vacancy factor and minus *all* expenses that would presumably affect the property in the coming year. All projections are computed on an annual basis.

The two most abused figures in exchanging are the management and the maintenance allotments. Larger properties must have an on-site manager. Smaller properties must have someone always available for any emergencies, and this information must be made public to all tenants, posted on the property. In addition, the property should support professional management. If the owners are managing the property, they should compute a management cost to compensate for their own time and effort.

Maintenance of the property should be looked at very closely. The property should be inspected to determine if there is sufficient money allotted to adequately cover the coming year's maintenance needs. Some of the major items to be checked include painting; asphalt repair; condition of the plumbing and electrical wiring; and replacement of hot water heaters, air conditioners, or furnaces. Many people use 5 percent of the scheduled gross income as a maintenance allotment, but this should be studied realistically to provide the actual dollar cost of such maintenance in today's marketplace.

Having arrived at the net operating income one can determine how much must be spent for financing and what is left for gross spendable income. One might need to use all the income for financing, thus producing a break-even property. At this point it is important to determine exactly what benefits the property can provide, such as spendable income or a leverage position.

LOCATING THE DESIRED PROPERTY

Now the exchange package is ready for presentation. At the various meetings the agent will receive preliminary offers from other agents. Each one of these preliminary offers deserves analysis, much in the same way that the property your client now owns has previously been analyzed. Only in this way can a proper comparison be made in selecting the most desirable property and the particular benefits which will accrue to a client from ownership of it. This is also the proper time to thoroughly analyze those terms and conditions of the offers which may or may not prove troublesome if the parties commit themselves to an exchange.

BALANCING EQUITIES

Earlier we discussed a two-way exchange, a two-way with cash out, and a multiple exchange. The first two are relatively simple to balance, but when an exchange grows into multiple legs, notes are being created and refinancing is generated to produce cash for a mutual sharing of the proceeds, and much more detailed accounting is necessary. A typical three-way multiple exchange would be simply structured in this way:

A takes B
B takes C
C takes A

Starting with the smaller property, and assuming that each party will add cash for costs and commissions, no refinancing would be necessary. Inventory of properties has established the following:

	A	B	C
Market value	$20,000	$100,000	$500,000
Existing loans	0	10,000	300,000
Equity	$20,000	$ 90,000	$200,000

Using the form for exchange recapitulation shown in Figure 25-3, we must first inventory the properties (or legs) of the exchange. The form was originally called a "have-and-get sheet" or a "spread sheet." By filling in the known information on lines A-1, B-1, and C-1 under the proper headings from columns 1 through 11, adjustments can be made on lines A-2, B-2, C-2. A number of assumptions must be made in our example:

1. No refinancing is being made in this exchange.
2. A will take B, B will take C, and C will take A.
3. Cash will be added by each party to cover all costs and commissions.
4. Each party has been counseled well.
5. Values have been established for each property.

On lines A-2, B-2, and C-2 the market value, existing loans, and equity amounts remain the same. Adjustments are usually made with cash or in "paper." However, they can also be made with other real property or with unlike property.

A-2 will have an equity in column 4 of $90,000. They are only entitled to $20,000 on line A-1, column 11. By subtracting line A-1, column 11,

PROPERTY 1	MARKET VALUE 2	EXISTING LOANS 3	EQUITY 4	CASH GIVES (IN) 5	CASH GETS (OUT) 6	PAPER GIVES 7	PAPER GETS 8	COMM. 9	TRANS. COSTS 10	NET EQUITY 11
A-1 LOT	20,000	θ	20,000	1,500				1,200	300	(20,000
A-2 Duplex	100,000	10,000	90,000			70,000				20,000)
B-1 Duplex	100,000	10,000	90,000	6,500				6,000	500	(90,000
B-2 8 units	500,000	300,000	200,000			110,000				90,000)
C-1 8 units	500,000	300,000	200,000	31,500				30,000	1,500	(200,000
C-2 Lot	20,000	θ	20,000				70,000 / 110,000			200,000)
D-1				39,500	θ	180,000	180,000	37,200	2,300	
D-2					37,200					
D-3					2,300					
D-4				39,500	39,500					

Figure 25-3   Exchange recapitulation.

from A-2, column 4, a difference of $70,000 is needed to balance the transaction for client A. By creating a "carry-back" or a junior mortgage or purchase money trust deed, the equities can be balanced.

If proper values are utilized from the beginning there should be no problem now with a realistic transaction. A is going in with a $20,000 equity in property presently owned and will conclude the closing with a $20,000 equity in the property being acquired.

As each leg is balanced a bracket is made around lines A-1 and A-2, column 11, to show that the horizontal balancing has been completed. Lines B-1 and B-2, then lines C-1 and C-2, are each balanced in this same manner until all the properties have a taker.

To ensure that the transaction is properly balanced the vertical columns 5 through 10 must now be totaled and cleared. Line D-1 will be the existing totals, starting with column 5 and working through to column 10. If columns 7 and 8 on line D-1 balance, showing all paper going into the transaction (column 7) and all paper going out of the transaction (column 8), then we can presume that these two columns are also cleared.

To clear column 9 the total figure is carried over to column 6 (cash out), line D-2. Column 10 can be cleared by carrying it over to the cash out column 6, line D-3. This will leave only columns 5 and 6 to be totaled on line D-4. If this proves to be true, then the transaction is in balance and the exchange agreement can be initialed by the parties. This form will also be used when the escrow officer drafts the exchange escrow instructions.

WRITING THE OFFER

The exchange agreement is the contract between the two parties to the transaction. Remember that, in exchanging, everything is done in couplets. Two-by-two the transaction is assembled, using first party and second party in the instructions.

The parties to the transaction should be listed just as they hold title. This information is available from the homework file. Either the grant deed, trust deed, or title insurance policy will give the proper vesting and legal description also. Insert property city, county, and state information in the correct blanks.

A notation as to what the property is—for example, a 40-unit apartment building in Florida or a mobile home park on State Street—will establish an identity which is useful in discussions and avoids confusion in the drafting and understanding of the escrow instructions. This type of designation should also be followed by the complete legal description and also the street address of the property.

Property offered to the second party can be subject to certain items which may or may not be of record, such as (1) current taxes; (2) covenants, conditions, reservations, restrictions, and rights of way or easements; (3) first mortgage or trust deed or contract; (4) junior mortgages or trust deeds; (5) month-to-month rental agreements or leases, and any other items which would pertain to this particular property. The preliminary title report would be the best source of information for things already of record.

For the second party the same basic information would be outlined. Remember, we are starting with the way title is presently held by the present owner.

The terms and conditions section is where all the adjustments of equity are made to consummate the transaction. Financing is usually the first item negotiated. New financing, refinancing, terms of the loans, assumptions or taking "subject to" an existing loan, the creation of junior financing, interest rates, due dates, and payment dates, all these should be detailed here.

What acts each party is responsible for follow. Depending on the type of property involved they might include approval of preliminary title report or of easements, new owner's inspection and approval of property, the issuance of termite clearances, or approval of rental agreements and leases or of existing loan documents which party will be assuming or taking subject to. Any action to be performed should have a time limitation specified in the exchange agreement and escrow instructions.

Other conditions might include the crediting of any advance rents and security deposits, an inventory of furnishings or equipment to remain on the property, laundry or vending machine leases, or any applicable governmental codes or licensing requirements which must be met. Each property will be different, so the agreement must be drawn with the idea that any item of future concern is covered in enough detail to be clear to all parties. The advice of the client's attorney and/or CPA should now be considered and included in the agreement.

The final commission arrangements should be indicated in actual dollar amount, by a percentage amount, or by the listing agreement instructions. After signature by the first party (exactly as they hold title) the exchange agreement is then handed to the cooperating agent who represents the second party.

If accepted, the parties may then go to escrow. But a counteroffer may be needed to clear up certain items or to arrive at a clarification of the terms and conditions and a true meeting of the minds.

If the property is not what the second party desires to own, it can still be accepted "in lieu of," so that a third leg can be found with a property which will qualify for satisfying the client's goals and needs. Sufficient time must be allocated to find the "up property," but when both agents are working diligently, the transaction will probably take place.

ESCROWING THE EXCHANGE

Once the parties have agreed to the terms and conditions that they desire to acquire the offered properties, the next step is to transfer title. The selection of a qualified exchange escrow officer is the next and most vital step. Unfortunately, most agents will go to the closest, least experienced escrow officer. This is a major error, since a multiple exchange in which most parties are vitally concerned with achieving a tax-deferred transaction requires the skills of a highly qualified and fully experienced exchange escrow officer.

Call in advance for an appointment to allow plenty of time to discuss the details and help the escrow officer to structure the transaction properly. All agents representing parties to the exchange should be present to dictate their portion of the transaction. A rough draft is prepared by the escrow officer for review by all the agents before a final set of instructions is made available and sent out for the clients' signatures.

Costs are a vital part of the escrow process. The escrow officer will be able to give a range of the expected costs so that the owners know what to expect at closing time. Most escrow officers will call for a stipulated amount to open the escrow to cover their initial costs for title reports, termite inspections, and drafting of documents and instructions. The anticipated closing date should be realistic, allowing for the intricacies of the transaction and the number of legs to the exchange. A good exchange officer will be very busy and must be given adequate time for preparation and processing of all papers. This is especially vital if any portions of the transaction deal with property in other states.

Many officers will have a checklist of all the various documents they will need to process the transaction. If you have done your homework well you should already have copies of most items needed. Provisions should be made to remove any contingencies in the exchange agreement or escrow instructions which might cause a delay in the closing date.

In some states the closing is somewhat different and will be performed by a title company and/or an attorney and will be concluded on the actual closing date. Regardless of the closing procedure used, an astute agent will remember that the escrow officer did that extra bit more which ensured that the transaction went smoothly. The commission check should be ready on time. Expressing your gratitude to the escrow officer (in the form of a floral display, theater tickets, or a dinner certificate) will go a long way toward making the next exchange a pleasant experience also.

FINALIZING THE TRANSACTION

Once the escrow has closed and title has passed to the new owners it is practical to go over the closing documents with your client, particularly the closing statement prepared by escrow. In the haste of closing the possibility of error always exists and can be corrected without too much trouble if detected immediately.

Make certain that your client is fully informed of any pertinent data, so that ownership can begin as a pleasant experience. Transfer keys and utilities promptly. Compile a list of repair and maintenance tradespeople who have served the previous owner well.

Arrangements for letters notifying the tenants of the change of ownership can be very helpful, especially when rent payments are mailed to a central office or a management firm.

A true professional knows that this is a crucial time for the client and will require some expert helpfulness and courtesy. The transfer of ownership can then be accomplished speedily, smoothly, and effectively.

How to Market a Real Estate Exchange

Jim Brondino   Realtor; Exchange Investment Counselor

The transferring and conveying of property, both real and personal, by exchange has been pursued for centuries. Essentially, it is the process of barter whereby one person obtains possession of another's holdings by giving up something. Of course the transaction would not culminate unless all parties to the transaction felt that they had equalled or improved their original position. The concept of exchanging can best be expressed as the giving or taking of one thing in return for another which is regarded as an equivalent. Exchanges and exchange transactions are animated by two stimuli—tax law and/or individual personal predicaments.

TAX ASPECTS OF EXCHANGES

Exchanging as an organized real estate activity gained impetus when the U.S. government instituted, in the early 1920s, a provision whereby taxpayers may negotiate a transfer of property without incurring a tax liability. This provision is now codified in the Internal Revenue Code under Section 1031. Section 1031 permits the deferral of all or part of the gain on the exchange of property provided that the statutory requirements are strictly adhered to. The primary benefit of a tax-deferred exchange is tax avoidance. Section 1031 reads as follows:

26-1

Exchange of property held for productive use or (a) Non-recognition of gain or loss from exchanges solely in kind. No gain or loss shall be recognized if property held for productive use in trade or business or for investment (not included stock in trade or other property held primarily for sale, nor stocks, bonds, notes, choses in action, certificates of trust, or beneficial interest, or other securities or evidences of indebtedness or interest) is exchanged solely for property of a like *kind* to be held either for productive use in trade or business or for investment.

Exchanges may involve partial taxability and partial deferral when qualifying property and unlike property are received. A completely tax-deferred exchange occurs when appreciated property held for productive use in a trade or business or for investment is exchanged solely for other property of a "like kind" to be held for productive use in a trade or business or for investment. When no taxes are to be paid, the taxpayer has more proceeds available to invest in another project. This may result in the acquisition of a larger property because the dollars which would have been siphoned off to pay capital gains tax can be reallocated to capture a larger investment opportunity.

It should be noted that if the basic characteristics of a qualified non-taxable exchange exist, the taxpayer cannot treat an exchange as taxable. The basic characteristics are:

1. There must be an exchange as distinguished from a sale and separate purchase.

2. Both the asset disposed of and the asset acquired must be held for business or investment purposes.

3. The exchange must involve property deemed to be of a like kind and the taxpayer must be restricted from actual or constructive receipt of unlike property such as cash, loan relief, notes, stocks, bonds, or the fair market value of personal property. However, personal property may be exchanged for other personal property of a like kind.

The like kind aspect relates to the character or nature of the property rather than its grade, use, or quality. Improved real estate is considered to be the same nature as unimproved real estate. Therefore, a farm or ranch for city property, a rental house for a store building, and apartments for land may all qualify as "like-for-like" exchanges. The underlying legislative rationale behind Section 1031 is based on the concept that the nature of the taxpayer's investment has not changed. Not to tax an exchange where the taxpayer has made a transition from one qualifying property to another and is continuing the original purpose, thereby avoiding any liquidation, remains the congressional intent.

For example, client A owns a parcel of land priced at $150,000. A's adjusted cost basis is $30,000, and A has received a full price cash offer to purchase. If A elected to take the sale, he or she would have $120,000 of recognized (taxable) gain. Client A prefers to use the provisions of

Section 1031 and to invest the proceeds, through a properly structured exchange, into other like kind property, in this case a warehouse. The warehouse, although different in grade, quality, and use, qualifies as like kind because client A intends to hold the property for investment. Meeting all the other requirements of a Section 1031 transaction, client A has at least two benefits from this transaction. First, she or he has deferred all the gain, thereby incurring no tax liability, and, second, A has moved from unimproved property to improved property.

Personal residences may also be exchanged, but somewhat different rules apply. The exchange of a taxpayer's primary residence for anything other than another principal residence does not qualify as a like kind exchange transaction. To avoid a taxable event when disposing of one's personal residence, one must either follow the provisions of the Code's Section 1034 or convert the residence to investment property. Section 1034 provides that the gain realized on the sale or exchange of the "principal residence" of the taxpayer is deferred as long as replacement property of equal or greater value is located within the prescribed 2-year period. Converting one's personal residence to investment property or a Section 1031 qualifying asset is achieved by renting the home or holding and offering the home for rent at a reasonable rental rate. In essence, the taxpayer is changing the nature and character of the residence to investment property, which would then allow Section 1031 treatment.

The use of Sections 1031 and 1034 is specifically designed to avoid or at least to defer taxes. But just as tax on some exchanges can be totally deferred, other exchanges may result in full taxation of the gain realized. Essentially, all transactions in which there is a conveyance are exchanges. Even the sale of property which involves the transfer of dollars for a deed is actually an exchange. Unfortunately, any gain realized on sale, unless structured as an installment sale, becomes immediately taxable to the extent of its fair market value because of noncompliance with the provisions of Section 1031. Contrary to the belief of some leading tax authorities, exchanges not only remain as a viable maneuver to avoid taxes and in some cases increased basis on the transfer of property but also may have gained greater impetus under the accelerated cost recovery system (ACRS). The recapture provisions under ACRS impose a rather onerous tax which can be postponed or eliminated by exchanging.

PROBLEM-SOLVING EXCHANGES

There is more to exchanging as a marketing philosophy than merely the techniques and technicalities associated with Sections 1031 and 1034 transactions. Encompassed in the philosophy is the attitude that people are more important than property. Out of the expanding acceptance of this attitude, a relatively new and dynamic real estate marketplace has arisen.

To understand and expand the concepts of exchanging is to ally oneself with a fraternity of "exchangors" who have formed marketing groups throughout the country. The focus of these groups is to maximize the probability of manufacturing an exchange transaction that meets the realistic investment criteria of the client.

These marketing groups' meetings *emphasize the needs* of clients as represented by their respective agents. The agents are seeking a transaction in cooperation with other agents to obtain the benefits agreed on by the agent and the client. This approach will most often result in a multiple exchange transaction. In this case, several agents representing a number of clients' will join in a cooperative effort to achieve clients' goals. The reasons for multiple exchanges are threefold:

1. The person receiving the offer does not want what is being offered but is willing to make a move under certain conditions.

2. The party receiving the offer cannot use the offered property but can use another parcel of property when it is presented.

3. The client receiving the offer will move only if she or he receives cash.

The use of the multiple exchange is often an absolute necessity in moving the original property.

Caution should be exercised before entering a cooperative exchange transaction that requires a cash "out." First, is the property offered but refused by the offeror convertible to cash at the asking price? Second, what credibility exists as to the agents involved regarding their ability to perform?

Obviously, although it is much more efficient to move directly from one equity position to another without converting to cash, the margin for success of a transaction decreases as the number of agents and principals participating in the transaction increases.

To manufacture an exchange transaction successfully requires broader knowledge than the mere techniques and academics of Section 1031. Aside from technical knowledge, it is imperative that the agent possess an understanding of the exchange marketplace and an in-depth knowledge of the client he or she will represent in that marketplace.

The scope of exchange marketing for most agents is literally staggering. Not all exchanges are prompted from a tax savings premise. Exchanging can and does accommodate tax-deferred motivations, but it has far wider application and presents unlimited opportunities to agents who wish to expand their marketing horizons.

Some of the unique aspects of using exchanges as a marketing philosophy include:

1. People are more important than property.
2. Value is determined through problem solving and the satisfaction of client needs.
3. Price is less important than benefits.
4. Benefits are the components of value.
5. Property location diminishes in relevance.
6. Product, either real or personal, can be integrated into a transaction.
7. Agents cooperate rather than compete.

A Change in Thinking

What transpires in the exchange marketplace embraces not only transfers of ownership providing tax benefits, when they are the major motivation, but also transfers of ownership which address a multitude of individual client motivations and client preferences. Engaging in exchanges necessitates a change in thinking from the selling of properties, which focuses primarily on generating cash and emphasizing price, to a concentration on benefits and how best to service and assist the client. Exchange marketing in a broader sense uses a problem-solving approach. A problem can be defined as any circumstance in which the property owner finds a need to change in some manner her or his ownership situation. The exchange marketplace concentrates on how best to improve the client's circumstances. This can be accomplished in a variety of ways. Those who may want to integrate the concept of exchanging into their practice as a marketing tool should realize that they will be working not with money but with real estate already owned by the client.

To comprehend exchanges is to comprehend the underlying philosophical differences between the typical buying and selling of real property as compared to exchanging real property. Buying and selling flourishes when property is easily sold. The sale market prospers when dollars are available from buyers and lenders are actively involved in providing funds for financing. On the contrary, exchanging is best suited to accommodate properties which are not so readily saleable and when economic conditions remove lenders from the marketplace. *Exchanges primarily deal in benefits, whereas the sales mentality is concerned with price.* The sale market has as its main consideration the generation of dollars. A sale is a direct conversion from the ownership of property to money, whereas an exchange involves a promise to agree to accept the other person's property under certain conditions. It is the conversion from one ownership position to an alternative ownership position.

Geographical Differences

Another difference between exchanging and buying or selling relates to geography. In most cases when a sale is required, the property and the client are in close geographical proximity. Exchanging on the other hand is less limited geographically. Properties and ownership circumstances from all corners of the world are represented in the exchange market. With proper investigation, structure, and management, the varying locations can be effectively and competently handled to the benefit of the client.

Identifying Benefits and Value

A cornerstone of the philosophy in exchange marketing is the knowledge and identification of benefits. Dictionaries define a benefit as anything which may be for the good of a person or thing. Benefits tend to be either receipt of things that give one pride, pleasure, or profit or relief from situations or things which cause pain, annoyance, or discomfort. Exchanging is indeed centered on problem solving. Therefore, it is incumbent on the agent to know how the client perceives her or his situation and whether the property owned by said client has sufficient quality interpreted by consumer demand to generate a solution to the problem at hand.

It is the process of identifying benefits that leads to the realization of value, since benefits are the components of value and value is directly equal to the sum of the benefits. A property can be valuable to some but poison in the hands of others. What else is value, then, but a measure of relative desirability? Real estate does not have value as an intrinsic or inherent quality. Real estate simply exists. It is only in relation to persons that real property may be said to have value.

People and their circumstances change, often far more rapidly than a property changes. Consider the value of a personal residence on the West Coast to a person transferred to the East. The only value is the buying power the western property will give the person on the East Coast. Leaving aside investment considerations and their problems, such a residence could actually be a severe liability to a person in this situation.

To say that the value of a residence is $100,000 does not mean that the mere existence of the property is the cause of that price. The price must be related to an individual's set of circumstances. The statement that a residence is worth $100,000 simply means that the rights of ownership to someone are worth that much for whatever reasons. Rather than the worth of a property, at best the price should be thought of as an approximate indicator of the length to which a person will go to gain control over a thing deemed valuable. Desirability and the individual's unique set of circumstances are what make a thing valuable.

Being Client-Centered

Productive exchange agents subscribe to the idea that cooperation is far more lucrative than competition. To impart accurate information using group brainstorming techniques, with the resolve to generate an offer or a solution with the other cooperating agent, is the essence of profitable marketing. This environment is best created when the agents involved in the marketing process agree that to be client-centered is more profitable than to be self-centered.

Being self-centered tends to make the agent talk excessively rather than listen attentively to the client, thereby reducing the pool of facts necessary to convey to fellow agents. It results in the agent telling more rather than asking appropriate questions of the client. This deters the agent from determining whether it is worthwhile to accept the listing responsibility from the client. The process of asking questions and listening to the client can save invaluable time and effort on the part of the listing agent and eliminates the abuse of the time and effort of cooperating agents who are working to solve the problem.

A dilemma is created for the self-centered individual when it comes to full disclosure. Failing to communicate with the client or other agents all the facts pertinent to the transaction, whether positive or negative, will significantly diminish the prospects of an otherwise perfect escrow. Unfavorable and sometimes disastrous transactions occur when the primary concern and motivation of the agent are focused on commission. The agent's vision becomes obscured as to what is in the best interests of the client, and the accuracy of the information conveyed to colleagues is distorted.

The closing of escrows will be facilitated when the agent maintains a client-centered perspective and develops respect for colleagues in the brokerage community. Full disclosure is a key component of respect, upheld when licensees recognize that time, money, and effort will be expended by other professionals on behalf of their respective clients.

The Human Factor

Limiting the concept of exchanging to Section 1031 inhibits the agent and is a disservice to the client. The basic philosophy of success in exchanging is to focus on the human elements. Exchanges are made between people, not between properties; therefore, price and selling techniques become far less important. Client motivation and the feasibility of designing a transaction which provides the benefits needed by the client are paramount.

Initially clients will assume that the equity in their real estate is cash. They presume that they can literally cash out of their current situations. Clients then demand from agents a new ownership position as if cash were being used as the acquisition commodity. When clients realize the extent to which cash transactions may be taxable, they may be stimulated to opt for an exchange. A problem arises when property is not cashable. A realistic assessment of client goals and the vehicle to be used must be made by the agent before committing to the listing responsibilities. Otherwise the agent will be negotiating from an unrealistic premise, and the chances of a completed transaction will be remote.

Clarifying Issues

Clarification should be of utmost concern to the agent. Client motivations are often numerous and conflicting. Although motivations fall into three basic categories, investment, tax, and psychological, it is incumbent on the astute real estate practitioner to identify clearly the most pressing of the motivations expressed by the client. Having the client give clear priorities is a useful approach. Next, the agent must determine whether in the current market a satisfaction for that motivation actually exists and whether that solution can be located directly or through steps using the property designated by the client. Although they may overlap greatly, the following are some of the reasons that motivate people to exchange. When exchanging for investment reasons, people frequently want to:

1. Use the equity for further investments
2. Protect holdings from immediate or anticipated economic, social, or psychological risks
3. Consolidate properties for reduced management
4. Divide property to spread risk
5. Add properties to diversify a portfolio
6. Balance an investment portfolio
7. Increase or decrease loan amortization

8. Increase leverage
9. Reduce or eliminate debt

When concerned with tax problems, people exchange to:

1. Avoid selling and thereby defer capital gains tax
2. Restore depreciation
3. Increase or decrease depreciation
4. Develop faster depreciation
5. Increase income
6. Decrease income

Some psychological or personal reasons for exchanges include:

1. Moving investment, business, or personal real estate from one location to another
2. Changing the type of investment or business
3. Appreciating capital through upgrading of property and/or through assumption of management
4. Changing investment location for safety or diversity or in anticipation of trends
5. Gaining immediate income
6. Building an estate
7. Avoiding breaks in the continuity of ownership
8. Getting away from a perceived problem
9. Taking advantage of a perceived profit

PREPARATIONS FOR MARKETING

Preparation for the marketing of an exchange is directly proportionate to the successful culmination of the transaction. There are three primary ingredients to professional preparation: (1) knowledge about the property, (2) knowledge about the client, and (3) knowledge about the objective sought by the client.

Property Knowledge

These ingredients are applicable not only to exchanges but to all real estate. The agent should be familiar with all the detrimental and beneficial physical aspects of the property being marketed. These include the physical condition, on-site and off-site management, current debt structure, potential or availability of new financing, zoning, access, income and expenses, demographics, or any other material facts associated with the property. The agent should be aware of all the opportunities and benefits which may accrue to a new owner which the present owner has exhausted or is unwilling or incapable of developing. Such considerations as a favorable land-to-building ratio for tax purposes; need for rehabilitation, development, and construction possibilities; management or lack thereof; climate conditions; changes in the neighborhood; user potential; and refinance possibilities which may lead to the generation of cash must be explored.

Client Knowledge

Knowledge about clients and what they are willing or unwilling to do to facilitate exchange transactions is vital. The agent should ascertain from the client what skills, talents, knowledge, and resources the client possesses so that, if necessary, they can be used as part of the problem-solving process. Amount and sources of income, managerial skills, past and present property ownership experience, development and contracting talents, accounting skills, capacity to service debt from current funds, and any other resources which can be committed to the transaction such as cash, additional real property, or personal property equities are important. Sources of labor or financing from family or acquaintances, geographical limitations, if any, and knowledgeable third-party influences should be explored. In other words, all facets of the human element which can contribute to or which can be integrated in the transaction process must be identified.

Client Needs

The third ingredient for successful exchanging is a thorough understanding of what the client *needs* to accomplish. What is the goal or objective? Difficulties arise because clients often will express what they *want* more readily than what they *need*. To want involves a wish or desire. In an investment, to satisfy a desire usually requires money. Satisfying a need on the other hand involves fulfilling a requirement or obligation. Fulfilling a need demands a realistic appraisal of the individual circumstances, an appraisal of the current market conditions, and knowledge of what can be used to achieve or reach the objective. In many cases the client is unclear or confused about what investment posture to take. The client's goals and objectives must be scrutinized as to their feasibility under current market conditions. It is a poor merchandising technique to enter the exchange market with a set objective or goal which is incompatible with the realities of the real estate market. The results are wasted time and a loss of the agent's credibility.

The goals or objectives must be agreed on by both client and agent.

Agents who merely "take the order" lack respect for their own time and that of their colleagues. Agents must be honest with themselves and their clients as to the feasibility of manufacturing transactions. Integration of one's knowledge of the marketplace, the details about the property being merchandised, a thorough understanding of the client, and a clearly identifiable goal are the issues to assess before accepting the obligation of the listing contract. The agent must decide whether to expend the time, energy, and money necessary to meet the objective. Once all the vital information has been gathered, the agent can move toward an assessment of how best to help the client.

EXCHANGING EQUITIES

Exchange transactions are actually creative selling. Instead of using cash or dollars, the exchangor is using equity. Therefore, the exchange specialist's skills lie in the ability to market the equity creatively. Before doing so, one must define what power the equity has in the marketplace. The first task is to ascertain how saleable the property in question is. Aside from consumer demand, the variable factors in this formula are the client and the time allocated to solve the problem. The extent to which the client will participate and the degree to which the client will contribute time, talent, and money to an exchange will greatly influence the negotiations and the ultimate benefits derived.

The *design* of the offer to the taker determines the power of the equity. It is the taker who will give the agent the tools to acquire the benefits sought by the client. Because equity is fluid it can be altered or adjusted to attract a taker with benefits needed by the client. For example, when client circumstances require purchasers with cash to vie for his or her equity, then the equity must be adjusted to attract the commodity of cash. Converting equity to cash equips the agent and client to compete effectively for other cash-oriented products or solutions. Realistic goals compatible with available alternatives in the current marketplace allow for practical transaction designs.

The Client's Equity Concept

The creative equity market can be awesome, complex, and a time-consuming place in which to operate. As noted before, the marketplace is founded on the principle that benefits are the components of value and that value directly equals the sum of the benefits. Confusion and misunderstandings arise when the agent attempts to integrate previous marketing technique (selling) with this environment.

The trouble stems from the incompatibility of the client's objective with the vehicle being used to acquire that which will satisfy the objective. In many instances the client has placed demands on the agent which the agent knows are unrealistic. When the agent conveys these demands to the marketplace she or he senses a lack of enthusiasm for the offered property. Both the agent and the client become disgruntled over the lack of activity, and ultimately the listing expires.

What is the solution? The roots of a productive, viable marketing program are grounded in agents with (1) well-counseled clients and (2) informed, educated colleagues. However, the essence of a good transaction is one that addresses the benefits sought by the client and is feasible to structure. The power of one's equity determines whether clients can demand what they want from the marketplace.

Defining Equity

To define the power of one's equity is to ascertain the saleability of that equity. An equity is saleable when an earnest buyer—a person shopping with cash—can be generated within 60 to 90 days of exposure of the property to the marketplace. A normal saleable circumstance would contain a buyer with a 20 to 30 percent cash down payment to a new loan or with carry-back paper at market interest rates. When these sale circumstances exist, the client and agent develop a so-called dollar mentality. This mentality presumes that even though a Section 1031 tax-deferred exchange is needed, the equity represented can be defined in cash. Therefore agents and clients perform as buyers when they examine the marketplace for alternate real estate investment opportunities.

There are essentially two types of equity transactions: (1) transactions involving equities that can be readily converted to cash and/or paper (saleable) and (2) transactions with equities not readily converted to cash and/or paper (nonsaleable). The astute agent, before entering the creative equity marketplace, must do the homework necessary to achieve a proper definition of the equity represented. Agents cannot effectively design transactions that will maximize the use of equity unless they know the power of that equity to capture or buy benefits.

When representing a client with an equity which is not readily saleable, it is imperative that a taker first be generated, whereas readily saleable packages have a built-in demand. The saleable situation allows the agent to shop for client benefits using cash or cash equivalents (cashable equities). This cash condition gives most strength to the equity. Anything less than a totally cashable equity diminishes the ability of the client and agent to demand dollar benefits. Obviously, any exchange which involves the purchase of a taxpayer's equity with cash can be structured properly to avoid tax consequences. Only when saleability, or lack thereof, is known both to client and agent can they be in a position to discover and to structure realistic transactions.

It is the agent's mentality as she or he approaches the marketplace which determines the ability to create a viable transaction. That mentality should be either a dollar mentality (saleable), in which case the appropriate economic analysis and comparisons will be employed, or an equity mentality (nonsaleable) which begs consideration for a taker/solution to the situation at hand. Until or unless the equity can be readily converted to cash within a reasonable time, the agent must realize that he or she is shopping the market with only equity. And equity is not cash. It is incongruous to make dollar demands with an equity that cannot be defined in dollars.

THE "THIRD LEG"

Defining the power of one's equity is a key determinant in whether to use the third "leg" or the "in lieu" concept of marketing. Each property in a transaction is referred to as a "leg." The "in lieu" situation arises when someone will take what a client has but that client finds little or no benefit in what is being offered in exchange. Yet, it may be in the best interest of solving the client's problem to use the offered property as a substitute vehicle to acquire the benefits sought by the client. The basic rule as to whether to engage in an in lieu situation is influenced by the quality of property being offered to the client and the competence of the other agent. If the property offered has equal or greater appeal in the marketplace, an in lieu may be advantageous. A competent in lieu agent has client management, is willing to commit time to the in lieu process, and understands its responsibilities.

The benefits of the in lieu transaction are twofold. First, it gives an equal or better vehicle to use to acquire client benefits. This may include neutralizing a client's position, as in the case of a property which has extensive deferred maintenance being neutralized by an offer of free and clear land. The unencumbered land will have greater market appeal than will the property in need of repair. The second benefit of the in lieu transaction is engaging other agents to help solve the problem. Involvement in a third leg transaction generally necessitates another agent. Now there are two or more agents actively seeking a solution to the client's problems. Caution should be exercised as to the credibility of the other agents and whether they indeed can 'or will make the contribution necessary to culminate the transaction.

DEVELOPING EXCHANGE CLIENTS

Developing a clientele oriented toward exchange transactions is a matter of exposure to those who have a need or perceive a problem with regard to their real estate portfolio. In understanding the various motivations people have in acquiring or disposing of real estate, client development becomes directly related to the agent's approach and positioning. Clients are readily available and will seek assistance when the agent is situated to allow the potential clients to recognize or begin to identify their needs. The creation of an environment where potential clients can associate the fulfillment of their needs with the skills and talents of the agent is the key. There are numerous circumstances where this can occur.

Sellers

A primary source of an exchange client is the individual who contacts the agent to sell a piece of property. The approach here is to discern whether the client actually needs a sale. The agent should ascertain what it is the client will do with the money in the event a sale can be negotiated. In many cases the client will express an interest to reinvest the proceeds into additional real estate. Then why not exchange it, thereby deferring taxation on the gain, preserving dollars for reinvestment, and maintaining continuity in the ownership of real estate? These are essentially the benefits of the Section 1031 exchange transaction.

Publicity

What other environments are conducive to client development? Speaking engagements are an invaluable source for clients. One method is to develop a 20- to 30-minute presentation on the broad range of benefits to be derived from exchanging. One can then deliver the talk to various service clubs and organizations in the community. Another method is to be placed on a speaker's bureau. This will give additional high visibility. On an individual basis one can also organize and conduct half-day seminars on the benefits of exchanging property and the problem-solving approach to real estate. This can be accomplished solo or in conjunction with a real estate attorney and/or accountant. Including other ancillary professionals broadens the scope of the presentation and demonstrates one's ability to work with other professions.

The written word carries a powerful message. Most opportunities which afford newspaper coverage will be beneficial to the practitioner. Maintaining communication with local newspapers often leads to free publicity. When possible, develop a column in the local press addressing some of the inherent benefits and detriments of real estate ownership. A question and answer format usually works best. Designing an informative newsletter focusing on current market trends, financing, and real estate tax updates has been successful in generating new clients. The newsletter is best directed to a specific audience such as educators, engineers, doctors, or pension plan trustees.

Apartment House Owners

Other than the single-family household owner, the apartment house entrepreneur is the second most prevalent improved property owner in the United States. Because these investors seem to have an insatiable appetite for information, the organization and leadership by an agent of an apartment house association is a practical approach to client development. It places the agent in a position of authority where she or he can act as a resource for information to the apartment house owners. And when a problem arises, the agent is the most visible helper in the mind's eye of the person in need. Development of a real estate management company leads to the same type of exposure. A qualified management company has direct input as to the operations and functioning of a property and a thorough ongoing dialogue with the owner. The agent is kept abreast of any needed changes in the conditions of the ownership and can respond appropriately when marketing skills become necessary.

Learned Investors

Most people are interested in pursuing some type of investment program, but they are confused by the various opportunities available— savings accounts, annuities, stocks, bonds, precious metals, gems, certificates of deposits, commercial paper, trust deeds, and, of course, real estate. There is a wealth of reading material available on each of these subjects. One can assemble a group of five to ten people into a "book group" which emphasizes the investigation of various investments. After each book is read, the participants examine the pros and cons of each opportunity and idea. Most readers will realize that real estate has historically proved the most viable and reliable of all investments. Here again they will turn to the real estate professional for help. The benefit to the agent, aside from increased clientele, is enhancement of one's overall investment knowledge.

Other Approaches

Essentially the approaches and methods herein described are indirect, contrary to the farming approach of knocking on doors. These approaches require the agent to construct a format in which information is shared, a need or problem is identified, and the skills and talents of a professional are recognized. Often overlooked by agents desiring clients are corporations, pension and retirement funds, and charitable institutions. Many corporations have acquired real estate through expansion or merger, and most corporations are unfamiliar with the alternatives available through the exchange marketplace. Although pension and retirement plans generally are liquid, the opportunities available for nontaxable profit in a creative exchange transaction are worth pursuing.

Schools, universities, churches, hospitals, and other nonprofit entities have portfolios of real estate ownership. A client can gain monetary and nonmonetary benefits from making a donation of real estate to an eleemosynary organization; also, once the realty is in its possession the organization will want to move it into a more passive situation. The nonprofit organization desires reduced management responsibilities and sufficient income to service the contract made with the donor. Creative exchanging can provide these benefits.

THE MARKETING PROGRAM

Understanding the philosophy of exchanges, which is essentially creative marketing of the equity, and having assembled the facts regarding the property and the owner allow one to design an intelligent marketing program. There are both traditional and innovative methods for marketing the exchange listing or "package." The most common approach is the multiple listing service. Unfortunately, multiple listing services are primarily geared for the buy/sell situation; hence, if the property in question is not readily saleable in the current market, the multiple listing is of little or no value from an exchange point of view. The multiple listing book best accommodates those properties which are readily saleable and require a Section 1031 tax-deferred exchange. When placing a listing in the multiple, it is advisable to document in the multiple book the intention for Section 1031 treatment.

Realty Boards

Another avenue for marketing the exchange is through the various realty boards. Many boards have investment and exchange divisions. They usually meet at the board office, where agents have an opportunity to communicate what it is they have available for exchange and what it is they wish to acquire in an exchange transaction. Presentations are brief and primarily focus on the property offered and that which the client *wants*.

Marketing Groups

A growing and far more productive approach to exchanges is the network of marketing groups which extends across the United States. These groups specialize in exchange marketing with an attitude that concentrates on solving problems. The formation of the exchange group was the brainchild of Richard R. Reno. He recognized the need to establish an environment where real estate agents could communicate openly with each other and work together in a cooperative effort to solve the problems of their respective clients. This concept has been perpetuated by many organizations. The National Council of Exchangors, the Society of Exchange Counselors, the Arizona Association of Real Estate Exchangors, and the Florida Real Estate Exchangors are but a few.

People need assistance in solving problems arising from real estate ownership as much as they need assistance in solving legal, medical, tax, and management problems. The exchange meeting or creative equity-marketing group is designed to generate successful transactions that fulfill client needs and meet client goals and objectives. Brainstorming, idea tracking, formal presentations, informal dialogue, skillful moderating, and group participation are among the methods employed in this marketplace. Most groups of this nature meet on a regularly scheduled basis. These meetings are held locally, regionally, and nationally. Some have rather stringent entry requirements; others are less restrictive.

The format for equity-marketing groups is relatively consistent. The three essential components are (1) an audience with a certain level of education in the techniques of exchanging, (2) a presenter who has a controlled and well-counseled client, and (3) a skillful moderator who asks questions which provoke the audience to think and participate. The meetings are organized as a forum for agents to present before an audience information concerning the property they represent and pertinent information about the client and the client's objective. This is commonly known as the stand-up presentation. Under the direction and guidance of the moderator, salient information is communicated to the audience so that they may respond with questions, pose solutions, or initiate an offer to acquire the property being presented. It is this cooperative environment, agents working together in a collective consciousness by sharing ideas and formulas, that is the most unique and beneficial aspect of transacting business in the exchange marketplace.

Moderators

The function of the moderator of these marketing groups is to gather information, clarify contradictions or ambiguities during the presentation, stimulate audience brainstorming, and facilitate the writing of offers to the presenter. The following is a list of the types of questions which may be posed by the moderator. The extent to which the presenter is prepared to respond intelligently to those questions will affect the potential for a successful transaction.

Property Questions

1. Which is more important, a tax-deferred sale per Section 1031 or creative marketing?
2. Briefly describe the property with information not already on the package.
3. What potential and/or opportunity may exist in the property that you feel can be achieved by a taker?
4. How much deferred maintenance exists?
5. Explain in detail the financing.
6. Where can current mortgages be moved?
7. What refinance possibilities exist?
8. How can management be handled?
9. What offers have been made or turned down and why?

People Questions

1. Relate facts about the client that will help agents solve her or his problem.
2. How and why was the property acquired?
3. How long has the client owned it?
4. Why does the client wish to exchange the property as opposed to selling it?
5. To what extent will the client accept reverse cash flow?
6. To what extent is there a third-party influence?
7. What is the client's cash and/or "can add" potential?
8. What are the client's geographical limits?

Problem Questions

1. How would you classify your client's needs?
2. Why has your client chosen to dispose of the property?
3. What solutions have you formulated that would move your client toward his or her objective?

4. What formulas have been discussed with the client?
   a. Creation of wealth
   b. Separate the interest
   c. Refinance
   d. In lieu of transactions
   e. Buy her or his way out
   f. Share the wealth
   g. Offsets
   h. Leaseback

Before and after Moderating

Depending on the number of participants at the marketing meeting and the volume of packages or client circumstances to be presented, it may be advisable to employ premoderating and postmoderating sessions. Most exchange marketing groups allocate to each presenter between 15 and 20 minutes of presentation time from the podium. When the meetings become too large and the presentation time must be reduced to 3 to 10 minutes to accommodate all those attendees who may want to present, premoderating is essential. In premoderating, the presenter meets with the moderator to discuss the package prior to the presentation. The prestaging of the presentation tends to condense and refine it so that time is not wasted. Essentially, it is a rehearsal for the final presentation before the audience. After the presentation the moderator, the presenter, and anyone from the audience who has an interest in the circumstances as presented from the podium can gather in the postmoderating room to explore in greater depth the possibilities of doing business together. Albeit an organizational effort, premoderating and postmoderating have produced highly beneficial results.

Packages

The participants at the marketing sessions keep track of the presentations by way of packages. Each participant receives a package for each presentation containing a brief description of the pertinent data regarding the property involved and the problems to be solved (Figure 26-1). On the reverse side of the package, should it be an income-producing property, is an income and expense sheet. When the property is unimproved, such as acreage or lots, a plat map showing the property's configuration and dimensions and general directions for locating the property and other logistic information is required.

Listing Date: Value: ($0.V.—WETV: $)
Fee Information: Loan: (Free and Clear: $)
Expiration Date: Equity: ($O.V—WETV: $)

Descriptive Title

Have: Concise description of property. Pertinent information that will help exchangors and the moderator understand what you have to offer.

Address: If definitive address is available, state it completely—street, city, state. If not (such as in recreational land) give enough information to locate from known landmarks. Have legal description in backup. A map is mandatory and should be printed on reverse.

Loans: Nature (first loan, junior paper, AITD, contracts), dollar amount of each, interest, payment amount, and payment period (monthly, quarterly, yearly). Lender: name and due dates. Itemize all loans.

Income: *Do not show on face of package.* On income rental property a complete income and expense statement is to be printed on the reverse of package.
               If package has no history of income, but there is potential income, provide projected income and expenses on reverse. Be prepared to back up all projections.

Objective: Divide into two catagories:
               (**1**) Short Term: State problem now confronting client and what immediate goal is.
               (**2**) Long Term: What are client's ultimate intentions?

Can Add: Be specific and be prepared. The same backup package is needed on the can adds as on the subject property. If adding cash, state the amount or give a range. Equity is to be stated on any can add.

Remarks: State all the items brought out through counseling that will stimulate audience brainstorming. Emphasize the benefits the client will add to enhance the property: leasebacks, buy backs, guaranteed rents, joint ventures, and subordination.

Client: Names of client and all principals having a vested interest in the property. Concise information that will lead to creative thinking.

Counselor: Name, address (including city, state, zip), and phone.

Disclaimer: A disclaimer is not a complete release of liability or responsibility for what is represented in the package but may prove helpful.

Figure 26-1   Instructions for preparing an exchange package at an exchange marketing session.

Country Store

In conjunction with the classical stand-up moderated presentation is the so-called country store method of marketing, developed by Murray Sobel. The country store allows agents to display all of the packages in their listing portfolios. Provided on the marketing meeting room walls, or in a separate facility, is a variety of designated property categories such as farms, apartments, commercial, industrial, lots, acreage, and so on. Under each category the appropriate property package is displayed for perusal by the attendees. When interest is stimulated after reviewing the package, the agents meet to discuss the possibilities of manufacturing a transaction. Obviously this marketing method is not nearly as effective as broadcasting from the podium, but used in concert with the stand-up presentation, it provides another marketing method.

Zander Board

The Zander board developed by Bud Zander is another useful and effective marketing tool. The emphasis of the Zander board is to develop from the audience a taker for the property being presented from the podium. Therefore, regardless of the client's needs or benefit structure, the Zander method first culls out any takers for the property. Once that has been exhausted the presenter must determine if the client would be a taker for anything that has been offered. This would result in a two-way exchange (Figure 26-2).

The next step is to generate from the audience solutions to the problem that has been presented. The solutions are to be revealed regardless of personal interest in the package presented. When a solution package accepts property in the taker column (column 1), a three-way transaction is formulated (Figure 26-3).

In some cases a third step is involved, that of the catalyst (column 2). The catalyst agrees to be a taker for any properties in column 1. The agent representing the solution (column 3) is then asked if she or he has any interest in the catalyst category, column 2. If so, a four-way transaction results (Figure 26-4).

The Exchange Offer

What transpires among the agents at the termination of a marketing presentation? It is hoped that offers will be made and submitted to the presenter. The offers come in the form of a preliminary exchange proposal, often referred to as the "mini" because it is actually a condensation of the formal long-form exchange offer. These preliminary proposals, which were originally developed by Don Eymann, are written "broker-to-broker" communiques or memos. The idea may require an exchange of equities or merely a thought which would not necessitate a conveyance. Many creative, valuable ideas are lost because they are not written down. The idea can be structured to benefit the client of the agent who has written the proposal, or it may result in a solution for the agent whose client has a problem. Generally, the minis, or prelims, are presented on three-part carbonless paper. Two copies are given to the other agent along with a copy of the offered package. The remaining duplicate offer is retained with

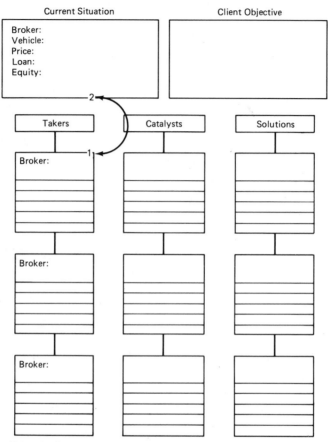

Figure 26-2   Using the Zander method to develop a two-way exchange.

the other agent's package. The mini provides the initial written instrument, which, after discussion with the other agent, can lead to a formal exchange contract. It also gives the receiving agent written documentation to present to the client. The preliminary exchange proposal is not a binding contract; rather, it is an agent-to-agent written memo which the client has the ultimate authority to accept, counter, or reject. The more thorough knowledge the agent possesses concerning the client and the problem, the more accurate and realistic will be the mini proposals that are written on behalf of the client (see Figure 26-5).

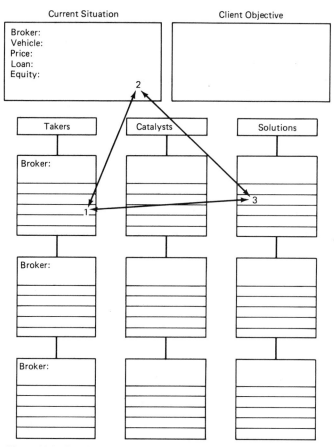

Figure 26-3 Developing a three-way exchange at a marketing meeting.

Other Avenues for Exchange

It is not only in these meetings that successful exchanges are negotiated. A real estate office staff can structure a viable exchange. Regular meetings to discuss office listings have a tremendous potential for exchanges. And, on a one-to-one basis, agents can arrange to meet other agents with whom they have previously worked or who are known for their proficiency in exchanging and creative thinking. Advertising in the local newspapers, direct contact with agents outside the field of exchanging, mailings, and personal correspondence are other merchandising alternatives.

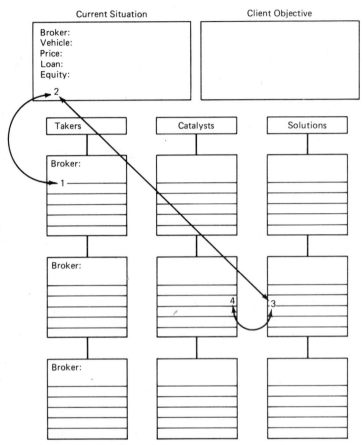

Figure 26-4 A four-way exchange.

FIDUCIARY RELATIONSHIPS AND OBLIGATIONS

The fees and commissions collected by real estate practitioners are the rewards for efforts expended in their business. In most real estate transactions all agents involved divide fees and commissions paid by the seller. Although this remains the most common method of handling fees, there are alternatives available which are being employed by a number of real estate professionals. In any case, the agent must know to whom he or she owes primary allegiance. Real estate agents know that they have a fiduciary relationship with all principal parties to a transaction. The fiduciary relationship is

```
┌────────────────────────────────────────────┐
│ ‖                                            │
│ F ──── Name, address, and phone number of    │
│ R ────                                       │
│ O      the agent initiating the proposal     │
│ M ────                                       │
│ ‖                                            │
└────────────────────────────────────────────┘

┌────────────────────────────────────────────┐
│ ‖      Name, address, and phone number of    │   At: Designates marketing meeting
│ T ────                                       │
│ O      the agent to whom the proposal is     │
│ ‖                                            │   Date ___ Date proposal is written
│        written                               │
└────────────────────────────────────────────┘
```

MY CLIENT: _____Name of agent's client_____

    Type of Property:___Brief description of___ Address:___Include street number,___
                          properties or commodities   street name, city, and state
                          being offered for exchange

    Subject to:___Detailed description of the loans of record___

YOUR CLIENT: _____Client to whom the proposal is written_____

    Type of Property:___Brief description of___ Address:___Include street number,___
                          properties or commodities   street name, city, and state
                          being offered for exchange

    Subject to: ___Detailed description of the loans of record___

TERMS AND CONDITIONS:___Basic structure of the exchange idea, generally includes the structure___
                              of the financing

NOTE: Other data on properties outlined herein as per sheets attached and submitted herewith. Final terms and conditions, if any, to be in subsequent offer and/or escrow instructions.

This offer is subject to my client's inspection and approval of the property and all pertinent financial information.

This proposal is subject to prior disposition of the above properties. It shall expire 15 days after herein date of submission.

This proposal is submitted as per client authorization and is subject to final approval of respective clients.

        Name of agent   Name of client
      Submitting Counselor   Client Acceptance

Remarks ___Included are any special provision such as leasebacks, guarantee of rents,___
             or contingency clauses. Used to document the intent of a Section 1031 exchange.

Figure 26-5 A typical exchange proposal (short-form approach).

defined in the *Division of Real Estate Reference Book of the State of California* as follows:

> An agent is a fiduciary. His obligation of diligent and faithful service is the same as that imposed upon a trustee. He is bound by law to exercise the utmost good faith, loyalty, and honest dealing in the execution of the duties of his agency. Because trust and confidence exist in such fiduciary relationships, it is the duty of the agent, in whom such trust and confidence is imposed by his principal, to make full disclosure of *all material* facts within his knowledge relating to the transaction of the agency, and any concealment of material facts is fraud.
>
> An agent is under a duty to use reasonable care and skill in his work, obey directions of his employer and to render an account on demand. A gratuitous agent cannot be compelled to perform his undertaking, but if he actually enters upon performance, he must obey instructions and is bound to exercise the utmost good faith in dealing with his principal.
>
> An agent or employee cannot compete with his principal on matters connected with the agency and, of course, cannot act as agent for a competitor.

Herein lies the potential for conflict. To whom does the agent owe fiduciary? There are esentially two types of fiduciary duties. First and primary is the duty to one's client, and second is one's general duty to all parties of the transaction. Encompassed in the definition of a fiduciary is the mandate under the aspect of full disclosure to disclose facts to all principals as to the condition of the realty involved. For example, an agent must inform a purchaser that although the property's use is currently commercial, due to down zoning, replacement of a commercial use building on the property would not be permissable.

Inclusive of this general duty to all principals is the broker's responsibility to reveal whether the agent is representing both the buyer and seller in the transaction. Another important material fact which bears on the agent's primary fiduciary is whether the agent stands to make a secret profit on the transaction.

As a result of the importance of one's fiduciary and as a step toward greater professionalism, the issue of single agency has arisen within the real estate industry. Single agency means that the agent will represent only one principal in any given transaction. Although dual agency remains as the primary method of representation throughout the country and certainly is not illegal as long as all parties to the transaction are informed of such agency, it appears to result in a conflict of interest. To represent all principals in a transaction equally is virtually impossible. Dual agency obscures the lines of representation and sometimes results in unnecessary conflicts between agents. The agent can become enmeshed in costly litigation and court battles.

If indeed the agent owes fiduciary to her or his client, what then is a client? A client is a person under the protection of another, a person who engages the professional advice or services of another. The client is the principal who employs the agent. How is client status different from customer status? A customer is a person who purchases goods or services. A customer enters the marketplace essentially unrepresented. Although the customer remains unrepresented, under the law of agency, the requirement of an agent is to disclose fully any detrimental aspects of the property which could affect the seller's decision to sell or the buyer's decision to purchase. Protection must be afforded to buyer or seller by the agent as to confidential information. Confidential information may include, but is not limited to, the willingness or ability to offer or accept a different price, terms, financing, or conditions.

In the case of an exchange transaction, when the employment agreement is executed it should state that the agent represents only one principal. This will avoid "pooling" and dividing of brokerage fees with any cooperating agents and will diminish the liability associated with dual agency.

In essence, the concept of single agency provides numerous benefits. The principal is assured of exclusive representation and is confident that the agent will negotiate on his or her behalf to secure the best price, terms, and conditions. Because each principal in a single agency transaction is responsible for the respective individual fee, she or he benefits by an expanded market which includes for-sale-by-owner properties and properties that are not available on the market. Aside from the monetary benefits which accrue to the principal under single agency, the principal so represented is the recipient of the loyalty, dedication, and honesty of the agent so employed.

For the agent, single agency affords the pleasure of working with a client. It provides a sense of security and allows the agent to be discriminating and selective in deciding whether to handle the responsibility of the listing contract.

Real estate exchange marketing is the most dynamic and expanding facet of the real estate business. Real estate practitioners should acquaint themselves with the exchange process to enhance their own transaction-making potential and to provide a necessary service to the public.

Chapter 27

The Delayed Exchange

Bruce B. Howey Realtor and Speaker for the National Institute of Exchange Counselors, Inc.

O ver the years one of the basic rules for a real estate exchange has been the requirement for a concurrent closing of each transaction. When deeding out of one property, the receipt of another like kind property should be made. Typically all documents are recorded in sequence at 8 A.M. thus fulfilling the simultaneous closing requirement.

A "delayed closing" is a matter of having located the exchange properties and having a short time interval on a nonconcurrent closing. In today's market it is not always possible to have the "up-leg" exchange property located or ready to close at the exact same time. In many cases a delayed closing is made wherein the properties are located but for some mechanical reason cannot be recorded at the same time. For instance, final signatures have been made but not received, a new loan has been approved but is not quite ready to fund, or some minor contingencies are not complete. In cases of this kind a day or two, or possibly a week or two, might elapse. This is not a good practice, but frequently it is better than some of the alternatives. The advice of a good real estate attorney is important.

A "delayed exchange" occurs when there is a taker for the exchange property but no property has been located to consummate the exchange, thereby necessitating a time lag to locate, process, and close the entire transaction. What is the difference between the time lapse of a few days or weeks in a delayed closing and a time lapse of up to 5 years in locating and processing the necessary exchange properties in a delayed exchange? The Starker cases addressed this issue.

In April 1967 Bruce Starker and T.J. Starker agreed to transfer Oregon forestry land to Crown-Zellerbach Corp. and Longview Fiber Co. In return the Starkers were to receive like kind property within a 5-year period.

Previously the IRS had taken the position that a delayed closing was unacceptable. In some older court decisions there were indications that nonconcurrent closings would qualify for tax deferment under the Internal Revenue Service (IRS) Code, Section 1031, but it was not until August 24, 1979, that the U.S. Court of Appeals, Ninth Circuit, "affirmed in part" the principle of a nonconcurrent closing.

For some 10 years the Starkers and the IRS were in various stages of discussion as to whether the Starkers had fulfilled the requirements of Section 1031 after acquiring like kind property within the 5-year time frame that had been stipulated. The cases involved were *Bruce Starker*, DC-Ore, 75-1 (U.S.T.C.), 9443, *T.J. Starker*, DC-Ore, 77-2 (U.S.T.C.), 9512, and *Starker v. United States* 602 F. 2d 1341 (9th Cir. 1979).

The concept of the delayed exchange made by the Starkers was that the Starkers would deliver their forestry property *now* for other like kind property to be delivered over a 5-year period (see Figure 27-1). The September 1977 issue of *News and Notes* (vol. 10, no. 9) for tax practitioners by the IRS again advised that *"transfers of real estate held for business or investment, where proceeds are held in some form of custodial arrangement* pending their use in acquisition of new property, do not qualify as nontaxable exchanges."

As a result of the *Starker* decision many individuals, companies, and/ or corporations have been formed to act as trustees to facilitate delayed exchanges. They work in cooperation with investors, brokers, attorneys, escrow companies, title insurance companies, accountants, banks, savings and loan associations, and other financial institutions.

The use of an individual as opposed to a corporation creates a problem, since an individual is subject to death, judgments, taxes, divorce, bankruptcy, unavailability, or a change of mind. The corporation as a

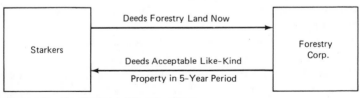

Figure 27-1 The Starkers' delayed exchange.

principal will (1) take title to the taxpayer's exchange property, (2) dispose of the property by sale or exchange, (3) acquire a satisfactory property of like kind, and (4) consummate the original exchange transaction by deeding the acquired property to the taxpayer. There is an interval of time while this all takes place. All transactions should be completed within the taxpayer's current tax year. If a longer period may be needed, then it is presumed that the tax deferment would be well worth any risk involved. The court approved, in the second Starker case, which had a time sequence completion date of 5 years. Any deviation from the *Starker* circumstances conceivably could be challenged by the IRS.

The holding corporation (or trustee) has no tax consequences, since there is no gain or loss in the transferring of properties between the taxpayer and the corporation. Any income received would be reported as ordinary income as to fees or interest. The benefit to the corporation is the use of all the cash.

The taxpayer is restricted as to the probable acceptance of any interest earned prior to reacquiring the acceptable exchange property to culminate the tax-deferred exchange. This is a gray area, and a qualified tax counsel should be consulted before deciding to accept any interest. Conceivably the acceptance of cash (interest) could destroy the tax-deferred status of the exchange. In addition, some corporations charge a processing and documentation fee going into (or out of) the overall transaction.

Selection of a corporation or "nominee" depends on:

1. Reliability
2. Knowledge
3. Experience
4. Tax counsel
5. Legal counsel

All these items are important. The transaction may never be audited, but, depending on how the transaction is reported on the taxpayer's return, it could be audited any time up to 3 years or indefinitely if fraud is alleged. In the event of a challenge, as in *Starker,* all the help that can be garnered is going to be necessary. Proper structuring and documentation at the outset should ensure a clean transaction.

Most corporations or nominees work in concert with the taxpayer's legal and tax counsel. They provide services on a noninterference basis with the existing escrow and/or broker-client relationships. The agent-client relationship is not disturbed but rather enhanced by the corporate services.

The sequence of a typical delayed exchange is:

1. Taxpayer's property (A) is deeded to the holding corporation.
2. Corporation takes title to taxpayer's property.
3. Corporation sells or exchanges taxpayer's property.
4. Corporation holds money or title in trust.
5. Corporation locates property (B) acceptable to taxpayer.
6. Corporation acquires property B with cash held in trust.
7. Corporation takes title to property B.
8. Corporation deeds property B to the taxpayer.
9. Taxpayer accepts property B, culminating the tax-deferred exchange.

Figure 27-2 is a simplification of a delayed exchange. Frequently there will be more properties, more people, and more problems. Assumptions are made that:

1. The taxpayer does not have unilateral access to any cash.
2. The taxpayer receives no cash, boot, or net mortgage relief.
3. Proper documentation is made.
4. Proper escrowing is done.
5. Proper legal advice is obtained.

All parties in a multiple exchange normally will not be able to defer taxes. Usually the up-leg or the cash-out property is the primary property that will incur acceptable tax consequences. If the benefits are such that they offset the taxes paid, then there is sufficient motivation to participate in the exchange.

The second *Starker* case was substantially enhanced by the Fifth Circuit's *Biggs* case [*Franklin B. Biggs*, 69 TC No. 78 (1978) and *Biggs v. Com* 12/15/80 (CA5)]. In this transaction Biggs orally agreed to sell his land subject to Powell acquiring a like kind property and deeding it to Biggs. Powell was unable or unwilling to take title to the Virginia farm that Biggs wanted, so an intermediary was set up. Title to both properties was deeded to the fourth-party corporation, who then re-

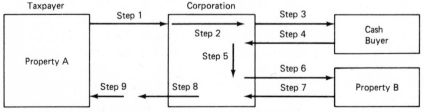

Figure 27-2 A delayed exchange.

deeded the respective properties. Biggs's property went to Powell, and the fourth-party corporation, having acquired the Virginia farm, deeded it to Biggs.

This is an oversimplification of the entire transaction, but the principle was enough of a parallel to give two major tax court opinions justifying the transfer of replacement property if not concurrently then at least in a reasonable period of time—"time" being unidentifiable as to the time frame of a delayed exchange.

The courts have been taking a liberal attitude toward exchanges and the various methods that are used today to close these transactions within the framework of Section 1031. The Fifth Circuit and the Ninth Circuit courts have both ruled in favor of the taxpayer.

The IRS has also taken somewhat of a permissive attitude, as in its Letter Ruling 793807. The IRS ruled in a specific instance that by putting the sale price in trust with an independent trustee one avoids the time delay factor of acquiring like kind property; thus it is a valid means of completing the so-called tax-free aspects of a nonsimultaneous exchange.

Letter Rulings serve only as a guideline, but they do give some indications of attitude in similar cases. They cannot be relied on, and therefore a qualified tax attorney should approve the transaction. After all, the transaction may be defendable but at what cost?

Section 1034 stipulates a time period for gain on sale of principal residence, and Section 1033 stipulates a time period on an involuntary conversion, but Section 1031 does *not* stipulate a time period. The courts, the taxpayer, and the IRS have agreed that a transfer "at or about" the time of sale is tax-deferred. Circuit courts have disagreed with IRS that a "substantial" period of time between divestment and acquisition of like kind property kills the tax-free exchange. To the taxpayer the issue is tax deferment; to the IRS the issue is taxability now; and to the courts the issue is time.

Part 6

Appraisal

Principles of Appraisal

Silas J. Ely   Independent Appraiser; formerly Principal Appraiser, Los Angeles
County Assessor's Office

Property valuation is a vital part of the decision-making process of all buyers, sellers, and users of real estate. Thus, appraisal lies at the heart of all real estate activity. Urban planning, zoning, taxation, and the management of our national resources also require a working knowledge of the basic principles of appraisal, if our most sensitive area of public control is to be administered efficiently.

NATURE AND FUNCTION OF APPRAISALS

Informal appraisals are simply opinions of value expressed by purchasers, sellers, investors, and managers of real estate. Such appraisals may be based entirely on intuitive judgment gained from prior experience. More commonly they depend, at least in part, on the recommendation and advice of experienced real estate practitioners and professionals.

Formal appraisals are more than mere opinions. Designed primarily to furnish value estimates that are independent of the parties to the transaction, professional appraisals require pointed market research, analysis of pertinent data, and the application of appraisal techniques deriving from an intimate knowledge of value theory as well as market attitudes and actions. When incorporated into written reports, such appraisals conform to the demanding standards of today's marketplace. They are designed to meet the legal requirements that govern corporate real estate activity and real estate lending as well as actions at law. They also stand behind or test property and estate taxation and other government activities involving real estate.

In broad terms, an appraisal can be defined as simply an estimate of value. Such estimate may be based either on a verbal opinion or on evidence presented in a written report. As we have seen, however, the usefulness and reliability of an appraisal depends on a degree of professional expertise, competence, and integrity on the part of the appraiser and the inclusion of certain concrete evidence to support the value opinion. Thus, a formal, professional appraisal can be defined as *a supported opinion of value for a defined property as of a specified date.* The value conclusion should be based on the processing and analysis of relevant data made available to the client. Formal appraisals are usually in written form.

Value Standards and Definitions

The word "value" generally means the utility or worth of some object to some person. However, dozens of different value definitions are encountered in common business usage. Depending on the purpose to be served any one may be a valid subject of appraisal.

Assessed value: Value for ad valorem tax purposes; often a percentage of market value as defined by law and estimated by the property tax assessor.

Actual cash value: Value for casualty insurance purposes (in most states). Sometimes related to the cost of replacement of the structures, actual cash value has now been interpreted by some courts to mean market value.

Book value: Usually defined as purchase price plus capital improvements less depreciation taken. This value is needed for certain accounting and income tax purposes.

Loan value: Value for loan purposes; most conventional loans are legally limited to a maximum percentage of value. Although this "value" usually refers to market value, it is also known by the ambiguous term "loan" value.

Inheritance tax value: The value determined for inheritance tax purposes; it is legally related to the market value of the property, but local practice varies.

Utility value or value in use: The value to the user, or the value for a specific purpose. It is a subjective value concept. A property may have different "values" for different purposes, as can be seen by the terms listed above.

Value in exchange: The value in the marketplace, that is, the amount of money, goods, or services the property will "exchange" for in the open market. It also means the value to people in general. That is why it is referred to as "objective" rather than "subjective" in nature.

Market Value

Because of the clear and objective conditions contained in its definition, market value is the standard most commonly used in professional appraisals. Institution loans, government actions, and court litigation revolving around real estate most often rely on market value appraisals. As buyers and sellers become more sophisticated, private as well as corporate investors require that appraisals clearly define the value sought as market value. Market value is defined as:

> The highest price in terms of money which a property will bring in a competitive and open market under all conditions requisite to a fair sale, the buyer and seller, each acting prudently, knowledgeably and assuming the price is not affected by undue stimulus. Implicit in this definition is the consummation of a sale as of a specified date and the passing of title from seller to buyer under conditions whereby: (1) buyer and seller are typically motivated; (2) both parties are well informed or well advised, and each acting in what he considers his own best interest; (3) a reasonable time is allowed for exposure in the open market; (4) payment is made in cash or its equivalent; (5) financing, if any, is on terms generally available in the community at the specified date and typical for the property type in its locale; (6) the price represents a normal consideration for the property sold unaffected by special financing amounts and/or terms, services, fees, costs, or credits incurred in the transaction. ("Real Estate Appraisal Terminology," published 1975.)

Market Value versus Market Price

Price and value are often confused. Very few have not heard the expression, "you can name the price if I can define the terms I am willing to pay in the purchase of your property." Market price is simply the amount actually paid or contracted for in a particular transaction. As such it may or may not be governed by prudent acts of the parties, unique financing agreements, or open market conditions. Innovative or creative financing has demonstrated in recent years the truism that the terms and conditions of a transaction determine the price. Sophisticated market appraisals must include these factors as surely as they do differences in location, size, or quality of the real estate.

Written Appraisal Reports

The type of report to be used in an appraisal depends on the needs of the client and the nature of the appraisal problem. The following are the three most common types:

1. The letter report is the least formal type of written appraisal report, most often used when supporting data are not required by the client. Consisting of a business letter of 1 to 10 pages, a letter report may simply identify the value problem, make a statement as to the scope of the study, and express an opinion of value.

2. A form or short-form report features a printed-page format for check-out completion by the appraiser. Lenders and other organizations that handle large volumes of appraisals prefer the form appraisal report because it has a standardized content and is easy to read and review.

3. A narrative appraisal report is the most formal and detailed of all written reports. It is preferred when the reader will likely need to follow the step-by-step logic of the appraiser. All data supporting the value opinion are included. Narrative appraisal reports are often required in connection with major investment property appraisals and in condemnation proceedings.

Since appraisal reports are a form of business correspondence, certain essential elements are necessary for the protection of both the appraiser and the client served by the appraisal. A discussion of the appraisal report and professional appraisal is found in Chapter 29.

REAL ESTATE, REAL PROPERTY, AND VALUE

A competent appraisal requires a thorough understanding of the physical and legal characteristics of real estate and the property rights available in our society. It also recognizes that the market value of real property reflects and is affected by the many forces that motivate and affect all human activity.

Physical and Legal Characteristics

It is an economic truism that land has no intrinsic value. Instead, its utility and value derive from the legal rights of its ownership and use. The distinction between real estate, real property, and personal property is basic in appraisals. "Real estate" refers to the physical land and everything that is permanently attached—buildings, structures, other improvements. "Real property" consists of the rights, interests, and benefits that are inherent in the ownership of the physical real estate. "Personal property" is anything that is not real estate or real property. It is generally movable, not permanently attached to the real estate. The courts have developed the so-called law of fixtures to determine whether an object is personal property or real estate. If it is a fixture, it is real estate for most legal purposes. Whether an item is a fixture or personal property depends on:

1. The intention of the parties
2. The degree of annexation or attachment
3. Whether the object is uniquely adapted to the land or building
4. Any agreement between the parties
5. The relationship of the parties

In many states the terms "real estate" and "real property" are legally synonymous, and thus they are used interchangeably. In its broader sense, real property consists of four elements, including both the physical real estate components and the legal rights that are ordinarily associated with its use:

1. Land: the surface, subsurface, and the air above
2. Permanently affixed objects:
   a. Buildings, structures, and improvements to land
   b. Fixtures: personal property that has been converted into real estate (see discussion of the five tests for a fixture)
3. Appurtenant or incidental rights: partial rights to other property, considered necessary to the use of the land
4. That which is immovable by law

Bundle-of-Rights Theory

The most complete ownership of real estate is referred to as the "fee simple estate." It consists of the greatest bundle of rights that is possible to legally hold. Such rights include the rights to occupy and use, encumber, sell, dispose, exclude, will, and bequeath.

The legal definition of real property implies that its ownership includes all rights to the use of land and everything attached and/or appurtenant to its intended use. However, four important powers of government limit this use:

1. Police power: The government may regulate the use of property to promote the safety, health, morals, and general welfare of the public. Examples include:
   a. Master plans and zoning ordinances.
   b. Building, housing, electrical codes.
   c. Flood and seismic safety zones.

    d. Environmental protection laws.

    e. Rent control.

2. Taxation: The government may impose whatever level and kind of taxes that are reasonable and necessary to fund government services.

3. Eminent domain: The government may take private property by condemnation when it is in the public interest to do so but must pay "just compensation" to the owner.

4. Escheat: On the death of the owner without a will or heirs, title and ownership of real estate revert to the government.

Rights to the use of real estate are often privately split up, divided, or restricted. Examples include a mortgage, assignment of rents, lease, or other real estate encumbrance. Easements, deed restrictions, and the like are also well known as private restrictions to the use of property.

Essential Elements of Value

Real estate is a basic and fundamental form of wealth. As we have already seen, however, its market value is a measure of the rights that the owners control. Such rights are transferred at prices set in the market. However, to enter the market, the rights involved must have the four elements of utility, scarcity, demand, and transferability. "Utility" defines the usefulness of any object, or its ability to satisfy human need or desire. "Scarcity" is lack of abundance. "Demand" is the desire for possession, coupled with the ability to purchase: purchasing power. "Transferability" suggests that value depends on whether a marketable good is transferable in ownership.

Broad Forces Affecting Value

Four broad forces maintain and modify real estate value. These important forces are physical, social, economic, and political in nature. In their numerous combinations and forms, these broad forces account for the dynamic nature of real estate and value. Physical forces include both natural resources and synthetic facilities of all kinds. Family size, neighborhood, population growth patterns, lifestyle, and attitudes of people comprise the major social forces. Economic forces include employment and income levels, money and credit, housing, and general business activity. Political forces derive mainly from governmental controls such as zoning, building and safety regulations, land use and development codes, rent control, public education and welfare, fiscal policy and taxation, government housing and finance, and regulation of business and industry.

ECONOMIC TRENDS AFFECTING REAL ESTATE VALUE

The broad forces affecting real estate value constantly change. Changes in the national economy tend to explain the forces at work in the region, community, and, ultimately, the neighborhood under study in an appraisal.

Understanding Economic Trends

An economic trend is a series of related changes in some aspect of the economy. At the national and international level, broad trends that reflect the supply of goods and services often affect purchasing power at all economic levels:

1. The balance of foreign trade
2. Commodity price levels
3. Wage and employment levels
4. The gross national product—the value of all goods and services produced in the nation
5. Interest rates and the availability of money

Some economic changes are seasonal in nature. These generally result from weather or custom. Examples include decline in construction activity during winter, increase in travel and recreational activities in the summer, and increases in retail sales when students return to school and at Christmas time.

Certain national and regional changes are cyclical in nature. Business and real estate activities tend to expand and contract in a recurring cycle. The business cycle describes recurring changes in employment, income, prices, and production levels. Business cycles generally follow a sequence from growing prosperity to stability, then decline and recession of the general economy, followed by a return to growing prosperity. The real estate cycle describes recurring changes in such real estate activities as new subdivisions, amount of new construction, and volume of sales. Real estate cycles tend to be related to supply and demand factors in real estate and to the availability of money.

Supply and Demand Factors

Economic trends can often be detected by the study of statistical supply and demand indicators (many are published by the U.S. Department of Commerce). Real estate supply factors include:

1. Housing supply: The national supply of some 80 million housing units is constantly decreased by conversion, disaster, and demolition as well as increased by new construction.

2. Volume and cost of new construction: This is a good index for judging the health of the real estate industry.

3. Availability of vacant land: From a theoretical point of view, this supply factor includes all available raw land at any particular location. However, zoning, land use, environmental, and subdivision laws affect time and money costs for public approval and development and thus effectively control land supply.

Real estate demand factors in the economy are suggested by:

1. Composition of population
   a. Birth rates, death rates, and inmigration
   b. Age and sex groups
   c. Education and income levels
   d. Occupations
   e. Makeup of households
2. Changes in the national labor force
3. Changes in the gross national product (GNP)
4. Estimates of disposable income
5. Availability of mortgage financing

The social and economic programs of the federal government critically involve real estate. As government changes its policies on housing, environmental protection, energy, monetary, and fiscal affairs, the supply, demand, character, and value of real estate change.

Neighborhood Analysis

A "neighborhood" is a grouping together of individuals in a community for similar interests, whether the purposes are residential, commercial, industrial, cultural, or civic in nature. All neighborhoods experience a life cycle of growth, stability, decline, and eventual renewal. The neighborhood is important to define and understand in an appraisal because it is the setting for the property under appraisal. Changes in the neighborhood predict changes in the subject property.

Since neighborhoods tend to be self-contained, they are often defined by physical boundaries such as rivers, hills, and freeways. Common services and city or zoning boundaries can help suggest neighborhood boundaries for an appraisal, because they often define the area of commonality that gives the community a sense or a name. To define the neighborhood defines the best search area for comparable market data. As the appraisal progresses, the search area may of necessity widen or contract within or beyond the defined boundaries. However, the comparative basis will have been established. Neighborhood analysis is more than a perfunctory chore to be performed as a requirement of the lender, buyer, investor, or other client served in the appraisal. Data sources for economic trends affecting the neighborhood and community include U.S. census reports, city and county population and demographic studies, city and county zoning and planning departments, school districts, public utility agencies, and tax assessors' offices.

ECONOMIC PRINCIPLES OF VALUATION

The economic principles of valuation form the basis of most of our appraisal methods and procedures. Since none is absolute, the principles interrelate. For better understanding, we present first those principles that relate primarily to real estate marketability and second those principles that relate to real estate productivity.

Principles of Real Estate Marketability

The principles of real estate marketability underlie the market and cost approaches to value. However, all value approaches share common theory.

Substitution: The value of any property tends to equal its cost of replacement. Indirectly, this principle underlies all three approaches to value.

Conformity: Maximum value results when land uses are compatible. A lack of conformity in improvement size, style, quality, or use can be detrimental to value, particularly in single-family residential properties.

Progression and regression: When a property does not conform in size or quality, its value tends to seek the level of the surrounding properties.

Change: Real estate values are constantly changed by the many social, economic, and political events that occur in our society.

Supply and demand: Real estate prices tend to increase when effective demand exceeds supply and tend to decrease when supply is greater than demand.

Competition: Market demand creates profits which in turn generate competition. Competition often decreases profits because new supply tends to overshoot demand.

Principles of Real Estate Productivity

The principles of real estate productivity underlie the effective use, management, and appraisal of income-producing and investment properties.

Agents of production: In economic terms all tangible and intangible benefits that come from real estate are described as real estate production. Such production derives from the use of labor, coordination, capital, and land; labor includes the costs of all operating expenses and all wages except management; coordination, or management, includes charges for management and entrepreneurial effort; capital includes all construction and equipment; and land includes the land, minerals, and airspace. Economically, land has the last claim on production revenues. For this reason returns to the land are sometimes referred to as "surplus" or "residual." The concept of economic agents of production underlies many of the principles that follow.

Surplus productivity, balance, and contribution: The net income that is available to land, after the other economic agents have been paid for, is known as the "surplus of productivity." The right balance of the agents maximizes the income available to land. The value of any agent is determined by its contribution to the total income.

Increasing and decreasing returns: Income and other real estate benefits may be increased by adding capital improvements up to the point of balance in the agents of production. Beyond that point, the increase in value tends to be less than the cost of the invested capital.

Principles of highest and best use and consistent use: The highest and best use of a property is that use that is most likely to return the greatest net income to land over the life of the improvements. It requires theoretical balance between land and building investment. The principle of consistent use requires that existing structures be appraised in recognition of the highest and best use of the land.

Anticipation: Value is said to be the present worth of future benefits, whether in the form of tangible (e.g., income) or intangible amenities. The principle of anticipation is fundamental to the income approach to value.

THE APPRAISAL PROCESS

A professional appraisal is an estimate of value that results from following an orderly procedure known as the appraisal process. The steps are: (1) define the appraisal problem, (2) plan the appraisal, (3) collect and analyze the data, (4) apply the appropriate value approaches, (5) arrive at a value conclusion, and (6) report the conclusion of value.

1. Define the appraisal problem.
    a. Identification of the property under appraisal.

       (1)   A complete street address.

       (2)   A complete legal description by lot block and tract number, metes and bounds or government survey.

       (3)   Brief description of the property to be appraised.

  b. Definition of property rights to be appraised.

       (1)   Fee simple.

       (2)   Property subject to a lease (lessor's or lessee's interest).

       (3)   Property ex of mineral rights.

       (4)   Other.

  c. The purpose of the appraisal and definition of the value sought.

       (1)   If the purpose is to estimate market value (for sale or loan purposes, for example) this intent should be made clear. The appraisal could be to estimate insurable value or others, for example.

       (2)   Failure to clearly state the purpose of the assignment might lead to a possible misuse of the appraisal.

       (3)   The type of value specified should be given a precise definition in terms that everyone will understand.

  d. The date of value.

       (1)   The date as of which the value estimate applies.

       (2)   For legal purposes the date of value may be as of a historic date.

2. Plan the appraisal.

  a. A preliminary inspection is made of the subject property and neighborhood.

  b. A preliminary estimate of highest and best use is made. The highest and best use is the most profitable use of the property considering zoning, location, and market demand.

  c. A list is made of data to be collected.

  d. An appraisal outline and work schedule are prepared.

3. Collect and analyze the data.

  a. The amount and kind of data depend on:

       (1)   The highest and best use of the subject property, as determined in an economic analysis.

       (2)   The type of property under appraisal.

       (3)   The purpose of the appraisal.

       (4)   The type and intended use of the appraisal report.

  b. Most appraisals require:

       (1)   General data on the region, community, and neighborhood.

       (2)   Specific data on the subject property.

       (3)   Specific data on comparable properties being investigated.

4. Apply the appropriate value approaches.
    a. Group the data according to their relationship to the three "approaches" to value:
        (1) Cost approach.
        (2) Market approach.
        (3) Income approach.
    b. Apply the approach or approaches that are the most pertinent to the problem.
    c. Some clients require that all three approaches be demonstrated in the appraisal.
5. Arrive at a value conclusion.
    a. Review all value estimates and reconcile their differences to arrive at a value conclusion.
    b. The reconciliation process considers and weighs the approaches according to the purpose of the appraisal and the adequacy and reliability of the data.
    c. Consider each approach as a check against the other.
        (1) The appraiser's conclusion should flow from the facts and their relevance to value.
        (2) The appraiser's conclusion seldom results from a simple average of the value estimates.
6. Report the appraisal conclusion—the type of report depends on the purpose of the appraisal and the needs of the client.

THE CLASSIC APPROACHES TO VALUE

As already suggested, the appraisal process requires the application of one or more of the three approaches to value. The market, cost, and income approaches incorporate classic and time-tested techniques for valuing real estate.

The Market Approach

Since it is the most direct of the three approaches, the market approach is considered the most important. This is especially true in single residential appraisals where comparable sales are usually the best evidence of value. Steps in the market approach are as follows:

1. Investigate current sales of comparable properties. Note conditions of sale, date, price, and terms.
2. Compare with the subject property as to time of sale, location, and other sales characteristics.

3. Make adjustments to selling prices to reflect differences between the subject property and the comparables.

4. Arrive at an indicated value for the subject property based on the results.

When comparing properties in the market approach, a good technique is to make selling price adjustments as follows:

1. List the features found in the comparables that are not present in the subject property.

2. Subtract the estimated value of such features from the respective selling prices of the comparables.

3. List the features found in the subject property that are not present in the comparables.

4. Add the estimated value of these features to the selling prices of the comparable sales.

The market approach is more fully discussed in Chapter 30.

The Cost Approach

The cost approach is used primarily in the appraisal of new buildings and in the appraisal of special use and public properties. The cost approach is also used as a check against the other approaches to value. Steps in the cost approach are:

1. Estimate the land value as if vacant.

2. Estimate the current cost of replacing the existing structures.

3. Estimate the accrued depreciation, or loss in value, as compared with a new structure.

4. Subtract the estimated depreciation from the cost as new.

5. Add the value of the land to the depreciated building cost. The result is the indicated value of the property by the cost approach.

In appraisals, cost estimates are made at current prices, not original prices. Also, typical costs are sought rather than actual costs. Techniques of the cost approach are discussed in Chapter 30.

The Income Approach

The income approach is emphasized in the appraisal of income-producing properties such as commercial, industrial, and residential income. The anticipated income is translated into an estimate of value by a process known as capitalization. Steps in the income approach are:

1. Estimate the gross income the property can produce.
2. Estimate typical vacancy and collection losses.
3. Subtract to arrive at effective gross income.
4. Estimate annual expenses and subtract from effective gross income to arrive at net income (or net operating income).
5. Analyze comparable investments to arrive at a capitalization rate and method.
6. Capitalize net income into indicated value.

There are a number of commonly used capitalization methods. These will be discussed in Chapter 30.

The Appraisal Report

Robert C. Mason   MAI, Independent Appraiser; formerly Chief Appraiser, Commercial Industrial Division, Los Angeles County Assessor's Office

I n our free market economy, questions of value often arise. Is a house worth the asking price? Is an automobile worth the asking price? Is XYZ stock a good buy at $25 a share? Because most of us work to obtain our money, we want to be assured that the price we are paying is a fair price if not a bargain price. In any event, we do not want to overpay. This is as true for giant corporations as it is for the individual of modest resources. Many times the question of value and price is easy to deal with because the price, such as the price of a bottle of milk, is often set by the state or some government agency. Or, for example, the price of cigarettes is nearly uniform from store to store. One may be uncertain as to whether one wants a bottle of milk or cigarettes, but there is little uncertainty as to the price of the item. The price is easily discovered, is stable over time, and is not negotiable.

The prices of some things sold in our market economy, however, are not easily discovered, are not stable over time, and are negotiable. In general, when a product is purchased for its style or artistic value, is custom made and not mass produced, or has such a long useful life that it can be owned by a succession of people, its value can be uncertain. It is then that we turn to an expert to help assure us that we are getting our money's worth.

A house is an item that is usually custom made, has elements of style and artistic value, and can serve a succession of owners. Likewise, an

29-1

automobile, although mass produced, has elements of style and is durable enough to serve a succession of owners. A certificate of stock ownership is also an item of value that can be possessed by a succession of owners. To help estimate value, we would employ a real estate appraiser if we were buying or selling a house, look in the "Bluebook" if we were buying a car, and consult with a stock broker about the future prospects of a company if we were buying its stock. Because of the uncertainty of the value of these items, various professional groups have developed who specialize in estimating the value of these things. The group we are going to focus on is the group of appraisers who estimate the value of real estate. We will look at what they do, for whom they do it, and how they do it.

WHO USES APPRAISERS

An appraiser is a neutral third party who estimates the value of real property when there is an existing or potential adversarial relation between two people who have an interest in the real property. The adversaries may be husband and wife during a divorce, landlord and tenant during lease negotiations, taxpayer and assessor, taxpayer and the Internal Revenue Service (IRS), borrower and lender, or buyer and seller. It is essential that the appraiser be an impartial judge of the property's value, or one or the other of the adversarial parties will be unfairly injured. The appraiser, unlike the lawyer, is not an advocate of the interest of the client even though the client pays the appraiser. Regardless of who pays the appraiser, the appraiser has a duty to render an impartial judgment as to a property's value.

In some instances, the appraiser is a full-time employee on the staff of an insurance company, a savings and loan association or a bank, or some government agency. These employers need an unbiased opinion of property's fair market value to conduct their business, and they believe that it can be most economically and reliably obtained from appraisers on their own staff.

Individuals in disputes or those making investments need appraisers only occasionally, and companies who lend or invest on a continuing basis need staff appraisers to assist in the conduct of their daily business. One of the largest employers of appraisers is the government. Federal, state, and local governments acquire property for public purposes; when they do this, they need an idea of a property's worth to set budgets and make offerings of purchase price to the owners. These appraisals are often made initially by staff appraisers. If the acquisition requires a court case, independent fee appraisers are also usually employed. Another large activity of government that employs appraisers is in the estimating of value for property tax purposes. Most of the modern law and theory of appraising has derived from these two activities of government: the acquiring of property for public purpose in eminent domain proceedings and the valuation of property for tax purposes.

WHO CAN BE AN APPRAISER

In most states, with some exceptions, notably Oregon and Connecticut, anyone can be an appraiser who can convince a client that the appraiser's services are worth paying for, because a license or certification by the government is not usually required. Although there is little government licensing or certifying of appraisers, there are private organizations that do certify the competence and experience of real estate appraisers. Probably the three best-known organizations are the American Institute of Real Estate Appraisers, whose members use the designation MAI; the Society of Real Estate Appraisers, whose members use the designation SRA; and the American Society of Appraisers, whose members use the designation ASA. There are additional designations within these organizations which designate senior or junior positions, but these are the main designations.

As can be expected, the requirements for membership vary, but they include consideration of past appraisal experience, general education, appraisal education, and demonstration of report writing. Appraising as an organized profession dates back to the 1930s when most of the aforementioned organizations were formed.

Over the years, there have been various efforts at state and federal levels to license or certify appraisers, but because they are so few in number relative to other professions, they are overlooked. The American Institute of Real Estate Appraisers, for example, has only about 5000 members in the entire country.

Some people question whether appraising is a true profession, but when examined closely, it does meet the general requirements of a profession. In general, professionals are hired to do their best. A doctor does not guarantee to save your life, and a lawyer does not guarantee to keep you out of jail. They just warrant that they will make their best effort to do so. It is because they have a license or a bar membership that you are willing to accept them as qualified to make a best effort. In the case of appraisers, membership in one of the better-known appraisal organizations substitutes for the license.

Where the appraisal profession does depart from other professions is in requiring the taking of educational courses provided by the appraisal organization issuing the designation. In most professions, such as accounting, medicine, and law, the required education can be obtained from a college or university. For many years, though, appraisal courses were not available at many colleges, so the appraisal organizations had to supply them. In recent years, efforts have been made to make appraisal education more available at the universities and colleges.

Not all appraisers who practice the profession are designated by one of the major appraisal organizations, and, of course, some of the non-designated appraisers are as competent as the designated appraisers. But, when one has no knowledge of the appraiser one is going to employ, obtaining a designated appraiser provides some minimum assurance of quality control, and that is the course that many users of appraisal service follow.

THE APPRAISAL CONTRACT

Like many professions, performance of service and payment for services performed rely mainly on the good faith of the contracting parties, since there is no written contract. And, in most instances, such is satisfactory. Occasionally, however, the appraisal task needs definition, a declaration of responsibilities between the contracting parties, and a statement of the fee and the manner in which it will be paid.

When the appraisal task involves a number of properties, will require court testimony by the appraiser, or is seeking the value of a specially defined real property interest such as a leasehold estate or leased fee estate, it is well to have these matters defined in a contract. Also, the date of value, whether it is a date current, a retrospective date, or a prospective and conditional date, should be set forth. Other matters that are dealt with in a contract include how many copies will be furnished, when and where delivered, and what information and data will be furnished by the client to the appraiser.

Sometimes, a contract is used only on a first occasion, and after mutual trust is developed between an attorney and an appraiser, for instance, a written contract is no longer used. Although practice varies, it is usual for the client to advance one-third to one-half the fee to the appraiser for any appraisal service that will require more than 1 or 2 days work by the appraiser. Fees for appraisers, like fees for attorneys, will vary, but on an hourly basis they will be similar to levels charged by attorneys. Some of the services performed by appraisers can, however, be performed in a very few hours, but where court testimony is required, the preparation time is commensurately longer.

REPORT DESIGN

The writing of an appraisal report really begins with the writing of the appraisal contract, because the contract determines what shall be done and how it shall be reported. In the appraisal contract, be it written or verbal, the appraiser and the client should agree as to what kind of a report will best serve the client's need. Appraisal reports, like other reports prepared for business use, come in all lengths and degrees of detail. Briefly, they divide into two major categories—the short form or check-off appraisal report and the longer form or narrative appraisal report. The narrative report further divides into the letter appraisal and the full narrative.

No matter what the length, the appraisal report is a report by an investigative reporter, the appraiser, to a reader who will take action based on the investigator's conclusion. Some business or legal decision is usually held in suspense until the appraisal report is submitted. To be useful, the report must:

Be of adequate scope to meet the client's needs of reliability and to meet any challenges that may be raised against the conclusion

Be written in an easily read manner, be logically sequenced, and be easily referenced

Contain sufficient data about the author's education, professional memberships, and experience so as to warrant confidence in the conclusion

Be typed or printed and properly bound

As one can see when reading this list, "adequate," "scope," and "sufficient" are words for which judgments must be applied. When is something adequate, how encompassing is scope, and when is something sufficient? These are not words with absolute limits, so they are best illustrated by example of what has been generally accepted by users of appraisal reports in the past. To some extent, they are like the lawyers referring to how a "reasonable" or "prudent" person would behave under like circumstances. (When you become a member of the bar, you are given the secret phone number of a reasonable person whom you can ask how he or she would behave in like circumstances!) An appraisal report is an argument that states premises, displays data, and presents a conclusion. It is of necessity an opinion, because value, like beauty, is in the eye of the beholder. Value has no objective existence, but what does exist are the actions of people in the marketplace. How they have acted and how they are expected to act in the future is what appraising is all about. This is what the appraiser is reporting to the reader.

Many business reports, of which an appraisal report is one, are written to persuade the reader to some course of action or conclusion. They are sometimes referred to as "illative" reports taken from the word "illation," which means the act of drawing conclusions or inferences from premises.

To write a good report, appraisal or otherwise, it is essential that the writer keep in mind two things: the level of comprehension of the readers on the subject being written about and the recognition that one is usually writing an argument. The conscious recognition that one is writing an argument assists one in deciding what to include in the report and the order in which it should be presented to the reader.

Over the years, through trial and error, some general rules have developed about what should be included in appraisal reports. Narrative appraisal reports divide into three main sections: the prefatory, the report body, and the addenda. The prefatory parts are those items that the reader must know to understand what is being read, why the report was written, and information which will assist in the understanding of the report. The prefatory parts are the title page, the letter of transmittal, the table of contents, and the report synopsis. Not all appraisers agree on this sequence, some believing that the letter of transmittal should precede the title page, since it is not a part of the report but is written merely to ensure delivery of the report to the proper party. The correct way to do it is, of course, the way that your employer or client prefers it. The federal government has one preference, and other levels of government sometimes have others. So, the first rule in writing a report is to design what your client or employer wants. In many instances, your client is not experienced in report writing and will leave it to your judgment, and this is when you should know what is acceptable form.

The Title Page

The title page, as its name implies, titles the report such as "Appraisal Report of Market Value," states the address of the property, recites who made the report, on what date, and for whom it was made.

The Letter of Transmittal

At a minimum, the letter of transmittal contains a restatement of the authorization to make the appraisal, identification of the property appraised, the opinion of its value, the date of the value, and the signature of the appraiser. In addition, if not covered elsewhere in the report, certifications, assurances, and limiting conditions can also be included. When this is done, the letter of transmittal takes on a larger role than its name implies, and it becomes a part of the body of the report.

The Table of Contents

A table of contents is required only in a longer report. There seems to be some agreement that if a report exceeds 20 pages in length, the assistance of a table of contents is needed. The table of contents is just a listing of the major topics or headings in the sequence in which they appear in the report showing on which page they are found.

Synopsis

As a courtesy to the reader, longer reports often have a précis, epitome, or summary of salient facts and conclusions. This is a page, near the front of the report, that gives the essential conclusions of the report so that the reader will not have to search through the report to recall the important conclusions. In an appraisal report, it recites the property type; the zoning; the optimum use of the property; the size, age, and condition of improvements on the property; the date of value; and the opinion of value. If the synopsis becomes too long, it becomes a report within a report and ceases to meet its purpose. The table of contents and synopsis work together to provide the reader quick access to essential data. The synopsis, like the table of contents, is appropriate in reports 20 pages or longer.

REPORT BODY

The report body is where the main argument as to a property's value takes place. It states or implies the value premises, displays the factual data processed in the value premises, and states the qualifications under which the conclusion is drawn. The report body consists of three main sections: property and environmental descriptions, valuation, and qualifications.

Property and Environmental Descriptions

Essential to the valuation of real estate is an intimate knowledge of the property being valued and of its environment. The description of the property in the report reveals to the reader how much knowledge about the property and its environment the appraiser has. The appraiser's knowledge of the property is important because the valuation procedures, the kind of data gathered to argue its value, and the appropriateness of the conclusion all depend on what is being valued. The property description recites the sizes and shapes of the land and the improvements on it as well as the age and condition of the improvements. The extent of detail is a judgment that must be made by the appraiser. For instance, in some properties view is important, in others it is not. In some cases the amount of sunshine received per day is important, and in others it is not. In some cases architectural style influences value, and in others it does not. Where ordinary utilities are present, this should be stated, and if some are lacking, they should be pointed out. If the appraiser believes that something influences value, it should be described. In addition to the physical aspects of the property, the appraiser should also describe the legal restraints on the use of the property, such as the zoning, deed restrictions, or leases that control use. To be sure there is a clear understanding as to which property is being described, its mailing address and legal description such as tract, block, and lot number should be included. Other identification used is the assessor's parcel number (often the assessed value is also stated).

Immediate neighborhood of a property has important influence on its value, and therefore the neighborhood and its boundaries should be described. In that description should be statements as to the approximate percentage of various types of improvements, the general price level of the properties in the neighborhood, observations as to the state of maintenance of neighborhood properties, and whether new construction is taking place. Neighborhood boundaries cannot always be easily discerned, but most commonly they are demarcations made by geographic factors such as rivers, oceans, and mountains or by changes in property types or major roads in the area. Political boundaries or school district boundaries also can define a neighborhood. Typically, though, the neighborhood boundary is determined by the age, quality, and type of the buildings; where the age, quality, and type of the buildings shift abruptly, a neighborhood boundary can be said to occur.

In some instances, the town, city, or state should be described. If one were appraising a large regional warehouse, railroad service, if present, would be described as well as the cities on the railroad which might be considered the neighborhood of the warehouse. In years gone by, some appraisers would include facts that had little bearing on the value such as the property is 125 miles north of the Mexican border, or the summer mean temperature is 70 degrees. Such data have meaning only if the properties to which the subject property will be compared in the valuation section have a different mean temperature or are a considerably different distance from Mexico. Such data are often taken from chamber of commerce brochures in which it is appropriate, because such brochures are often circulated countrywide to attract new industries. Statistical data on direction of population change, either rising or waning, can provide a general background as to future demand for property, so it may have some pertinence in an appraisal report.

As in so many other parts of an appraisal, the appraiser must decide what should be included in the report. When making those choices the appraiser should have some compassion for the reader by not including information that is irrelevant to the task of estimating the value of the property. There is a good chance that the reader is at least as smart as the writer, if not smarter, and is likely to resent the time spent on irrelevancies.

Valuation

The valuation section is the heart of the report, and it is here that you make or break the appraisal. It is divided into three general topics: the property's highest and best use, the value measurements, and the conclusion of value.

The highest and best use of the property is by definition that use which has the greatest net return of income or savings over time or which creates the greatest value in the land. In the report, the appraiser will state what the appraisers opinion of the highest and best use is and why. In general, the existing use of the property is its highest and best use because people do not intentionally design noneconomic uses. Highest and best use becomes a problem when the property is in a transitional stage and there is the possibility of converting the property to another use. Conversion of a neighborhood from single-family houses to apartment houses is a typical example. It may be obvious from the conversions that have already taken place and the zoning that apartment use is the use to which the subject property will be converted, but when the conversion will take place may still be uncertain. The appraiser relies on extrapolating rates of conversion from the past, and thus some indication of the interim period remaining between the date of value and the future conversion can be estimated. A typical highest and best use statement in an appraisal report would be:

> Based on the rate of conversions from single-family residences to multiple residential use of an average 3 percent per year for the past 5 years in this neighborhood, and recognizing that the subject property is one of the older and smaller buildings in the neighborhood, making it a good candidate for conversion, it is my judgment that the property can be sold for development to apartment house use in the next 5 years.

Another statement might be:

> Based on the present zoning of the property for single-family use, the good maintenance of the single-family houses in the neighborhood, and the ready market and higher trending prices for houses in the neighborhood, it is my judgment that the highest and best use of the property is to continue its use as a single-family residence.

When appraising commercial property, especially vacant commercial property, the highest and best use analysis might be much more elaborate. If one were appraising vacant land for shopping center use, for example, a full feasibility study might be necessary to determine the highest and best use. Feasibility studies are a separate and additional task from that required in a typical appraisal report. They require the projections of sales, future competition, population growth, and a host of hazardous estimations. They would not be done at all if there were a better way to analyze the chances of success of a shopping center, but at present there is not.

The highest and best use section of the report is important because the type of value measurements to be made are based on the highest and best use conclusion.

In appraising real estate, there are three primary measures of value. Briefly they are the cost approach, which implies that value is equal to or nearly equal to the cost of creating a property; the income approach, which implies that value is equal to the capitalized value of the net income produced by the property; and the market approach, which implies that the value of the subject property is equal to the selling price of other properties similar to the subject that have sold near to the date of valuation. The last measure, the selling prices of other similar properties, is regarded as the premiere measure and would be used exclusively except that in some markets at some times other similar properties have not sold, either because the market is slow or because there are no other similar properties. Then one has to use the other value measures. In addition, even when there are other market data, the income and cost approaches are useful checks on the conclusion indicated from the market approach.

There are essentially two premises of all value measurement. One is that if house A is physically and legally equal to house B, and house B has recently sold, then house A should sell for a similar price. The other is that if house D is inferior to house C and superior to house E, and houses C and E have recently sold, then the reasonable expected price for house D is going to be in between the prices of houses C and E. The first premise is based on equalities, and the second premise is based on ordinalities. In the real world, the second premise is usually encountered, because in most cases, with exception of some condominiums, properties are only equal to each other in the broadest sense. Appraisers, however, have developed systems of adjustment which increase equality between properties by adjusting away the differences. This is done because market data for some kinds of properties and for all properties at some times are scarce.

In the appraisal report, the reader is entitled to see what value-measuring procedures the appraiser used and some explanation as to why they were selected. In most appraisals one of the approaches is primary and the others are secondary and tertiary. In general, if a property is purchased for its income-generating ability, the capital value of the income generated is the most important measure followed by the comparative sales approach and the cost to create approach. On the other hand, in the appraisal of a lodge building or a church, the cost approach might be primary. These kinds of property usually do not generate net income and rarely sell. The cost approach is the fall-back position because almost all properties that have structures on them or contemplate structures can be measured by this approach. It has notorious weaknesses in the measuring of accrued depreciation, but at times it is the best available value measure. Given the type of property and the data available, the appraiser makes his or her best effort to measure its value using generally acknowledged procedures. Sometimes the appraiser is inundated with data and must select the best to avoid redundancy, and other times poor data are all that is available.

In a good appraisal report, the appraiser will tell the reader the scope of the data search and the results of the search and will comment on the quality of the data. Most sales data are obtained from public records, buyers, sellers, and brokers. To some people, asking them about the purchase or sale of their property is regarded as a personal affront. Others like to discuss what they paid or sold a property for. In recent years, because of the influence of buyers from Europe and Asia, where sales are considered a very private matter, the verification of selling price has become more difficult. Of course, when the appraiser is appraising for a case that will go to court, the power of subpoena can be used by the attorney working with the appraiser. If a sale is essential evidence and can be so shown, the court can order it presented.

In the valuation section of the report, the amount of data displayed will depend on the complexity of the appraisal, the need of the client, the time available for the appraisal, and the quality of the data. If one is appraising the effect of an inverse condemnation of an avigation easement over a leasehold estate, the appraiser will have to use a certain amount of the report just explaining to the reader what the meaning of those words is and how the effect on value, if any, can be measured. On the other hand, the appraisal of a tract house might be done on a simple form or a short letter.

Comparative Approach

In general, the reader of the report should expect to find the comparable sales measure of value in the valuation section or an explanation as to why the comparative measure is not appropriate. As an old English ditty says, "The worth of thing is the price it will bring," and the price it will bring is best measured by the price of similar things that have recently sold. So, the first duty of an appraiser is to discover if there are sales of similar properties. The information reported on the sold properties that are used as the measure of value of the subject property can vary, but typically there will be a data sheet in the report for each sale. If there are no sales, and there may not be if you are appraising the only high-rise office building in your city or the only shopping center, then the appraiser must resort to the other measures of value, the cost of creating a similar property or the capital value of the income generated by the property.

Even when such sales are available, the other two measures of value are often used as a confirming test of the indications produced by the comparison measure of value. This is especially true if the sales are drawn from a volatile market and some new factor influencing value, such as a change in mortgage interest rates, has intervened since the sales took place. Or, there may have been a sudden explosion in the cost of construction. But, usually, the recent sales of similar properties are a rebuttable presumption of the measure of the value of the property being appraised, and in most appraisals they are the premiere measure.

Cost and Income Approaches

When the other measures of value, the cost approach and the income approach, are used, the appraiser should cite the source of the cost estimation. If a cost engineer prepared the cost estimate or if it was derived from one of the several cost-estimating manuals that are published, this should be stated. The costs produced are for the costs of a new building, and often what is being appraised is an old building, so some adjustment, depreciation, has to be estimated. This is the weakest link in the cost approach chain. Depreciation can be derived from market studies, but if there are enough market data to measure depreciation, there are enough market data to measure the value directly by comparison. What is usually done to estimate depreciation is to consider the buildings a wasting asset that declines in value over time. If the building will last an estimated 100 years and it is 50 years old, then it is presumed that only 50 percent of its cost new value is remaining. Obviously, this has some shortcomings, but it is a procedure which, when applied over a great number of properties, has a high correlation with market value. A more sophisticated approach is to use tables derived from generalized market studies by property class. These usually take the form of a curve looking somewhat like a reverse shallow

"S." Little depreciation takes place in the early years followed by a fairly rapid midlife decline and then a slow decline in the later years. The cost approach as a measure of value should be taken for what it is: a not-too-persuasive measure of value but better than no measure at all and one that can be universally applied to all improved properties. What it lacks in precision it makes up for in its universality. In spite of its lack of precision, it is a good error test for the other measures, because if there is a large departure in the results of the measures, it is time to review.

The income approach, or the capital value of net income generated, is a better measure, and, in the case of income-producing properties, it might be the premiere measure. It is a procedure that substitutes the comparison of the physical features of a property for the comparison of the economic features. In the income approach, it is assumed that if the net income generated has the same size, duration, and risk, then one property is a substitute earning stream for the other. It does not matter that one earning stream is produced by a warehouse and the other by an apartment house. Physical similarity is not as important as income similarity. But again, as in the cost approach, important elements needed can only be extracted from market data. And, like in the cost approach, if market data are available, why not use the sales to directly measure the value of the property? The answer is that often the real estate market data are unobtainable, but financial market data such as mortgage rates and long-term bond rates are available, and the capital value of the property can be found using these rates. Studies show a high correlation between the long-term bond market rate and the real estate rate. It would appear the added management burden and risk that real estate entails is offset by the tax shelter and capital gain opportunity, so the overall rates for long-term bonds and real estate remain about the same.

In the appraisal report, then, the appraiser may use all three measures of value, the cost approach, the market or comparative sales approach, or the income approach, and all may be used in various degrees of complexity.

The market approach may include a multiple regression analysis wherein all the obvious variable value characteristics are statistically weighted, or it may be a simple recitation of the sales data, which are presumed to be self-evident measures of the subject property's value. The income approach may be a simple gross multiplier or an elaborate discounted cash flow scenario. The cost approach may be a simple cost factor from a manual adjusted for depreciation and summed to the estimate of land value, or it may involve many efforts to measure the various causes of depreciation if they can be identified and an elaborate engineering study of the costs. The report is tailored to the needs of the client, and the scope should be set out in the contract or verbal understanding at the time the appraiser is employed.

Once the value evidence is displayed in the report, the final step is the conclusion of value from the evidence. In the conclusion, the appraiser will summarize briefly the evidence, qualify the evidence, and tell why the conclusion is in the amount that it is. Usually, readers will know from the report which is the most substantive evidence and will have drawn their own conclusions. This is especially true if the report is prepared for someone who reads many appraisal reports such as a lender or investor. In the conclusion, the appraiser refers back to the evidence and argues the value conclusion from it. If the report is well done, the reader will concur with the appraiser's conclusion.

ADDENDA

In many reports, there are data that should be available for reference or verification of statements made in the report which are bulky and would detract from the essence of the report if they were in the main body of the report. Legal descriptions can sometimes run pages long of metes and bounds; if placed in the body of the report, they would divert the reader from following the appraisal. The long description should be placed in the addenda; thus if there is a question about the legal description, the information is available but does not interfere with the easy reading of the report. To provide legal description in the report body when the description is long, a map of the parcel should be provided.

As is often the case in writing, there are no hard-and-fast rules as to what should be in the main report body and what should be in the addenda or exhibits, but statistical data, blueprints, zoning codes, and other material referred to in the report usually should be in the addenda. Sometimes charts or tables can be shown on the page facing the narration wherein the chart or table is discussed in the body of the report. Since most appraisal reports are printed on one side only, the back of the previous page is available for chart or table display.

Because of the complexity of the properties appraised, the needs of clients, and the potential challenges which may be raised against the value conclusions, appraisal reports vary immensely in length and content. For some purposes a printed form appraisal such as the standard Federal National Mortgage Association form 1004 is very adequate for the purpose of valuing a single-family home for a lender's security for a loan. For a complex appraisal of air rights, a minority property interest, or a condemnation case, the narrative appraisal which is custom tailored to the appraisal needs is required. To obtain a satisfactory report, the most essential act is for the client and the appraiser to each have a clear understanding of what is to be done, of the scope of the appraisal, and of how the appraisal will be used and for what purpose. If this understanding can be obtained, a satisfactory result will usually follow.

Applied Techniques of Appraisal

Silas J. Ely   Independent Appraiser; formerly Principal Appraiser,
Los Angeles County Assessor's Office

To apply the principles of appraisal to either the most routine or the most complex appraisal assignment, one must understand first the economics of land and then something of the design, construction, and utility of the building improvements that make up the remainder of the typical real estate entity.

SITE ANALYSIS AND VALUATION

The analysis of land is an integral part of the use, management, and valuation of real estate. In several appraisal procedures, land and buildings are treated as separate economic components. The cost approach requires an estimate of site value. To such an amount, the estimated value of the improvements (that is, the cost new less depreciation) is then added. The market approach requires a knowledge of land value as a variable among the comparable sales in size, shape, location, and other respects. Some techniques in the income approach require a separate site value estimate. The income and value contribution of land and buildings may need to be separately processed for capitalization purposes.

Certain tax laws require a separation of land and building values. Income tax laws generally require that a purchase price be allocated to

30-1

land and improvement values when depreciation is claimed in real estate investments. Depreciation is figured only on improvements. Ad valore (or "according to value") property taxes are usually imposed on land and improvements as two separate amounts. Different tax rates sometimes apply.

Highest and best use: Whether improved or vacant, land value is economically a function of its highest and best use. Highest and best use is defined as *that reasonable and profitable use that will support the highest land value as of the date of the appraisal.* When estimating the highest and best use of land, follow these guidelines:

1. Estimate as if the land were vacant.

2. Consider only those uses that are legal or for which there is a reasonable probability of legal approval.

3. Consider only the uses that are profitable at that location.

4. Consider only those uses that are physically possible.

Ultimately the highest and best use of land will depend on a careful consideration of the many legal, locational, and physical factors that must be identified and analyzed by the appraiser.

Legal factors of site analysis: To understand the nature of the appraisal problem and rights being appraised, the data required for site analysis should include the following legal information:

1. Legal identity.
    a. Legal description and plat map.
    b. Legal interests involved. A deed and/or title search may be required to identify these with certainty.
    c. Legal entity:
        (1) Detached land parcel.
        (2) Planned unit development where ownership includes both the lot and common areas.
        (3) Condominium where site consists of airspace plus common area interests.

2. Public and private restrictions.
    a. Public restrictions include:
        (1) Zoning regulations and the general or master plan. These generally regulate permitted uses, density, set-back or yard requirements, height restrictions, parking requirements, and the like.
        (2) Building and safety regulations. These regulate construction methods, materials, and engineering standards for structures.

(3) Environmental protection laws and other developmental restrictions or moratoriums.

b. Private restrictions include deed restrictions, easements, leases, and other encumbrances.

3. Taxes.

a. Since local property taxes are a burden on real estate, the level or rate of taxation affects value.

b. Some properties are subject to special assessments for public improvements.

Locational influences to be considered include:

1. Community and neighborhood setting: social, economic, and political factors

2. Relationship of the site to neighboring properties, streets, alleys, transportation routes; access to the site

3. Conformity of the site to the typical site in the area

4. Utilities available

5. Climate

Physical characteristics of the land also affect the appraisal. The following factors should be included in an appraisal:

1. Size and shape of the site.

a. Area is usually described in square feet or acres.

b. Useful or net area is the gross area less future streets, easements, etc. Used for market comparison.

c. Shape refers to the general configuration of the site boundaries or relationship between the width and depth of the lot. Shape often affects relative utility.

d. Frontage is the length of the side facing the street. Often affects the potential and economic use of a commercial site.

e. Excess depth refers to a rear or interior portion that is relatively low in utility or market demand.

f. Plottage refers to the improved utility that may result from combining two or more sites into one.

2. Type of lot: the site's location relative to nearby lots and streets.

a. Interior lot: any lot fronting on only one street.

b. Corner lot: a lot that fronts on two intersecting streets. May or may not command a higher price in the market.

c. Keyed lot: a lot with several other lots backing onto its side yard (usually a disadvantage).

    d. Cul-de-sac lot: a lot at the end of a dead-end street; has the advantage of privacy and large backyard but the disadvantage of reduced street frontage.

    e. Flag lot: a rear lot, with a long, narrow flagpole-like access drive to the street.

3. Orientation: how the lot is situated relative to the sun, wind, climate, views, or to surrounding land features. It affects both design and use of structures.

4. Topography, soils, and drainage: these all affect building costs, maintenance, and safety of the site for habitation.

5. Site improvements: these include grading, filling and compaction, retaining walls, drainage systems, and other improvements treated as part of the land.

6. Off-site improvements: these improvements are located outside the land boundaries. They include common area improvements as well as curbs, gutters, sidewalks, streets, alleys, etc. Utilities are sometimes included.

METHODS OF APPRAISING LAND

There are four accepted ways of estimating land value: (1) the market comparison method, (2) the allocation or abstraction method, (3) the development method, and (4) the land residual method.

The Market Comparison Method

1. Sales and listings are obtained and compared with the subject property as if it were vacant and available for its highest and best use.

2. All sales comparisons should be recent sales of vacant sites comparable as to location, physical characteristics, zoning, and potential use.

3. The sales should be investigated as to open market exposure, price, and terms of sales. Ideally, verification should be made with a party to the transaction.

4. Data sources include title insurance company records, public recorders' and assessors' offices, private data sources, realty boards, and the appraiser's personal files.

5. Make adjustments to selling prices to recognize differences between the subject site and the comparables. Typically, adjustments are made for:

    a. Terms of sale; terms may determine the price.

    b. Time of sale; value may change with time.

c. Location.

d. Physical characteristics.

6. Common units of comparison include:

   a. Price per square foot, front foot, or acre.

   b. Price per unit that can be developed (as in raw acreage or residential income–zoned land).

7. Adjustments may be made in plus or minus percentage or lump sum dollar amounts. Always adjust from the comparable toward the subject. For example, if the comparable location is inferior to subject, a plus adjustment to price is in order.

8. An example follows, showing the use of three comparable sales.

Price	Terms	Time	Location	Topography	Adjusted price	Per square foot
$50,000	0%	+2%	0%	+5%	$53,500	$10.50
75,000	−10	+5	−10	0	63,750	9.25
62,500	−5	+3	+5	−5	61,250	12.00

9. Giving the most weight to the sale that required the least adjustment, a 6400-square-foot site under appraisal would be valued on the basis of sales adjustment and comparison as follows:

$$6400 \times \$10 = \$64,000$$

The Allocation or Abstraction Method

The allocation method is used in built-up areas where there are no vacant sales.

1. Allocate the total sales price between land and buildings. Three methods are available:

   a. Use a value ratio discovered in similar areas for similar properties. For example, where the site represents 25 percent of the total value, a $100,000 sale would indicate a site value of 25 percent or $25,000.

   b. Use the local assessor's allocation between land and improvement values. Multiply the sale price of each comparable sale by the percentage of land assessment to total assessed value. Then compare each with the subject site. This is an inferior method, but it may sometimes be used for accounting purposes.

   c. Use an abstracted site value, subtracting an estimate of the improvement value from the total price.

2. Using the abstracted value method, assume we are analyzing a $200,000 improved sale. If the appraiser estimates a depreciated

cost of $120,000 for the building, a land value of $80,000 would be "abstracted" merely by subtraction: $200,000 − $120,000 = $80,000.

The Land Development Method

The land development method is used to appraise raw acreage that is ready for subdivision when comparable sales are not available. It may be used to appraise land for any potential residential, commercial, or industrial use. The method requires a market study to indicate what the land will be worth after development. The land development method requires the following steps:

1. Estimate how many lots can be developed.
2. Project the total dollar amount of gross sales, based on market study of current prices for finished lots.
3. Subtract all direct and indirect costs of development, promotion, and sales. Developer's profit may be treated either as a percentage of gross sales or as a percentage of capital invested in raw land.
4. Conclude the value of the raw land by an analysis of the results.

As an example, assume that a 30-acre parcel of land can be developed into 100 single residential lots. At the time of appraisal, developers require 20 percent of gross sales as payment for entrepreneurial efforts. Nearby lots of this type are selling at $75,000 each. You project as follows:

Development costs:
Indirect

Required studies and reports	$ 15,000	
Financing	425,000	
Taxes	100,000	
Administration	200,000	
Advertising and sales	250,000	
Subtotal		$ 990,000

Direct

Design and engineering	$ 60,000	
Clearing and grading	300,000	
Utilities, street improvements	1,500,000	
Subtotal		$1,860,000
Total development costs before profit:		$2,850,000

Projected sales:
100 lots at $75,000 = $7,500,000
Net proceeds before profit:

$7,500,000 − $2,850,000 =	$4,650,000

Less developers profit:
$7,500,000 × 20 percent =   — $1,500,000
Indicated value of the raw land: $3,150,000

The Land Residual Method

The land residual method may be used in feasibility studies to estimate site value for commercial, industrial, and residential income properties, either vacant or improved. It is the preferred method for valuing income property when comparable land sales are not available. When using the land residual method, use the following steps:

1. A net income is projected for the site as if it were developed to its highest and best use.
2. A return on investment in improvements is subtracted to calculate potential land income.
3. The income attributed to land is capitalized into an indicated site value.

The land residual method is further described as a part of the income approach to value.

BUILDING DESIGN, CONSTRUCTION, AND UTILITY

The professional appraiser needs a working knowledge of building design and construction. Whether residential, commercial, industrial, or special use property is involved, appropriate design, materials, style, and quality of the improvements affect the utility and market appeal of the real estate package.

Standards of Design and Functional Utility

Good architectural design can be defined as the use of appropriate materials in a proper scale and in harmony with the setting. Good architectural design and functional utility work together. Functional utility sums up the usefulness and attractiveness of a property. Functional utility of a structure depends on how well it is placed on the site, the general suitability of the floor plan or layout, and the sufficiency and convenience of the equipment. A functional design provides the most benefits for a given cost.

A residential structure should be placed on the site to take advantage of the sun, weather, view, and natural topography. Such orientation should also provide adequate front, back, and side yards, as well as air, light, privacy, and access to the street. Provision for parking, storage, refuse areas, and recreational facilities also contributes to property acceptability.

Inside the residence, the floor plan is an important factor. Easy access to each room, a good traffic flow, separation of areas of different use, wall space for the placement of furniture, cross ventilation, and adequate storage space are sought. Plumbing, baths, heating, and/or air conditioning should be adequate and energy efficient. Layout of the kitchen and good access to yards and utility areas also affect the appeal and marketability of a home. For one- and two-family dwellings, Federal Housing Authority (FHA) standards of property acceptability generally require:

1. Safe, secure, healthful, and attractive living facilities

2. Ease of circulation and housekeeping

3. Visual and auditory privacy

4. Appropriate light and ventilation—all bedrooms should have cross ventilation

5. Fire and accident protection

6. Economy of maintenance and space use

7. Accessory services

8. Sanitation facilities

In income-producing properties, functional utility can best be measured by using economic standards. Design features that are in demand by tenants and also help maximize investment return are the functional ideal. The cost, durability, and ease of maintenance of a building depends in part on the type of construction and building materials selected.

Construction Type or Classification

In standard building codes and construction cost manuals, buildings are generally classified by the type of basic frame, wall, floor, and roof construction involved.

Class A buildings have fireproof structural steel frames and reinforced concrete or masonry floors and roofs. Many institutional and high-rise buildings fall into this category.

Class B buildings have reinforced concrete frames with concrete or masonry floors and roofs. Three- to five-story residential, commercial, and industrial buildings are typical for this class.

Class C buildings have masonry exterior walls and wood or exposed steel floor and roof structures. One- and two-story buildings of all use types are included in this classification.

Class D buildings have wood or light steel frames and roof structures. Perhaps the largest number of single residential buildings are in this class.

Selection of Materials

Materials used for structural, "finish," and mechanical components of buildings traditionally depend on:

1. Climate, soil, and seismic conditions
2. Availability and cost
3. Style and function
4. Durability and ease of maintenance
5. Energy efficiency
6. Building code requirements

Rating for Quality and Market Appeal

General guidelines for single-residence building quality are as follows:

1. Low cost: minimum or substandard building; plain and inexpensive finishes on both interior and exterior
2. Average: medium standard of quality; meets Veterans Administration (VA) and FHA standards
3. Good: good architectural design, work quality, and materials; usually has two or more bathrooms, central heating, and built-in kitchen appliances
4. Very good to excellent: custom design, using high-quality materials and execution; incorporates many extra features

Popular Architectural Styles

Architectural styles are often associated with historic and locational traditions. They may characterize the design of either residential, commercial, or institutional structures. Some popular architectural styles include:

Contemporary: features a flat roof, low profile, and a floor plan oriented to the outdoors.

California ranch: a low, rambling style; features gable roof with roof overhang, and wood, brick, or stone trim.

Colonial: includes many different early American architectural styles such as New England, Cape Cod, Dutch, Southern, and Georgian.

Colonials are rectangular, stately, and symmetrical buildings. They usually have shutters, dormer windows, and steep gable roofs.

Spanish: features thick-appearing walls, a heavy frame, and red-tile roof. The exterior is often sand-finished stucco or adobe.

Monterey or Monterey Spanish: a version of the Spanish-style residence that features a second-story porch or balcony in the front of the house.

English half-timber: characterized by steep-pitch roof and plaster, half-timber, and heavy masonry exterior walls. Windows are usually casement style.

Victorian: a multigabled wood exterior style, ornately trimmed with wood detail. Style is reminiscent of the turn of the century.

French Provincial or French country: usually a large house on a sizeable plot, with a very high, steeply pitched hip roof and formal, stately features.

THE MARKET APPROACH TO VALUE

When comparable sales are available, the market approach is the most direct of the three approaches and therefore the most reliable. Following the principal of substitution, the appraiser applies the market approach by comparing the subject property to similar properties that have recently sold. After analysis of differences in sale conditions, terms, and property characteristics, the appraiser makes appropriate adjustments to sale prices and thereby arrives at a probable selling price or market value for the property under appraisal.

Data Requirements

The data collected in the market approach are often basic to all three approaches to value. There are three general categories: general data, sales transaction data, and physical and legal data.

General data on the region, community, and neighborhood should indicate trends and factors relevant to the appraisal problem at hand. (See prior discussion of economic trends.)

Sales transaction data should be collected about each comparable to be investigated. Verification should ideally be made with a party to the transaction. Pertinent data include:

1. Date of sale. (The date that the sale price was agreed on may be preferred to the date of recording.)
2. Sales price and terms of sale (type of financing, etc.).

3. Legal description, rights acquired, encumbrances of record.
4. Name of grantor (seller) and grantee (buyer).
5. Identification of any items of personality in the sale.
6. Any special motives of buyer and seller.

Physical and legal data include property characteristics that are the most important in the marketplace both for the subject property and for the comparables:

1. Size, shape, and topography of the land
2. Age and square-foot area of improvements, type and number of rooms, rental units, suites, or other areas
3. Design, layout, and quality of improvements
4. Special features and amenities such as pools, patios, appliances, equipment, energy-saving devices, view, etc.
5. Condition and modernization at time of sale
6. Zoning and general plan
7. Taxes and special assessments
8. Public and private restrictions, easements, etc.

Sources of Data

Sale transaction data and pertinent property data are available from the following sources:

Public records: Ownership change records are usually available at the county clerk or recorder's office. They typically include the names of grantor and grantee, the documentary transfer tax (often indicative of price paid), date of deed recordation, and mailing address of the buyer. The legal description and property conveyed may be obtained from a copy or abstract of the recorded deed. Assessment roll information is available at the county assessor's office. Indexed by assessor's parcel number, the records often include much of the same transaction data cited, plus parcel maps, age and area of buildings, and lists of current sales in the area.

Realty boards and multiple listing offices: Most listing services publish a cumulative summary of listings and sales available to members and subscribers. Some offices can furnish computerized data on comparables by location, size, and other property parameters.

Local data services: A number of data services sponsored by savings and loan associations and appraisal associations publish monthly and quarterly summaries of sales data on residential, income, and commercial properties. Some services offer computer access and analysis as well.

Parties to the transaction: Brokers, lenders, buyers, and sellers are most often the best source of information about sales.

Appraisal office data files: Current sales information is often maintained in the appraiser's private files.

Elements of Comparison

In comparing sales or other market data with the subject property, it is necessary to identify and compare differences between the sale property and the subject property as to:

Terms of the sale: Terms often determine the price. Favorable seller or assumable financing often results in a higher-than-typical price.

Time of sale: This must be considered to adjust for gradual price trends in the market.

Location: Location factors covered in the discussion of neighborhood and site analysis are considered.

Physical features: Salient land and building characteristics should be considered in light of their probable impact on price and value.

Sales Adjustment Methods

The adjustment process is designed to consider all important differences between the comparable sales and the subject property by quantifying the estimated amount that a feature unique to either the sale or the subject property would affect its selling price. Lump sum dollar or percentage amounts may be determined by one of the following methods:

1. Using the direct comparison, or matched pair, method, two sale properties are compared to discover the market response for a single feature that differentiates them. The dollar or percentage difference in the selling prices would suggest the premium paid for an extra feature or amenity—say a swimming pool or an extra large lot.

2. The depreciated cost method bases the amount of adjustment on the depreciated cost of a building feature being adjusted. For example, an adjustment for an extra bath costing $5000 in a 20-year-old house would be $5000 less an allowance for age. If loss in value were estimated at 1 percent per year, the adjustment amount would be as follows:

Item cost new	$5000
Less age allowance	
20 percent × $5000	− 1000
Amount of adjustment	$4000

3. In many appraisals, adjustments are made by the direct comparison and depreciated cost methods used in combination. Here, either lump sum or percentage amounts are worked out and then applied as appropriate to the sales. (See Table 30-1.)

Sales adjustments may be made without relying directly on either dollar or percentage adjustments. Two methods are available.

Unit of Comparison Method. The unit of comparison method takes an important overall aspect of the sale properties and uses it to compare the sales. The price per room and square foot are examples. To calculate the price per square foot for each sale property, for example, divide the sale price by the number of square feet of main area.

TABLE 30-1 Sales Comparison Example
(Adjustments Simplified for Illustration)

Assume that the subject property is a medium-quality, 25-year-old home with a two car garage. The home size is 1600 square feet. The appraiser locates three similar homes that recently sold in the neighborhood on typical market terms. All have similar square footage, quality, and number of rooms. Dollar adjustments have been arrived at by the direct comparison and depreciated cost methods. Because all were recent sales, no time adjustment was necessary.

Market study:

Date	Comparable A	Comparable B	Comparable C
Price paid	$168,500	$140,000	$143,500
Terms	Equal to subject	Equal to subject	Equal to subject
Location	Better than subject	Equal to subject	Equal to subject
Lot size	Equal to subject	Larger than subject	Smaller than subject
Improvement size	Equal to subject	Smaller than subject	Equal to subject
Overall condition	Better than subject	Equal to subject	Inferior to subject

Dollar adjustment factors:
Location difference	$7500
Lot size difference	5500
Improvement size	6000
Overall condition difference	4000

Adjustments:

Date	Comparable A	Comparable B	Comparable C
Price paid	$168,500	$140,000	$143,500
Terms	0	0	0
Location	− 7,500	0	0
Lot size	0	− 5,000	− 5,000
Improvement size	0	+ 6,000	0
Overall condition	− 4,000	0	+ 4,000
Indicated value of subject property	$157,000	$141,000	$152,500

Conclusion: Giving somewhat more weight to comparables B and C, the appraiser concludes a value of $150,000.

Then use the typical or appropriate value per square foot to value the property under appraisal. Economic units of comparison include gross rent multipliers, price per apartment or rental unit, and price per unit that can be developed; the latter is an adjustment method for appraising land.

Units of comparison should *not* rely on an assumption that the value is in direct relationship with the unit being compared. For example, on variably sized homes on uniform-sized lots, the price per square foot usually varies inversely with the square-foot area of the house. As the house gets significantly larger, for example, the price per square foot tends to decline, all other things being equal. This is because the constant land value is being absorbed in a larger and larger building size. A graph can assist in the analysis of units of comparison. In Figure 30-1, the analysis of sales price versus square-foot building size suggests a subject property value of:

$$\$87.50 \times 2650 \text{ square feet} = \$231,875$$

Linear and Multiple Regression.   Both linear and multiple regression discover statistically the relationship between a series of numbers representing property characteristics and selling prices and calculate a formula for the relationship. Important characteristics of each sale property (price, square foot of area, age, etc.) are entered into the equation or program. A mathematical procedure produces a special formula that can be used to value the subject property.

When a single variable, such as square-foot size of improvements, is

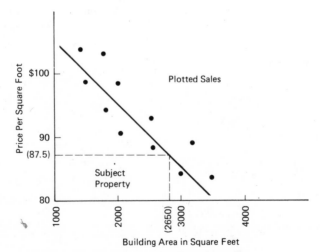

Figure 30-1   Price per square foot of liveable area.

found among the sales, a linear regression program featured in some financial calculators can be used to graph or solve for probable selling price of the subject. Regression analysis can also be used to validate or test a sales sample as to whether a comparable is typical for a particular market.

Adjusting for Sale Terms

Professional appraisals must recognize the influence of financing on real estate prices by making adjustments for sales with financing that is superior or inferior to that available for the subject property. When the terms of a sale cannot be adjusted by market comparison, a more indirect method may be used:

1. Subtract from the selling price any loan points or charges paid by the seller.

2. Subtract the "premium" value of a favorable loan (usually a lower-than-typical rate) that is assumed by the buyer or taken back by the seller. If the loan is inferior to available financing, add the "penalty" value.

3. Estimate premium or penalty amounts by an analysis of market discount rates from the trust deed market or from "annuity" capitalization procedures. In the latter, one technique is to multiply the monthly benefit or disadvantage in loan payments by the annuity factor found for current money rates over the remaining term of the loan. Financial calculators can perform this present value operation.

Reconciling the Results of Sales Adjustments

If the sales are analyzed and adjusted using market-related percentage, dollar amounts, or units of comparison, there should be a fairly close range of values indicated for the subject property. A wide spread may suggest an erroneous inclusion of a sale involving uninformed parties or perhaps unique or urgent motives on the part of the buyer or seller, or it could suggest faulty data or unreasonable adjustments made in the sales analysis procedure. Ultimately, the greatest weight should be placed on the comparables that require the fewest adjustments and those represented as open market transactions by the most reliable sources. A simple average of the results of the sales adjustment procedure is not recommended. However, in statistically validated studies, the median result may be logically concluded.

TECHNIQUES OF THE COST APPROACH

The cost approach is based on the principle of substitution. The value of an existing property is compared to the cost of creating a new property that is equally desirable. First, land value is estimated, preferably from comparable sales. Second, the reproduction or replacement cost of improvements is estimated. Then an allowance is made for age and obsolescence of improvements. Lastly, the land value is added to the depreciated building cost to form the total value indicated by the cost approach.

The cost approach serves three main purposes in appraisals: (1) to estimate the value of new property; (2) to appraise unusual properties not commonly selling in the open market; (3) to serve as a check against the other value approaches.

The cost approach has definite limitations. Some cost elements are difficult to identify and estimate. Also the estimate of accrued depreciation can be quite subjective. The cost approach is usually weak in the appraisal of older buildings.

Basis of Costs in Appraisals

A separate estimate of structure costs can be an important element in each of the three approaches to value. Therefore it is important to note that all cost estimates used in appraisal relate to current costs, not "book" costs or historic costs. For appraisal purposes, costs include all direct and indirect cost elements required to place the building at the consumer level.

Direct cost elements include all elements involved with the physical development of the structure. These include (1) labor paid by builder or subcontractor, (2) materials and equipment, (3) design and engineering, and (4) subcontractor's fees for professional services other than labor and materials. Indirect cost elements are all other necessary costs such as (1) legal fees, appraisal fees, permits, and licenses; (2) interest on construction financing; (3) liability and casualty insurance; (4) property taxes during construction; (5) administration and management (overhead); (6) interest on investment during construction; (7) rental loss during fill-up period; (8) builder's and developer's profit; and (9) selling costs.

"Reproduction cost new" is the estimated cost of constructing a duplicate or approximate replica building on the date of value. All physical components are included. This procedure has the advantage of being a clear representation of structural content and quality. If obsolescence is present it is separately allowed for. The disadvantage of using reproduction cost is that changes in construction technology since the date of construction are difficult to represent. However, lenders prefer reproduction cost estimates in single-family appraisals. "Replacement cost new" is the estimated cost of constructing a building which would effectively replace the utility of the existing one. Modern methods, design, and materials are projected. The advantage of this estimating system lies in its simplicity; the disadvantage lies in the subjective nature of the cost estimate. If obsolescence is involved, it is not always pointed out by the appraiser. Replacement cost is the basis most often chosen by appraisers because it is easier to apply.

Methods of Estimating Cost

The following methods are used singly or in combination to estimate cost of construction:

1. The comparative square foot method estimates building cost by applying the typical cost per square foot of a comparable new building. It generally relies on published cost data. The square foot, square meter, or cubic foot method is the most widely used and the most practical method of estimating construction costs.

2. In the unit-in-place method, individual building components are priced by their "in-place" cost per square foot, per surface foot, or in lump sum amounts. Such costs may be developed for the floors, walls, roof, and mechanical components of a structure and then added up for a total cost estimate. Applied to separate components, this method is used to refine the comparative square foot method.

3. The quantity survey method involves a complete construction cost breakdown like that used by contractors. All required quantities of labor, materials, profit, and the like are itemized, priced out, and summed up. This method should not be attempted without expert knowledge of current construction.

4. The index method adjusts known original or historic costs to current cost levels by the use of published cost index numbers. Although not generally recommended, this method is sometimes used to cost unique buildings or to do mass appraisal work where historic costs are available.

Construction Cost Variables

The following physical design features have the most notable effect on construction costs; therefore, most cost manuals are designed to reflect them as the major cost variables:

1. Design or use type: categorizes buildings according to their intended use: residential, commercial, etc.

2. Construction classification: the type of frame, wall, roof structure, and fireproofing—has a most important influence on construction costs. In general, class A is the most costly construction and class D the least.

3. Quality of construction: the overall quality of materials and workmanship—is often considered the most difficult cost variable to estimate.

4. Size: total cost increases with the overall building size. However, square-foot costs tend to decline with size.

5. Shape: refers to the number of corners and linear feet of building perimeter compared to area. Increased shape causes greater cost for walls, doors, and windows and generally greater overall square-foot costs.

6. Story-height: the typical floor-to-ceiling height of a building is fairly standardized, but higher ceilings usually mean higher costs.

7. Yard or site improvements: garages, parking areas, walkways, drives, outside lighting, sprinkler systems, pools, patios, fencing, and landscaping—increase the overall cost of a project.

The following is an example of a cost estimate using square-foot and unit-in-place costs:

You are using a published cost manual to estimate the reproduction cost of an average-quality dwelling with three bedrooms and two baths. There are 2000 square feet of living area and six perimeter corners in the building exterior. The specifications of a similar house in your cost manual are like those of the subject except for the built-in appliances and air conditioning found in the subject house. The floor area and shape adjustments are obtained from the cost manual. Proceed as follows:

Base cost factor from cost manual:	$70.00 per sq. ft.	
Area and shape multiplier:	× 0.973	
Base cost factor, adjusted:	$68.11	
Base cost: 2000 square foot × $68.11 =		$136,220
Plus:		
Built-in appliances:	$3400	
Air conditioning:	4800	
Total additives:		+ 8,200
Equals: Estimated total cost of house		144,420
Plus: Garage and yard improvements cost		+ 20,000
Equals: Total reproduction cost new		164,420
Rounded:		$164,500

After estimating reproduction or replacement cost new of improvements, an estimate must be made of accrued depreciation. Such amount must be deducted from the cost new estimate; finally, to complete the cost approach, add the value of the land.

ESTIMATING ACCRUED DEPRECIATION

It is important to distinguish depreciation as estimated in appraisals from depreciation as used in accounting. In accounting, depreciation is an annual expense or deductible charge against the value of improvements before calculation of income taxes. Also, for accounting purposes, depreciation is often calculated on the historical acquisition cost, or "cost basis," of the improvements. As used in appraisals, "depreciation" refers to loss in value as compared with cost new. Thus, it is an amount to be deducted from an estimated *current* reproduction cost of improvements. In appraisals then, depreciation refers simply to estimated loss in value to be deducted from the reproduction cost new estimate of improvements in the cost approach.

Causes of Accrued Depreciation

There are three categories that describe the value loss that buildings typically experience as they become old and/or obsolete: physical deterioration, functional obsolescence, and economic obsolescence.

Physical deterioration describes wear and tear caused by usage and the action of the elements or structural integrity that is impaired through neglect, vandalism, or lack of maintenance. Physical deterioration may be divided into curable and incurable categories that refer to whether the loss in value can be economically restored.

Functional obsolescence is loss in utility from faulty design, out-of-date equipment, changes in construction methods and styles, or changes in market preference. It is a defect within the property itself. In new buildings, functional obsolescence can be an immediate result of underimprovement or overimprovement of the site. Functional obsolescence may be either curable or incurable.

Economic obsolescence results from factors outside the bounds of the property, for example, changes in zoning or land use patterns that adversely affect the value of the subject improvements. Economic obsolescence is generally incurable.

Methods of Estimating Accrued Depreciation

The following discussion includes the use of four methods for estimating accrued depreciation: the straight-line, or age-life, method; the cost-to-cure, or observed condition, method; the sales data method; and the capitalized income, or rental loss, method.

In the straight-line, or age-life, method, annual loss in value is assumed to be proportional to the total life of the improvements. Thus, a building with a life of 25 years would depreciate at the rate of 4 percent per year. If such building is presently 10 years old, its accrued depreciation would be 10 × 4 percent = 40 percent. Depreciation allowance is generally based on effective age, which is the age of a building with similar condition, utility, and marketability. A 30-year-old building might have an effective age of only 20 years if modernization and superior maintenance enable it to compete with 20-year-old buildings on the market, for example. The straight-line method is preferred by appraisers because of its simplicity. However, buildings seldom depreciate at a constant rate, and economic life cannot be estimated with any degree of accuracy.

The cost-to-cure, or observed condition, method is used in conjunction with the straight-line method. The cost-to-cure method estimates the loss in value as the amount required to make all the repairs necessary to restore to a "like-new" condition. If incurable functional or economic obsolescence is found, the loss in value is estimated as the capitalized rental loss from the condition.

The sales data, or market, method is based on the premise that value loss is constantly measured in the market by buyers and sellers. Older buildings typically sell at lower prices than new ones. To estimate accrued depreciation by the sales data method:

1. Subtract the land value for each sale (preferably by market sales of vacant land) from selling price. The result is the abstracted building value.

2. Deduct the abstracted building value from an estimated reproduction cost new in each sale. The result is the accrued market depreciation indicated for each sale property.

3. Divide the accrued depreciation by the estimated reproduction cost new. The result is the percentage of value loss for each sale property.

4. Divide the value loss percentage by the age of the improvements involved to indicate the annual rate of accrued depreciation.

5. Apply the results to the subject improvements.

Example: Analysis of a 40-year-old house sale

Reproduction cost of improvements		$150,000
Sale price	$140,000	

Estimated land value	− 50,000	
Abstracted improvement value		− 90,000
Accrued depreciation		$ 60,000

$60,000 ÷ $150,000 = 40 percent = 1 percent per year value loss

Any time the value of a property can be related to the income it produces, the loss in value can be estimated, either in total or in part, using the capitalized income, or rental loss, method.

To estimate the total loss in value: (1) Estimate the building value by capitalizing the income that can be attributed to the improvements. (Such procedure is described later as the building residual capitalization method.) (2) By subtracting the estimated building value from the cost to reproduce the same building new, an estimate of accrued depreciation results. To estimate the loss in value from a single cause, a poor floor plan, for instance: (1) Estimate the rental loss that results from the problem. (2) Capitalize the rental loss to discover the amount of value loss attributed to the obsolescence factor. A gross rent multiplier may be used instead of a capitalization method if preferred.

The following is an example using the gross rent multiplier: A single-family home has a poor floor plan causing functional obsolescence. You estimate that it would rent for $100 less per month than competitive properties because of the defect. If a gross multiplier of 150 is suggested by a market study, the loss attributed to the functional obsolescence is as follows:

$$\$100 \times 150 = \$15,000$$

Summary of the Cost Approach

When the depreciated improvement costs are added to the land value, the cost approach is completed. The following example uses the cost estimate shown in the last section.

Total reproduction cost new		$164,500
Accrued depreciation (assuming effective age is 40 years)		
Normal physical deterioration 1 percent per year		
(from sales data method):		
40 × 1 percent = 40 percent × $164,500 =	$65,800	
Functional obsolescence:		
Curable (old style kitchen)	8,000	
Incurable (small rooms)	2,000	
Economic obsolescence (adjacent to		
new industrial park)	10,000	

Total accrued depreciation	− 85,800
Depreciated cost of improvements	$ 78,700
Land value from comparables	+ 65,300
Total property value from the cost approach	$144,000

THE INCOME APPROACH

The income approach attempts to measure the present worth of future benefits in the form of income anticipated from ownership of the property. Thus, the method is adaptable only to income-producing property.

Appraisers' versus Owners' Viewpoints

In general, income or investment properties are viewed subjectively by their owners as a type of holding that best suits their investment and business strategy. First, the equity or down payment, rather than the entire property value, is generally viewed as the investment. Second, the loan payment or debt service is considered an expense of owning the property, with the deduction of loan interest and building depreciation offsetting such expenses. Further, the typical owner anticipates the possibility of profitable resale or exchange at a higher price or with a favorable tax advantage. In commercial and industrial property, more and more purchases are made for the location of family or corporate business enterprises. In such cases, the owner-users anticipate the security of being their own landlord and have the advantage of operating a business identified with a fixed location.

The appraiser deals with the many subjective motives of buyers and sellers by attempting to recognize their collective effect on the market in general. Thus, the income approach relies primarily on an estimate of the income-producing capabilities of the property and the capitalization of such income at rates discovered in the general marketplace. The total property is valued, not just the equity. When expenses are estimated, only those that are attributed to the real estate are considered. Expenses strictly related to the debt or tax position of the owner are not taken into account in the income approach unless the purpose of the appraisal is to discover investment value instead of market value.

The steps in the income approach are to (1) estimate the gross income the property is capable of producing, (2) estimate typical vacancy and rent losses, (3) subtract vacancy and rent losses from gross income to arrive at the effective gross income, (4) estimate annual expenses and subtract from effective gross income to determine net income (or net operating income), (5) analyze comparable investments to arrive at a capitalization rate and method appropriate for the subject property, and (6) capitalize the net income into an indicated value.

The capitalization technique appropriate for any appraisal depends largely on the character of the property being appraised and the data discovered in the market study. (These will be discussed later.)

Estimating Gross Income

The term "gross income" refers to the total anticipated rent, assuming 100 percent occupancy. This also includes service income, the money received from incidental sales and services to tenants.

Economic Rent. Economic rent (or market rent) is the most common rent looked for in appraisals. It is the potential gross rent in an open market, assuming that the facilities are unencumbered by any lease. It assumes good management. The purpose of an economic rent estimate is to measure all of property rights, not just those available to a purchaser. Differences can be accounted for later.

Contract Rent. Contract rent is the rent the tenants are currently paying. It may be more or less than market rent. Types of tenancies include month to month, short-term leases (1 to 5 years), long-term leases (10 years and up). The most common lease types encountered are the straight lease, where the rent remains constant throughout the term of the lease; the step-up lease, where regular increases are scheduled in the lease; and the percentage lease, where rent is a percentage of gross volume of business or sales. Types of rent involved in leases include minimum rent—the base rent in a percentage lease; overage rent—the amount paid over the minimum rent; and excess rent—the amount by which total contract rent may exceed economic rent. Landlord and tenant agreements determine responsibility for expenses.

Economic rent should be based on a survey of competitive properties in the neighborhood. For each property surveyed, complete data should be gathered as to location, physical description of facilities (that is, number of units, age and condition, quality, amenities, and so on), and a schedule of existing rents.

The rent survey should also include types of units (one or two bedroom, for instance), dates of occupancy, dates of rent control adjustments if any, deposits and/or gratuities, tenant obligations for utilities, services provided to tenants (furniture, utilities, and the like), and the typical vacancy factor. Rents are usually compared by rent per apartment, rent per square foot of living area, net rentable area, or rent per front foot (as in some strip commercial appraisals).

After completing the rent survey, the appraiser should construct a complete new schedule of rents for the subject property, considering the results of the rent survey and the existing schedule of rents for the subject property. Be sure to correct omissions, such as rent for owner's unit, that may be later deducted as part of operating expenses.

The effective gross rent is the market rent projected for the subject property less allowance for vacancy and rent losses. It is the prediction of rent that will actually be collected. The vacancy and rent loss allowance should be based on typical rates for this type of unit in the study area.

The Gross Rent Multiplier Method

The gross rent multiplier method is generally used as a substitute for the income approach in single-family appraisals. In the appraisal of multifamily and other income properties, gross rent multipliers are sometimes considered a part of the market approach. However, for clarity we present them here. The gross rent multiplier (GRM) is simply the relationship between sales price and gross rent, as shown in the displayed formula. As such, it can be an inaccurate measure of value when vacancy rates or expenses vary among the comparables or between the subject property and the comparables.

$$\text{GRM} = \frac{\text{sales price}}{\text{gross rent}}$$

To appraise an income property using gross rent multipliers follow these steps:

1. Find at least three recent sales of comparable properties. Comparables should be in the same location and have similar amenities to the subject. Number of units, size per unit, and type of services (e.g., utilities, furniture, security) should also be comparable to the subject.

2. Estimate for each the market rent at the time of sale. This may be different from the existing rent. Actual rent should not be used except where the units are under rent control or where the schedule is found to be in line with the typical in the area at the time of sale.

3. Divide each selling price by the monthly or annual gross rent, as shown in the formula.

4. Arrive at an appropriate multiplier for the subject property considering sales data analyzed.

5. Multiply the gross scheduled rent of the subject property by the chosen multiplier.

6. The result is the indicated value of the subject property.

Example: A six-unit apartment under appraisal has an economic rent that averages $400 per unit per month. Recent sales of similar buildings have been at 10 times the annual rent. Our value estimate is as follows:

Gross annual rent:	6 × $400 × 12 =	$28,800
Gross rent multiplier:		× 10
Indicated market value:		$288,000

Estimating Annual Expenses

For appraisal purposes, annual expenses include all those expenses necessary to produce the effective gross rent. As mentioned earlier, owner's expenses such as loan interest and tax write-off depreciation are not to be charged. As part of the income approach, annual expenses will be deducted from effective gross income to derive the net income to be capitalized into an indication of value.

Operating Expenses. Operating expenses are day-to-day, "out-of-pocket" expenses that include management, payroll, and contracted services, supplies, grounds maintenance, utility costs, painting and decorating, repairs, maintenance, and cleaning.

Fixed Expenses. Fixed expenses are lump sum amounts that occur annually with somewhat greater predictability than operating expenses. They include insurance premiums (fire, extended coverage, liability, special coverages) and property taxes. In jurisdictions where property taxes are increased on transfer of title, property taxes should be estimated at the new level.

Reserves for Replacements. Reserves for replacements are projected expenses that are required to keep the building equipment and furnishings in working order. Replacement items usually include roof replacement, built-in kitchen equipment, carpeting, furniture and accessories, boilers, air conditioners, and replacement of other machinery and equipment. Replacement costs are projected on an annual basis by (1) estimating the expenditure required for each individual item as replacement is necessary and (2) dividing its projected cost by the anticipated useful life of the item. The result is the annual expense allocation for the item.

When estimating expenses, the appraiser should consider the property's past operating expenses as well as typical expenses reported for similar buildings. Assume efficient management. Remember to exclude invalid items such as interest of loan, loan payments, income taxes, and depreciation charges. Capital additions must also be excluded. Remember to include a charge for management or any other service that may be performed by the owner but not reported on the operating statement.

Net Income

When annual expenses are subtracted from the effective gross income, we arrive at an estimate of the net income for the property. The capitalization rate and method to be applied at this point in the income approach depend on an analysis of the relative safety of the investment, the durability of its income stream, and other factors to be discussed.

INCOME CAPITALIZATION

Income capitalization is the mathematical process of converting an income stream to its capital equivalent. For example, a savings account earning $100 per year at a rate of 10 percent "capitalizes" to an amount of $1000 ($100 ÷ 0.10 = $1000). This is the necessary dollar amount on deposit required to return an annual income of $100 at 10 percent interest. Discovering real estate value is based essentially on the same process. The mathematical formula is:

$$\text{Value} = \frac{\text{income}}{\text{rate}} \quad \text{or} \quad V = \frac{I}{R}$$

Capitalization Rates: Note that the capitalization rate is the connecting link between the income and the value. It follows that selecting the appropriate rate is a critical part of the income approach. For appraisal purposes, there are four types of rates, all important in the analysis of income properties and the capitalization process: (1) The interest rate is the rate of return on invested capital. The term is synonymous with yield rate and discount rate. (2) The overall capitalization rate is the relationship between net income and value for the total property (or the ratio of net income to value). Theoretically, this allows for both return on investment and recapture of investment capital, but the proportions are usually unknown. (3) The recapture rate is the rate at which invested funds are being returned to the investor, and (4) the composite capitalization rate is a rate composed of interest and recapture, in separately determined amounts.

Methods of Estimating Rates

Capitalization rates may be estimated by the direct comparison, band of investment, or summation methods.

The Direct Comparison Method. The direct comparison (or comparative sales) method is the preferred method of deriving a capitalization rate. Recent sales of similar properties are analyzed, and in each case the net income is divided by the sales price. The result is the indicated overall capitalization rate (OAR) for each sale. For example:

Net income:	$ 50,000
Divided by selling price:	÷500,000
Overall rate	10 percent

The Band of Investment Method. The band of investment is a weighted average between a rate for mortgage loan money and a rate for the investor's equity. The relative importance of each rate depends on the percentage of the purchase price provided by the loan and the equity down payment.

Example: Assume that the prevailing loan terms for a particular type of property include 16 percent interest, with a maximum loan of 75 percent of the property value. The equity down payment will thus be 25 percent of the value. For this investment assume that equity yield expectations are found to be 6 percent.

Loan:	$0.75 \times 0.16 =$	0.12
Plus equity:	$0.25 \times 0.06 =$	0.015
Property interest rate		0.135

Another type of band of investment calculates an overall capitalization rate for the property instead of an interest rate. It uses the mortgage constant rather than the mortgage interest rate and the equity cash-on-cash (or dividend) rate instead of the equity yield rate.

The Summation Method. The summation method calculates an interest rate by combining or adding up amounts for the separate theoretical elements that help determine yield rates. The base is usually the so-called safe rate—for example, the going rate for U.S. government bonds; investment risk, lack of liquidity, and management burden components are then added, and, in turn, advantages of tax shelter and potential appreciation, for example, may be subtracted. Although the summation method is perhaps too theoretical for everyday use, it can be helpful in estimating a rate for a unique investment.

Several other methods of estimating rates are available. An interest rate can be converted to a composite capitalization rate by adding a component for recapture. Using another method, an interest rate can be converted into an overall capitalization rate by adding or subtracting a component for anticipated future value change. The so-called Ellwood method can be used to adjust overall rates derived from the band of investment to reflect the equity buildup from loan amortization and/or anticipated changes in property value. This latter method is primarily an investment analysis tool.

Allowing for Capital Recovery

The net income may provide both a return on and a return of the invested capital in a building. The return of the investment is described as "capital recovery." There are three methods that include a specific provision for capital recovery in income capitalization. The straight-line and sinking funds methods specify recapture provisions, either in the capitalization rate or in an adjustment to annual income. The annuity method includes recapture within the capitalization technique.

The Straight-Line Recapture Method. The straight-line recapture method assumes that equal annual recaptured payments will be provided out of the annual net income. The annual payment may be treated as an expense in dollars, or it may be handled as a component of the capitalization rate.

The Sinking Fund, or Hoskold, Method. The sinking fund method assumes that the annual investment recapture amounts are deposited into a sinking fund where they earn interest and compound at a "safe rate."

The Annuity, or Inwood, Method. The annuity method assumes that invested capital is recovered from the level annual income in the same manner as a loan is paid off. Since annual recapture amounts are capable of earning compound interest at the yield rate of the property under appraisal (rather than at a safe rate as in the Hoskold method), a higher capitalized value results.

In each of these three methods, the recapture of invested funds takes place over a period of time representing either the term of the lease or the estimated remaining economic life of the improvements. The period of recapture depends on the age and condition of the improvements, the risk of building obsolescence, and the like.

Income Capitalization Techniques

Income capitalization techniques are based on the principle that any single component of the property can be valued by measuring its contribution to the total net income.

The Direct Capitalization Technique.   Direct capitalization is the simplest method of income capitalization and generally the most accurate. It is recommended for use when there are adequate numbers of comparative sales relatively similar to the subject in size, character, and the ratio of land value to building value. This technique is sometimes called the "property residual method" because it capitalizes the income to the total property. The following is an example of direct capitalization:

Net operating income:	$63,000
Divided by overall capitalization rate:	÷ 9 percent
Indicated Value	$700,000

The Building Residual Technique.   The building residual technique can be used to capitalize income when there are enough data to support an accurate estimate of the land value but building value is unknown. The technique is sometimes useful when older buildings are being appraised and the sales data are inadequate to estimate overall rates for the direct capitalization technique.

There are four steps to follow if we assume straight-line recapture of the investment in improvements: (1) Calculate the income needed to provide a return on the land investment by multiplying the land value by the estimated interest or yield rate. The resulting income is referred to as the "land charge." (2) Subtract the land charge from the total net income to discover the income that can be attributed to the improvements. (3) Capitalize the income to the improvements by using a composite building capitalization rate that combines both interest and recapture. (4) Add the value for the improvements to the value indicated for the land to obtain the total property value.

Example: Assume that an investment property has a remaining economic life of 25 years, a land value of $100,000, and that investment capital requires a 6 percent return. What is the indicated property value by the income approach?

Annual net income		$60,000
Less return required on land ($100,000 × 0.06)		−6,000
Net income to improvements		$54,000
Divided by: composite rate		
interest rate	0.06	
plus recapture rate	+0.04	
composite rate		÷ 0.10
Indicated improvement value		$540,000
Plus land value		+ 100,000
Property value		$640,000

The Land Residual Technique.   The land residual technique may be used when the building value can be estimated but the land value is unknown. The improvements should be new or nearly new and also clearly the highest and best use of the land. Steps in the land residual technique providing straight-line recapture are: (1) Estimate the value of the improvements by using their reproduction or replacement cost less accrued depreciation. (2) Multiply the improvement value by a composite rate to include interest and recapture. The result is known as the "building charge," or the income needed to provide the return of, and return on, the building investment. (3) Subtract the building charge from the net operating income. The result is the net income that can be attributed to the land. (4) Divide the net income to land by the yield or interest rate. The result is the indicated value of the land. (5) Add the estimated values of land and building to calculate the indicated value for the total property. Feasibility studies often project alternative improvement concepts to discover land value under the highest and best use.

Example: Assume that a new office building costing $750,000 to construct represents the highest and best use of the land and is leased at a net annual income of $100,000. Solve for land value assuming a 9 percent yield requirement and an economic life of 50 years.

Annual net income		$100,000
Less income to building		
Improvement value	$750,000	
Multiplied by composite rate		
Interest rate 0.09		
Plus recapture rate 0.02 = composite rate	× 0.11	
Income to building		− 82,500
Income to land		$ 17,500
Divided by interest rate		÷ 0.09
Land value		$194,440
Plus improvement value		+ 750,000
Property value		$944,440
Rounded		$945,000

The Equity Residual Technique. The equity residual technique analyzes the income available from a property after deduction of debt service required by any proposed or existing loans. Primarily an investment analysis method, this technique can result in a valid market value estimate when there is a positive cash flow and when financing and equity rates are considered typical of the market. The steps to follow are: (1) Subtract annual loan payments from the net operating income to determine the "cash flow" to the investor. (2) Divide the cash flow amount by the equity cash-on-cash (dividend) rate required. (3) Add the indicated value of the equity to the total amount of mortgage obligation. The result is the indicated value of the property.

Example: An investor is considering the purchase of an income property with a net operating income of $70,000. A $400,000 loan is available that repays at an annual 15 percent constant. We will solve for the warranted down payment (equity value) for an equity cash-on-cash return of 5 percent to be realized.

Net operating income	$70,000
Debt service at 0.15 × $400,000	− 60,000
Equity cash flow	$10,000
Divided by equity rate	÷ 0.05
Indicated equity value	$200,000

The analysis suggests a total sales price of $600,000 for the property ($400,000 loan plus $200,000 down payment).

RECONCILIATION AND FINAL VALUE CONCLUSION

Reconciliation of the different indications of value derived through the analysis of the market, cost, and/or income data in an appraisal leads to a final value estimate or conclusion.

Review of Appraisal Procedures

The first step in the reconciliation process is to review the appraisal procedures applied and the completed work. All data should be verified as to the accuracy and consistency of application throughout the appraisal. Assumptions should be reviewed for reasonableness and for their impact on the final results. Also, all calculations should be reviewed for accuracy.

Applicability of Approaches

The second step is to judge and weigh each approach as to applicability, adequacy of data, and the range of value indicated. In single-residence property, the greatest weight is usually given to the market approach. In income-producing property, such as residential income, commercial, and industrial, the income approach should be given considerable weight if the comparables clearly indicate the yield or capitalization rate required by the market. If the improvements are nearly new and represent the highest and best use, the cost approach deserves major emphasis.

The Purpose of the Appraisal

If the appraisal purpose is other than to estimate market value, the most relevant approach may be suggested by the assignment itself. The cost approach is usually stressed in insurance appraisals, for example. Valuations for sale, purchase, exchange, condemnation, or estate settlement usually require market value appraisals that stress the approach or approaches described as the most applicable for the type of property involved.

Final Value Conclusion

The final value conclusion should be the logical result of the appraisal data presented in the approaches to value and reviewed in the reconciliation process. A single value estimate is usually required, although a stated value range is called for in some assignments.

The final value conclusion should *not* be a simple average of the figures arrived at by the individual approaches. The final value most often is reached by placing primary weight on one approach or the other. For this reason the final value conclusion nearly always falls within the value range of the two or three approaches applied. Any result to the contrary would require extensive explanation.

Example: Assume that you have applied the three conventional value approaches to a fairly unique commercial property located in the suburb of a major city. Improvements are almost new and appear to represent the highest and best use of the land. Results are as follows:

Indicated value from the cost approach:	$750,000
Indicated value from the market approach:	875,000
Indicated value from the income approach:	650,000

Although the market approach ordinarily is the most indicative of value, we cannot give it major weight in this appraisal because our comparables require significant adjustment for quality, design, and age. Because of well-established land values and rental rates for similar properties, we emphasize the results of the cost and income approaches for the modern property under appraisal. Thus:

Market value conclusion:	$725,000

Part 7

Marketing Real Estate

Chapter 31

Getting Started in Real Estate

Barbara Phillips   G.R.I., Real Estate Broker; Instructor,
Pasadena City College

Now that you have your license, you want to further your career in the real estate business. You are like a teenager who has been given a gun and hunting license—you are dangerous! To keep you from hurting yourself and others you need additional training. With little or no money you have been able to get your license and enter a field with the largest inventory of goods in the world. You have no inventory tax, and you do not have to "floor-plan" it. Your tools in this inventory are the multiple listing book and the computer. You can, in some cases, sell anywhere without leaving your community. You have help in the form of buyer desire, since so many people want to own real estate (perhaps not what you are showing them, but something). You are now dealing with numbers, since the national average turnover of houses and other real estate is once every 5 years, even faster in Florida and California. That turnover is business for you. To equip yourself to sell this commodity, to make those income levels that everyone hears about, to enjoy the prestige and feeling of success after a good transaction, you need a combination of training and hard work. Successful salespeople generally work 50 to 60 hours per week, including weekends and evenings.

HOW DO YOU SELECT AN OFFICE?

To select an office, first interview several offices in the area in which you wish to work. Investigate that office's reputation with your friends,

31-1

people who have dealt with it, the Better Business Bureau, and the chamber of commerce. All offices are different, and you need to find one that you will be comfortable in. Do you feel more comfortable in a three-person office, a twenty-five-person office, or in a very large company with many branches? Many companies now have two or three interview patterns with some giving psychological tests to determine aptitude for real estate. Question the following items.

Training Program

The training program is critical and should not be a training by rote or "just listen" type of program. Agents need to be developed. The broker needs to look at where the salesperson will be at the end of 3 months, 6 months, and 1 year. How is the training given? Many times an intense 2-week program just leaves the agent bewildered. No one can absorb all that information and knowledge at once. A more practical way is to have classroom instruction on 3 half-days a week and then to send the trainees out to practice what they have learned. The four steps to training are:

1. Theory or pure teaching of necessary information
2. Examples, role playing, and going into the field
3. Case work: measure a house, fill out a listing, and write up deposit receipts
4. Drill for skill: give theory of cold canvasing; show students how to canvas; have them show how to canvas; students go out and knock on ten doors; students return to class to discuss problems, successes, and failures

Commission Scale

The commission scale varies considerably. Some offices work on a graduated scale—perhaps from 50 percent of what you bring into the office to as high as 80 percent after you bring in a set amount in commissions. Very few offices will start a new person with a "draw" to keep them going till they make a sale. Some percentages go back to the bottom level at the beginning of every year. Some offices will keep you on a higher plateau once you have consistently done well. Many offices pay less for a listing commission than for a sale because of the high costs of processing and advertising the listing.

Expenses

You will probably pay your own board dues and multiple listing (MLS) fees and possibly those for business cards and mail-outs. Many offices now share phone and advertising expenses as well. A certain level of insurance on your car will be required.

Advertising

Can you pick up a local paper and easily find the company advertising? Is it a regular feature? Do they have institutional advertising as well as strip columns? Are they in any "home magazines"? Do they pay for flyers for your listings or do you?

Job Description

Are you an independent contractor or an employee?

Floor-Time Scheduling

Floor-time scheduling can be a problem no matter how many people are in the office. Do they have all-day shifts, two 4-hour shifts, or three 3-hour shifts? Is there a backup system?

Policy and Procedure Manual

Even as an independent contractor you will have to know company policy on many matters. A policy and procedure manual can be in the form of a looseleaf book or printed on the contract you sign.

Supportive Services

Is the office fully staffed with receptionist, secretary, bookkeeper, ad writer, answering service, microfiche system, copier machine, computer systems, membership in more than one board or MLS, conference rooms, and extended or WATS telephone lines?

Assistance

Do they have a good listing inventory and desk space or do you share with others? Do they restrict your buying and selling on your own account? Do they have help available in the form of an assigned "buddy" or available manager or broker?

Understand yourself. Are you a loner or a joiner? Do you prefer a friendly, social office or are you strictly business? Do you *have* to win a contest? Many offices have them and want you to participate in competing for top number of listings or sales.

According to a very recent survey by a large franchise company, brokers were asked "How many sales associates would you replace for lack of production, if you had someone qualified to replace them?" Sixty-four percent of the brokers would replace 50 percent of their sales associates, and 18 percent would replace 30 percent of them. They all felt it was still 20 percent of the people doing 80 percent of the business. Would you be a replacement or a replacee?

WHAT ARE YOUR RESPONSIBILITIES?

First and foremost, you must understand company policies, procedures, and goals. Once you put your license with that office, your loyalty is to that broker. You can help contribute to the real estate business by working on board and MLS committees and by wholeheartedly participating in the seminars and meetings that are offered. You are expected to dress in a businesslike fashion, have a clean automobile, and share in the community activities where you work. Cooperation with other brokers is the way agents help each other. Without it there would be far fewer sales. If there are certain procedures in handling papers—for instance, turn in listings to the manager, with flow to the ad writer, then to the secretary who makes copies for the "up-desk" and also sends them to the MLS—be sure to avoid disrupting this flow. If commission checks are handed out at weekly meetings, do not try to get the bookkeeper to write you a check an hour after the commission check comes in. Follow office procedure.

You have certain legal, contractual, and ethical responsibilities to your broker. A wrong action on the part of a salesperson could not only cause revocation of the salesperson's license but might place the broker in jeopardy as well. Most contracts between broker and salespersons spell out what the agent will pay in case of legal action against him or her and/or the company. The real estate business works with the golden rule, and, if you apply it, you will be on your way to a successful career.

FINANCIAL RESPONSIBILITIES AND MONEY MANAGEMENT

Most real estate agents are independent contractors. As such, their broker/employer does not withhold federal, state, FICA, or other taxes from their commission checks. If you do not know at the beginning of the year whether sales will be tight due to a slow economy or whether you will be a member of the multimillion-dollar club, then you must base your quarterly payments on an estimated amount from the previous year. If you underpay, or do not pay in at least 80 percent of the tax on your current year's income by January 15 of the following year, the Internal Revenue Service (IRS) will assess a strong penalty in addition to regular income taxes due, figured on each quarter of underpayment. As the payments become due, the payments together with the form 1040ES voucher should be filed with the IRS center for your state. If your state has a similar state tax, then it is mailed to the state tax center at the same time. The IRS can give you advice and forms to help you figure out your liability. Your best investment is a good professional tax advisor, who can save you money in showing you what your credits and deductions can be and how to set up proper recordkeeping for your expenses and income. Documentation is the most important item, and every receipt should be kept in its categorical file.

Real estate agents spend a great deal of time in their automobiles, and the IRS does allow them to take the car and its related expenses as income tax deductions. There is a choice of two ways: one is a deduction for the actual expenses pertaining to the business use of the car, and the second is based on the standard mileage rate. Your tax advisor can work out examples for you showing which would be more beneficial.

The IRS is currently allowing deductions for business use of the home, but with stringent restrictions. Whatever part of the home is used must be used exclusively and regularly for it to qualify.

Business entertainment and gifts are a large part of your costs. The lunches and dinners for clients and other business contacts and the gifts for referrals and to buyers and sellers can be deducted. The IRS sets monetary limits on gifts.

Educational expense is another large item in your costs. If taken to renew a license or to maintain or improve skills required in performing the duties of your business, educational expenses may be deducted. You may also take the expenses for travel and transportation to the course site, tuition, fees, and meals away from home if you are gone overnight.

You may deduct your business supplies, conventions, phones, licenses, accounting fees, and board and MLS dues. A large item often forgotten is the cost of postage and subscriptions to books and magazines related to business.

All these items must have documentation, receipts, and cancelled checks and must be kept for 3 years from the date the return was filed or due. Good recordkeeping is a must—use an account book, appointment book, and/or a record book, which is stored in the car, for recording your business mileage. Since you are in the real estate business, which is dependent on the economy, it is very difficult to estimate the year's income. If you have gone through a training session with your company, they probably stressed the need to plan your time to generate the most business. Often the company has a chart that shows how many buyer/seller contacts must be made before a listing or sale is generated and how you can schedule your time to contact as many people as possible. From that you can work out the number of contacts needed to make X number of sales to make X dollars in income. There is no easy way to make a good income in real estate. It takes hard, continuous work. As the commissions come in, you must follow a budget carefully. An annual budget made up and then divided into the following 12 months must be adhered to. As the commissions come in, an amount for basic living expenses is put into a checking account and the balance into a savings account. The budget will show which month is scheduled for the car insurance payments, IRS payments, property taxes, and other large payments. The saying that you cannot spend a commission until you get it is painfully true. A failed escrow produces no money, and if you do not have the necessary funds for living expenses in the savings account, you will become one of the "fall-outs." As you progress in the field and become successful, invest in your product. You will be able to spot good buys and build up your own real estate portfolio so that, in time, it will take care of you. If you do not believe in real estate enough to invest in it, you should not be selling it.

SUMMARY

After you get your license and start interviewing for an office, you must also find an accountant or CPA, plan your budget, set up your bank accounts, deposit at least 3-months living expenses in a savings account, and go through a sales training course paying particular attention to managing your time and finding out how to make the most contacts for possible sellers and buyers. Discuss with the broker you choose what expenses you will be liable for, including business cards, mail-outs, postage, long-distance calls, stationery, board and MLS dues, errors and omissions insurance, sign costs, and at least $300,000 in liability insurance on your car. All these figures go into your budget, parceled out in a monthly amount. Find out what the average yearly earnings are in the company to give yourself a goal. The broker has a large overhead and wants to see you succeed. If you are undercapitalized and feel you must go on a part-time basis, discuss this with the broker. Usually the part-time people work weekends and are assigned a partner who will take care of all work that must be done during the week. There is generally a commission split or referral fee in such cases. The broker's policy manual and independent contractors agreements will have all these factors spelled out along with a job description. If you agree with these documents and your goals are their goals, then you will have a happy relationship. Your broker, in many states, will have you covered with workers' compensation insurance in case of a work-related accident. You may be able to get health insurance through your board of Realtors at a group rate, and it is helpful to have disability insurance coverage in case you are unable to work for any length of time.

Chapter 32

How to Market Residential Property

Augustine Sodaro   Resident Manager, Coldwell Banker, Claremont, California

I n this chapter we will assist sales associates and brokers in marketing real estate (houses) by explaining the whole marketing process rather than simply a piecemeal view. The key to marketing residential real estate is to first market the salesperson. It is only from this background that salespeople will achieve what they so earnestly want—a whole series of "sold" signs.

MARKETING YOURSELF

Marketing a salesperson begins with knowledge, specifically product knowledge.

Product knowledge is an extremely important aspect of effective real estate marketing. It is difficult, at best, to know "all" about real estate. Basic knowledge forms an excellent skeleton on which to expand. Magazines, newspapers, and real estate periodicals keep you up to date and broaden your base of real estate understanding. Do not "get into" real estate, let real estate "get into you." Really involve yourself in the business, and the results will be an increased desire to be more professional.

Daily review of the financial market, the economy as a whole, and local market conditions is necessary. Take your real estate temperature daily. Know what is affecting your industry and ultimately your marketing programs.

You should be able, with both written proposals and verbal presentations, to convincingly detail the services available through you and your company. Marketing of self and property has three main goals:

1. Sell sellers on yourself and your services.
2. Sell sellers on your company and its ability to meet their needs.
3. Sell property for sellers to qualified buyers.

HOW YOU FEEL ABOUT YOURSELF

Successful marketing of property is preceded by how you see yourself. We are all a mirror for our clients to look into. Will they see optimism or pessimism, interest or disinterest, enthusiasm or boredom? These feelings are expressed by us daily in many ways. Obvious to clients is our body language and manner of speaking, which speak loudly about our inner feelings.

How we feel about this industry can affect our feelings of self-esteem. Sellers will mentally question our ability when we lack that self-confident air. They will be reluctant to risk perhaps thousands of dollars of their equity to work with someone who is unsure of his or her competency.

We need to practice liking ourselves for a good mental attitude to come through. Spend time taking courses that will improve your skills, which will, of course, include motivational courses as well. Such sessions can also be fantastic recharging sources, giving that mental battery a real lift.

Remember, however, that we must practice self-motivation and work at pulling it out of ourselves. Others can motivate us temporarily, but daily attention to our goals is necessary to spur us on to succeed.

Sometimes market conditions, property values, and other factors can discourage us unless we have set our goals and planned for achievement. Ups and downs will always exist in the real estate profession, but the professional salesperson can weather the storms of change. Today's unusual market will probably be the normal market of tomorrow. We also need to feel good about the people with whom we work and the company that we represent. This will be reflected to our sellers.

FINE TUNE YOUR MIND

Continually sharpen your selling skills. Look for courses that share new ways to work the basics of real estate, advanced financing programs, legal questions, and more. These will again pull up from within us the feeling of confidence of knowing how to handle each situation.

Courses that help us to understand people, psychology, and body language seminars are a necessary asset to a well-trained professional. How can we properly service a client's needs if we cannot communicate effectively?

Learn to be a good listener. We learn most about people when we listen. Little, if anything, can be gained from a one-sided conversation. We may feel we have control of the situation but little is gained for the client's benefit. Often, we feel that the client must know everything about our abilities and expertise. This usually presents itself by talking much and listening little.

OVERCOMING RESISTANCE

Most of us have a natural resistance to strangers, but in real estate sales we must shed this fear and talk and listen to strangers to achieve success. Once we recognize the basis for our hesitation, we can work toward overcoming this resistance.

Some of us may find the transition difficult. We rationalize that calling on the telephone may be an imposition and knocking on doors not only demeaning but again an invasion of privacy. We must remember that how we feel about certain things does not necessarily represent the way the rest of the world feels. A salesperson who believes she or he is an imposition leaves room for a successful salesperson to step in and work with people on the telephone and in person.

HANDLING REJECTION

Rejection enters our minds on a regular basis. No one wants to hear a "no," even if that no might be in his or her best interest. We take these negatives personally instead of for what they really mean, such as, "I'm really not interested in buying or selling at this time." We would rather hear a "maybe" which leads to a no sale and only playing at real estate. The result is that we waste time for sellers and buyers and we earn nothing.

TOO MANY VOICES

We are influenced by ourselves. That is the little something within us which tells us when we feel good, bad, should or should not make decisions and generally can make chaos of our career if we "hear" the wrong things. If we are not on guard, that voice will tell us how inadequate we really are and why we are not more successful. The voice will also agree with others (well meaning or otherwise) when they attempt to advise us. These people, along with that little voice, are often dream stealers. Do not let anyone rob you of the success you know you can achieve. Practice liking yourself to the point that your goals and objectives are what drive you and not others' goals and objectives.

ATTITUDE: A KEY

You are important! You are successful! Attitude is what we are talking about—your attitude needs to be healthy and positive, so that others will notice this when they come in contact with you. They will gravitate toward you, the positive personality, rather than toward the negative thinker and negative doer. They will want to work with you, for your enthusiasm is contagious! Choose positive attitudes which will bring professionalism to the forefront for your clients to see. It takes little effort to be smiling and positive. You will be more attractive to your potential clients with this positive attitude.

Attitude is a big factor in real estate success. Goal planning will only be successful if we have an attitude that says, "I will succeed." Attitude can be described as a state of mind, belief, a faith, as it were, in one's ability.

We may believe that we are special and we do have something to contribute to others' success as well as our own, or we may have an attitude that we are a nobody and are unable to accomplish anything worthwhile. We meet people daily who are bent on failing. These people are unable to assist anyone to sell or buy property because they convince others that they cannot meet those needs. Their negative attitudes are like quills on a porcupine. They can hurt when we come close to them. This type of person will not last long in real estate sales.

Attitude can be seen when we enter the room. We need not say anything for others to pick up our "vibrations" or even our body language. As mentioned before, we reflect our attitude to others. This also tells observers whether we believe in ourselves, our product, our company, and so on. Attitude might be described as charisma. One need not be extremely outgoing to have a charismatic personality. Project yourself outside the boundaries of conformity to develop charisma. Check your "feeling" temperature in front of a mirror prior to meeting people for the day. What you see is what you will project for the day. Work on that positive mental attitude so that you feel good with what you see.

HABIT

We often hear people in our profession say that we need to have a good attitude, but they fail to describe what they mean. Attitude becomes a habit, and habits can be changed. When we sense the need for change and have the self-discipline to follow through, the result is positive change. Practice attitude change regularly, as often as brushing your teeth. Before long feeling positive will require no effort.

Once we come to grips with attitude as something that affects others as well as ourselves we can then modify our attitude to take advantage of each situation.

We have all heard the phrase "you get better results with honey than with vinegar." It takes little effort to be pleasant and pleasing, but we must work at being miserable. Unfortunately, some people seem to naturally look on the dark side of everything. This is no doubt as a result of role models to which they have been attached either by choice or by family ties.

We sometimes see corrective criticism from our parents as rejection. Our memory has stored that information, yet we do not consciously recognize that it is there. When it emerges in actions we do not see its roots. However, when someone says to us "You are just like your father" we hear that but it may not register. Introspection is a valuable tool to analyze our actions—use it. Be careful, however, not to rely too heavily on feelings that are generated by self-analysis. This introspection can be beneficial toward positive attitude when we recognize again that feelings of rejection are part of our attitude.

GUILT

Self-analysis may turn us away from effective results by making us feel guilty or more rejected than before. We must guard against discouragement. A good balance is required. A sense of humor is also an asset. Choose friends who project positive attitudes. Associate with those people whose goals are most like your own or who are sympathetic to your direction and goals. You should associate with real estate professionals who are equally motivated in a positive way.

Recognize that physical beauty is not important. We have been led to believe that beautiful people are the most successful, but inner beauty is what others really see. Have a pleasing look to others in dress, cleanliness, and manner. Your positive attitude will overshadow any physical characteristics that you consider undesirable.

BRAINWASHING

Keep your inner self clean. Practice brainwashing daily. Put your mind through a daily exercise of removing anything that cannot be effectively taken care of that day. There is no point in worrying about something that may happen tomorrow; those thoughts will serve only to keep us from being effective with today's efforts.

Spend some time daily making others happy. It is not only good for them, you will reap rewards from it too.

Fill your mind with productive thoughts. Avoid depressing activities and depressing news on radio, television, and in the newspapers. You will get enough from negative people without searching for more. Always end the day by reading, listening to soft music, or just relaxing. Avoid listening to late news or reading the newspaper before retiring for the night. You will rest much easier and wake refreshed, ready to meet your next appointment.

It has been said that even in good times real estate is a down business. Perhaps this is true. Interest rates, buying power, and other market forces will always be pressing on this profession. Recognize that times are always difficult for people who make them so. Then go on with your plan to succeed.

LEADERSHIP

Prior to moving off the subject of attitude, motivation, and self-confidence, it is important to mention the value of good leadership in the real estate office. As many managers and brokers know, the success or failure of a real estate operation will be heavily affected by the quality of the management person or team in charge.

You are a mirror image of your manager/broker. His or her style of leadership is what you have chosen. That style can be a factor in whether you will fail or succeed. If your manager drags into the office and treats each day as a chore, what do you think your attitude will be? If your manager is not success motivated, can you be? If your manager looks like he or she is "lemoncoly" (facial expression that looks like they are sucking on a lemon), will you feel the same way? Chances are fair to good that you will reflect this attitude.

Remember this important factor when you are developing your marketing plan. It might be that you will now change real estate offices because of what you see in your manager.

INVOLVEMENT

Become an active member of your local multiple listing service (MLS). The exposure will be important for your visibility, and can offer further assistance which may benefit not only your sellers but other members of the real estate board as well.

Attend regularly scheduled meetings. This is a good time to meet other salespeople and affords you an excellent opportunity to share your marketable properties. Often guest speakers from mortgage companies and other related industries will impart timely information.

As many brokers and sales associates know, we have an excellent opportunity to share properties when the telephone rings or salespeople, brokers, and managers come into our offices to transact business. Do not make the assumption that because your property is available in the local publications or on a computer that every salesperson knows about its existence. Use the opportunity to share your enthusiasm for the property and for its unique qualities. This adds exposure and thus more possible chances to sell the property.

Often sales associates and brokers calling or dropping in have figurative "blinders" on when it comes to knowing about other real estate offices' inventory. Also, when a new property comes on the market it may take 7 to 10 working days before it appears in the MLS book. If on computer, it may only take 1 day. Most computer "hot sheets" do not contain enough information without a call to the listing agent. Do a good selling job on that property to the other members or the service especially during the first few days of the availability of the property.

The more interaction there is between sales associates and brokers, the more available properties are exposed, and the better we get to know each other, the more we will see increased sales as a result.

VISIBILITY CREATES SUCCESS

Several things happen when you are visible daily in your market area and among potential clients:

1. Your credibility increases because you interact with people concerning real estate, the economy, market conditions, and elements of real estate which interest them.

2. Showing an interest in your clients as well as knowing what is going on in your field will many times lead to referrals.

3. Your visibility keeps you abreast of what is happening in your geographic (farm) area. Knowing current prices of properties, who lives and works in the area, and neighborhood plans for the future is part of creating an image of a competent salesperson.

4. Visibility indicates that you care about the job you perform. Sales associates are not very visible sitting at a desk waiting for the telephone to ring. They must be out among people daily. You will need to interact with potential clients at least two to three times before they will begin to remember who you are.

LOOKING GOOD AND FEELING GOOD

One area of real estate marketing that is least discussed is your physical appearance when you meet the public. You know if you look good, you will feel good. But what about the impression you make when they see you casually dressed promoting property? Are they apt to list their property for sale with you if you look carelessly dressed? Will your relationship with them be casual as well? It is recommended that both men and women in real estate sales and management dress as professional business people. If your company has a particular attire, wear it and keep it looking sharp. If your company has no particular dress attire, men should be in shirt, tie, and jacket with optional vest. Women should wear dresses or tasteful pants suits that best describe your professional status. Provocative clothing is fine for social occasions, but it is not appropriate for professional salespeople meeting clients. If you are well dressed, feel good, and look good you will feel much more in control of yourself and in turn will be in control of the contact and your marketing program.

INVEST YOUR TIME

Real estate is one of those professions which needs many hours of attention. Sometimes those hours may not be strung together. Being available or on call is a must. Client availability may be only on evenings, weekends, or holidays. This is where the full-time sales associate has it over the part-timer. A full-timer is described as a sales associate who has no other profession other than real estate. Responding to a buyer or seller at a moment's notice may mean the difference between a sale or no sale. Time planning is a very important aspect of availability.

A commitment to your job is a must. Time *is* money, and planning its wise use will make the difference at the end of the year when those commission checks are totaled up.

Being available means having your days planned in advance. Schedule at least 1 month ahead with time blocked for sales meetings, training meetings, home previews (also known as caravans), floor assignments, prospecting for new clients, and so on. When that all-important client calls, adjustments in your schedule should be made easily. If your schedule is tight, and it should be, ask the clients to adjust their schedule to yours. They will appreciate you more.

I am not suggesting that you abandon your schedule each time a client calls; rather, work as a team with the client to come up with a mutually agreeable appointment. Your schedule indicates that you are a busy sales associate, and busy people have time for people and are successful. Be sure to be busy doing the right things. Work smart, not hard!

Because availability is so important, being a part-time sales associate is difficult. The person who is able to work at another profession and still devote enough time to efficiently work real estate sales and marketing strategies is rare.

Part-time associates may do a disservice to other members of the real estate office where they work by putting an added burden of otherwise shared office responsibilities. They also have difficulty making sales meetings, previewing new properties, and in general keeping up with the real estate market.

EFFECTIVE PLANNING

Effective marketing begins with a plan. No project can reach an effective conclusion without planning. It would be like planning a vacation without looking at travel brochures or even a road map.

To have any successful marketing, one must plan to succeed with that plan—a commitment, as it were, to success. This is not mere chance, or "luck" as some would call it, but a definitive approach for a period of time which contains signposts to recognize when change must be made and when success is being achieved.

Possibly the reason planning is neglected so often is because it requires quality thoughts and time to put an effective strategy together. There are no shortcuts to planning.

Planning is nothing more than deciding (1) what you want to accomplish, (2) when you want it accomplished, (3) what it will take to complete the elements, and (4) how you can measure the success. The barometer of success is the end result. We look back for guides to the future and forward to completion of our goals.

Without planning we are unable to chart where we have come from and where we are going. It has been said that many of us are not really aware of what is going on around us. Possibly nowhere is this more true than in real estate today.

Most of us are not taught how to plan. We travel along in life occasionally succeeding, not recognizing why. Many people attribute success to luck. Luck is really the residue of design or planning. All too often we stumble along hoping everything will happily fall into place. However, results will be directly related to the effort expended. We can become disappointed with such results and in the end avoid planning because "it really didn't work anyway."

PLAN TO PLAN

The following steps are needed for an effective marketing strategy:

1. A designed plan to properly list a marketable property with a formal presentation to get that listing.
2. A plan to market that property with respect to the tools that are available: signs, advertising, lock boxes, open houses, and so on.
3. A strategy to interact with clients and brokers and sales associates on promoting the property.
4. Determine what elements are needed to have the results you desire from the marketing plan.

A good strategy will work many times on many different properties with slight modifications.

Planning Backward

Determine the end result desired *first!* Then work backward on paper and ask, "What needs to happen before that element can be accomplished?" Continue doing this backward motion until you reach the obvious starting point. Follow each step to its obvious conclusion. The end result will assist you in determining what needs to be modified to be more successful the next time the plan is implemented.

Example

You want to effectively market a new property that you have taken in a well-planned area of your city. The property is priced right, and the seller will assist in financing the sale. You need to ask specific questions in the planning process. Where will the buyer likely come from? How much exposure will be required to get the property sold? How motivated are the sellers to sell?

The backward strategy works this way: the property is sold. What has to take place before that can happen? The buyer must make an offer. What has to happen before that? Agents and brokers need to be made aware the property is available, and the terms of sale. What happens before that? Special marketing items may need to be employed to get the word out.

Flyers, open houses, brokers' open houses, sharing at multiple listing service meetings, newspaper advertising, and the like are all important. Before this can happen, you must know the special features of the property and what is motivating the seller to sell. Before that you must make a listing presentation to "sell the sellers" on using your services to market their property. Now we come to the starting point: The presentation must be made ready to share with the seller.

TAKING THE FIRST STEP

Each program begins with the first step. In the beginning we are all a bit fearful. This is the "I don't want to fail" fear. Recognize that immediate fear for what it is: the uncertain feeling that your plan will not work. Adequate preparation will do much to alleviate this fear.

Motivation to work the plan will be directly related to the desire to be effective and reach the goals you have set. A daily commitment to act may be required. For some of us a slight push is all we need to be off and running. For some, a daily prod is required. Still others will take all the pushing and shoving we can provide, and still we discover that they really are not motivated.

Desire will be present until a goal is reached or until attitude or conditions change relative to that goal. Upon attainment, new goals need to be implemented. This becomes an endless productive cycle and should be recognized as such.

Remember to use your daily time planner, your calendar of events, so to speak. If you do not use the daily planner your days will slip by with little accomplishment. We tend to waste time on unnecessary tasks when we have not set priorities on our activities. *Remember that the urgent is seldom important.*

ACTIVITIES OF PLANNING

In your planning, write first the activities that occur on a regular basis:

1. Floor time
2. Staff meetings
3. Training sessions

4. New home previews
5. Related MLS activities

Now schedule time to advertise the properties, meet new clients, and participate in activities that place you in the public eye. These should be scheduled at least 5 days a week. Set priorities based on your planning and goals and do not deviate unless it is necessary.

If you have to move a segment of marketing activity, reschedule to return to the daily effort you have planned. It may mean doubling up on an activity. If you feel guilty about having missed an activity you might naturally procrastinate. Procrastination can cost you dearly.

An example of a good day's activities should include:

1. Two hours in your geographic market area
2. One hour of telephoning to new potential clients (referred to as cold calling)
3. One hour of direct-mail follow-up
4. One hour of calls and visits to the clients you are working with

This sounds like a lot of time spent! However, with this schedule you have only blocked out 5 hours, 5 days per week!

SCHEDULING DIRECT-MAIL FOLLOW-UP

The direct-mail follow-up may be done at home early in the morning or late at night when your other activities cannot be accomplished. Do not waste valuable hours doing direct mail. Often you can do the direct-mail work while on floor duty waiting for the telephone to ring or when sitting at an open house.

Too often one or more of the areas mentioned will be neglected. These are, however, basic to the real marketing effort. They are generally replaced by coffee breaks, weather, general chatter about how bad real estate really is, and office procedures that are really used more as an excuse for not doing them then anything else. Frequently the up-and-down cycle of real estate sales is directly related to the up-and-down activity of the sales associate or broker and not the real estate market! Any plan or goal worth achieving takes daily implementation to be successful.

BALANCE PROMOTING

Promoting one property or dozens involves the same basic elements. No one technique will succeed on its own. A total marketing program is required. The advertising, flyers, open houses, sign on the property, and so on are all part of the complete picture. Balancing these efforts to the individual property is necessary:

1. Organize your strategy for using these marketing tools (and others you develop) based first on the type of property to be sold.
2. Consider the types of financing that are available for that property.
3. Solicit the cooperation of the seller in assisting you with your marketing plan. It is important to make sellers feel they have an important part in the marketing of their property. In today's ever-changing real estate market this is especially true.

FOLLOW THE RULES

Keep your multiple listing service rules and regulations in mind when developing your marketing strategy. Also remember your department of real estate responsibilities and your legal and moral responsibility to the sellers.

THE BASIC PLAN

It is a good idea to have a basic plan ready even before you have listed a property. For example, you list a property in your geographic market area, you decide to call all the neighbors around the subject property to inform them of its availability. This should be a normal practice! (You will not find many sales associates doing it though!) You then invite them to a special open house and suggest they bring interested friends and relatives to view the property in the event they might be interested. This also becomes a good tool to get additional sellers to recognize your availability and ability.

You develop a well-written and illustrated flyer (printed, not run on a copy machine), remembering to put in only enough information to make them curious. Hand carry the flyer to cooperating brokers and sales associates offices and interact with these associates in person!

Do not be afraid to use some of your creativity to develop and distribute these flyers and motivate yourself and the associates you encounter.

Involve the Seller

To inspire your sellers to cooperate and assist you in selling their property you have to be sufficiently motivated to work hard in their behalf. You can create in your sellers a positive attitude by your own enthusiasm.

Be prepared to assist them beyond what they expect of you. Be ready and willing to go the "extra mile," to answer questions, calm fears, or do whatever else might be needed. Remind yourself to keep your schedule up to date so that the sellers cannot make unreasonable demands on your time. Control them and your time schedule!

Listen

Be a good listener when your clients are talking. Good listening habits so often need to be acquired. Being a good listener will reap the reward of improved relationships, not to mention dollars in your pocket. Good listeners can evaluate a client's needs. Good listeners seldom have communication problems with clients!

Take Care

Caring real estate professionals are known for their personal involvement with the needs of their sellers. Nothing is more important than follow-up and regular communication with them. A note of caution, however: beware of becoming emotionally involved with them. Be sincere, but be professional!

Do Not Be a Know-It-All!

Not knowing an answer to a client's question is not poor professionalism unless you try to cover up with a made-up answer. The best response is to admit you are uncertain but that you do know where to find the answer. Honesty in your dealings is of utmost importance.

Probe the Seller

There should be a time of thorough probing when you are first asked about listing the property for sale. The purpose of this questioning session is to determine the seller's motivation and need. Often, as many brokers and sales associates know, the important questions that should be asked during the initial listing stages are left unasked or unanswered until the marketing effort has run aground. Do not be afraid to ask about finance, moving plans, property condition, mortgage instruments on the property, or any element that could affect marketability of the property.

Always ask questions which need explanation. As we have said previously, try to avoid questions that can be answered yes or no! The listing process might go faster, but you won't learn the necessary facts.

The proper questioning and restating of sellers' answers will ensure that you understand what they are saying. This will also eliminate any interpretations that you might draw that will cloud the situation. Avoid as much miscommunication as possible. The key is to communicate!

Determine Motivation

Another factor in successfully selling a property is the seller's motivation. In today's market there is little or no room for the seller who is adamant about price and terms and who is determined to make you do all the convincing to a buyer. You may make a conscious decision not to list a particular property when the wrong motivation is apparent or when the seller is just testing the market. Your first listing will be the one that violates this principle. That is alright provided that listing is marketed in such a way as to give it the proper exposure for you, the company, and the seller! The result will be other buyers and sellers for you and good reputation for the company. A by-product will be good feelings from the seller because you tried. Make no mistake, however; be up-front with your sellers about the chances that their property will sell!

Above all, know what is a good property to list and what is not. The seller-questioning session may take place in the comfort of their home. However, it would be better in your sales office. This puts you more in control of the session with no distractions and no interruptions. The MLS books and computers are at your service.

Prior to completing the forms required by your company and the MLS, explore the marketing potential with the seller to maximize that first exposure step. Be prepared to identify you and your company, the property's marketability, and your strategy for marketing the property. Be confident and motivated during this process. Asking the questions "Where are you going?" and "When do you have to be there?" not only will give you seller motivation but could lead to a referral to another city and additional compensation.

Did you ever wonder why the seller did not call the salesperson from whom she or he bought the property? That associate did not have a plan, did not work at it, and did not follow up on the client after the sale closed. Planning does not stop after the sale!

Remember that the marketing of yourself and your company is rein-forced by a good presentation of your marketing plan during the questioning session. Credibility will say to the seller, "We do not need to look any further for help in selling our property."

The first indication of an inadequate presentation during the listing effort is the seller saying, "We want to interview other brokers and agents before we list." Shopping for a real estate company should be eliminated when they know you are aware of their needs and can respond with a plan to successfully sell the property.

Polish the Presentation

A good presentation should take about 2 to 2½ hours including the filling out of all required forms. That may or may not be accomplished on your first visit. You probably will need to preview the property and return with comparables of properties sold, of those on the market, and of expired listings to reinforce the selling price and terms prior to listing.

Do not rush the presentation, or the sellers will want to talk to other real estate sales associates prior to putting the property on the market with you. Practice your presentation before going on that call! The more you practice, the better your presentation will be and the more confidence you will gain.

At the end of the session your seller should be assured that your presentation has answered all questions and that you have interacted enough to proceed with the marketing effort on the property.

Your marketing efforts should vary from property to property, but only slightly. Your basic strategy should be the same with those modifications that will expose and sell that property.

Some suggestions as to what should be part of your plan are:

1. Research information about the property that will assist you during the listing presentation.

2. Write up the required information to list the property.

3. Determine (with the seller) the location for the "for sale" sign, for maximum visibility. Avoid flower beds and special areas in lawns that could be a problem if you just stick the sign anywhere.

4. Determine where the lock box should go for accessibility by other agents and brokers. (If your area does not use lock boxes, you will need to be sure to have extra keys in the office for other brokers and agents to use.)

5. Note any special features that should be mentioned about the property. This would also include any special financing options.

6. Determine what should be said in the MLS book and computer about the property. Again, the seller can assist you with this and will enjoy doing it.

7. Determine in which Boards of Realtors the listing should appear and in what sections of their books.

8. Determine whether open houses should be held and how often.

9. Determine what items should be checked about the property for improvement.

10. Determine when real estate offices can preview the property and coordinate with the seller and those offices to avoid embarrassment for the seller.

11. Determine if the property should be scheduled for a broker's open house during the week or on a weekend.

12. Determine if a photo of the property will enhance its salability in flyers and in advertising that could be developed.

13. Determine whether newspaper advertising would get the telephone to ring at the office. (Special features of the home, special financing, low price, and so on, will make the telephone ring.)

14. Determine the type and style of flyer to be printed to distribute to members of the local MLS and possibly adjoining Boards of Realtors.

15. Discuss with the seller any ideas they may have about special promotions. Involve the seller in these items and in some cases discuss why certain items may or may not be in their best interest.

Your enthusiasm for the property and its salability will assist you in properly selling the sellers and the contacts you make that will lead to a sale.

Now that the property is listed for sale make weekly visits and pick up the business cards of sales associates and brokers that have either previewed the property or shown it to a potential buyer.

A friendly call to these salespeople will give you additional insights into the showability and salability of the property. During the call, determine whether they previewed the property to possibly show to a client or if they actually did show it to a potential buyer. Question them about price, condition, and what they think of the property, recognizing that all the input is designed to get the property sold.

Radiate Your Enthusiasm

During your calls to sales associates and brokers who have seen the property be sure to radiate enthusiasm for the property. Share the unique properties of this offering. It may lead that associate or broker to return for another look. As mentioned earlier, radiate your motivation to the seller too!!

Record and Report

Keep thorough records of activity on each property. Make a file that you can keep with you that tells you when you held the last open house and the results, contacts with other brokers and agents about the property, and other activity to remember when sharing the marketing results with the seller.

Call the sellers immediately after you hold an open house to advise them of the results (even if poor) and your feelings about why it was or was not successful. If you have suggestions for improvement of the property be sure to do it face-to-face and not over the telephone or in a note. The seller could misunderstand your intention if you attempt to leave a note.

Open house time is generally when we notice more fully the things that could be improved about the property. Also, guests that come through the open house will be verbal about improvements that need to be made.

A thank-you note left at the property after the open house is also a good idea. A thank-you note when you drop by to pick up those business cards is also appropriate.

Communicate

Make regular communication—open and honest communication with no puffing to make yourself look better. The regular communications will increase your credibility.

Generally agents and brokers will not communicate as regularly as they should, usually because nothing is happening with the property. It is not being shown, interest is not generated by other brokers and agents, or for many reasons it is being avoided. All the more reason to communicate frequently.

Silence might give sellers the idea that you do not care about them or their property. Weekly calls with information or encouragement should be a minimum frequency.

Stop at the property when the seller is home so that you can interact as has been mentioned earlier. Do not look for future business from a seller that you have not contacted regularly. Remember that a report of no news is still better than avoiding a seller because you have nothing to offer.

PREPARING THE PROPERTY

Certain steps are necessary to prepare the property for daily showing. Advise the sellers to put valuable items out of sight. Coin collections, stamps, or any rare items that could be carried off easily should be hidden away. Gun collections are also better off hidden and locked up. All these, plus wallets, purses, and keys, should not be left lying around.

(This can be a delicate area because the seller might assume that someone is waiting to steal things the minute you put up the for sale sign. Your professionalism can have an opportunity to shine here when you say, "we do not expect thieves, but we do not want to put out the welcome mat either.")

Small objects of decor may become a problem of potential damage with small children coming into the property with parents. Be observant when previewing the property for these areas and be ready to make suggestions to the sellers.

Signs of ceiling leaks, water damage, dripping faucets, or other items that may be called "deferred maintenance" should be discussed. Ask the seller, for example, "did the roof leak at one time?" Has it been repaired? These are questions a potential buyer will ask. Refer to it in this manner when asking questions.

The walking inspection of the property is an excellent opportunity to share ideas on how to enhance the features of the property. Give the property that "warm" comfortable feeling. The first impression is extremely important.

Arrangements of throw pillows, setting the dining room table, mood lighting, and fragrant candles add touches that will increase desirability for the potential buyer to "emotionally move in." Your inspection might also turn up things that need only soap and water or possibly some touch-up paint.

Suggest the use of your office staff to preview and help make recommendations for improvement or even pricing suggestions. If suggestions come from many of your coworkers it will be taken as constructive because they are also professionals. Also others may see things that you have missed. Sellers often do not realize simple improvements that could be made. It is our responsibility to tactfully share ideas.

We should provide the seller with a market evaluation. This is a collection of statistics on properties sold, properties currently on the market in the area, or expired properties.

In today's market accurate evaluations are made easy through use of computers. Many multiple listing services employ this tool. Use comparable books and computers to evaluate the results on those properties sold that are close in size, design, and amenities to the property you are working on. Recognize that you do not get exact copies of the property you are going to market. That is why your market evaluation is strictly an estimate. It is not an appraisal. Keep reminding yourself that the property will only sell for what a willing buyer will pay, based on other similar properties in the area that are for sale. The sold comparables will assist your seller in setting a sales price that will begin to draw buyers.

SLOPPY PROMOTION—SLOPPY RESULTS

Sometimes real estate salespersons consider promoting property as putting up a for sale sign, running an ad in the local newspaper, holding an occasional open house, and possibly making a copy machine (handwritten) flyer to mail to other real estate offices. Efficient marketing is much more than that.

As indicated previously, accurate market evaluations are a key factor in proper marketing right from the start. A market evaluation that inflates the property to impress the seller will lead to a longer marketing effort to get the property sold and could bring discredit to the sales associate as one who takes "overpriced turkeys." Again, remember the sellers set the asking price, but help them to be realistic about what they will ask. If you inflate the price to make the seller feel good, you will only have to explain your actions later when the property does not sell.

Another key ingredient to good marketing is the location. Will traffic driving by see the sign? Is it a heavily traveled area? If it is on a dead-end street seldom traveled, drive-by contacts will be few. You will have to develop strategies for getting the other agents and brokers and general public to come by the property. It is true that many properties are sold from people seeing the for sale sign.

Sellers in difficult locations should be talked to openly and frankly about the marketing potential of open houses. A special brokers open house, with directions, may be the only way to get people up to the property.

Is this particular property unique? Is it different from surrounding properties? Will it appeal to a special buyer? If so, will you need to employ special incentives to reach those agents and brokers to find those unique buyers? For example, consider a bonus to the selling agent!! Perhaps a trip, an appliance, or an antique. Use your imagination with respect to promotion. Sellers can participate in many of these special incentives and usually enjoy doing it. Agents and brokers sometimes use door prizes to lure sales associates to come to an open house. Business cards will be dropped in a special container for a drawing at the end of the day.

What about Advertising?

Consider whether advertising in the local newspapers or big metropolitan papers will be useful. The object here is to get the telephone to ring at your real estate office. Buyers rarely buy from an ad in the paper, but curious buyers reading interesting ads will call. What they are really saying is "I am interested in buying, can you help?" Often sales associates indicate to sellers that they will advertise their property only to find the manager or broker does not because they must advertise unique-sounding properties which will get the telephone to ring. Value pricing of a property will also get the telephone to ring. Share with your sellers during the listing presentation just what the purpose of advertising is. The greatest value advertising has is for the institution you represent.

What about Financing?

In today's economic climate it may be necessary for a seller to carry some of the equity in the property in the form of paper carried for a specified period at an agreed-upon interest rate. This can be a good selling feature for an ad in the newspaper. The seller who wants all their cash out of a property may wait a very long time for the buyer willing to get new financing, and thus the traditional 20 percent down, 80 percent financing may not work in today's real estate sales.

Lenders are reluctant to extend financing for 30 years when the market conditions fluctuate so rapidly. This makes the type of terms available on a property a very important marketing tool. Talk with your sellers to determine to what use they will put their equity. Many sellers realize that they may have to leave some of the equity behind, and your guidance will assist them early in the listing period in determining the most feasible financing options.

What about Property Condition?

If maintenance has been deferred, the seller may need to invest some money to bring the property up to potential. The seller may choose to reflect the need in a reduced price or in allowances for such things as carpet, drapes, or landscaping.

You cannot move the property to a different location, so you need to evaluate it where it stands. As many brokers and agents know, many property owners do not see the little improvements that can be made to make a property more saleable. They may have been seeing it that way for years. Shampooing carpets, painting trim, and washing windows can make a great difference in the first impression, resulting in an interested client.

A Seller Checklist

Provide your seller with a checklist of items that will bring maximum exposure. The home should be tidy and neat during the listing period. First impressions last and mean a lot to a buyer who may see himself or herself as the new owner. General neatness is a must—beds should be made, closet doors should be closed, and clothes should be put away. This area may be difficult to discuss for some sales associates. However, when discussed early as part of making the property more saleable, the seller should be receptive. Share these things as suggestions. Selling today is a joint venture between the seller and sales associate. You use the best marketing tools at your disposal, and sellers help with the tips we have been mentioning.

Flyers

As mentioned earlier, flyers should never be run on a copy machine. They should be printed professionally on quality paper. They should be brief and descriptive enough to get the reader's attention and make him or her want more information. Use words that create interest such as value, under market, well-maintained, and so on, words that create pictures for the reader to see.

Create eye-catching flyers by using creative writing and attractive layout of the information. Many print shops will assist you in properly designing the flyer for photographing and printing.

Typical flyers are boring, full of information, and leave nothing to the imagination. They are factual and nothing more. Ask yourself, "What is going to make the reader want to see this property?" Then proceed to develop the flyer. One final note on flyers: Your enthusiasm will show itself here also!

Use Some Energy

Take those flyers to the people that are most likely to have access to a buyer. Many agents and brokers mail them to offices and hope they get distributed to other agents and brokers. Remember what was said earlier about hand carrying them and meeting the people!

Too often the sales associate at an open house will "hide" behind the flyer by giving it to potential buyers and suggesting that if they have any questions to call at their leisure. The obvious result is that the sales associate loses an opportunity to gain a buyer.

The plus side of an attractive brochure or flyer is that it is given after a definite appointment to work with that client is established.

The For Sale Sign

Two basic types of for sale signs are used. The stake sign can be installed by a sales associate on the property with little effort. Carry a hammer and a railroad spike (or tent stake) to install this type of sign. This can also be used to install open house signs and flags. Use the railroad spike to make the beginning hole where you want the sign (or flag if it is an open house) and drive the spike into the ground with the hammer. Remove the spike and replace it with the sign or flag. It will save your signs and flags, since most of them cannot take being hit very hard with any tool.

Take caution to use the hammer with care as metal to metal contact can be dangerous. Take care not to interfere with sprinkler system pipes and special garden treatments. The sign should be visible from as many directions as possible. Signs should be painted on both sides for maximum exposure. Take care that the sign is in good shape and not rusty. These may or may not be the responsibility of each salesperson depending on the company policy.

Post signs are generally installed professionally by a person contracted to do so. This person is usually responsible for the maintenance of the signs and posts so that they look good when installed. The sign installer may look to you, the sales associate, for suggestions as to location and best visibility. Expect to give this advice.

The Sign Rider

Many real estate companies allow the market area specialist (the farmer) to post a sign rider above the post sign or stake sign. This identifies the person to call for information about the property. They generally say "call Joe" or "call Nan." It may or may not be the market area person assigned to that area's listing, but it does add a personal touch to the marketing effort of a sales associate. Sign riders are generally made to specifications required by the real estate company and are the responsibility of each agent or broker to purchase and maintain. When you own it you tend to take better care.

Another form of sign rider would be descriptive of the property for sale. The sign might read "olympic pool," "horses OK," or "owner will help finance." These types of sign riders may be used to draw additional special attention to the property.

Access to the Property

Lock boxes allow a sales associate or broker access to a property to show or inspect while the owner is away or if the property is vacant. These boxes are very secure and make showing, previewing, and selling much easier than having to call a real estate office each time a property is to be shown. This item should be one of the first sales tools that a sales associate can share with a seller to install on the property.

The three other options open to an agent or broker are:

1. Keys kept in listing office for pickup to show property.
2. Listing agent must accompany potential buyers and their agent and they alone have the key.
3. Property must be shown by appointment only, usually with 24-hour notice required.

Each of these has a built-in problem. Will a potential buyer want to see the property (1) when you can get the keys, (2) when the seller is home for appointment only, or (3) when the listing agent is available to meet the potential buyers and their agents? Obviously, from a marketing perspective, availability is severely hampered by these last three approaches.

When convincing sellers that they need a lock box, sell them on the benefits of having easy access to show and sell the property. Another key advantage is that they do not have to be home for it to be shown.

When installing the lock box be sure to install it where it can readily be seen by potential selling agents. Keep it out of the bushes and crawl spaces as much as possible. A special note: attach any special instructions to the keys, for instance, where the burglar alarm can be turned off, or which is the dead bolt key and which is for the main lock.

A key box in the listing office is an added benefit for the rare occasions when the keys disappear or the keys in the lock box will not work. They are also handy for termite inspectors, appraisers, repairpersons, and others who need to get into the property but the lock box key needs to remain in its place ready for that next showing. The key box in the office should be locked away at night, and each key should be tagged and cataloged for ease of location.

When agents come into your office to get keys to your available properties, get some kind of identification before handing out the keys. It is a good idea to put their business card into the key box so the next person knows who has the keys to that property.

WORKING WITH TENANTS

Very often a seller will be selling a property that is occupied by a tenant. It is important that you work with the seller to get maximum cooperation from the tenant. It is the sellers' responsibility to inform the tenant that they will be selling the property and solicit their cooperation from the outset. The seller needs this cooperation to head off problems, for example, if the tenant will not let agents or brokers and potential buyers into the property except when convenient, or if the tenant will not allow a lock box or for sale sign on the property. (This is a very touchy area and should be handled at the time the listing is taken to avoid tenant friction when the sign goes up.)

The seller will need to get the cooperation of the tenant to keep the property in showing condition. Again, the key word is *communicate.*

PREPARING FOR AN OPEN HOUSE

Visit the neighbors around the subject property during the week prior to the open house and invite them to attend. Invite them to bring friends and relatives that might be interested in the property. Using the telephone to invite them will work well if they have met you and know your efforts in the neighborhood.

There are two main reasons for an open house: (1) to expose the community to you and your company's services and (2) to acquire clients for this property and others. Post a sign a day early to "precondition" the neighbors to the open house.

Your sellers should mow and trim their yard in anticipation of the open house. Good "curb" appeal will result.

Brief the seller on the elements necessary to hosting a good open house. We indicated earlier that location is an important factor to a successful open house. The traffic potential of the open house will be important.

The physical condition of the property for open house is very important. As mentioned earlier the seller should do a good job preparing the home for showing: straighten up, put things away, close closet doors, and so on. You may need to assist the seller with suggestions that will help the property show at its best. All these elements will lead to a good feeling when potential buyers enter the property.

Ask the sellers to be away during your open house period. If they stay around they will inhibit your ability to "close" on a client, and you might feel uncomfortable about what you are doing. Sellers have the desire to sell their property to everyone who comes in the door. We know that everyone looking at open houses is not a buyer, but the seller tends to hope that everyone who enters wants to buy their home. Also, hard feelings can be avoided if a buyer makes a comment about something in the property and the seller takes it personally. The seller has emotion invested in the property and may react negatively to off-hand comments.

Always keep the front door closed during the open house so that potential buyers will ring the bell and you can greet them properly at the door. Have a guest book for buyers to sign as they enter the property. Request that they sign the book as a courtesy to the seller. A good idea is to have a name already signed in so the first party through the property will be encouraged to sign. You might also want to draw names for a door prize. That will be additional incentive to sign the guest book!

After they have signed into the guest book indicate any special features in the property that you might want to bring to their attention. Now, let them preview the property while you follow close behind to answer any questions they may have. Let them talk, and you listen to what they are saying. Many times this listening period will give you clues as to what they are looking for and how this property fits their plans. Your main objective in listening to these potential buyers is so that you can close on them for an appointment to determine just exactly what they are looking for in a home.

Avoid using the open house as the probing tool to get the potential buyers qualified for a home. Make that appointment for later in the day or possibly for the following day.

If you tell a seller that you will hold her or his property open from 1 P.M. to 4 P.M. be sure to arrive early and leave late. During the summer months when it stays light later you might want to keep the property open longer into the evening. Avoid closing an open house early to show a potential buyer property prior to any type of qualifying. It is difficult to tell a seller why you left early when your responsibility is to that seller and that property.

Be sure when posting directional signs that you get permission from the owners where you wish to place the signs. Also, know the city rules about signs in the area you are working. Some cities do not allow any form of directional sign. When this happens you may have to resort to special open house features in the newspaper along with maps and flyers at your real estate office and offer them to potential buyers to pick up for their convenience. Check with your manager to know what to do about local ordinances.

Do not waste a directional sign if another agent or broker has already placed one in the direction of your open house. Just put one where you want them to turn to get to the property you are holding open.

Always be sure to leave the house as you found it. Doors and windows should be secured, lights turned off, music off, and any other items that were added to create a good open house feeling for potential buyers.

Often sellers are given the impression that by holding an open house you will sell their property. Reporting back to a seller after a poor showing on a Sunday afternoon is usually difficult for any agent. Reaction of the seller is, "Why didn't you do what it takes to get people out? You told me holding an open house would attract people. What happened?"

What happened was that you did not plan the open house properly. A few basic questions were in order during the listing presentation period. These questions should be asked of yourself and shared with the seller:

1. Is the property well located (will people find it even if they do not know the area)?
2. What about drive-by traffic (will there be a lot or a little)?
3. Can we attract other brokers or agents to see this property?
4. Does the property conform to others in the area (is it a tract home or one of a kind)?
5. Is it unique? Will it attract attention?
6. What effect will the property's condition have on holding an effective open house?

Again, planning enters the picture. Just running to a corner and putting up a directional sign and a couple of flags is not open house marketing.

You cannot assume that because you put a sign up that people will see it and be able to find the property. During the week decide on the best sign locations. Plan how you will dress up the property to get attention. Plan how you will get people out to see the property. Do not rely on one open house ad in the Sunday classified ads to get the people out.

Use the open house opportunity to learn more about potential buyers who drop by. Your goal for each of them is to get an appointment for some time after the open house.

Refreshments at your open house are a good idea. Something simple such as punch and cookies is ideal. You might want to take a frozen pie, bake it while in the home, and then leave it with a note to the sellers thanking them for allowing you to hold their property open.

CONCLUSION

Marketing of self and property takes planning, goal setting, motivation, and the mental attitude that you are someone important capable of selling yourself and your client's home.

Little remains for you, if your product is ready to sell and you are not. Do not take shortcuts to your goal, which is to sell a home and make a commission and make a buyer and seller happy. Stay motivated about your profession, challenged by the changes that affect it, and positive about your ability to succeed.

Chapter 33

Office Management for Brokers

Barbara Phillips G.R.I., Real Estate Broker; Instructor,
Pasadena City College

You have been a successful real estate salesperson, saved your
money, taken the courses leading to a broker's license and some
extended courses in office administration, and now want to spread your
wings and open your own office. There are now some specific items to
consider.

MANAGEMENT EXPERTISE

Can you direct other people? What type of a broker do you want to be?
A "selling broker" manages the staff and continues to sell as a primary
source of income. "Sales manager brokers" manage staff and spend the
majority of their time in management with some listing and selling, but
they want their primary income to come from the company. "Administrative brokers" have a sales manager to supervise the staff, do little or
no selling, oversee the daily operation, plan for the future, and derive
all income from the company.

MANAGEMENT TRAINING

Do you have experience as a manager? Many of the large franchises
have management training programs. There are excellent courses of-

fered through the Realtors National Marketing Institute which lead to a professional designation. Many community colleges have office administration courses, and others are offered by state associations and private sources.

BUSINESS STRUCTURE

Are you going to be the sole owner? Perhaps a partnership could be better financially and for the sharing of responsibilities. You must know if you can work in a partnership situation. Will it be a general or limited partnership? Look at what each form might have to offer. Do you want to be a corporation? If so, consult with your accountant and attorney as to the benefits of a regular one or a subchapter S corporation (which is taxed similar to a partnership). Would a franchise be helpful? If so, investigate those available in your area. Franchisers are helpful in many ways when you are starting an office, since your success is their success.

SIZE

What is the best number of sales associates for your community? If the site you chose is expandable, will you want to add other income-producing fields? These could include an escrow office, financial services, insurance, appraisal, and others that tie in with real estate.

RECRUITING

Are you going to start out alone, or will you want other salespeople working with you to build a larger company? Do you want experienced sales associates with a following of clients or would you rather have a new licensee that you can train and work with to help become successful? Many offices use a personality test as a screening system, with two interviews, including one with a spouse to make sure that the spouse understands the long hours and hard work that go into the making of a successful real estate agent. Will you advertise for associates, hold open house for prospective real estate licensees, visit licensing schools, or have an ongoing program to attract the type of person you want working with you?

OPERATING CAPITAL

What do you have available in your own savings and in your ability to borrow for future operating costs and expansion? General estimates say that you should have a minimum of $25,000 to $35,000 plus personal living expenses in your capital reserve. If you are going to borrow, remember it must be paid off plus interest on an ongoing basis. If you are looking for a 15 percent profit, the interest paid could eliminate the profit. You will have a period of time, perhaps up to 6 months, with no income before any commissions are received. You may project your first year to have a loss, the second year to break even, and a profit on the third year. Any classes in business administration and accounting will help in planning your finances.

BUDGET

Have you had experience in preparing a budget for a year and for 5 years? NAR has charts that will start you off and the Small Business Administration will supply help in preparing your start-up costs and continuing expenses. A budget is basically a forecasted financial statement. You must work with uncertainties, either with your budget or without it. The annual budget may be broken down by quarters and months. A continuous budget whereby a month is added in the future as the month just ended is dropped keeps you always a year ahead in planning. The budget covers selling, administrative, and other expenses. These expenses are either fixed or variable. The fixed expenses are rent or property payments, property taxes, insurance, board and multiple listing service (MLS) fees, payments on office furniture, legal and accounting fees, salaries, and perhaps sales training. Other expenses change with the volume of sales and usage such as utilities, advertising, telephones, postage, sales commissions, and repairs. These figures must be compared with actual results so that their planning and control effectiveness is useful to you. You must project your production reports monthly in what you expect in listings and sales. Allow for noncompleted sales and "co-op" sales. This is the area that helps you judge fair commission percentages to your sales associates. After the commissions are paid out, the amount left is the "company dollar" to run the company. This amount will relate to the quality of the facilities and services provided by the company to salespeople and clients. When your budget figures for fixed and variable expenses are totaled and then divided by your desks (or salespeople) you will have "desk cost." Although it varies considerably from area to area, it will give you a figure that each associate should produce as a minimum and help you evaluate whether to keep a marginal producer or to raise commissions for high producers.

BANK ACCOUNTS

Your trust account is for handling of clients' checks. With it, a log book is needed for logging in a check as soon as it is received. A copy for the file is generally made. One person should be responsible for the check log and handling of deposits of clients' checks. The general account will be used for all office expenses and commissions in and out. If your accountant sets up the books on a cash basis and you (or a staff member) do the monthly entries, you will be able to have a monthly operating statement to compare with the budget.

EXPENSES

The percentages from your company dollar will depend on the company's efficiency, size, the real estate market, and your community activity. Advertising is a large percentage, and your policy will be based on factors such as cost of local newspapers, type of area (city, resort, farm area, or small town), and your determination of what reaches the most people effectively. Many offices have a "company identification" ad, usually a long column or special quarter or half page. If you are in a franchise, you may be included in their full-page ads. You will have smaller scatter ads in the various specialty columns. You may be in neighborhood throwaways and home magazines and perhaps some radio time. Your signs are part of your advertising, on duty 24 hours a day.

Are you allowing for a receptionist, a secretary, a bookkeeper, or a sales manager? Will the sales manager get a salary and/or commission override?

Office costs can include the furniture, decor, map books or a microfiche system, stationery, business cards, all the artwork for your company logos, and answering service. Business licenses, the costs of a DBA (or fictitious business name), and any legal filing must be considered here. The net profit is the figure left after all other expenses are covered. If you are active in listing and selling, then those commissions should go to you, just as any other salesperson. Putting them into the net profit figure gives a false picture. If you are actively managing, then a salary or override should reflect that in expenses. The final step is to consider the net profit figure as to its income tax effects.

POLICY MANUAL

Every company should have an office policy manual outlining company procedure. It should be drawn up in the start-up phase of the company and can and should be flexible. This will give clarification of all your policies and procedures couched in terms such as "we recommend" or "we suggest" so that you do not step into the employer realm. There can be parts of this in your independent contractors agreement also. The sections should include the following:

1. Staffing hours for both office staff and sales staff, responsibilities for lights, machine turn-offs, floor time, supplies, forms, and other office procedures

2. Listing policies and procedures, sales policies and procedures, forms to be used in these, and the processing flow

3. Advertising policies, diagramming who writes the ads, how they are processed, and the handling of direct mail and cards

4. Communications, including taking of messages for others, answering procedures for phones, use of telephones, answering services, and the obligations of checking with the office and clients

5. Dress codes and automobile requirements

6. Days off and vacation time

7. Buying and selling of property by sales associates

8. Other items such as commission schedules, availability of special rates on health insurance and group investment programs, property management, and company training programs

Commission schedules should spell out the amounts for listing, sales, and in-house versus outside broker sales, increased percentages for higher production, any differences if the associate is buying or selling for their own account, and when commissions are paid. If commissions go back to a base level at the end of each year, that should be shown at what the levels would be. Your base level should cover all your desk costs; once they are covered for the year, then the commission percentages can go up. If they stay up for the beginning of the next year, how will you cover your expenses?

What kind of a training system will fit your office? The simplest is a videotape course that your salespeople can watch in half-hour sessions. If you are in a large franchise, there will be a training program for your area set up in a central location. The franchise may have a traveling trainer who comes into the area at regular times. There are real estate boards and state associations that give training classes as well as the community colleges.

A good training program will "drill for skills," and the trainer will go over a subject such as door-knocking and prospecting. The trainees will then go out and actually do the assignment with follow-up reports on their progress. Good training will enhance a qualified sales associate, but no amount of training will help a person who is not suited for the demanding real estate field.

Property and/or contents insurance, car insurance, with certain requirements for sales associates with the broker as an "also-insured" based on your insurance agent's recommendations, are important. Since the real estate business is a frequent target for lawsuits, errors and omissions insurance is needed. Due to the high cost, many offices require the salespeople to pay a prorated portion of this. A competent insurance agent and legal adviser can help structure your business practices to avoid problems.

The status of real estate salespeople has been the main source of controversy regarding coverage by workers' compensation insurance. Many states say that for the purposes of this coverage, real estate brokers are employers of sales agents and must carry a policy on them. If the broker is uninsured and there is an "on-the-job" accident, she or he must defend not only any costs but also penalties, sanctions, and losses that could destroy him or her financially. There are certain requirements in posting and notifying the real estate agents of their rights.

Most companies ask that the sales associate take out certain amounts on liability and property damage with the company as also-named insured.

The broker just starting an office should have an attorney to advise on forms, contracts, and any partnership agreements or equity sharing with investors. Some brokerages pay a monthly retainer fee to a lawyer, which enables them to call for minor legal problems that arise. In some cases there is an agreement between broker and sales associates as to who pays what in case of a legal action.

THE FUTURE

Your management must allow for planning for the future, including expansion into branch offices and allied fields such as construction, property management, insurance, and relocation programs. You need to take the time to plan your long-term goals. By discussing these goals with your staff you may find several possibilities that could be implemented by using previously untapped skills within the company. Perhaps someone has expertise in exchanging and/or syndication and could start a division to specialize in investments. Someone else may be handling rentals for clients and could parlay that into a property management division. The possibilities are only limited by lack of imagination. As you grow and have agents three to a desk, it is time to consider a branch office.

The location of a branch office is a prime consideration and must be carefully researched. Do you have a name identification in the area? Have you had listings and sales there? Is there a high volume of sales in the area? Is the area saturated with other offices? Do you have enough capital to keep the office open in the first year when it may lose money? Will the office be large enough for a manager? Will that person have to be on salary until commissions reach a point of providing a good override? The broker who takes a high producer and puts that person in as manager may be doing both a disservice.

The timing of your expansion is crucial. What is the economy doing? Is it going up, sliding down, or holding its own? If you have been growing well and planning for expansion when the economy goes into a slump you may do far better to stay put and plan for the loss of some associates who will not be able to survive in a slow market. Your plan should be to survive in the worst market and grow with a rising economy.

FRANCHISE OR INDEPENDENT?

Many brokers feel it is better to start with a franchise adding its support to the ability of the broker. The possibility of starting out with a known and accepted name of a franchise added to the broker's name so that there is instant market identification is very appealing. The growth of real estate franchises has been extremely rapid since 1970. Although it appears to have leveled off recently, the strength of numbers of brokerages who have joined makes them a potent force in the real estate market. The broker will be included in the mass advertising at discount prices and often will have instant referrals. Franchises are offering many management services, including salesperson training, management training, setting up a department for relocations services, and setting up financial services. The fee structure should be gone over thoroughly when contemplating an affiliation. If you feel they are too high, consider what you could do to offer the same services with that amount of money. In general, the smaller offices have not joined as readily or with as happy results as the larger offices. If you have good management techniques and good office procedures and a way you want to train your salespeople, you may derive very few benefits from the affiliation. If you have good name recognition in your area, the name value of the franchise may not add to your ability to get a larger share of the market. The National Association of Realtors did a survey in 1981, "Profile of Real Estate Firms," that gives much information on franchising and the satisfaction of brokers who joined one or dropped out of one. It may be obtained from their Economics and Research Division for $10.

Chapter 34

Marketing Rental Property

William C. Weaver   Real Property Consultant, Dallas, Texas

This chapter is written especially for those people who find or expect to find themselves involved with the day-to-day marketing of real estate. Owner-managers will find this chapter of immense practical value.

This material is oriented toward the small owner-manager, the beginning resident manager, and the student in this area. It does not discuss problems associated with multimillion-dollar regional shopping centers nor does it cover skyscraper management. It does discuss, in detail, small residential marketing management—the very down-to-earth, practical things people need to know to successfully market their own property or to be an on-site person for a property management company.

The large emphasis placed on apartment management is justified in two ways. First, it is where the need is! Most owner-managers of real estate are concentrated in the residential area: small apartments or rented houses. Second, many of the marketing skills needed for success in residential marketing management are easily transferable to other types of properties. The emphasis here is on practical knowledge that is immediately usable.

MARKET INTELLIGENCE

"Know thyself" is all inclusive—it means knowing your properties' strengths *and* weaknesses. You do not really need to know all the construction details, but, for example, you certainly should know about soundproofing. How are the common walls constructed so as to avoid the transmissions of sound from one apartment to the next? You should know the answers to questions about the following:

1. Size of apartment, size of each room
2. Number and type of closets and their size
3. Number of and equipment in bathrooms
4. Floor plans
5. Equipment, such as types and brands of stove, refrigerator, disposals, heating and air conditioning, furnishings, if any, and so on
6. Amenities such as pool, laundry facilities, club rooms, saunas, extra soundproofing, burglar and fire alarms, self-cleaning ovens, ice makers and trash compactors; in short, all the possible "extras" that may be in your apartment complex
7. Whether cablevision is available
8. Types of carpet available, color, and so on
9. Provision of pest control service
10. Pet policies
11. Children policies
12. Apartment security

One big amenity that small apartments may have as compared to the big complex is their smallness. They may be able, if designed and managed well, to offer the resident more privacy, a more "homey" atmosphere, and a better location. You should maximize this very valuable amenity. Plan the landscaping, decking, porches, and the like to take maximum advantage of this.

You should know every possible advantage your property has, and for *each* advantage you should be able to relate *several benefits* to your prospective tenant. Large rooms? Do not simply say, "See how large the bedroom is?" Rather, say, "These huge bedrooms mean that your king-size furniture will fit nicely with room to spare." Or, perhaps, "These extra-large bedrooms give you room to spread out—no cramped feeling here." Stress benefits to your prospective tenant, not facts.

Know Your Competition

The best way to gain knowledge of your competition is to visit them! Take a look, not once but regularly. Your competition can be divided into two kinds—direct and indirect. The closest and most obvious competition is, of course, those other apartments much like yours that offer basically the same accommodations at about the same price. The indirect competition will be other apartments that do not attract the same market. Either their units are priced quite a bit higher or lower or they appeal to other types of people. You may be able to arrange a working relationship with your indirect competitors. They can be of help to you and you may be of help to them.

You should arrange to swap leads—even swap names of repairpersons and workers. The direct competition should be "shopped" regularly. Any advertising material used by your competitors as well as their newspaper ads should be collected and saved for reference.

To shop competitors, start by collecting data such as advertising material and ads in the newspapers. Next, visit to "look-em over." A competitor form should be filled out on *every* competitor. Remember that the more you know about the competition the better able you are to "sell" your own units. This marketing approach may not seem too important when the market is firm with few if any vacancies. But, when the trends change, as they inevitably do, you will find that to be competitive you need to know this information.

You may even ask a friend or relative to be your comparison shopper and to assist you in filling out the competition offers and what they charge. If you keep up to date, you will know when prices change and can react at once. One other advantage of this exhaustive survey is the mental advantage it gives you. You are psychologically prepared to meet the prospective tenant because you know your strong points and weak points and just what your competition offers.

Know the Community

The other set of data you need, in addition to knowing all about your own complex and your competitors, is a thorough knowledge of your community. If an apartment owner or manager can tell a prospective tenant all about the community—especially if she or he can relate it to that complex—the owner-manager has a much better chance of leasing up quickly and remaining 100 percent occupied. Usually the leasing decision is not made on any one point but is the result of several little things. The more professional you seem in your management the more assured your prospective tenant will be concerning good management. Many people have a good deal of experience with apartment living, and they place more and more importance on adequate management.

Community Survey.   The best way to approach a community survey is to have a map of your area posted on a bulletin board in a common room or area of your complex if possible. If your apartments are not large enough for this, be sure that you go to the trouble to memorize the distance to various community services. The following list, by no means exhaustive, is a suggestion of some of the data that you need to know:

1. Income level—what type of people live in area
2. View (if any)
3. Shopping
4. Transportation
5. Schools
6. Churches
7. Employment
8. Fire and police
9. Medical and dental emergency services
10. Recreation facilities
11. Child care services
12. Local government offices—with a list of things to do (drivers licenses, voting registrations)
13. Utilities services (if needed)
14. Liabilities of area (if any)
15. Points of interest and amenities in area
16. Noise level in area

For example, if you have a view, be very sure to use it! Do not assume that your prospective tenants can see it. Point it out. Make sure that they know what they are looking at—not just the mountains but Rich Mountain or Ski Mountain. If you do not have a particularly exciting view, point out other advantages. Perhaps you have a nice yard with flower beds or large private patios. Remember, be aggressive in showing your property. Is it clean and well maintained, is the lawn well sodded and cut? If you have done your job well you should have no need of apologies for the property and should be proud to show it off.

Immediate Community.   What kind of people live in your immediate area—students, older people? Is the area residential, apartment, mixed, or commercial? Close to a university? What is the average person in your area like? Remember, people usually prefer to live around people like themselves—students prefer to live close to other students, older people close to other older people, and so on.

PROPERTY MARKETING

It is highly artificial to separate marketing from other aspects of good management. In fact, this separation is only made in writings such as this—never in reality. With this in mind we will proceed to examine the methodology of marketing in more detail. The first requirement has been to gain knowledge—knowledge about yourself, your competition, and your community.

Renting an apartment should be approached with thought. The way you place it on the market may well determine whether it rents well. How do you "place" an apartment on the market? The very first step in this process is to decide to whom you want to rent. It is usually not wise to simply say, "Here it is, the rent is $225 per month." It is far better to pick the type of resident that you want to attract and to then design a marketing campaign to attract that particular group of people. Technically this is called "market segmentation." All it really means is that you feel that you can more effectively market your complex to a smaller group of people who have some common characteristics. For example, you may decide to appeal to students, older retired couples, or young married couples with small children. Can you see that you might do things differently in appealing to these three groups? Your advertising copy would be different, it would be in different places, even your rent schedules may be set differently. All successful apartment complexes aim at specific markets or groups of people rather than a "shotgun" approach. An apartment cannot be all things to all people —you must design it with one group, or, at most, a few groups or types of people, in mind.

Once you have decided whom you want to rent to, you immediately narrow your decision problems. You cannot design effective advertising without knowing the target. When writing any advertising copy—newspaper, bulletins, radio, T.V., whatever—there is a vital point to keep in mind. This is the difference between features and benefits.

Features and Benefits

All apartments have features: large 12-foot by 15-foot bedrooms, tiled baths, brand new units, tile floor in baths, carpet in other rooms, storage rooms or attic storage, and so on. Features are details about your complex—usually physical. *Features do not sell!* Benefits sell. Benefits result from features.

To use the previous examples, a large 12-foot by 15-foot bedroom does not really sell your apartment. But, if you say "lovely 12-foot by 15-foot bedrooms allow plenty of space for your king-size bedroom suite," you are more persuasive. "The beautiful ceramic tile is easily cleaned" sells an apartment more effectively than a simple statement of fact. Convert your features into benefits for your customers. Do not make them do *your* work.

Now that you have an idea of *whom* you are selling to and *what* you are selling, it is time to go to work!

Advertising of apartments does not sell (or should not)! No ad in any paper *ever* rented an apartment. Advertisement merely brings people to your property or causes them to phone for more information—its main purpose. *You* are supposed to sell the apartment, not the ad. You want interested prospects to come look and thus give you an opportunity to sell to them. How do you convince them to call or drop by?

Attention, interest, desire, and action are the four words to live by. Any ad must attract a prospect's *attention;* it must cause him or her to become *interested* after that. If it is good enough it will generate a *desire* for more information, thus causing the prospect to take *action*—a phone call or a visit.

The ad's headline grabs the prospect's attention via a wanted and believable benefit. (Your knowledge of to whom you are appealing makes it easier to pick a benefit that is "wanted.") With good layout, correct use of white space, and proper positioning, the headline reaches out and grabs the reader's attention. A picture or line drawing sometimes helps.

Your message, or "copy," should provoke first interest and then desire. It should prove your headline benefit and translate the benefit to your reader's interest. If possible, additional benefits should be presented in the same way—strong subheads, then the expansion of the statement. Be careful not to put too much data in the advertisement.

The action element of the model can be very specific—"call Mr. Bill Weaver at 262-2147 today." It may simply be implied by listing the address and phone number.

For this attention/interest/desire/action model to work for you, the copy should use emotionally motivating words. Each benefit must be described so that your reader feels a strong emotional pull to your property. The following list is intended to be a guide in your thinking—see how many more you can add.

Atmosphere	*Atmosphere (cont.)*
Luxury or deluxe	Cheerful
Quiet	Picture window
Artistic	View of bay, ocean, lake, etc.
Fine view	Secluded
Attractive	Professional and business people
Set in garden	New area
Charming neighborhood	Residential
Resort	Friendly
Luxurious	Unusually large
Spotlessly clean	Casual luxury

Atmosphere (cont.)

Convenient
Sunny
Lovely
Executive
Pleasant
Restful
Desirable
Exciting
Delightful
Excellent planning
Quiet and countrylike
Picturesque and exclusive
Many luxury extras
Efficient management
Individual privacy
Gracious living
Uniquely designed

Atmosphere (cont.)

True adult living
Centrally located
Space and quality
Newly landscaped
Easy, relaxed living
Homey feeling
Charming setting
No pool, quiet adult living
Restful and secluded
New fashion in modern living
Desired quiet
Sunny and cheerful
Restful
Peaceful
Carefully planned
Flexible living room
Security patrol

Location

Easy commuting
Easy access to freeway
Bus at door
Near shops
Near schools
Hillside view
Above reproach
Easy to shopping
Near university or college

Condition

Newly furnished
Redecorated
New building
Sound conditioning
Newly painted
Very clean
Sparkling

Luxuries

Private balcony or terrace
  or patio
Enclosed garage
Maid service
Dressing room
Air conditioned
FM music
Switchboard
Elevator
Built-in stove and oven
Phone jacks
Parking attendant
Heated swimming pool
Garden patio

Decor

Chinese modern
Artist studio
Smartly furnished
Modern oriental
Open beam
Beam
French modern
Smart
Wood-paneled
Nylon carpeting, etc.
Custom drapes
Custom furniture
Knotty pine
Decorate to suit

Luxuries (cont.)
Play area fully equipped
Near recreation
Game room
Recreation room
Color TV in lobby

Recreation
Overlooks pool
Sports-minded
Patio
Barbecue
Sunny area
Exercise room
Billiards
Sauna bath
Putting greens
Social activities

Others
Spacious
Split level
View
Quiet

Decor (cont.)
Provincial
Styled by interior decorator
Sliding glass doors
Like home

Conveniences
Forced-air heat
Electric kitchen
Gas kitchen
Automatic washer and dryer
Telephone service
Free parking
Off-street parking
Private garage
Extra closets
Built-in TV antenna
Private entrance
Double entrance
Private storage
Extra telephone outlet

MEDIA ADVERTISING

There are many sources of advertising in the rental market. The professional must choose the most effective media source for the least cost. Because there is such a variety you must use thought in selection. Your prospective resident profile can help. Select the media to reach the people you want as residents in your apartments. The following is a list of advertising media available to apartment owners and managers (in approximately the frequency used):

1. Newspaper (classified and display)
2. Apartment signs
3. Highway signs
4. Banners
5. Flags and streamers
6. Directories
7. Brochures
8. Other outdoor and directional signs
9. Shopper publications

10. House organs
11. Radio and television
12. Magazines
13. Car cards
14. Bench cards
15. Flyers
16. Postcards
17. Advertising cards
18. Manager's card
19. Letterheads and sales letters
20. Word of mouth
21. Apartment locating services
22. Miscellaneous

No matter which medium or combination of media you choose, your copy should follow the model of attention, interest, desire, and action. The use of emotionally motivating adjectives will assist you in gaining interest. The design and structure of the ad will do the rest.

Newspaper

There are two general types of newspaper advertising: classified sections and display advertising. The classifieds are the single most useful and popular medium in use today because they are confined basically to the area that you are trying to reach (geographic area) and they are repetitive (every day). In addition, people are "trained" to look there when they are in search of an apartment. Thus your message gets to the people that you want to communicate with. Prospective renters use this medium as their number one source of available units.

Classified advertising is usually inexpensive relative to the exposure, but an apartment complex can sink a good sum into this area in a short time with little to show for it. One way to cut cost is the knowledge and use of *discounts*.

Most newspapers offer three types of discounts: cash, quantity, and frequency. In general, the more space you use the less expensive each column inch is. The same idea applies with the frequency concept. The more insertions of a particular ad, the less expensive the ad is. A cash discount, often expressed as 2 percent 10 net 30, for example, simply means that if you pay your bill during the first 10 days you receive a 2 percent discount. The full amount of the bill is due after 30 days. The amount of these discounts can be determined by obtaining the standardized publisher's advertising rate card from the newspaper advertising office. The newspaper sales office will supply you with rate cards as well as with other data concerning deadlines for receiving copy and extra charges for special services. Some can even give you data about readership audiences. Be sure that you use the current rates!

Attention is the single most important factor in any classified ad. Your copy is competing with hundreds of others. You must have some method of directing attention to your copy rather than to the competition's.

The three basic methods are (1) size of type, (2) white space, and (3) headlines. Attention methods can be listed and discussed separately, but they should always be used together. Make your type size different from that around your ad, use attention-getting headlines, and put white space or blank space on the top, bottom, and sides in a creative manner to grab the reader's attention.

Why is it so important that your ad stand out? Research has shown that the average apartment hunter picks out only a few ads that look especially attractive to call. If, after the phone conversation, they are still interested they go and see the apartments. Make sure that your number is one of the first that they call!

In addition to the wise use of the three methods of gaining attention, be very careful with the use of abbreviations. Take a look at most classified ads—often there are too many "ar's," "br's," "rms," "tl.fl.'s," and so on. Many times an ad can be made totally incomprehensible with the use of abbreviations. "BR" for bedroom is about the most commonly accepted abbreviation and should be the *only* one used. Why try to save a few cents and possibly lose your reader?

Remember that most apartment hunters will pick a few very attractive ads and then call about them. You must be prepared to sell your apartment on the phone when they call. Make sure that you have all the necessary data close at hand if you have not committed them to memory.

One last point to remember in classified ad design is that it is not good to advertise several apartments in the same ad. Much research shows that when two or more apartments (such as "one, two, and three bedrooms") are listed in the same ad, it loses much of its impact. People may wonder why you have so many vacancies. Most responses are negative to multiple apartment ads. Take a look at the really successful large complex. Many run separate ads for each apartment size and in separate locations (down the page or in another column altogether).

The other newspaper ad variety is what is known as the display ad. It can be found throughout the newspaper in any area. It can be any size up to two facing pages and often has great variety of type and illustrative work. Although the display ad can be quite expensive, it has a much better chance of gaining attention due to its placement (away from competing copy), size, and copy. Display ads are not used in everyday promotion unless problems are encountered in renting units. Openings, new units on the market, or attempts to reposition a complex in the market are typical reasons for using display ads.

Professional help is suggested for display ad composition, especially if artwork is required. An ad agency is usually a helpful source—many take a commission from the newspaper and thus are free (some will charge a small amount for the actual art layout). Many newspapers employ people to give you assistance in this area—check both before making a decision.

A constant check should be made on competitive advertising, especially display ads. They may serve as a tip-off to important changes in policies, rent schedules, market strategies, and the like.

Many newspapers have special sections that feature housing or even apartment housing. This is usually a good section to use because the people reading it are preselected. They are interested in housing or they would not be reading that section. Place display ads in this section if possible. Positioning your display ad is important, and the professionals can give you helpful advice. Sometimes special placement is more expensive, but, if you are going to the trouble and expense to have a display ad, then the extra placement charge is worth every cent.

Signs

One of the most important media for any apartment, large or small, is the sign. The sign on the premise states emphatically that "This Is an Apartment House." This is a very specialized area because the message must be short, distinctive, and understood in a very short period of time. Good design of an apartment sign is difficult and should be approached with much thought if not done by a professional.

Your sign should transmit an image that fits with the previously developed customer profile. Probably 70 percent of the signs now used are tasteless, ineffective, and unattractive—*and they do not work!*

It is surprising that a developer will spend a million dollars on a large complex and then use the cheapest, most ineffective sign obtainable. Signs should be refurbished or replaced at the first sign of wear! Cheap, weather-worn signs turn off prospects just when they need reinforcement—at the first sight of your property.

All signs should be integrated into the property. They should look built-in rather than tacked on. Your signs should look as if they belong. One of the most effective ways to accomplish this is by the use of a structure—a clock tower kind of building. If the property is large enough, some sort of entrance gate or structure can serve as an excellent location for a well-designed sign. The sign structure should be architecturally integrated into the style of the buildings or building that it advertises.

Good, effective lighting can and should be used to highlight your signs. Rather than flashing neon lights, tasteful spotlights tied in with landscaping efforts can create a sign that is even more effective at night than during the day. Any sign should be designed with enough flexibility to allow changes and updates.

Always check with your local zoning board and research the sign ordinances before ordering a sign. It can be expensive to erect a sign, and then have an official drop by with a request to remove it.

Another type of sign is the highway sign. It can be a large billboard or a smaller sign on the side of a local highway. The billboard is usually too expensive for an apartment complex for the results it can generate. The smaller signs, however, can be extremely useful. Commonly known as directional signs, these smaller signs can be a help in directing traffic to your location. It is not uncommon for people who were looking for another property to stop at a complex whose directional signs are clear and effective. Usually these signs are owned by the complex and space is rented near main travel routes. The sign should be professionally done, weatherproof, and *very* clear as to directions.

Banners and Streamers

Banners are little used in the apartment business, because they usually do not fit into the image that you are trying to establish. Banners tend to be cheap looking. Use them, if you must, for initial openings only.

Streamers are much like banners—they should be used only at openings or at upgradings where you are trying to convey the idea that what you are offering is new. They do attract attention—especially with a breeze—and can be useful in special situations. They are not for everyday use.

Directories

There are two kinds of directories: the familiar Yellow Pages, and, in some cases, special apartment guides published to help people locate apartments. Usually you are asked to purchase space—the guide is then filled with useful information about the community and distributed free from area motels, restaurants, and other locations. This can be a good buy if the advertising cost is low.

The Yellow Pages is yet another source of advertising. You will rarely gain new prospects from such a listing, but it aids in establishing your property in the market. A display ad is relatively expensive, but in a very competitive market one can be a good purchase.

You are entitled to a one-line listing in the Yellow Pages if the complex has a business phone. For a small extra charge, you can have it placed in bold-face type—a good buy.

Brochures

One of the most useful elements in advertising media is the brochure, defined as printed material about an apartment. The most popular size is 8½ by 11 inches (standard letter size) although almost every size imaginable has been successfully used. The letter size will fit into standard envelopes, packets, and racks with ease and usually offers enough space to get your message across. It is also the least expensive size to print.

The brochure faces all the problems that any other advertisement faces—it must cover features and benefits about your property in a tasteful way. Any image can be produced; professional advice may be needed if you desire a very special image that is a cut above the competition. Photographs of common areas will say more about your property far better than any copy. Pools, tennis courts, and other recreational areas can be marketed far more effectively with a photograph. Save the copy for benefits inherent to each apartment (ice makers, self-cleaning ovens, dishwashers, and so on).

Always have a map to show your location. The name, phone number, and address should also appear on any brochure. Almost any format can be used effectively, from one-sheet brochures to a 5- or 10-page booklet. The larger the property, the more space needed—especially if the amenities are large in number.

Remember to supply *every* prospect with a brochure! Never let a "looker" leave without taking one, since lookers often become buyers later on. They often can influence others to consider your property just by showing them the brochure. People will often shop several locations and then sit quietly at home and discuss the advantages and disadvantages of each before making a decision. A good brochure will help them to remember all the advantages of your property.

Shopper Publications

Shopper publications are largely an unexplored area. Given the opportunity, give them a try and see what kind of results you get. Be sure that you use the same guidelines in writing copy that you would use for any newspaper ad.

House Organs

House organs, or publications by a company for its employees, can be very helpful if you can get space in them. These periodicals do not, as a general rule, accept advertising. Your best chance is at opening time or when you are announcing a new project. Any kind of human interest story will usually be accepted if it pertains, somehow, to either the subject company or one of its employees. This is usually very fine advertising if you are able to secure it.

Radio and Television

Normally neither radio nor television serve our purpose. They do not reach the audience that is searching for a home. They reach too large an audience over too large an area and require too large an outlay from our advertising budgets.

In smaller towns with lower air costs, a local radio station (AM or FM) may be considerably more helpful. If the copy is well designed the image of your property may be improved significantly. Always use radio on weekends—it is much more effective than midweek. Use it for the last 2 weeks of the month, not the first 2. People who shop for an apartment usually do so during this last 2-week period.

Magazines

Magazines are very rarely used for apartment advertising, since they also reach the wrong audience.

Car Cards

Car cards are advertising done on buses or streetcars in urban areas. The advertiser leases space from the transit company for a message. Costs are relatively high because of design cost and lease cost, and coverage is spotty. Bench card advertising is much the same except the message is painted on transit car seats. These two media are definitely to be avoided for medium- or higher-priced units but may be effective in reaching the lower-priced segment of the market.

Flyer

A flyer is a less expensive brochure designed to be distributed in quantity—an announcement medium. Usually flyers are inexpensive handouts designed to be spread around in all sorts of places—gasoline stations, laundry facilities, motels and hotels—any high traffic area. Make sure that your flyer is printed not mimeographed. Printing looks much better and costs only pennies more.

Postcards and Advertising Cards

Useful in promoting the image of a complex, the glossy postcard is lithographed in full color with a high-gloss photograph of your complex.

It has the photo on the face and a short sales message on the reverse side. These postcards are usually distributed to motels, hotels, residences, and so on. Each time they are used you receive good word-of-mouth advertising. Advertising cards are much like the high-quality postcard but less expensive because of the absence of the photograph. Depending on the segment of the market that you are trying to capture, either type of card can be effective.

The Manager's Card

The manager's business card can be very effective in promoting your property. All resident managers should have cards with the name of the property, address, phone number, and, of course, their name. If you use a fold-out card you have plenty of room for a message, map, if needed, list of benefits, and the like. Be sure to have it done by a professional—you want it well designed; use a quality printer.

Letterhead and Sales Letters

Depending on the type of market you are trying to reach, letterhead stationery can be of tremendous value. If you are oriented toward the top end of the market, tasteful, well-designed letterhead stationery distributed to your present residents can be one of the best media available. Every time a resident writes a letter to a friend in town you receive good advertising to the very group of people that you want to reach (people like your present residents). Printing letterhead in large quantities costs relatively little per hundred and will make a very impressive holiday gift from the management to the residents. This will assist in promoting good word of mouth. A little public relations effort on your part will pay off in better resident relations and, at the same time, provide great promotion possibilities. This same letterhead can be used to develop a sales letter to groups of people—newlyweds, companies, professionals, and so on. This medium can be extremely useful if well done.

Word of Mouth

In the long run, this is one of the most powerful advertising media available to anyone. Word of mouth, if it is good, can persuade people to move into your property more effectively than any other medium. People believe other people, especially friends, above any other media. If your present residents are "plugging" for you, you will have a step on any competition. Many complexes reward their residents for bringing in their friends by free rent or even cash. Whatever method you choose, if any, make sure that your residents are *for* instead of *against* you and your property.

Apartment Locating Service

In some areas, especially urban areas, there are firms that specialize in helping people find suitable housing. They operate on a no-charge basis to their client, and they are paid by the apartment owners. If your area has these types of services, make sure that you know every one of them. More important, make sure that each and every one of them know *you* and your property. Sell them on your apartments. The more sold they are on your property the better they will be able to sell their clients. It is hard to overestimate the value that these people have to the average apartment complex. Apartment managers usually are only too anxious to cooperate in hard times with apartment locating services, but they tend to become less than cooperative when occupancy rates are high. In the long run it is best to remain on good terms all the time.

Miscellaneous

The professional apartment owner or manager will come to know many people in the process of managing a property. The following are some of the persons you should call on.

Personnel directors of area companies or anyone involved in relocation services for local industries and businesses should be contacted. The professional manager should have a planned program of *personal* calls to meet and develop all these contacts. Sell your property to these people. Work with them. If they need an apartment for one of their new executives for a month or two, provide it if possible. Bend a little for them and they may help you quite a bit.

Have you ever met a couple who were just going to stay a couple of months to house hunt and, a year later, are still looking? And still renting? It happens!

Many companies have training programs—they bring several employees in for months at a time. Once the first group leaves a new crew comes in. It may even be possible to rent several units at a time for a long-term period at higher than normal rental rates to groups like this.

Hotel and motel personnel can help send you prospects. New people come into town and stay at area motels. If the management has advertising materials available they can often refer prospects to you. Return the favor!

Moving companies and neighborhood merchants should have a personal call from the professional manager. These people can often put in a good word for you if approached properly. It may be possible to work out advertising deals with these local merchants so that you distribute special coupons for these merchants to your residents. This adds to the image of your apartment property.

If your properties are near military reservations or military bases, it is wise to meet the base officer in charge of housing. Many times officers require off-base housing, and if you have built up a good relationship with the housing officer you may get more than your share of the business. You need a military lease for this. It is simply a conventional lease that allows the lessee to break the lease with no penalty if their orders move them from the city.

One last point about the various media: local newspapers can be useful if you are able to give them a usable copy. A well-written story (with several glossy 8- by 10-inch photos) about your new complex or about a new opening of a recreation building, child development center, or the like is always welcome. You can usually purchase low-cost reprints to use as handouts for traffic passing through the property.

Proper use of the various media in your particular situation depends on how well they perform for you. *Always* find out how well each ad works. Ask each person that comes to you, "How did you find out about our apartments?" Keep tabs on the answers. They tell you how well you are spending your advertising budget.

Provided that you use good copy in effective media, you will cause a prospect to either visit your property or call for more information. This phone call is your chance to sell the prospect not on your apartment but on a visit to your property. Rarely, if ever, will you rent an apartment over the phone. You must convince the prospect to visit your property and try to gain some information concerning the prospect's needs.

The telephone company has developed a set of helpful hints for building effective telephone techniques:

1. Be alert; do not act sleepy or uninterested.

2. Be pleasant; no grumpy "hello, who is this?" *Smile*, it will show up in your voice.

3. Be natural; use normal words—no slang or technical terms.

4. Be expressive; do not speak in a monotone—vary the pitch and volume of your speech.

5. Be distinct; try not to slur words or speak with too much of an accent.

6. Be polite.

Always answer the phone with the name of your apartment and then your name: "Good morning, Old Town Apartments, Bill Weaver speaking." End this greeting with a rising inflection in your voice and it will almost always generate a very positive response. You have given the caller information that he or she needs—the name of your apartment house and your name. You will find it easy, now, to ask the caller's name.

Always have paper, pencils, a map, and your latest advertisement control form by your phone. Write down the caller's name and, as the conversation develops, jot down any additional information that you get—where caller is from, names of children, name of employer; you might even have a small pad printed with a short form.

SELLING

Once you have the prospect at your property you have the opportunity to go to work. How do you sell an apartment? You don't! An apartment should sell itself, with a little help from you.

The first step is to sit down and list every feature of your property (Figure 34-1).

After examining each feature, place a +, a 0, or a − beside each. In short, is this feature better than, less than, or equal to that of the competition? By looking down this list and adding up the symbols, you can get a quick idea of how your property compares with its competition.

Once you have a complete list of your features, develop a series of benefits for each feature (Figure 34-2). Benefits, as you remember, are expansions of features. For example, an ice maker is a feature. Benefits of one would be (1) plenty of ice for parties, (2) lots of ice for homemade ice cream, (3) ice always available with no messy breaking of cubes out of ice trays. Further expand each benefit by telling just what the benefit will mean to the prospect. Use the sample form to come up with at least three benefits for each feature. Know these benefits, and use them in describing your property.

Never merely say that "the bedroom is 13 feet by 16 feet." Say instead that "the 13-foot by 16-foot bedroom is so large that you can have a complete king-size bedroom suite and still have plenty of room for a love seat or easy chair and reading table." This brings the message home. Many people have trouble visualizing a room's size even if they are looking at a vacant one. Your visual picture of a large bedroom with certain furnishing is not only more appealing but easier to comprehend.

There are always some good features to talk about, and there usually are some bad ones as well. You must be able to unsell the bad features just as well (or better) as you sell the good ones. List your bad features

	+		0		−
Pool					
Private patio, balcony, terrace					
Tennis court					
Laundry facilities					
Enclosed garage					
Maid service					
Putting greens					
Dressing rooms for pool					
Air conditioning					
FM music system					
Switchboard					
Elevators					
Barbecues for residents					
Children's plat areas					
Baby-sitting service					
Child development center					
Refrigerator (+ for larger than average, − for smaller)					
Stove (+ for deluxe, − for less than average)					
Dishwasher					
Garbage disposal					
Trash compactor					
Game room for adults					
Recreation room (bar, etc.)					
Exercise room					
Saunas					
Open beam construction					
Carpets					
Closets (+ for larger than average, − for smaller)					
Bedrooms					
Living rooms					
Dining rooms					
Kitchen					
Built-in television antenna, cable					
Double entrance					
Private storage					
Security patrol					
Others					

Figure 34-1 Market comparison.

just as you did the positive ones and design at least three logical ways of handling each one. It is vital to anticipate tough questions and to have a ready answer.

Any apartment has positive features. Any apartment has negative features. Be able to maximize your positive features with long lists of benefits. Also be able to minimize your negative features. How you do

Features: _____

    Benefit 1. _____

              _____

              _____

    Benefit 2. _____

              _____

              _____

    Benefit 3. _____

              _____

              _____

Features: _____

_____

_____

Figure 34-2   Unit benefits.

this is critical. Try to turn a negative into a positive: "No, Mr. Prospect, we do not have townhouses—all our apartments are designed without steep stairs. No stairs to climb a dozen times a day and no worry about falling."

CLOSING

Although there are many different closing methods, perhaps one of the most effective and easiest is to assume that the sale is made. Once you have shown the grounds and the model merely pick up a copy of your lease, hand it to your prospect, and say, "Why don't you look over this while I get this application form filled out?" If you say it as if it were commonplace, very casual and low key, it will work well. This is a low-key, high-pressure close. Low key because the prospect does not feel that you are pressuring her or him, and high pressure in that you are forcing the prospect to decide one way or another. If the prospect says nothing continue with your personal data questions and get a signature on the lease. If the prospect objects, act surprised and ask why not. The prospect will then come up with an objection—a reason for not renting. If it is an easy objection (one arising out of a misunderstanding or from a fact that you failed to discuss) answer it directly and return to the close. If it is a difficult objection, minimize it by stating some offsetting advantages and then return to the close. Your prospect may come up with several objections—handle them all in this manner, always returning to the close. Eventually the real reason for not renting will surface. If you recognize that it is a really important objection, concentrate especially hard on your answer. Recap the features and benefits that seemed to appeal to your prospect and then close in the same manner.

This sale-is-made technique is quite powerful in *any* sales situation (more information may be obtained from *Salespersonship* by William C. Weaver). It should be practiced until it is second nature.

Once a prospect is sold there is but one last step—that of processing the application. Never heard of an application? Always just filled out the lease right on the spot? How much money has your property lost due to poor tenant selection, lost rents, legal fees, time lost, and just plain bother? Tenant selection is as important to profits as the sales process. It is not profitable to fill up your property and then have to evict people right and left for one reason or another. It also is costly to your image. It is far better to concentrate on selecting good people initially. If you follow good marketing practices, you will have plenty from which to make your selection.

Tenant selection process is a three-step process: (1) a prospective resident signs the lease (you do not), fills out a personal credit and data form, pays a deposit, and receives a receipt; (2) you or a credit agency checks out the person's background as thoroughly as possible; (3) you notify the prospective resident whether she or he is accepted and either give him or her the signed lease or return the deposit.

You are using your lease as a closing tool. You hand the prospect the lease while you fill out a rental application. You should have a printed lease that looks professional and is legal. As you might surmise, the lease should be very tight and binding. Lessee and lessor should go over each section carefully, rather than hiring a lawyer to take care of a misunderstanding that was caused either by a weak form or by your not covering something that should have been covered.

While the prospect is looking over the actual lease you should be filling out the tenant information sheet. You can fill out the prospect's name, last address, bank, employer, and so on. Just go down the form asking questions and printing the answers. Once you have completed the form, hand it to the prospect to verify the correctness of the data and sign it. You then proceed to fill out the lease. After completing the lease go over each basic item entered by hand and explain just what is there and why. Then go over each section of the lease. Explain in plain terms what the lease says. Hand the prospect the lease and a pen and *shut up!* Do not talk at all until the prospect either signs or asks a question. Answer the question if asked and again shut up. This approach forces the prospect to make a decision; if you approach this closing technique with confidence it will be successful 90 percent of the time!

When your new residents sign the lease, give them a receipt for the deposit and whatever prorated rental that is agreed on. Be sure to ask them to write on the check, "For $_____ deposit on apartment #_____ and for prorated rental from _____ to _____." This is the best receipt available once you have cashed it.

Once you have a signed lease (signed by all parties who will live there), a properly completed application form, and a deposit, check on the applicant. This credit and "behavioral pattern" check is the most important step in the process. This is where you weed out the undesirable—not via an eviction suit. You can either do it yourself or have it done. You may want to investigate the local credit agencies and see if they can furnish the information that you require. You want some idea of their creditworthiness and of their past behavior. If credit agencies can supply all the data you need, you may find it less expensive in the long run to let them do it.

If the information you need is not available from an agency, then the job falls to you. There are five areas to investigate.

1. What debts are outstanding—can the prospect afford to pay rent in addition to other debts?

2. Are all parties employed? Where? Can you verify employment? Are jobs short term or long term? How long have they been employed there? What is gross income?

3. Check the bank references—what kind of account does the prospect have? Has the prospect ever had insufficient funds to cover a check? What is the average balance in the account?

4. Where are the prospects living now; where did they live before that? The last is important, since the previous manager may give a more accurate report of behavior than the present one.

5. Check out personal references. Who are they? What kind of people are they?

Never use this behavior and credit check to discriminate against any minority, no matter how easy it appears to be to do so. If you are going to use this resident selection concept at all, it *must* be applied across the board. You should have a definite list of requirements to be met. You may want to attach a small form to each receipt given to prospective residents that says that all applications will be checked and the reasons they will not be accepted are the following:

1. No job
2. Job less than 1 year

3. Income less than four times monthly rent
4. More than four in the family
5. Bad credit report
6. No credit at all
7. Incorrect information on application
8. Bad reference from former manager

This is just a sample list. Remember that you must treat everyone alike. If you turn away one family because of poor credit, you must turn away all who have poor credit.

Realistically, it is a value judgment on your part as to who has poor credit, but, with a systematic approach, you will have documentation that you follow the open housing law to the letter.

ACCEPTANCE OR REJECTION

The last step in the tenant selection process is the ratification of acceptance or rejection via a form letter. You can write a simple note saying that all the paper work has been completed and that the application has been approved. In the letter you should mention the date that the prospects are to take occupancy, the amount that they have paid as a deposit, the rent, and the due date. In rejecting an application you must protect yourself from legal action if at all possible. The form letter should be short and to the point. "Dear _____, The information we have does not meet our requirements for tenancy at this time. We are enclosing your deposit which was made by your check #_____, dated _____ in the amount of _____." Never put the reason unless the applicant requests it. If possible, discuss reasons in person rather than in writing.

Two points to remember in the resident selection process: Keep copies of everything and keep all information confidential. Never give out specifics about a prospective resident to anyone. For that matter, never give out specifics about a present resident to anyone. If someone inquires (a credit bureau, for example) about a resident (present or past) give only general details: tell them that the person either has or has not lived up to the lease agreement. Period. No specific details.

CONCLUSIONS ON MARKETING

We have discussed what is necessary to successfully market an apartment property. You must know not only your own property and surrounding community but your competitor's property as well. Once you have these basic facts in mind you can start developing a profile of the ideal resident. The more you know about this person the better your marketing efforts can be. This is called "segmenting" the market. Breaking the market down into smaller groups of people that are closely alike and orienting your total marketing effort toward them is one of the more frequent consulting assignments that any marketing person has. It is important to know your target market so that you can correctly orient your advertising media with the rest of the marketing effort. This is of *prime* importance in complex development and design. Pick a target market (one that meets certain criteria), design the amenities just for the segment, and prerent 90 percent of your units!

The discussion of advertising media touched on a few practical points to remember about the various media. Make certain that your use of media matches your resident profile; that is, be sure to advertise in places that are most likely to be read by the type of person that you want as a resident.

Finally, have a good, legally binding lease, explain it throughly to your residents, and then live by it!

MANAGEMENT AND MARKETING

Every apartment house has certain rules and regulations—or should have. These should be formalized and printed in quantity to hand out to each new resident. One of the best ways to do this is in the form of a letter welcoming the new family and outlining the regulations; for example:

> This letter is to welcome you to Old Town, your new home. The owners and management wish you to have a comfortable and pleasant home here and have provided several features to help accomplish this. These features were designed for *you* and we would like to take this chance to tell you about them:
> Car washing—We have set aside an area where *all* car washing must be done. Water and hoses have been provided for your convenience. Please wash down the area after you have finished so that it is clean for the next person.

This is just the start of what can and should be a rather lengthy list of suggestions and regulations. For example, these are some areas that may need coverage:

1. Regulations for visitors
2. Storage space—how used

3. Delivery service
4. Laundry room—where, rules
5. TV antennas—OK?
6. Signs
7. Window coverings
8. Additional light fixtures
9. Pets OK? rules?
10. Phone installation—extra
11. Salespersons permitted
12. Children's toys
13. Availability of vacuum cleaners and waxers
14. Vacation—notify if away for long period
15. Extra locks OK?
16. Bicycles OK? where?
17. Pool regulations
18. Keys—lost? more?
19. Maid service
20. Parking regulations
21. Water beds permitted? rules?

All these areas should be discussed if they apply. Since these areas are so important you may want to send the letter via registered mail so that new residents must sign for it. The little additional cost is worth impressing residents with the importance of the material.

Residents with children often have special problems. You may consider preparing a special sheet of regulations just for people with children regarding toys, play areas, special pool regulations, and so on. If this is done in a manner that reflects management concern over the health and safety of the children, then it will be well received by the new family.

When you give residents the keys to their new home, take them to the apartment and give them an orientation tour. Show them that they are receiving the apartment in good repair. Show them the circuit breaker box and how it works. Show them any reset buttons on any of the appliances in the apartment (garbage disposal, water heater, and so on). Explain the air conditioning controls, timer units, parking spaces—everything that they need to know to live in their new home. This tour may take an hour or so, but it is time well spent.

The better oriented the resident is, the less trouble he or she will have, the less trouble you will have, and the longer he or she will stay. It is far better to have a person renew than for you to have to rent the property again.

To achieve a high renewal rate make sure that your present residents are happy. Once a year send in a painter to touch up the walls with fresh paint. Have the carpets steam-cleaned regularly. Respond to maintenance requests rapidly.

The last subject discussed under resident policies is rent collection. This is, by its very nature, a recurring problem. A specific policy should be established and followed.

The first step in collection of late rent begins before you rent an apartment. Tell the prospect that the rent is due and payable on a certain date each month. Read the area in the lease that discusses the rent, emphasizing again the due date. When the resident is notified of acceptance, repeat the rent due date. On the orientation tour of the new home, repeat again when the rent is due, where, and what it will cost if it is late.

Let every resident know that you stand firm on late rent collection. If a resident is a day late, he or she must pay the late charge. Once you take this attitude, keep it up. Once the residents find out that you mean it, you will be paid on time.

However, from time to time, you will find a few who will not pay on time. You should have specific procedures to follow in this case. For example:

1.   A phone call 2 days after the deadline to remind the residents
2.   A written notice 5 days after the deadline
3.   A written notice (registered) 10 days after the deadline

The phone call can be a friendly call just to remind the person who is forgetful. If the resident promises to "send it in right away" but does not, the written note is more formal and legal sounding. "As per our phone conversation on _____ you promised to send in your rental payment of $_____ for the month of _____. We have not received it. We are required to report to the owner at once, thus we are requesting immediate payment."

This note usually brings immediate response if the phone call failed, but you should have a third and last letter ready just in case: "We still have not received your rental payment for the month of _____ for $_____. We have talked with you by phone, written you a note, and still no results. This oversight on your part will not permit you to remain as an acceptable resident. If your rent of $_____ plus $_____ late fee (plus any other fee your lease calls for) is not received in this office today, we are required to enter into the legal proceedings necessary to protect the owner's interests." The wording plus the special delivery status usually works.

Although a strict collection policy and a very formal timetable are important, flexibility should be built in. If a resident comes to you with a reason why the rent cannot be paid (providing it is not a frequent occurrence) and asks for time, if possible, give it—but only once!

There are times when a resident will pay with a bad check. If this happens, the following procedure may be used: (1) Call the bank and make sure it is not their mistake and ask if the check will be honored now. If so, take it down personally, at once, and cash it. If this is the first time it has happened with this resident, do not mention it to them. Keep a record, however. (2) If the check will still not clear go directly to the resident. Tell her or him that the check was returned and ask if the check will clear now. (Do this just after your conversation with the bank—you know that the check will *not* clear.) Once the resident answers you can get an idea of the character of the person. If the person says, "Yes, it will clear now," you can then ask, "Have you made a deposit today? I just called the bank and they said that there are insufficient funds!" This puts the resident on the hot seat and you will usually get the truth! (3) If the reason for the bad check is a short supply of money, arrange some method of partial payment. In the future you may want to require cash or certified checks. Remember not to come on too strong the first time. Insist that any late charges be paid, but do not require cash and so on. Your response should be a graduated one—gentle at first but getting stronger and stronger. If you do take a partial payment, be sure that the receipt describes, in detail, the situation.

In general, a set of definite rules and regulations contributes to the well-managed property. The better your residents follow the rules, the happier everyone will be. Do not, however, interfere in the residents' rights and privileges under the leasehold. There can be too many rules, and they can be too strict and thus oppressive.

RECORDKEEPING

Once a property has been successfully marketed, a property owner must maintain current information concerning operations to manage the property, ensure maximum return on the investment, and prevent waste or theft. Other than a personal, physical inspection of the property, an owner's only guide comes from analysis of the records of operations.

The owner's bookkeeper or tax accountant should establish an initial set of books to record the original acquisition of the property and to provide an accounting record of operations for tax purposes. This should include establishing depreciation methods and bases tailored to the owner's particular financial position. A chart of accounts can also be established at this time.

A minimal set of records designed to give maximum control with a minimum of clerical work follows. Maintain all records on an up-to-the-minute basis.

1. The rent receipt is prepared by the manager whenever rent is received. Use standard triplicate receipt forms. Be sure to void bad copies. The resident gets the original, the duplicate is posted to an apartment record card and monthly rent report and then, together with bank deposit receipt, sent to owner. The third copy should remain in receipt book.

2. The bank deposit is prepared for each deposit on a bank-supplied form that provides for a detailed listing of each check or money order. Give the original to the bank, have the duplicate stamped by bank, and forwarded to the owner with duplicate rent receipts. Keep the third copy for on-site property records.

3. The apartment record card is a permanent record of all information regarding each apartment, its tenant, receipts, major expenditures, and so on. The card is prepared from the lease when a new resident moves in. Post rent receipts to this from duplicate rent receipt and all major expenditures from the job work order.

4. The monthly rent report is prepared by the manager to provide control of income and occupancy. It should be posted monthly from rent receipt. Owner should get the original, duplicate goes to accountant, and triplicate is a file copy.

5. The job work order is prepared by the manager to control work of maintenance, repair, cleaning, and so on. This should be for other than normal upkeep and special maintenance requirements. The original goes to the owner, the duplicate to workers. Maintenance workers record what was done, materials used, and cost, and return it to the manager. This is then posted to the apartment control card and then sent to the owner.

6. The weekly vacancy report is prepared by the manager once a week to report vacancies and collections. The original goes to the owner. The copy is kept by the manager as a file copy.

7. The petty cash report is prepared by the manager to report reimbursement of petty cash expenditures. The owner gets the original, the copy stays in the manager's file.

8. The furniture inventory control is prepared and maintained by the manager to control stock of furniture not in use.

9. The stock control card is prepared and maintained by the manager to control stock of consumable supplies and equipment.

Chapter **35**

Marketing Condominiums

Ray Watt   Chairman of the Board and Chief Executive Officer, Watt Industries

O ur company began working with condominiums in the latter part of 1959, when we discovered that we were having a problem building a home that people could afford. There were two aspects to this: price and financing. We discovered that through the development of condominiums we could deliver a product that was price competitive and for which buyers could more readily qualify.

To familiarize ourselves with the concept, we went on tours of those parts of the country, specifically Baltimore and New England, where there had been condominium development. We also researched what the costs were and whether we could develop workable management arrangements. Ultimately what we were searching for was a method of selling the product to the consumer.

The biggest problem revolved around lenders. In particular, we had difficulty convincing West Coast lenders that condominiums would sell. (In fact, we originally intended to build co-ops on the West Coast. When we discovered how reluctant lenders were to loan on them, we decided to go with condominiums.) We spent a great deal of time with Home Savings and Loan and Southern California Savings and Loan associations. They were enthused by the idea, and we launched our first condominium programs.

At the time, in the early 1960s, there were very few people involved in the industry. Initially there were about five major builders interested in condominium development. After some preliminary work, we discovered that interest had mushroomed.

There had been so much publicity about condominiums (condos) that builders thought they were going to be a panacea for their housing problems. By 1964 a great many lenders began making loans. We began working with the Federal Housing Administration (FHA) and the Veterans Administration (VA) and got them to modify their regulations so that they would also make loans.

NEED

The basic need for condos came from the fact that the building industry could no longer build a product that the consumer could afford to buy. As land prices continued to go up and as municipalities upgraded and put greater fees and charges on individual lots, builders needed new techniques to maintain a sales price people could afford. This brought about pressures to form more communal living, and the result was the condominium.

PUBLIC ACCEPTANCE

The consumer initially resisted condo living. It was only in the inner areas of the city where land costs were high that there was any affirmative response, and that was to "townhouses." In the suburbs, however, people would not buy condos unless they were priced about one-third below the price of comparable single-family homes.

However, by the middle to late 1970s condos could be sold for prices comparable to houses in suburban areas. Of course by then lot prices had gone up fourfold in southern California, and building single-family homes became unrealistic in many areas.

Today the consumer has totally accepted the condominium, because it is a product the consumer can afford. However, benefits (recreation such as horse facilities, swimming, tennis, golf, and so on) to make consumers purchase are still necessary. Because of the desire for privacy, many consumers still feel that they are giving up something when they buy a condo. Active condominium home owners associations that create successful condo projects have been a marketing necessity. The home owners associations decide how they want to run the development, how they want to assess themselves, and what kind of social programs they should develop for the benefit of all. Because of the work of the home owners associations, the consumer can enjoy condo living in any price category, if he or she wants to participate. In today's condominium development, the overall family has much more to receive because of the nature of a planned community (which offers recreational and other activities).

FUTURE PROSPECTS

In the future the heaviest development of condos will be in the inner cities and in the sun belt. Condominium development will continue to grow and will provide an ever greater percentage of the housing market. Ultimately there will be just two forms of housing: the single-family lot and the condo in its many forms (townhouses, elderly citizen communities, single communities, resort communities, and so on).

My own experience has been that we need to spend a lot of time developing the home owners association. Builders and purchasers must develop management teams to realize the benefits inherent in condominium living. It may be simpler to build single-family homes. Nevertheless, if we are going to continue in the business as merchant builders, we have to supply this form of development and cope with the related problems.

Chapter 36

The Real Estate Office of Tomorrow

Thomas W. Dooley   Director of Graduate Studies, College of Business, Lewis University, and President, TWD and Associates

Describing the real estate brokerage office of the future is akin to predicting what the stock market will do in forthcoming months and years. Pundits proliferate to predict whether the market will ascend or descend along its vertical financial axis. Prognosticators of the future of real estate are prone to similar gyrations.

With many stocks likely to move upward, downward, and sideways, the stock analyst will fashion a projection by attempting to predict the movements of a widely accepted barometer of measurement such as the Dow Jones Industrial Average or the Standard & Poor's broader stock index. In doing so, he or she will deal with averages derived from widespread input which may or may not be representative of a particular stock.

A parallel situation exists in spotlighting the real estate office of the future. In focusing on average situations, as one must, an observer is going to be off target when extremes are examined. This phenomenon is especially likely to occur in applying futuristic visions to real estate brokerage operations, because the options are many and relatively varied.

So, instead of concentrating our efforts on *the* real estate brokerage of the future, let us propose several alternatives and suggest that the vast majority of realty offices (albeit not all) will soon be found in one or another of the suggested categories. There are good and ample reasons to conjecture that most real estate brokerage offices of the future may be positioned in one of the following categories:

- Local offices of major national conglomerate real estate entities
- Franchisees of national franchise firms
- Franchisees with regional and local franchise firms
- Local firms with national (nonfranchise) marketing or referral network affiliations (large, medium, and small local firms)
- Totally independent local firms without any affiliation (a size subdivision also may be required in this category)

CURRENT CONGLOMERATES

Local offices of major conglomerates, most represented in the early 1980s by Coldwell Banker (also known as Sears) and Merrill Lynch Realty, may well constitute a very major segment of the real estate brokerage community of the future. Such offices will be affiliated as wholly owned or controlled subsidiaries of some of the major corporations of the United States, each looking for either the magic of synergism or the dynamics of diversification.

It is logical to assume that many of the parent firms of these local realty entities will be financial service companies. With Sears, a self-proclaimed new entry in the field of financial services, and Merrill Lynch, a veteran in the arena, each offering real estate brokerage as a profit-oriented activity, dare others be far behind? Doubtful, indeed! Rather, one can envision a host of Sears and Merrill Lynch financial competitors engaging in the real estate brokerage business. Probably only the general recessionary decline in real estate market activity during the early 1980s prohibited an early "keep up with the Joneses" entry. As soon as industry conditions improve, look for an avalanche.

Moreover, it appears likely that Congress is bent on liberalizing legislation to permit savings and loan associations (S&Ls), and probably banks, to operate their own real estate brokerage offices on the same premises as the financial institutions. The suggestion to buy your home and acquire your financing in the same place will be rather pronounced.

While this trend is materializing the entire structure of the savings and loan industry is changing as it becomes apparent that, by and large, the small entrepreneur cannot survive. Thus, through mergers and acquisitions, S&Ls are becoming big business. Many have been acquired by the same type of financial conglomerates that will acquire real estate companies—more evidence of conglomerate presence in real estate brokerage.

Although the newly pronounced main mission of Sears is financial services there are those who still recognize the company more readily as a merchandising colossus. Among such observers are such major competitors of the Sears merchandising empire as J.C. Penney, Montgomery Ward, K-Mart, Federated, Allied, and so on. Should Sears appear to have discovered a cost-efficient use of store floor space by opening a real estate department, will the other marketing giants lag behind? Probably not. Through a series of acquisitions and, perhaps, company-owned start-ups, the other retailers also will offer customers a chance to buy a home while shopping for a suit of clothes or a garden hose.

OTHER CONGLOMERATES

The ranks of potential conglomerates entering real estate brokerage do not stop with just financial service entities and department store chains. At least two other fields of business are likely candidates, and each is closely related to real estate as a purveyor of services to current practitioners. They are the *third-party corporate relocation companies* and the *computerized multiple listing service (MLS) companies.* Each is so close to the daily operations of real estate brokerage as to seriously consider the synergistic benefit of being *in* rather than *aligned with* the brokerage industry.

The trend is already somewhat noticeable with third-party relocation contractors. Although no third-party company has, in effect, acquired or started its own real estate brokerage network, several have become affiliated with or acquired by multifaceted conglomerates that have real estate brokerage elsewhere in their operational portfolio.

Once again leading the field is Sears, which, through ownership of Executrans, is able to incorporate corporate relocation assistance and third-party buyouts with its Coldwell Banker brokerage services. Not far behind is the Control Data/Commercial Credit operation, which, through its controlling interest in Relocation Realty Service and Electronic Realty Associates (ERA), is able to blend third-party buying with brokerage.

The remaining independent kingpins in the third-party corporate relocation business are dwindling in number as they tend to merge one with another. One recent example is the acquisition by Equitable Relocation Corporation (a subsidiary of Equitable Life Assurance Company) of Employee Transfer Corporation, a spinoff by Chicago Title and Trust and its "parent," the Lincoln National Insurance Company.

Not to be outdone is Merrill Lynch, which operated its Merrill Lynch Relocation Services division even before it entered residential brokerage acquisitions, having taken over the third-party subsidiary formerly operated by TICOR (Title Insurance Company of America) in the early 1970s. The other major entry in the third-party field is Home Equity, a wholly owned subsidiary of Patterson, Howell & Heather, leasing specialists headquartered in Baltimore.

Thus all the majors in this field are affiliated with large acquisition-minded companies. Some already are part of an umbrella structure that includes real estate brokerage. It is not too farfetched to imagine that the others will either follow suit or will structure their own real estate identification in the years ahead, perhaps by firm-by-firm acquisition in major markets, or, more likely, through purchase of a major franchise or marketing network.

THE MLS PURVEYORS

The computer service companies are another potential source of conglomerate acquirer. It is interesting to see how they arrived at such a possible position: The direct ancestors of the computerized MLS purveyors of today were the printing firms that produced card system or book system multiple listing services for most boards of Realtors around the nation no longer than 15 years ago.

Riding on the wave of computerized technology, many of these MLS printers converted their operations and their customers, first to MLS books that were computer typeset and then to a fully computerized management information system stored in data banks and accessed through a plethora of portable and permanent terminals in the possession of real estate agents.

Virtually all the MLS service firms that made the transition most successfully were entrepreneurial in nature, owned and operated by individual founders. They bore such names as International Graphics Corporation, R.L. White Company, Realtron, Realtronics, and the like. Today they are known as Moore Corporation, McGraw-Hill, Planning Resources, Inc., all large publicly owned entities that acquired the MLS firms as the need for capitalization outpaced internal generation of funds.

Whereas the original owners of MLS service companies were seeking an entrepreneurial and highly segmented niche in the vast panorama of real estate operations, the modern corporate owners are acquisition- and expansion-minded, preferring to see (or own) the forest, not just an individual tree therein. Although top management in the MLS purveyor industry profusely deny it, there are those industry soothsayers who predict that the establishment of a brokerage organization by these firms might not be surprising, especially if some of the other conglomerate giants initiate their own computerized systems that take business away from the service companies.

WHO ARE THE ACQUIREES LIKELY TO BE?

A major premise in the argument for expanded conglomerate presence in the real estate brokerage business is that acquisition-minded (for the most part, not real estate–related) corporations will be acquiring independent real estate companies, much in the manner that Coldwell Banker and Merrill Lynch have done.

One should not forget that it takes two to tango. For every acquisition there must be an acquiree as well as an acquirer. So, it is logical to speculate whether independent real estate brokerage firms will be inclined to swoon to the offers of corporate suitors. Our bet is that many of them will—enough certainly to satisfy the basic needs of all acquirers.

Such a prediction could be challenged, especially by those who remember the obstacles Merrill Lynch encountered when it first proposed to about fifty leading independent firms around the country (who, more than incidentally, happened to be large-scale recipients of Merrill Lynch corporate relocation listings) that they accept the opportunity of a business lifetime and sell to Merrill Lynch only to discover many of the firms considered the invitation an affront.

The passage of time, however, has a way of establishing individual perception of inevitabilities. As time goes by, more real estate brokerage proprietors are evaluating acquisition possibilities by large conglomerates as quite viable opportunities.

To be sure, there is still a general trepidation about losing identity, personal prestige, and operational control of the business, but, with increasing frequency, these negatives are being offset by perceived benefits. Most frequently identified are three key potential attributes of acquisition: (1) establishment of value for the business, and conversion of that value to liquid assets; (2) a provision for succession and continuity in the operation of the business; and (3) infusion of sufficient capital to remain competitive in the marketplace.

Establishing a value on a real estate brokerage business has long been a process of confusion and frustration. A commonly accepted price-to-earnings ratio or similar measurement has rarely been agreed on by industry experts. In effect, the presence of large-scale acquirers is establishing such a value system and is giving respectable independents an opportunity to convert a balance sheet asset into net spendable dollars with relative ease.

Many brokers, having established a substantial business, have found themselves without proper human resources to project an active continuance of the business beyond the days of their personal operational involvement. Except in family, partnership, and rather unusual corporate structures, real estate proprietorships have traditionally lacked an automatic line of succession of management. Conglomerate acquisition overcomes this dilemma, often assuring the selling proprietor of a continuing personal involvement in the organization to the extent he or she desires while also establishing solid successors.

Competitive challenges in the field of real estate brokerage are probably more pronounced than ever before. They promise to get even more intense as real estate practitioners increasingly use macro- rather than micromarketing. Nowhere is this fundamental change more obvious than in the realm of advertising and promotion. Whereas the successful real estate marketer of the past relied almost solely on a well-organized campaign of newspaper classified advertising use, buttressed occasionally by a print media display ad, the practitioner of today and the future frequently uses and will use the "hot" media of broadcasting, with particular emphasis on television.

Compare the costs of ample television (or even radio) coverage with saturation-type print media. Many brokers have, and they have found it so disproportionate as to be beyond their financial capabilities. Nor does concentrated use of this new medium eliminate the use of the print elements.

A quite graphic example, advertising is but one of a host of cost elements in operating the real estate brokerage firm of the future in a competitive manner. These cost elements have grown to be so sizable as to convince many independent brokers that they need operating capitalization far beyond their personal capabilities to survive and prosper: another endorsement for acquisition.

All things considered, then, it is totally logical to expect that there will continue to be a sizable demand on the part of conglomerate acquirers, both those currently in the field and new entrants, to engage in the real estate brokerage business. And acquirees will join forces with the large giants for a number of self-serving reasons. The net result, one can predict, will be a noticeable domination of the real estate brokerage field of the future by local entities affiliated with national conglomerates.

Sizable though this penetration of the marketplace will be, it will not encompass the totality of brokerage operations. There will remain a very considerable number of independent brokers who either ignore or oppose the intrusion of the giants or who do not fit the acquisition standards set by the conglomerates. Many of these firms will be troubled about the invasion of the national companies and quite concerned about their own future profitability and, maybe, survival. Thus, they will seek help of a different type.

Convinced of the merits of the truism, "In unity there is strength," they will join forces with other independent brokers while retaining a certain amount of independence and operational control of their offices.

THE SCOPE OF THE FRANCHISES

Throughout the latter half of the 1970s and into the 1980s, this trend was obvious in the gravitation of thousands of firms throughout the nation to the ranks of franchise organizations. This trend will continue into the future, although both its pace and direction may be altered.

Franchise organizations like to present themselves as offering independent real estate brokers the best of two worlds. While gaining the national identity and promotional muscle required to cope with the corporate giants, the franchisers argue, a franchisee still maintains a basic independence of ownership, control, and decision making. Many individual real estate brokers have perceived the situation in much the same terms and sought the haven and/or advantages offered by franchise organizations. As might be expected, expectations were met and exceeded by some franchises and thwarted by others. On balance, however, the concept of franchising as a method of survival and success for independent brokers is well enough established to make it one of the highly viable structures in the real estate brokerage scene of the future.

Franchise organizations of the future, however, are quite likely to be somewhat dissimilar from those of an earlier era. Perhaps the most significant change will be in the organizational structure of the franchiser. The pioneering days of national real estate franchising seem to have faded into history rather rapidly. Time was when new franchises, alleging to be national in scope, blossomed forth virtually every month of the year. Most of them were brainstorms of independent entrepreneurs, a good number of whom were themselves independent brokers. Names like Art Bartlett and Marsh Fisher (Century 21), Tony Yniquez (Red Carpet), and John Nothnagle (Gallery of Homes) are renowned in the history of real estate franchising because these individuals started with little more than an idea and structured it into sizable national networks, using their own inventiveness and, in most cases, their own capital.

This opportunity is unlikely to continue in the future. First of all, the costs connected with properly launching a national franchise with any hope of ultimate success have expanded so as to be virtually out of the reach of individual financing. Thus, any new future franchise is more than likely to be under corporate sponsorship, perhaps even the same corporate sponsorship which also has ownership positions as a real estate conglomerate. Such a situation is already visible in the case of Coldwell Banker/Sears. Realizing that acquisition and corporate operation of major firms is probably viable only in major markets throughout the nation, Coldwell Banker now is using the franchise route to extend its name and presence into secondary markets where there is no desire for company ownership. The only other relatively recent franchise of a true national nature is Better Homes and Gardens. It too functions under large corporate ownership and capitalization, with Meredith Publishing being the parent company.

Even those franchises initiated by the entrepreneurial pioneers have realized the need for conglomerate corporate sponsorship to remain progressive and competitive. One by one, they have merged with or been acquired by Fortune 500 companies. Century 21 was one of the first to go the corporate route, acquired by Trans World, Inc., after a previous flirtation with H&R Block had been dashed. ERA followed suit by coming under the umbrella of Commercial Credit/Control Data. Realty World sold a substantial amount of stock and control to the security brokerage firm Thompson McKinnon. Red Carpet got its capital infusion through an acquisition by the West Coast investment group of Oakland/Financial/Frank Scott Enterprises, as did Gallery of Homes. But rumors abound that as of this writing Gallery is again on the sales block actively seeking an acquisition offer.

There are several anticipated key results of these blendings of the independent franchiser organizations into the corporate complex. The first is to further solidify the notion that in the future no independents will start national franchises. If new groups do appear on the horizon, they will be under the banner of some well-known and well-heeled organization.

Second, the notion that many large-scale organizations will explore the opportunity to start franchises is doubtful. With the market for potential members limited and with the competition for those members quite severe most national corporations with real estate brokerage aspirations are much more likely to buy firms than to franchise them.

Third, from the point of view of the franchisee who joins the franchise network for competitive muscle and directional advice and counsel as well as for national identity and some form of national referral network, there will be pluses and minuses. Because of economies of size and financial ability, the major corporations should be able to promote the franchise in such a way as to maximize membership and public exposure, thus expanding the potential market for each franchisee. However, the disadvantages of organizational bureaucracy are likely to take effect with individual franchisees finding a growing amount of control and direction insisted on by the franchiser, allegedly in the interest of uniformity and quality control.

To assess the impact of national franchisers on real estate offices of the future, certain assumptions might be made, which, if accurate, chart the course for accurate predictability. One key assumption is that when it comes to acquiring additional franchisees from the existing real estate brokerage field, the franchise industry is at the full maturity stage of its life cycle. Unless there is a significant alteration in external, noncontrollable environmental conditions, it is unlikely that large numbers of current real estate brokers suddenly will discover virtues in franchise that they have overlooked while being courted by sales representatives for the past decade or more. Some will come and some will go, of course, but the net change in the number of franchise offices among existing real estate firms will be little or nothing.

There will be internal shifting among those firms that are convinced of the general merits of belonging to a franchise but not convinced that they currently belong to the correct one. Already there is a considerable cadre of real estate firms that are in their second or third generation of affiliation with different franchise groups.

If there is a sizable net increase in the number of total franchise real estate brokerage offices, that growth is likely to come from entrepreneurs opening their real estate firms for the first time, seeking instant recognizability and public acceptance.

On balance, then, those real estate offices of the future that elect to join a national franchise will be less of a percentage of the total realty office population than at present; those who are in the franchise movement will probably be more of a factor in their individual marketplace because of the support of the franchise by major corporate powers. Overall, the franchise movement probably will be eclipsed by the conglomerate ownership movement as a major new venture of real estate operation.

Local and Regional Franchises

Not all franchises of the present, and assuredly not of the future, will be national in intent and/or actual scope. As the price of admission to the national franchise market continues to climb, entrepreneurs financially frozen out of the national market may well initiate new franchise movements directed to small numbers of franchisees. It is likely that most such segmentation will be along geographic lines, with regional, sectional, statewide, and, in some cases, even metropolitan franchises. There will also be a place for segmentation along areas of principal concentration of interest or business activities. Franchises that offer memberships only to brokerage firms that specialize in resort properties, vacation homes, retirement centers, or even condominiums will arise and, in some instances, prosper.

The effectiveness of these smaller-scale entities in the franchise field will vary. Some will be very powerful big fish in the size pond of their own choosing. They will compete valiantly with the whales of the corporate conglomerate sphere and the larger-scope franchises. Other localized franchises will be little more than local cooperative movements among real estate practitioners attempting to control advertising and promotional costs by negotiating group "franchise" rates with their principal media. Overall, these smaller-scale franchise representatives will not be a vitally important force in the real estate field, but, in particular circumstances, situations, and locations, they might well be major, or even dominant, factors.

Having accounted for those firms that will dress in the corporate conglomerates' colors and those that will fly under either national or less than national franchise emblems, it seems that the only remaining group is those real estate offices that, failing to go either of the group routes, elect to travel alone as fierce and sometimes fiery independents. However, such is not totally the case.

Marketing and Relocation Networks

Many firms of the future that steadfastly refuse to join a franchise or sell to an acquirer may nonetheless realize the need for some form of unified strength and mutual benefaction to be derived from joining forces in some sort of an alliance with other independent brokers in similar situations. Unions of this type, less than franchises but more than just professional friendships, will be nothing new. They have existed since at least the late 1960s, usually under the generic title of *marketing networks* or, in the case of some groups banded together for more specific purposes, *referral* or *relocation networks*. There are important differences between the marketing groups and the relocation networks. Marketing groups' principal missions are to develop and share ideas, techniques, practices, and strategies across a whole spectrum of real estate operations. Usually the greatest concentration of effort on the part of marketing networks is in the fields of education, advertising, promotion, conventions, data exchange, and referral generation and exchange. Over the years, various real estate groups have identified themselves as, and urged others to recognize them as, marketing networks. Among the more prominent names of the past or present in the category are AIMS, ARMS, Homes For Living, Realty USA, the Master Minds, and the California Brain Trusters.

Relocation networks in their purest sense devote their sole efforts to fostering, improving, and expanding the exchange of referral and relocation clients and customers among members. Some powerful names of the past and present in this realm are RELO (at one time known as Inter-City), All Points Relocation Service, InterCom, Translo, and City-to-City.

The distinction between the marketing networks and the relocation groups is quite fuzzy, because most marketing networks work hard to make referral activity one of the principal services offered to members, whereas many relocation networks have, from time to time, expanded their activity to forms of advertising, promotion, and other marketing efforts designed to increase and improve referrals.

Regardless of which label is used, most independent brokers of the future will establish, maintain, and promote affiliation with one or another group. They will do so in some cases out of a desire and expectation to profit from the services rendered by the group and in other instances for the ability to share ideas with brokers in situations similar to their own, and to exchange clients and customer leads whenever the occasion warrants. Still another important reason for such membership is because the buying and selling public has come to expect it.

With the visible domination of the marketplace by conglomerates and franchisers, people expect a broker to belong to some organization, usually one connected with relocation services. Not too many persons outside the real estate industry make a distinction between types or sizes of franchises, between referral and marketing networks, or even between corporate conglomerate offices and the rest. What they do know when they are selling their homes is that there are structures in real estate that permit their property to be merchandised throughout the nation as well as throughout the local community. And when they are moving from one section of the world to another, they have some distant or proximate understanding that there is a system whereby a broker in the city they are leaving alerts brokers in the area where they are going so that they can, in advance, identify and assemble listings for their viewing that are compatible to their needs and expectations.

This client-customer perception alone is enough motivation for most independent brokers to seek affiliation with either a marketing or a relocation network and, having established affiliation, to promote and extol the affiliation highly to impress prospects and customers.

Small- and medium-sized independent firms in general will be rather highly dependent on the leadership and services offered by the networks. Larger firms may be more inclined to relegate their network memberships to a position where they are but one of a number of marketing devices used to retain competitive position. Thus, to a certain extent, networks of independent brokers will be a minor factor in the realty profession of the future.

Independents

Finally, there will be those offices of the future that steadfastly refuse to join anything or align themselves with anyone, preferring instead resolute independence until their dying days—which, under the circumstances, may not be too far away.

With no national identity, no referral programs, and a poor public image, totally independent offices, be they large, medium, or small, may suffer. These are difficult obstacles. In fact, there are only two basic ways in which a totally independent office might overcome these shortcomings. One way is to totally ignore them. To do so without suffering bankrupting consequences, the independent will have to segment its marketplace so narrowly and differentiate itself so obviously that within its own narrow sphere of market operation there is no challenger. Opportunities to establish such a position in the market are not frequent. Even when they do appear, many brokers are slow to notice them or reluctant to exploit them. Instead, far too many of the independents try to cover a broad waterfront, attempting to do battle with competitors whenever and wherever the occasion may arise, without the competitive armaments necessary for success. It is better to fight a small but successful skirmish on a "turf" that one controls than to wage a multifaceted competitive war across a wide spectrum controlled by the competition. Those independent brokers that are ready to admit *and* follow this pragmatic philosophy have some small chance for survival in the future.

The other way that an independent office might choose to overcome the realities of the future is to reduce its operation to "bare bones" overhead. Becoming a one- (or two- or three-) person operation may stay the day for some independents, but only if they tend to have an established clientele that will provide them with an abundance of personal referral business. Most brokerage offices that elect to follow this path must be content to do most of their business on a cooperative basis, selling a good number of other broker's listings and having the few listings they generate sold by other firms. Thus, this type of firm must adjust to living on the split commissions generated by cooperative sales.

On balance, the fully independent offices of the future will be relatively few in number and fundamentally weak in their influence on the marketplace. Their task will be to survive rather than to succeed.

SUMMARY

Piecing together these random glances into the real estate crystal ball to create a panoramic perspective of the future, one sees a brokerage industry dominated more and more by big-size operations, either conglomerates or franchises. This dominance will not be total, as knowledgeable independents, mostly with the assistance of their marketing network affiliations, will continue to render professional services in many communities, and the holdouts against any form of organized unity will grapple and grasp for continuance.

Even among the successful independents, however, value judgments, strategy development, and practical implementation of strategic plans will be significantly influenced by what the giants of the conglomerate and franchise world are doing. Independent offices will be, for the most part, reactive, while the giants of the industry establish the basic environmental conditions under which the brokerage business is to be conducted.

However, all firms, regardless of size, location, or affiliation, will be involved in the process of rapid change. That change need not be detrimental to real estate offices, but it surely can be under some circumstances. Those firms that attempt to ignore or struggle against change, longing for a return to the stability of the "good old days," will find their wishes granted as the firmness and stability of rigor mortis sets into their business. By contrast, those firms that recognize change as an opportunity to be innovative, progressive, and nontraditional will be the winners of the future. For them, change will represent not a curtailment of things past but rather a commencement of future excellence and success.

Index

1